THE INVENTION OF
ENTERPRISE

THE INVENTION OF ENTERPRISE

**ENTREPRENEURSHIP
FROM ANCIENT MESOPOTAMIA
TO MODERN TIMES**

EDITED BY

DAVID S. LANDES, JOEL MOKYR, & WILLIAM J. BAUMOL

PRINCETON UNIVERSITY PRESS · PRINCETON AND OXFORD

In the United Kingdom: Princeton University Press, 3 Market Place, Woodstock,
Oxfordshire OX20 1SY

Library of Congress Cataloging-in-Publication Data

The invention of enterprise : entrepreneurship from ancient Mesopotamia to modern times /
edited by David S. Landes, Joel Mokyr, and William J. Baumol.
    p.   cm.   (The Kauffman Foundation series on innovation and entrepreneurship)
  Includes bibliographical references and index.
  ISBN 978-0-691-14370-5 (cloth : alk. paper)
  1. Entrepreneurship—History.   I. Landes, David S.   II. Mokyr, Joel.   III. Baumol,
William J.
  HB701.I58 2010
  338'.0409—dc22   2009034315

British Library Cataloging-in-Publication Data is available

Published in collaboration with the Ewing Marion Kauffman Foundation and
the Berkley Center for Entrepreneurial Studies, New York University

This book has been composed in Sabon

Printed on acid-free paper. ∞

press.princeton.edu

Printed in the United States of America

10 9 8 7 6 5 4 3

Contents

Foreword

THE IMPORTANCE OF HISTORY to understanding entrepreneurship cannot be underestimated. Through history, we see the power, the resilience, and the complexity of this phenomenon. We gain a better understanding of the changing nature of entrepreneurial activity over time. We learn more about the complex web of social and institutional influences on entrepreneurship. And we develop a broader awareness of the impact of entrepreneurship over time—on individuals and on society as a whole.

Historical work in this area complements the increased attention to entrepreneurship among economists in recent years. Among many other topics, economists have elucidated a great deal about firm formation, growth, and death; the institutional influences on entrepreneurship; the demographic and personality characteristics of entrepreneurs; and the important role of entrepreneurship in economic growth. While economic theory and models offer a great deal of insight, history offers a different lens to view entrepreneurship. It allows us to understand specific examples at a deeper level, to probe the varied nature of the activity, to understand the environments in which entrepreneurs have thrived, and, perhaps most importantly, to see patterns and understand the evolution of innovation and entrepreneurship through the years.

The Ewing Marion Kauffman Foundation, the world's leading foundation in increasing understanding of and encouraging entrepreneurship, has directed significant resources in recent years toward the study of entrepreneurship among academics, with a particular focus on economics and history. Recognizing that entrepreneurship has long been absent from both history and economics textbooks, we initially sought to create a place for a new discipline among academics. The work we have seen in recent years has gone far beyond our early goals. Interest in the study of entrepreneurship has flourished throughout the academic community, and the wealth of information gleaned has both taught us a great deal and inspired us to learn more. At the Kauffman Foundation, we believe that if the public is to understand the importance of entrepreneurship to economic growth today, people will need to learn more about the role entrepreneurship played in economic growth throughout history.

This volume, in particular, breaks new ground as the first book to trace the history of entrepreneurship throughout the world since antiquity. Spanning the ages and covering the globe, this volume takes us from Mesopotamia and Neo-Babylon to the present. It offers insights from the Middle East, Asia, Europe, and the United States. The work presented in this volume testifies not only to the prevalence of entrepreneurial activity throughout history, but also to the changes in this activity over time and to its role in economic change and growth more generally.

While the entrepreneurial activity described during each historical period varies greatly, commonalities and themes emerge. At a detailed level, this work gives us great insight into the variables that affect entrepreneurship. We see the varied impact of culture and religion on this important phenomenon, in some cases inspiring individuals to pursue entrepreneurial dreams and in others making these dreams nearly impossible. We gain a greater understanding of the institutions that drive entrepreneurship, from contract law to the patent system. We understand the tension between productive entrepreneurship that enhances the growth of the economy and unproductive entrepreneurial activity that exploits opportunities for personal gain. And, finally, we see the distinction between the replicative entrepreneurs who simply create more new businesses like those they see around them and the truly innovative entrepreneurs who create new products and services and change the very nature of the market. It is this understanding that allows for the public policy lessons we draw from history. We come to learn how to promote innovative, productive entrepreneurship today by discovering the catalysts for and the impediments to entrepreneurial activity in the past.

On a broad scale, these accounts go even further: they offer us a window into the seemingly innate impulse for innovation and entrepreneurship that cuts across cultures and time periods. The diversity of the accounts is illuminating, but it is the commonalities that ultimately offer us a means of understanding human nature and the entrepreneurial impulse. We see here that people have been inspired to create, to innovate, and to market their productive abilities since the early years of recorded history. And we understand that it is this drive that has allowed our society to reach its current level of sophistication and complexity.

This comprehensive consideration of entrepreneurial activity throughout recorded history strikes out in new directions and encourages us to move further down this path. Each of these chapters, in fact, is an entrée into a much deeper, more complex story of entrepreneurs in a particular time and place. Learning more about each of these unique periods will give us a better understanding of the drivers of entrepreneurship, the barriers that impede it, the impact it creates, and, ultimately, human nature.

This volume also serves as an outstanding second contribution to the new Kauffman Foundation Series on Innovation and Entrepreneurship. A collaborative effort between the Kauffman Foundation, the Berkley Center for Entrepreneurial Studies at New York University, and Princeton University Press, this series of books will explore entrepreneurship and innovation from a wide range of disciplines and approaches. As one of the earliest works in this important collection, this volume both sets a high standard for the quality and depth of work in the series and suggests a broad research agenda for other historians. Indeed, further research on entrepreneurship is not only necessary for insight into policy matters; it is this study that allows us to understand who we are and how we have arrived at this point in time.

CARL J. SCHRAMM

Preface

The Entrepreneur in History

Wherefore rejoice? What conquests brings he home?
What tributaries follow him to Rome...?
                    —*Julius Caesar*, Act 1, Scene 1

The Central Objective of the Book

For readers who are not historians, history can nevertheless make fascinating reading. For one thing, the plots are often more improbable and more daring than a work of fiction. But entertainment is not the purpose of this book. Rather, it was written to investigate several hypotheses that are of considerable importance for the general welfare of society, hypotheses that, unfortunately, resist testing by standard procedures such as statistical analysis or controlled experiment. Only history seems to offer any promise of providing evidence for their verification or rejection.

In brief, the first hypothesis asserts that the practical utilization of inventions and their indispensable contribution to economic growth (at the very least, the rate of such growth and hence the level of per capita income) will be well below the levels they might otherwise have achieved without the intervention of entrepreneurs. But the entrepreneur's contribution is much more than this. If entrepreneurship were just "another factor," far more inventions would have been born to blush unseen. That is, without them, we would have basically nothing of the unprecedented growth miracle of the recent centuries. The second hypothesis goes in a direction rather different from the first. It asserts that entrepreneurial activities are not always productive and growth enhancing. Indeed, they may sometimes sabotage growth and prosperity. The third hypothesis is that the direction taken by entrepreneurial activity depends heavily, at any particular time and in any particular society, on the prevailing institutional arrangements and the relative payoffs they offer to entrepreneurial activities that promote growth and those that do not, or those that even handicap it. The research underlying this book was undertaken out of general interest in the subject, but also with the goal of shedding light on these three hypotheses.

The remainder of this preface will go a bit further in explaining the hypotheses and the reasons why history is the most promising way to test them; that is, why the more standard procedures used in empirical testing are not likely to work in this arena.

Fundamental Differences among Enterprising Activities: The Hypotheses

We consider individuals to be engaged in enterprising activities if they devote their own independent efforts to the acquisition of wealth, power, and prestige. They do not do so as employees of others, and, in the entrepreneurial process, they display initiative to a considerable degree. It seems clear that two primary avenues have been followed in this undertaking, which we label, for convenience, *redistributive entrepreneurship* and *productive entrepreneurship*. Examples of the first are obvious: aggressive warfare, larceny, bribery and rent-seeking litigation, among many others. Here it is important to distinguish between sanctioned or legal forms of redistributions such as lobbying for protective tariffs and unsanctioned ones, such as violent crime. It is practitioners of the former who can prosper and garner respect even in highly organized and "well-governed" societies. And it is to be noted that many such undertakings were once considered commendable and some still are. Indeed, those who undertook some of them were deemed heroic and were celebrated accordingly. A few centuries before the Industrial Revolution, this began to change. In some societies merchants and financiers were already quite appreciated, notably in Florence and Antwerp. The problem was that these societies were typically small and came under pressure from predatory neighbors, a particularly pernicious form of redistribution. Before that period, however, entrepreneurial activity that was both innovative and productive, that is, activity that increased the productive capacity of the economy, seems to have been relatively rare and not highly valued.

Aside from cultural attitudes that valued the successful warrior and looked down upon productive effort, there is another clear reason that favored redistributive undertakings. By its very nature, the payoff to success in redistributive entrepreneurial activity is clear and often immediate. The capture of territory from a rival monarch, the acquisition of a wallet by a pickpocket, or the bribe given to a corrupt bureaucrat are all unambiguous gains to the recipient. This is in marked contrast to the rewards that accrue to the productive entrepreneurs, whose contributions may well have largely accrued to free riders in the past and, indeed, to a considerable extent, still do.[1] To someone who adds to the economy's capacity to produce, the magnitude of the gain is usually far from obvious, nor is the lag entailed easily estimated; moreover, the gainers, who will reap much of the benefit, may not emerge until much later, and even then, their identity may be far from clear. Indeed, if the system works well, a good deal of the gain, and perhaps its preponderance, goes to consumers—often foreigners.

The work of Douglass North indicates that institutional arrangements play a crucial role in determining the structure of payoffs—the relative rewards offered by different entrepreneurial occupations in the society under examination. If North's conclusion is indeed valid, and it seems difficult to believe otherwise, then it follows that those institutions are among the primary influences that determine the allocation of entrepreneurial activity between the redistributive and the productive occupations. It would appear that until about the time of the British industrial revolution the prevailing institutions in most countries and in most periods were such as to favor redistributive activity by the economy's enterprising individuals. The change in the structure of payoffs that emerged with the appearance of capitalism can then plausibly be taken to contribute to the unprecedented growth rates that emerged thereafter. It would appear that never before in history have per capita incomes risen so quickly for so long a period, and the long era of slow growth surely requires explanation. Astonishing periods of invention were not absent, as we recognize. Then why did productivity and production remain so low and grow so slowly? A central purpose of this book is to shed light on such critical issues—light that can be helpful to today's impoverished economies and can guide the wealthier societies in the future.

But Why a Historical Approach?

It has already been suggested that no source of evidence and analysis other than that offered by study of history is promising for testing of hypotheses against the facts in this arena. It is worth recapitulation of the reasons why this is so. But first it must be emphasized that the obstacles to statistical analysis of matters related to entrepreneurship are easily exaggerated. There has, in fact, recently appeared a rich empirical literature on topics such as the personal characteristics of the entrepreneurs, their activities, their financial needs, their psychological propensities, and their earnings. However, such material has not been used to test hypotheses derived from formal or informal theory, and notably no broad hypotheses about the fundamentals of innovative entrepreneurial behavior and their consequences, such as those that have been proposed above.

The primary reason for the absence of such investigations is the indispensably essential attribute of an invention: it necessarily is something that was never available before. Of course, many if not most innovations are close substitutes for things already on the market. Yes, they are of course heterogeneous, but like snowflakes, even if they are all different we may find it useful to do some kinds of statistical analysis (e.g., on patents, or the biographies of great inventors) to look for empirical regularities. Nevertheless, invention must be the ultimate heterogeneous product. This impedes both standard approaches to statistical analysis: both a time series and a cross-sectional procedure. Or put more generally, the foundation of statistical analysis of relationships is the availability of a sufficient number of homogeneous observations to ensure that any observed interrelationship in the behavior of two such sets has a very low probability of having been fortuitous. But for the behavior of the innovative entrepreneur on the matters here under discussion, such internally comparable data sets are not generally available.

It may be noted that a similar difficulty impedes the optimality analysis that underlies most microeconomic theory, and helps to account for the absence of a formal microtheory of entrepreneurship. An optimality calculation entails at least an implicit comparison among the available choices for the decision at issue, while the innovating entrepreneurs normally deal with no set of well-defined substitutes among which they may choose on the basis of their attributes that are quantifiable and comparable. In contrast, standard theory of the firm analyzes well-defined choices of management among comparable options in fully operational enterprises in which the entrepreneur has already completed his or her job and left to create other firms.

With these impediments to both theory and data analysis, we can only return, without apology, to what we can learn from history. Of course, we are aware of the handicaps with which this option is beset. Most serious of all is the inability to perform anything analogous to a controlled experiment, so that any observed event or historical period is sure to be governed by complex interactions of a multitude of determinants, thereby preventing anything like direct evaluation of any one of them. Nevertheless, study of history provides much information and insight not otherwise obtainable. Most notably it allows us to look at environments very different from our own and see how these people coped. It is much like paleontology; only a minute fraction of all the interesting species that were ever alive are extant now, so how would we know anything about the physiology of giant lizards or ten-foot sloths? Yet no method in economics is without its shortcomings and impediments, and history has no reason to be deemed an unworthy approach.

Accordingly, this book turns to history, to find out what it can teach us about entrepreneurs, invention and its dissemination and utilization, and their implications for economic growth.

Some Observations That Emerge

The policy designer who reads this book will find a number of lessons that are likely to be helpful in suggesting what institutions and institutional modifications promise to contribute to the general welfare and to invention and innovation. But it can be hoped that the general readers will find much to inform, surprise, and delight them. For example, one conclusion that seems to emerge is that before the modern era the societies that were most creative in the generation of productive inventions were often poor performers in putting them to use. Abraham Lincoln cited the Roman case, with its production of a working steam engine, invented by Heron of Alexandria, and its failure to put the breakthrough to use as anything but a toy. Military inventions were, of course, put to use, and so were gadgets, many contributed by Heron and provided to the Roman priests as means to convince their flocks of their divine powers. Even more striking is Tong and Sung China, with its flood of inventive contributions, the spinning wheel, a magnificent astronomical clock, printing, playing cards, and much more. True, many of the Chinese inventions were put to use, such as printing, spinning, shipbuilding, and hydraulic technology. Yet the institutional arrangements did apparently lead toward a dead-end of sorts. In striking contrast is the much earlier Mesopotamian regime, and that of Europe in the later Middle Ages (notably the twelfth and thirteenth centuries) with its striking architectural inventions and its inventive use of the water mill to—in addition to grinding grain— saw lumber, hammer metal, contribute to the cloth-finishing process, pit olives, and much more, using so many water mills that they blocked traffic on the Seine. Our basic hypotheses would appear to account for this paradox that those who possessed the inventions seemed often to be only moderately capable of putting them to effective work. These hypotheses suggest that the reason for the failures to put inventions to use is that the payoffs were not available there but rather were offered for other things. In all these periods the prime payoff was offered for military invention: better armor, better castle design, and an improved stirrup for the war horse to permit more effective use of the lance. Though it is often argued that there were spillovers or (more persuasively) that the lines between military and civilian technology were more blurred than now, in the sense that iron, horses, construction, hydraulics, and even food preservation were all "common" technologies. In other cases, there was a payoff from the religious authorities who sought equipment with which to impress their flocks by their magic.

But these remarks, in a similar vein, are offered to induce the prospective reader to read on. For what this preface has offered is only a few samples of the ideas to be found in this book and the insights that it offers.

WILLIAM J. BAUMOL

Note

[1] Thus, Nordhaus has provided spillover calculations that show how little of the efficiency rent goes to innovators: "Using data from the U.S. non-farm business section, I estimate that innovators are able to capture about 2.2 percent of the total surplus from innovation. This number results from a low rate of initial appropriability (estimated to be around 7 percent) along with a high rate of depreciation of Schumpeterian profits (judged to be around 20 percent per year).... the rate of profit on the replacement cost of capital over the 1948–2001 period is estimated to be 0.19 percent per year" (2004, 34).

Reference

Nordhaus, William D. 2004. "Schumpeterian Profits in the American Economy: Theory and Measurement." NBER Working Paper No. 10433, April. Cambridge, MA: National Bureau of Economic Research.

Acknowledgments

THE IDEA FOR THIS BOOK arose in a conversation between Bob Strom and Will Baumol when the former accepted an invitation to teach a course in entrepreneurship. As we discussed material for the course and approaches that would place the topic in historical context, the idea for this book emerged.

As neither of us is a historian, the need for help was clear. We were determined to seek editors who were second to none, and our thoughts turned first to David Landes and Joel Mokyr. It seemed miraculous that both scholars accepted our invitation immediately. They thoughtfully assembled an outline for the volume, and Joel compiled a list of promising contributors. Once again, we were delighted to find that most of the authors quickly accepted the invitations and were enthusiastic about this project.

In order to ensure that the volume was not a mere collection of miscellaneous papers with little relation to each other, we, the editors, set out a list of topics that the authors would be asked to address—with some degree of flexibility, of course. At an authors' conference at New York University in October 2006, drafts of the chapters were discussed both in terms of their substance and their coherence to this list of topics. With another year of revision and editing, we hope that what has emerged is indeed a volume that is illuminating, readable and cohesive.

Though it sometimes entailed hard work, the task has been a great pleasure, and the enhanced friendship with our two editors has been a rich reward. In addition to what is owed to their efforts, we must also recognize the invaluable contribution of Alyse Freilich, who read the manuscripts closely, edited them with care and understanding, and finally shepherded them to the publisher. She stepped in to rescue us after the very sad passing of Sue Anne Blackman, our beloved colleague of many years, who had been expected to oversee the preparation of this volume. She and Janeece Lewis, Baumol's very capable associate at NYU, deserve much of the credit for the final emergence of the volume.

We must also express our gratitude to our colleagues at Princeton University Press, with whom we have worked before, so that their helpful contribution came as no surprise. Finally, we must acknowledge our tremendous debt to the Ewing Marion Kauffman Foundation, not only for its very encouraging support of this volume, but perhaps even more for giving it one of the inaugural positions in the Kauffman Foundation Series on Innovation and Entrepreneurship.

WILLIAM J. BAUMOL AND ROBERT J. STROM

THE INVENTION OF
ENTERPRISE

Introduction

Global Enterprise and Industrial Performance: An Overview

WESTERN ENTREPRENEURSHIP AND TECHNOLOGICAL PROGRESS go back centuries and have changed the world for the better. That, at least, is one assessment of the historical record—one with which not everyone would agree. Some scholars there are who, disapproving of Western triumphalism or solicitous of Asian (mostly Chinese) pride and prowess, would date the Industrial Revolution as a late phenomenon in the history of entrepreneurship and treat it as lucky accident (or unlucky, depending on one's sense of values). It could have happened anywhere, they say; it just fell to Europe's or Britain's lot, in large part owing to political fortune, reinforced by overseas dominion. And globalization, in the sense of worldwide diffusion of trade, industry, and technology, came even later: after World War II.

Yet newer research and reflection on comparative world history make it clear that global trade goes back more than a millennium, back to Asian and then European economic development in the later Middle Ages, back to the opening of the world with the turning of Africa and penetration of European vessels into Asian waters and to the contemporaneous European invasion of the Americas.[1] The centuries that followed saw the West grow richer than other regions of the world, pull away from the onetime leaders, establish empire in distant lands—all of this on the basis of superior scientific knowledge, industrial technique, and business enterprise. Much of subsequent history has been profoundly influenced by this gap and the reaction to it of lagging areas—these last resentful of patronizing, condescending, charitable and uncharitable, advantageous and predatory Western dominion.

They see this gap between rich and poor as the fault of the rich; they see their own weaknesses and shortcomings as someone else's doing. In particular, they feel that advanced industrial nations have used their power not to help, but to exploit and plunder the weak. In this scenario, success and empire are forces for evil.

Nonetheless, the gains made by the more precocious industrializers incited other, slower nations to imitate and emulate. There was money to be made by these new ways. But wanting was not necessarily doing. Emulation required knowledge, the ability to organize and rationalize production, intelligent and active entrepreneurship, laws protective of property and change. The countries best equipped to undertake the task were to be found in parts of the West, such as Ireland, Scandinavia, pieces of central and eastern Europe, Canada, some bits of Latin America—places that had earlier been barred from the pursuit of new ways by political misfortune and cultural impediments.

In general, the countries and regions that have done best are precisely those that have taken advantage of the opportunities offered by active trade and entrepreneurial freedom, often in the face of official constraints. These are the countries that have most attracted foreign advances and investment. But they have not done so by following the formulas proffered or imposed by experts from richer lands. The essence of successful enterprise lies in creative imagination and initiative.

The older centers of hither and farther Asia—the Islamic world, India, China—lacked the cultural and institutional foundations on which entrepreneurship rested. Worse: they tended to cling to tradition in a world of disturbing and disagreeable challenge.[2] Both China and the Arabic Middle East offer pungent case studies of this resistance to innovation and the subsequent national revenge against those they blamed for the economic disparities that ensued. Both impoverished themselves by insisting on their cultural, moral, and technical superiority over the barbarians around them, by refusing to learn from people they scorned as inferiors, by simply refusing to learn. Pride is poison, and as the proverb puts it, pride goeth before a fall.

China was once the richest and proudest of civilizations. Faced with pretentious eager, greedy barbarians, the Chinese did badly, nursing feelings of superiority that blinded them to opportunity.[3] Angus Maddison's (1991, 10) estimates, shown in table I.1, tell a clear, unmistakable story.

Their refusal to exchange ideas with others cost them some four hundred years of potential progress. Western sinologues (really sinophiles) try to comfort the Chinese by dating the Western advance as late as possible, by reducing it to happy accident, by minimizing its extent and impact. I emphasize the "Western." The Chinese themselves know better. Because they know better, they are now doing something about it.[4]

One can tell a similar story about the Muslim Middle East, Arabic and Ottoman.[5] This had once been a world center of economic growth based on scientific and technological priority, a teacher of the West. But religious values confounded with political ideology grievously hurt productivity and justified self-impoverishment, insofar as it was not blamed on others. The result has been an angry ossification and resentment that has led much of Islam to reject the West and turn back to the allegedly superior values of Mohammed's time.

TABLE I.1
China versus Western Europe and Its Overseas Extensions

	Gross domestic product per head (1985 dollars)		Population (millions)	
	Western Europe	China	Western Europe	China
1400	430	500	43	74
1820	1,034	500	122	342
1950	4,902	454	412	547
1989	14,413	2,361	587	1,120

Thus many Muslim countries and societies have strenuously opposed Westernization, which they see as a process of material corruption, a sacrifice of traditional virtue on the altar of self-indulgence. This defensive closure has cost them their place in the world. After all, Muslim civilization was once the intellectual and cultural leader—and Muslims the masters—of the Eurasian world. As one wit put it, if there had been Nobel prizes a thousand years ago, they would have gone, just about all, to Muslims (Pipes 2002, 4). (In this sense, the Nobels serve as something of a barometer of current and potential scientific and industrial performance. Look at Japan: four prizes in the last three years.)[6]

So what went wrong with Muslim performance?[7] We have here a case study in defensive refusal to learn, a systematic suppression of curiosity, a pursuit, instead, of revenge and return. To be sure, Islam has its diversity and variety. Muslim Turkey, Malaysia, and Indonesia are very different from the Arab Middle East, Algeria, Pakistan, or the northern Sudan. (I shall come back to this.) Yet almost everywhere, rule is autocratic, with little patience for opposition or obstruction. The rulers and the powerful have succeeded in silencing the open-minded dissenters, who have come to realize that their very physical safety depends on their discretion or their departure to more open cultures—and sometimes not even then.

As a result, many Muslim countries and societies, particularly those of the Arab heartland, have found themselves slipping steadily, one might almost say inexorably, backward, in political strength and material wealth. The process is somewhat mitigated and concealed by the accidents of geography, in particular by the possession of major resources of that invaluable engine and motor fuel, petroleum. They have given the Arab countries a political role far exceeding what their population and wealth, to say nothing of their behavior, might have warranted.

The Muslim world's response to challenge and decline has not only been one of refusal, but an intensification of the traditionalistic, often crippling aspects of the culture. This has been particularly true of the response to European technological and commercial achievement, which has been seen as a ruthless betrayal of moral justice and an undeserved reversal of proper historical relations. The Muslim reaction, as befits a virile, honor-based society, has ranged from angry violence to smoldering, sulky resentment. Within the Islamic world, such a negative response to challenge and opportunity has its spiritual and psychological consolations. But the economic consequences can be disastrous, for anger and inequality kill trust. Trust is wanting among strangers, setting a limit on potential expansion of business ventures and enterprises. Trust is especially wanting between Muslims and non-Muslim minorities.

To be sure, the Muslim world does have its bright spots—Indonesia, Malaysia, and Singapore (all Asian), for example. But their success owes much to the relative looseness of their religious strictures, their multicultural populations, above all to the large presence of non-Muslim Chinese émigré entrepreneurs. They might normally be the object of systematic hostility by way of reserving the economy to good Muslims—the kind of exclusivity that has been a principle of Turkish economic policy, for example. But Asians have learned the value of open and free entrepreneurship. Still, Islam matters, and in Malaysia the tacit understanding is that non-Muslim (Chinese) entrepreneurs shall maintain a position of silent modesty. The economy grows, in large part owing to the Chinese contribution; and the Muslims take the credit.

There remain Latin America and Africa, both laggards. Latin America is a mixed picture. A few countries have done well: Brazil, Argentina (yes and no), Columbia, Chile. Such successes have been based, as in the Middle East, on nature's accidental generosity: precious raw materials, prairie lands especially well suited to mass cultivation of cereals; jungle plants of industrial value, rubber particularly. Still, these are nations that have largely failed to combine increasing product with a higher standard of living and a leveling up of incomes. They are countries of a few rich and many poor, stuck in unbalanced arrangements that go back to colonial times, where minorities of privileged white conquerors ruled over the beaten survivors of indigenous peoples and then took in poor immigrants, preferably and often compulsorily Roman Catholic, to do the dirty work of painfully and tediously urbanizing societies. These nations are legally democratic and parliamentary, but practice often diverges from principle, and internal peace and order are precarious. One finds the same discrepancy with the market and entrepreneurship: the recent difficulties in Argentina testify to the intrinsic instability of an economy that was once envied and admired by the world's advanced industrial nations. Latin America remains a big question mark.

Africa offers the most extreme examples of economic failure. To begin with, the geographical environment is not favorable to work and effort. Air conditioning would make a big difference, might even attract enterprise and labor, but air conditioning costs money and the African peoples do not have it. Philanthropic progressives put hope in subsidies by the rich, especially investments in productive capital. Yet such hopes for now have been food for disappointment, in large part owing to political mismanagement and corruption. Africa has been a place of flight and exit; success in Africa, a ticket for departure.

Meanwhile the more advanced countries, comfortable in their technological and political superiority, have been increasingly tempted by the opportunities to export work to places of cheap labor. This sort of thing happens all the time now, because entrepreneurs are in it for the money, and they can make more money with a lower wage bill. Just read the story of James Dyson, inventor of the bagless vacuum cleaner. Dyson's British company made more than 8 million of these machines in less than a decade; had sales of $316 million in the year 2000 alone; had built capital to an estimated value of $700 million. By 2002, however, it was planning to move production of all vacuum cleaners to Asia. Needless to say, the decision brought howls of protest. But Dyson dismissed such objections as irrational: "I put £40 million of my money into this business to try and make manufacturing work here. But I have to regard the law of economics. If we are to survive as a business, we have to go where manufacturing is economical. I am not betraying anybody."[8]

Or take the story of Polaroid film, made for years in a factory in Waltham, Massachusetts. This plant closed in the summer of 2002, and the work moved to new plants in Mexico and the Netherlands. The decision to move came from an investment group that bought Polaroid and prefers profits to sentiment. Needless to say, the workers were unhappy. Some had been employed by Polaroid for decades and never dreamed the company would ever leave Massachusetts. The Massachusetts secretary of state began investigating the company program that required employees to buy shares and then sold them without consent. His comment: "I think it's been fairly sinister the way the company has been cut apart like a stolen car at a chop shop while the employees are left holding the spare tire."[9]

Nor are the initiatives toward job export limited to the advanced industrial nations of the West. When Honda Motors of Japan announced its intention of building plants in China, to make cars not only for the Chinese market but for export around the world, they defended the action by announcing that quality of product would match that of autos made in Japan, but costs would be 20 percent lower.[10]

This process of job transfer ("outsourcing") is a central aspect of contemporary entrepreneurship and globalization. This last is a terrifying word for many, to the point of violently negative response. If one were to judge by the recent proliferation of writing on the subject, one would think that globalization was an invention of the late twentieth century, a turn of the exploitation screw, an international attack on peace and happiness. Yet as we have seen, it is a process that goes back centuries and varies in intensity with technological and social possibilities, the ups and downs of business enterprise, the ever-changing uncertainties of war and peace. It is not a cause, not an ideology. It is simply the pursuit of wealth.

We today are living in a period of particularly active globalization of economic activity. This is a good thing, especially for those poor nations that build on these imports of activity to catch up. It is the way the backward learn, the way the poor can escape from poverty. Given these generally (ultimately) beneficent effects, why then the resistance and resentment? Why the angry riots? Why the flood of criticism?

One reason is disappointment with the results. "Poverty," writes Dani Rodrik in a luminous and eloquent essay, "is the defining issue" (2002, 29). The poorest countries have not done well, in spite of strenuous efforts by economists and government institutions in the rich countries of the West (thus the IMF and World Bank) to get them to do the things that are supposed to promote development. Almost all of Africa is sinking into a morass of failure, corruption, and disease. The countries of Latin America have known alternating prosperity and failure and seen growth rates fall below their historical averages. A number of former socialist and communist countries, which might be expected to flourish in newfound freedom, closed out the twentieth century with falling income per capita. Even the so-called miracle economies of South and Southeast Asia have met with reverses.

To be sure, on the global level, poverty has diminished, and this because the two most populous nations in the world have done well. China has averaged almost 8 percent annual growth of GNP since the late 1970s; India has gone from 1.5 percent to 9 percent in 2005–6. These two nations hold more than half the world's poor and make the overall result positive. What do these gains mean for the people of these lands? Just look at life expectancy. In 1960, the average Chinese could expect to live only thirty-six years; by 1999 this figure had risen to seventy years, almost as high as in the United States.

Many if not most Third World countries, or the South as against the North, see globalization as a device or pretext for imposing postimperialist domination and exploitation by the West of the Rest. This must be true, for the gap is apparently growing, and who else could be responsible? Even more vexing is the cultural conquest and destruction that accompany material triumphs: the cinema, the music, the art and architecture, the heroes and heroines, the styles, furnishings, fast-food cuisine, manners. Globalization swallows all, leaving no place for those outside it.[11]

These reactions are reinforced by the sense that history has done the losers wrong; that where once they were leaders and standard-bearers, they have now been pushed aside, reduced, humiliated. The West, say the self-proclaimed victims, rules the world, does as it pleases, commits crimes at will. Formal empires may have dissolved, but the school of imperialism has continued to breed war criminals. Witness, they say, the bullying and oppression of Afghanistan, Iraq, Palestine, Lebanon, Syria. Hence an abiding, festering hatred of Americans and Jews (or Israelis, seen as agents of the United States). Hence infinite indulgence for barbaric crimes, defended as the legitimate, unavoidable recourse of weak against strong. Hence the deliberate killing of civilians, the use and celebration of child suicide bombers using weapons designed to hurt and maim noncombatants. The weak, this reasoning goes, can do no wrong.

What is to be done? We know no foolproof answer, and certainly no single remedy that always works. But part of the answer, if it can be made politically feasible, is the adoption of enhanced incentives for domestic enterprise. Indispensable is enterprise that is prepared to learn from the successes of others, and to adapt appropriate foreign practices and rules of the game to the needs of domestic circumstances and cultures. For it is only by introduction of more effective mechanisms to enhance domestic productivity and production that poverty can be contained. This, of course, is hardly all that it is needed, but historical evidence suggests that it is not easily dispensed with. This book is designed to bring together some of the relevant history and to suggest some of the lessons the history implies. We hope that it will offer interesting insights to the reader and make for good reading as well as valuable knowledge.

Notes

[1] For a new and important approach to early trans-Eurasian trade and development, see Gordon 2008.
[2] On China particularly, see Landes 2006.
[3] See Chan, chapter 16 in this volume, for a broad discussion of the history of entrepreneurship in China.
[4] For an anti-Eurocentric, romantically sinophilic point of view, with abundant barbs at David Landes, see Wright 2000, chap. 12, "The Inscrutable Orient." Even more romantic is the new book by William Menzies, *1434* (2008).
[5] For a more detailed discussion of Muslim entrepreneurship, see Kuran, chapter 3 in this volume.
[6] *International Herald-Tribune*, October 14, 2002, 4.
[7] This is the title of the book by Bernard Lewis: *What Went Wrong?* (2002).
[8] *International Herald Tribune*, February 22, 2002, 1.
[9] *Boston Globe*, April 20, 2002, C2.
[10] James Brooke in the *New York Times*, July 11, 2002, W1.
[11] I take this from a talk by Abbas Beydoun, director of the cultural pages of the Lebanese newspaper *Assafir*, to the Policy Forum of the German Foundation for International Development in Berlin, March 4–5, 2002.

References

Gordon, Stewart. 2008. *When Asia Was the World*. Cambridge, MA: Da Capo Press.
Landes, David S. 2006. "Why Europe and the West? Why Not China?" *Journal of Economic Perspectives* 20, no. 2: 3–22.
Lewis, Bernard. 2002. *What Went Wrong? Western Impact and Middle Eastern Response*. New York: Oxford University Press.

Maddison, Angus. 1991. *Dynamic Forces in Capitalist Development: A Long-run Comparative View*. New York: Oxford University Press.

Menzies, William. 2008. *1434: The Year a Magnificent Chinese Fleet Sailed to Italy and Ignited the Renaissance*. New York: William Morrow.

Pipes, Daniel. 2002. *Militant Islam Reaches America*. New York: Norton.

Rodrik, Dani. 2002. "Globalization for Whom?" *Harvard Magazine*, July–August, 29–31.

Wright, Robert. 2000. *Nonzero: The Logic of Human Destiny*. New York: Pantheon.

Chapter 1

Entrepreneurs: From the Near Eastern Takeoff to the Roman Collapse

MICHAEL HUDSON

A CENTURY AGO ECONOMISTS could only speculate on the origins of enterprise. It seemed logical to assume that entrepreneurial individuals must have played a key role in archaic trade, motivated by what Adam Smith described as an instinct to "truck and barter." When a Mycenaean Greek site from 1200 BC was excavated and storerooms with accounting records found, the building accordingly was called "a merchant's house," not a public administrative center.[1]

There was little room for Max Weber's idea that a drive for social status might dominate economic motives. Materialist approaches to history both by Marxist and by business-oriented writers assumed that economic factors determined status and political power, not the other way around. The basic context for enterprise was deemed to consist of timeless constants: money, account-keeping to calculate gains, credit, and basic contractual formalities. To the extent that public institutions were recognized as economic actors, they were assumed to be an overhead, incurred at the expense of enterprise, not as means of promoting it. There was little idea of temples and palaces playing a catalytic role, much less a key one in production or providing money and provisioning commercial ventures. There was even less thought of rulers regulating markets, canceling personal debts, and reversing land transfers as a way to enhance prosperity.

Translation of cuneiform records over the past century has changed these attitudes. A veritable explosion of colloquia over the past decade has analyzed the emergence of enterprise in Mesopotamia and its neighbors (in particular Dercksen 1999; Bongenaar 2000; Zaccagnini 2003; Manning and Morris 2005; and, earlier, Archi 1984, in addition to the compendious *Civilizations of the Ancient Near East* [Sasson et al. 1995]). Our own working group, the International Scholars Conference on Ancient Near Eastern Economies, has held colloquia dealing with the public/private balance (Hudson and Levine 1996), the emergence of urban and rural land markets (Hudson and Levine 1999), debt practices and how societies handled the economic strains they caused (Hudson and Van De Mieroop 2002), account-keeping and the emergence of standardized prices and money (Hudson and Wunsch 2004). These conference volumes have been bolstered by many books and articles presenting a complex view of the emergence of commercial enterprise.

The vast supply of Near Eastern tablets and inscriptions dealing with economic affairs is being translated free of the past generation's ideological split over whether the economic organization of classical Greece was "ancient," "primitivist," and "anthropological" in character, as asserted by Karl Bücher, Karl Polanyi, and Moses Finley, or "modern," as asserted by Eduard Meyer and Mikhail Rostovtzeff. (The basic documents in the century-old debate are collected in Finley 1979. For a recent discussion see Manning and Morris 2005.) Half a century ago, Polanyi and Finley criticized "modernist" views of antiquity by claiming that it operated as part of a system more "traditional" and bureaucratic than entrepreneurial. The quasi-Marxist theory of Oriental despotism was even more extreme. But the past few decades of scholarship have seen the pendulum swing back away from such views, finding many innovative economic practices in the ancient world (Hudson 2005–6).

It is now recognized that most of the techniques that would become basic commercial practices in classical antiquity were already developed in the third millennium BC in the temples and palaces of the Bronze Age Near East—money, along with the uniform weights, measures, and prices needed for account-keeping and annual reports (Hudson and Wunsch 2004), the charging of interest (Van De Mieroop 2005; Hudson and Van De Mieroop 2002), and profit-sharing arrangements between public institutions and private merchants ranging from long-distance trade to leasing land, workshops, and retail beer-selling concessions (Renger 1984, 1994, 2002). Assyriologists now apply the term *entrepreneur* broadly to Assyrian and Babylonian *tamkarum* "merchants" from early in the second millennium BC down to the Egibi and Murashu families of Babylonia in the seventh through fifth centuries BC, who created novel commercial strategies to manage estates and provision the palace and its armed forces.

These practices initially were developed to create an export surplus of textiles, metalwork, and other labor-intensive products to obtain the stone, metal, and other raw materials lacking in southern Mesopotamia (what is now Iraq). During the second millennium these techniques diffused westward via Ugarit and Crete to Mycenaean Greece. After the long Dark Age that followed the collapse of Mycenae circa 1200 BC, seafaring merchants brought them to Greece and Italy, where they were adopted circa 750 BC in a context less conducive to enterprise and with fewer institutional checks and balances on debt, dependency, and economic polarization. Clientage came to be viewed as a natural state of affairs as economic attitudes changed from those in the Near East.

Wealthy Greek and Roman families controlled handicraft production, trade, and credit directly rather than coordinating these activities via the temples and palaces. Yet classical antiquity's aristocratic attitude viewed commercial enterprise as demeaning and corrupting. The details of trade and enterprise typically were left to outsiders or to slaves and other subordinates acting as on-the-spot managers, organizers, and middlemen for their backers. Most enterprising individuals were drawn from the bottom ranks of the social scale, typified by the fictional but paradigmatic freedman Trimalchio in Petronius's comedy dating from the time of Augustus. "The greater a man's *dignitas*," D'Arms (1981, 45) has pointed out, "the more likely that his involvement [in business] was indirect and discreet, camouflaged behind that of an undistinguished freedman,—client, partner, 'front man,' or 'friend,' " and leaving management of their affairs to slaves or other subordinates. When such lesser individuals were able to accumulate fortunes of their own, they aspired to high status and prestige by sinking their money into land and obtaining public office. The freedman Trimalchio "immediately ceased to trade after amassing a fortune, [and] invests in land and henceforth talks and acts like a caricature of a Roman senator" (D'Arms 1981, 15; see Dio Chrysostom, *Or.* 46.5).

Although we might expect Romans at the high end of the economic spectrum to have enormous personal fortunes corresponding to the city-state's great riches (parasitic as these may have been), Heichelheim (1958–70, 3:125) notes that its leading families spent beyond their means, running up catastrophic debts in their drive for status and power. This behavior "finds no analogy at the time of the Golden Age of Greece either among private individuals or among princes."

The history of enterprise in antiquity therefore falls naturally into two periods. First is the development of economic practices in Mesopotamia circa 3500–1200 BC. By the end of antiquity we find gain-seeking shifting away from productive enterprise to land acquisition, usury, profiteering from political office, and extraction of foreign tribute by force. To begin the story of enterprise in this later classical epoch thus would be to ignore the fact that most commercial practices already had a pedigree of thousands of years by the time Near Eastern traders brought them to the Mediterranean lands in the mid-eighth century BC.

What led communities to develop a commercial ethic in the first place? Who were the beneficiaries, and how were the benefits shared? Why did this ethic, which seems so natural to us today, take so long to emerge in the ancient world, only to be overwhelmed by less economically productive, more corrosive social values? To answer these questions it is necessary to address the transition from interpersonal gift exchange to bulk trade at standardized market prices, that is, from "anthropological" to "economic" exchange and production.

The Revolutionary Entrepreneurial Gain-Seeking Ethic

Trade extends back deep into the Paleolithic, but modern tribal experience and logic suggest that the most archaic trade probably occurred via reciprocal gift exchange, whose primary aim was to promote cohesion among the community's members, and peaceful relations among chiefs of neighboring tribes. (Mauss's *The Gift* [1925] is the paradigmatic study along these lines.) Anthropological studies have documented that the typical attitude in low-surplus communities living near subsistence levels is that self-seeking tends to achieve gains at the expense of others. Traditional social values therefore impose sanctions against the accumulation of personal wealth. The economic surplus is so small that making a profit or extracting interest would push families into dependency on patrons or bondage to creditors. The basic aim of survival requires that communities save their citizenry from falling below the break-even level more than temporarily. In antiquity, for example, losing land rights meant losing one's status as a citizen, and hence one's military standing, leaving the community prone to conquest by outsiders.

The result is that while low-surplus economies usually do produce surpluses, archaic political correctness dictated that they should be consumed, typically by public display and gift exchange, provisioning feasts at major rites of passage (entry into adulthood, marriage, or funerals), or burial with the dead. Status under such conditions is gained by giving away one's wealth, not hoarding or reinvesting it. It long remained most culturally acceptable to consume economic surpluses in public festivals, dedicate them to ancestors, and, in time, to supply provisions for the construction of temples and other monumental structures.

Concentration of the Economic Surplus at the Top of the Social Pyramid

When tribal communities mobilize surpluses (usually as much via warfare as by trade), they tend to be concentrated in the chief's household, to be used, at least ostensibly, on behalf of the community at large. And as part of their role as the community's "face" in its commercial or military relations with outsiders, this "household" tends to absorb runaways, exiles, or other unattached individuals. The ethic of mutual aid calls for chiefs, in turn, to act in an open-handed way.

Some surplus normally is needed for specialized nonagricultural production. In such cases either the chief or leading families may administer a sanctified, corporately distinct cult charged with capital-intensive production such as metalsmithing. Such occupations often involve a particular class of workers, who need to be supplied with raw materials, and either with their own self-support land or with food from the chief's household or from land leased out by the specialized group. Such groups tend to institutionalize themselves on the model of families, but to have an essentially public identity.

Profit-seeking "economic" exchange was so great a leap that initially it seems to have been conducted mainly in association with public institutions, at least nominally. The first documented "households" to be economically managed were those of Mesopotamia's temples. To be sure, Lamberg-Karlovsky (1996, 80ff.) has traced their evolution out of what began as the chief's household from the sixth through the third millennium, followed by palaces that emerged from temple precincts circa 2750 BC. These large institutional households developed a community-wide identity, especially as they absorbed dependent labor such as that of the war widows and orphans, the blind or infirm taken out of their family environment on the land, and also slaves captured in raiding. It is in them that the first standardized bulk production was organized to yield a commercial surplus.

Temples of Enterprise

Southern Mesopotamia was in a uniquely resource-dependent position. Its land consisted of rich alluvial soil deposited by rivers over the millennia, but lacked copper, tin, lapis and other stone, or even much hardwood. The region needed to obtain these materials from distant sites ranging from the Iranian plateau to central Anatolia. In the mid-fourth millennium BC the Sumerians created fortified outposts up the Euphrates to the north, but archaeologists have found that they had to be abandoned after a century or so. Military conquest was too expensive a means to obtain distant raw materials and transport them to the southern Mesopotamian economic core.

Sumerian cities fought among themselves in the fourth, third, and even second millennia BC, but acquisition of foreign materials in large quantity over long distances had to be organized on a reciprocal and voluntary basis with Anatolia and the Iranian plateau, while trade with the Indus Valley was conducted mainly on the island of Dilmun. Peaceful trade meant enterprise, requiring southern Mesopotamia—Sumer—to have exports to offer. Because of the large sums involved, city temples and palaces played the dominant role as producers and suppliers of goods. Ships and overland caravans were outfitted and provided with textiles and other products to exchange for the raw materials lacking in the Sumerian core.

In recent years, Assyriologists have reconstructed how this system worked, using as evidence royal inscriptions and the archives of palace officials and merchant-entrepreneurs. Imperial conquerors in time imposed the payment of tribute and taxes on defeated populations, but city-temples and palaces did not levy taxes as such. Rather, they supported themselves by their own workshops, large herds of animals and means of transport, and by leasing out fields and workshops, much as Athens later would do with its Laurion silver mines. Their dependent labor force produced textiles for export, and beer for domestic sale.

The absence of either export or local sales documents suggests that the temples and palaces advanced these commodities to merchants for later payment upon the return from a voyage, after a five-year period, or at harvest time for domestic sales for payment in crops. In the early stages of long-distance trade they were given rations or "salaries" and supplied with donkeys by the temples, a sure sign of their public role (Frankfort 1951, 67). In time these merchants accumulated capital of their own, which they used along with that of private backers (typically their relatives). Most of their archives have been excavated in temple or palace precincts, indicating that there was no idea of conflict of interest with regard to their position in the temple or palace bureaucracy, which seems to have remained mainly in the hands of leading families. Their personal business archives are found along with public administrative records. It is clear that the way to become an entrepreneur was to interface with these large institutions. That is what made Mesopotamian economies "mixed" rather than statist (run by public bureaucracies such as the "temple state" postulated in the 1920s) or strictly "private enterprise," as assumed by the older generation of economic modernists.

The public institutions established relationships with well-placed individuals, whose title—Sumerian *damgar*, Babylonian *tamkarum*—usually is translated as "merchant" or, by Babylonian times, "entrepreneur." Applying Israel Kirzner's (1979, 39) definition of the entrepreneur's role, Johannes Renger (2000, 155) points out that it is a seventeenth-century French term denoting "a person who entered into a contractual relationship with the government for the performance of a service or the supply of goods. The price at which the contract was valued was fixed and the entrepreneurs bore the risks of profit and loss from the bargain." An entrepreneur seeks economic gain either with his own money or, more often, operating with borrowed funds or managing the assets of others (including public institutions) to make something over for himself by cutting expenses or creating a business innovation. In Babylonia, the palace leased land and workshops at stipulated rents, and advanced textiles and other handicrafts to merchants engaged in long-distance trade. In the process of developing this enterprise, administrators and entrepreneurs created the managerial elements for large-scale production and market exchange to squeeze out an economic surplus and reinvest it to obtain further gains.

Debt Relationships

One sees traces of a tug of war between local magnates and the central palace, not unlike that between the barons and the kings of England in the twelfth century of the modern era. An important role of palace rulers, for instance, was to prevent interest-bearing debt—and subsequent foreclosure, especially by palace revenue collectors—from stripping away the citizenry's basic means of self-support. Royal "clean slates" preserved economic solvency by annulling agrarian "barley" debts (but not commercial "silver" debts), reversing land forfeitures, and freeing debt pledges from bondage. This meant that indebted citizens could lose their liberty and self-support lands only temporarily.

Ancient historians found the logic for these policies to be recognition that the infantry was drawn from the citizen body composed of landowning males. Hammurabi's laws, for example, assigned charioteers their own self-support lands, kept free from foreclosure. To have left these men to become prey to creditors expropriating their land and shifting to cash crops would have put Babylon in danger of conquest by outsiders.

The Near East thus managed to avert the debt problem that plagued classical antiquity. Although debt forced war widows and orphans into dependency and obliged the sick, infirm, or others to pledge and then lose their land's crop rights to creditors at the top of the economic pyramid, such forfeitures were limited to merely temporary duration (viz., the Jubilee Year of Leviticus 25 and its Babylonian antecedents). But they became permanent in Greece and Rome, reducing much of the population to the status of bondservants and unfree dependents. This is primarily what distinguishes the Greek and Roman oligarchies from the Near Eastern mixed economies. It proved much easier to cancel debts owed to the palace and its collectors in Mesopotamia than to annul debts owed to individual creditors acting on their own in classical times. (Even Roman emperors occasionally canceled tax arrears in order to alleviate widespread debt distress.)

Debt was the lever that made the land transferable in traditional societies, which usually had restrictions to prevent self-support land from being alienated outside of the family or clan. (Hudson and Levine 1999 gives examples.) By holding that the essence of private property is its ability to be sold or forfeited irreversibly, Roman law removed the archaic checks to foreclosure that prevented property from being concentrated in the hands of the few. In practice, this Roman concept of property is essentially creditor-oriented, and quickly became predatory. But as in the Near East, commercial law freed sea captains from debt liability in the case of shipwreck or piracy.

Documentation of Early Entrepreneurial Activity

Our sources oblige us to rely almost exclusively on archives and inscriptions from Babylonia, Assyria, and the neighboring lands for documentation regarding early economic organization. Little early primary data survive from Egypt, which in any event remained much more commercially self-contained than other parts of the Near East, save for its military incursions. We know from pictorial sources that there were markets, but according to Bleiberg (1995, 1382–83) the normal Egyptian state of affairs was a redistributive economy. The hints of entrepreneurial behavior are limited to "intermediate periods," transitions in which the pharaoh's power weakened and economic life became less centralized (as also occurred in Mesopotamia). "One recent exponent of the belief that there was a place for the private merchant in ancient Egypt is Morris Silver," comments Bleiberg. "Not surprisingly, the evidence that he adduces for private traders comes from the First Intermediate Period and the end of the Ramesside period, both times of weak or nonexistent central government. The existence of such traders is never attested in Egyptian sources from periods when the economic apparatus of the central government was functioning well."

No written records exist for the Indus Valley, although archaeological evidence shows that it traded with southern Mesopotamia via the island of Dilmun (modern Bahrain) in the third and second millennia BC. Phoenician society and its colonies to the west in Carthage and Spain in the first millennium are also undocumented. The syllabic record-keeping found in Crete and Mycenaean Greece from 1600 to 1200 BC pertains only to the collection and distribution of products, not enterprise as such.

The largest archives dealing with entrepreneurs are from Neo-Babylonian times. Nothing remotely as sophisticated is available in Greece or Rome even for the brief period in which economic magnitudes are recorded. "Since it was a part of upper-class etiquette for a rich man to pretend that he was not really well-to-do," D'Arms (1981, 154) points out, "the character and degree of senators' involvement in money-making ventures usually resist precise documentation." Andreau (1999, 17) notes that "when Brutus' money was loaned to the people of Salamis in Cyprus through the intermediaries Scaptius and Matinius, these two were the sole official creditors. Until Brutus revealed his hand in the affair, neither the people of Salamis nor Cicero knew that the sums loaned belonged to him." We would not know either, if not for the political exposés, lawsuits, and prosecutions that illuminate how predatory fortunes were made in Greece and Rome. (Matters may not be so different today. Former New York attorney general Eliot Spitzer's prosecutions and reports by congressional committees on investigations have done more to describe corporate and banking practices than a generation of management textbooks has done.)

Economic details are available only for about two centuries of Roman history, circa 150 BC to AD 50. Business archives are lacking, as the focus is mainly military and political. After Augustus, MacMullen (1974, 48) notes, "Among thousands of inscriptions that detail the gifts made by patrons to guilds, cities, or other groups, only a tiny number indicate where the donor got his money." For Greece, the window of economic visibility is several centuries earlier, with lawsuits here too being major sources of information. In any event, it was the Near Eastern forerunners of Greece and Rome that provided the models and literally the vocabulary of commerce and banking, contractual formalities, and other preconditions for market exchange and enterprise.

Productive versus Corrosive Enterprise

In light of this *longue durée*, the problem for economic historians is to explain why commerce and enterprise yielded to a Dark Age. What stifled enterprise thousands of years after the Near Eastern takeoff? For a century the culprit was assumed to be state regulation. But it was the temples and palaces of Sumer and Babylonia that first introduced most basic commercial innovations, including the first formal prices and markets. The collapse of antiquity can be traced more to oligarchies capturing the state and dismantling the checks and balances that had kept economies in the Near East from polarizing to so fatal an extent between creditors and debtors, patrons and their clients, free men and slaves. The ascent of Rome saw laws become more creditor-oriented and property appropriations more irreversible, while the tax burden was shifted increasingly onto the lower orders.

Hereditary landed wealth tends to gravitate toward corrosive forms of enterprise, and the Greek and Roman mode of gain seeking was more military than commercial. It was as if the privileged aristocrats who inherited favorable economic and political status felt embarrassed at having to try actively to gain wealth by commercial activity (especially retail trade with social inferiors) instead of producing it (and consuming or distributing it) on their own estates. Much like sex in Victorian England, everyone seemed to be doing it, but it did not add to one's prestige. That stemmed from autonomy, not commerce. The classical ideal was to remain self-sufficient and independent on large estates, not to dirty one's hands by engaging in trade and moneylending. It therefore seems somewhat ironic that, on an economy-wide scale, the oligarchy depleted the home market. Its members stripped away much of the land from the community through debt foreclosure, reduced the population to bondage, and brought commerce and even the money economy to an end, leading to western Europe's Dark Age.

The oligarchic ethic preferred seizing wealth abroad to creating it at home. The major ways to make fortunes were by conquest, raiding and piracy, slave capture and slave dealing, moneylending, tax farming, and kindred activities more predatory than entrepreneurial. Gaining wealth by extracting it from others was deemed to be at least as noble (if not more so) than doing so commercially, which was deemed to be equally exploitative without the exercise of personal bravery. "When I was young it was safe and dignified to be a rich man," complained Isocrates in Athens during that city-state's struggles between democracy and oligarchy; "now one has to defend oneself against the charge of being rich as if it were the worst of crimes" (*Antidosis* 159–60, quoted in Humphreys 1978, 297). The result of this disparaging attitude is that although entrepreneurs stood at the economy's fulcrum points—managing estates, organizing shipping and public construction, operating workshops, and provisioning armies—they worked in an environment less and less conducive to such activities over the course of antiquity, and sought to become more leisurely rentiers and philanthropists. The broad effect was to exhaust the regions absorbed into antiquity's empires.

The moral is that what is most important for society is the institutional set of rules and social values that govern how entrepreneurs gain wealth. The path does not always lead upward toward higher productivity, to say nothing of greater efficiency for social development or even survival. There are many ways to seek economic gain. "Indeed," observes Baumol (1990, 894), "at times the entrepreneur may even lead a parasitical existence that is actually damaging to the economy." By classical antiquity the three most lucrative areas of gain seeking were tax farming, public building contracts, and provisioning the palaces, temples, and army. Building a fortune involved interfacing with the state under conditions where the surplus took the form of tribute, usury, land grabbing, and profiteering from public administrative position. The domestic surplus, and ultimately the land itself, was obtained increasingly via interest-bearing debt (often via foreclosure or forced sale) and by conquest.

If enterprise is defined as part of an overall social system that sets its rules, one finds a shift occurring from the Bronze Age Near East to classical Greece and Rome from productive to unproductive enterprise. "If entrepreneurs are defined, simply, to be persons who are ingenious and creative in finding ways that add to their own wealth, power, and prestige," Baumol concludes (1990, 897–98), "then it is to be expected that not all of them will be overly concerned with whether an activity that achieves these goals adds much or little to the social product or, for that matter, even whether it is an actual impediment to production (this notion goes back, at least, to Veblen 1904)."[2]

Rome's wealthiest and most prominent families sought to make as many clients, debtors, and slaves as dependent as possible through force, usury, and control of the land. This predatory rentier spirit led to the century-long Social War (133–29 BC) that saw the Republic polarize economically, paving the way for the subsequent empire to give way to serfdom. One looks in vain for the idea that profit-seeking enterprise might drive society forward to achieve higher levels of production and living standards. No major minds set about developing a policy for society or even the oligarchy as a class to get rich by economic growth and development of an internal market.

Some Myths regarding the Genesis of Enterprise

If a colloquium on early entrepreneurs had been convened a century ago, most participants would have viewed traders as operating on their own, bartering at prices that settled at a market equilibrium established spontaneously, in response to fluctuating supply and demand. According to the Austrian economist Carl Menger, money emerged as individuals and merchants involved in barter came to prefer silver and copper as convenient means of payment, stores of value, and standards by which to measure other prices. But instead of supporting the Austrian School's individualistic scenario for how commercial practices developed—trade, money and credit, interest and pricing—history shows that they do not emerge spontaneously among individuals "trucking and bartering." Rather, investment for the purpose of creating profits, the charging of interest, creation of a property market and even a proto-bond market (for temple prebends) first emerged in the temples and palaces of Sumer and Babylonia.

It now has been established that from third-millennium Mesopotamia through classical antiquity the minting of precious metal of specified purity occurred under the aegis of temples or other public agencies, not private suppliers. The word *money* itself derives from Rome's temple of Juno Moneta, where it was coined in early times. Silver money was part of the pricing system, developed by the large institutions to establish stable ratios for their account-keeping and forward planning. Major price ratios (including the rate of interest) initially were administered in round numbers for ease of calculation (Renger 2000, 2002; Hudson and Wunsch 2004).

Rather than deterring enterprise, administered prices provided a stable context for it to flourish. The palace estimated a normal return for the fields and other properties it leased out, and left managers to make a profit—or suffer a loss when the weather was bad or other risks materialized. In such cases shortfalls became debts. However, when the losses became so great as to threaten this system, the palace let the arrears go, enabling entrepreneurs to start again with a clean slate (Renger 2002). The aim was to keep them in business, not to destroy them.

More flexible pricing seems to have occurred in the quay areas along the canals. Rather than a conflict existing between the large public institutions administering prices and mercantile enterprise, there was a symbiotic and complementary relationship. Liverani (2005, 53–54) points out that administered pricing by the temples and palaces vis-à-vis *tamkarum* merchants engaged in foreign trade "was limited to the starting move and the closing move: trade agents got silver and/or processed materials (that is, mainly metals and textiles) from the central agency and had to bring back after six months or a year the equivalent in exotic products or raw materials. The economic balance between central agency and trade agents could not but be regulated by fixed exchange values. But the merchants' activity once they left the palace was completely different: They could freely trade, playing on the different prices of the various items in various countries, even using their money in financial activities (such as loans) in the time span at their disposal, and making the maximum possible personal profit."

A century ago it would have been assumed that the state's economic role could only have taken the form of oppressive taxation and overregulation of markets, and hence would have thwarted commercial enterprise. This is how Rostovtzeff (1926) depicted the imperial Roman economy stifling the middle class. But Jones (1964) has pointed out that this was how antiquity ended, not how it began. Merchants and entrepreneurs first emerged in conjunction with the public temples and palaces of Mesopotamia. Rather than being despotic and economically oppressive, Mesopotamian religious values sanctioned the commercial takeoff that ended up being thwarted in Greece and Rome. Archaeology has confirmed that "modern" elements of enterprise were present and even dominant already in Mesopotamia in the third millennium BC, and that the institutional context was conducive to long-term growth. Commerce expanded and fortunes were made as populations grew and the material conditions of life rose. What has surprised many observers is how much more successful, fluid, and also stable these arrangements are seen to be as we move back in time.

What led many generalists to trace the origins of commercial practices less than halfway back from the modern era to Mesopotamia's takeoff two thousand years earlier was the idea of *Western* as a synonym for private sector. For a century, Near Eastern development was deemed to lie outside the Western continuum, which was defined as starting with classical Greece circa 750 BC. But what was novel and "fresh" in the Mediterranean lands was mainly the fact that the Bronze Age world fell apart in the devastation that occurred circa 1200 BC. The commercial and debt practices that Syrian and Phoenician traders brought to the Aegean and southern Italy around the eighth century BC were adopted in smaller local contexts that lacked the public institutions found throughout the Near East. Trade and usury enriched chieftains much more than temples or other public authority set corporately apart to mediate the economic surplus, and especially to provide credit.

Growing awareness of the fact that the character of gain-seeking became economically predatory has prompted the past generation to take a more sociological view of exchange and property in classical Greece and Rome (e.g., the French structuralists, Kurke 1999, and Reden 1995), but a more "economic" post-Polanyian view of earlier Mesopotamia and its Near Eastern neighbors.

Morris and Manning (2005) survey how the approach that long segregated Near Eastern from Mediterranean development has been replaced by a more integrated view (e.g., Braudel 1972 and Hudson 1992), in tandem with a panregional approach to myth and religion (Burkert 1984 and West 1997) and art (Kopcke and Takamaru 1992). The motto *ex oriente lux* now is seen to apply to commercial practices as well as to art, culture and religion.

Some Contrasts between Enterprise in Antiquity and Today

A number of differences between antiquity's economic practices and those of the modern world should be borne in mind with regard to the changing context for enterprise. Rather than being autonomous, handicraft workshops were located on basically self-sufficient landed estates, including those of the large public institutions. Such industry was self-financed rather than using credit, which was extended mainly for long-distance and bulk trade.

From Babylonian times down through imperial Rome, commercial earnings tended to be invested in land. Yet there was no land speculation based on rising prices. At most, subsistence land was shifted to growing cash crops, headed by olive oil and wine in the Mediterranean, and dates in the Near East, harvested increasingly by slaves working at lower cost.

We do not find banking intermediaries lending out people's savings to entrepreneurial borrowers. Throughout the Near East, what have been called "banking families" such as the Egibi (described by Wunsch in this volume) are best thought of as general entrepreneurs. They did hold deposits and made loans, but they paid the same rate of interest to depositors as they charged for their loans (normally 20 percent annually). There thus was no margin for arbitrage, and no credit superstructure to magnify the supply of monetary metal on hand. (See the discussion in Hudson and Van De Mieroop 2002, 345ff.) Promissory notes circulated only among closely knit groups of *tamkaru*, so a broad superstructure of credit was only incipient, and did not come to fruition until modern times with the development of fractional-reserve banking from the seventeenth century onward (see Wray 2004, especially the articles by Ingham and Gardiner). Most lending either was for commercial trade ventures—in which the creditor shared in the risk as well as the gain—or took the form of predatory agrarian loans or claims for arrears on taxes or other fees owed to royal or imperial collectors. Down to modern times, small-scale personal debt was viewed as the first step toward forfeiting one's property, a danger to be entered into only unwillingly. The dominant ethic was to keep assets free of debt, especially land. In any case, property almost never was bought or sold on credit in the modern sense, although sometimes a short delay in payment secured by an asset might be permitted.

Moneylending in classical Greece was mainly in the hands of outsiders, foreigners such as Pasion in Athens, and in Rome low-status individuals headed by freedmen and slaves. The Roman elite left banking in the hands of freedmen, ex-slaves who "confine[d] their activities to bridging loans and the provision of working capital," operating only "on the margins of trade and industry" (Jones 2006, 245).

Throughout antiquity entrepreneurs tended not to specialize but to pursue a broad range of activities organizing and managing voyages, fields, workshops, or other productive units. They rarely acted by themselves for just their own account but as part of a system. Traders and "merchants" tended to work via guilds, such as those organized by Assyrian traders early in the second millennium, and in the Syrian and "Phoenician" trade with Aegean and Mediterranean lands by the eighth century BC. Balmunamhe in Old Babylonian times, Assyrian traders in Asia Minor (Dercksen 1999, 86), the Egibi in Neo-Babylonia, Cato and other Romans spread their capital over numerous sectors—long-distance and local trade, provisioning the palace or temples with food and raw materials, leasing fields and workshops, moneylending and (often as an outgrowth) real estate.

Even as late as the second century BC when we begin to pick up reports of the Roman *publicani*, they had not yet begun to specialize. Despite the fact that collecting taxes and other public revenue must have required a different set of skills from furnishing supplies to the army and other public agencies, most *publicani* acted opportunistically on an ad hoc basis. "What the companies provided was capital and top management, based on general business experience," observes Badian (1972, 37), probably with a small permanent staff of assistants and subordinates. An entrepreneur might run a ceramic workshop, a metal workshop, or the like, as well as dealing in slaves or renting them out. As Jones (1974, 871) concludes: "The term *negotiator* was widely interpreted, including not only merchants, shopkeepers and craftsmen but moneylenders and prostitutes."

There was no such thing as patent protection or "intellectual property" rights, and little thought of what today would be called market development. Artistic styles and new techniques were copied freely. Finley (1973, 147) cites the story, "repeated by a number of Roman writers, that a man—characteristically unnamed—invented unbreakable glass and demonstrated it to Tiberius in anticipation of a great reward. The emperor asked the inventor whether anyone shared his secret and was assured that there was no one else; whereupon his head was promptly removed, lest, said Tiberius, gold be reduced to the value of mud...neither the elder Pliny nor Petronius nor the historian Dio Cassius was troubled by the point that the inventor turned to the emperor for a reward, instead of turning to an investor for capital with which to put his invention into production." Finley holds discouragement of an entrepreneurial ethic along these lines to be largely responsible for the fact that antiquity never embraced or even formulated the modern goal of achieving technological progress and economic growth. "What is missing in this picture," he concludes (1973, 158), "is commercial or capitalist exploitation. The ancient economy had its own form of cheap labour and therefore did not exploit provinces in that way. Nor did it have excess capital seeking the more profitable investment outlets we associate with colonialism."

As noted above, however, the most recent generation of economic historians has criticized Finley for being too extreme in doubting the existence of gain-seeking investment and "modern" economic motivation. There are many examples of Baumol's "productive enterprise," especially in the Near East. What remains accepted is that usury and slavery became increasingly predatory and corrosive practices, and that wars were fought mainly to strip the wealth of prosperous regions as booty to distribute at home.

Entrepreneurs, Predators, and Financiers

How many of these activities were truly entrepreneurial in the productive and innovative sense understood today? The key to defining productive entrepreneurs should be their contribution to generating an economic surplus, not merely transferring it or, even worse, stripping the economy. War making and piracy to seize booty and slaves were common predatory activities, and the largest fortunes known in antiquity were made by conquering or administering foreign lands and collecting taxes from defeated populations. So not all fortunes were amassed through enterprise, and not all managers were entrepreneurs.

Even when entrepreneurs played a nominally productive role, they worked in a war-oriented environment. A major source of fortunes was provisioning of the army, mainly with food but also with manufactured goods. Frank (1933, 291) notes that during 150–80 BC "we hear of only one man...who gained wealth by manufacturing, and that was in public contracts for weapons during the Social War (Cicero, *in Pis*. 87–89)." On the retail level, Polanyi's paradigmatic example of free price-making markets was the small-scale food-sellers who followed Greek armies. Provisioning food was indeed the main activity, but much more economically aggressive were the public contractors who supplied Roman armies on the wholesale level. Contracts were let out at auctions that became notoriously "fixed" by the first century BC.

Financial extraction is a form of enterprise very different from industrial investment. Evolving largely as a by-product of collecting public fees and taxes in Babylonia, moneylending grew from a side activity of the *tamkaru* to a major focus of the Roman *publicani*. Weber (1976, 316) refers to Rome's publican companies as enterprises, but most writers today depict them as predatory. MacMullen (1974, 51–52) notes the increasingly agrarian focus of moneylending, citing Rostovtzeff's calculation that mortgage loans yielded "either fields foreclosed or interest in the neighborhood of 6 to 8 per cent. The rate compared favorably with the 6 per cent (at least in Italy) that one might reasonably hope for from money invested in agriculture. At that, one's money doubled in a dozen years. Why take a chance in trade?" The effect was to divert capital to agriculture and usury.

There may be a fine line demarcating an investor from an entrepreneur, but the latter certainly must play a more active managerial role than rentiers such as the Old Babylonian *naditu* heiresses investing their inheritance by making loans and buying revenue-yielding properties (although Yoffee 1995 refers to these women as entrepreneurs and some no doubt acted in this way). Cato's treatise on agriculture acknowledged that trade and usury were more lucrative than farming, but warned that commerce was risky and moneylending was considered immoral. Landowners needed managerial talent, but are not usually deemed entrepreneurs. A rental levy or property foreclosure is not profit earned in production, except to the extent that land use is upgraded (which did indeed occur, to date palms in the Near East and to olive growing in Italy).

The key to whether engaging in a trade was entrepreneurial depends on the degree to which one worked for oneself or as an agent or employee sharing directly in the profits of buying and selling. And furthermore, although self-employed craftsmen often doubled as sellers of their wares, they would not qualify as entrepreneurs unless they also acted as managers and organizers of a complex system. Humphreys (1978, 153) points out the problem of deeming craftsmen entrepreneurial:

> To run a workshop in an "entrepreneurial" spirit would have required supervision by the owner. Instead, the workshops of which we know details were managed by slaves or freedman, and the owner drew a fixed income from them. There was no interest in expansion.... Demosthenes' father owned two workshops, one making beds and the other knives: there was no connection between them. Pasion's bank and shield-factory were equally unconnected and it is significant that while Pasion, an ex-slave, evidently devoted considerable energy and personal attention to the bank, his son Apollodorus (who received Athenian citizenship with his father) acquired three estates, preferred the shield-factory to the bank as his share of the inheritance, and devoted his energies to politics and the showy performance of liturgies, in the style of an Athenian gentleman. As metic traders and bankers became more important to the prosperity and food-supply of the city, the most successful of them were rewarded with citizen privileges, came under pressure for gifts and contributions to the *demos*, and tended to adopt the ethos of the rich citizens rather than encourage the latter to venture into new fields of investment.

There was a basic conflict between social ambition for high status and the aristocratic antipathy to engaging directly in business ventures. "Although Aristotle asserted that 'unnatural' *chrematistike* (money-making) knew no bounds," Humphreys concludes, "the general impression given by our sources is that the majority of Athenians were quite ready to give up the effort to make money as soon as they could afford a comfortable *rentier* existence, and that even the few who continued to expand their operations could not pass on the same spirit to their sons. The result was small-scale, disconnected business ventures, assessed by the security of their returns rather than their potentiality for expansion."

The most typical form of enterprise remained long-distance trade. Its organizational pattern changed little from the epoch when Mesopotamia's temples and palaces provided merchants with commodities or money. Drawing a parallel with the medieval Italian *commenda* and *compagnia*, as well as the Arabic *muqarada* practice, Larsen (1974, 470) views such entrepreneurs as administering advances of money or inventories from their backers.

Opportunities for making money evolved as a by-product of this mercantile role. In Old-Sumerian documents, Leemans (1950, 11) notes, "damkara are only found as traders. But when private business began to flourish after the beginning of the third dynasty of Ur [2112–2004 BC], the *tamkarum* was the obvious person to assume the function of giver of credit." By the time of Hammurabi's Babylonian laws, in many cases "*tamkarum* cannot denote a traveling trader, but must be a money-lender." Leemans concludes (22): "The development from merchant into banker [that is, a moneylender or investor backing voyages and similar partnerships] is a natural one, and there is no essential difference between these two professions—surely not in Babylonia where in principle no distinction was made between silver (money in modern terms) and other marketable stuffs. In a society whose commerce is little developed, trade is only carried on by merchants, who buy and sell. But when commerce increases, the business of a merchant assumes larger proportions."

As merchants rose to the position of being able to supply money to agents and subordinates, after the model of the early temples, these varied functions were telescoped into the word *tamkarum*. But none of them involved banking in the modern sense of the term. *Tamkarum* merchants did not lend out deposits, but worked with their own funds. By the same token, individuals who accumulated savings had to invest these personally or participate in partnerships. Although merchants formed guilds to coordinate their trading activities in foreign regions, there were no formal money managers outside of families.

Over time, financial backers gained ascendancy over on-the-spot traders, largely because trade was a risky and speculative business in which wrecks or piracy ate up much of the gain. By the late Roman Empire, explains Jones (1964, 867–68), "so much depended on an intimate knowledge of shippers and their ships [that it] did not appeal to the ordinary investor and was usually conducted by men, often retired sea captains, who specialised in the work." A specialization of functions developed, although nothing like the large trading companies found in England and Holland in the seventeenth century, for instance (the Russia Company, the East India Company, and so forth). "In maritime commerce a distinction must be drawn between the shipper (*navicularius*), the captain (*magister*) and the merchant (*mercator*, *negotiator*) or his agent. All these roles might be, and very commonly were, filled by one man, the owner of a vessel which he navigated himself and which he loaded with cargoes which he bought and sold. There were, however, shipowners who did not navigate their own ships."

Reflecting the disdain in which active participation in money-seeking commerce was held by antiquity's aristocratic ethic, most of the shippers engaged in Rome's maritime trade were foreigners or ex-slaves owning one or two small sailing vessels. Whether the shipper was wealthy or a petty tradesman, explains Jones (1964, 868), he "rarely depended on his own capital, exclusively, preferring to raise nautical loans, which would partially cover him against loss by storm. For such loans, since the creditor stood the risk of losing his money if the ship were wrecked or the cargo jettisoned, the rate of interest was subject to no legal limit, until Justinian in 528 fixed the maximum at 12 per cent. per annum, as against 8 per cent. for ordinary commercial loans and 6 per cent. for private loans."

Undertaking risk does not in itself make an activity entrepreneurial. Nearly everyone was subject to risk, and laws took a pragmatic approach in recognizing this fact. Cultivators and sharecroppers faced the possibility of drought, flooding, and military hostilities. At least in the Near East, rents and fees owed to the large institutions and other creditors were annulled in such circumstances. In the commercial sphere, when ships were lost at sea or their caravans were robbed, commercial laws from Babylonia down through Roman times freed traveling merchants from the obligation to repay their backers.

The well-to-do accordingly spread their risk by taking partial investment shares in many ventures, much as Lloyd's insurance does in modern times. Plutarch describes Cato as "requir[ing] his borrowers to form a large company (*epi koinonia*)," summarizes D'Arms (1981, 39), "and then when there were fifty partners, and as many ships for security, he took one share in the company himself and was represented by Quintio, a freedman of his, who accompanied his clients in all of their

KAUFFMAN FOUNDATION SERIES ON
Innovation and Entrepreneurship

*Boulevard of Broken Dreams: Why Public Efforts to Boost
Entrepreneurship and Venture Capital Have Failed—
and What to Do About It,* BY JOSH LERNER

ventures. In this way his entire security was not imperiled, but only a small part of it, and his profits were large."

Plutarch describes Cato as anticipating what Weber would call the Protestant ethic. He was a stingy and self-abnegating man who did not enjoy the riches he made, refusing to buy expensive clothes or food for himself, preferring to drink the same lowly wine as his workmen, and turning out old and worn-out slaves when they no longer could do enough work to justify their support. In his public role he cut costs, opposed corruption, and increased the price that Rome received for farming out its taxes while minimizing the prices given out in public contracts. "To incline his son to be of his kind of temper, he used to tell him that it was not like a man, but rather like a widow to lessen an estate. But the strongest indication of Cato's avaricious humor was when he took the boldness to affirm that he was a most wonderful, nay, a godlike man, who left more behind him than he had received." The emphasis that Plutarch gives to his behavior suggests that such economic calculation was exceptional.

To sum up, entrepreneurs either headed wealthy families or sought fortunes by managing other people's money, which typically was provided subject to a stipulated return. Regardless of the source of their capital, they coordinated a complex set of relationships whose institutional structure evolved throughout the second and first millennia BC.

Social Status of Merchants and Entrepreneurs

In Babylonia after about 1800 BC, Renger explains (2000, 155; see also 1984, 64), the entrepreneurs to whom the palace leased fields, herds, and workshops tended to be "members of the elite or upper classes." The title of *damgar* or *tamkarum* merchant presupposed social status and connections to the palace or temple bureaucracy, administering franchises in "a form of economic management termed by F. R. Kraus as 'Palastgeschäft.'" Some managers worked in the palace bureaucracy, but others worked entirely on their own account. Renger (2000, 178) notes that the prominent Balmunamhe was a private *tamkarum* merchant, not a palace functionary. (Van De Mieroop 1987 surveys the archive recording his activities.)

By contrast, the absence of public entrepreneurial institutions and indeed, the less trade-oriented aristocratic ethic prevalent from Greece through Rome, led foreigners to play a leading commercial role throughout most of the Mediterranean. It was Syrian and Phoenician traders who brought Near Eastern commercial and economic practices to Greece and Italy in the ninth and eighth centuries BC, and by the end of the Roman Empire only Near Eastern traders were left, as commerce in the West shrank to a small scale. During the interim, the westward shift of antiquity's military and political center was associated with a lower status for commercial enterprise, mainly because its association with aliens and low-status individuals deterred high-status individuals from taking a direct role. Apart from the Near Easterners, slaves and freedmen played the leading role in Greece and Rome. Humphreys (1978, 148) describes them as becoming "foremen, managers of shops and workshops, captains of trading vessels and bailiffs of estates; slaves acquired legal capacity in lawsuits concerning banking and trade; they increasingly often lived and worked independently, paying a fixed sum to their masters and accumulating surplus earnings, if they could, toward the purchase of their freedom;...in banking, where success depended heavily on experience and goodwill, a slave could rise to citizenship and the highest level of wealth," gaining status by acting as a philanthropist or public official.

Commenting on the link between the scale of business and social prestige, Cicero expressed the prevalent attitude of his time (*De officiis* I, 150–51): "Public opinion divides the trades and professions into the liberal and the vulgar. We condemn the odious occupation of the collector of customs and the usurer, and the base and menial work of unskilled laborers; for the very wages the laborer receives are a badge of slavery. Equally contemptible is the business of the retail dealer; for he cannot succeed unless he is dishonest, and dishonesty is the most shameful thing in the world. The work of the mechanic is also degrading; there is nothing noble about a workshop. The least respectable of all trades are those which minister to pleasure." He seems to be representative of his time and place in explaining that "business on a small scale is despicable; but if it is extensive and imports commodities in large quantities from all over the world and distributes them honestly, it is not so very discreditable; nay, if the merchant, satiated, or rather, satisfied, with the fortune he has made, retires from the harbor and steps into an estate, as once he returned to harbor from the sea, he deserves, I think, the highest respect. But of all the sources of wealth, farming is the best, the most able, the most profitable, the most noble."

It helped to be born rich and with much land. And when one was rich enough to purchase a governorship, it was reputable and almost a source of pride to squeeze as much as one could out of the provinces. In modern terms, the Roman ethic preferred "bad" or unproductive enterprise, asset stripping, and hoarding over more economically productive modes of gain-seeking.

This set of economic values went hand in hand with highly stratified Roman commercial roles with respect to nationality and political and economic status. Entrepreneurs played a subordinate role, as the aristocracy preferred dealing with high finance on the public plane and involving itself with commerce only as rentiers. Emphasizing the linkage between landownership and the financing of commerce, Weber (1976, 316) points out that the publican companies "were the largest capitalist enterprises in Antiquity.... Participation in these enterprises was limited to men with vast capital holdings in slaves and cash. They also needed to have extensive landed possessions, preferably with Italic status (which was privileged and therefore at an economic advantage), since they had to offer land as security when bidding for contracts. This last condition, by which only land enjoying full privileges under Roman land law could be offered as security, had the effect of giving the capitalist class in the Roman state a distinctively national character. It was much more so than had any similar class been in the Near East. Under the Ptolemies, for example, the publicans seem to have been mainly foreigners, and in Greece the smaller states actually encouraged foreign capitalists to make bids in order to have more competition."

What made Rome unusual, continues Weber (1976, 317), was that despite the fact that "exclusion of aristocrats from direct involvement in industry was common throughout Antiquity," in Rome "this exclusion was extended to include tax farming and shipping; a senator might possess ships only of a capacity just sufficient to transport the products of his own estates. As a result, senators could gain wealth only from political office, from the rents paid by their tenants, from mortgages assumed through the agency of freedmen (though this was forbidden, it was commonly done as early as Cato), and from indirect investment in commerce and shipping. On the other side was the class of capitalists [the publican class of equestrian knights], the men who participated directly in capitalist enterprise. They were excluded from the Senate.... From the time of Gaius Gracchus they formed a legally constituted order," increasingly detested for profiteering at society's expense. A widening divide emerged between the various ways to make fortunes.

The Public Context in Which Entrepreneurs Operated

By the time Assyria developed far-flung trade relations with Asia Minor in the nineteenth century BC, private merchants had come to play a much larger role than in the south, in Sumer and Babylonia. Larsen (1974, 469) describes the Assyrian trade as "venturing, *i.e.* all shipments were sent abroad without the sender being guaranteed a certain price for them in advance." He adds: "The economically decisive element in the Assyrian society is not found on the 'state level,' even though the role played by the temples is still somewhat obscure. Instead, the trade is clearly organized via a great number of large kinship-based groups, called 'houses,' which we may provisionally describe as 'firms.'" Mercantile guilds functioned as trade associations representing merchants vis-à-vis local authorities, reducing the risks involved by creating an "underlying pattern of permanent representation, partnerships, and 'factories.'"

Moving westward from the Near East to the Mediterranean we find more predatory and corrosive economic strategies as society became more "individualistic," that is, oligarchic. Yet even in Rome, where the links between positive commercial enterprise and the state were looser than elsewhere (Weber 1976, 316), the most successful entrepreneurial path was to work in conjunction with public institutions. Contracts for public works and services have been traced back to the fourth century BC, first to provide supplies for religious rituals, public building, and similar civic projects, and then for the operation of public enterprises (from fields to mines and workshops) and collection of public fees and revenues. Provisioning the army soon became the largest category of contracts, along with collecting taxes from defeated lands.

Lacking a permanent public or royal bureaucracy such as characterized the Near Eastern mixed economies, the government needed private suppliers for services it could not perform itself and relied on private individuals to collect its taxes and administer its domains. Rome's absence of civic oversight or even significant taxation of business enabled businessmen to profiteer at public expense. "The publican's chief profits came from the *ultro tributa* (contracts for goods and services, especially army supplies)," summarizes Badian (1972, 24). In view of the scale involved, even a small rate of profit could produce a large fortune. But Rome's financial knights were most notorious for their predatory behavior. Livy (XLV 18, 4) complained famously that "where there was a *publicanus*, there was no effective public law and no freedom for the subjects." Describing how publican tax collectors enslaved debtors, selling many in the market on Delos, Badian (1972, 33) cites the report of Diodorus (V 38) regarding Spain's fabulously rich iron and silver mines, where publican managers "literally worked [slaves] to death as quickly as possible, to produce the maximum of profit in the shortest possible time." The resulting economic polarization was aggravated as mines passed into private hands during the Republic, many into those of Crassus (Frank 1933, 374).

A comparison of antiquity's leading families with the Forbes lists of today's richest individuals in many countries shows a common basis of well-placed families taking control of the land, mineral rights, and other enterprises from the state, and leasing them for a stipulated rent to be paid to the civic authority. State monopolies for salt, mining, and even the postal service were farmed out down through medieval European times. In due course rent-seeking individuals took direct possession of these assets, especially in lands that were conquered. In Egypt, Johnson (1946, v) finds: "The Romans apparently surrendered the Ptolemaic monopolies to private enterprise, and Alexandria developed as one of the most important centres of trade and industry in the empire." The Romans themselves sought not so much to gain via workshops and industry (Frank 1933, 291) as to profiteer from the state and the provinces it conquered. The time frame of merchants and financial rentiers always has been notoriously short—and shortened further as debt bondage, asset stripping, and economic polarization dried up domestic markets.

Financing Enterprise

Many economic historians (e.g., Andreau 1999, 151–51, and earlier Humphreys 1978, 151, and Larsen 1974, 470) have cited the terms of commercial lending in Babylonian times as prototypes not only for classical antiquity but for the Italian *commenda* loans of medieval Europe. Such loans combined interest-bearing debt with a profit-sharing partnership agreement. And often the senior partner was the palace or a temple—or, in classical times, the relevant civic authority.

Hammurabi's laws spell out how creditors shared in the debtor's risk under such contracts. Paragraphs 98–107 show the typical Babylonian arrangements governing trade. Merchants were to split their profit fifty-fifty with their backers, keeping strict books recording their activities. Paragraph 100 explains the normal procedure: "If a merchant gives silver to a trading agent for conducting business transactions and sends him off on a business trip...[and] if he should realize [a profit] where he went, he shall calculate the total interest, per transaction and time elapsed, on as much silver as he took, and he shall satisfy his merchant" (translation Roth 1995). If he reports no profit, he must give his backer(s) double the original advance (par. 101). If he makes a loss, he still has to return the original capital sum (par. 102). However, paragraph 103 stipulates that he shall be free of debt if he is robbed or if a ship sinks and its cargo is lost. But a merchant is liable for triple damages if witnesses claim he has testified falsely about how much he has been advanced (par. 106).

Most commercial loans throughout antiquity took the form of such shipping loans. They paid a high return (20 percent in the Near East, plus a share of the trading profits) because of the risk that the ship might not reach port safely. From Sumer down through Rome, the merchant's debt was canceled if his ship was lost at sea or raided by pirates, or if a caravan was robbed. This gave such borrowing the character of marine insurance to the shipper, while limiting such backing to experienced professionals down through Roman times.

Veenhof (1999, 55) describes the drive for financial gain by Assyrian caravans bringing "tin and woollen textiles into Anatolia in order to convert them, directly or indirectly, into silver, which was invariably shipped back to Assur. After necessary payments had been made (expenses, taxes, debts, interest, dividend), much of what remained was again used for commercial purposes, either directly, by contributing to or equipping a new caravan, or indirectly, by investing it in a firm or issuing a loan to a trader." This trade developed such modern credit innovations as "promissory notes which do not mention the creditor by name, but refer to him as *tamkarum*, 'the merchant/creditor.' In a few cases such notes add at the end the phrase 'the bearer of this tablet is *tamkarum*.' This clause suggests the possibility of a transfer of debt-notes and of ceding claims, which would make it a precursor of later 'bearer cheques'" (Veenhof 1999, 83).

Most agrarian debts were owed to royal collectors of rents, fees, and taxes or managers of public enterprises (including "ale women" who sold beer apparently advanced by the temples or palaces). Royal clean slates alleviated the risk that they might not be able to pay their debts as a result of natural disaster or warfare. Hammurabi's laws prescribed that if lands were flooded, the cultivator was freed from the obligation to pay rent. Annulling these debts also canceled those which royal agents and leaseholders owed to the palace. In times of weak rulers, it seems that these individuals were able to keep the rents and other fees in any event.

With respect to the situation in classical antiquity, Finley (1973, 141) cited three characteristics making the Greek and Roman economies premodern. First was the absence of productive loans—a view that subsequent economic historians have found extreme, to be sure, especially when the spread of Near Eastern models is recognized. Second was the fact that although "there was endless moneylending among both Greeks and Romans...all lenders were rigidly bound by the actual amount of cash on hand; there was not, in other words, any machinery for the *creation of credit* through negotiable instruments.... In Greek law sales were not legal and binding until the sale price had been paid in full; credit sales took the form of fictitious loans." Finally, most loans were short-term, mainly to finance voyages or overland trading expeditions.

There has been a tendency to assume that what Finley is describing must have been the "primitive" case from the outset. But as noted above, these generalities do not well apply to the Near East, especially for the complex financial arrangements found in Neo-Babylonian practice. The Egibi archive in particular stands in sharp contrast to the view by the past generation of economic historians of classical Greece and Rome, who find almost no productive lending for tangible capital investment. The Egibi took out antichretic loans—that is, advances where the collateral that secured the loan generated the interest being charged. This is the same strategy used by many real estate investors today, as expressed in the motto, "Rent is for paying interest." The family also pledged urban property (the "House of the Crown Prince") to obtain a commercial line of credit. Finally, their partnerships sometimes extended over more than one generation, as described by Wunsch in this volume.

The inability of historians of Greece and Rome to find anything so sophisticated makes the classical economies appear as the end-result of decay into more rudimentary financial arrangements. As Finley (1973, 108) famously noted in the most extreme statement of this view:

> There was no clear conception of the distinction between capital costs and labor costs, no planned ploughing back of profits, no long-term loans for productive purposes. The import in this context of the short-term loan (like the short-term tenancy) cannot be exaggerated. From one end of antiquity to another, one can easily count the known

examples of borrowing on property for purposes of purchase or improvement. The mortgage was a disaster ("mortgaging the old homestead"), a short-term personal loan designed to "cover deficiencies in the supply of necessities occasioned generally by some emergency which has made unexpected demands upon the resources of the borrower," not a deliberate device for raising money at a low rate in order to invest at a higher rate, [which is] the main function of the modern business mortgage.

Andreau (1999, 147–48) finds a few scattered examples of Roman business-men borrowing to tide their operations over or making delayed payment of a final balance owed to buy a business. However, he sums up: "Did Roman financiers direct most of their efforts towards economic life in order to create an effective instrument for investments? Did any financial establishments specialize in the promotion of productive loans? The answer to both questions must definitely be no."

One deterrent was the fact that Greek and Roman enterprises were organized as partnerships, as would characterize most trading companies throughout Europe down to the seventeenth century. "Every partner was held liable for the full amount of any debt and...the partnership came to an end at the death of any partner," Frank explains (1940, 217). "Under such strict limitations large business enterprises were not apt to prosper." Walbank (1969, 48) likewise cites the absence of permanent joint-stock corporations as discouraging enterprise: "Because of the risks entailed, it was always costly to raise capital for a trading venture; interest rates were high because the risk run was personal." Roman law did recognize that the large sums involved in public building projects required corporate organization, and on much the same logic the *publicani* knights also were empowered to organized companies to conduct public enterprise (including tax farming), above all that associated with military provisioning and other imperial spending. (Nicollet 1966 and Badian 1972 describe these activities.) However, notes Frank (1933, 350), "Roman law persisted in discouraging joint stock companies with limited liability in business not directly serving the state," and "firms dealing in state contracts were given business for only five-year terms." (See also D'Arms 1981, 41.)[3]

Also limiting the potential takeoff was the absence of paper credit. There was no public debt to manage. Budget deficits prompted the Roman emperors to adulter-ate the coinage, not to monetize their spending by creating public credit as national Treasuries and central banks do today.

These institutional constraints limited the buildup of capital reserves in mer-cantile undertakings and gave them an ad hoc character. The result, summarizes Frank (1940, 28), was that "partnerships based on the full liability of each member could hardly grow to great size." Under the empire, "We hear of no bankers of importance.... In the houses of the nobles the old custom still prevailed of trusting financial matters to personal slaves and freedmen, so that there was little room for investment banking; and in Rome's economic structure there was no place for cor-poration banking." This "led to business success not being held in any esteem...the only occupations befitting senators were agriculture, and civil or military office. Lucrative business in shipping, industry, and banking rested almost entirely in the hands of foreigners and freedmen. And to such people social position did not come, whatever the scale of their profits."

Freedmen played a key role in Roman enterprise and became some of Rome's most successful entrepreneurs when elite families provided them with a *peculium*, observes David Jones (2006, 244–45), but "did not produce a 'middle class' of businessmen." After getting their start, "non-economic values held sway." The sole upward mobility that ex-slaves enjoyed was to ape the landed aristocracy as best they could. "Trimalchio made a seamless transition from trading in mixed cargoes ('wine, bacon, beans, perfumes and slaves') to settling down on a country estate and providing finance for another generation of ex-slave entrepreneurs." This simply emulated what the philosopher Seneca "described [as] the characteristics of the 'fortunate man': a handsome family, a fine house, plenty of land under cultivation and plenty of money out on loan (*familiam formosam habet et domum pulchram, multum serit, multum fenerat*). Elsewhere he says that the rich man 'has gold furniture... a large book of loans (*magnus kalendarii liber*)... plenty of suburban property...' [Sen., *Epist*. 41.7; 87.7, cited in Jones 2006, 173.] And it was land and money out on loan that made up Seneca's own wealth."

Describing the freedmen who became bankers in Puteoli, the grain and export emporium on the Bay of Naples, 170 miles south of Rome, Jones (2006, 165) finds: "The business of the Sulpicii was built around the provision of small, short-term secured loans. There is no evidence in the Murecine archive to suggest that the Sulpicii or their depositors made medium- or long-term loans for capital projects such as the construction of ships, buildings or workshops. Nor is there any sign that the Sulpicii or their depositors lent money for high-risk, high-reward maritime ventures. Furthermore the bank operated on a local basis." Their loan market was local, despite the fact that they took in deposits and lent cash to members of the imperial household. "There is no suggestion that the acquisition of additional funds by the elite furthered, or could have furthered, the expansion of trade and industry," he concludes (2006, 174). "It was taken for granted by Roman commentators and their audiences that the Roman elite took no interest in commercial activities and did not consider investment in trade and industry as an appropriate use of their capital." It was a rather thoughtless extractive spirit with little concept of economic growth. This explains the feature of ancient enterprise noted by Baumol: the failure to commercialize technology, which began only in medieval times.

Entrepreneurs, Debt Abuses, and Shifting Property Relations

"Stretching the envelope" of what is deemed legal always has been most pronounced in the financial sphere. It was debt foreclosure that first turned family self-support land into absentee-owned property. Plutarch's melodramatic depiction of a Spartan father disinheriting his son and bequeathing his land to an acquaintance finds its counterpart over a thousand years earlier in Babylonia. To circumvent the traditional sanctions that prevented (and indeed, protected) citizens from alienating their subsistence land outside of their families, Babylonian creditors (and also those of Nuzi to the northwest) hit upon the tactic of getting their debtors to adopt them as "sons" and hence legitimate heirs to their land in payment for debt. These "fake adoptions" enabled creditors to start monopolizing the land, disenfranchising citizens and hence the community's fighting force.

The laws of Hammurabi (1750 BC) and his dynasty's "economic order" (*misharum* or *andurarum*) proclamations, culminating in that of Ammisaduqa (1648 BC), sought to preserve stability and a strong military capability by annulling agrarian and personal debts, preventing creditors from reducing citizens permanently to debt bondage. No equally broad context for the law is found in Greece or Rome. Without "divine rulership" or other central authority to check narrow self-interest, Rome in particular became harshly creditor-oriented and oligarchic.

Retail trade always has been notorious for cheating, and crooked practices such as using false weights and measures are rife from Babylonian "wisdom literature" down through biblical proverbs. But what is most noteworthy in classical times is large-scale fraud. The earliest description of the Roman *publicani* appears in a senatorial prosecution. When the Treasury was strapped during Rome's war with Carthage, suppliers obtained a government agreement to insure all supplies once they were loaded onto ships. Two eminent Etrurian contractors, T. Pomponious and M. Postumius, loaded "worthless goods on board unseaworthy ships and [claimed] the insurance sum for army supplies when the ships sank." Badian (1972, 17–18) remarks that "the incident...shows the *publicani*, on practically their first explicit appearance in our record, already organized as an extra-legal pressure group, already putting private profit above the public interest, and willing to defend a member of their class, no matter how bad his case." Cicero's surviving defense pleadings show the *publicani* continuing to stick together in a tacit compact of mutual support. There thus was little peer pressure to behave better—and if anything, mutual support for the most rapacious practices.

Rome's major attempt to prevent commercial abuses occurred in 133 BC, when Gaius Gracchus established a system of checks and balances whereby the Senate and the *publicani* knights were to act as mutual checks by prosecuting each other's misdeeds. But instead of the financial class turning into the "jury" class, the knights colluded with provincial administrators for mutual gain. The case of Verres in Sicily showed how crooked governors and businessmen made corrupt deals together. Cicero depicted him as a bad apple, and a time-honored strategy of businessmen has been to single out an individual as a scapegoat to be punished conspicuously so that the others can go about their business as usual. Verres became the sacrificial lamb, immortalized by Cicero's eloquent Verrines speeches. But the system itself had gone bad, culminating in the excesses of Brutus, Caesar, and other patricians looting Rome's provinces by levying extortionate taxes and tribute and then charging exorbitant interest on payment arrears. Badian (1972, 107) describes publican companies forming a cartel that "must have included the whole upper order of society and of the State, except for a few traditional aristocrats." The money was spent mainly on buying domestic Roman political support, as public administration and the right to loot ended up being a lucrative source of wealth—the antithesis of productive enterprise. It was said that a provincial governor "had to make three fortunes during his year's administration, one to pay his debts, another on which to retire, and a third to bribe the jurors in the inevitable trial for extortion" (Walbank 1969, 7). The Senate proved too weak and indifferent to stop such abuses. And inasmuch as the richest sources of loot were the most productive regions, the effect was to strip their capital and stifle economic growth wherever the empire reached.

From Commercial Entrepreneurship to Oligarchy

What is widely described as the individualistic spirit of Greece and Rome was primarily a military and increasingly oligarchic ethic of status and prestige. It relied on conquest and moneylending as the main sources of gain, disdaining profit-seeking commerce. The Theognid poetry of Greece in the seventh and sixth centuries BC reflects the conservative aristocratic ethic:

> ...this city is still a city, but truly the people are different.
> Those who, in the past, knew neither justice nor laws
> but wore out the goatskins which covered their sides
> and grazed like deer on the outskirts of the city,
> now these men are the nobles (*agathoi*)...
> and those who before were of the nobility (*esthloi*)
> now they are inferiors (*deiloi*).
> (Theognis 53–58, in Figueira and Nagy 1985, 16)

Commerce seemed akin to money-grubbing, a violation of the aristocratic ethic reflected in Aristotle's attitude finding "natural" self-sufficient householding more socially acceptable than commerce (*kapelike*). Humphreys (1978, 144) finds this spirit reflected in "the Theban law that anyone who had traded in the market within the last ten years could not hold political office [and] in the hostility against traders as foreigners callously exploiting the hardship of others which flared up in Athens when corn prices rose. A type of interaction in which each party was expected to consider only his own immediate economic advantage was a flagrant contradiction of every conception of social life: the man who lived by such transactions could only be an 'outsider.'" The irony is that a major factor stifling the Greco-Roman economic takeoff was the aristocratic disdain for enterprise, productive as well as predatory.

The Romans are credited with a genius for organization, but they devoted it mainly to organizing their army. The city's historians described its founders, Romulus and Remus, as feral children nurtured by a wolf, establishing a city of refuge between its two hills to attract exiles, refugees, and criminals who in due course became the basis of its citizen army. By the sixth century BC the city had built substantial defensive walls and the largest temple in Italy. The preconditions for a commercial takeoff were present, but a patrician oligarchy gained dominance through usury and land acquisition, with little thought that reducing much of the population to bondage would destroy the home market needed to grow.

Roman affluence—literally a "flowing in"—stemmed largely from slave capture and booty hunting, usury, and tribute from defeated realms. Military to the end, as Frank (1933, 399) summarized, "the larger fortunes during the last fifty corrupt years of the Republic [80–30 BC] came, not from business, but from military returns, from dealing in confiscated goods, and from various abuses of power. To these sources are traceable the wealth of Lucullus, Caesar, Pompey, and Crassus, who were the richest Romans of the period."

In today's economic terminology this was classic rent-seeking behavior. Instead of having a commercial strategy, "The aristocracy that directed Roman policy during the Republic was almost wholly agrarian-militaristic," Frank concluded (1940, 295). "Clearly, it was not less moved by an economic drive, by self-seeking, and by greed than the commercial societies of today. But the gain sought was of a different kind. The trade and commerce of the Mediterranean were then largely controlled by old seafaring peoples with whom the Roman nobles, wedded to agriculture, could not compete with success, or by ex-slaves accustomed to trade, who had no influence in shaping the politics of government. By the Augustan day the important men of the state had placed their investments in provincial real estate and mortgages, not in industry or commerce."

The Decline of Enterprise

"Before Caesar's death Rome was probably the financial center of the Roman world," remarks Frank (1933, 350). "Yet no dominating banking firm grew up." Andreau (1999, 137) attributes this striking fact to the shortcomings of the oligarchy. Most moneylending was predatory. Rome's *publicani* lent abroad to appropriate the wealth of others, not to finance enterprise. "The generation that came to maturity under the Julio-Claudian emperors provides one of the best examples known to history of an upstart aristocracy that abused the benefits of prosperity," Frank (1940, 29) sums up. Without much productive investment from the second century BC onward, Rome could consume only by taking booty from foreign lands—tribute and usury from Asia Minor, Spanish mine output (dug out largely by slaves), and the looting of Egypt that continued even long after the tribute demands of Mark Anthony and Caesar.

Replacing the *publicani* knights with an imperial bureaucracy hardly helped matters. By the time of Septimius Severus (AD 193–211), regional armies were fighting among themselves for the Roman throne, plunging the empire into economic as well as military instability. "With the exception of a few military 'houses' who still succeeded in recouping their fortunes abroad, few families managed to remain in the wealthiest group for long," writes Humphreys (1978, 146). Rostovtzeff (1926, 399) quotes the *History* by Herodian (VII 3, 3–6) (AD 180–250) as using similar words to those used by Theognis at the outset of the Greek takeoff: "Every day one could see the wealthiest men of yesterday beggars today. Such was the greed of the tyranny which used the pretext that it needed a constant supply of money to pay the soldiers." The resulting military state stifled enterprise while shifting the tax burden onto the lower orders, paving the way toward the Dark Age to come.

In contrast to Near Eastern policies such as clean slates to restore a balance between debt and liberty by freeing bondservants (and other unfree labor throughout the Roman Empire), Diocletian tried to save matters by imposing price controls and a "totalitarian economics" (Frank 1940, 303), to which Herodian added a distinctly Roman coda: "When Maximinus [235–38], after reducing most of the distinguished houses to penury, found that the spoils were few and paltry and by no means sufficient for his purposes, he attacked public property. All the money belonging to the cities that was collected for the victualling of the populace or for distribution among them, or was devoted to theaters or to religious festivals, he diverted to his own use; and the votive offerings set up in the temples, the statues of the gods, the tributes to heroes, all the adornments of the public buildings, everything that served to beautify the cities, even the metal out of which money could be coined, all were melted down."

"Commerce was at a standstill, and consequently industry was much reduced," concludes Broughton (1948, 912) in describing the third and fourth centuries AD; "all fortunes dependent upon loans, notes, mortgages, and such forms of investment were practically wiped out. Those dependent upon real estate, urban and nonurban, although reduced in number and amount by imperial collections and confiscations, probably retained some proportion of their value but for a time provided no income at all, or only a small one in kind. A tendency in the country to revert to a form of feudalism was an almost inevitable result. Thus the reign of Gallienus [253–68] brought to a climax all the miseries of the century," debasing the silver content of the coinage from about 15 percent to less than 2 percent in the final eight years of his rule.

By the late Roman Empire, industry ended much as it had begun, concentrated in public-sector potteries, mints, textile production, iron foundries, and armor workshops to supply the army's needs. "For some time," summarizes Walbank (1969, 78ff.), "the State (or Emperor) had been the largest landowner; now it became the largest owner of mines and quarries and the greatest industrialist." But in the empire's shrinking economy these state enterprises could only afford to pay their workers in kind, and ended up tying them to their professions on a hereditary basis.

Fortunes dried up as the economy was stripped of money. Most of it flowed eastward, increasingly to India. Handicrafts and industry moved from the cities to the villages and self-sufficient country estates, partly to escape the fiscally predatory militarized state. "By making everything on the spot," explains Walbank (1969, 56–57), "the late Roman precursor of the feudal baron would eliminate the most costly item in his bill of expenses," transportation. Large estates became "the symbol of the decline of urban civilization, and both the result of the general decay and a factor in hastening it...each estate, in proportion as it became self-sufficing, meant so many more individuals subtracted from the classical economic system, so many less potential consumers for those commodities which still circulated in the old markets."

The largest landowners were able to obtain exemption from imperial taxes, shifting the fiscal burden onto mercantile activity (Hudson 1997). "Influential people could wangle immunity either as individuals or as a class," summarizes MacMullen (1988, 42): " 'the registrars of the municipalities through collusion are transferring the burden of the taxes of *potentiores* to *inferiores*,' Constantine angrily declares in 313; or again, in 384, the entire body of senators in Thrace and Macedonia are excused from paying anything at all on their lands."

The empire expanded by economically slashing and burning an ever-widening area, stripping populations of their potential to serve as a market. It took four centuries to exhaust the supply of booty and slaves. Rome's richest province, Asia Minor, failed by the end of the third century as the temples spent their resources on charity under permanent emergency conditions (Broughton 1938, 912). Piracy became prevalent again, and almost the only documented building was for walls to protect against robbers. The best that can be said is that in the West the epoch of Roman conquest was ended by the barbarian invasions. The northerners always were there, of course, but the imperial economy had become too weak to resist.

Conclusion

Past events make us pay particular attention to the
future, if we really make thorough enquiry in each
case into the past.
                    —Polybius (XII 25e, 6)

Mesopotamia's lack of basic raw materials prompted even military rulers such as Sargon of Akkad to boast that they had extended long-distance commerce. By contrast, the Mediterranean aristocracies sought local self-sufficiency. This became the condition into which the western Roman Empire sank as economic life retreated to landed estates, while prosperity lasted longer in Egypt and the eastern half of the Roman Empire ruled from Constantinople.

The fact that Near Easterners were the first to develop the basic repertory of business practices poses the question of what is distinctly Western. Classical Greece and Rome have long been depicted as representing a fresh start, in contrast to the allegedly stagnant Near Eastern economies. Yet the Near East enjoyed superior prosperity from the beginning to the end of antiquity, as well as better economic balance and stability. What has long been viewed as a fresh spirit of individualism turns out to be a product of the breakdown following the devastation that swept the eastern Mediterranean after 1200 BC. The ensuing interregnum brought a free-for-all that never developed an ethic of steering gain-seeking along productive rather than predatory and extractive lines.

When Syrian and Phoenician merchants organized Mediterranean trade in the eighth century BC, they brought standardized weights and measures, money, a financial vocabulary, and interest-bearing debt to Greek and Italian communities. Local chieftains applied these practices in a smaller, more localized context that lacked the checks and balances found in the Near East to save economies from polarizing between creditors and debtors. Apart from Solon's *seisachtheia*, Greece and Rome had no tradition of annulling debts to prevent creditors from foreclosing on the land and reducing much of the citizenry to debt bondage. Just the opposite: Greece and Rome measured success by the ability of creditors to achieve social status through landownership with its patronage power over tenants and clients. There was no attempt to justify wealth and property by attributing it to the labor expended by its owners. Land was obtained by inheritance or through foreclosure on the impecunious, or taken from the public domain by military conquest or insider dealing. Bondage became harsher and more inexorable, with more than a quarter of the Roman population falling into servitude by the fourth century AD, increasingly on large slave-stocked estates.

Rome's economic history provides a leading example of Arnold Toynbee's conclusion in *A Study of History* that the cause of imperial collapse invariably is "suicidal statecraft." It is the same contrast that Baumol has drawn between productive and unproductive enterprise. Foreign relations *in particular* aimed at extorting tribute and indebting local populations. The short time frame of Roman imperial administrators did not allow replenishment of the resources stripped from the provinces. And instead of promoting domestic market demand at home, Rome let debt service and taxes siphon off purchasing power and dry up commercial enterprise, debasing the coinage to deal with the fiscal crisis that culminated in feudalism.

In these respects classical antiquity must be viewed as an unsuccessful mode of exploitation. Nobody voiced a program of raising general living standards, labor productivity, or technology by developing a home market. Charity by the wealthy seemed the best that could be hoped for. It remained for John Locke and other Enlightenment political economists to justify property morally by the labor that went into its acquisition (an idea that, Locke acknowledged, applied only on the small scale of self-sufficient holdings). But for this labor theory of property value to apply, the political and fiscal context for enterprise had to be transformed.

And indeed, a new world did emerge out of Rome's collapse into a Dark Age. The transition from slave labor via serfdom to free labor transformed the social character of enterprise. Commerce began to revive with the Arab and Moorish trade across southern Europe to Spain. In 1225 the looting of Constantinople by the Crusaders, financed by the Venetians as a paying venture for a quarter of the loot, drew vast sums of monetary bullion into western Europe. It was enough to provide the basis for an expansion of credit. The Schoolmen permitted loopholes for bankers to charge interest in the form of *agio* on foreign payments, mainly to finance trade— along with royal war debts.

It was in the late medieval period, and more so during the Renaissance and Enlightenment, that economic gain-seeking took the form of expanding production. Trade became the means of obtaining the monetary metals, and credit came to be monetized on the basis of national treasuries and central banks. Bankruptcy laws became more humanitarian and debtor-oriented, at least until quite recently.

And yet the history of antiquity shows that evolution is not inevitably carried upward by economic or technological potential automatically realizing itself. Entrepreneurs have obtained surpluses through the ages, but often in ways that injure society as a whole. Predatory loans mounting up to strip capital, and economies living in the short run by asset stripping are universal deterrents to long-term investment. Many vestiges of the rentier ethic that culminated in the post-Roman feudal period are still with us, weighing on the present like a dead hand (lit. *mort-gage*). Much as classical antiquity plowed its commercial gains and the extraction of interest into the land, many enterprises today find land (along with financial speculation and corporate takeovers) more attractive than new capital formation.

Modern observers have criticized Rome's legal framework for not replacing commercial partnerships with permanent limited-liability joint-stock companies. Trading profits had to be paid out each time a partner died or a new one joined, and often paying out profits at the end of each voyage. But today's stock-market raiders appear to be reverting to the short-term perspective that historians have blamed for blocking Rome's economic takeoff. The economic environment that most effectively contributes to prosperity is one that induces entrepreneurs to gain by investing in new means of production, not by rent-seeking, redistributive property expropriation, debt foreclosure, and insider dealing. Successful enterprise helps economies grow by contributing to output, or adding to efficiency by innovations that minimize costs, not by a proliferation of debt and property claims. The moral is that the race is not always to the strong or economic victory to the most productive. The economic course of civilization has not always been uphill, as historians who focus more on technology than on the institutions of credit and property tend to imply. That is the main lesson taught by a review of the history of enterprise, positive and negative, over the course of antiquity.

Notes

[1] I discuss the public and private role of merchants and enterprise in Hudson 1996a and 1996b.

[2] In fact, Livy, Diodorus, and Plutarch blamed the decline and fall of the Roman Republic on usury and related oligarchic greed, and on the use of political violence against populist leaders such as the Gracchi brothers, whose murder initiated Rome's Social War.

[3] The commercial activities for which corporations could be organized remained limited to state projects, including the exploitation of subsoil resources in the public domain. "At some point," notes Jones (2006,

208), "the *societas vectigalis* was granted a form of corporate entity, according to the jurist Gaius in the second century (Digest 3.4.1): 'Partners in tax farming, gold mines, silver mines, and saltworks are allowed to form corporations.... Those permitted to form a corporate body consisting of a *collegiium* or partnership...have the right, on the pattern of the state (*ad exemplum rei publicae*), to have common property, a common treasury and an attorney or legal counsel through whom, as in a state, what should be transacted and done in common is transacted and done.'"

References

Andreau, Jean. 1999. *Banking and Business in the Roman World*. Trans. Janet Lloyd. Cambridge: Cambridge University Press.

Andreau, Jean, P. Briant, and R. Descat, eds. 1994. *Économie antique: Les échanges des l'Antiquité, le rôle de l'État*. Saint-Bertrand-de-Comminges: Musée archéologique départemental.

Archi, Alfonso, ed. 1984. *Circulation of Goods in Non-palatial Context in the Ancient Near East*. Rome: Edizioni dell'Ateneo.

Badian, Ernst. 1972. *Publicans and Sinners: Private Enterprise in the Service of the Roman Republic*. Ithaca, NY: Cornell University Press.

Baumol, William J. 1990. "Entrepreneurship: Productive, Unproductive and Destructive." *Journal of Political Economy* 98:893–921.

Bleiberg, Edward. 1995. "The Economy of Ancient Egypt." In *Civilizations of the Ancient Near East*, editor in chief Jack Sasson, 1373–86. Peabody, MA: Hendrickson.

Bongenaar, A.C.V.M., ed. 2000. *Interdependency of Institutions and Private Entrepreneurs: Proceedings of the Second MOS Symposium (Leiden 1998)*. Istanbul: Nederlands Historisch-Archaeologisch Instituut te Istanbul; Leiden: Nederlands Instituut voor het Nabije Oosten.

Broughton, T.R.S. 1938. "Roman Asia Minor." In *An Economic Survey of Ancient Rome*, ed. Tenney Frank, vol. 4, *Roman Africa, Syria, Greece, and Asia*. Baltimore: Johns Hopkins Press.

Burckert, Walter. 1992. *The Orientalizing Revolution: Near Eastern Influence on Greek Culture in the Early Archaic Age*. Trans. Walter Burkert and Margaret E. Pinder. Cambridge: Harvard University Press.

Calhoun, George M. 1965. *The Business Life of Ancient Athens*. Studia Historica 20. Rome: "L'Erma" di Bretschneider.

Cartledge, Paul, Edward E. Cohen, and Lin Foxhall, eds. 2001. *Money, Labour, and Land: Approaches to the Economics of Ancient Greece*. London: Routledge.

Casson, Lionel. 1984. *Ancient Trade and Society*. Detroit: Wayne State University Press.

Charpin, Dominique. 1982. "Marchands du Palais et Marchands du Temple à la Fin de la Ire Dynastie de Babylone." *Journal Asiatique* 270:25–65.

Cohen, Edward E. 1992. *Athenian Economy and Society: A Banking Perspective*. Princeton: Princeton University Press.

D'Arms, John. 1981. *Commerce and Social Standing in Ancient Rome*. Cambridge: Harvard University Press.

Dercksen, J. G., ed. 1999. *Trade and Finance in Ancient Mesopotamia: Proceedings of the First MOS Symposium (Leiden 1997)*. [Istanbul]: Nederlands Historisch-Archaeologisch Instituut te Istanbul; Leiden: Distributor, Nederlands Instituut voor het Nabije Oosten.

Diakanoff, Igor M., ed. 1991. *Early Antiquity*. Trans. Alexander Kirjanov. Chicago: University of Chicago Press.

———. 1992. "The Structure of Near Eastern Society before the Middle of the 2nd Millennium BC." *Oikumene* 3:7–100.

Figueira, Thomas J., and Gregory Nagy, eds. 1985. *Theognis of Megara: Poetry and the Polis*. Baltimore: Johns Hopkins University Press.

Finley, Moses. 1973. *The Ancient Economy*. Berkeley and Los Angeles: University of California Press.

———, ed. 1979. *The Bucher-Meyer Controversy*. New York: Arno Press.

Frank, Tenney, ed. 1933. *An Economic Survey of Ancient Rome*. Vol. 1, *Rome and Italy of the Republic*. Baltimore: Johns Hopkins Press.

———, ed. 1938. *An Economic Survey of Ancient Rome*. Vol. 4, *Roman Africa, Syria, Greece, and Asia*. Baltimore: Johns Hopkins Press.

———. 1940. *Rome and Italy of the Empire*. Baltimore: Johns Hopkins Press.

Frankfort, Henri. 1951. *Kingship and the Gods: A Study of Ancient Near Eastern Religion as the Integration of Society and Nature*. Chicago: University of Chicago Press.

Garnsey, Peter, Keith Hopkins, and C. R. Whittaker, eds. 1983. *Trade in the Ancient Economy*. Berkeley and Los Angeles: University of California Press.

Gress, David. 1998. *From Plato to NATO: The Idea of the West and Its Opponents*. New York: Free Press.

Heichelheim, Fritz. 1958–70. *An Ancient Economic History: From the Palaeolithic Age to the Migrations of the Germanic, Slavic, and Arabic Nations*. Rev. ed. 3 vols. Leiden: A.W. Sijthoff.

Hudson, Michael. 1992. "Did the Phoenicians Introduce the Idea of Interest to Greece and Italy—and If So, When?" In *Greece between East and West*, ed. Gunter Kopcke and I. Tokumaru, 128–43. Mainz: Verlag Philipp von Zabern.

———. 1996a. "The Dynamics of Privatization, from the Bronze Age to the Present." In *Privatization in the Ancient Near East and Classical Antiquity*, ed. Michael Hudson and Baruch Levine, 33–72. Cambridge, MA: Peabody Museum of Archaeology and Ethnology.

———. 1996b. "Privatization in History and Today: A Survey of the Unresolved Controversies." In *Privatization in the Ancient Near East and Classical Antiquity*, ed. Michael Hudson and Baruch Levine, 1–32. Cambridge, MA: Peabody Museum of Archaeology and Ethnology.

———. 1998. "Land Monopolization, Fiscal Crises and Clean Slate 'Jubilee' Proclamations in Antiquity." In *Property in Economic Context*, ed. Robert C. Hunt and Antonio Gilman, 139–69. Lanham, MD: University Press of America.

———. 2000. "How Interest Rates Were Set, 2500 BC–1000 AD: *Máš, tokos* and *fœnus* as Metaphors for Interest Accruals." *Journal of the Economic and Social History of the Orient* 43:132–61.

———. 2005–6. Review of *Autour de Polanyi: Vocabularies, théories et modalities des échanges*, ed. Ph. Chancier, F. Joannès, P. Rouillard, and A. Tenu (Paris: De Boccard, 2005) and *The Ancient Economy: Evidence and Models*, ed. J. G. Manning and Ian Morris (Stanford: Stanford University Press, 2005). *Archiv für Orientforschung* 51:405–11.

Hudson, Michael, and Baruch A. Levine, eds. 1996. *Privatization in the Ancient Near East and Classical World*. Cambridge, MA: Peabody Museum of Archaeology and Ethnology.

———, eds. 2000. *Urbanization and Land Ownership in the Ancient Near East*. Cambridge, MA: Peabody Museum of Archaeology and Ethnology.

Hudson, Michael, and Marc Van De Mieroop, eds. 2002. *Debt and Economic Renewal in the Ancient Near East*. Bethesda, MD: CDL Press.

Hudson, Michael, and Cornelia Wunsch, eds. 2004. *Creating Economic Order: Record-Keeping, Standardization, and the Development of Accounting in the Ancient Near East*. Bethesda, MD: CDL Press.

Humphreys, S. C. 1978. *Anthropology and the Greeks*. London: Routledge and Kegan Paul.

Joannès, Francis. 1995. "Private Commerce and Banking in Achaemenid Babylon." In *Civilizations of the Ancient Near East*, editor in chief Jack Sasson, 1475–86. Peabody, MA: Hendrickson.

Johnson, Allan Chester. 1936. *Roman Egypt to the Reign of Diocletian*. Baltimore: Johns Hopkins Press.

Jones, A.H.M. 1964. *The Later Roman Empire, 284–610: A Social, Economic, and Administrative Survey*. Norman: University of Oklahoma Press.

Jones, David. 2006. *The Bankers of Puteoli: Finance, Trade, and Industry in the Roman World*. London: Tempus.

Kirzner, Israel M. 1979. *Perception, Opportunity, and Profit: Studies in the Theory of Entrepreneurship*. Chicago: University of Chicago Press.

Kopcke, Gunter, and I. Tokumaru, eds. 1992. *Greece between East and West*. Mainz: Verlag Philipp von Zabern.

Kurke, Leslie. 1999. *Coins, Bodies, Games, and Gold: The Politics of Meaning in Archaic Greece*. Princeton: Princeton University Press.

Lamberg-Karlovsky, Carl. 1996. "The Archaeological Evidence for International Commerce: Private and/or Public Enterprise in Mesopotamia." In *Privatization in the Ancient Near East and Classical World*, ed. Michael Hudson and Baruch A. Levine, 73–108. Cambridge, MA: Peabody Museum of Archaeology and Ethnology.

Lambert, Maurice. 1960. "La naissance de la bureaucratie." *Revue Historique* 224:1–26.

Larsen, Mogens Trolle. 1974. "The Old Assyrian Colonies in Anatolia." *Journal of the American Oriental Society* 94:468–75.

Latouche, Robert. 1961. *The Birth of Western Economy: Economic Aspects of the Dark Ages*. Trans. E. M. Wilkinson. London: Methuen.

Leemans, W. F. 1950. *The Old-Babylonian Merchant: His Business and His Social Position*. Leiden: E. J. Brill.

Liverani, Mario. 2005. "The Near East: The Bronze Age." In *The Ancient Economy: Evidence and Models*, ed. J. G. Manning and Ian Morris, 47–57. Stanford: Stanford University Press.

MacMullen, Ramsay. 1974. *Roman Social Relations, 50 BC to AD 284*. New Haven: Yale University Press.

———. 1988. *Corruption and the Decline of Rome*. New Haven: Yale University Press.

Manning, J. G., and Ian Morris, eds. 2005. *The Ancient Economy: Evidence and Models*. Stanford: Stanford University Press.

Nicolet, Claude. 1966. *L'Ordre équestre a l'Epoque républicaine*. Paris: E. de Boccard.

Parkins, Helen, and Christopher Smith, eds. 1998. *Trade, Traders, and the Ancient City*. London: Routledge.

Postgate, J. N. 1992. *Early Mesopotamia: Society and Economy at the Dawn of History*. London: Routledge.

Reden, Sitta von. 1995. *Exchange in Ancient Greece*. London: Duckworth.

Renger, Johannes. 1984. "Patterns of Non-institutional Trade and Non-commercial Exchange in Ancient Mesopotamia at the Beginning of the Second Millennium B.C." In *Circulation of Goods in Non-palatial Context in the Ancient Near East*, ed. Alfonso Archi. Rome: Edizioni dell'Ateneo.

———. 1994. "On Economic Structures in Ancient Mesopotamia." *Orientalia* n.s. 63:157–208.

———. 2000. "Das Palastgeschäft in der altbabylonischen Zeit." In *Interdependency of Institutions and Private Entrepreneurs: Proceedings of the Second MOS Symposium (Leiden 1998)*, ed. A.C.V.M. Bongenaar, 153–83. Istanbul: Nederlands Historisch-Archaeologisch Instituut te Istanbul; Leiden: Nederlands Instituut voor het Nabije Oosten.

———. 2002. "Royal Edicts of the Babylonian Period—Structural Background." In *Debt and Economic Renewal in the Ancient Near East*, ed. Michael Hudson and Marc Van De Mieroop, 139–62. Bethesda, MD: CDL Press.

Rostovtzeff, Mikhail. 1926. *The Social and Economic History of the Roman Empire*. Oxford: Clarendon Press.

Roth, Martha T. 1995. *Law Collections from Mesopotamia and Asia Minor*. Atlanta: Scholars Press.

Sasson, Jack, editor in chief. 1995. *Civilizations of the Ancient Near East*. Peabody, MA: Hendrickson.

Scheidel, Walter, and Sitta von Reden, eds. 2002. *The Ancient Economy*. Edinburgh: Edinburgh University Press.

Scott, William Robert. 1912. *The Constitution and Finance of English, Scottish, and Irish Joint-Stock Companies to 1720*. 3 vols. Cambridge: Cambridge University Press.

Stolper, Matthew. 1985. *Entrepreneurs and Empire: The Murashu Archive, the Murashu Firm, and Persian Rule in Babylonia*. Leiden: Nederlands Historisch-Archaeologisch Instituut te Istanbul.

Van De Mieroop, Marc. 1987. "The Archive of Balmunamhe." *Archiv für Orientforschung* 34:1–29.

———. 1992. *Society and Enterprise in Old Babylonian Ur*. Berlin: D. Reimer.

———. 2005. "The Invention of Interest." In *The Origins of Value: The Financial Innovations That Created Modern Capital Markets*, ed. William N. Goetzmann and K. Geert Rouwenhorst, 17–30. Oxford: Oxford University Press.

Veblen, Thorstein. 1904. *The Theory of Business Enterprise*. New York: Scribner.

Veenhof, Klass R. 1972. *Aspects of Old Assyrian Trade and Its Terminology*. Leiden: E. J. Brill.

———. 1997. "'Modern' Features of Old Assyrian Trade." *Journal of the Economic and Social History of the Orient* 40:336–66.

———. 1999. "Silver and Credit in Old Assyrian Trade." In *Trade and Finance in Ancient Mesopotamia: Proceedings of the First MOS Symposium (Leiden 1997)*, ed. J. G. Dercksen, 55–83. [Istanbul]: Nederlands Historisch-Archaeologisch Instituut te Istanbul; Leiden: Distributor, Nederlands Instituut voor het Nabije Oosten.

Walbank, F. W. 1969. *The Awful Revolution: The Decline of the Roman Empire in the West*. Liverpool: Liverpool University Press.

Weber, Max. 1976. *The Agrarian Sociology of Ancient Civilizations*. Trans. R. I. Frank. London: NLB.

West, M. L. 1997. *The East Face of Helicon: West Asiatic Elements in Greek Poetry and Myth*. Oxford: Clarendon Press.

Wray, Randall, ed. 2004. *Credit and State Theories of Money: The Contributions of A. Mitchell Innes*. Cheltenham, UK: Edward Elgar.

Yoffee, Norman. 1995. "The Economy of Ancient Western Asia." In *Civilizations of the Ancient Near East*, editor in chief Jack Sasson, 1387–1400. Peabody, MA: Hendrickson.

Zaccagnini, Carlo, ed. 2003. *Mercanti et Politica nel Mondo Antico*. Rome: "L'Erma" di Bretschneider.

Chapter 2 ———————————————

Neo-Babylonian Entrepreneurs

CORNELIA WUNSCH

THE NEO-BABYLONIAN EMPIRE under the so-called Chaldaean rulers[1] lasted nearly a century, from 626 to 539 BC. It ended when Cyrus the Great conquered Babylonia and made it part of the much larger Achaemenid Persian empire. Its center and power base was southern Mesopotamia, from where it controlled large parts of the Near East. Babylon, its capital, was situated on one branch of the Euphrates River, circa 75 km to the south of the modern-day Iraqi capital Baghdad.

From 626 BC on Nabopolassar gradually had seized and consolidated control over Babylonia until his troops, with help by Median allies, finally defeated Assyria and destroyed its capital Nineveh in 612 BC. Babylon then became the capital of a large empire, reversing the effects of its prior military devastation and subjugation under Assyrian rule. Tribute flowed into it rather than being drained from it.

Nabopolassar's famous successors Nebuchadnezzar and Nabonidus used these resources to finance large-scale building projects, such as renewing, renovating, and expanding temples and palaces, extending city fortifications, and expanding the irrigation system. Nebuchadnezzar followed the Assyrian policy of relocating substantial parts of the local population from conquered regions by settling them in Babylonia.[2] This helped stimulate economic growth under relatively peaceful domestic conditions resulting in sustained population growth and relative prosperity.

Cyrus' conquest in 538 BC marked the end of Babylonia's sovereignty and therefore a hiatus in its political history, but it did not cause a break in Babylonian administrative or legal institutions. The transition was made smooth by the early imperial Persian policy of relying as much as possible on existing legal and economic structures in the conquered areas.[3] The Achaemenids[4] typically superimposed their own administrative layer on preexisting structures. With its much larger scope, their empire afforded new business opportunities, although Babylon no longer was the center of power; the royal court resided elsewhere.

Babylonia's economic capacities were a major asset to the Persians, providing a third of the empire's tribute, as Herodotus reports.[5] Resources thus were drained, as had been the case under Assyrian rule, but economic growth helped soften the impact.[6] Despite Babylonia's wealth, privileges and relatively independent local power, the yoke of the Persian rule was increasingly resented. Attempts to cast it off were triggered whenever the succession to the Persian throne was fought over. When political unrest ensued after the death of Darius in 486 BC, two pretenders (presumably from prominent Babylonian families and well connected with the local Persian administration) temporarily gained power over northern Babylonia. This fight prompted the victorious Xerxes to punish their backers and reorganize the way in which Babylonia was governed. As a result, many archives of the traditionally leading Babylonian families do not survive beyond his second regnal year.[7]

Subsequent sources, such as the business archive of the Murašû family from Nippur in the fifth and early fourth centuries, portray a different kind of entrepreneurial activity as compared to the sixth century, organized around the administration of large Babylonian estates held by members of the Persian aristocracy. As a result we have a fairly homogeneous picture for a period of over 120 years or five generations, until around 485 BC. Rich sources attest to economic continuity through the dynastic change, as well as a continuity of administrative and legal institutions. The subsequent period is less well documented—and by different types of sources—indicating that more than merely minor details have changed.

Periodization in terms of broad political history thus will not do justice to the socioeconomic dynamics at work. In the absence of a more accurate terminology—and to avoid long hyphenated terms, hybrids, or acronyms—the term *Neo-Babylonian* (unless applied to the empire as such) in the course of this study will tacitly include the first decades of Achaemenid rule (until about 485 BC) as well as the preceding period of the Neo-Babylonian empire (626–539 BC).

Primary information about Neo-Babylonian economic activity comes from business records in Akkadian, a now defunct Semitic language related to Hebrew, Aramaic, and Arabic. It was written in cuneiform script on clay tablets, created by pressing a writing implement into the wet medium in numerous combinations of wedge-shaped impressions. Tablet shapes and sizes vary, depending on their purpose. The majority of Neo-Babylonian contracts fit in the palm of a hand, with fifteen to twenty-five lines of text. Because clay is a durable material, tablets easily can survive millennia once they are buried in the ground, be it accidentally or on purpose. Museums around the world house nearly 100,000 such tablets and fragments from the Neo-Babylonian period alone; about 16,000 are published.[8] Most of them were dug up by local people or licensed excavators in the late 1800s, before controlled excavations by modern standards began.

These Neo-Babylonian tablets predominantly come from two temple archives (Uruk to the south and Sippar to the north of Babylon) and from private archives of some well-to-do urban families and entrepreneurs from several places. Only a few remnants of the royal archives have come to light so far, thus inevitably biasing our view of this period.[9]

The last two decades have seen a surge in Neo-Babylonian archival studies with dozens of small- to medium-size private archives studied and published, or at least made accessible thanks to a more generous attitude of museums granting access to their materials. Scholarly effort has resulted in the publication of new source material, leading to a new level of sophistication in interpreting these sources.

Our discussion will focus on the activities of the Egibi family, which left the largest private archive, containing more than 2,000 tablets (including fragments and duplicates) from five generations covering nearly the whole time span under discussion.[10] To be sure, an average between one and two records per month seems meager as compared to the legacy of one single fourteenth-century Italian merchant from Prato, of about 150,000 papers in total.[11] Even if the Egibis had generated only

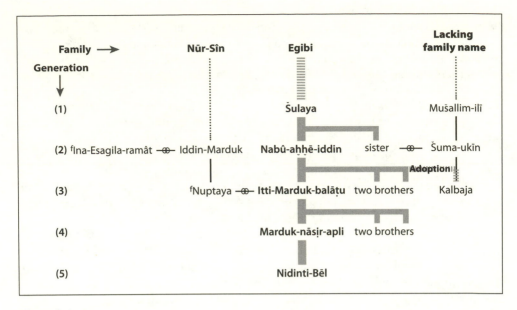

Figure 2.1

one-tenth of this amount, our known records would represent such a small fraction as to fall below the margin of significance. To make matters worse, the wording of cuneiform tablets is notoriously formulaic and terse, revealing mere bare-bone facts without any hints at the intentions or motives of the parties involved and rarely including descriptions of previous proceedings. We therefore only get glimpses and have to rely on a few exceptionally well-documented transactions as explanatory models where the evidence is sketchy.

Nevertheless this archive reveals much about Neo-Babylonian entrepreneurs and their activities, involving commodity trade, food processing, agrarian credit, and tax farming. On the one hand it serves as a key to understanding other, even more tersely documented archives. On the other hand, some smaller archives elaborate on details that are spelled out less clearly in the Egibi tablets and otherwise would remain obscure.

The Neo-Babylonian Economy[12]

Natural Conditions

Southern Mesopotamia is an alluvial plain with limited natural resources. It lacks metal deposits, stone, and hardwood suitable for building material, and therefore is completely dependent on raw-material imports. Although the soil is fertile, average rainfall cannot sustain regular crops. The Euphrates and Tigris carry abundant waters for irrigation, but they tend to flood their plains and—unlike the Nile in Egypt—do so when water is least needed: at grain harvest time. Irrigation therefore is a precondition for farming in southern Mesopotamia. It requires a large-scale and sophisticated system of dams, dikes, and sluices both to supply water and to protect the fields from floods. Because the rivers also carry large amounts of silt, these structures need constant supervision and regular maintenance work. With irrigation in place, grain yields can reach proverbial abundance, while water-logged areas of low ground unsuitable for tilling or gardening yield fish and fowl. The alluvial plains are surrounded by steppe land and mountain ranges providing pasture.

The Large Institutions

The crown. The royal administration is not well documented, as only minuscule remnants of the central archives have come to light so far, and provincial administrative archives are lacking. Therefore most of what we know stems from the interface of the royal administration with temples or private individuals.

The king as the single most important landowner controlled large domains all over Babylonia. Other land was held by members of the royal family (e.g., a distinct "house of the crown prince" is known from cuneiform sources)[13] and high officials, such as the royal treasurer.[14] We can assume that the management of large estates was organized in a similar way to that of temple land described below. Large tracts of land, especially newly claimed areas along the canals, were parceled out to settle diverse population groups as small landholders in return for military service.

The royal administration needed managers to oversee domain lands, to collect taxes and user fees for irrigation, canal transport, and other public infrastructure, and to organize and supervise the corvée, a duty on landowners to provide labor for public projects. This involved provisioning a widening range of forced labor as well as free hired workers who, temporarily or permanently, needed to be fed and supported. Distribution, marketing, and conversion of crops into money equivalents offered major opportunities for enterprise. This required the creation of synergies to facilitate the payment of taxes and fees to the palace. A complex set of relationships developed among the royal, temple, and city administrations, involving large movements of commodities and personnel.

Temples as landholders. Although most temple land was in the vicinity of the cities, some was more outlying, and of diverse quality. Efficient agriculture was possible only along the irrigation canals. Digging and maintaining them was a royal task, and the temples provided manpower and resources to build and maintain infrastructure such as watercourses, dams, locks, and roads. Land was abundant, but the temples were short of people and draft animals to cultivate it.

Much temple land was worked by unfree dependent personnel (oblates).[15] Such temple farmers typically were organized in plow teams based on extended family groups for grain farming, but they often were given larger work assignments than they were able to till. Temples also employed tenants on a sharecropping basis, with the portion of the harvest to be delivered depending on the quality of the property.[16] Eventually, to increase productivity and achieve a stable income, temples introduced rent farmers, who would take on part or all of the temples' grain fields or date orchards, including personnel and equipment, in exchange for a fixed delivery quota of commodities and cash.[17] On the one hand, temples introduced certain incentives more beneficial than usual to the rent farmer, expecting him not only to contribute a considerable amount of time and effort, but also to invest his personal means in desperately needed equipment, and therefore taking considerable personal risk. On the other hand, temples had to make sure that he would not use such arrangements to their detriment. This was a difficult balance to maintain.

It is far from obvious whether such seemingly entrepreneurial activity always was undertaken voluntarily. In ancient Greece, for example, the wealthiest citizens were subject to special fiscal burdens such as the *trierarchy* (equipment and maintenance of a battleship), to finance the staging of dramatic choruses and other expensive civic duties. The tendency seems to have been for most of these individuals to use this tax as a vehicle for prestige rather than seeking to make money of it. Rostovtzeff has described this problem in late Roman time.[18]

This raises the question of whether Babylonian rent farmers were always eager participants or had to be pushed into these arrangements. The records disclose that even temple officials doing tasks within their normal "scope of employment" often were held personally liable for accidents or shortfalls that occurred. Many examples exist of people compelled to sell assets to the temple in lieu of their backlogs due for barley, dates, sheep, or wool deliveries. Such deficits could be considerable, indicating that these temple debtors were not small farmers or shepherds but major players.

In one case a notorious entrepreneurial temple official named Gimillu either refused to accept or returned a rent-farming license because an insufficient inventory of draft animals and personnel for seed plowing came with it.[19] Someone else eventually took up the license, but only after having negotiated for twice the amount of draft animals so as to make the arrangement more profitable. In another situation a rent farmer returned his rent-farming license to the temple authorities because he had substantial arrears that he clearly had difficulty meeting, and therefore he felt he no longer could afford to continue the venture.[20] We have little way of knowing whether his backlog (and those of other rent farmers) came from especially difficult years with a poor harvest, or whether rent farmers generally worked on tight margins. In other words, we do not know whether such backlogs were accidental and occasional, or systematic and regular.

One might postulate that temple authorities used debts arising from such shortfalls as a way to keep certain families from growing too rich and powerful, much as kings attempted to keep the temples' power in check by imposing extra duties on special occasions. Allowing entrepreneurs to accumulate a large backlog may also have constituted a capital infusion, increasing the rent farmer's working capital by letting him use the commodities or silver owed for other business. Temples in any event were always crucial credit institutions in the ancient Near East.[21] But to understand the exact meaning of these large backlogs, each case needs to be assessed individually, where the context permits.

Babylonia's growing population, its incorporation into the much larger Persian Empire, and its heavier tax duties called for intensified agricultural activity. Temples responded by moving away from subsistence farming, increasingly focusing on cash crops, and delegating more tasks to entrepreneurs, who either came from the rank and file of temple officials, or were outsiders, much in the vein of modern outsourcing practices.

Animal husbandry was of special importance in the south. In Uruk raising animals was the main cash crop.[22] Herds were entrusted to shepherds, who might be temple dependents or independent contractors. Temple sheep and goats would roam freely in the steppe and be driven large distances from one season to the next, being brought back at shearing time. Shepherds had to account for their flocks and deliver a specified quota of lambs for sacrificial purposes, and hides and wool to be processed in the temple workshops.

Dairy products were of minor importance because the sheep and goats were unavailable most of the year. Cattle were difficult to maintain and feed over the summer. As a result, they were a scarce resource and hence of eminent importance to the temple administration. The major use of cows and oxen was as draft animals for plowing.

The swampy areas unsuitable for tilling or gardening provided fish and fowl. In those areas under temple authority, fishing and fowling were done by temple personnel; the involvement of outside entrepreneurs is not attested so far. The temples tried to control access to these resources within their domains by licensing systems.[23]

Temples and their cities. Southern Mesopotamia's temples were institutions of long tradition as vital economic centers, not just cultic entities. At the very least they were in charge of the implements and services required for the care of the gods, maintenance of the temple site, and support and care of its personnel. In addition to providing for the religious needs of the community by housing, feeding, clothing, and maintaining the gods, the temples controlled vast amounts of land and personnel. As a result, temples and their cities formed a symbiotic unit: Cities thrived around the cultic center, and the temple in turn needed the city and its region for support.

The prebendary system. Prebends were entitlements to shares in the temple revenue in return for priestly services and professional work required for the cult. Prebendaries prepared and served ceremonial meals, created and mended cultic garments, cleaned, dressed, and moved around the cult statues, performed rituals, and maintained the inner sanctuary. These tasks not only required certain skills, but the status of a person was important in the sense of his being fit for his particular service, that is, being "pure" in a cultic sense. Thus many craftsmen working for the temple were prebend holders, not dependents or slaves. Prebendaries represented society's free, skilled urban elite, and the prebendary system integrated these oldest and most important local families with the temple.

Remuneration for prebendary service usually comprised commodities such as barley, dates, and beer, as well as leftovers of the meals of the gods, and thus generated a steady and dependable income stream. Such offices originally were associated with certain families and were inheritable. Duties were broken down into monthly and daily units, and in the process of inheritance divisions ran even further to fractions of days.

Enterprise versus Rival Avenues to Wealth: Opportunities and Costs

Economic attitudes and mentalities of the propertied urban classes in Babylonia can be described in terms of two basic (although necessarily idealized) models: a *rentier* type and an *entrepreneur* type.[24] Rentiers seek to obtain a reliable income from mostly inherited positions and resources with little risk, by exploiting prebends and landed property. Entrepreneurs tend to engage in highly profitable but also risky venture businesses in a competitive environment.

Many families linked with the temple through prebendary duties and entitlements had a rentier attitude, being the civil servants of the ancient world. Their office was hereditary and although prebends became tradable in time, only certain individuals could perform the core duties in the inner sanctuary. This meant that prebendaries were indispensable, but were restricted in assigning such duties to anyone but their colleagues. But although such offices were not in and of themselves key entrepreneurial situations, some did provide opportunities for enterprise, especially those involving food preparation.

For example, prebend holders could have their slaves perform the prebendary task for them, so long as it did not require a certain status, such as in the direct presentation and care of the gods. This freed up the prebend holder for other gainful activity. Ownership and the service could be bifurcated by sophisticated business contracts for prebendaries outsourcing services for payment of a share in the prebendary income.

The commercialization of prebends made some more desirable than others. Those with long duties and no chance to delegate them might entail prestige, but were a burden from an economic rationale by preventing their holders from more profitable activity. This is indicated by one record where a father urges his youngest son (not the eldest!) to perform his duties as a temple singer and take care of him. In exchange, the father grants this son an extra share in the inheritance. Even if this mainly was meant to reward him for caring for his elderly father, it shows that this prebend cannot have been much of an asset.

During the Neo-Babylonian period a polarization among the traditional urban propertied classes can be observed, as their wealth declined in relative terms, unless they embraced enterprise. The economic potential must have been enormous, although not for all of them: some entrepreneurs went bankrupt. But one example shows that prior to this they had amassed large real estate in a very short time.[25]

From the city of Borsippa a group of private archives of traditional temple-related families indicates that while some used their position and income to become entrepreneurs, others did not.[26] No clear-cut pattern emerges to show which course prebend holders might take. There probably was a special incentive for younger sons who inherited very little to become entrepreneurs. But that route took a robust mental disposition, good health, and possibly a business drive that not everyone had.

The Status of Entrepreneurs

The historical record makes it clear that entrepreneurial activity was socially rewarded, not considered beneath anyone's social status. There is no indication that enterprise was considered "dirty business" or something to be delegated to an underling as in Roman times. A temple's rent farmer often came from the ranks of its officeholders or prebendaries. But in general relatively few entrepreneurs came from well-established urban families already endowed with wealth, offices, and good connections.

Of those who did, our records unfortunately do not indicate just how these families rose to their level of fortune and influence, because they already were important by the time our textual evidence resumes at the beginning of the sixth century BC after centuries of extremely sparse documentation. We find members of these families as prebendaries or in the higher echelon of the temples for several generations prior to the business transactions documented in our records. One such example comes from the Ēṭiru family: By the time of king Neriglissar one of their members held a butcher's prebend at the main temple, and was married to the daughter of a royal judge, but at the same time was involved in a venture business.[27]

Belonging to an important family—however loosely connected—certainly helped in developing business contacts and prospects. But not all branches of these families were rich and influential. For instance, by the end of the seventh century the Egibi family had firmly established itself in several Babylonian cities, holding both prebends and offices. But the Babylon branch that left the impressive five-generation archive rose from humble beginnings, initially owning neither real estate nor prebends.

The majority of entrepreneurs seem to have been ambitious social climbers. Characteristically, they were men without a family name; that is, they did not belong to the urban establishment. Many made their mark within the royal administration or developed significant links to it. As soon as they achieved some measure of financial success, they sought to affiliate themselves with influential families, much as ambitious eighteenth- and nineteenth-century Europeans married into less glamorous branches of noble families. For instance, Itti-Šamaš-balāṭu from Larsa, an entrepreneur "of no name," engaged in tax farming, agricultural contracting, and presumably trading, married his daughter into a well-known prebendary family from Larsa.[28] Marriage links thus helped to achieve status and widen one's access to financial opportunities.

Marriage and entrepreneurial strategy. Advancing business connections through marriage has been a constant for most of recorded history. Certainly in the case of the Egibis, this can be demonstrated by their marriage patterns. In the earliest instance we find a daughter married to a man of some means, but without a family name. He did business with his brother-in-law and seems to have had good connections to, or even a position in the royal administration. This marriage link helps explain some aspects of the Egibi's takeoff, whose early stages are largely undocumented. The Egibi brother-in-law claims to have taught his sororal nephew to read and write cuneiform among other skills, and later adopted him, but without granting him an inheritance share beside his three natural sons. This indicates that the purpose of the sister's marriage was to advance the Egibis' business, while the adoption served to mend her son's handicap of being "of no name" as a result of her marriage.

In the following generations the eldest sons married upward, to women whose fathers were of "good" families, had good connections, and provided rich dowries. By contrast, their daughters were married off to business partners with dowries that typically cost only a fraction of what their eldest sons received, reflecting the Egibis' superior status in relation to these in-laws.[29]

Reputation of lenders. Creditors have a poor reputation in ancient societies in general, as can be seen from biblical sources. We know little, however, about the social standing of creditors in the Neo-Babylonian period. Our terse records generally disclose no information about emotional attitudes toward creditors. Literary sources occasionally urge creditors to be kind to their debtors. We also have a tablet where a creditor is said to have taken mercy upon his debtor.[30]

The Entrepreneur's Activities

Several areas of entrepreneurial activity are significant in addition to the rent farming discussed above.

Agricultural enterprise and changing land use. Throughout antiquity a person's landownership was the criterion on which his political, fiscal, and social status was based. Land provided for a family's basic self-sufficiency and supported dependents and clients. What was true of most Roman traders—that as soon as they had made money, they would put it into land as a prestige good—also applies to the Neo-Babylonian period.

The Egibis invested their business profits in farmland and rented it out on a sharecropping basis. Their perspective was long term. For instance, their leasing arrangements gave tenants an economic motive to invest in cultivating more capital-intensive crops, shifting from grain to dates. In return for planting date palms, the Egibis allowed their tenants to pay little rent in the early years, foregoing short-term grain rent in order to obtain higher long-term returns from date trees, which take several years to mature and yield a crop. They also require good irrigation and maintenance, and thus can be grown only in areas close to a water supply.

Over the course of three Egibi generations, date cultivation on one specific plot along the New Canal increased from just one-thirtieth to one-quarter of the terrain.[31] Much of the land beyond the orchard was suitable for grain, but the part furthest from the canal could not be reached by irrigation. Therefore the tenant was granted especially favorable terms if he would cultivate and water it by bucket.

Niche products. Specialization on a niche product was the key to success for Iddin-Marduk from the Nūr-Sîn family. He focused on onions, which were grown as a by-product alongside the canals. Shipment and distribution certainly required more effort as compared to the same value in grain or dates, but his strategy worked.

Transport and marketing opportunities. There is a tendency to think of entrepreneurs primarily as promoting new industrial technologies. But transportation and marketing have been equally important throughout history (e.g., most recently the Walton family's Wal-Mart stores). In the sixth century BC, major opportunities for enterprise lay in organizing the flow of commodities and payments between cultivators and large institutions.[32] Managers had to establish market relations among the rural areas where cultivators had to pay rent, taxes, and fees for irrigation and other necessities, the urban areas where commodities were needed, and the temple and royal institutions that needed cash or bulk deliveries to support their personnel.

The problem was that tenants and owners of small plots had limited means to ship their crops to the cities and sell them there. The key to linking these spheres was to develop arrangements to collect and ship crops from the countryside to urban consumers, palace dependents, the army, and the temple. Contracts demanding delivery in kind suited the needs of rural farmers as the contracts guaranteed that their crops would be accepted as money equivalent. The traditional Mesopotamian practice was to draw up debt contracts to deliver a given volume of crops at harvest time, in payment for money advanced for seed or draft animals, fees for irrigation water, kindred taxes, or similar items. In this respect early enterprise benefited from arbitrage opportunities associated with creating an articulated system of market relations that helped stimulate market-oriented production above the subsistence level. Almost from the outset, quite modern practices emerged as part of this system.

Tax farming. Tax farming is an arrangement whereby an individual undertakes to collect the taxes due from a given region, in exchange for paying a lump sum to the institution entitled to extract them. The amount is based on the expected tax revenues from that area. Tax farmers make their money by the margin of the collection over payment, and the ancillary lending opportunities that usually go with this activity—most notoriously, rural usury to cultivators who lack the ready cash to pay on the spot.

A high rate of collection was the tax farmer's chief goal, and the business incentive that drove the enterprise. Such activity has the danger of being corrosive unless it is accomplished in a way that sustains the tax base and leads to higher or more efficient production. Tax farming in the ancient Near East could have a positive effect when linked to transport and marketing opportunities.

One of the major problems for small producers was that taxes were increasingly payable in money rather than commodities. Given the limited marketing possibilities in more remote regions, farmers were burdened with produce they could not sell. The Neo-Babylonian tax farmer often established himself as the go-between, accepting commodities for the tax payment from the small rural cultivator, converting the crops to cash through transport and sale, thereby linking the producer and consumer, and then delivering the tax money to the crown. This stimulated market production by linking the producer and consumer and by organizing transport. The tax farmer made his profit in two ways: first, by collecting taxes in excess of what he paid the state, and second, by marketing the crops to consumers to raise the money. An increasing number of people lived in cities and hence had to buy commodities. Intermediaries therefore became critical to a well-functioning economy.

The Egibi family focused their tax-farming business in rural areas along the canals, hiring boats and boatmen to transport goods. Landowners, including the temples, had to pay specific rates to maintain the canals and irrigation system. Establishing contacts with the local official responsible for maintaining the canals and collecting fees from their users, the Egibis supplied him with money to pay the palace in return for the right to extract these fees in kind. They then would establish lending, crop-purchase, and delivery arrangements (all of which were drawn up as debt contracts) that called for cultivators to bring their crops to loading sites along the canal by a specific date as tax payment. Boats were scheduled to deliver the harvest in Babylon, and if the crop was not delivered at the canal by the specified date, the debtor-cultivator was obliged to deliver it in Babylon at his own expense. This tax-farming system enabled the Egibis to transport their crops to Babylon for a flat payment to the local canal official rather than having to pay the retail rate for individual deliveries.

While the Egibis increased access to commodities for trade, their effective control over such toll-collecting points enabled them to obtain a major part of their profit margin at the disadvantage of competitors, much in the way that John D. Rockefeller built up his Standard Oil monopoly by negotiating favorable freight rates with the railroads. Tax farming probably was not their main business purpose, but dovetailed efficiently with other aspects of their commodity trade. Once they had built up a strong shipping, storage, and food-processing network, they had an interest in keeping the supply moving. Whether tax farming was the primary or a secondary profit motive, the family fit into the tax system as intermediaries, advancing money to pay royal taxes against an equivalent amount in the form of crops, spurring agricultural and consumer activity while enlarging their profit margin through market control.

The family appears to have maintained its position as tax farmers even in periods of dynastic change, for example, from Nabonidus to Cyrus (539 BC). To preserve their role, Itti-Marduk-balāṭu journeyed to the Persian court and sought out other high-ranking Babylonians, evidently to befriend the officials responsible for administering taxes under Persia's empire. The result was that when the Persians took over the Babylonian tax system, they delegated responsibility to local officials and businessmen such as the Egibis and other important Babylonian families who knew how the system functioned.

Lending activities. Individuals borrowed money for a broad number of reasons. The less affluent, of course, often borrowed money to cover their subsistence expenses as long as they had some assets that could be used for collateral. When private individuals borrowed, it generally was to pay taxes or to bridge temporary shortfalls. They also might borrow money to pay a hireling to perform their military or corvée service.

Entrepreneurs borrowed to increase liquid capital, raw materials, equipment, personnel—and, in the case of farmers, seed. But unlike the modern world, we find no cases of buying houses or arable fields on credit. There was no mortgage market and hence no financial inflation of property prices A Neo-Babylonian entrepreneur could raise the price of real estate only by actively improving the land, for example, by putting buildings or dwellings on urban plots or planting date palms on irrigated land.

Food processing, distribution, and marketing. Commodity traders tended naturally to extend their activities to processing and distribution down the line to consumers. For example, date traders might have dependents who brewed date beer.[33] The result was an increasing degree of vertical integration.

Textile production. Textiles were a major Mesopotamian export. The Egibis, or at least their relatives, were involved in this trade. Documents show that they bought the wool income of Belshazzar, the crown prince of Nabonidus, enabling them to participate in textile production and export.

The Entrepreneurial Use of Slaves

Slave labor is expensive as compared to free labor, unless the supply is so abundant as to keep replacement costs low.[34] Many Roman slave-owners worked their slaves to death at an early age, but such a practice could be sustained only for a limited period of time. Neo-Babylonian slaves were precious commodities, not easily replenished, and sold for an equivalent of several years' income of a hired worker. They might originate in foreign lands as war captives or through slave trade. Exposed children or those sold by their parents could be brought up as slaves. House-born slaves also were utilized or traded. Slave women typically were given as a dowry to help daughters in the household and in rearing their children. Slaves had to be fed and clothed, which was not cheap.

It made economic sense to raise the value of slaves by training them in professions and renting them out. This is an early example of "human capital," although it took the form of a return on an investment by the owner rather than by the individual being educated. Family members often assigned administrative duties to slaves who showed good business ability. This involved employing them in mercantile trade or delegating management of the family business to them.

Few families voluntarily sold their slaves. Sales usually were preceded by pledging the slave for debt. Slave families typically were sold together, and children were separated from their mother only when they had reached working age. Personal treatment and living conditions certainly were harsh for most of them, but there was no Babylonian anticipation of Rome's slave-stocked latifundia. In agriculture, slaves usually appear as tenants rather than as forced laborers. Most agricultural work, as well as maintenance of the irrigation system, required diligence, foresight, and care. It was more practical to give slaves contracts to work independently so that they would have an interest in the result. Again in contrast to Roman experience, there was little problem of slaves rebelling and using their agricultural tools as weapons. However, some of the inventories made by business partners, or by families for inheritance divisions, report that slaves had run off.

Slaves could live and work independently of their master by paying him a *mandattu* fee. They basically were hiring or renting themselves from their master. As they had to earn much more than an average hireling, this was an option only for clever and well-trained slaves. In addition to paying their own *mandattu*, some privileged Egibi slaves also paid that of their wife so that she could accompany them. Other slaves entered partnerships as junior partners. Such business arrangements will be discussed in more detail below.

As in Greek practice, some Neo-Babylonian slaves acted as proxy for their masters and managed their affairs, but unlike the case in Greece, Neo-Babylonian slaves apparently did not engage in large-scale moneylending. Perhaps this is because in Babylonia there was no moral stigma attached to the practice, which might have prevented their masters from doing it themselves.

Itti-Marduk-balāṭu of the Egibi family entrusted at least three of his slaves with running his on-the-spot affairs during prolonged periods of his absence. Their letters address the master as "my lord," while he addresses his slave as "my brother." One such slave is known to have started a business of his own with five minas of silver and two junior partners.[35] By contrast, Itti-Marduk-balāṭu seems not to have trusted his own brothers in business matters.

In contrast to Roman practice, no evidence exists for Babylonian slaves buying their liberty with money they earned through their enterprise, no matter how rich they became. Manumission was a voluntary act that only could be initiated by the master. In Babylonia manumission normally was connected with the obligation to care for the aging master and mistress until their death. Manumission therefore occurred most often near the end of the slave's working life.

Neo-Babylonian Economic and Legal Institutions: Property and Contract Law

Over a century ago J. B. Say remarked: "English economists almost always confuse under the name of *profit*, the return that the *entrepreneur* obtains from his industry and his talent, and that which he derives from his capital."[36] The contrast between entrepreneurs and more passive financial backers is spelled out in remarkable clarity in Neo-Babylonian *harrānu*[37] contracts that organized trade and business partnerships on a debt/equity basis.

These partnerships commonly were formed between a senior financial backer (the sleeping partner) and an on-the-spot junior partner who did the actual work.[38] Drafted as an interest-free debt contract, they implied that the backer would recoup his original capital upon the dissolution of the business, so that only the profits were shared and either reinvested or distributed in regular intervals. Such partnerships were neither new nor unique, as similar forms of enterprise already are known from the beginning of the second millennium BC under the name of *tappûtum*, especially in long-distance trade. A stipulation in the laws of Hammurabi (ca. 1750 BC) reads:[39]

> If a man gives silver to another man for investment in a partnership venture, before the god they shall equally divide the profit or loss.

The way in which such partnerships are set up corresponds to the principles of the Islamic *muḍāraba*,[40] Italian *commenda*, and the Hanseatic trade partnerships, of which they may be considered ancient ancestors. What is new in Neo-Babylonian times is the scope and the field of activity: many people are doing it, applying its business principle to intraregional trade.

Success would allow junior partners to gradually pay off their backer and reap the fruits of their efforts in full. One such contract, *Nbk* 216 from the thirtieth year of Nebuchadnezzar (575 BC), illustrates this process:

> "Six minas (= 3 kgs.) of silver, (the working capital owed) to person A (is) at the debit of person B, for a *harrānu* (business venture). (Of) whatever he makes (with it) in city and country, one half of the surplus person B shares (lit. "eats") with person A. The(se six minas of) silver are the remaining (unpaid balance of the original) *harrānu* debt note of eleven minas from the twenty-fourth year of Nebuchadnezzar (that was) at the debit of person B."
> Names of three witnesses and the scribe, place and date.[41]

In this arrangement person A was the senior financing partner and person B the junior working partner. The latter would have to share equally with the senior partner whatever profit he made through his own efforts and use of the senior partner's capital. He returned nearly half the original venture capital (in this case amounting to eleven minas of silver) to the venture capitalist over the course of six years.

Such partnerships typically divided the profit equally, as in the above example. But this legal instrument was flexible, and could be adapted to different circumstances depending on the number of partners, their function, and the ratio between capital and work-input.[42]

Such arrangements enabled well-to-do individuals to play the role of venture capitalists by finding capable partners to manage their *harrānu* businesses. There must have been many individuals eager to establish business but without enough capital to set themselves up on their own—for instance, younger sons who did not inherit much. Some Neo-Babylonian archives show such men entering a business as junior partners, working with money put up by a backer, and making enough to rise to the position of senior partner, financing other newcomers to work for them.

One such example is Kāṣir from the Nūr-Sîn family. He started out as a junior partner in 581 BC with eleven minas (ca. 5.5 kg) of silver, and in six years was able to repay his backer nearly half of the original capital out of his earnings.[43] He then was joined by his younger brother Iddin-Marduk from 576 to 572 BC. They already (if possibly only partially) were working with their own funds, and employed an acting partner, although at least on one occasion not successfully.[44] The brothers' business profited from Iddin-Marduk's marriage, as he put seven minas (3.5 kg) of his wife's dowry silver into their risky affairs.[45] Creditors must have had substantial claims against the two of them and their father, for Iddin-Marduk's father-in-law in 571 BC urged him to transfer all his property to his wife as security for her dowry silver that he had invested in his family's business. He dutifully signed over two slave women and their five children—evidently all his property not tied up in the business.[46]

Occasionally two or more partners would pool funds, acting as partners on equal terms in order to achieve·a critical mass for business. *Dar 97* from the Egibi archive (518 BC) is an example of this kind of arrangement:

> "Five minas of A and five minas of B they have put together for a *harrānu* (business venture). (In) whatever they make from these ten minas, they (have) equal (shares)."
>
> Names of at least four witnesses and the scribe, place and date.[47]

We find this type of arrangement also in the affairs of the aforementioned Iddin-Marduk. Ultimately separating himself from his brother's business, he entered into a *harrānu* venture with another person, first as junior partner but soon shifting to a parity arrangement that lasted seven years. Simultaneously, he employed junior partners of his own. In this manner he still did part of the field work himself, while spreading his risks and testing the capabilities of his underlings. His career was typical of entrepreneurs of the time, and is exceptional only because of his remarkable success.

The returns to *harrānu* enterprise typically were high. They had to be, given the customary annual interest rate of 20 percent. This was the "opportunity cost" of capital—what backers could get simply by lending out their money against security. Because the return had to be shared, a *harrānu* venture would make sense for the financial backer only if it promised to return at least 40 percent annually, twice the 20 percent interest rate on secured loans.

The junior partner's objective was to return the venture capital out of his earnings so that he might come to own the business outright. Even after establishing a business with his own equity, however, he might borrow money from the former senior partner or other individuals at interest to bridge a short period or even to expand his operations.

Harrānu ventures might last beyond an entrepreneur's own lifetime when sons inherited and carried on the business. Whereas the relatively short-term Greek and Roman commercial partnerships normally divided up the proceeds upon the completion of each voyage or other venture, the Egibi archive includes one partnership that lasted over forty-two years from one generation to the next. The heirs did not dissolve and divide up the business until such time as the managing partner grew too old to continue running it any longer.[48] Even so, for at least three more years both parties jointly shared the income from a field purchased with business proceeds.

Entrepreneurial Efficiency: A Case Study

How the Egibi family rose from junior partners to large financial entrepreneurs. The Egibi family represents an outstanding example of Schumpeter's idea that the main entrepreneurial opportunities for profit or quasi-rent lie in creating new business practices. The key to their far-flung operations was the ability to turn commodities into money by creating a marketing plan that integrated agricultural production, tax payments, and the shipment of crops to the cities along Babylon's canal system.

It took many years for the founders of the family fortune to accumulate enough money to become backers of their own operations. The archive does not document who provided the money for their earliest ventures. Evidently they were able to find (or be found by) backers, starting out as junior managing partners in profit-sharing *harrānu* ventures. Over a span of two generations the family built up its relationships with some royal officials responsible for collecting taxes and fees linked to land ownership. By the third generation the family is documented maintaining close relations with the governor of Babylon, who was in charge of collecting taxes, organizing corvée labor and the military draft.

Account-keeping and enterprise. Once established, the Egibi family typically conducted its business in partnership arrangements with others, usually on-the-spot entrepreneurs whom they found and backed, just as their own family's business founders were once backed. These partnerships involved a specific activity, such as brewing date-beer or buying local crops and selling them in Babylon. The Egibi prepared regular accounts for these ventures to calculate the surplus.

These businesses usually maintained their working capital at a steady level, distributing profits to the individual partners to do with as they chose. Rather than using them to expand the joint venture, partners typically took their profits out of the business to invest in their own. Their detailed accounts show how much each party put into specific enterprises, and the records assign property and its income to the partners of each venture. The level of detail is comparable to those of Europe's Hanse towns some two thousand years later.

Economic innovation. At the beginning of Nabonidus' reign (555 BC), or maybe even earlier, the Egibis are known the have developed a special relationship to the chief administrator of the crown prince's household. After they had acquired a house adjacent to the crown prince's palace, the Egibis leveraged this real estate investment by borrowing against the house. They arranged a loan-rental mortgage transaction, by borrowing the funds from the man who rented the house, with the rent corresponding to the customary interest charge of 20 percent—the modern definition of equilibrium between asset price, rent, and carrying charges. In other words, the Egibis borrowed to buy a prestigious house, and then turned around and rented it out to their creditor.[49]

Antichretic credit arrangements (where use of the pledge is granted to the creditor in lieu of interest payments) were not new in themselves, but normally they were used in a different context. When an individual in need of cash had pledged his house or field as security to a creditor, but at a certain point could not catch up with the interest payment, he would relinquish to his creditor the right to use the pledged asset, in lieu of the interest payment. This typically was the final, and sometimes long-lasting, stage before transfer of ownership. The Egibis, in contrast, were not debtors in distress. They rather used this legal instrument to acquire title to the house but kept its value liquid for other business ventures, a clear sign of their creative approach to a given legal framework. The brilliance of this arrangement was that it involved the administrator of the crown prince's palace as creditor-tenant, who thus could make use of the premises. For the Egibis, this transaction essentially was an interest-free loan, and did not require any real flow of funds until the debt eventually was repaid. This loan/rent contract was occasionally renewed and remained in place under four different rulers and through the dynastic change, from the reign of Nabonidus to Darius. This was important in view of the standard 20 percent per annum rate of interest on secured loans, which did not allow profitable real estate speculation—a major factor keeping real estate prices fairly stable, except as they reflected economic growth and prosperity.

Moneylending and the question of banking. Late nineteenth-century literature, written shortly after the Egibi archive was discovered, described them as bankers of Jewish descent. Their family name was thought to derive from Hebrew *Jacob*. This fit contemporary perceptions (or rather misconceptions) about Jews and their role in banking. Even today some publications apply these labels without explanation, though the ideas both of "bankers" and the allegedly Jewish ethnicity of the Egibis were shown to be inappropriate many decades ago. The family name *Egibi* is of straightforward Sumero-Babylonian origin,[50] and the business of the branch that left the famous archive fits the description of *entrepreneurs* rather than being associated with deposit banking.[51]

Investment of business profits. Successful business operations yielded high profits, but it made sense to add this gain to the working capital only under conditions where a healthy expansion could be achieved. Partners typically chose to retire some capital by distributing it among themselves, to buy land, houses, slaves, and luxury goods whenever opportunities were available. This generated further income and helped build up their prestige while serving as a store of value that could be collateralized for a loan when necessary. One set of Egibi records regards the sale of assets worth fifty minas of silver to settle debts that were probably accumulated backlogs.

When the Egibi inheritance was divided among the fourth-generation sons in 508 BC, the family owned sixteen houses in Babylon and Borsippa and more than one hundred slaves, not to mention agricultural land not inventoried on this occasion.

Economy-Wide Efficiency of Enterprise

Rent and tax farming are much like the privatization of modern public utilities: they may or may not be efficient. The motive for institutions to privatize is understandable. They need reliability, stability, and accountability, which they may be unable to get internally for one reason or another. Entrepreneurs, of course, get into the arrangement for the money. In such cases the question is always whether the private entrepreneur can serve the public better and more efficiently than a public institution or its officials. Will the profit motive invite efficiency, or become corrosive as investors extract as much profit as possible in as short a time as possible, leaving the business in ruins? However we may answer such questions, it seems that Neo-Babylonian society found the outsourcing of various royal and temple functions to be an important and productive economic practice. But constraints were put on them.

Incentives and Disincentives for Innovation

Two obstacles to enterprise can be identified: the effort needed for political lobbying and the inheritance system.

Political lobbying. Businessmen engaged in rent or tax farming depend upon certain political institutions and officials. Such undertakings demand care of political relationships. Rent or tax farmers may have had to spend a great deal of time establishing and maintaining such contacts, and expended resources on prestige goods to give as presents, incentives, or bribes. This is inherently risky business because the entrepreneur never can be fully sure that powerful benefactors will not turn against him. Itti-Marduk-balāṭu traveled to Persia for extended periods to secure his tax-farming business. These trips were apparently strenuous and dangerous, as he made his will before he left the first time. They were critical to his success, as they were to other Babylonian families.

Inheritance divisions. Inheritance rules often are blamed as business disrupters by causing productive assets to be divided between many heirs, each receiving a share too small to be profitable. This happens under traditional Islamic law and has been cited as one of the reasons why capitalist development did not occur in Islamic societies in the same way as in the West.[52] In Neo-Babylonian practice, sons were the only heirs, who excluded collateral relatives, and women could not inherit through intestate succession. Furthermore, at least half of the legacy remained in one hand, as the law provided that the eldest son receive twice as much as his brother, or half of the estate if there were more than two sons.[53] This middle-of-the-road approach assured that none of the brothers went penniless, while keeping the core business intact.

Moreover, Neo-Babylonian society had the institution of "undivided brothers" comparable to the Hindu joint family,[54] allowing the business to be kept running as a single entity for a considerable period of time after the father's death. Without any need for legal formalities, the eldest son succeeded to his father's business and represented the heirs collectively. This delayed the inheritance division—an essential condition for a smooth transition. As long as brothers did not divide their father's inheritance, all business proceeds belonged to all of them according to their shares in the inheritance, regardless of who did the actual work.

Such arrangements were not always without conflict. Evidence again is glimpsed from the Egibi records. When Itti-Marduk-balāṭu's eldest son finally sorted out the family business with his two brothers, some fourteen years after his father's demise, he tried to claim certain objects on the ground that they had been bought with money of his wife in her own name. The brothers refused to accept his claim, as the dowry's usufruct lay with the husband's father, and subsequently with his heirs as long as they maintained their undivided status. In the end everything had to be included in the division.[55] In sum, Neo-Babylonian inheritance rules had some dysfunctional business consequences as compared to primogeniture, but did not cause the same level of disruption found in many other systems that practice partible inheritance or include a wider circle of heirs.

Lessons for Contemporary Innovative Entrepreneurship

The Neo-Babylonian political and economic environment provided ample room for innovation toward higher levels of productivity in an agriculturally based economy. It permitted and required entrepreneurs to function as intermediaries between the basic level of agricultural production and consumers on the one hand, and between the individual landholder and all levels of royal or temple administration on the other. As intermediaries they helped extend and intensify agricultural production and processing of raw materials. By extending credit and monetizing commodity payment-in-kind into money-taxes they helped monetize and integrate different sectors of production.

The moral is that new technologies and equipment are not the only important ways to increase productivity. Critical aspects of entrepreneurial success include the way relationships are established, the way labor and profit is shared, the methods of financing, and the manner of product marketing and distribution.

Notes

[1] Nabopolassar (21 years, 626–605), his son Nebuchadnezzar II (43 years, 605–562), the latter's son Evil-merodach (2 years, 562–560; murdered), Nebuchadnezzar's son-in-law Neriglissar (4 years, 560–556), followed by the latter's son Laborosoarchod, who only reigned for two or three months until Nabonidus usurped power. His son Belshazzar was left in charge of Babylonia when Nabonidus spent several years in the Arabian desert, but was never recognized as king; hence all contemporary Babylonian records date to the reign of Nabonidus (17 years, 556–539).

[2] The best-known example is the biblical account on the Judaeans in Babylonian captivity. Tablets excavated in the southern palace of Babylon document the issuing of commodities to high-profile captives or hostages (Weidner 1939). Among the recipients are dignitaries from Judah, most prominently King Jehoiachin (cf. 2 Kings 24.8–12; 25.27–30; 2 Chr. 36.9–10; for an easy-to-find summary of the Babylonian sources see www.livius.org/ne-nn/nebuchadnezzar/anet308.html). Recent tablet discoveries allow a glimpse of the lives of ordinary Judaean people, deported and settled in rural Babylonia. For an overview see Pearce 2006; a full edition is being prepared by her and the present author.

[3] On this transition see most recently Jursa 2007 with previous literature.

[4] Cyrus (9 years, 539–530), his son Cambyses (8 years, 530–522), and Darius (from a side branch of the Achaemenids, 36 years, 522–486). The short-lived reigns of Smerdis (alias Bardiya, also called Gaumata) and the usurpers Nebuchadnezzar III and IV date to 522 and 521.

[5] Herodotus, *Histories I* (Kleio), 192.

[6] This has been suggested by van Driel 2002, 164–65, 318–19, and discussed by Jursa (2004), who argues that an increase in productivity and export volume offset the negative effects of Persian taxation. Babylonia must have exported textiles and food to obtain the silver paid to Persia. Productivity increase can be demonstrated for institutional agriculture, although probably it was not enough to offset the increasing tax burden in the long run.

[7] For the dates of the Babylonian revolts against Persian rule and their political consequences, as well as a thorough study and interpretation of the phenomenon of the end of these archives, see Waerzeggers 2003–4, with discussion of previous literature.

[8] According to Jursa 2005, 1.

[9] Jursa (2005, 57–152) provides an overview in English of Neo-Babylonian archival documents according to provenance and excavation history, as well as a brief summary of their contents.

[10] For an overview see Wunsch 2007 (in English); more detailed in Wunsch 2000a, esp. 1–19 (in German).

[11] Francesco di Marco Datini (1335–1410); most of them business letters (Origo 1997, 8).

[12] Jursa 2007 provides the most recent and reliable overview in English on the economic situation of Mesopotamia during the first millennium BC.

[13] Known as *bīt redûti* "house of succession" or *bīt mār šarri* "house of the king's son" in sources from Neo-Babylonian as well as Achaemenid times, this institution seems to have survived the political and dynastic change virtually unchanged.

[14] Akkadian *rab kāṣir*, Persian *ganzabara*. Estates of this official are known from the vicinity of Babylon, and the Egibi family was involved in managing them.

[15] The term *oblate*, derived from Latin *offerre* "to offer," essentially means the same as Akkadian *širkū*, i.e., a person given or presented to a religious institution, although the concepts behind the terms differ a bit. Babylonian temple dependents (also referred to as "temple slaves") were bound to live and work in their temple or on its land (much as the serfs of Indian temples), but in contrast to Christian oblates they were encouraged to live in families to reproduce and allowed to own personal property. Nevertheless, living conditions must have been harsh for most of them, as temple records constantly report on escaped personnel.

[16] These were better conditions than granted to temple oblates. The temple administration had to deal with the fact that their dependents tried to rent out portions of their (usually too large) assignments in outlaying areas where administrative control was less effective; see Janković 2005.

[17] On details of rent farming in the temple context see Cocquerillat 1968 (concerning date orchards of Eanna in Uruk [in French] and Jursa 1995 (on arable land and date orchards of Ebabbar in Sippar [in German]).

[18] See Hudson, chap. 1 in this volume.

[19] Van Driel 1999 discusses this dossier of texts.

[20] The tablet dates to the eighth year of Darius (514 BC). See MacGinnis 2007, text no. 1.

[21] This does not mean banking. Banking in its narrow definition refers to taking in deposits, giving out credit, and living off the interest differential. That did not happen until the third century, as Jursa 2007 has shown.

[22] See Kozuh, forthcoming, for details.

[23] Fishing is best documented in the Eanna archive of Uruk; see Kleber 2004 (in German).

[24] This was spelled out by Jursa 2004, based on ideas of Vilfredo Pareto and Max Weber.

[25] The example of the Šangû-Gula family is treated by Wunsch 2000a, 139–50.

[26] The evidence has been studied by Caroline Waerzeggers and presented at a conference in 2004; the results will be included in a forthcoming study. This summary is based on her communication.

[27] Wunsch 2004, 370–71.

[28] See Jursa 2005b, 108–9, sub 7.9.1.1. for an overview of the archive of Itti-Šamaš-balāṭu and the Šamaš-bāri file with a brief discussion on their connection. Itti-Šamaš-balāṭu's activities are covered in greater detail by Beaulieu 2000.

[29] Roth 1991.

[30] References are discussed by Jursa 2002, 203–5.

[31] This land probably was claimed early in Nebuchadnezzar's reign, in 2,000-meter-wide strips on both sides of the canal, subdivided into units of 1/50 and 1/1000. The Egibis bought it in 559 BC from the heirs of a former governor of Babylon.

[32] See Cocquerillat 1968 (for Eanna at Uruk) and Jursa 1995 and 1998 (for Ebabbar at Sippar).

[33] This is known from the Egibi and Bēl-eṭēri-Šamaš archives.

[34] Compare Goody 1980. In some societies slavery existed for considerations of prestige: "By supporting slaves who might be less productive than hired workers the masters are, in effect, displaying their wealth for all to see.... The exhibition of idleness may be the slave's only real duty but this has to be extracted like any other service" (Watson 1980, 8).

[35] *Nbn* 466 (Strassmaier 1889b; 545 BC): Nergal-rēṣua. He still nominally belonged to Ina-Esagil-ramât (the wife of Iddin-Marduk and mother-in-law of Itti-Marduk-balāṭu), and probably was the son of one of her dowry slaves.

[36] Say 1803, book 2, chap. 5; 1972, 352. English translation after Charles Gide, "Jean Baptiste Say," *Palgrave's Dictionary of Political Economy* (London, 1926).

[37] Originally meaning "path, road," the term broadened to include all sorts of road travel, such as "military campaign, expedition, business trip, caravan." Its use as a legal term designates a special kind of partnership venture and the capital provided for it.

[38] Lanz (1976) studied the legal aspects of these partnerships. For additional details see Jursa 2005a, 212–22 (both in German). A comprehensive study of the economic aspects of such partnerships (including the source material published after 1976) is much desired.

[39] The translation follows Roth 1995 (p. 99, gap ¶ cc; in other editions counted as §98).

[40] See the contribution by Timur Kuran, chap. 3 in this volume.

[41] *Nbk* 216 (Strassmaier 1889a) from 21/ix/30 Nebuchadnezzar = 25.10.575 BC, edited in Wunsch 1993 as no. 5. The conversion of Babylonian dates into the Julian calendar is based on Parker and Dubberstein 1956.

[42] As pointed out by Jursa (2004), who discusses the many possibilities.

[43] *Nbk* 216; see translation above at note 38.

[44] BRM 1 49 (Clay 1912), edited in Wunsch 1993 as no. 7.

[45] *Nbk* 254 (Strassmaier 1889a) (572 BC, edited in Wunsch 1993 as no. 9) reads: "The account balance concerning the silver that PN_1 (the father-in law) has put as dowry at the disposal of PN_2 and that is at the debit of PN_2 and PN_3 (the brothers) they have not yet finished."

[46] *Nbk* 265 (Strassmaier 1889a), edited in Wunsch 1993 as no. 13.

[47] *Dar* 97 (Strassmaier 1897) from 14/xii/3 Darius = 12.3.518 BC.

[48] First partnership contract: *Nbk* 300 (Strassmaier 1889a; 569 BC). The dissolution in the third year of Cambyses is mentioned in BM 31959 (edited in Wunsch 2000a as no. 10; for more detail see 1:99–104).

[49] For details see Wunsch 2000a, 103–4.

[50] Egibi is an abbreviation of Sumerian E.GI-BA-TI.LA, the full form being used occasionally in the archival records. In a learned text on the meaning of their most ancient family names Babylonian scribes equate it to the Babylonian name *Sîn-taqîša-libluṭ*, which can be translated as "O Sin [the moon god], you have granted (us this child), may he now live and thrive," which follows a well-attested Semitic name pattern. The Assyriologist F. E. Peiser already in 1897 pointed out that it had nothing to do with *Jacob*, and occurs in cuneiform records in the eighth century BC, long before the time of the Babylonian captivity.

[51] R. Bogaert's exhaustive 1966 study on early "banking" shows that the essential characteristic of taking money as a deposit and lending it out at a higher rate cannot be found.

[52] See Timur Kuran's contribution to this volume for details.

[53] These rules are derived from practical texts such as records of inheritance divisions, property transfers, wills, etc., as law collections covering this topic comparable to the Codex Hammurabi from the early second millennium are not preserved from this period. The preferential double share for the eldest son also features in pre-Neo-Babylonian times. The fact that the eldest of more than three sons takes one-half of the inheritance (i.e., more than a double share) has been a recent discovery; see Wunsch 2004, 130–31, 144–45. A comprehensive study of inheritance law in first-millennium Mesopotamia is being prepared by the present author.

[54] Joint families consist of several generations, with all the male members being blood relatives. The family is headed by the pater familias, usually the oldest male, who makes decisions on economic and social matters on behalf of the entire family. All property is held jointly with virtual shares assigned according to each member's inheritance rights. As long as the undivided status remains, all income achieved by any of the members accrues to all of them proportionately.

[55] The record on the inheritance division is *Dar* 379 (Strassmaier 1897) from 508 BC. It contains the following stipulation (ll. 55–56 and 59–60): "(Concerning) all their fields, as many as there are, including the fields that...(the eldest son) has bought in in his (own) name, (in the name of) ..., his wife, or in the name of someone else:...(the eldest son) will take a half share, and... (the younger brothers) will take a half share (of the aforementioned assets)."

References

Abraham, Kathleen. 2004. *Business and Politics under the Persian Empire. The Financial Dealings of Marduk-nāṣir-apli of the House of Egibi*. Bethesda, MD: CDL Press.

Baker, Heather D., and Michael Jursa, eds. 2005. *Approaching the Neo-Babylonian Economy: Proceedings of the START Project Symposium Held in Vienna, 1–3 July 2004*. Alter Orient und Altes Testament 330. Münster: Ugarit-Verlag.

Beaulieu, Paul-Alain. 2000. "A Finger in Every Pie: The Institutional Connections of a Family of Entrepreneurs in Neo-Babylonian Larsa." In *Interdependency of Institutions and Private Entrepreneurs: Proceedings of the Second MOS Symposium (Leiden 1998)*, ed. A.C.V.M. Bongenaar, 43–72. Istanbul: Nederlands Historisch-Archaeologisch Instituut te Istanbul; Leiden: Nederlands Instituut voor het Nabije Oosten.

Bongenaar, A.C.V.M., ed. 2000. *Interdependency of Institutions and Private Entrepreneurs: Proceedings of the Second MOS Symposium (Leiden 1998)*. Istanbul: Nederlands Historisch-Archaeologisch Instituut te Istanbul; Leiden: Nederlands Instituut voor het Nabije Oosten.

Cocquerillat, Denise. 1968. *Palmeraies et cultures de l'Eanna d'Uruk (559–520)*. Ausgrabungen der Deutschen Forschungsgemeinschaft in Uruk-Warka 8. Berlin: Mann.

Clay, Albert T., ed. 1912. *BRM 1. Babylonian Records in the Library of J. Pierpont Morgan*. Part 1. New York, privately printed.

van Driel, Govert. 1999. "Agricultural Entrepreneurs in Mesopotamia." In *Landwirtschaft im Alten Orient (CRRAI 41, 1994)*, ed. Horst Klengel and Johannes Renger, 213–23. Berliner Beiträge zum Vorderen Orient 18. Berlin: Reimer.

———. 2002. *Elusive Silver: In Search of a Role for a Market in an Agrarian Environment. Aspects of Mesopotamia's Society*. Istanbul: Nederlands Instituut voor het Nabije Oosten.

Goody, Jack. 1980. "Slavery in Time and Space." In *Asian and African Systems of Slavery*, ed. James L. Watson, 16–42. Oxford: Basil Blackwell.

Janković, Bojana. 2005. "Between a Rock and a Hard Place: An Aspect of the Manpower Problem in the Agricultural Sector of Eanna." In *Approaching the Neo-Babylonian Economy: Proceedings of the START Project Symposium Held in Vienna, 1–3 July 2004*, ed. Heather D. Baker and Michael Jursa, 167–81. Alter Orient und Altes Testament 330. Münster: Ugarit-Verlag.

Joannès, Francis. 2000. "Relations entre intérêts privés et biens des sanctuaires à l'époque néo-babylonienne." In *Interdependency of Institutions and Private Entrepreneurs: Proceedings of the Second MOS Symposium (Leiden 1998)*, ed. A.C.V.M. Bongenaar, 25–41. Istanbul: Nederlands Historisch-Archaeologisch Instituut te Istanbul; Leiden: Nederlands Instituut voor het Nabije Oosten.

Jones, David. 2006. *The Bankers of Puteoli: Finance, Trade, and Industry in the Roman World*. London: Tempus.

Jursa, Michael. 1995. *Die Landwirtschaft in Sippar in neubabylonischer Zeit*. Archiv für Orientforschung, Beiheft 25. Vienna: Institut für Orientalistik.

———. 1998. *Der Tempelzehnt in Babylonien vom siebenten bis zum dritten Jahrhundert v. Chr.* Alter Orient und Altes Testament 254. Münster: Ugarit-Verlag.

———. 2004. "Grundzüge der Wirtschaftsformen Babyloniens im ersten Jahrtausend v. Chr." In *Commerce and Monetary Systems in the Ancient World: Means of Transmission and Cultural Interaction. Proceedings of the Fifth Annual Symposium of the Assyrian and Babylonian Intellectual Heritage Project Held in Innsbruck, Austria, October 3rd–8th, 2002*, ed. Robert Rollinger and Christopf Ulf, 115–36. Melammu 5. Stuttgart: Franz Steiner Verlag.

———. 2005a. "Das Archiv von Bēl-eṭēri-Šamaš." In *Approaching the Neo-Babylonian Economy: Proceedings of the START Project Symposium Held in Vienna, 1–3 July 2004*, ed. Heather D. Baker and Michael Jursa, 197–268. Alter Orient und Altes Testament 330. Münster: Ugarit-Verlag.

———. 2005b. *Neo-Babylonian Legal and Administrative Archives: Typology, Contents, and Archives*. Guides to the Mesopotamian Textual Record 1. Münster: Ugarit-Verlag.

———. 2007a. "The Transition of Babylonia from the Neo-Babylonian Empire to Achaemenid Rule." In *Regime Change in the Ancient Near East and Egypt: From Sargon of Agade to Saddam Hussein*, ed. Harriet Crawford, 73–94. Proceedings of the British Academy 136. Oxford: Oxford University Press.

———. 2007b. "The Babylonian Economy in the First Millennium BC." In *The Babylonian World*, ed. Gwendolyn Leick, 220–31. London: Routledge.

Kleber, Kristin. 2004. "Die Fischerei in der spätbabylonischen Zeit." *Wissenschaftliche Zeitschrift für die Kunde des Morgenlandes* 94:133–65.

Kozuh, Michael. Forthcoming. *The Sacrificial Economy: On the Management of Sacrificial Sheep and Goats at the Neo-Babylonian/Achaemenid Temple of Uruk*.

Lanz, Hugo. 1976. *Die neubabylonischen ḫarrânu-Geschäftsunternehmen*. Münchener Universitätsschriften, Juristische Fakultät. Abhandlungen zur rechtswissenschaftlichen Grundlagenforschung 18. Berlin: J. Schweitzer.

Leick, Gwendolyn, ed. 2007. *The Babylonian World*. London: Routledge.

MacGinnis, John D. 2007. "Fields of Endeavour: Leasing and Releasing the Land of Šamaš." *Jaarbericht van het Vooraziatisch-Egyptisch Genotshap Ex Oriente Lux* 40:91–101.

Origo, Iris. 1997. *"Im Namen Gottes und des Geschäfts": Lebensbild eines toskanischen Kaufmannes der Frührenaissance*. Trans. U. Trott. Berlin: Klaus Wagenbach. First ed. in English under the title *The Merchant of Prato: Francesco di Marco Datini* (London: Jonathan Cape, 1957).

Parker, Richard A., and Waldo H. Dubberstein. 1956. *Babylonian Chronology, 626 B.C.–A.D. 75*. Brown University Studies 19. Providence, RI: Brown University Press.

Pearce, Laurie E. 2006. "New Evidence for Judeans in Babylonia." In *Judah and the Judeans in the Persian Period*, ed. Oded Lipschits and Manfred Oeming, 399–411. Winona Lake, IN: Eisenbrauns.

Roth, Martha T. 1991. "The Women of the Itti-Marduk-balāṭu Family." *Journal of the American Oriental Society* 111:19–37.

———. 1995. *Law Collection from Mesopotamia and Asia Minor*. Writings from the Ancient World—Society of Biblical Literature 6. Atlanta: Scholars Press.

Say, Jean Baptiste. 1972. *Traité d'économie politique ou simple exposition de la manière dont se forment, se distribuent ou se consomment les richesses* (1803). Collection Perspectives de l'économique—Les fondateurs. Paris: Calmann-Lévy Éditeur.

Strassmaier, Johann Nepomuk. 1889a. *Inschriften von Nabuchodonosor, König von Babylon (604–561 v. Chr.)*. Babylonische Texte, vols. 5–6. Leipzig.

———. 1889b. *Inschriften von Nabonidus, König von Babylon (555–538 v. Chr.)*. Babylonische Texte, vols. 1–4. Leipzig.

———. 1897. *Inschriften von Darius, König von Babylon (521–485)*. Babylonische Texte, vols. 10–12. Leipzig.

Waerzeggers, Caroline. 2003–4. "The Babylonian Revolts Against Xerxes and the 'End of Archives.'" *Archiv für Orientforschung* 50:150–73.

Watson, James L., ed. 1980. *Asian and African Systems of Slavery*. Oxford: Basil Blackwell.

Weidner, Ernst F. 1939. "Jojachin, König von Juda, in babylonischen Keilschrifttexten." In *Mélanges syriens offerts à Monsieur René Dussaud...par ses amis et ses élèves*, 2:923–35. Paris: P. Geuthner.

Wunsch, Cornelia. 1993. *Die Urkunden des babylonischen Geschäftsmannes Iddin-Marduk. Zum Handel mit Naturalien im 6. Jh. v. Chr.* Cuneiform Monographs, 3 A and B. Groningen: STYX.

———. 2000a. *Das Egibi-Archiv. I. Die Felder und Gärten*. Cuneiform Monographs, 20 A and B. Groningen: STYX.

———. 2000b. "Neubabylonische Geschäftsleute und ihre Beziehungen zu Palast- und Tempelverwaltungen: Das Beispiel der Familie Egibi." In *Interdependency of Institutions and Private Entrepreneurs: Proceedings of the Second MOS Symposium (Leiden 1998)*, ed. A.C.V.M. Bongenaar, 95–118. Istanbul: Nederlands Historisch-Archaeologisch Instituut te Istanbul; Leiden: Nederlands Instituut voor het Nabije Oosten.

———. 2003. "Mesopotamia: Neo-Babylonian Period." In *A History of Ancient Near Eastern Law*, ed. Raymond Westbrook, 2:920–44. Handbuch der Orientalistik 72. Leiden: Brill.

———. 2004. *Urkunden zum Ehe-, Vermögens- und Erbrecht aus verschiedenen neubabylonischen Archiven*. Babylonische Archive 2. Dresden: ISLET.

———. 2005. "The Šangû-Ninurta Family." In *Approaching the Neo-Babylonian Economy: Proceedings of the START Project Symposium Held in Vienna, 1–3 July 2004*, ed. Heather D. Baker and Michael Jursa, 355–416. Alter Orient und Altes Testament 330. Münster: Ugarit-Verlag.

———. 2007. "The Egibi Family." In *The Babylonian World*, ed. Gwendolyn Leick, 232–43. London: Routledge.

Chapter 3 ——————————————

The Scale of Entrepreneurship in Middle Eastern History: Inhibitive Roles of Islamic Institutions

TIMUR KURAN

AT LEAST FROM THE NINETEENTH CENTURY ONWARD, certain observers have viewed Islam as a religion that discourages entrepreneurship by fostering fatalism, conformism, and conservatism.[1] Leading Muslim reformers of the nineteenth century, including Jamal al-Din al-Afghani (1839–97), believed that this view confuses a perverted form of Islam, which counsels passive resignation to events, with authentic Islam, which holds individuals responsible for their acts and requires the use of God-given talents (Hourani 1983, 128–29).

Islamism, which emerged through the works of Sayyid Abul-Ala Mawdudi (1903–79), Sayyid Qutb (1906–66), and Muhammad Baqir al-Sadr (1931–80), generally agrees that Islam encourages entrepreneurship. Islam promotes creative experimentation, Islamists hold, at least in regard to science, technology, and economics. Islamic economics, a doctrine ostensibly based on the fundamental sources of Islam, highlights Islamic institutions designed to stimulate entrepreneurship.[2] Islamic banking, the most salient achievement of Islamic economics, is meant to finance entrepreneurs without regard to their ability to post collateral.[3] Islamic economics texts routinely cite scripture interpreted as encouraging entrepreneurship, such as the following: "When the prayers are ended, disperse and go in quest of Allah's bounty" (Qur'an, 62:10) (Sadeq 1990, 25, 36).

The uninitiated may wonder whether these interpretations relate to the same region or religion. In fact, each draws a caricature. Islamic economics effectively equates a selective reading of Islamic doctrines with Muslim practices, failing to recognize the existence and historical persistence of Islamic institutions inimical to economic creativity. One contributor presents Islamic banking, which emerged in the 1970s, as testament to the adaptability of Islamic law, neglecting to address why under Islamic law institutions of private finance stagnated for close to a millennium (Ahmed 2006). Al-Afghani characterizes as corruption the deficiencies of Muslim practices, without explaining why "authentic Islam" proved corruptible. For their part, observers who consider Islam fatalistic and conservative overlook that for much of Islamic history the Middle East was considered prosperous. Although the anti-Islamic diatribes of premodern Europe faulted Islam for many things, they did not treat it as a source economic backwardness (Rodinson 1987, esp. 18–23). Visitors of the sixteenth century did not consider the Middle East lacking in entrepreneurship.

With the partial exception of Islamic economics, the foregoing intellectual traditions overlook that decisions to innovate depend on institutions. No matter how motivated people are to take chances, if they cannot raise capital, or their entrepreneurial rewards are insecure, they will turn their energies elsewhere. To an outsider, they will seem fatalistic, wedded to tradition, and uninterested in improving their living standards. By themselves, then, such traits as fatalism and conservatism do not explain the underdevelopment of today's Arabs, Middle Easterners, or Muslims. Insofar as antientrepreneurial traits are ascribed to Islamic teachings, there is the further problem that Islam has a rich heritage capable of supporting sundry causes and lifestyles. If antientrepreneurial attitudes are dominant, it is necessary to explain why one particular interpretation of Islam has prevailed.

To its credit, Islamic economics recognizes that the institutional nexus affects entrepreneurial incentives. Yet what it offers as the ideal set of institutions is an oversimplified interpretation of classical Islamic law, which took shape between the seventh and tenth centuries. It assumes, in effect, that institutional efficiency is invariant to context.[4] Accounts of Islamic history that point to attitudinal handicaps share this characteristic: in ignoring the infrastructure of exchange, they effectively treat it as irrelevant to entrepreneurial performance.

In fact, the supply of entrepreneurship depends on the suitability of incumbent institutions to the prevailing challenges. As I will show, Middle Eastern institutions well suited to personal exchange—the global norm in the medieval era—became a source of retardation with the transition to impersonal exchange. Though continuing to support small-scale entrepreneurship, they inhibited larger-scale entrepreneurship. Removing obstacles to entrepreneurship is itself among the tasks of entrepreneurs. But certain obstacles are harder to overcome than others. A satisfactory account of links between Islam and Middle Eastern entrepreneurship must make sense not only of the observed entrepreneurial record but also of the associated institutional history.

Entrepreneurship and Its Dependence on History

Entrepreneurship is a concept often used imprecisely. Here it refers to the activities of people who are extraordinarily alert to opportunities for gain and unusually eager to exploit them. Like everyone else, entrepreneurs receive more information than they can process. What sets them apart is that they notice opportunities that most others miss. Their responses dampen disequilibria, as Friedrich Hayek (1937) and Israel Kirzner (1979) emphasized. They also lessen inefficiencies, as Harvey Leibenstein (1968) stressed. As a by-product, entrepreneurial responses generate new disequilibria and inefficiencies, creating, as Joseph Schumpeter (1934) argued, exploitable opportunities for others.

With respect to an economy subject to natural shocks, and situated in a dynamic global economy, these varied observations correspond to facets of a single process of decentralized transformation. Fusing them into a single theory of entrepreneurship, as Mark Casson (2003) has attempted, makes entrepreneurs appear at once as initiators, exploiters, and managers of change. They create new markets, but also enhance their productivity in existing ones. They generate new forms of organization, find novel ways to deploy the new forms, and initiate refinements.

This integrative view of entrepreneurship implies that it can feed on itself. With every active entrepreneur unwittingly creating opportunities for others, innovations can stimulate further innovations. A society that has experienced many recent innovations will feature disequilibria in many markets, presenting myriad opportunities to alert people. Their entrepreneurial activities will then beget new dislocations, presenting opportunities to a fresh set of entrepreneurs. By the same token, if entrepreneurship is somehow deficient, the deficiency need not be self-correcting. Precisely because of the paucity of entrepreneurship, exploitable disequilibria will be scarce, and the condition of limited entrepreneurship will perpetuate itself. A long-stagnant social system will experience few dislocations. Hence, its entrepreneurs will find few opportunities to put their talents to use. A society can stagnate, then, simply because it was stagnant in the past. It can find itself trapped in a lethargic state characterized by low entrepreneurship, not because it lacks risk takers but because of its entrepreneurial history.

The social unit experiencing persistently low entrepreneurship need not be as large as an entire civilization, or even a nation. It could be an economic sector or geographic region. One sector may appear structurally stagnant, and its members lethargic, conservative, and fatalistic, even as another displays creativity and vigor. The contrast will be compounded insofar as entrepreneurs are mobile. In search of higher returns to their talents, they will flock to the relatively dynamic sector.

Scholars who characterize the Middle East or the broader Islamic world as deficient in entrepreneurship usually have in mind its commercial sectors. This emphasis has a sound empirical basis. Historically, the state displayed considerable flexibility in domains critical to its own immediate survival. For instance, methods of taxation changed repeatedly in response to new conditions (Løkkegaard 1950; Darling 1996; Coşgel 2005). By contrast, neither Islamic contract law nor Islamic commercial practices changed significantly between the tenth and seventeenth centuries.[5] This institutional stagnation went hand in hand, we shall see, with a slip in the relative global significance of Middle Eastern entrepreneurial feats. The challenge ahead is to identify the sources of this relative decline.

Entrepreneurial Activity in the Medieval Middle East

The emergence and spread of Islam in the early seventh century CE, like the development of other great religions, involved entrepreneurial acts of immense ingenuity. Muhammad displayed remarkable social, political, economic, and military ingenuity in securing the earliest conversions, moving with his coreligionists from Mecca to Medina to establish a rudimentary state, and then defeating his pagan opposition by taking control of the region's commercial arteries. Over the next few centuries the development of Islamic norms, standards, rules, laws, practices, organizations, belief systems, and reward mechanisms entailed a creative synthesis based on the appropriation, but also the refinement and modification, of pre-Islamic institutions.

Of particular interest here are institutions designed to facilitate entrepreneurship. Entrepreneurs commonly lack the resources to carry out their ambitions. To succeed, they depend on the capital and labor of others. Classical Islamic law harbors a law of contracts that offers entrepreneurs various contractual templates, each suitable to a distinct range of objectives (Udovitch 1970; Nyazee 1999). This law provided peoples all across the Islamic world, which by the eighth century stretched from the Atlantic Ocean to the shores of China, an essentially uniform legal system enforceable wherever Muslims ruled.

The indebtedness of Islamic contract law to other civilizations is a matter of controversy, as are its influences on the institutional evolution of Mediterranean Europe. What is settled is that around the tenth century it was at least as advanced as its analogues prevalent elsewhere. Not surprisingly, at the time Islam was still spreading to far corners of the world, sometimes through the sword, but also through mercantile colonies operating under Islamic law. It was merchants who carried Islam to many parts of East Africa, India, China, and, later, Indonesia. Their trading posts attracted diverse professionals. In addition to privileged access to their services, the incentives for converting to Islam included acceptance into Muslim trading networks, preferential treatment in Islamic courts, eligibility for high administrative positions, and sometimes also lower taxation.

The commercial missions that contributed to Islam's expansion generally entailed forays into the unknown. Prior to the emergence of Muslim-Chinese colonies, boarding a ship or joining a caravan headed to China required courage as well as a taste for adventure. Ordinarily an individual who undertook such a voyage sought outside financing under Islamic contract law. Securing the necessary financing was itself a challenge requiring creativity. The missions also required collective action, to achieve both security in numbers and bargaining power in negotiations. Although information on Islam's early commercial expansions is scant, we know that when a ship carrying Middle Easterners arrived in a foreign land, representatives of its passengers negotiated with the ruler's side over trading privileges and settlement rights.

The voyages that carried Middle Eastern merchants to uncharted foreign lands often resulted in the opening of new markets (Ashtor 1976, chap. 3; Abu-Lughod 1989, chap. 8; Chaudhuri 1985, chap. 2). The early waves of Middle Eastern settlers in East Africa introduced new commodities into the continent. Where commercially less advanced societies were involved, the process of market opening also required the diffusion of certain Middle Eastern institutions. Thus, in connecting parts of tropical Africa with global markets, Muslim merchants carried commercial regulations into places without written laws. They also introduced arithmetic, which simplified accounting, and metal coins, which facilitated payments and wealth accumulation. Further, they spread Arabic as a commercial lingua franca—a facilitator of communication, and thus exchange and cooperation, among areas previously segregated by linguistic differences. Each such facet of Islam's commercial expansion involved one or more forms of entrepreneurship. Transplanting institutions across regions, organizing commercial trips with uncertain outcomes, building commercial links with unknown territories, establishing new markets, and introducing people to new commodities are all entrepreneurial activities par excellence.

By the standards of the time, the Islamic commercial expansion represents an immense accomplishment. Numerous giant commercial centers of the age owed their prominence to Middle Eastern settlers. They include Mombasa and Mogadishu in Africa, and Calicut, Malacca, and Canton in Asia. In many such centers Islam became the dominant religion, although their Middle Eastern settlers also included Christians, Jews, and Zoroastrians. The Middle Easterners who moved to certain faraway places formed huge communities. When bandits captured Canton in 878 and slaughtered its local population, the victims included 120,000 Middle Eastern immigrants, mostly Muslims (Hourani 1995, 61–79; Chaudhuri 1985, chap. 2).

The establishment of Muslim-dominated trading centers in tropical Africa, the Asian subcontinent, and East Asia is all the more remarkable considering that the natives of these regions did not build trading colonies of their own, or spread their commercial institutions, in the Middle East. The asymmetry has been attributed to the cyclical rhythms of the monsoon winds and seasonal crop patterns. But the peoples of other regions, for instance the Chinese, could have overcome any climactic disadvantages precisely by establishing trading colonies in the Middle East, along with appropriate institutions. With respect to China, another view, often appended to the climactic argument, is that its emperors did not need foreign trade, as its internal economy provided an adequate tax base (Chaudhuri 1985, 21–29, 188). Putting aside the implausibility of the claim that Chinese rulers had bounded ambitions, one must ask why so few Chinese merchants pursued commercial opportunities in the Middle East, as they did in Southeast Asia. The reason probably lies in the first-mover advantage of the Middle Easterners who came to dominate various trade routes. Where Islam had already achieved a significant presence, the local population would not have had incentives to welcome settlers, unless they had superior commercial institutions. Chinese institutions were not noticeably superior.

If Middle Easterners of the early Islamic centuries established institutions favorable to the sort of entrepreneurship that fueled commercial expansion under Islamic law, a major reason is that the Muslim jurists who incorporated them into Islamic law were themselves businessmen. In the Arab heartland of Islam, during the ninth and tenth centuries 75 percent of all religious scholars (ulama), whose ranks included all jurists, earned a living primarily from business. Although most were artisans or producers, many participated in commerce as investors or, less commonly, as traveling merchants (Cohen 1970, table C-1). Born into a merchant-dominated tribe, Muhammad himself was a merchant by profession. Such factors did not guarantee that Islam would promote institutions supportive of entrepreneurship. However, they ensured that during its formative period people familiar with entrepreneurial needs, even entrepreneurs themselves, held influential positions.

The Onset of Entrepreneurial Ineffectiveness

The early centuries of Islamic history stand out as a time of remarkable commercial feats by Middle Easterners. Subsequently, the global significance of Middle Eastern commercial accomplishments dropped noticeably. In the sixteenth century, some Arabs still went to India; few traveled as far as China. By the eighteenth century even the region's spice trade with India, once a source of fabled wealth, had lost its importance. Spice caravans between the Indian Ocean and the Mediterranean became a spectacle of the past because Europeans developed and monopolized a cheaper route around the Cape. Middle Easterners continued to dominate certain trade routes in Africa a while longer. However, in the nineteenth century Europeans made inroads even into regions of Africa once commercially tied to the Middle East.

By the middle of the second millennium, Middle Easterners were playing at best a secondary role in the expansion of global commerce. The global explorations and conquests associated with names such as Vasco da Gama, Christopher Columbus,

Ferdinand Magellan, and Hernán Cortés were planned, financed, and executed with only peripheral Middle Eastern involvement. Likewise, in the half-millennium preceding the Industrial Revolution the myriads of institutional innovations that laid the infrastructure of today's modern economy came primarily from Western merchants, financiers, statesmen, and other professionals. In contrast to the medieval period, their Middle Eastern counterparts played no leading role in the early modern phase of the protracted institutional transformation that led to industrialization.

To be sure, even after the development of the global marketplace came to be spearheaded by Westerners, every generation of Middle Eastern merchants, financiers, and producers included unusually innovative people. Ismail Abu Taqiyya, an Egyptian merchant active in Cairo between 1580 and 1625, offers a shining example. He was born at a time when the use of coffee as a beverage was spreading across the Middle East through Sufis, who drank it in order to stay awake during nocturnal worship services. Puritanical religious scholars found the new beverage objectionable, formally on the ground that it causes intoxication—sinful, in their view—but in all likelihood also because of its association with a liberal interpretation of Islam. Nevertheless, the consumption of coffee spread among the general population, largely through coffeehouses. Rulers had a motive of their own for fanning anticoffee opposition and persecuting violators—even, in some cases, as they themselves acquired a taste for coffee. Political activity was integral to the social life of coffeehouses, which posed a threat to public order (Hattox 1985, chaps. 1–3, 7).

In this environment, Abu Taqiyya, along with various partners, started importing coffee to Egypt from Mocha, Yemen. Anticipating Starbucks by several centuries, he also promoted coffee consumption by building scores of coffeehouses. If the profit opportunities were great, so were the risks. For one thing, mobs had destroyed coffeehouses. For another, future demand was dependent on the social and political climate, both uncertain. Abu Taqiyya exhibited a similar entrepreneurial spirit in trying to revive Egypt's sugar industry. Sensing a potential for dramatic market expansion and corresponding price increases, he financed the planting of sugarcane, established refineries, and sold the output at home and abroad (Hanna 1998, 78–95).

Other examples could be given, from Abu Taqiyya's time or later, of Middle Eastern merchants who adapted to emerging market opportunities and took shrewd initiatives to improve products or create new markets. In the seventeenth century an Armenian network based in New Julfa, Iran, managed to link markets as far apart as Venice, Russia, India, and China (Curtin 1984, chap. 9; McCabe 1999, chaps. 4, 8–9; Aghassian and Kévonian 1999). Meanwhile, faced with a flood of fine Indian fabrics, Iranians, Turks, and other groups developed and marketed a wide range of substitutes, using dyes from various places, including India itself (Veinstein 1999). But most of their contemporaries in the world of business followed well-beaten paths. With few exceptions, accounts of commercial life in particular cities and times describe routine business activities.[6] The merchants who left traces of their careers were less ambitious and less creative.

Scale and Longevity of Middle Eastern Enterprises

We will return to the typical pattern on the eve of the Industrial Revolution. Yet Abu Taqiyya's colorful and impressive career affords additional insights into his region's

entrepreneurial capacity. His accomplishments went beyond entrepreneurial successes in the coffee and sugar markets. However, just as Sherlock Holmes solved a
crime by noticing that a dog did not bark, we can learn also from identifying what
Abu Taqiyya did *not* achieve.

Abu Taqiyya's biographer based her study entirely on several hundreds of
court cases in which he appeared as a litigant or witness. She did not have access
to financial ledgers, order books, by-laws of his companies, minutes of his strategy sessions with partners, or even his occasional correspondence. Such sources are
available in abundance to historians of the English Levant Company (1583–1825),
which operated in the Eastern Mediterranean (Wood 1935). Like the overseas trading companies of the English and other north Europeans, certain Italian companies of earlier centuries left elaborate archives. Surviving financial statements of the
Florence-based Medici enterprise (1397–1494) are sufficiently rich and systematic
that modern scholars use them to reconstruct its business practices (De Roover
1963). In principle, the unavailability of a private Abu Taqiyya archive could reflect a
chance event, such as a fire or flood. Nevertheless, it fits a general pattern. Few private
commercial records of the region have survived from before the nineteenth century. In
a 262-page book devoted to historical sources on the Ottoman Empire, to which
Egypt belonged in Abu Taqiyya's days, a distinguished historian devotes less than
a page to "private archives" (Faroqhi 1999, 58). A basic reason is that few private
archives were formed in the first place, let alone maintained for generations.[7]

It absorbs resources to save, classify, and preserve documents. Hence, a merchant will go to the trouble only insofar as the expected benefits are sufficiently
large. If record keeping is an essential activity of modern firms, this is because they
have long lives, enter into long-term contracts with many individuals, and face lawsuits requiring the consultation of agreements made in the distant past. Shareholders
may claim rights based on founding documents registered, literally, centuries earlier.
Hence, it is no coincidence that business historians of Italy and England have access
to the records of large enterprises that lasted for many generations. The Medicis and
the Levant Company left orderly records because their expected longevity and the
complexity of their activities justified the costs of forming archives.

In his career that spanned half a century, Abu Taqiyya operated through myriads
of independent partnerships involving geographically dispersed people. Each partnership was based on a separate contract designed for a narrowly defined purpose,
such as financing a farmer's sugarcane planting for one season, or transporting a
load of coffee beans from Mocha to Alexandria, or operating a coffeehouse in Da-
miat. The partnerships pooled limited resources; usually they were also short-lived.
For these reasons, none presented a need for indefinite record keeping. Tellingly,
Abu Taqiyya's conglomerate did not outlast him. After his death, some of his associates took over certain components of his conglomerate. Although the fate of his
coffeehouses is unknown, many of them probably survived under different owners
and new financial arrangements. But he took with him a web of connections formed
over several decades, and no person or organization inherited his regionwide commercial reputation. His commercial capital, too, got dissipated. His heirs did not
maintain the conglomerate, to say nothing of enlarging it. Therein lies the fundamental reason why his biographer found no Abu Taqiyya archive. If he anticipated
his conglomerate's demise after his death, he would have felt no urge to keep orderly
records.

A basic motive for record keeping is indeed to assist later generations of owners and managers. Yet the Islamic inheritance system made it difficult to preserve a successful enterprise. By premodern standards the Islamic inheritance system is highly egalitarian. It mandates individual shares for all members of the nuclear family, male and female, and in certain circumstances also for the decedent's more distant relatives. Thus, for all its distributional advantages, it led to the fragmentation of successful enterprises. In principle, one could recombine the shares of a deceased businessman's capital. However, ordinarily it took just one or two financially strapped or recalcitrant heirs to block that outcome. The problem was particularly acute for highly successful businessmen, because they tended to have more children, often from multiple wives. Abu Taqiyya's heirs consisted of eleven surviving children and four surviving wives. Although a few of his inheritors tried to consolidate their shares of the estate, within a decade family squabbles, illnesses, and additional deaths took their toll (Hanna 1998, 161–64).

Another unintended effect of the Islamic inheritance system was a reduction in the scale and expected longevity of commercial enterprises. Merchants, producers, and investors minimized the probability of having to deal with the heirs of their partners by forming small and ephemeral partnerships. In the process, they also minimized the expected costs of untimely liquidations (Kuran 2003, 414–46). Like so many other successful businessmen of his time, Abu Taqiyya operated through a plethora of partnerships, all mutually independent from a legal standpoint, and each claiming a minute slice of his capital, usually for at most a year or two at a time.

The absence of an Abu Taqiyya archive is symptomatic, then, of a fundamental characteristic of the premodern Middle Eastern economy: its dependence on atomistic and generally ephemeral commercial enterprises. If Abu Taqiyya did not establish a formal conglomerate that his descendants could maintain, and thus had no need for elaborate record keeping, a basic reason is that the prevailing commercial institutions of his region made it optimal to work through simple, small, and short-lived private enterprises.

Absence of the Corporation

The identified obstacles to forming large and durable partnerships under Islamic law do not fully explain why Abu Taqiyya's conglomerate did not outlast him. Institutional limitations are not necessarily insurmountable. Abu Taqiyya might have overcome the limitations of Islamic contract law through an organizational form akin to the business corporation—an enterprise that enjoys legal personality, is capable of a perpetual existence, and is owned jointly by people who may transfer their shares to others. Had he amalgamated his activities into a corporation, his conglomerate would have had an existence apart from his own. Moreover, his descendants wishing to convert his estate into cash could have transferred equity without necessarily endangering the conglomerate itself. Shares of the corporation could have been passed on across generations, with the enterprise living on under a changing membership.

However, Islamic law recognizes only flesh-and-blood persons; it lacks a concept of legal personhood (Kuran 2005b). This stood as an immense obstacle to introducing the corporation into the Middle East. Abu Taqiyya would have had to reform the judicial system, in addition, of course, to convincing his partners to operate within a radically new business structure. Such mega-innovations are rare in any field. When the Levant Company obtained its corporate charter, it was at the forefront of an unfolding commercial transformation. But its institutional leap was far smaller than the one that Abu Taqiyya would have had to make. Outside of business, the corporate form had seen use in Western Europe for more than half a millennium. England's Levant Company did not have to invent legal personhood, or develop its applications from scratch, or deal with judges unfamiliar with the concept.

Had Abu Taqiyya lived in the twenty-first century, he could have established a holding company to rival such enterprises as Orascom Telecom and EFG-Hermes, each traded on both the Cairo and Alexandria Stock Exchange and the London Stock Exchange. Today's leading Egyptian companies use organizational forms inconceivable in Abu Taqiyya's milieu. They also benefit from economic institutions unknown to him, such as secondary share markets, banks, and a business press, to name a few. Egypt's present economic institutions, like those of the wider Middle East, are based on far-reaching reforms, launched in waves from the mid-nineteenth century onward. Successive reforms narrowed the jurisdiction of Islamic courts and introduced new legal norms based, in part, on foreign models. By no means is the Egyptian economy of the early twenty-first century a model of efficiency. But four centuries earlier, Abu Taqiyya's organizational options were incomparably more limited.

The Middle East's golden age of entrepreneurship was over long before Abu Taqiyya came on stage. This is not to endorse the view, popular in some circles, that the region experienced an economic decline in some absolute sense. Although Abu Taqiyya did not travel to China, he and his fellow businessmen operated within an economy at least as large as that of a few centuries earlier, and through organizations every bit as advanced. What differed is the wider global economy. Europe's commercial institutions had undergone cumulatively revolutionary transformations that were about to turn much of the remaining world, including the Middle East, into an underdeveloped zone.

There was a decline in economic performance, then, only in a relative sense. Abu Taqiyya's exploits, phenomenal when viewed through the lens of a specialist in Middle Eastern studies, look less impressive to a business historian familiar with the scale, longevity, and structural complexity of coeval businesses in England and Holland. By Abu Taqiyya's time, Middle Eastern entrepreneurs were already institutionally disadvantaged vis-à-vis their Western contemporaries. Their handicap was to worsen for another quarter-millennium, until the initiation of fundamental reforms.

During the period when the organizational handicap of the Middle East worsened, the challenges that its entrepreneurs faced in the private economy were smaller than those of their Western counterparts. In effect, it was caught in an equilibrium trap whereby the absence of major entrepreneurship perpetuated itself by limiting the range of disequilibria; and, in turn, the paucity of disequilibria limited the range of opportunities for basic innovations in production and commerce. Had merchants of Abu Taqiyya's generation attempted, say, to establish direct commercial relations with the Americas, the consequent challenges in finance, navigation, and communication alone would have created major opportunities for innovation. The resulting entrepreneurship might have created further dislocations, stimulating additional creative responses.

Effects of Islam on Attitudes toward Innovation

We have seen that certain distinctly Islamic institutions played critical roles in the broader institutional stagnation of the Middle East. The Islamic inheritance system limited incentives to modernize Islamic contract law, which assumed its classical form around the tenth century. Traditional Islamic contract law was well suited to the personal exchange prevalent in the medieval global economy. However, it became increasingly dysfunctional as global commerce, and then gradually commerce within the Middle East, became progressively more impersonal. Over the ages, then, Islam influenced the supply of entrepreneurship and productivity of entrepreneurs by shaping the capacities to pool capital, expand commercially, engage in long-lasting ventures, and preserve successful businesses.

In the medieval era, such effects would have been considered favorable. This is clear from the diffusion of Islamic law to areas far removed from Islam's heartland. During the half-millennium preceding the Industrial Revolution, the same effects turned into handicaps, which became crippling when technological progress boosted the advantages of institutions supporting complex economic exchange. Reformers who subsequently transplanted modern economic institutions to the Middle East were motivated by the very same impulses that drove the earlier diffusion of Islamic law: preserving and improving economic competitiveness.

The proposed relationship between Islam and entrepreneurship conflicts with arguments that invoke fatalism or conformism as fundamental Islamic attributes. Whereas they presume a permanent handicap integral to Islam's ethos, the present mechanism highlights the effects of changing circumstances. Islamic contract law became a handicap for entrepreneurs only as people outside the region developed the institutions of impersonal exchange. But one can reject the empirically untenable "religious fixity" claim without eliminating the possibility of attitudinal effects rooted in religion, or mediated by it. In principle, attitudes harmful to innovation, creativity, or risk taking could have emerged at any time, early in Islamic history or much later.

In Abu Taqiyya's time, coffee producers, traders, and consumers encountered opposition based, formally, on the notion that "black water" amounted to *bid'a*—a harmful innovation incompatible with Islam. This term entered Islamic discourse in the early days of the religion, to characterize practices unapproved in the brief period up to the Prophet's death in 632. It is thus the converse of *sunna*—standards introduced by Muhammad and his pious companions. In its strictest form, *bid'a* served to dismiss as un-Islamic every commodity, habit, and idea unknown in Arabia during Muhammad's lifetime. Over the ages, conservatives and traditionalists have castigated as *bid'a* a wide range of innovations, including the table, the printing press, and football (Talbi 1960; Lewis 1993, 283–84). The charge that coffee drinkers reap hell-fire represented neither the first nor the last time that opponents of innovation have sought legitimacy from Islamic tradition.

Yet the Islamic opposition did not keep Abu Taqiyya from developing the Egyptian market for coffee. Over the long run, in fact, the anticoffee campaign failed momentously. In sixteenth-century Arabia many clerics urged their congregations to destroy coffeehouses. A half-millennium later, leaders of Saudi Arabia's puritanical Wahhabi sect proudly serve coffee to their guests, treating it as an ancient Arab delicacy, usually without an awareness of the history of Arab and Islamic resistance to this now-cherished custom. Numerous other innovations have gained Islamic legitimacy following a period of fervent resistance. In the early 1960s Wahhabi leaders opposed television. It violates the Islamic ban on graven images, they said, and might encourage idolatry. Wahhabites led riots that the Saudi police was able to quell only by firing on demonstrators. Once Wahhabi leaders understood television's immense potential as an instrument of religious indoctrination, they promptly discovered that it falls, after all, within the *sunna*. "Someday a man will be able to see his brother standing on the other side of the mountain," they found that Muhammad had said, thus blessing television almost fourteen centuries in advance.[8]

The use of traditionalist rhetoric to discredit innovation is not unique to Islam. Every society, past and present, harbors groups who defend the local culture, or a local industry, or a way of life by characterizing innovators as unpatriotic, irreligious, or enemies of the local culture. Witness the French campaigns against McDonalds, fought not for reasons of health but on the ground that it threatens the "French way of life."[9] Just as Sunni religious scholars of Abu Taqiyya's Cairo portrayed coffee as un-Islamic to weaken their Sufi rivals, so Parisian restaurant owners wrap themselves in the French flag to intimidate the new fast food industry and its patrons. In and of itself, then, episodes involving accusations of *bid'a* do not make Islam particularly inhospitable to entrepreneurship.

In any case, just as opponents of innovation may invoke religion, so too can its promoters. The term *bid'a* rarely appears in the Qur'an, and none of its usages carries the pejorative connotation that it would acquire. On that basis, supporters of particular innovations, and of receptivity to innovation in general, have sought to turn the tables on religious conservatives by arguing that the concept of *bid'a* is itself *bid'a* (Talbi 1960, 73–76). Others tried to restrict the meaning of the concept to exclude useful innovations that are not demonstrably un-Islamic. Al-Shafi'i (767–821), the leading contributor to one of Islam's four major schools of law, held that *bid'a* encompasses innovations that contradict the Qur'an, the *sunna,* and the consensus (*ijmā*) of the Muslim community. It does not subsume uncontested innovations. By this logic, all *bid'a* is blameworthy, but not all innovation is *bid'a* (Talbi 1960, 62–63). Still other theologians amend the meaning of *bid'a* to allow for a distinction between "bad *bid'a*" and "good *bid'a*." In their view, bad *bid'a* involve sinful errors that lead to hell. Novelties beneficial to the Muslim community are good *bid'a*.[10]

Throughout Islamic history, then, there have existed religious functionaries willing to give entrepreneurs religious support for their innovations. As coffee was spreading through Cairo, one center of opposition was al-Azhar, the city's main college and congregational mosque. Although a renowned al-Azhar preacher declared coffee forbidden, other al-Azhar clerics sided with the proponents of legalization. Adopting an experimental approach, a judge of the Hanafi school of law held a council where he offered coffee to all participants, and then waited for signs of intoxication such as slurred speech, drowsiness, and melancholy. Finding none, he ruled, to the delight of the bourgeoning coffee sector, that coffee is permissible under Islamic law (Hattox 1985, 39–40).

The printing press offers another example of an innovation whose proponents were able to counter religious opposition through religion itself. For more than two centuries after the invention of the printing press in Europe (1450), Middle Eastern guilds of scribes opposed the establishment of local printing presses (except by minorities, to print books in their own languages). Authoritative knowledge could only be transmitted, they said, from person to person, for example, a calligrapher to the buyer of the hand-copied book. Printing, by giving the producer anonymity in the eyes of buyers, would weaken the authority of the learned class and, hence, Islam itself. The demand for books being very low, for numerous generations no significant counterpressures arose. By the early eighteenth century, however, such a lobby did emerge. It argued that the printed book would preserve, if not strengthen, existing patterns of religious authority (Robinson 1993, esp. 239–42; Berkes 1998, 36–50; Babinger, 9–11). Asked to rule on the legality of the printing press, an influential Istanbul cleric said the following:

> God knows what's best! If someone cognizant of printing technology and capable of manufacturing fonts can reliably reproduce hand-written texts, and if his enterprise offers the advantages of speedy production, easy copying, and prices low enough to put books within everyone's reach, and, finally, if proficient proofreaders are available, the enterprise is praiseworthy and deserving of support. (quoted in Babinger 2004, 13; my translation)

Charges of *bid'a* undoubtedly had a retarding effect on the diffusion of some innovations. They would also have dampened the incentives for entrepreneurship. However, in and of themselves they cannot explain why, after several centuries of innovative Muslim rule, the Middle East lost some of its institutional dynamism. After all, the concept of *bid'a* was already present in the golden age of Middle Eastern entrepreneurship. It was available to opponents of innovation in the eighth century when Muslim entrepreneurs replaced fragile and expensive papyrus with Chinese paper, and then founded paper mills to produce Baghdadi paper, a fine substitute (Ashtor 1956, 99–100). Likewise, it was present during the ninth century as Muslim jurists were continuing to develop what was to become classical Islamic contract law. Since the organizational forms used by Abu Taqiyya and other towering entrepreneurs differed from those used by Muhammad and his companions, they could have been castigated as un-Islamic. If *bid'a* charges were indeed made to prevent organizational development in the early Islamic centuries, the evidence has not survived. What we do know is that the partnership forms used by Abu Taqiyya gained full legitimacy in the eyes of Muslim authorities.

Stabilizing Effects of Islam's Self-Image of Timeless Perfection

If one channel through which Islam influenced the supply of entrepreneurship was the doctrine of *bid'a*, a possibly more significant channel involved the teaching that Islam instituted a permanently ideal social order. Islam holds that the Qur'an, which was revealed to the last of a long line of prophets, embodies the unaltered words of God. As such, it outlines a way of life that cannot possibly be improved upon. In certain contexts, this presumption of perfection has served as a rationale for immobility: in an already flawless social order, innovations cannot yield benefits and may well do harm.

As a matter of practice, of course, no one has ever acted as though the social order is beyond improvement. In the face of changing circumstances, novel opportunities, and new challenges, successive generations of Muslims have routinely responded with fresh thinking and creative solutions. Moreover, such solutions have commonly gained acceptance from Islam's schools of law. They have also gained an association, in the popular imagination, with traditional Islam. Islamic contract law offers a case in point. It took more than a quarter-millennium for the key features of Islam's contracting principles to assume their classical forms. Along the way, diverse refinements occurred, many of them in response to practical problems that could not even have been imagined during Muhammad's lifetime, let alone solved (Udovitch 1970, esp. chaps. 1, 7). In actuality, therefore, Islamic contract law was constantly in flux. Understandings of what is properly Islamic gradually evolved. In this context, as in others, the evolution of Islamic doctrine involved reinterpretations of the Qur'an, along with additions to compendia of Muhammad's remembered words and deeds.

The challenges often differed across localities, which led to variations in the adopted solutions. Some of these variations translated into differences among the major schools of law: Hanafi, Maliki, Shafi'i, and Hanbali. On the specifics of contract law, for instance, these schools did not always rule identically (Udovitch 1970, chaps. 2, 4–5; Nyazee 1999, chaps. 7, 10–16). In certain domains, attachment to doctrine was always tenuous to begin with, so variations across time and space were particularly pronounced. Temporal and geographic variations in the resource base inevitably led to wide variations in tax practices. What a wheat grower paid in taxes differed greatly between, say, Turkey and Egypt, and, in either country, between the sixteenth and eighteenth centuries (İnalcık 1994, 55–154).

However, neither the transformations of practices associated with Islam nor their geographic diversification received formal approval. On the contrary, a steady rhetoric of institutional fixity effectively denied legitimacy to the process of innovation. Moreover, the fabrication of ostensible Islamic precedents for diverse innovations erased from the collective memory the innovativeness of past Muslims as well as the dynamism of Islamic history. The consequent metamorphoses of the collective memory then kept new generations from appreciating how much more comfortably they themselves lived than earlier generations of Muslims, including the first Muslim community in seventh-century Arabia.

The process of absorbing changes and borrowings into Islam without conceding the plasticity of Islamic civilization also denied status to innovators. The founders of the Middle East's paper industry were not remembered or celebrated as entrepreneurs who spotted a useful Chinese commodity, marketed it locally, and then developed a technology for manufacturing a local variant. Nor, for that matter, were the generations of jurists who developed Islamic contract law remembered as institutional architects. They were treated as interpreters rather than innovators, as discoverers of an all-encompassing, fixed, and eternally perfect legal system rather than as creative legislators in their own right. Islam's rhetoric of institutional fixity would have discouraged entrepreneurship both by underrating its social significance and by denying social rewards to individual innovators.

From antiquity to the present, towering social thinkers have observed that the esteem of others influences human actions.[11] Insofar as Islam's self-image of timeless perfection required the denial of esteem to Muslim innovators, it would have limited incentives to develop new commodities, invent new production processes, and concoct legal reforms.

Clerical Impediments to Innovation

Before the modern era, Middle Eastern entrepreneurs operated within a legal system based, in principle, on divine revelation. In practice, jurisconsults (muftis), some of whom lacked ties to political authorities, extended and modified the law through advisory opinions (fatwas) regarding dilemmas brought before them. Meanwhile, state-appointed judges (kadis) found creative solutions to daily conflicts (Masud, Messick, and Powers 1996).

Traditionally neither innovative religious opinions nor the creative judgments of Islamic courts were treated as legal advances of broader relevance. No system existed for publicizing the evolution of the law to produce general precedents. One result was a duplication of judicial effort: judges had to resolve common disputes by going back, at each occurrence, to first principles. Although news of judicial decisions could travel, the lack of a system of granting authority to precedents would have hamstrung legal development. It would also have reinforced the above-discussed perception of institutional fixity. The former effect would have limited entrepreneurial capabilities; the latter would have dampened the rewards.

Where the prevailing interpretation of the law posed great inconveniences, a common response was casuistry (*hiyal*). For example, in places where the ban on *ribā*, an ancient Arabian institution, was treated as a generalized prohibition of interest, interest-bearing loans were made through a double sale, or by disguising interest charges within currency exchanges, or by overpricing an exchanged commodity, among other such stratagems. The use of casuistry to meet common needs elevated transaction costs (Kuran 2005a, 597–602).

It is the effects on entrepreneurial opportunities that matter here. Although casuistry provided a cheap method for legitimizing simple financial arrangements, it was of little use with regard to complex contracts involving large groups pooling resources for indefinite periods. The parties to such contracts would generally insist on transparency, which is precisely what casuistry is meant to overcome. Had Abu Taqiyya attempted to form, say, a corporation, potential shareholders would have wanted its charter to specify their rights. They would also have insisted on credible measures to monitor its financial flows and enforce its promises. Casuistry and surreptitious reinterpretation were poorly suited, then, to institutional modifications and innovations of the extent necessary to establish the infrastructure for impersonal exchange.

The point may be supported through the greatest privately initiated Middle Eastern institutional innovation of the half-millennium preceding the Industrial Revolution: the emergence of a "cash waqf" sector. A *waqf* is an unincorporated trust established under Islamic law to provide a designated social service in perpetuity. Traditionally, its corpus had to consist of real estate; no portion of an endowment could be liquid. Because every waqf was considered sacred, endowed assets gained considerable immunity against expropriation. For this reason, and also because founders and their families could claim part of its income, the waqf became a very popular wealth shelter. Around the sixteenth century, depending on the area, waqfs owned between a quarter and half of all arable land and urban real estate (Kuran 2001).

As far back as the eighth century, which is when the waqf of immovables emerged, professional moneylenders, whose wealth was largely liquid, sought to bend the adopted rules by forming waqfs with liquid endowments. Uncommon for many centuries, in the fifteenth century cash waqfs started spreading rapidly, mainly in Turkey and the Balkans. Their rising popularity provoked intense religious controversy, not unlike today's clashes over abortion. In the minds of conservative clerics cash waqfs violated both waqf law and the presumed ban on interest. Liberal clerics, some of whom invested in cash waqfs themselves, defended the innovation on the basis of its apparent usefulness (Mandaville 1979, 297–300, 306–8).

The vast majority of all cash waqfs were minuscule as measured by assets, and they lent primarily to consumers for short terms (Çizakça 2000, 48). As with a bank, a cash waqf could maintain capital in perpetuity. Unlike a bank, it could not lend on a large scale by pooling the savings of multiple individuals. In principle, it could have metamorphosed into a financial institution akin to a bank. Clerics could have looked the other way as it effectively acquired legal personhood. They might also have reinterpreted waqf law to facilitate waqf mergers. Specifically, just as the traditional restriction on waqf assets was effectively rescinded under pressure from moneylenders, so the waqf rule requiring assets to be used in strict conformity to its founder's stipulations might have been relaxed to allow asset pooling on the part of later generations of caretakers (*mutawallis*).

The key difference between the two challenges—legitimizing the cash waqf and allowing flexibility in the use of capital—lay in the externalities involved. The act of endowing liquid capital produced no obvious negative externality. Indeed, no one could claim credibly to be harmed directly from broadening the range of endowable assets. By contrast, waqf mergers would have drawn objections from the designated beneficiaries of individual waqfs. Some beneficiaries would have argued, within reason, that mergers placed their entitlements at risk. Transforming the waqf sector into a veritable banking sector would have required, then, collective action on a large scale to counter the inevitable resistance. This is probably one reason why the moneylenders who used the waqf of immovables as the basis for a new financial institution did not take the next logical step of forming banks.[12]

The cash waqf was well suited to personal exchange. Its caretaker made loans to members of trust-based networks, and ordinarily he lent only to people known to him personally. A bank belongs to a more complex economy in which impersonal exchange is becoming, or has become, the norm. So obstacles to transforming the cash waqf into a veritable bank would have hampered the scale of entrepreneurship by restricting the supply of credit. Insofar as clerical concerns were to blame, they thus harmed entrepreneurial performance, leaving Middle Easterners handicapped in the evolving modern economy, in which the efficient exploitation of new technologies required large-scale investments.

Because the cash waqf did not metamorphose into a bank, establishing a financial system suitable to industrialization required fundamental legal reforms through either a massive reinterpretation of Islamic law or legal secularization on matters pertaining to commerce and finance. It is the latter option that Middle Eastern reformers ultimately took in the nineteenth century (Kuran 2005b, 608–12). The timing of the reforms speaks volumes. Territorial losses, political instability, and protracted economic crises had lowered popular resistance to broad reform.

The State's Impact on Entrepreneurial Capabilities

All states help to solve collective action problems. Thus, both before and after the rise of Islam, Middle Eastern states protected property rights, administered justice, defended borders, and spearheaded campaigns of territorial expansion. In pursuing such goals they routinely learned from their mistakes, embraced new technologies, and made organizational adaptations.[13] Although subjects benefited unequally, most did better than in a Hobbesian world of anarchy. In principle, states might also have assisted the advancement of commercial institutions. They could have taken steps to facilitate, say, large-scale entrepreneurship involving long-term investments. In England, home to some of the earliest business corporations, the Crown assisted their development through charters.

Had a similar scenario played out in the Middle East, it would have marked an exception to a general pattern: minimal state support to private economic activity. Traditionally, Muslim-governed states monopolized the provision of law and order. They also raised taxes, where possible directly, more often indirectly through tax farmers who purchased collection rights through auctions. However, after Islam's initial period, Middle Eastern states pursued no major initiatives to develop the institutional infrastructure of commerce. Until the nineteenth century, when efforts to codify Islamic law were launched, the judges of Islamic courts interpreted contracting rules in a decentralized manner, without state direction.

Nor did states of the region play the leading role in the provision of social services. In the great cities of the medieval Middle East, social services were supplied largely by waqfs. It was through waqfs that schools, hospitals, soup kitchens, fountains, and even roads and parks were ordinarily financed and maintained. The caravanserais (fortified inns for caravans) found on the region's commercial arteries were usually organized as waqfs. True, rulers were not indifferent to the allocation of waqf resources. Aware that the waqf system's vast assets could serve their strategic objectives, they induced waqf-founding elites, especially their relatives, to favor particular regions and sectors. Nevertheless, until modern times many services now provided centrally through such agencies as municipalities, highway administrations, education boards, and water departments were supplied in a remarkably decentralized manner. In this respect, the governance of premodern Middle Eastern societies conformed to the ideals of modern libertarianism (Kuran 2001).

Just as Mamluk, Ottoman, and other Middle Eastern rulers sought to use the waqf system to their own advantage, so in various contexts they tried to benefit from the activities of merchants and producers. Political stability required major cities to remain well stocked with staple commodities, so protections were extended to businessmen belonging to relevant supply chains. Rulers also imposed economic restrictions to alleviate perceived threats to favored constituencies. For instance, certain guilds and traders were awarded court-enforced monopoly or monopsony powers.[14] There are examples, finally, of rulers protecting long-distance traders with whom they formed partnerships. Ayyubid and Mamluk sultans extended financing as well as commercial privileges to the Karimi traders who in the twelfth and thirteenth centuries dominated the Indian Ocean spice trade (Ashtor 1956). Shah Abbas I of Iran (r. 1587–1629) and several of his successors invested in the cross-continental silk trade of Armenian merchants based in New Julfa. Iranian rulers also gave the New Julfa Armenians military and diplomatic support (Curtin 1984, chap. 9; McCabe 1999, esp. chap. 4).

Strikingly absent are state initiatives to improve commercial capabilities in general. The building of centralized urban markets, or grand bazaars, is the major exception that proves the rule. One motive for establishing grand bazaars was to stimulate commerce. However, rulers wanted also to facilitate the monitoring of trade flows for the purpose of taxation. In principle, the lure of a larger tax base could have led sultans to improve the organizational capabilities of merchants operating under Islamic law. They might have encouraged clerics to reinterpret the Islamic inheritance system in a manner helpful to the preservation of successful businesses, or to introduce into Islamic law a formal distinction between natural and legal persons. However, if any premodern statesmen detected the advantages of such reforms, they took no initiatives that left historical traces. During financial emergencies, rulers doubled their efforts to locate untapped sources of wealth. But they did not pursue institutional innovations to stimulate wealth creation. Until the nineteenth century, they did not consider the prevailing means for resource pooling, or the scale of entrepreneurship, a problem calling for state intervention.

On the contrary, at times they actively opposed institutional innovations aimed at enhancing commercial capabilities. In 1695, faced with a budget crisis in the midst of military retreats, the Ottoman government converted a large number of short-term tax farms into life-term tax farms (*malikanes*). The goal was to borrow against future revenue by raising the down payment required to purchase a tax farm. Of interest here is that the lengthening of the tax-farm terms induced a potentially far-reaching innovation in financial markets. In order to meet the higher payments required to win auctions, tax farmers took to forming partnerships meant to last many years. Predictably, personal emergencies and business opportunities made certain members of these partnerships attempt to sell their rights. Under Islamic law, strictly interpreted, the transfers were illegal; at each withdrawal the preexisting partnership became null and void, requiring the negotiation of a new contract. However, tax farmers and the state had a common stake in the transferability of shares. Accordingly, an officially tolerated but informal market in tax farm shares took hold (Çizakça 1996, 159–86).

Had this development run its course, the region might have developed organized stock exchanges organically, rather than through top-down reforms involving the transplanting of foreign institutions. However, the Ottoman government began to fret, on the one hand, about keeping track of ownership patterns and, on the other, about the growing clout of tax farmers. In the early nineteenth century it restricted the divisibility of tax farm ownership, and then started confiscating tax farms. These moves alleviated pressures for further innovations in private financial markets. The empire's first organized stock markets went into operation in 1866, in a period when the region saw the establishment of its earliest local banks, the adoption of modern accounting, and the founding of secular courts to operate alongside traditional Islamic courts.[15]

The Ottoman government's opposition to the transferability of enterprise shares, like so many other state policies in Middle Eastern history, is commonly attributed to the economic conservatism of ruling elites (Genç 2000, pt. 1). Moreover, conservatism on the part of rulers is often treated as a basic determinant of entrepreneurial deficiencies. Yet the ideological tendencies of political elites were not formed or maintained in a vacuum. Nonstate actors such as craftsmen, shopkeepers, traveling merchants, and moneylenders contributed to their development. Hence, a full explanation for the economic conservatism of state officials, or of their indifference to the institutions governing entrepreneurial capabilities, must take account of factors shaping ideologies prevalent within the business community.

For reasons already identified, commercial sectors of the premodern Middle East were atomistic. Enterprises formed through contracts among nonkin were usually small and ephemeral. Exchanges tended to take place among people known to one another. Accordingly, the worldviews of merchants, investors, and producers were shaped by the exigencies of personal exchange. And in the absence of fundamental changes in commercial and financial practices, these groups did not get habituated to thinking about new institutional possibilities. Their own contentment with the institutional status quo would have limited the stimuli inducing statesmen to think about commercial reforms. Had businessmen been more creative in regard to the structure of commerce, they would have initiated debates on institutional alternatives, forcing statesmen to ponder the desirability of reforms. At least some political elites would have discovered the long-term advantages of measures to enhance the scale of entrepreneurship.

The observation that Middle Eastern statesmen were economically conservative is often advanced alongside the view that in western Europe, fount of the modern economy, statesmen were relatively more enlightened on economic matters. English and French rulers of the seventeenth century certainly helped their merchants advance globally. Also true is that their Ottoman and Safavid counterparts, insofar as they tried to assist merchants, were relatively ineffective. Yet, in and of themselves, recorded differences in official ideology do not explain the observed gaps in commercial performance. In both the West and the Middle East, the economic worldviews of statesmen coevolved with those of the business community. Moreover, in each region the evolution of commercial institutions affected ideological development.

Given the immense economic weight of the waqf sector in the premodern Middle Eastern economy, no inquiry into the region's entrepreneurial capacity would be complete without an investigation of how the waqf shaped economic creativity. Among the literal meanings of *waqf* is "to stop" and "to make dependent" (Wehr 1980, 1091–94). These meanings convey one of the basic principles of the waqf: "static perpetuity." It entails the immobilization of endowed assets for the purpose specified in the waqf charter. If a waqf was established to build and then maintain a fountain, ordinarily its assets had to serve that purpose in perpetuity. There were conditions, of course, under which the assets could be reallocated. If the neighborhood around an endowed fountain got deserted, a judge might allow the reallocation of the underlying assets. Under less severe changes in economic conditions, however, the principle of static perpetuity commonly locked resources into inefficient uses (Kuran 2001, 861–69).

When a successful merchant established a waqf in order to gain material security, resources got transferred from a sector in which they were mobile to one in which more or less enforced allocational restrictions, and therefore additional obstacles to entrepreneurship, came into play. If Middle Eastern merchants were held back by inadequate means for forming large enterprises, the caretakers of waqfs were generally barred altogether from pooling their resources. Assets that flowed from the commercial sector into waqfs harmed entrepreneurial capacity in two additional ways. Because courts had supervisory authority over waqfs, as a matter of practice caretakers trying to preserve the value of waqf assets had less freedom than managers of private portfolios. Waqf rules limited institutional change also by barring the use of resources for political purposes.

The waqf is not among Islam's original institutions. Its history extends only to the eighth century, a century after the advent of Islam. Although little is known about its emergence, it came to serve as an antidote to weak property rights, for the benefit of high state officials, many of them major landowners. In modifying and enriching Islamic law, state officials thus helped to solve a social problem that they themselves aggravated through predation. If for a millennium resources then flowed into a sector that limited allocational flexibility and institutional creativity, this is an unanticipated consequence of that particular institutional choice.

Are the waqf's effects on the supply of entrepreneurship rooted, then, in Islam or in state policies? These two effects cannot be disentangled. State policies influenced the specifics of Islamic waqf law. By the same token, the state itself governed in the name of Islam, which accepts no formal separation between religion and state. The antimercantilist tendencies of premodern Middle Eastern states, the immense popularity of the waqf as a wealth shelter, and the region's growing entrepreneurial deficiencies in the face of global economic transformations are all manifestations of several mutually enforcing social mechanisms.

Recapitulation and Implications for the Economic History of the Middle East

The foregoing arguments discredit both of the extreme views on the links between Islam and entrepreneurship in Middle Eastern history. Neither the categorically negative view nor the categorically positive view stands empirical scrutiny. The region's entrepreneurial performance in relation to the prevailing global standards has varied over time. Although Islamic institutions undergirded the variations, the mechanisms at play have differed from those commonly invoked.

The historical record belies the claim that Islamic conformism or fatalism has impeded entrepreneurship. For the better part of the past fourteen centuries, the Middle East has not appeared deficient in entrepreneurship. Moreover, even in recent times Middle Easterners in general, and Muslims in particular, have undertaken the sorts of activities we associate with entrepreneurs.

The diametrically opposed view, promoted most vocally by Islamists, that Islam offers institutions necessarily beneficial to entrepreneurship flies in the face of the Middle East's economic modernization campaigns. Islamic institutions that served innovators well in the medieval global economy became dysfunctional as the world made the transition to impersonal exchange. In the process, the relative entrepreneurial performance of the Middle East slipped. The observed deficiencies would have been greater, in fact, had the region not responded by transplanting various institutions of foreign provenance to supplement or supplant their counterparts grounded in traditional Islamic law.

Making sense of variations in the region's relative entrepreneurial performance requires a nuanced analysis focused on the dynamics of entrepreneurial capabilities and possibilities. State policies are among the determinants of entrepreneurial opportunity. Although in Islam's early centuries Middle Eastern states assisted commercial development, subsequently they did little to improve entrepreneurial performance. For a millennium they left the provision of services relevant to entrepreneurial capacity largely to waqfs, which came to control vast economic resources. Thus, the caravanserais that enabled merchants to travel long distances were financed mostly through waqfs, as were schools that provided literacy and numeracy. Because the waqf sector was designed to immobilize resources for particular ends, and thus to limit flexibility and innovation, its absorption of resources led to their concentration in a sector particularly inimical to entrepreneurship. The state fueled waqf formation insofar as its penchant for expropriation and arbitrary taxation made the wealthy seek to shelter assets. Islam played a role as well, and what secured its assets is their presumed sacredness.

Islam influenced Middle Eastern entrepreneurship also through several other channels. One entails the influence of clerics. Every generation of Muslim clerics included individuals opposed to one innovation or another. Their agitations imposed barriers to entrepreneurship, which would have lowered its supply. However, this resistance was never decisive, for broadly beneficial innovations always drew clerical support as well. The effects of clerical resistance may be likened to those of modern environmentalism. Land developers now face opposition from environmentalists who require them to prove, through costly legal procedures, that the environment will not suffer. The antigrowth campaigns of environmentalists have reduced investment in land development schemes, but hardly to the point of extinction. The lure of hefty gain makes investors overcome the opposition through countercampaigns. Similarly, where Middle Eastern businessmen have considered innovation sufficiently profitable, opposition in the name of Islam has usually had only a retarding influence.

Opportunities for beneficial innovation are never self-evident. People with the requisite talents and motivations must first notice a problem, sense the possibility of creating a new demand, or discover that an existing demand may be met more efficiently through a new technology or combination of resources. Whether entrepreneurs spot emerging opportunities depends partly on how well public discourse prepares them to do so. This brings us to another channel through which Islam has affected entrepreneurship. Islam's self-image of timeless perfection required the Muslim learned community to downplay, even actively conceal, the dynamism responsible for its successes. It had to trace new developments to early Islam, promoting the fiction that Muslim generations after the first interpreted the Qur'an and drew lessons from the wisdom of the Prophet without innovating in any fundamental sense. Prior to mass communications, this myth, taught in schools and propagated through mosques, would have trained people to seek personal advancement through replicative activities. Hence, it would have dragged the Islamic world from the state of relatively high entrepreneurship characteristic of its first few centuries to one of relatively low entrepreneurship, under which the sense of fixity became more or less self-fulfilling.

The myth of timeless perfection helped, then, to destroy a social equilibrium whereby people experienced structural changes and witnessed advances in the private sector, replacing it with one that sustained a perception of continuity. This transformation depended critically on yet another linkage between Islam and entrepreneurship. Certain elements of Islamic law dampened individual incentives to build larger and longer-lasting commercial organizations, thus limiting entrepreneurial possibilities. Specifically, Islam's egalitarian inheritance rules encouraged merchants and investors to keep their operations small and ephemeral; and, in turn, those organizational choices dampened incentives to refine traditional partnerships and develop techniques of impersonal exchange. Any entrepreneur who noticed the limitations of Islamic partnerships and went looking for a more complex organizational form would have been stymied also by the lack of an Islamic concept of the corporation. Such organizational limitations jointly dampened the pace of structural change in commerce and finance, thus facilitating the entrenchment of the myth of timeless perfection. The scale of commercial operations remained small in the

Middle East even as Europeans developed the means for producing and exchanging on a massive scale. The waqf system, which controlled vast assets, offered no substitute for modern economic institutions, for it was designed to serve rigid goals.

The question of why the Middle East has experienced entrepreneurial deficiencies relates to the broader question of why the region fell behind the West. In his voluminous writings, Max Weber invoked several factors as explanations: the inflexibility of Islamic law, failure to achieve legal formalization, arbitrary personal rule, and lack of an ascetic streak fueling "salvation anxiety" (1978, 572–76, 818–22, 1231–34). The empirical relevance of the last factor has been discredited (Turner 1978, chap. 1). But the first three have been invoked here as well, though using different terminology. Viewing them as fixed attributes of Islamic civilization, Weber suggested that they suppressed entrepreneurial drives. Here I have proposed that Weber asked the wrong question about the origins of Middle Eastern underdevelopment. The fundamental question is not which factors harmed economic advancement but why economically disadvantageous traits proved so persistent. Until the modern era, these traits were mutually reinforcing, and they drew strength also from laws limiting the scale and longevity of entrepreneurial projects.

Lessons for Innovative Entrepreneurship in the Modern Middle East

Motivations, beliefs, laws, regulations, and practices are all malleable. As such, any element of Islam that somehow came to harm the Middle East's relative entrepreneurial performance was always subject to reconsideration and modification. The massive reforms of the nineteenth century testify to the possibility of institutional change within domains long regulated in the name of Islam.

Those reforms enabled individual entrepreneurs to borrow from banks, establish organizations with indefinite lives, and track complex financial flows through standardized accounting. They thus removed the obstacles that kept Middle Eastern enterprises atomistic and ephemeral. As of February 2007, *Fortune*'s Global 2000, a list of the world's 2,000 leading publicly traded companies, included 14 companies from Malaysia, 11 from Turkey, 5 from Saudi Arabia, 3 from Egypt, 2 from Pakistan, and 1 from Jordan, for a total of 36 companies headquartered in a predominantly Muslim country.[16] The geographic diversity of this distribution shows that it is now possible to form giant private companies all across the Islamic world. Were Abu Taqiyya to come back to life, he would be bewildered by the new opportunities for pooling resources and preserving enterprises. He would recognize that modern organizational forms provide entrepreneurial capabilities unimaginable in seventeenth-century Egypt.

Throughout the Middle East, even in its poorest corners, institutional reforms of the past two centuries have removed obstacles to forming modern enterprises. Many of these replaced ancient Islamic institutions with ones that emerged or reached maturity in Western countries. Following Al-Afghani, today's Islamists often claim that Muslims lost economic standing when they ceased to practice authentic Islam. In fact, Muslims did not suffer economically as a result of transplanted institutions developed outside the purview of Islamic law. On the contrary, they expanded their entrepreneurial capabilities by leaps and bounds, thus contributing visibly to advances in the region's absolute living standards. None of today's Global 2000 companies could exist or operate under Islamic law.

Al-Afghani claimed also that European Christians gained economic strength because they were not really Christian (Hourani 1983, 129). There are grains of truth here. Although a majority of the Venetians, Dutch, and English who pioneered new commercial techniques or production methods practiced some form of Christianity, seldom did they look to the Bible or to ecclesiastical laws for solutions to business problems. The separation of church and state early in the second millennium enabled European entrepreneurs to develop institutions within an essentially secular space, and generally without worrying about clerical reactions.

The history of Christianity is not, of course, a story of uniform or unilinear secularization. Eastern Christians responded to the meteoric rise of Islam not by trying to understand the socioeconomic factors behind the new religion's success but generally by treating it as punishment for their own wickedness, or that of their brethren. They inferred that God was instructing them to become better Christians (Kaegi 1969). Following an analogous script, today's Islamists claim that to overcome the economic backwardness of the Islamic world, Muslims must first and foremost return to being good Muslims. In regard to economic life, they say, Muslims must reinstitute early Islamic practices. This preoccupation with purity and authenticity is blinding Islamists who take such claims at face value, along with assorted multiculturalists, to the incompatibility between Islam's traditional economic institutions and the modern global economy. It is also diverting the efforts of energetic and potentially creative Muslims from open-ended thinking about improving productivity to sterile debates about what is properly Islamic. In certain spheres of life, innovators are fretting about whether they will be accused of introducing forbidden practices, still known in certain circles as bid‘a.

Not everyone in the Islamic world shares the Islamist agenda. Resistance from secularists of various shades fuels political instability. As the experiences of Afghanistan, Iraq, Sudan, and Algeria demonstrate, people with skills and initiative move out of politically volatile areas, carrying along their entrepreneurial talents. Although relatively pragmatic forms of Islamism are associated with upward mobility, its militant forms are manifestly harmful to entrepreneurial performance.[17]

To observe that today's entrepreneurs have access to modern organizational forms is not to say that the organizational history of the Middle East no longer matters. The persistently small scale of premodern profit-oriented enterprises blocked the development of civil society, as did limitations on the use of waqf assets. In most parts of the Islamic world, authoritarian regimes have filled the resulting political vacuum. Facing scant resistance from private organizations, these regimes have been able to pursue interventionist economic policies that discourage private initiative and weaken the rule of law.

The foregoing observations suggest that entrepreneurship in the Middle East can be stimulated through a multipronged strategy. Steps that reinforce the rule of law would help, as would policies that strengthen the private sector and civil society in general. Educating the public about the causes and dynamics of the Islamic world's slip in economic standing would serve to build a consensus in favor of such reforms. Obstacles to entrepreneurship can be lowered also by publicizing the direct and indirect effects of Islamist efforts to reinstitute medieval economic practices.

What is not required is to familiarize the region with organizational forms conducive to entrepreneurship on a large scale. Nowhere do the organizational options of entrepreneurs remain limited to Islamic partnerships.

Notes

I thank Wilfred Dolsma, Naomi Lamoreaux, Debin Ma, and Jan Luiten van Zanden for useful discussions and constructive feedback on an earlier draft; and Hania Abou Al-Shamat for able research assistance. The Ewing Marion Kauffman Foundation provided helpful research support. The chapter draws on data generated through a much appreciated grant from the Templeton Foundation and the Metanexus Institute to the University of Southern California Institute for Economic Research on Civilizations.

[1] For three variants, see Patai 1983, 310; Sayigh 1958, 123; and Lewis 2002. The latter source stresses the closing of the Muslim mind between the ninth and eleventh centuries.

[2] Mannan (1970) offers an introduction. Extensive treatments of entrepreneurship are found in Siddiqi 1979, chap. 2; and Sadeq 1990, 24–29. For a critique of Islamic economics and an account of its history, see Kuran 2004, chaps. 1–5.

[3] In reality most Islamic banks operate like ordinary commercial banks; their Islamic features are mostly cosmetic. See Kuran 2004, 7–19, 43–49; and El-Gamal 2006, 7–25.

[4] For detailed critiques in this vein, see Kuran 2004; and El-Gamal 2006.

[5] Goitein (1967) offers evidence on contractual forms used in tenth-century Egypt. My own data set of commercial cases handled by Istanbul's Islamic courts between 1602 and 1696 shows that the contractual forms did not differ fundamentally. Reviewed court registers (*defter*s): Galata 24, 25, 27, 41, 42, 130, 145; Istanbul 1, 2, 3, 4, 9, 16, 22, 23.

[6] See, for instance, Marcus 1989; and Abdullah 2001, both on the eighteenth century.

[7] Faroqhi attributes the paucity of Middle Eastern private archives to "wars and civil wars." But western Europe, too, endured destructive political instability, which suggests that a more fundamental factor lies in interregional differences in incentives to maintain records.

[8] Lackner 1978, 84–88; and Boyd 1973, esp. 107–9. For broader analyses of religious opposition to technological change in Saudi Arabia, see Al-Rasheed 2002, chaps. 2–4; and Steinberg 2005.

[9] For critical perspectives on modern campaigns against cross-cultural fertilization, see Lowenthal 1996; and Cowen 2002.

[10] We know of such revisionist views partly through treatises that sought to discredit them. See Fierro 1992; and Labib 1970.

[11] For a recent example, see Brennan and Pettit 2004.

[12] A possible objection to this interpretation is that new cash waqfs could have been granted flexibilities without threatening any existing beneficiaries directly. True, but a ubiquitous threat was that of concessions eroding public morality in general. Indeed, the fear of the "slippery slope" has been a common theme of resistance to Islamic reinterpretation. Mandaville (1979, 304–6) documents that it was an element of the conservative rhetoric exhibited during the cash waqf controversy. For examples from other contexts, see Zilfi 1988, chap. 4.

[13] Ágoston (2005) develops all these points in his analysis of the Ottoman arms industry. For complementary observations, see İhsanoğlu 2004, chaps. 2–3.

[14] For evidence see the following cases from Istanbul court register no. 9, which covers the period 1661–62: 56b/1, 64a/5, 121a/1, 125b/2, 171b/2, 190b/3, 262b/3.

[15] For overviews of these developments, see Liebesny 1975; Anderson 1968.

[16] http://www.forbes.com/lists. The regularly updated list is based on sales, market value, assets, and profits.

[17] Kuran 2004, chap. 2. On the role of economically helpful effects of Islamism, see also Singerman 1995, chaps. 3–4; and Özcan and Çokgezen 2006.

References

Abdullah, Thabit A. J. 2001. *Merchants, Mamluks, and Murder: The Political Economy of Trade in Eighteenth-Century Basra*. Albany: State University of New York Press.

Abu-Lughod, Janet L. 1989. *Before European Hegemony: The World System, A.D. 1250–1350*. New York: Oxford University Press.

Aghassian, Michel, and Kéram Kévonian. 1999. "The Armenian Merchant Network: Overall Autonomy and Integration." Trans. Cyprian P. Blamires. In *Merchants, Companies, and

Trade: Europe and Asia in the Early Modern Era, ed. Sushil Chaudhury and Michel Morineau, 74–94. Cambridge: Cambridge University Press.

Ágoston, Gábor. 2005. *Guns for the Sultan: Military Power and the Weapons Industry in the Ottoman Empire*. Cambridge: Cambridge University Press.

Ahmed, Habib. 2006. "Islamic Law, Adaptability and Financial Development." *Islamic Economic Studies* 13:79–101.

Al-Rasheed, Madawi. 2002. *A History of Saudi Arabia*. Cambridge: Cambridge University Press.

Anderson, J.N.D. 1968. "Law Reform in Egypt: 1850–1950." In *Political and Social Change in Modern Egypt*, ed. P. M. Holt, 209–30. London: Oxford University Press.

Ashtor, Eliyahu. 1956. "The Kārīmi Merchants." *Journal of the Royal Asiatic Society* pts. 1–2: 45–56.

———. 1976. *A Social and Economic History of the Near East in the Middle Ages*. London: Collins.

Babinger, Franz. 2004. *Müteferrika ve Osmanlı Matbaası: 18. Yüzyılda İstanbul'da Kitabiyat*. Trans. Nedret Kuran-Burçoğlu. Istanbul: Tarih Vakfı.

Berkes, Niyazi. 1998. *The Development of Secularism in Turkey*. Reprint. New York: Routledge.

Boyd, Douglas A. 1973. "An Historical and Descriptive Analysis of the Evolution and Development of Saudi Arabian Television, 1963–1972." Ph.D. diss., Department of Mass Communication, University of Minnesota.

Brennan, Geoffrey, and Philip Pettit. 2004. *The Economy of Esteem: An Essay on Civil and Political Society*. New York: Oxford University Press.

Casale, Giancarlo. 2006. "The Ottoman Administration of the Spice Trade in the Sixteenth-Century Red Sea and Persian Gulf." *Journal of the Economic and Social History of the Orient* 49, no. 2: 1–29.

Casson, Mark C. 2003. *The Entrepreneur: An Economic Theory*. 2nd ed. Cheltenham, UK: Edward Elgar.

Chaudhuri, K. N. 1985. *Trade and Civilisation in the Indian Ocean: An Economic History from the Rise of Islam to 1750*. Cambridge: Cambridge University Press.

Cohen, Hayyim J. 1970. "The Economic Background and the Secular Occupations of Muslim Jurisprudents and Traditionists in the Classical Period of Islam (until the Middle of the Eleventh Century)." *Journal of the Economic and Social History of the Orient* 13:16–61.

Coşgel, Metin M. 2005. "Efficiency and Continuity in Public Finance: The Ottoman System of Taxation." *International Journal of Middle East Studies* 37:567–86.

Cowen, Tyler. 2002. *Creative Destruction: How Globalization Is Changing the World's Cultures*. Princeton: Princeton University Press.

Curtin, Philip D. 1984. *Cross-Cultural Trade in World History*. Cambridge: Cambridge University Press.

Çizakça, Murat. 1996. *A Comparative Evolution of Business Partnerships: The Islamic World and Europe, with Special Reference to the Ottoman Archives*. Leiden: E. J. Brill.

———. 2000. *A History of Philanthropic Foundations: The Islamic World from the Seventh Century to the Present*. Istanbul: Boğaziçi University Press.

Darling, Linda. 1996. *Revenue-Raising and Legitimacy: Tax Collection and Finance Administration in the Ottoman Empire*. Leiden: E. J. Brill.

De Roover, Raymond. 1963. *The Rise and Decline of the Medici Bank, 1397–1494*. Cambridge: Harvard University Press.

El-Gamal, Mahmoud A. 2006. *Islamic Finance: Law, Economics, and Practice*. Cambridge: Cambridge University Press.

Faroqhi, Suraiya. 1999. *Approaching Ottoman History: An Introduction to the Sources*. Cambridge: Cambridge University Press.

Fierro, Maribel. 1992. "The Treatises against Innovations (*Kutub al-bida'*)." *Der Islam* 69:204–46.

Genç, Mehmet. 2000. *Osmanlı İmparatorluğunda Devlet ve Ekonomi.* Istanbul: Ötüken.

Goitein, S. D. 1967. *A Mediterranean Society.* Vol. 1, *Economic Foundations.* Berkeley and Los Angeles: University of California Press.

Hanna, Nelly. 1998. *Making Big Money in 1600: The Life and Times of Isma'il Abu Taqiyya, Egyptian Merchant.* Syracuse: Syracuse University Press.

Hattox, Ralph S. 1985. *Coffee and Coffeehouses: The Origins of a Social Beverage in the Medieval Middle East.* Seattle: University of Washington Press.

Hayek, Friedrich A. 1937. "Economics and Knowledge." *Economica* n.s. 4:33–54.

Hourani, Albert. 1983. *Arabic Thought in the Liberal Age, 1798–1839.* Rev. ed. Cambridge: Cambridge University Press.

Hourani, George F. 1995. *Arab Seafaring.* Expanded ed. Princeton: Princeton University Press.

İhsanoğlu, Ekmeleddin. 2004. *Science, Technology, and Learning in the Ottoman Empire: Western Influence, Local Institutions, and the Transfer of Technology.* Aldershot, Hampshire, UK: Ashgate.

İnalcık, Halil. 1994. "The Ottoman State: Economy and Society, 1300–1600." In *An Economic and Social History of the Ottoman Empire, 1300–1914,* ed. Halil İnalcık with Donald Quataert, 9–409. New York: Cambridge University Press.

Kaegi, Walter E. J. 1969. "Initial Byzantine Reactions to the Arab Conquest." *Church History* 38:139–49.

Kirzner, Israel M. 1979. *Perception, Opportunity, and Profit: Studies in the Theory of Entrepreneurship.* Chicago: University of Chicago Press.

Kuran, Timur. 2001. "The Provision of Public Goods under Islamic Law: Origins, Impact, and Limitations of the Waqf System." *Law and Society Review* 35:841–97.

———. 2003. "The Islamic Commercial Crisis: Institutional Roots of Economic Underdevelopment in the Middle East." *Journal of Economic History* 63:414–46.

———. 2004. *Islam and Mammon: The Economic Predicaments of Islamism.* Princeton: Princeton University Press.

———. 2005a. "The Absence of the Corporation in Islamic Law: Origins and Persistence." *American Journal of Comparative Law* 53:785–834.

———. 2005b. "The Logic of Financial Westernization in the Middle East." *Journal of Economic Behavior and Organization* 56:593–615.

Labib, Subhi. 1970. "The Problem of the Bida' in the Light of an Arabic Manuscript of the 14th Century." In *Proceedings of the Twenty-Sixth International Congress of Orientalists, New Delhi, 4–10th January, 1964,* vol. 4. New Delhi: International Congress of Orientalists.

Lackner, Helen. 1978. *A House Built on Sand: A Political Economy of Saudi Arabia.* London: Ithaca Press.

Leibenstein, Harvey. 1968. "Entrepreneurship and Development." *American Economic Review* 58:72–83.

Lewis, Bernard. 1993. *Islam in History: Ideas, People, and Events in the Middle East.* 2nd ed. Chicago: Open Court.

———. 2002. *What Went Wrong? Western Impact and Middle Eastern Response.* New York: Oxford University Press.

Liebesny, Herbert J. 1975. *The Law of the Near and Middle East: Readings, Cases, and Materials.* Albany: State University of New York Press.

Løkkegaard, Frede. 1950. *Islamic Taxation in the Classic Period, with Special Reference to Circumstances in Iraq.* Copenhagen: Branner and Korch.

Lowenthal, David. 1996. *Possessed by the Past: The Heritage Crusade and the Spoils of History.* New York: Free Press.

Mandaville, Jon E. 1979. "Usurious Piety: The Cash Waqf Controversy in the Ottoman Empire." *International Journal of Middle East Studies* 10:298–308.

Mannan, Muhammad A. 1970. *Islamic Economics: Theory and Practice.* Lahore: Sh. Muhammad Ashraf.

Marcus, Abraham. 1989. *The Middle East on the Eve of Modernity: Aleppo in the Eighteenth Century*. New York: Columbia University Press.

Masud, Muhammad Khalid, Brinkley Messick, and David S. Powers. 1996. "Muftis, Fatwas, and Islamic Legal Interpretation." In *Islamic Legal Interpretation: Muftis and Their Fatwas*, ed. Muhammad Khalid Masud, Brinkley Messick, and David S. Powers, 3–32. Cambridge: Harvard University Press.

McCabe, Ina Baghdiantz. 1999. *The Shah's Silk for Europe's Silver: The Eurasian Trade of the Julfa Armenians in Safavid Iran and India (1530–1750)*. Atlanta: Scholars Press.

Nyazee, Imran Ahsan Khan. 1999. *Islamic Law of Business Organization: Partnerships*. Islamabad: Islamic Research Institute.

Özcan, Gül Berna, and Murat Çokgezen. 2006. "Trusted Markets: The Exchanges of Islamic Companies." *Comparative Economic Studies* 48:132–55.

Palmer, Monte, Abdelrahman Al-Hegelan, Mohammed Bushara Abdelrahman, Ali Leila, and El Sayeed Yassin. 1989. "Bureaucratic Innovation and Economic Development in the Middle East: A Study of Egypt, Saudi Arabia, and the Sudan." In *Bureaucracy and Development in the Arab World*, ed. Joseph G. Jabbra, 12–27. Leiden: E. J. Brill.

Patai, Raphael. 1983. *The Arab Mind*. Rev. ed. New York: Charles Scribner's.

Robinson, Francis. 1993. "Technology and Religious Change: Islam and the Impact of Print." *Modern Asian Studies* 27:229–51.

Rodinson, Maxime. 1987. *Europe and the Mystique of Islam*. Trans. Roger Veinus. Seattle: University of Washington Press.

Sadeq, AbulHasan Muhammad. 1990. *Economic Development in Islam*. Petaling Jaya, Malaysia: Pelanduk Publications.

Sayigh, Yusif A. 1958. "Toward a Theory of Entrepreneurship for the Arab East." *Explorations in Entrepreneurial History* 10:123–27.

Schumpeter, Joseph A. 1934. *The Theory of Economic Development: An Inquiry into Profits, Capital, Credit, Interest, and the Business Cycle*. Trans. Redvers Opie. Cambridge: Harvard University Press.

Siddiqi, Muhammad Nejatullah. 1979. *The Economic Enterprise in Islam*. 2nd ed. Lahore: Islamic Publications.

Singerman, Diane. 1995. *Avenues of Participation: Family, Politics, and Networks in Urban Quarters of Cairo*. Princeton: Princeton University Press.

Steinberg, Guido. 2005. "The Wahhabi Ulama and the Saudi State: 1745 to the Present." In *Saudi Arabia in the Balance: Political Economy, Society, Foreign Affairs*, ed. Paul Aarts and Gerd Nonneman, 11–34. Washington Square: New York University Press.

Talbi, Mohammed. 1960. "Les Bidaʿ." *Studia Islamica* 12:43–77.

Turner, Bryan S. 1974. *Weber and Islam: A Critical Study*. London: Routledge and Kegan Paul.

Udovitch, Abraham L. 1970. *Partnership and Profit in Medieval Islam*. Princeton: Princeton University Press.

Veinstein, Gilles. 1999. "Commercial Relations between India and the Ottoman Empire (Late Fifteenth to Late Eighteenth Centuries): A Few Notes and Hypotheses." Trans. Cyprian P. Blamires. In *Merchants, Companies and Trade: Europe and Asia in the Early Modern Era*, ed. Sushil Chaudhury and Michel Morineau, 95–115. Cambridge: Cambridge University Press.

Weber, Max. 1978. *Economy and Society: An Outline of Interpretive Sociology*. Ed. Guenther Roth and Claus Wittich. Trans. Ephraim Fischoff et al. 2 vols. Berkeley and Los Angeles: University of California Press.

Wehr, Hans. 1980. *A Dictionary of Modern Written Arabic*. Beirut: Librarie du Liban.

Wood, Alfred C. 1935. *A History of the Levant Company*. London: Oxford University Press.

Zilfi, Madeline C. 1988. *The Politics of Piety: The Ottoman Ulema in the Postclassical Age (1600–1800)*. Minneapolis: Bibliotheca Islamica.

Chapter 4

Entrepreneurs and Entrepreneurship in Medieval Europe

JAMES M. MURRAY

THE FIRST USE OF THE WORD *ENTREPRENEUR* comes to us from the late Middle Ages when this French loan word was used to describe a battlefield commander. Only very gradually was the word's meaning extended to the battlefield of business. Along the way it was used to describe the "director or manager of a public musical institution," before the late-nineteenth-century economist Richard T. Ely rather sniffily wrote in his *Introduction to Political Economy* that "we have been obliged to resort to the French language for a word to designate the person who organizes and directs the productive factors, and we call such a one an entrepreneur." The *Oxford English Dictionary* goes on to trace the ready adoption of the word by subsequent economists, including Keynes and of course Schumpeter, before it became worthy to be studied and cultivated in schools and institutes of higher learning.[1]

But surely if the word is modern, the activities it describes are not, for "productive forces" and their directors are as old as civilization. Yet the European Middle Ages—traditionally defined as the millennium from 500–1500 CE—I will argue deserve a special place in the history of entrepreneurship, for it was at the end of those thousand years that unique and characteristic qualities of behavior and character were assigned to a particular social group. These "merchants" by the fourteenth century were described in the Germanic languages as skilled in the art of the merchant, which in Flemish and German was *Coopmanscepe* or *Kaufmannschaft*, etymologically related to English's *salesmanship* but with a meaning much closer to our word *entrepreneurship*. Dante Alighieri, himself a product of the merchant city of Florence, also offers merchants a special circle in Hell where the sin particular to their profession (usury) is punished in picturesque and pungent fashion.[2] In other words, by the end of the medieval period, merchants came to direct many of society's "productive forces" within cities and were subject to the corrective judgment of a society still bound to Christianity's mission to heal the rift between God and humanity and gain individual salvation for all the baptized.

From Ancient to Medieval (1–500 CE)

Edward Gibbon famously attributed the end of the ancient world to the triumph of barbarism and Christianity, as if those elements were foreign to Roman civilization by circa 500 CE. But in fact, Christianity in its Romanized form was the medium through which the migrating Germanic tribes came to know and desire the benefits of Roman civilization. For better or worse, the distilled essence of several millennia of Mediterranean civilizations, from ancient Mesopotamia to Egypt, was expressed in Christianity, that offspring of Judaism; and the central Italian city from which the most successful Mediterranean-based empire of the ancient world had its beginnings, served as the cult center for a new civilization whose political and economic foundations would take shape in areas relatively little influenced by the ancient Roman Empire except in memory. However aimlessly and unintentionally, the early medieval world took shape from the decayed remains of the Roman provincial world.

The Economics of Lordship

Karl Marx and others have famously labeled the Christian/German hybrid that arose after 500 CE as a "feudal economy," without, however, agreeing on a precise definition of this invented term. Much recent controversy notwithstanding, it is still useful to label as feudal a legal and social system whereby a religious/military elite exercised control over a largely servile peasantry through both a monopoly of armed force and a compelling vision of human society and its purpose. Inspired by the threefold nature of their God, western European society was to consist of three sorts of people: those who prayed, those who fought and, most numerous, those who worked. Its mission was individual and collective salvation brought forth through preparation for Christ's Second Coming. From the eleventh century, this vision of "Right Order in the World" became a program of a reforming papacy under whose leadership internal discipline was preached and to a more limited degree enforced, while the boundaries of Christendom were pushed outward into lands held by Muslims, Slavs, Greeks, and Celts (Duby 1982).

Though theologically inspired, western Europe never became a theocracy chiefly because of the complementary but somewhat competing ideology of the warrior elite of Europe, who by the twelfth century called themselves knights and their common culture, chivalry. Built upon a series of military improvisations designed to repel a highly mobile adversary (Vikings, Magyars, Saracens) the chivalric class ("those who fought") monopolized the technology of fighting on horseback with lance, sword, and shield, acting in formation under structures of command, and enforcing their will through the practice of castle building. Medieval knights insisted upon a divine sanction for their own power independent of that of popes, priests, and monks. Its expression assumed a variety of forms, from the literature of epic and romance, to tournaments and crusades, and a culture of conspicuous consumption proper to the ideal of "living nobly" (Keen 2005).

Entrepreneurial Lordship

Though differing slightly in mission, lords spiritual and lords temporal alike depended on a collection of rights and rents owed them by workers whose labor produced the material basis for this civilization. These "serfs" (from the Latin *servi* or slave) settled mostly in village communities in an institutional form historians call manorialism, which is best understood as the sum of man-made productive forces brought to bear on the fields, forests, and pastures of the European countryside. In return for possession—though not outright ownership—of land, European peasants owed their lord labor on his land, and they owed various in-kind and monetary payments as well. Thus they were obliged to have their grain ground in the lord's mill, their bread baked in the lord's oven, and were not free either to choose the crops they raised or to pick up stakes and migrate elsewhere without their lord's permission. On the other hand, a peasant household, unlike a slave's, could not be broken up and sold by the lord; serfs had rights to remain on the land and had customary rights against outright confiscation of the products of their labor on the land.

This new labor system was deployed to furnish the lords of Europe a diet and material existence shaped by their mixed cultural past. On the one hand, Romans had long subsisted on grain, especially wheat, usually baked into bread or cooked as a porridge; accompaniments could be a bit of meat, vegetables, with wine as the preferred beverage. Germanic peoples had long been pastoralists and expected meat and other animal products on their table. Thus a mixed farming system of cereal cultivation and animal raising took root across the arable midsection of western Europe and was transplanted in turn to the new European colonies in central and eastern Europe, Ireland and Spain, even to the semifrozen expanses of Greenland and Iceland. But a number of practical problems faced the generations of lords and farmers in the first medieval half-millennium (Hunt and Murray 1999, 250).

The dissolution of the Roman Empire in the west had been preceded and accompanied by wholesale neglect of much of the agrarian infrastructure. The majority of the grain consumed in Italy and elsewhere was grown in North Africa and Sicily on slave-worked plantations, and was acquired on contract by urban governments for public distribution. Undercut by large-scale agriculture and depopulated, much of the Italian and cisalpine countryside reverted to marsh and forest. Huge swaths of northern Gaul were never farmed at all because the soil type was foreign to Mediterranean cultivation methods and investments in technology and labor were never feasible. Providing incentives to peasants and investing in labor-saving technologies were the hallmarks of the largely anonymous revolution produced by enterprising lords.

Investment in technology by European lords consisted of the major implements needed to till the fields. In the north of Europe, these, as well as the draft animals needed to propel them, were a considerable investment, involving a stout iron plowshare, a moldboard to turn over heavy clay soils, and a team of two to four oxen, or more rarely horses (Langdon 1986). Such heavy, wheeled plows more than justified their expense, and by the eleventh century were the standard tillers of the fields across most of northern Europe. And by this time, the large swath of plains from central France to Poland was well on its way to becoming the breadbasket of Europe.

A second implement provided by the lord but benefiting all was the watermill. Like the heavy plow, watermills had been known and used by the Romans. But medieval lords faced with labor shortages in the countryside invested in the construction of innumerable mills across Europe—England in 1086 had some 6,082—and this spared peasants the work of milling their own grain, so that their labor could be directed to more productive ends. This was especially true for women's work, which had traditionally included the hand milling of grain for domestic consumption. By the twelfth century, the windmill had joined the watermill as a flexible and effective technology that could be put to many uses (Lucas 2006; Langdon 2004). These uses went well beyond milling of grain and included mills that sawed lumber, mills that hammered metals, mills devoted to fulling of cloth, and on and on.

Improvement in technology and land use alone could not have produced the surge in production achieved in Europe by the turn of the millennium. Enhanced production of cereal crops and animals demanded more lands beyond what had been settled islands of traditional village communities often surrounded by forest. The conquest of the medieval forest frontier from the ninth to the thirteenth century is perhaps the best demonstration of the power of entrepreneurial lordship: lords provided capital and incentives to peasants in order to capture their labor for a variety of objectives. Here lords—monasteries, princes, bishops, and so on—offered special privileges and power over newly won agricultural land. Such incentives caused settled rural communities to chip away constantly at the surrounding wasteland, bringing more and more of it under the plow.

The second form of lord-peasant cooperation that helped revolutionize agriculture was the recruitment of settlers to lands newly obtained by conquest. To secure colonists, lords often drew up agreements with representatives of prospective settlers, offering terms far more favorable than those of the old population centers. In exchange for payment of a small tax per homestead, such colonists received much more power over the land they farmed as well as rights that amounted to personal freedom. One example was Wichmann, archbishop of Magdeburg (1152–92) who sent out *locatores* to make the pitch for settlers from among the relatively crowded countryside of Flanders and Holland. The attractions were considerable: freedom from all forced labor on the lord's land, and possession of land in return for a relatively small rent. By the late twelfth century, German speakers were settled in eastern Europe from Estonia to the Carpathian Mountains. Nor all were farmers. It was Germans who worked the gold and silver mines that were developed to exploit the mineral deposits discovered in the Slavic midsection of Europe (Bartlett 1994).

What explains the dynamic growth at the core of rural Europe in the centuries from the end of Roman civilization and the High Middle Ages? Certainly neither form of lordship—seigneurial or ecclesiastical—had entrepreneurial growth as its raison d'être. Yet intended or not, Europe's escape from backwardness was driven by demand generated by lords great and small, from the most obscure bishop to the holder of the most isolated castle. This demand was both inherited from the Roman past and developed from the Germanic roots of chivalry, yielding a sophisticated and often expensive level of material culture given to conspicuous display and consumption. Dietary expectations, for example, were a remnant of the Mediterranean-based expectations of bread and wine, with olive oil as the edible fat of choice. Transplanting such a diet to the soil and weather conditions of Europe north of the Alps became the central challenge of Dark Age agriculture, and resulted in a hierarchy of bread grains produced, from wheat for the lords, to barley, rye, and spelt for the peasant. Beverages were most often grain-derived ale for commoners, with wine reserved for the wealthiest even among the lords. Stock raising always remained an adjunct to grain farming in the medieval countryside, with pork the favorite meat and cattle and sheep distant runners-up (Biddick 1989; Berman 1986).

Yet the requirements of diet were only the starting points of lordly desire. Churches and monasteries required vestments and relics, buildings and books.

Knights required horses and armor, swords and lances; and castles themselves became ever more elaborate in materials and design from their beginnings as wood palisades, which were replaced by stone structures after 1100. And all Christians felt the compulsion to journey on pilgrimage in search of spiritual and physical healing, with the greatest sinners obliged to travel the longest distances.

The following are a few examples of enterprise conspicuous before the turn of the medieval millennium. Ecclesiastical demand kept a long-distance trading network alive throughout the Dark Ages. Some of the remarkable variety of items traded are unsurprising, thus common liturgical goods such as incense; and silk textiles; and other spices used for medicinal purposes (McCormick 2001, 291–93). What is surprising is the frequency and quantity of relics of Mediterranean provenance that came to form major collections in the ecclesiastical heartland of Francia. By the year 1000, for example, the surviving collection at Sens in Burgundy numbered over 600 items. A significant number originated from Mediterranean saints' shrines, and many of those came from the distant eastern Mediterranean. A second Frankish relic collection, this one at Chelles (Ile de France), reached its height slightly later in time, therefore showing more evidence of trading contact with Italy (especially Rome) and the Holy Land. Thus recent research shows the endurance of long-distance communication and trade links in Francia from 500 to 750 CE.

Even by charitable estimate, the world of the early Franks was profoundly underdeveloped by the standards of the Muslim and Byzantine states that surrounded it. Yet entrepreneurs remained at work in the interstices of those cultures and economies, supplying the one western commodity much in demand across the Mediterranean from the eighth through the tenth centuries: slaves. Fragmentary records attest to slave hunting and transport, with Anglo-Saxon slaves captured and conveyed to markets in southern France, northern Italy, and Rome. Volume swelled under the Carolingians after 750, when conquests in central and eastern Europe brought heathen Slavs to market, leaving that name *sclavus* as the permanent marker of this source of captives. By the eighth century, Venice had become a great slave port, with Venetian traders functioning as middlemen in the sale of slaves to southern and eastern Mediterranean markets. Michael McCormick is bold enough to insist, "The European commercial economy in the Mediterranean was born precisely in the dynamic centers of the slave trade with the Arab world, in Naples and Amalfi, and in Venice" (2001, 736–39, 776; and see Schwarcz 2003, 279–82).

For all the accomplishments of European lords in the two centuries before the turn of the millennium, by far their greatest creation was the medieval city. This was a creative effort of unparalleled size and geographical extent, and it produced a new form of urban community, one that would serve as a laboratory for entrepreneurship until the end of the twentieth century. This urban revolution occurred across the long twelfth century, roughly 1050–1220, during which time urban Europe expanded both in absolute numbers of towns and cities, and in the size and extent of older communities. Most impressive is the fact that European population probably doubled in the period 950–1200, but the number of urban areas quadrupled (Nicholas 2003, 1–23).

Generalizing about this revolution is difficult, given the variety and number of urban foundations. In southern Europe few new cities were actually founded in the Middle Ages, but their enclosed areas and populations expanded exponentially, with the northern half of the Italian peninsula excelling the south in the number and importance of its cities. Thus Genoa, Venice, and the new upstart inland city, Florence, had no ancient antecedents. Elsewhere, particularly in the new European colonial areas of Spain and Slavic and Celtic Europe, lords founded new enclaves, often on site of previous settlements or for particular political ends. In Spain, new settlements were founded as defensive strong points against the Muslims. In Ireland, the Normans used fortified urban areas as their way to settle and domesticate the countryside. In Flanders, the counts founded a series of towns, but only a handful ever became significant. And in Germany east of the Elbe River, a large number of urban plantations became significant after the thirteenth-century revival of the Baltic trade. Thus cities as distant and disparate from one another as Munich and Lübeck owe their origins to princely founders.[3]

Abundant and messy as the details of this urban wave may have been, two permanent changes to the contours of economic life resulted. First, the urban map became more or less fixed by 1220, with two poles of intense urbanization, one in the European south, the other in the north, stretching from southeast England through Paris, and across the plains of Picardy and Flanders to Cologne, the great city of the Rhine. Second, these communities evolved from seigniorial to merchant centers, where demand for a wide variety of goods—not just luxuries—fueled the medieval entrepreneur. Lords by no means withdrew from these developing market centers, for many European cities became the seats of important bureaucracies, for town lords both bought merchants' goods and brought capital to the towns, and often their grant of privileges and monopolies was critical to urban growth. Such transitions could be turbulent, as urban residents, called bourgeois or burghers, often agitated for change and increased autonomy over the opposition of bishop, count, abbot, or cathedral chapter. But despite some spectacular flare-ups of violence, Europe's first urban revolution was relatively peaceful (Nicholas 2003, 92–97).

The signal service of lords in this transitional age was to function as a site of consumption and therefore as a pole attracting entrepreneurial interest. Most eleventh-century settlements that became centers of long-distance trade had communities of resident Jews, who loaned money to the town lords and may have contributed capital to the industries that began to flourish in the suburbs. The twelfth century was the high point of Jewish involvement in capital formation and concentration in the cities. Thereafter changes such as princely persecution, plus a new wave of Christian moneylenders employing more sophisticated financial techniques (whose purpose was to evade the church's usury proscription) effectively took over this early Jewish entrepreneurial impulse.

The two urban poles of Europe provided the congeries of markets and networks that resulted in what Peter Spufford has described as a "critical mass, so that qualitative as well as merely quantitative changes in the nature of commerce began to take place" (2002, 19, 388–89). The sum of these changes is known in economic history as the "commercial revolution," which must be understood as the result of enterprise in the two distinct urban laboratories north and south; and more importantly as the result of the interaction of the two from the thirteenth century to the early modern period. It can be fairly said that most of the innovations and hallmarks of European business and economic history were developed in this bipolar urban network, stoked with bullion from the gold and silver mines of central Europe.

The Super-Company Phenomenon

The most significant achievement of medieval southern businessmen was the super-company, a form of enterprise that most effectively combined the possibilities of profit in the thirteenth century and thus may serve as a suitable case study for our purposes. These organizations were unusually large and qualitatively different, engaged simultaneously in an exceptional range of activity—general trading, commodity trading, banking, and manufacturing—over a wide geographical area for an extended period. They all took root in the fruitful commercial soil of Florence, amid a competitive and contentious archipelago of cities. The demand for food generated by these urban populations challenged the entrepreneurs who formed these companies, which pooled capital in order to lock up long-term grain contracts with the Angevin rulers of southern Italy, and from that base diversified into long-distance trade and local manufacture alike. How were these large firms organized? Like most Italian firms of significant size, they were quasi-permanent multiple partnerships that did not dissolve upon the death or removal of the managing partners. Even upon "dissolution" partnerships were instantly renewed. Partnerships lasted as long as was found suitable, from two to twelve years in practice, and often had a core of closely related individuals as the major providers of capital. Often the company (derived from the expression "those of one bread") took the name of this family clan—for example, Bardi, Peruzzi—though at no time was the company composed exclusively of family members. For example, the Peruzzi Company of 1300 incorporated with seven family members and ten outsiders who combined in a 60/40 ratio to amass a capital of 85,000 florins, a staggering sum for the time (Hunt and Murray 1999, 105). Partnerships could be diversified even further, as in the Bardi company of 1310, which consisted of fifty-six shares, each transferable and survivable, and company capital could be further augmented by deposits by outsiders carrying fixed rates of interest much like modern debentures. Like contemporary hedge funds, the medieval ancestors of "high net-worth individuals," be they aristocrats or wealthy merchants, invested their excess cash with one or more of these companies (Spufford 2002, 22–23).

Such quantities of relatively cheap capital opened a world of possibilities. Each company deployed its resources differently, though all established branches or supported representatives in the key cities of European commerce, often staffed by shareholders under the authority of a managing board headed by the *capo* or chairman, who was almost always a leading member of the family whose name formed part of the company title. The presence of these men both at home and in foreign posts gave assurance to their clients that the company was an enduring organization, notwithstanding the frequent dissolution of partnerships. This sense of permanence was enhanced by the use of a company logo of distinctive or heraldic design (Spufford 2002, 44, 46).

Although there is no direct evidence that any of the great companies had drawn up formal divisions of responsibility or lines of authority, the many references in the surviving records of the Peruzzi company to the various parts of the company's operations in Florence and abroad offer a reasonable idea of how they worked in practice. They suggest that the Peruzzi had a form of organization that permitted a degree of decentralization at the operating level, but reserved important areas of decision-making to the powerful chairman's office in Florence. Operations in

Florence were fairly centralized, with several subsidiary companies reporting directly to the chairman. Roughly speaking, the so-called *tavola* (literally "table") dealt primarily with banking operations managed in Florence, and the *mercanzia* with trading and logistics outside Florence. The *drapperia* controlled a small textile contract manufacturing operation. "Special accounts" oversaw directly from Florence such important foreign customers as the Order of the Hospitalers and certain church dignitaries. The *limosina* was simply an account through which the company's charities were channeled. About 2 percent of the company's capital was set aside for "God's work," from which the *limosina* received allocations of profit (Hunt 1994, 76–100).

Employees numbered in the hundreds for these large firms, from the 133 employed by the Peruzzi in the 1330s to the 346 who worked for the Bardi in the period 1310 to 1345. Very few of these men were related to the family whose name the company bore, which suggests that nepotism was not the dominant criterion for selection and advancement. Interfamilial alliances were the rule, however, as family members of rival companies were not found among the employees, suggesting that the mercantile elite sent its brightest sons along well-worn paths of patronage and mutual obligation. Young men were often schooled in the secrets and practices of a particular company by foreign postings, returning to Florence as mature and accomplished merchants with enough wealth to start their own families and enterprises.

Tools of Trade

Super-companies both inherited and developed a toolkit of business practices that sought to overcome constraints on trade posed by both society and distance. One of the most pervasive problems besetting medieval entrepreneurs was the rigidity of the money supply, and some of the most creative innovations were directed at alleviating that problem. In the thirteenth century, money in circulation was overwhelmingly in the form of minted coins. Some lower-value coins might be minted from base metals and bear more a fiduciary value as small change for daily purchases. Most money in use in trade consisted of coins of intrinsic value, made primarily of silver, and also, from the middle of the thirteenth century, of gold. The money supply was therefore profoundly affected by physical phenomena associated with precious metals—the production of mines, losses from wear and hoarding, diversion into objects of art, and constant exports to cover trade imbalances with the East. The European economy could afford the siphoning off of great quantities of specie as long as mining output remained high. In fact, the effects of such a trade in bullion could be downright positive by stimulating general trade and reducing inflationary pressures. But when mining output faltered and exports continued, Europe experienced the deflationary effects of repeated "bullion famines" in the fourteenth and fifteenth centuries (Spufford 1988, 339–62).

Entrepreneurs were happy to move precious metals from place to place either as export commodities or as materials for minting if they could realize a profit. Moving coins as money, however, was a business expense that added no value to the transaction. The expense of tolls, security, and transport could be considerable. And the annoyance of sending messengers with coins across urban markets must have been considerable, particularly if the bullion content of each and every coin had to be measured. One solution to the inconveniences of coin was the money changer, who was a ubiquitous figure in markets across Europe, and was the originator of medieval banking. These changers performed the useful service of bringing order into a coin-dominated economy, through their skills in assessing the weight and fineness of coins. They also supplied service to governments as the main suppliers of bullion and used coins to the mints. Their superior knowledge of bullion prices and exchange rates of foreign coins gave them commercial advantage over their fellow merchants, but also imposed an obligation for fair dealing. Some changers acquired sufficient customers and enough specie on deposit that they recorded such deposits for safekeeping in terms of a standard money of account. Such "book" money began to be traded by merchants in place of the real thing (Murray 2005, 119–77).

In this manner, merchant money changers gradually became merchant-bankers, executing payments, not by issuing checks (at least not before the fourteenth century), but by transferring charges and credits in the accounts of their clients. This was the so-called giro system (from the Italian *girare*, to rotate), still in use in contemporary Europe. The system worked because the bankers and their merchant clients knew each other and gave their instructions orally at the banker's table, so that the entries could be made on the spot. The personal nature of the business and the fact that the banks also took deposits for safekeeping inevitably led to the extension of credit by means of overdrafts. This lending on the principle of fractional reserves in effect created additional money supply, albeit only in a very few leading commercial cities (de Roover 1948).

The most important financial innovation of the commercial revolution was the bill of exchange, which combined three attributes of great value to the international entrepreneurs who traded within western Europe. It avoided the cost of transporting specie; it provided a practical mechanism for international credit and currency exchange, and it finessed the church's prohibition of usury. The bill of exchange found its definitive form by the end of the thirteenth century, after evolving from the notarized exchange instrument first used in the Italian port city of Genoa (Murray 2005, 65; Spufford 2002, 34–35). The fully developed bill of exchange made it possible for one party to receive a sum of money in one currency in one place on one date and repay it in another currency at another place at a later date. The transaction involved four parties, the borrower and lender in the town of issue and the borrower's correspondent (the payer) and the lender's representative (the payee) in the town of repayment. The difference in dates, called "usuance," normally reflected the generally accepted time required to move goods between the two locations, such as sixty days between Venice and Bruges and ninety days between Venice and London. The bills, of course, could move much more quickly, and we know of specialized courier services maintained between the cities of Tuscany and the Champagne fairs from the 1260s (Spufford 1988, 25). Besides the destination and the date of issue and redemption, the bill specified the currency exchange rate, with the objective of giving the issuer a reasonable profit on the deal. The lender's representative might be instructed to use the foreign exchange to buy merchandise, or to convert it into the lender's own currency by drawing up a new bill in the opposite direction. And although the bill of exchange was developed by merchants for merchants, its advantages were enjoyed not only by merchants but also by the great institutions of the church and government (Murray 2005, 66 and n. 9; Spufford 2002, 37).

A second significant entrepreneurial breakthrough of Italian merchants was in accounting. A vast range of merchants and bureaucracies had long used single-entry accounting. This form of bookkeeping had the advantage of providing at low cost a rational basis for decision-making, as credits and debts could be easily tracked. Its disadvantage was that it failed to account for profits automatically and it could not provide a separate measurement of capital and revenue. Most significant, however, it made concealment of fraud easy, thus requiring frequent audits and other antifraud measures. The complexities of super-company trade and accounting led to the double entry of cash receipts, first discharging the account of the debtor, then charging the account of the cashier, thereby permitting the establishment of cross-references. By 1300 the new system had spread widely among Italian firms and quickly reached a sophisticated level of development, providing balance sheet data and separate accounting of capital and revenue, and had introduced useful concepts such as accruals and depreciation.

Tools for managing risk were also a signal development of this great age of enterprise. Previous to 1300 merchants had often separated their merchandise among several ships, and often maritime property was divided among multiple owners to shield any one person from catastrophic loss. Primitive forms of spreading risks in the form of the insurance loan date from the thirteenth century. This involved two parties, the shipowner, who advanced the merchant shipping goods with him a sum equal in value to the whole or part of the goods entrusted to his ship. If the cargo arrived safely, the merchant repaid the loan/advance with an extra charge to cover the costs of freight and risk. If the freight was lost, the merchant kept the advance as compensation for the loss. Marine insurance as we understand it began in the first half of the fourteenth century in Genoa, when premiums were charged explicitly to insure against loss and recorded in notarial instruments. By the end of the century insurance underwriters were at work in Pisa, Venice, and elsewhere in Italy assessing risk and quoting insurance rates based on a host of variables affecting risk. By the late fifteenth century marine insurance was available at all the major European ports including those of the Netherlands (Spufford 2002, 33).

But the fate of the Florentine super-companies shows that not all risk was insurable and that changes in the business climate could topple even the most elaborate business edifice. The foundation of these firms had always been the very profitable grain trade with southern Italy, which was racked by weather-related difficulties, and these increased government interference in price setting and supply. Even the famine of 1329, far from being a boon to grain distributors, was so severe and widespread that the great companies were forced into a classic price squeeze. They were required to supply grain at politically tolerable prices while scrambling for supply in a seller's market. By the 1330s, city governments were stepping in as grain purchasers, thus cutting out the companies from provisioning a number of cities, and population was falling across Italy even before the advent of the Plague in 1347. The bankruptcies of both the Bardi and Peruzzi within a thirty-month period shocked Europe and led some contemporaries to blame the unpaid debts of the English king as the cause. Yet the real culprit was a change in economic conditions that made such giant firms unnecessary. The fact that many of their techniques and innovations continued as standard business practice shows the long-term success of short-term failure.

The European North

The north developed in different and distinct ways from the south, although the north could not escape the power and influence of southern, mostly Italian, entrepreneurs and entrepreneurial techniques. Yet it would be a mistake to underestimate the sophistication of northern European business or to consider it merely derivative. Indeed the entrepreneurial innovations that in many ways began with the Champagne fairs, that great meeting ground of south and north, were eventually captured and urbanized in Bruges by the fourteenth century, to be passed on and expanded by Antwerp and Amsterdam in turn.

A critical difference between northern and southern urban communities was the early movement of industry to northern towns, especially the manufacture of woolen textiles. With the invention of the treadle-operated horizontal loom in the eleventh century, probably in Flanders, economies of scale and vast improvements in quality became possible. Quality was further enhanced with the replacement of the horizontal loom with the broadloom in the thirteenth century. Weaving became primarily a male occupation, centered in the cities and subject to regulatory control. Immigrants from the surrounding countryside provided abundant labor, although some clothmaking crafts such as wool cleansing and spinning remained rural occupations. Expanding production created demand for raw materials, chiefly wool and dyestuffs. By the twelfth century, the towns of Flanders and the pastures of England had been integrated, so that large quantities of wool from English sheep were turned into finished cloth by Flemish weavers, fullers, and dyers. Demand for Flemish cloth came from far distant economic areas, necessitating periodic markets where cloth could be exchanged for spices (including dyestuffs). Thus were the fairs of Champagne born (Nicholas 1992; Munro 2003).

The six Champagne fairs are an interesting example of the constraints and opportunities within which northern entrepreneurs worked. Roughly equidistant between the Low Countries and Italy, the twin poles of European urbanism, the county of Champagne was ruled by a series of counts eager to initiate and maintain trade by granting fair privileges to local communities as well as by guaranteeing the physical security of those journeying to the county. By circa 1175, medium grades of cloth were commonly brought south by Flemish merchants, to be sold to Italian merchants who made of European woolen textiles an important export commodity throughout the Mediterranean. Over the next century the rhythm of the six fairs and constant attendance of merchants created a financial system of credit and payment that formed the beginnings, however tentative, of merchant banking. Capital-rich Italians not only granted credit to be repaid at future fairs, they also advanced money to be repaid in Italy. Besides the Italians, the great beneficiaries of the Champagne-centered economy were the cloth entrepreneurs of a number of northern French/Flemish cities, notably Arras, Lille, Cambrai, Tournai, and Valenciennes, and Arras emerged as the financial center of the region (Spufford 2002, 144–47).

This distribution of industrial production, finance, and exchange left a permanent mark on northern entrepreneurs. They tended to band together in merchant guilds—Henri Pirenne conjectured that this was a result of traveling together in caravan from fair to fair. By the twelfth century, merchant group consciousness was carried over into important social and political functions in cities from England to Germany. By long habit, then, northern merchants formed shorter-lived, more dynamic business relations with each other than did southerners. Fewer of these would be based on extended family, in favor of more fluid relationships formed by the merchant guild. And it was along these associative links that investment capital, even urban finance, tended to flow. It was not until well into the fifteenth century that northern merchants began to imitate the joint-stock companies of the Italians, and even then the northern merchant often acted alone or in company with a few others, often in single business ventures. These tendencies were to find full expression in the streets and marketplaces of Bruges.

Through a series of changes and perturbations, Bruges emerged as the new focal point of exchange after 1300, and for the first time the city also became the center of finance for the entire north, including the larger cities of Paris and London. Bruges's new status owed much to a favorable geographical position as the traditional port of entry for English wool, and its situation at the intersection of eastern, western, and southern overland trade routes. The city benefited enormously by the shift in transport preference to ships, and Bruges became the destination point for Mediterranean trade fleets, which first docked there in the 1280s. Because of its traditional role in the English wool and Flemish cloth trades, Bruges was able to provide profitable return cargo for the Italian ships. And the "Easterners," as German and other Hanse members were called, were themselves attracted by the merchandise conveyed by the Italians and by the chance to sell their own regional products: furs, wax, honey, amber, and later grain, beer, and metal. Another reason to journey to Bruges was to take advantage of the demand generated by the wealthy hinterland of the Low Countries and northern France. So Bruges became the natural distribution point of the luxuries consumed by the rulers of Flanders, Brabant, and Hainault, and by the principalities of western Germany. As a key transshipment point, the city attracted colonies of foreign merchants, including large numbers of English, Germans, and Italians from a variety of cities, as well as Catalans, northern Spaniards, and Portuguese (Murray 2005, 95–97).

Coinciding with the this shift in patterns of trade was the displacement of the Flemish by Italians as the middlemen in the export of English wool to the continent. War played some role in this substitution, as the English kings retaliated against their French rivals by instituting a series of embargoes, retaliatory confiscations, export taxes, and acts of piracy, which placed Flanders, essentially part of France yet tied economically to England, in the crossfire. The Italians also brought large amounts of cash, with which they purchased future wool clips and financed the English war effort (other Italian companies financed the French king). Step by step, the Flemish were forced to reorient their efforts away from the transport and direct trade in commodities, favoring instead the sedentary and stable role of broker, partner, and entrepreneur.

The government of Bruges furthered this reorientation by sparing neither effort nor expense in building up the city's business infrastructure. Even before the city had a proper town hall, it boasted two major commercial buildings, several municipal scales, and the huge man-powered crane made famous by generations of Flemish artists. Bruges was also the first city in the Low Countries to ban thatched roofs in the heart of the city in an effort to contain that curse of medieval towns, outbreaks of fire. The many impressive works in support of business no doubt added to the city's luster, but its most important attraction was the web of human relationships that offered lodging, banking, brokering, and business contacts to the foreign merchant (Hunt and Murray 1999, 160–64).

Essential to Bruges's success was the system of book transfers and complementary payment services offered by the city's innkeepers and money changers. This intricate and far-reaching system of book transfers permitted those merchants with an account in Bruges to make payments for goods and services far beyond the city's walls. In effect, the Bruges money changers extended the giro transfer system to foreign trade as well as to local transactions. One nearby example was the ability of merchants residing in Bruges to draw upon their Bruges accounts while visiting Antwerp during its trade fairs. As important as money changers were, they were in most respects the junior partners of the innkeepers, who provided multifarious services to their foreign merchant customers, from legal representation before the city aldermen to financial and other business. But most of all, Bruges innkeepers were financiers investing capital entrusted with them by their customers, organizing partnerships and pursuing opportunities on their own account. Thus were the payment and financial systems, previously divided between the fair towns of Champagne and financial centers like Arras, brought together in one city (Murray 2005, 216–58).

This was a centralized economic system only insofar as its intersection was in Bruges, where all significant long-distance merchants had to have a presence, if not be actually present. Thus rather like a node in a computer network, Bruges brought together distinct geographical and financial systems—from Tuscany to the remotest town of the German Hanse—and made it possible for these merchants to exchange and cooperate. This was the essential background to the Bourse of Bruges, a public square that in the course of the fifteenth century was set aside for merchants to gather and do business. The connection to innkeeping and brokerage was explicit in the name *Bourse*, which was taken from the family name of a prominent inn that stood on that public square. These "merchants of the Bourse" gathered to exchange information, upon which exchange rates were based, and thereby bills of exchange were drawn up. For nearly a century, this was the leading money market of Europe (Murray 2005, 178–215).

Societal Constraints: Usury, Chivalry, and Guilds

Christian teaching and church authority affected day-to-day business activity in profound ways, given that business and personal values were so closely intertwined. Evidence of the pervasiveness of religious attitudes appears in the most mundane of commercial documents. A company's books normally opened with a prayer for the success of the business and the health and safety of its personnel. Flemish bankers initiated their account books with the words "To the Glory of God." Christian scriptures and church (or canon) law were more than merely ornamental; they constituted a vital part of the fabric of entrepreneurial life. The medieval concept of "just price," formalized in the thirteenth century, had its basis in Christ's injunction in Matthew's Gospel "so whatever you wish that men would do to you, do so to them, for this is the law and the prophets." This message was especially relevant to the agrarian and small-town cultures of western Europe, where life was seen as a zero-sum game in which one person's gain came inevitably at the expense of others. Church theologians and lawyers closely examined all kinds of economic transactions and pronounced on their morality and legality. During the commercial revolution the number and diversity of such pronouncements increased, keeping pace with the growth in commerce.

The issue most affecting the entrepreneurial climate of Europe was the treatment of usury. The medieval doctrine of usury, with roots in both the Old and New Testaments, regarded any interest, not just excessive interest, as a mortal sin. Church councils recalled this prohibition in the fourth through ninth centuries, and even the emperor Charlemagne promulgated a usury ban upon both clerics and laymen.

And in lengthy restatements of usury doctrine in the thirteenth century, scholastic theologians drew upon the views of Aristotle, who regarded lending money at interest as contrary to natural law. Church and civil penalties for those practicing usury were issued from the late twelfth century through the fourteenth century, depriving usurers of burial in consecrated ground, sacraments, even the ability to make a valid will (Armstrong 2003).

It was the two chief mendicant orders, the Franciscans and Dominicans, who took the church's virulent antiusury position to the people. Francis was himself the son of a Tuscan cloth merchant, and his horror of money and commerce gave a special edge to the generations of Franciscan preachers who fanned out through Europe to tend to the spiritual needs of Europe's urban classes. Dominicans were the medieval preachers par excellence, and they lent intellectual rigor to church doctrines regarding money and its use. Both Thomas Aquinas and Albert the Great wrote penetratingly about the essential nature of usury, which both viewed as theft. And all Europeans must have become familiar with the lurid exempla promulgated to illustrate the eternal horrors that awaited the rapacious usurer. These achieved literary expression in Dante's *Commedia*, with usurers occupying a particularly low niche in hell alongside murderers, blasphemers, and sodomites.

The main problem with church teaching on usury for the medieval entrepreneur was that it did not distinguish between loans for consumption and loans for productive purposes: all loans at interest were sinful. As the need for credit swelled business finance from the twelfth century, tension developed between what was licit and illicit moneylending. On the one hand, providers of consumption credit were marginalized—both Jewish and Christian pawnbrokers and casual moneylenders suffered legal and social penalties for their profession. But even "legitimate" merchants such as money changers and others did not escape the taint of usury, as many merchants made restitution of gains in their wills, despite having cloaked interest profits in bills of exchange. Yet the absolute prohibition of usury was eroded in the writings of several theorists such as Peter John Olivi and Bernardino of Siena, who argued for certain types of nonconsumption loans as licit because of loss of earnings for the lender—an early conception of the time-value of money (Little 1978; Hunt and Murray 1999, 70–74).

The Chivalric Ethos

One of the oldest stereotypes in European history is the leisured aristocrat who abhors commerce as derogatory and beneath his social status. Being "in trade" was considered ignoble, and in some European countries before the eighteenth century, notably France, titled aristocrats were legally barred from any business but farming, government (royal) service, and warfare. As the "noble life," that is, the material and social comforts of elite status, always remained the goal of the few socially mobile individuals across the medieval and early modern centuries, this ethos would seem to pose a powerful countervailing force to entrepreneurial endeavors. But, as with so much else in the history of economic growth in the Middle Ages, this obstacle was more apparent than real.

A story from chivalry's formative century is a good example. In an epic poem celebrating the life of William Marshal (ca. 1146–1219), the hero was traveling in northwest France accompanied by his squire when he by chance encountered a monk and a young noblewoman who were eloping. When interrogated by William, it turned out that that their plan was to live together in an unnamed city outside the reach of the young woman's family, upon the proceeds of a sum of money to be invested with local moneylenders. William did nothing to stop the pair from riding on, even though he knew the young woman's family and could not have approved of her actions. Before he let them pass, however, he confiscated the money they intended to live on, thus "saving" them from the sin and scandal of usury. Even though this might appear a transparent excuse for theft, it does reveal the abhorrence that a paragon of chivalry shows for the misuse of money. To live upon interest was unthinkable for a nobleman; but William's use of money is significant as well. Upon his return to his entourage at a local inn, he had his squire count out the money (he would not deign to touch it himself) and distribute it to his retinue, while also paying for an elaborate round of drinking and eating. In other words, money was intended to cement personal bonds and enhance status, not as an end in itself.[4]

Yet knights had a complicated relationship with money even if they did not care to amass or invest it in trade. Again, William Marshal provides a telling example of knight as entrepreneur. As a younger son of a family of lesser nobles, William had no legal share of the family lands and possessions; nor did his father make any special provision for him in his will, as sometimes happened for younger sons and daughters. After completing his training in arms in the household of a wealthier and more powerful relative, William took to the road to ply and perfect the craft of fighting in that mélange of combat, sport, and commerce called the tournament. Marshal's career commenced just as the tournament gained respectability among kings and at least grudging acceptance from the clerical establishment, which had at first excommunicated all participants and refused burial rites to anyone killed in a tournament. Tourneying had also become a big money sport owing to its sponsorship by great lords and the wealth that could be gained by capturing and ransoming adversaries. Indeed, some clerics used the same word for both tournaments and trade fairs, which must have appeared quite similar to the uninitiated (Crouch 2002, 192–99).

William Marshal was an unmatched moneymaker in his sixteen-year career as a tourneyer, unhorsing opponents right and left and turning his victories into silver payment in return for the freedom and equipment of the vanquished opponent. So lucrative did this pursuit prove, that Marshal joined forces with another knight in a veritable fighting company with Marshal's kitchen clerk serving as accountant. In the course of two years of hard fighting, with tournaments across France and Flanders at intervals as short as two weeks during the season, these knightly entrepreneurs took as many as 500 knights captive. The wealth Marshal gained thereby was expended on entertainment, equipment, and lavish gifts for those around him, all investments in his reputation and social standing. Ultimately, this once landless knight became regent of England and its chief general in the years after the death of King John. This was a rich return indeed for the greatest knight of the age (Crouch 2002, 194).

Medieval Guilds

Guilds have traditionally been high on the list of impediments to entrepreneurship, and even if contemporary historians no longer subscribe to this assessment, the myth of guild obstructionism still holds sway in popular histories. This is an unfortunate result of an older historiography that relied too heavily on literal interpretations of guild statutes as well as on a too blind adherence to Marxist and liberal ideologies. The last half-century of research has added considerable nuance to the traditional picture, and has shown that craft guilds could be a force for innovation and economic change, as well as insurers of the status quo. Much depended on the industry and market conditions of the particular guild, as well as the geographical location and political context within which the guild operated (Black 1984; Stabel 2004).

The first myth to be dispelled is that guilds functioned as monolithic institutions, staunchly protected by legal monopolies and impenetrable social structures. As we know now, the very demography of medieval cities made unwavering stability of any institution impossible owing to the extremely high mortality rates that affected all sectors of the population. High death rates due to infant mortality, infectious disease, crime, and military action meant that medieval guilds had to be open to immigrants in order to remain viable in a market economy. Openness to newcomers seems to have been greatest among guilds whose products were involved in long-distance trade, such as the cloth industry of the Low Countries and northern Italy. In fifteenth-century Bruges, for example, more than three-quarters of the masters in several guilds were either foreigners or unaffiliated locals. Those guilds that did tend to restrict mastership to sons of masters were concentrated in the less dynamic, food-centered trades, which depended on control of stalls in local sales halls (Stabel 2004, 194).

Craft guilds could also be important partners with merchant entrepreneurs in reorganizing an industry in the face of competition and changes in market conditions. As organizers of the labor force and guarantors of product quality, guild masters often collaborated with others in reorienting production. This fluidity and collaborative ability was aided by the power structures in medieval cities, which brought together leaders of guilds and merchant groups in the exercise of urban authority. Thus in medieval Flanders, a profound reorientation of output was achieved in the great cloth cities through specialization in production of high-quality textiles, abandoning some cloth types and enforcing elaborate content and quality standards. This profound shift was a result of long-term negotiation with merchant-traders and guild leaders of the cloth crafts in response to market data and changes in the security of long-distance transportation networks. Higher-priced textiles, the products of a complex, guild-orchestrated production process, were better able to withstand the higher transaction costs imposed by a war-torn Europe. A variation of this guild-organized enterprise is found in the textile industry of northern Italy, which was able to challenge the supremacy of northern textiles by imitating their quality while reducing costs (Hunt and Murray 1999, 166–70).

Conclusions

The history of entrepreneurs across the medieval millennium (500–1500) is instructive on a number of counts. First is the lesson that medieval society could be entrepreneurial (i.e., effective in achieving economic growth) often without visible individual entrepreneurs. This flies in the face of modern notions of the triumphant individual who grasps and exploits economic opportunities, quite apart from, indeed often challenging, social and political norms. What drove growth across the era was not individual profit maximization, but dedication to a variety of communal goals, all of which emanated from a church-defined mission of a Christian society. Within that framework, church institutions, such as the papacy and monasteries, were able to expand their economic reach to encompass an expanding Europe, so that by 1200 Benedictine and Cistercian monasteries organized agricultural production from Ireland to Silesia, and Sicily to Norway, and revenues from these areas and those in between flowed to papal Rome in Europe's first long-distance financial network. Moreover, medieval aristocrats, in taking up their God-given vocation to protect Christendom, both expanded the geographical borders of Europe and invented a way of life that required horses, arms, armor, as well as the leisure to master their use. The potent combination of lordly demand and investment in the means to obtain it fueled the waves of agrarian growth beginning in the ninth and tenth centuries and continuing even across the downturns of the fourteenth century.

This early medieval entrepreneurship without entrepreneurs was responsible for crucial investments in agrarian machinery, that is, water and windmills, techniques of capturing animal power (plows and harnesses), and techniques of productive land use. Monasteries pioneered in management and record-keeping technologies, often overlooked, that refined and improved seeds and crops as well as the domestic animals so critical to maintenance of soil fertility. It was not accidental that monks tended the largest flocks of sheep in England, as well as the most valuable vineyards of France by 1200. Income from these innovations supported grand construction projects, investments in religious culture, and the trading networks that brought gold, silks, and spices to the liturgies and refectory tables of monastic Europe. Quintessentially long-term institutions, monasteries provided the important admixture of stability and investment necessary to settle and transform the European countryside across the medieval centuries.

The greatest entrepreneurial institution of all, the medieval city, owed its beginnings to the actions of lords, both clerical and secular, in generating the demand for goods and services that enabled economically specialized communities to gather around castles and monasteries. And beyond being customers, lords granted a variety of liberties and exemptions that unfettered trade in incipient towns, and lords acted as guarantors of markets and courts that served to attract outsiders and their money. This combination of production and distributive trade against a background of relative freedom and legal guarantees of property and exchange was the common denominator of the return of urban communities to Europe. Moreover, unlike cities in the Roman or Greek past, medieval towns and cities had at their center an entrepreneurial essence that made them the leading laboratories of economic innovation down to the present day. They also produced by the later Middle Ages the first clear individual entrepreneurs in European history, as well as encouraging the merchant-artisan community whose values both defined and limited the horizons of the medieval entrepreneur.

Individuals from the leading commercial cities of Europe could become immensely rich from their entrepreneurial endeavors, but wealth was almost never the ultimate goal of their ambitions. Wealthy merchant dynasties like the Medici of Florence used money as a means to dominate local and regional politics in Italy, in the process benefiting the arts as well, all to enhance their status. The wealthy English merchant William de la Pole became a powerful government official and royal financier, but he was the only entrepreneur in a family that joined the lower aristocracy in the next generations. The examples could be multiplied, and all show strategies designed to enhance power and social status, not to gain permanent business or economic advantage. Already by the fourteenth and fifteenth centuries, the pattern of wealthy urban families intermarrying with destitute aristocratic clans became widespread. Thus social advancement in the Middle Ages was defined by the aristocracy, not by successful entrepreneurs. This was true all over Europe and well into modern times.

Study of the medieval entrepreneur cautions us against making any universal claims for some kind of eternal entrepreneur who acts independently of time and context. In many (if not most) times and places, the creative destruction in the name of economic progress that Joseph Schumpeter posited was neither present nor desirable. And equally significant, the relative absence or unimportance of the stand-alone entrepreneur did not preclude economic growth. The economic historian must be aware of and alert to the unique proclivities of other times and cultures, and this should encourage a healthy skepticism of sweeping generalizations or excessively abstract models.

Notes

[1] This essay owes much to my earlier work in Hunt and Murray 1999, copyright © 1999 Edwin S. Hunt and James M. Murray. Reprinted with the permission of Cambridge University Press.
[2] *Divine Comedy*, Canto XVII.
[3] Nicholas 2003, 11; globally more towns through growth than foundation except in Spain and Germany.
[4] Duby 1985; but note the corrections and elaborations of David Crouch (2002).

References

Armstrong, Lawrin. 2003. "Usury." In *Oxford Encyclopedia of Economic History*, ed. Joel Mokyr, 5:183–85. Oxford: Oxford University Press.

Bartlett, Robert. 1994. *The Making of Europe: Conquest, Colonization, and Cultural Change, 950–1350.* Princeton: Princeton University Press.

Berman, Constance H. 1986. *Medieval Agriculture, the Southern French Countryside, and the Early Cistercians: A Study of Forty-three Monasteries.* Philadelphia: American Philosophical Society.

Biddick, Kathleen. 1989. *The Other Economy: Pastoral Husbandry on a Medieval Estate.* Berkeley and Los Angeles: University of California Press.

Black, Anthony. 1984. *Guilds and Civil Society in European Political Thought from the Twelfth Century to the Present.* London: Routledge.

Crouch, David. 2002. *William Marshal: Knighthood, War, and Chivalry, 1147–1219.* 2nd ed. London: Longman.

Duby, Georges. 1982. *Three Orders: Feudal Society Imagined.* Chicago: University of Chicago Press.

———. 1985. *William Marshal, the Flower of Chivalry.* New York: Pantheon.

Hunt, Edwin S. 1994. *The Medieval Super-companies: A Study of the Peruzzi Company of Florence.* Cambridge: Cambridge University Press.

Hunt, Edwin S., and James M. Murray. 1999. *A History of Business in Medieval Europe, 1200–1550.* Cambridge: Cambridge University Press.

Keen, Maurice. 2005. *Chivalry.* 2nd ed. New Haven: Yale University Press.

Langdon, John. 1986. *Horses, Oxen, and Technological Innovation: The Use of Draught Animals in English Farming from 1066–1500.* Cambridge: Cambridge University Press.

———. 2004. *Mills in the Medieval Economy: England 1300–1540*. Oxford: Oxford University Press.

Little, Lester K. 1978. *Religious Poverty and the Profit Economy in Medieval Europe*. Ithaca, NY: Cornell University Press.

Lucas, Adam. 2006. *Wind, Water, Work: Ancient and Medieval Milling Technology*. Leiden: Brill.

McCormick, Michael. 2001. *Origins of the European Economy: Communications and Commerce, AD 300–900*. Cambridge: Cambridge University Press.

Munro, John H. 2003. "Medieval Woolens: Textiles, Textile Technology and Industrial Organisation, 800–1500." In *Cambridge History of Western Textiles*, ed. David Jenkins, 1:181–227. Cambridge: Cambridge University Press.

Murray, James M. 2005. *Bruges, Cradle of Capitalism, 1280–1390*. Cambridge: Cambridge University Press.

Nicholas, David. 1992. *Medieval Flanders*. London: Longman.

———. 2003. *Urban Europe, 1100–1700*. New York: Palgrave.

de Roover, Raymond. 1948. *Money, Banking, and Credit in Mediaeval Bruges*. Cambridge: Mediaeval Academy.

Schwarcz, Andreas. 2003. "Some Open Questions." *Early Medieval Europe* 12, no. 3: 279–82.

Spufford, Peter. 1988. *Money and Its Use in Medieval Europe*. Cambridge: Cambridge University Press.

———. 2002. *Power and Profit: The Merchant in Medieval Europe*. London: Thames and Hudson.

Stabel, Peter. 2004. "Guilds in the Late Medieval Low Countries: Myth and Reality of Guild Life in an Export-Oriented Environment." *Journal of Medieval History* 30:187–212.

Chapter 5

Tawney's Century, 1540–1640: The Roots of Modern Capitalist Entrepreneurship

JOHN MUNRO

The Weber-Tawney Thesis on Protestantism and Capitalism: The Role of Protestant Dissenters in the Scientific and Industrial Revolutions (1660–1820)

One of the very most remarkable features of the Industrial Revolution era is that Non-Conformists or Dissenters—those Protestants who refused to conform to the officially established Church of England[1]—accounted for a remarkably high proportion, perhaps one half, of the scientists and inventors listed in the Royal Society (founded 1660) and the related Lunar Society of Birmingham (founded 1764).[2] Even more important for the history of entrepreneurship is the fact that they also accounted for at least half of the known entrepreneurs (and other business leaders) of the Industrial Revolution era itself, up to circa 1820. Yet Dissenters were then a very small minority: consisting of about 1,250 congregations in later eighteenth-century England, comprising about 5 percent and certainly under 10 percent of the population.[3]

There is no agreed upon explanation for this extraordinary phenomenon. Some various hypotheses will be offered in the subsequent discussion of the role of religion in the early-modern English and Scottish economies, in the context of the very well known, and still hotly debated Weber-Tawney thesis. For a variety of reasons that will soon become apparent, the focus of this discussion is on Richard Tawney (1880–1962), unquestionably one of the very most important economic historians that England has ever produced: in particular, on his role in seeking to explain the emergence of modern capitalist entrepreneurship in what is now commonly called "Tawney's century," 1540–1640.[4] The central thesis of this current study, however, is that all of the events and turning points leading to the rise or dramatically significant expansion of modern forms of capitalism, per se, of a truly modern capitalist ethos, and thus of entrepreneurship, took place, not in Tawney's century, but rather in the following century, 1640–1740, the one preceding the modern Industrial Revolution era. Indeed, this thesis is indicated by the very statement that begins this study.

With deeply held Christian and Fabian socialist views, Tawney had become fascinated with the relationship between Protestantism and the emergence and development of modern capitalism, and implicitly of modern capitalist entrepreneurship.

That led, in 1926, to the publication of his most famous book: *Religion and the Rise of Capitalism*. While highly esteemed for the vast amount of new information that it supplied on both religion and society in sixteenth- and seventeenth-century England, the book's chief importance lies in explaining, elaborating on, and propagating the much earlier thesis on this issue, initially published (in 1904–5) in German: Max Weber, *The Protestant Ethic and the Spirit of Capitalism*.[5]

Neither author, it must be stressed, ever proposed that Protestantism was responsible in any way for the actual birth of European capitalism, for they were well aware that its origins were purely medieval. Furthermore, they were far from being the first scholars to make a link between Protestantism and modern capitalism, a linkage involving a wide variety of theories. Their goal was instead to provide an analytical framework, in the context of historical sociology, to explain how one particular form of Protestantism—Calvinism—ultimately influenced the development of the "ethos" or "spirit" or *mentalité* of modern European capitalism, in ways that distinguished it from earlier forms of capitalism.[6] Weber and Tawney both agreed that Calvinism (ultimately) played such a role by the socio-psychological consequences of its three essential doctrines or components.

The first is the doctrine of predestination, which in essence stipulates that God, being omnipotent, determines (has determined, will determine) who are the very few to be the so-called Elect: those who shall enjoy eternal salvation with God. All the rest of mankind, because of original sin and free will, have and will have condemned themselves to eternal perdition in hell, and thus they are completely incapable of gaining salvation on their own.[7] Even for the most devout of faithful Calvinists, such a bleak doctrine must have seemed unpalatable, indeed horrifying. But Calvin scorned those who sought to find positive signs of their Election, replying that to do so was inherently sinful. A century or so later, however, that strict Calvinist view could and did no longer prevail: perhaps because of pressure of public opinion in predominantly Calvinist lands (see Pettegree, Duke, and Lewis 1994; Riemersma 1967; Little 1969), and perhaps because of the evolving impact of the other two doctrines of this Calvinist triad: in Weber's terminology, the "calling" and "worldly asceticism."

The doctrine of the calling was also based on the principle of God's omnipotence, so that obviously the world existed according to his will, as he had ordained it; and thus it was the duty of every man and women to serve God by fulfilling his or her calling—in whatever honorable (nonsinful) occupation one had gained—to exercise his or her utmost ability, in order to achieve the greatest possible degree of success in doing so.[8] Calvin himself had been trained as a lawyer, and deemed that to be an honorable calling, as were not only those of other professional persons (e.g., doctors, professors, theologians), but also businessmen, and thus entrepreneurs. Indeed that list implicitly includes merchants, financiers, industrialists, retailers, storekeepers, and also industrial craftsmen or artisans, all so necessary for the maintenance and prosperity of a well-ordered civil society.

For many businessmen, what better, more tangible sign of success in one's calling could be found than profit? That meant profit maximization, which surely is the very essence of modern microeconomics. As so many came to believe, such proof of success in one's calling should also mean a positive, indeed certain, sign of one's Election. In turn, to the extent that so many in Calvinist societies came to equate such success in their calling with Election, that society in turn came to view such success, and success in profitable business enterprises in particular, with far greater approval, as a socially desirable goal, than ever before, in medieval society.

Nevertheless, by the seventeenth and eighteenth centuries, an individual entrepreneur or businessman's success in his calling, when measured by profits (or "the bottom line," as many would say today), was strictly conditional on how that person utilized those profits, in terms of the Weber-Tawney concept of "worldly asceticism." If profits were spent largely on "conspicuous consumption," such an individual risked incurring social opprobrium: that is, for worshipping Mammon,[9] and not God. If consuming profits in this fashion was sinful, then the obvious and most laudable alternative—both socially and theologically—was to reinvest those profits in the business enterprise: that is, to increase the capital stock and scale of the enterprise, better enabling the entrepreneur to innovate and to increase subsequent profits, and thus better able to be dedicated to one's calling, for the greater glorification of God.

The Weber-Tawney thesis has, of course, engendered an enormous amount of debate from the 1920s, continuing to the present day; and a reexamination of that debate would serve no useful purpose in this study.[10] In my own view, whether or not the Weber-Tawney thesis has any real significance for the history of entrepreneurship in England, and for the evolution of a more truly "capitalist" economy, the relevance will be found not in "Tawney's century" itself—when so many Calvinists seemed to be hostile to capitalism (and usury)—but rather in the succeeding century, 1640–1740.[11]

First, during the era of the English Civil War, Commonwealth, and Cromwell's Protectorate (1642–59), Calvinists—both Puritans and Scottish Presbyterians—played a very major role in winning that war against the Crown and the Cavalier or royalist factions; and furthermore, in then governing England during the Commonwealth-Protectorate era and in altering the nature of the established Church of England.[12] In 1659, the year after Cromwell's death, the army terminated the Protectorate of his son Richard, and then forced the dissolution of the Long Parliament. The new parliamentary Convention that replaced it in April 1660 then invited Charles II (1660–85) to resume his throne. The ensuing Restoration Parliaments enacted two statutes to rid England of any Calvinist, and therefore Republican, influences within the English church and governments (national and local): the Corporation Act of 1661 and the Test Act of 1673.[13]

Together these statutes required anyone seeking to hold any church or government-related position (including the army, local justices, education, etc.) to swear oaths to conform to the Thirty-nine Articles of the Church of England and to take communion annually within the established church. As noted earlier, those Protestants who refused to do so were thus known as Non-Conformists or Dissenters. Along with Calvinists and Presbyterians, this group included such other Protestant sects as Baptists, Quakers, Unitarians, and later the Methodists.[14] When, however, the Catholic King James II (1685–88) was deposed in the Glorious Revolution, his successors, his daughter Mary II (1689–94) and her husband the Dutch prince William III of Orange (1689–1702), insisted that Parliament protect the religious rights of his Calvinist coreligionists, in the Toleration Act of 1689 (not including Catholics or Unitarians).[15] That act did not, however, annul the provisions of the Corporation and Test Acts, so that Dissenters remained barred from all the aforementioned government, and government-related and church-related, positions and schools.

Do these sociopolitical events and circumstances themselves explain why Dissenters came to play such a vital and clearly disproportionate role in the ensuing age of the Scientific Revolution (from 1660) and then in the Industrial Revolution era itself? Or should the answer be sought in the socio-psychological evolution of Calvinist Protestantism, as indicated in the Weber-Tawney thesis? Or are there yet other, alternative if complementary explanations?

Certainly one obvious explanation for that disproportionate role, to be sought in the first hypothesis, is the Dissenters' minority status: yet one without the burden of true oppression, in enjoying that "halfway" house of full religious but only partial social toleration. Thus their obvious challenge. Finding themselves excluded from the normal avenues of wealth, power, and social prestige, now available only to members of the established Church of England, the Dissenters instead sought to succeed and prosper in alternative avenues that did remain open to them: namely, in the worlds of business enterprise, commerce, finance, and industry (but also commercial agriculture). Perhaps they also experienced a deep psychological compulsion and social drive to prove themselves, both in their own eyes and in the eyes of society: so that such minority status did not mean inferior social status.

Another explanation, one that T. S. Ashton has offered, is "the fact that, broadly speaking, the Nonconformists constituted the better educated section of the middle classes," which was chiefly due to the role of the so-called Dissenting Academies (1948, 19). They were the educational institutions that the Dissenters had been forced to establish, after having been barred from the traditional church- and state-sponsored schools and universities. Many of these academies were modeled after Scottish Presbyterian schools, which, in Ashton's view (endorsed by many others), were "in advance of that of any other European country at this time," as were Scottish universities.[16] Such schools focused upon or emphasized mathematics, the physical and biological sciences, and modern languages (English, French, and German especially). Also included in the curriculum were such practical subjects as accounting, surveying, and engineering. Necessarily eschewed—if only on grounds of opportunity cost—were the traditional subjects long favored by Church of England schools, "public" (i.e., private), and state grammar schools: Greek and Latin language and literature, philosophy, theology, and history. Even if history and Latin were also taught in the Dissenting academies, they were not taught within the same framework (theological) and emphasis; for indeed many Dissenters viewed Latin with some suspicion as still the fundamental language of the Catholic Church.

In Ashton's view, and certainly in the view of many other historians, the education offered by the Scottish schools and the English Dissenting academies was one more in tune with the objectives of the post-1660 Scientific Revolution and then of the British Industrial Revolution, and one more likely to inspire profitable innovations and entrepreneurship in both. Nevertheless, this Ashton thesis does not really tell us why these schools were so different from and better than the traditional schools: why in particular they were so much oriented to the worlds of science and business. One answer may be that those designing the curriculum in the Scottish schools and Dissenting academies were not encumbered by centuries of tradition and church-sanctioned and aristocratic social requirements. Another may be market demand: most of the students came from predominantly middle-class families that were then involved in the world of business, commerce, finance, and engineering.

Even to the extent that both explanatory models are valid, they do not permit us to discard the essence of the Weber-Tawney thesis, in particular the *subsequent* ways in which English society, in the later seventeenth, eighteenth, and early nineteenth centuries, came to interpret the Calvinist doctrines discussed above. For a better historical perspective, let us recall that in France, in 1685—just four years before William III's Toleration Act—King Louis XIV had revoked the Edict of Nantes, which Henry IV (a Calvinist forced to convert to Catholicism to gain the throne), had promulgated in April 1598, in order to grant full religious rights and full civil liberties to France's Protestant Huguenots, thereby ending the country's horribly divisive and destructive Wars of Religion (1562–98). The revocation of the Edict of Nantes soon led to the expulsion or emigration of a high proportion of the nation's Huguenots, many of whom were, like the Dissenters, disproportionately active in trade, commerce, and banking.[17] While many refugee Huguenots fled to Protestant Holland and Protestant German states, some also came to England, where they made valuable contributions to the growth of the English business community, in trade and banking in particular (see Crouzet 1991).

Stanley Chapman, in his impressive monograph *Merchant Enterprise in Britain* (1992), provides much additional supporting evidence for the unusual economic and social role of the Dissenters in the Industrial Revolution era, stressing in particular the importance of their international mercantile connections with coreligionists abroad (especially in the American colonies), indeed the vital importance of both their family and religious ties for providing the necessary trust involved in "the transmission of credit and trading reports." For all economic transactions involving principal-agent relationships—perhaps accounting for the majority of economic transactions in European economic history—have vitally depended on trust and confidence between all participants, in order to obviate the high transaction costs of enforcing agreements and monitoring a multitude of activities. Certainly, most economists would quickly recognize the importance of principal-agent relationships that were based on both knowledge of and trust in those with common religious, social, and business activities, and a common need of coreligionists and family members to unite for protection against hostile forces. Or as David Landes has so cogently and pithily observed: "In banking [and trade], connections count."[18] Finally, Chapman contends that economic ideology played almost as important a role in the striking mercantile success of the Quakers and Unitarians in the eighteenth and nineteenth centuries (1992, 43–47).

There are, of course, many other possible or hypothetical relationships between Protestantism and the development of modern forms of capitalism and of capitalist entrepreneurship in particular that have concerned a wide variety of historians and sociologists, but cannot be considered in this study.[19] That question of relationships includes a deeper sociological analysis of the Protestant "work ethic," which pertains as much to artisans, tradesmen, and professionals, as to entrepreneurs. One other possible relationship, and a major difference between Protestantism and Catholicism, that has not been so well studied is the question of confession and guilt. Well known, of course, is the power and prevalence of the Catholic confessional, in which the penitent, in confessing his or her sins by the sacrament of penance, to a hidden priest, receives absolution or formal remission of sin: that is, forgiveness and thus the (temporary) removal of guilt. Protestants had and have no such confessionals, and no such absolution and thus no such removal of the stain of guilt. To what extent were Protestants, and not just Calvinists and other Dissenters, motivated to achieve success in order to absolve themselves of guilt—not so much guilt for actual sins committed but guilt for not living up to their ingrained ideals, including those of the Protestant "work ethic"?[20]

Protestants in England's Glorious Revolution and the Ensuing Financial Revolution

Finally, any analysis of the relationship between Protestantism and capitalism, and the role of the Dissenters, in the century from the end of the Civil War and Cromwell era to the beginnings of the Industrial Revolution, must also be seen in the context of major constitutional and institutional changes. Those were principally the product of the aforementioned Glorious Revolution: the overthrow of King James II (1685–88), and his replacement by Mary II and her Dutch *stadhouder* husband William III of Orange. Well known is the 1989 article of Douglass North and Barry Weingast on the consequences of this Glorious Revolution. Those consequences included not just the quasi-religious freedom offered by the Toleration Act of 1689, but more so the final establishment of the supremacy of Parliament—of the House of Commons over finances. That in turn also brought about the establishment of judicial independence and the rule of law and property rights, as much in the market economy—greatly reducing transaction costs (as defined by North)—as in the political sphere and civil conduct. The most specific and immediate example was the 1689 Bill of Rights, establishing the rule of law over royal supremacy.[21]

Perhaps of equal importance, especially for this study on entrepreneurship, is what the British still call the Financial Revolution, whose chief institutional features were clearly imported from William's Dutch Republic (The United Provinces).[22] That led to the establishment of a permanent funded national debt—the responsibility of Parliament, not of the Crown—based on the government's sale of fully negotiable perpetual annuities (Dutch *renten*), traded on the London and Amsterdam stock exchanges, and financed by the levy of excise (consumption) taxes authorized by Parliament.[23]

Any such seemingly radical reinterpretation of economic history, on critical "turning points," has naturally and recently provoked a considerable reaction in the periodical literature (see Sussman and Yafeh 2006; Stasavage 2003, 2007). Though I do not believe that the critics have succeeded in negating the North-Weingast thesis, the nature of this study on British entrepreneurship, along with lack of space, precludes any further analysis of this debate, except to note one relevant point: the relationship between a major religious issue, for Protestants as well as Catholics—the usury doctrine, and the origins and nature of the Financial Revolution.

As I have contended elsewhere, those origins lie in the vigorous resuscitation of the antiusury campaign in the early thirteenth century, following the Church Council Lateran IV, in 1215, and the contemporary establishment of the two mendicant preaching orders—the Franciscans and Dominicans—preaching hellfire and damnation for those guilty of the mortal sin of usury: both for those who exacted and those who paid any interest on a loan. There is considerable evidence that, from the 1220s, in many towns in northern France and Flanders, more and more merchants and financiers, fearing such damnation, preferred to accept much lower returns on annuities (*rentes, renten*) purchased from urban governments than the far higher interest rates that they would have earned on loans or debentures. As the papacy soon determined, as early as 1251 (Innocent IV), the *rente* or annuity was not a loan, and hence not subject to the usury doctrine, because the purchaser had surrendered his capital in perpetuity to the seller, and thus had no right to redeem or reclaim his investment, while the seller could later choose to redeem the annuity at par. By the sixteenth century, the sale of annuities (*rentes*) was displacing loans as the predominant form of public borrowing in western Europe: thus, providing the precedents for England's own Financial Revolution (Munro 2003a, 2008c; Tracy 1985, 1995, 2003).

The relevance for seventeenth-century England is simply the fact that most Protestants had continued to be as hostile to usury as most Roman Catholics had been, and probably even more so. We have been led to believe, however, that after Elizabeth I's Parliament of 1571 had amended the usury laws to permit interest up to 10 percent—so that henceforth usury came to mean any interest charges above that limit—public hostility to "normal" interest waned. But such a view is far from the truth. Even Elizabeth's statute used hostile language in stating (in an almost contradictory fashion) in its preamble that "all Usurie" was "forbydden by the lawe of God."[24] In fact, Elizabeth had merely restored her father's statute of 1545 (Henry VIII), which had then been repealed under the even more Protestant regime of Edward VI, in 1552: "Usurie is by the worde of God utterly prohibited, as a vyce moste odyous and detestable."[25]

Furthermore, John Calvin (1509–64) and Martin Luther (1483–1546), the two major initiators and leaders of the Protestant Reformation, did not really have the more liberal views commonly attributed to them on the usury issue. Only grudgingly did these religious leaders accept interest payments: but only on investment loans and only to a maximum of 5 percent.[26] Calvin himself clearly voiced his disapproval in stating that "it is a very rare thing for a man to be honest and at the same time a usurer."[27] He had also contended that all habitual usurers should be expelled from the church (Noonan 1957, 365–67); and indeed in Holland, the Calvinist synod of 1581 had decreed that no banker should ever be admitted to communion service (Parker 1974, 538). Subsequently, in the seventeenth century, an English Puritan minister observed that "Calvin deals with usurie as the apothecarie doth with poyson";[28] and early in that century the renowned Sir Francis Bacon (1561–1626) had contended that "Usury is the certainest Meanes of Gaine, though one of the worst."[29] According to Richard Tawney, the English Puritan clergy continued to preach against the "soul-corrupting taint of usury" to the very eve of the English Civil War (Wilson 1925, 106–34, esp. 117; Tawney 1926, 91–115, 132–39, 178–89).

It is thus important, in the early-modern history of usury laws and the origins of England's own Financial Revolution, to note that, although Elizabeth I had set the maximum interest rate at 10 percent (1571), subsequent Parliaments lowered that legal maximum, evidently in accordance with the long-term decline in real interest rates: to 8 percent in 1623, to 6 percent in 1660, and finally to 5 percent in 1713, the rate that continued to prevail until Parliament finally abolished the usury laws in 1854.[30] Hence another point of significance about England's Financial Revolution, in establishing its own permanent funded national debt: it was entirely based on annuities, and not on loan instruments (bonds and debentures), and thus it was also fully exempt from these usury laws, with such a low legal maximum.[31] One indication of the success of the Financial Revolution was the fall in the interest rate on government borrowing from the 14 percent return on the Million Pound Loan of 1693 (in fact a lifetime annuity, marking the inception of the Financial Revolution) to the 3 percent return on consols in 1757, with the completion of Pelham's Conversion.[32]

That reduced considerably the extent to which government borrowing, principally to finance warfare, "crowded out" capital investments for private enterprise; and the fully negotiable consols themselves provided British entrepreneurs with an exceptionally valuable form of collateral in borrowing capital, both working and fixed capital.[33] Few entrepreneurs were and are able to survive without borrowing at some time in the development of their business enterprises.

Tawney's Thesis on "Agrarian Capitalism" and the "Rise of the Gentry" Debate

Tawney had first achieved academic fame, not with *Religion and the Rise of Capitalism,* but much earlier, in 1912, with his study on the enclosure movements and the evolution of "agrarian capitalism" in Tudor-Stuart England: *The Agrarian Problem in the Sixteenth Century*. Subsequently, almost three decades later, in 1941, he achieved even greater fame, but then trenchant opposition, opprobrium, and misfortune, with his famous article on "The Rise of the Gentry." His goal was to explore both the social and economic origins of the English Civil War, and also of modern capitalism. In his view, the English gentry were or largely became agrarian "capitalists," who were imbued with an entrepreneurial spirit and profit-maximizing motivations, far more so than typical members of the traditional, military-oriented, aristocracy—or, more properly speaking, the peerage: that is, dukes, archbishops, marquesses, earls (= European counts), viscounts, and barons.

The term *gentry* has to be understood as a unique English social institution, in its relation to the genuine aristocracy.[34] For the English aristocracy differed in many important respects from continental forms. In the first place, only the eldest son, by the law of primogeniture, inherited the noble or aristocratic title, along with the attached estates, and thus the right to sit as a peer in the House of Lords. All other offspring were commoners under law (even if having a lifetime courtesy title of Lord), while on the continent they would have been considered members of the aristocracy. Therefore, many members of the English gentry were the younger sons and relatives of these peers; and consequently—as Tawney was really loathe to admit—they were generally indistinguishable economically, socially, and politically from the peers. Certainly they were not a separate social class. Furthermore, while all knights (cavalry horse soldiers) were considered to be aristocrats on the continent (*noblesse d'épée*), they were all legally commoners in England; and they were also the major component of the House of Commons in medieval and early-modern England. The English gentry also consisted of those second-generation gentlemen farmers whose fathers—often of bourgeois or even yeomen origins—had purchased manorial estates and who then bred their children to emulate the lifestyles of a lesser landed nobility, though without (in Tawney's view) losing their bourgeois acquisitive and entrepreneurial instincts.[35]

Tawney's thesis begins again with the question of Protestantism: namely, Henry VIII's break with Rome to establish an independent Church of England, in 1534 (Act of Supremacy), a break that was solidified with the dissolution of the monasteries in the years 1536–41. Initially, most of the monastic lands, accounting for perhaps 20 percent of the developed arable lands of England, were either given as rewards or sold to Henry's aristocratic supporters—to ensure that they would support him against Rome. But during the following century—from 1536 to the outbreak of Civil War in 1642—about 90 percent of those monastic lands (according to most estimates) passed into the hands of the gentry.[36]

In Tawney's view, the economic mechanism that lay behind this vast transfer of land to the gentry was the Price Revolution: in particular the variety of responses to this long sustained inflation, commencing just before 1520 and lasting until the mid-1650s.[37] Tawney contended that the traditional feudal aristocracy were suffering from three related problems during the Price Revolution era. First, most aristocrats' estates were in the form of hundreds or more manors scattered across not just England, but across the British Isles. That scattering made estate management very difficult to undertake, all the more so since much of their estate income was in the form of fixed feudal dues and relatively fixed (nominal) rents for both freehold and copyhold peasant tenures. Consequently, their estate incomes did not rise with inflation.

The second problem was that many of the aristocracy were still imbued with a feudal mentality that scorned any thought of commercial estate improvements and profit-maximization—certainly not any form of "agrarian capitalism," as Tawney envisaged it—and also any thought of seriously disrupting the lives of their tenants, many so loyal to their lords over many generations. The third and related problem was that their political, military, and social statuses, so necessary to maintain their aristocratic rank, were becoming increasingly expensive to maintain, especially when many such costs—chiefly military and court services—were rising faster than the consumer price index, or the overall price level.[38]

Whether all or most of these factors were really true of the Elizabethan aristocracy, clearly many did opt for the line of least resistance in coping with inflation: namely, to live off their capital by selling lands, especially recently acquired lands that were not governed by aristocratic estate entails. That meant chiefly their lands of monastic origin, though many aristocrats were also finally forced to sell patrimonial estate lands as well. The Tudor and early Stuart monarchs were similarly forced to sell off crown lands, for the very same reasons.[39]

Many of the gentry, on the other hand—again, in Tawney's view—did not face such enormous demands on their time and energies. Furthermore, in having far smaller estates, often with only a few manors, they had a commensurately greater ability to engage in rational estate management, and indeed to engage in the enclosures that became so prominent in Tudor-Stuart and Hanoverian England, so that by the early eighteenth century about 70 percent of the cultivated arable land of England had been enclosed.[40] Such enclosures eliminated communal peasant tenancy rights and permitted the engrossing or amalgamations of the scattered plow strips constituting the former peasant tenancies into compact farms under single unified management, whether undertaken by the landlord himself or by his tenants, who leased lands at market rentals. That allowed both gentry landlords and their major tenants, now freed from peasant property rights and their communal constraints, to engage in the New Husbandry, most of which was imported from the Low Countries. Thus much of the gentry, whether they managed their own estates, as capital farms, or let their enclosed lands to tenant farmers, on relatively short-term leases, were able to capture much more of the economic rent (Ricardian rent) that accrued with the steady rise in the real values of most agricultural commodities—economic rents that would otherwise have been captured by those freehold and copyhold tenants enjoying fixed, nominal money rents.

What is the current evidence for the extent of such land transfer? According to statistics from various sources (unavailable to Tawney), presented in table 5.1, the gentry's share of English arable lands rose from about 25 percent in 1436—thus indicating that the gentry had already "risen" long before 1536—to 45 percent in 1690, and to 50 percent by 1790.

Those gentry gains, up to 1690, appear to have come chiefly from the Church and the Crown, whose share fell from 35 percent in 1436 to just 10 percent in 1690, while the shares for the peerage (aristocracy) fell only from 20 percent in 1436 to 18 percent in 1690. But these figures are highly misleading, in not revealing that a considerable proportion of aristocratic land holdings in 1690 consisted of estates that were held by many former gentry who had acquired peerages after 1660 (when the ranks of aristocrats had been seriously depleted, for various reasons). As this table indicates, and as H. J. Habakkuk had contended, they undoubtedly provided a major reason why this rejuvenated aristocracy, so vastly different from that of the Elizabethan era, was able to regain its share of land holdings to about 25 percent, a century later, in 1790. Note, from this table, that the gains in both aristocratic and gentry landholdings, from 1690 to 1790, came chiefly at the expense of yeomen freeholders.

We should not assume that these new peers had shed their former gentry customs, culture, and socio-economic and especially entrepreneurial outlooks. Indeed, many of them—such as Norfolk's Second Viscount Charles Townsend of Rainham (1675–1738), known as Turnip Townsend—were major proponents and practitioners of the New Husbandry.[41] Of course one can find many variations, with some gentry who failed as capitalist farmers, or those who simply failed to engage in rational estate management, and contrary examples of some aristocratic landowners who did cope with inflation and prospered—though most such examples are really found among the aristocracy of gentry origins, in the post-Restoration era.

In general, the Tawney thesis on the "rise of the gentry"—even if the gentry had risen long before Tawney's century—deserves more support and credit than most

TABLE 5.1
Percentage of Land Held by Various Social Groups in England, 1436, 1690, and 1790

	1436	1690	1790
Church and Crown	35%	10%	10%
Peerage (aristocracy)	20%	18%	25%
Gentry	25%	45%	50%
Yeomen freeholders	20%	27%	15%

Sources: Mingay 1976, table 3.1, p. 59, based on Cooper 1967; Thompson 1966, table 3.1.
Note: Figures adjusted, to add up to 100 percent.

historians seem willing to grant it. For unquestionably, Tudor-Stuart England did experience the transfer of a vast amount of productive lands into the hands of those more likely, more able, more willing, and certainly more predisposed to engage in rational estate management, and other commercial enterprises, indeed to engage in entrepreneurial profit-maximization.[42] Furthermore, as Tawney and many others have noted, a high proportion of these gentry, especially in the seventeenth century, were Puritans—the most renowned example being Oliver Cromwell himself (see Cliffe 1984, 1988).

The extent to which at least a significant number of the English gentry and their major leasehold tenants did become or act as genuine "agrarian capitalists," employing significant innovations in market-oriented mixed husbandry (i.e., combining the cultivation of grain and other arable crops with livestock raising, both sheep and cattle), with the aim of maximizing profits, has yet to be fully explored. But consider, for example, the ingenuity and entrepreneurship of the Herefordshire gentleman farmer Roland Vaughan, who, in 1589, invented and then popularized the "floating meadow" (or water meadow). This capital-intensive innovation involved the use of sluice gates, dykes, and canals to divert water from streams or rivers to flood the meadows or parts of the arable in November, and then to drain them in March. That provided a thermal blanket, under the ice, to protect the underlying soil from freezing and to promote far earlier and more intense germination, yielding as much as an eightfold increase in hay production.[43]

Certainly the very character of English agriculture did change dramatically from this period, especially with the far more widespread diffusion of convertible husbandry, which led to major increases in agricultural productivity. In essence, convertible husbandry meant the alternation in the use of agricultural land between arable and pasture (as opposed to the previous regime of permanent arable and permanent pastures) over a cycle of five or more years, the cultivation of a wider variety of crops, including far more powerful nitrogen-fixing legumes (clover, alfalfa-lucerne, sainfoin), other fodder crops, and industrial crops, thereby eliminating the need for fallowing parts of the arable. It also provided far more efficient pastures and thus a far more productive form of livestock raising. That in turn vastly improved livestock feeding (with more fodder crops from the arable) and the size of cattle and sheep herds. Equally important, enclosures and convertible husbandry also permitted selective breeding of livestock, which had been virtually impossible with the previous communal grazing system of open field peasant agriculture. Convertible husbandry became the very heart of the later so-called Agricultural Revolution, in providing the most efficient and productive form of agriculture before the advent of modern chemical fertilizers.[44]

The greatest and most widespread diffusion of convertible husbandry, especially with the cultivation of the new legumes, came during the period of an agrarian recession, from the 1660s to the 1740s, when the behavior of relative prices promoted a shift from grain growing to fodder and industrial crops, and especially a much greater shift to livestock products. At the same time, a fall in grain prices, while wages and other farm costs were rising, created a price-cost squeeze, which in turn provided a strong incentive for farmers to increase efficiencies per unit of labor and per acre of land. Convertible husbandry, along with the introduction of floating meadows, required very large infusions of capital, which were generally obtained by mortgaging enclosed lands; and mortgaging was also virtually impossible to undertake with communal peasant open field farming. Those landowners and tenants-in-chief who did engage in mortgage financing, and those who succeeded in vastly increasing rents and profit margins, certainly were entrepreneurs, in any sense of the word, and well deserve to be called agrarian capitalists.[45]

One may cavil, however, that while many such gentry did become, in Tawney's terminology, genuine agrarian capitalists and were responsible for promoting important innovations in agricultural productivity, such developments are not really relevant to a study on entrepreneurship—even if they did promote English economic development. The proper response is that the Tawney thesis on agrarian capitalism is highly relevant, in two respects, if we may now draw on the wisdom of Joseph Schumpeter (1883–1950).

Schumpeter on Entrepreneurship

First, many of us who have written on this theme have been inspired by the work of Schumpeter: especially his classic essay on this subject, but also his many other publications.[46] His views on the historical development of entrepreneurship do not seem to be confined merely to the worlds of industry, commerce, and finance. In my view, he would have implicitly accepted Tawney's "agrarian capitalism" (if he accepted the thesis itself) as an integral part of the evolution of modern entrepreneurship. Indeed, his definition of entrepreneurship is exceptionally broad: that which succeeds in "transforming or combining factors into products [and services]." Schumpeter comments further: "If there is not necessarily any sharp dividing line between entrepreneurial activity and ordinary management," nevertheless, "the distinction between adaptive and creative response to given conditions may or may not be felicitous, but it conveys...an essential difference." For Schumpeter, an apt synonym for an entrepreneur is a business innovator—someone who proves successful in introducing and maintaining productive and profitable economic changes in his or her enterprise. Especially important for this study is Schumpeter's view that "the entrepreneurial function need not be embodied in a physical person or, and in particular, in a single physical person" (Schumpeter 1949, 254–55).

Certainly in this study one basic objective is an investigation of the economic, social, and cultural forces that induce profitable innovations as the key to economic growth. A related objective is to demonstrate that innovations, especially technological innovations, have been fundamentally the products of capitalist entrepreneurship, in all four key sectors of the economy, including agriculture. Above all, we must always be clear in distinguishing between mere inventions—many of which were never successfully applied in their day (e.g., Hero of Alexandria's steam pump, of circa 60 CE)—and entrepreneurial innovation: the successful, productivity-increasing, and profit-maximizing application of new techniques and new technologies in some business enterprise, including agricultural enterprises.

Another justification for examining the role of the early-modern English gentry in such entrepreneurial innovations is simply the long-accepted fact that many gentry landowners did not draw even the greater share of their incomes from leasehold rentals. Nor did they confine their enterprises to agriculture. For they also invested in mining, metallurgy, and textiles. We must remember that many capitalistic industrial enterprises—in mining and metallurgy especially—were necessarily found on gentry estates; and much of the capital investment in these enterprises came from gentry landowners, for clearly they had a disproportionate amount of the nation's wealth to make such investments (see in particular Simpson 1961). The extent to which they financed and promoted or engaged in English industrial development in the early-modern era is yet another avenue of research that needs to be more fully explored, despite several important recent studies.[47] Even more important would be a fully-researched historical analysis of those gentry, and especially the well-educated and the socially, economically, and politically well-connected sons of gentry who became successful, profit-maximizing entrepreneurs in business itself, as usually the term is understood: in industry, commerce, and finance.

The Hamilton-Keynes Thesis on Profit Inflation and the Rise of Industrial Capitalism during the Price Revolution Era, and the Gould Alternative

Pre–World War II scholarship on economic issues in Tawney's century (1540–1640), especially those involving the Price Revolution, includes two other scholarly names, once renowned, if not so much today, for clearly neither had Tawney's intellectual caliber. Yet both remain important for raising very important issues for any scholar analyzing the origins of early-modern industrial capitalism and related issues of capitalist entrepreneurship. We simply cannot dismiss them for supposed defects in their scholarship, if they did succeed, in this fashion—that is, by investigating such critical issues—in promoting our understanding of the evolution of early-modern English entrepreneurship, and industrial capitalism.

The first was Earl Hamilton (1899–1989), professor of economics at Chicago (1949–69), and President of the Economic History Association in 1951–52. His chief claim to fame in economic history is in providing some statistical foundations for an explanation of the inflation of the European Price Revolution era based on a quantity theory of money, in many publications, from 1928 (Hamilton 1928, 1929a, 1929b, 1934, 1936, 1942, 1947, 1952). Since the time of the French philosopher Jean Bodin (1566) a majority of scholars had in fact assumed that the primary cause of the Price Revolution was the influx of silver from the Americas (Bodin 1946; Wiebe 1895). That inflation had in fact begun much earlier—in Spain, England, the Low Countries, Italy: from at least the 1520s, long before any significant amounts of Spanish-American silver had arrived in Europe. Some economic historians, on discovering this fact, unfortunately leapt to the false conclusion that the true, fundamental cause of this inflation was instead population growth. In fact the initial causes were monetary, but in the form of the south German–central European silver mining boom (ca. 1460–ca. 1550) and a financial revolution in the 1520s, issues that need not detain us here, except to note that Hamilton himself had also perceived the importance of these two issues, and did not (contrary to popular opinion) contend that the influx of American silver provided either the initial cause of the Price Revolution or the predominant cause of Spanish inflation during its final phase, in the first half of the seventeenth century.[48]

Hamilton's second claim to fame, and the one far more relevant to the theme of this study on entrepreneurship, was his 1929 thesis that the inflation of the Price Revolution was fundamentally responsible for the birth of modern industrial capitalism through the mechanism of "profit inflation." In truth, Hamilton really owed his fame to the fact that the eminent economist John Maynard Keynes (1883–1946) had so strongly and publicly endorsed Hamilton's thesis; and indeed it was Keynes himself who actually coined the term *profit inflation* (in 1930).[49]

In essence, Hamilton and Keynes argued that in this era industrial wages lagged behind prices, particularly in England (but not so much in Spain), thereby producing growing profits, the bulk of which English entrepreneurs chose to invest in larger-scale, more capital-intensive forms of manufacturing industries and other industrial or commercial enterprises, for example, overseas joint-stock trading companies (see below).

To be sure, in England, as in many other European countries, nominal or money wages generally did lag behind consumer prices; and such a phenomenon can be found in many other eras as well (including the twentieth century). Unfortunately for Hamilton, however, he used wheat prices to measure the price level. From the 1950s, most economic historians have instead preferred to measure changes in the price level by following the model of Henry Phelps Brown and Sheila Hopkins: by constructing a weighted "basket of consumables" consumer price index. In their index, about 80 percent of the commodity weights consist of foodstuffs: wheat, rye, peas, barley, malt (for beer), butter, cheese, meat, and fish. The remaining 20 percent is in common industrial products: chiefly textiles and fuels.[50] In all price indexes for this era, grain prices rose the most, by a very substantial degree, followed by those for wood fuels, and livestock. Prices for industrial manufactures did rise, as well, but by a far lesser degree. It is far from clear that in various individual industries prices of manufactures rose more than did the wages for those who produced them.

Under such circumstances, one may ask why English industrial entrepreneurs would have necessarily, by the Hamilton model, invested their supposed extra profits, if any, in larger-scale, more capital-intensive forms of industry, when labor had become relatively so cheap, and, in real terms, had become even cheaper. Furthermore, if the real wages of industrial labor had declined, from a rise in their cost of living, industrialists in general would have achieved market gains only if the real incomes of those engaged in other economic sectors—agriculture, commerce, and finance—experienced a more than compensatory rise. That was an important issue that neither Hamilton nor Keynes (nor indeed most other historians) ever really considered.

With the now better-observed long-term behavior of relative prices and wages in early-modern Europe, we may confidently assert that Hamilton and Keynes were not justified in contending that industrialists enjoyed any verifiable profit inflation. Indeed, no economic historian can make such a contention without measuring, industry by industry, the long-term relationships between industrial wages and the wholesale prices for the manufactures that wage-earning employees produced. For the later sixteenth- and seventeenth-century southern Low Countries, arguably then one of the most advanced industrial regions in Europe, I myself have found evidence for the very opposite of profit inflation: a rise in industrial wages (for building craftsmen) that was, overall, greater than the rise in the industrial price index. And yet that did not seem to impair the profits and fortunes of most industrialists and entrepreneurs in the seventeenth-century southern Low Countries (Munro 2002).

Whether or not, in this and other eras, inflation reduced the factor cost of labor in this and other sectors of the economy may seem to be an interesting if moot question. Yet this question raises two very important and more major issues: (1) what has been the historical impact of inflations and deflations upon all factor costs of production; and (2) how have industrial entrepreneurs reacted to such changes in their real factor costs: that is, have such changes proved to be yet another spur to entrepreneurial innovation?

One of the very few economic historians to explore this vital issue was John D. Gould, though regrettably without much success in affecting historical interpretations. In a now all but forgotten article, published in 1964, Gould contended that inflation generally reduced an arguably even more important factor cost: namely, the cost of capital. Thus, insofar as early-modern entrepreneurs had borrowed funds for capital investment by contracts that specified the payment of annual interest and finally the repayment of the principal, in current money-of-account terms, the inflation of the Price Revolution era had cheapened the costs of previously borrowed capital. Any contrary contention that lenders of this era—when annual rates of inflation were still low by modern standards—had responded by raising their interest rates is fully negated by abundant evidence that nominal interest rates were continuously falling in the sixteenth century (in Flanders, from 20.5 percent in 1511–15 to 11.0 percent in 1566–70), so that in fact, with inflation, real interest rates fell even further.[51]

Finally, we may observe that insofar as the Price Revolution did cheapen capital costs, it did so in ways that more directly promoted larger-scale, more capital-intensive forms of manufacturing industries. One may also argue that it similarly promoted larger-scale capital-intensive agricultural and commercial enterprises.

Perhaps, however, the real significance of the ill-formulated Hamilton thesis is that it provoked his colleague John Nef into producing an alternative thesis to explain the early-modern origins of genuine industrial capitalism in Tudor-Stuart England, and one that certainly involved rational if risk-taking innovative entrepreneurship.

The Nef Thesis Revisited (with Wrigley and Hatcher): The Tudor-Stuart Energy Crisis and an Early Industrial Revolution

John Nef's counterthesis on this same theme was that England experienced a veritable "energy crisis" in Tawney's century, 1540–1640, and one that entrepreneurs largely resolved (in Nef's view) in the form of an "early industrial revolution." This "revolution" involved very significant industrial innovations, specifically important technological innovations in fuel consumption, and also necessarily in the form of far larger-scale and genuinely capitalist forms of enterprise.[52]

The traditional medieval and early-modern industrial economies had been fundamentally wood-based—for both fuels and construction. In Nef's view, the energy crisis took the form of soaring wood and wood charcoal prices, rising as much as or even more than grain prices, and certainly to a far greater extent than industrial prices. The implicit culprit was population growth. Indeed, as we now know (and better than Nef), the population of England and Wales well more than doubled in this era: rising from about 2.250 million in the 1520s to reach a peak of 5.773 million in the mid-1650s.[53] That demographic expansion, combined with a disproportionate growth in urbanization, and a rapid growth in shipbuilding for overseas trade, led to a far more extensive deforestation than was experienced in any other region in northern Europe.

Furthermore, as Nef contended, England enjoyed a singular advantage over any other European region afflicted by a similar fuel crisis: in enjoying an abundant supply of readily accessible, relatively cheap coal, easily transportable by water (river or seaborne) in much of England. Thus a continuing divergence between wood char-coal and coal prices provided industrial entrepreneurs with a strong cost-price and profit incentive to shift from wood fuels, or wood charcoal, to coal. This contention subsequently, from the mid-1950s, aroused considerable, and generally very hostile, criticism from a wide variety of scholars.[54]

In this respect, two very important defects in Nef's analyses of fuel prices must be noted, though they were not defects that his opponents fully, clearly, and convinc-ingly dealt with. First, as many opponents indeed noted, he made the absurd claim that England had suffered a "national" energy crisis during this century, when there were no national markets for wood, wood charcoal, or coal and when available evi-dence for some regional markets indicates often significant disparities in fuel prices. Nor could there have been any national market with such serious deficiencies in overland transportation and commercial facilities. Charcoal, it should be noted, was not a commodity that could then have been easily transported, chiefly because of its friable nature: that is, its physical instability, such that any agitation or disturbance causes the charcoal to crumble into unusable dust. Instead, in Tudor Stuart England, there were purely regional, local markets: in some such markets, wood remained abundant—and there charcoal was typically created at the forest site. In other re-gions, it soon became scarce and expensive, especially in relation to coal.

The other defect was to state, on the basis of insufficient data samples, that a serious divergence in charcoal and coal prices had already occurred by the later six-teenth century. My detailed comparative analysis of various sets of wood, charcoal, and coal prices in the same regional markets (see figure 5.1) indicates that, for a wide variety of such regional markets, the most marked divergence in relative prices did indeed take place—contrary to the assertions of some critics—but generally not until after the 1640s, when coal prices starting falling while charcoal prices (nominal and real) generally continued to rise.[55] Nevertheless, for some specific local markets, such as Cambridge and Westminster, the price of a ton of coal was well under half the price of a ton of charcoal—when both had about the same calorific (heating) utility—indeed before the 1640s.[56]

If an industrial shift from charcoal to coal, purely on the basis of relative prices, were the only story to be told, it would not be worth serious consideration in a history of early-modern English entrepreneurship. The real interest lies in the en-trepreneurial responses in the form of technological innovations, and consequent increase in industrial scales, that such a change in the choice of fuels necessitated: made necessary in the sense that without such innovations many industrial entrepre-neurs would have faced failure and bankruptcies. The basic technological problem involved in choosing coal over wood charcoal lies in the fact that coal is a very dirty fuel that contaminates most products with which it comes into contact. Charcoal, conversely, is a form of pure carbon, and the purest of all available fuels, explaining its worldwide use over many millennia.

There were two possible solutions to the fuel contamination problem. For this early-modern era, the first and indeed only technological solution was the construc-tion of a reverberatory furnace to separate the coal fuel, and its noxious fumes, from the manufactured product. The second solution, which came much later, only with the advent of the Industrial Revolution era, was the distillation and purification of coal, transforming it into coke. That process in turn proved successful only after long, arduous, and costly experimentations, which themselves reveal a true entrepre-

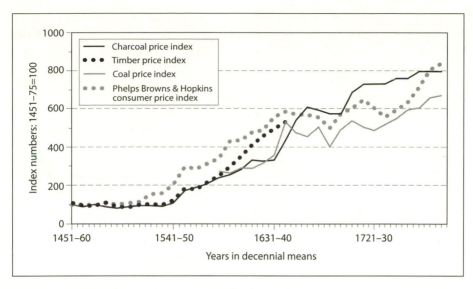

Figure 5.1. Price Relatives for Fuels (Wood, Charcoal, and Coal) and the Phelps Brown and Hopkins "Basket of Consumables" (Revised Version), 1451–60 to 1781–90, in decennial means. Base 1451–75 = 100 for all indexes.

neurial spirit among many industrialists, in the course of the later seventeenth and early eighteenth centuries.[57]

The first solution, the reverberatory furnace, is first described in Vanoccio Birunguccio's *De la pirotechnica*, about 1540, though we do not know who were the original inventors or entrepreneurs, those who first succeeded in achieving this vital technological advance. It was a very large-scale and complex brick kiln furnace that transmitted heat by convection and reflection ("reverberation")—reflecting heat from the roof of the furnace onto the product being manufactured, while isolating the coal fuel itself and the fumes by eliminating the chimneys and using underground pipes to exhaust the fumes and to draw in fresh air.[58] This new furnace also required hydraulic machinery, with large water-powered leather bellows, in order to inject air into the burning coal fuels to achieve the required high levels of combustion. Such technologically complex furnaces obviously required a quantum leap in the scale of capital investment. That in turn meant a dramatic change from simple artisanal production to true industrial capitalism, employing not traditional artisans (owning their own capital), but wage-earning laborers, indeed factory workers.

Would this far more costly furnace technology have threatened the profit margins of the new industrial capitalists? Whatever their initial fears and expectations, the answer is no. For Nef's so-called industrial revolution in fuel technologies in fact entailed three separate sets of cost reductions. First, this new and very capital-costly fuel technology required a commensurately large increase in industrial scale, which in turn ultimately meant a sharp fall in the marginal costs of production. Those changes in scale economies, however, had to be based upon and justified by a very large increase in market sales, from both a general population growth and disproportionate urbanization (discussed below) and an expansion of the market economy itself with the requisite commercial-financial institutions (also discussed below). In other words, the success of this industrial innovation depended upon a large enough increase in production and sales to distribute the initially high fixed costs over the production run, so that unit costs fell. Second, industrial capitalists achieved gains in transaction, organizational, and labor costs by concentrating production in one centralized, factory-like unit. Third, of course, they benefited by substituting relatively cheaper coal for ever more costly charcoal, at least generally so from the 1640s. Nef's chief point, therefore, is that industrial entrepreneurs, facing this "energy crisis"—even if Nef misdated the real era of crisis—could have survived to prosper only by engaging in a technological change that in turn demanded radical changes in industrial and commercial organization, to achieve much larger economies of scale.

What examples of the new "industrial capitalism," specifically for early-modern (later Stuart-Hanoverian) England, did Nef and other historians of the British coal industry, such as John Hatcher, provide? The chief examples are the following innovative industries: glass (perhaps the first such industry, ca. 1610),[59] beer (brewing with hops), bricks, clay tiles, pottery making, lime-burning (construction and agriculture), soap, paper, gunpowder, brass wares, salt (seawater evaporation), alum and dyestuffs, sugar refining (post-1660). In the field of metallurgy, the new coal-burning industries included those of calcining ores (burning out impurities before smelting); copper-based industries, especially those making brass and bronze alloys; metallic processes in separating silver from lead; the final finishing of many metals, for example, in drawing wire or making nails. None of these was truly new, of course, in terms of the product, but rather in terms of industrial technology; and many did become important as import-substitution industries.

To reiterate the other key point: such industries could have been successful in achieving the necessary scale economies only if they had found sufficient mass markets to consume these products. Such was not the case for export markets, for none of these "new" industries was responsible for any significant exports (except a few industrial products exported to West African and American markets). They were far more successful in the domestic market: thanks to the aforementioned population growth. Although, as noted earlier, the population of England and Wales had reached a seventeenth-century peak of 5.773 million in 1656, and although that population thereafter did experience some decline and stagnation, it rose again from the 1720s to reach a level of 6.757 million in 1761, on the eve of the modern Industrial Revolution era. But far more dramatic and certainly far more important was the growth of London itself. Having been relatively insignificant in 1500, with a population of only about 50,000, it had grown to 200,000 by 1600, to 350,000 in 1650—when it had become indisputably the largest city in Europe—and to 550,000 in 1750. That provided a concentrated mass-market with much lower transaction costs from the very density of sales.[60]

Equally important was the fact that such products as glass, bricks, soaps, dyestuffs, beer, brass- and bronze-wares enjoyed significant price elasticities of demand, so that cost and then competitive price reductions ensured a more than proportional increase in the quantity demanded and consumed. The same effect was achieved, in this era of steadily rising real-wage incomes, from the 1650s, for those products that similarly enjoyed a high income elasticity of demand.[61]

Other major manufacturing industries of this era did not, however, enjoy any such changes and benefit from this new furnace technology. Woolen textiles, which collectively remained by far England's most important manufacturing industry, producing by far its overwhelmingly dominant exports until the eighteenth century (92.5 percent by value, to the 1640s), did not undergo any truly significant technological changes, not even with the rise of the so-called New Draperies, until the true Industrial Revolution of the later eighteenth century, that is, from the 1760s.[62] Indeed productivity in the eighteenth-century woolen industry remained about the same as that documented for the fifteenth century (Munro 2003b, 1988).

Furthermore, England's other major and growing industry, iron manufacturing, proved to be unable to use the new furnace technology. Until the early eighteenth century, it remained fully dependent on charcoal (and also on water power). The technological reason for that is very simple: smelting iron ore requires the direct contact of the ore, as ferric oxide (Fe_2O_3), with the fuel, so that the carbon in the charcoal unites with the oxygen in ferric oxide to liberate the iron (Fe) while producing carbon dioxide: CO_2. The initial solution to that problem, and at the same time, the previously indicated second solution to the overall "coal problem," came in 1709–10 with Abraham Darby's development of coke fuels. That fuel was the successful result of distilling coal into coke in an airless furnace, as a virtually purified form of carbon.[63] It did not, however, then produce an "industrial revolution," because initially coke fuels were more expensive than charcoal fuels, and coke-smelting also required extra refining costs, to eliminate the silicon (which, however, improved the quality of cast iron). Coke-smelting became fully cost-effective and thus successful, indeed "revolutionary," only with application of John Smeaton's piston air pumps (replacing bellows, ca. 1760) and then James Watt's steam engine to power them, in 1776. It should be noted that most of the trenchant opposition to the Nef thesis concerns his views—and those of T. S. Ashton—on the supposed "tyranny of wood and water," in curbing the growth of early-modern iron industry. This is a story beyond the scope of this chapter, belonging to the study of the eighteenth-century Industrial Revolution.[64]

In summary, and in all these respects, it is fair to criticize the Nef thesis by contending that no industrial revolution took place in Tudor-Stuart (or even early Hanoverian) England: there was no significant growth of the industrial sector, whether in terms of outputs, exports, or employment. Furthermore, no significant transfers of labor and resources from the agrarian to the industrial, commercial, financial, and service sectors took place in either Tawney's century or the following century: none to compare with those of the later eighteenth and nineteenth centuries.

Nevertheless, we must not overlook the important fact that coal was assuming an ever greater role in the British industrial economy from the sixteenth to eighteenth century, well before the onset of the Industrial Revolution. John Hatcher has contended that "in the latter half of the seventeenth century, sweeping changes occurred in the pattern of industrial coal consumption," so that "by 1700 coal was the preferred fuel of almost all fuel consuming industries, and access to coal supplies had already begun to exert a determining influence over industrial location" (1993, 450, 458). Even if the aforementioned textile industries did not, as noted earlier, undergo any significant technological changes in this era, certainly none involving power, nevertheless they also experienced a major growth in coal consumption for many of their industrial processes: from combing to dyeing to finishing; and in the production of dyestuffs and mordants (Tann 1973; Wrigley 1988, 78; Hatcher 1993, 442–44). Hatcher estimates that British coal output (England, Scotland, Wales) had expanded almost twelvefold: from about 227,000 tonnes in 1560 to about 2,640,000 tonnes in 1700, when it was supplying about half of England's fuel needs (1993, table 4.1, p. 68). Anthony Wrigley has furthermore observed that British coal output was then at least five times greater than the combined output in the rest of the world. By 1800,

British coal output had expanded at least fivefold, to about 15 millions tonnes a year, which was at least five times greater than the aggregate coal output in continental Europe.[65] By 1830, according to Michael Flinn's estimates, Great Britain was producing 30.861 million tonnes (34.024 million tons), almost twelve times as much as Britain had produced in 1700.[66]

The aforementioned rapid and dramatic growth in London's population itself had a major impact on the English coal-mining industry and trade, for that growth could have occurred only with and because of massive imports of coal, especially for domestic heating, chiefly by sea from Newcastle, into London. Certainly London could not have imported enough wood to supply the city's need for both domestic and industrial fuels. As Wrigley has pointed out, a ton of coal produces "about twice as much heat as the same weight of dry wood." Furthermore, noting that an acre of woodland then produced only about two tons of dry wood a year, he contends that the heat produced by one million tons of coal (mined and seaborne) would have required one million acres of forested land.[67]

Coal, as so many historians have contended, became the essential core of European industrialization in the eighteenth and nineteenth centuries, both promoting and permitting very major technological changes, which, by their very nature, were also entrepreneurial changes.[68] Indeed, Wrigley has put forward the seminal thesis that English economic growth and the Industrial Revolution both depended upon a shift from an "organic" (wood) to a "mineral"-based economy (coal).[69] Coal, distilled into coke, replaced charcoal almost everywhere in metallurgy (amalgamating smelting and refining, with vastly increased scales of production); coal-fired steam engines ultimately replaced water-mills, while later coal-fired steam turbines produced a new and very cheap form of power in electricity. And finally, coal also subsequently, and much later, became the fundamental base for a new set of very innovative chemical industries that also constituted part of the so-called Second Industrial Revolution, especially from the 1870s.

In sum, and in retrospect, Nef had supplied the essence of a good case for explaining why England was the birthplace of the modern Industrial Revolution: its entrepreneurial, technological, and industrial primacy in using coal, as the essential ingredient for modern industrialization. But he seriously compromised his case by using poor data, and by exaggerating his claims of growing industrial output in Tudor Stuart England. Perhaps his most serious fault was one of chronology. To reiterate the primary thesis in this historical analysis of English entrepreneurship: the Nef thesis, and Tawney's theses as well, have a much greater validity for the century following Tawney's century—the century preceding the Industrial Revolution. Those innovative entrepreneurial developments in that century indeed do help us better to understand the nature of the forms of the ensuing Industrial Revolution, from the 1760s, especially, and thus obviate concerns about a temporal gap between Tawney's century and the Industrial Revolution.

Overseas Expansion and Changes in Commercial-Financial Structures

The Atlantic Ship

There remains, however, one further set of English economic and entrepreneurial developments in Tawney's century—actually beginning in the previous century, but in the Iberian peninsula—that demands our attention in this study: the age of overseas maritime exploration, colonization, and trade. That in turn ultimately brought about economic "globalization." The combination of technological innovation and entrepreneurial ingenuity that physically and economically made this possible—indeed in a very major form of industrial capitalism for this early-modern era—was the development of the so-called Atlantic ship or full-rigged ship.[70] Portuguese shipyards, responding to demands from those oceangoing mariners who had been unable to cope with the Atlantic trade winds off the African coast, had initiated this industrial and commercial transformation by copying and adapting the triangular lateen-sail rigging of the Arabic coastal ship, in fact, a very small boat, known as the *dhow*; but the result was a much larger ship (40 to 200 tonnes) known as the *caravel*, with correspondingly much larger masts. It was that lateen-rigging that provided the caravel with the maneuverability to cope with these Atlantic trade winds, and allowed Portuguese mariners, from 1434, to advance south of Cape Bojador (26° N), and thus to commence their commercial and colonial acquisitions along the West African coast, and ultimately to Asia (India and the East Indies) in a highly successful search for both gold and spices, with the aid of a much improved oceangoing ship.

Subsequently, some unknown Iberian shipyards made the next advance in ship rigging, perhaps in the mid-fifteenth century, by combining the large square canvas sails of the northern Hanseatic *cogge*—providing power and speed—with the caravel's lateen sails: a small lateen spritsail on the bow, the square sails in the middle, and a large lateen sail on the rear or mizzenmast. These full-rigged or Atlantic ships, better known as *carracks* and *galleons*, were much larger than the Portuguese caravels, expanding in size to 600 tonnes in the early sixteenth century and then to 1,500 tonnes by the 1590s. A major factor in that increased scale was the addition of naval artillery: up to fifty or sixty cannons, placed both on deck and below deck. It was this large, full-rigged, heavily armed ship that allowed Europeans to dominate the world's oceanic trade routes up to the nineteenth century. Indeed, it may be considered, along with Gutenberg's printing press (ca. 1450), as the most important technological innovation of the fifteenth century—certainly a marvel of European entrepreneurship.

Another major aspect of this new age of overseas expansion was, of course, the vast influx of Spanish American treasure, silver, especially, which did so much to fuel and promote the ongoing inflation of the Price Revolution era (see Munro 2003c). But surely the more important economic function and consequence of that vast influx was in providing Europeans with essential means of expanding their trade with Asia: all the more so, since silver generally commanded a higher value in relation to both gold and goods in Asia than in Europe. That in turn was the prime consideration in western Europe's subsequent achievement of economic globalization.

The Crises in English Trade with the Antwerp Market in the 1550s

If we date the beginnings of this new era of overseas expansion with Portugal's capture of the Moroccan port of Ceuta in 1415, and then with the Portuguese and Spanish acquisitions in Africa, Asia, the Atlantic islands, and the Americas, to, say, the 1520s, the English appear to have been remarkably slow to seek out these new overseas business opportunities. One reason may have been that English exports, once predominantly in the form of raw wool, were by the 1520s almost entirely in the form of woolen cloth—accounting (as indicated earlier) for at least 90 percent of the total value of all exports. Almost all of this export trade was directed to the cross-Channel port and market of Antwerp.

Indeed, the original "tripod" or three-legged foundation upon which Antwerp had gained its role as the preeminent commercial, financial, and industrial center at the dawn of the modern era, from circa 1460 to circa 1560, had consisted of first, English woolen cloths; then, south German metals (silver, copper), fustians, and banking; and finally, from 1501, the Portuguese royal staple for the spice trade from the East Indies. English cloth merchants, having been excluded from Flanders, the Baltic, and the Mediterranean, had found only this one available outlet, in the Antwerp market (the Brabant fairs), where German merchants avidly sought their woolens, and had them finished in the Antwerp region, as their chief return cargo, just as the Portuguese later sought south German silver, copper, and banking to conduct their new African and Asian trades (see Munro 1994, 1999).

The English cloth trade boom, from circa 1460 to 1552—almost entirely co-inciding with the Tudor enclosure movement (then chiefly for sheep pastures)—reached its culmination, followed by disaster, in the Great Debasement of 1542–52, which Henry VIII and his successors had undertaken to finance their wars. Then, in mid-1552, Northumberland's Protectorate government abruptly revalued the English coinage by 253 percent (a 3.5-fold increase in silver contents). The obvious consequence of this drastic revaluation was a sharp rise in the foreign exchange value of the pound sterling, and hence a sharp increase (if not fully proportional) in the overseas cost of buying English woolens, whose sales soon plummeted on the Antwerp market.[71]

Since the previous debasements had provided such a stimulus to cloth exports, the Antwerp market may have already experienced a glut, so that exports might have fallen even without the revaluation (though probably not as much). From 1546–50 to 1551–55, London's quinquennial mean cloth exports had fallen by 10.4 percent: from 123,780 broadcloths to 110,888 broadcloths; and in 1560s London's mean exports fell to just 85,952 broadcloths (an overall decline of 30.5 percent).[72] By the end of that decade, the outbreak of the Revolt of the Netherlands (1568–1609) made Antwerp quite inhospitable to English trade. But long before those events, the English had already undertaken their new search for alternative trading ports, and that involved a radical change and transformation in business organization in the form of the joint-stock company.

The New Joint-Stock Companies of the Later Sixteenth and Seventeenth Centuries

The very first such overseas joint-stock trading company, the Muscovy or Russia Company, was established in May 1553, in the direct aftermath of the Antwerp crisis.[73] It is also the first (historically verifiable) joint-stock company, a revolutionary new form of business organization.[74] The founders of this new venture subscribed a capital sum of £6,000 through the sale of stock, that is, shares of ownership, with a par value of £25 (i.e., 240 shares). This capital was then invested, with additional expenditures of £4,000, in the purchase of three ships and trading goods. Two ships were lost in the ice of the White Sea en route to Russia (which then had no Baltic port); but the third, under Richard Chanceller, the expedition's leader, did reach Archangel. He successfully negotiated a trade treaty with Czar Ivan IV ("The Terrible"). On his return, Chancellor obtained a royal charter that incorporated the new company "as one bodie and perpetuall fellowship and communaltie," with a monopoly on all trade with Russia and adjacent regions in Asia. By 1563, the capital stock had been increased to £33,600, with permission to call upon a further £60 from each of the 240 shareholders (i.e., an additional £14,400 to bring the total capital to £48,000).[75]

The revolutionary nature of this new form of business organization can best be understood by comparing it with that of the famous Merchants Adventurers Company, first established in 1407, for the English cloth export trade, but given a royal charter for that trade in 1505.[76] This earlier enterprise was a "regulated company" in the sense that it possessed such a charter and certain monopoly rights, whose enforcement required a governing council with an appointed governor and his assistants and a court in its overseas headquarters at Antwerp. But the actual commerce, the cloth-export trade, was conducted by a large number of private firms—family firms and simple partnerships—that operated on their own account under the protective umbrella of the Merchants Adventurers. They raised their capital by pooling funds of family members or those of the partners, generally limited to six members. Other capital was raised by borrowing, often by mortgaging properties. Because of the nature of their trade—the very short cross-Channel trade between London and Antwerp—their capital requirements, both in terms of fixed and working capital, were small. Rarely did such merchants own and operate their own ships; and generally they bought their woolens, on credit, at Blackwell Hall, and simply leased space on small ships for this cross-Channel journey. With a succession of cloth sales at Antwerp, and with the investment of the proceeds in the purchase of various goods from the Brabant fairs, for importation into England (on behalf of the Mercers Company of London), these Merchants Adventurer enjoyed very quick turnovers of cargoes and business transactions—a matter of a few weeks at most, permitting them either to reinvest profits in this bilateral trade or to invest them by purchasing a bill of exchange from other merchants about to embark on their own Antwerp-based trade.

The Russia (Muscovy) Company, in sharp contrast, was established to conduct very long-distance, truly overseas trading ventures, each of which required a year or more to be conducted and return a profit. That was indeed true of all the new overseas trading companies. Such a very large-scale, long-term enterprise, requiring large initial fixed-capital investments, could hardly have been financed by the traditional methods of pooling funds from family members and a few partners. Instead the necessary capitals for such firms could have been raised only by the sales of stock (shares), often to hundreds of investors.

The origins of this form of business organization remain obscure. They may have been Italian, in that medieval *commenda* contracts were often divided into shares, or *loca*; but *commenda* contracts were undertaken for only one maritime venture.[77] For this early-modern English business organization, the term *joint stock* meant that the capital stock was held collectively by all of the stock- or shareholders, as joint owners of the company. It was a collective business venture with a common capital, invested in the company, and not in the individual participants. Each shareholder had the right to vote for the directors of the company, based on the number of shares that each investor held. Shareholders received a share of the profits, in the form of dividends declared per share. Equally important, they had the right to sell their shares to other investors, and thus potentially to reap substantial capital gains as well.

The sale of shares or the death of shareholders in no way affected the life and operations of the company, as was the case with a partnership. A partnership existed only so long as all of the partners continued to own the firm. Thus the withdrawal or death of a partner necessitated the legal cessation of the firm, which could continue only with a new partnership contract. In contrast, a joint-stock company continued to exist as the same business venture, until such time as the shareholders voted to wind up the affairs of the company, and to distribute the invested capital among the existing shareholders.

The other two major joint-stock companies in overseas trade, established in the later sixteenth century, were the Levant Company, originally created in 1581 as the Turkey Company, and then reorganized in 1591, under its new name; and the East India Company, created in 1600, with a royal charter and a monopoly on trade with South Asia (that is, with those parts of Asia not included in the Russia Company's monopoly charter).[78]

Certainly by far the most important of the new overseas joint-stock trading companies, for the later sixteenth and early seventeenth centuries, was the Levant Company. It represents England's very first and remarkably successful entry into the still far more lucrative Mediterranean trade.[79] The circumstances that led to this English success, and the establishment of the Levant Company, were somewhat fortuitous: the Ottoman Turks' seizure of Cyprus in 1570–71, thereby gaining control of the Aegean Sea from Venice; and then, in October 1571, the crushing victory of the Venetian-led coalition of European fleets over the Turks at the Battle of Lepanto. That ended forever the European fear of Ottoman naval supremacy in the Mediterranean and enabled the English to exploit European differences in dealing with the Turks. Note that the Levant Company was founded just ten years after the Battle of Lepanto.

What the Turks wanted was a new European ally—one more reliable than the French had been. They also wanted a secure supply of guns, munitions, and above all other European textiles, but most especially fine English woolen broadcloths, to reduce their recent dependence on Venetian woolens, especially since the Turks were so often at war with Venice. What the English wanted was not just a general entry into Mediterranean trade, but more specifically a new and more profitable market for their own woolens, in view of the serious difficulties still afflicting Antwerp and other potential northern markets. English merchants also wanted a guaranteed access to the even more lucrative import trade in raw silk (Turkish and Persian) and Asian spices.

The brilliant entrepreneurial success of the Levant Company was due principally to two factors. The first was skilful diplomacy, especially in negotiating better commercial relations and commercial services, in supplying better-quality textiles than those offered by its European and especially Venetian competitors.[80] The second was much superior naval technology and naval tactics. By the mid-seventeenth century, the English were building far larger, far stronger oak-based carracks and galleons, which were also more heavily gunned than were those of any of their rivals in the Mediterranean basin. They proved to be largely invincible to both pirates and Muslim corsairs—which had for so long menaced the Mediterranean shipping lanes. While their freight rates were perhaps 10 percent higher than those of their competitors, their insurance rates were far lower—and above all the Levant Company's galleons offered the virtual certainty of delivering their cargoes.[81]

In 1600, some leading entrepreneurs in the Levant Company were also instrumental in the establishment of what ultimately became an even more important overseas joint-stock trading company: the East India Company. Its objective was to compete with the Dutch, in a desperate race to establish a direct sea link, via South Africa (the Cape route), with the Indian Ocean and East Indies spice trade, at a time when warfare was disrupting the spice trades of the then two principal participants: Venice and Portugal.

In the early seventeenth century, however, the English seemed destined to lose this competition, especially after the Dutch, in 1623, had forcibly evicted the English from Amboyna (modern-day Ambon), one of the key East Indies spice islands, in the Moluccas, thereby allowing the Dutch to gain virtual control of this region's trade. The Dutch victory was due to superior capitalization and superior organization in its own joint-stock company, the Vereinige Oost-Indisch Compagnie (United East India Co.: VOC), and to its superior military power, with a government support that was largely unavailable to the English East India Company. The English East India Company directors then decided to "suboptimize" by focusing their commercial, political, and then military activities on gaining control of the Indian subcontinent. But they were certainly not successful in doing so, nor in expanding their Asian commerce, until at least the 1660s. But if the export of silver, the chief export of both companies to Asia, is a measure of relative success, the English exports had exceeded those of the Dutch by 1720.[82] Certainly by that time, both East India companies had proved successful in terminating forever the role of both the Venetians and the Portuguese in the Asian spice trades.[83]

Growing hostility in late Elizabethan and Stuart England to monopolies, in both domestic industry and overseas trade (since most demanded and enjoyed royal monopoly rights)—and a growing mercantilist hostility as well to exports of "treasure" (gold and silver)—hindered the creation of new joint-stock companies. Thus not until after the Civil War and Commonwealth-Protectorate era, and with the Restoration under Charles II in 1660, were new and important joint-stock companies created, in particular (1) the Royal African Company in 1662, reorganized with a new charter in 1672; (2) the Hudson's Bay Company in 1670; (3) the Bank of England in 1694; (4) the New East India Company in 1698 , which was established by a large loan to the government, as rival to the original East India Co.; but in 1709 it was absorbed by and merged into the original company; and finally, (5) the South Sea Company in 1711 (Scott 1912, 1:263–421, 2:228–40; Cawston and Keene 1968, 154–243).

Only from the 1660s did the joint-stock overseas trading companies prove truly successful in both altering the structure of English foreign trade and in establishing economically viable commercial-colonial empires for Great Britain. They did so, fundamentally, by shifting their trade from spices, precious metals, and luxury silks into a new reexport trade in more mass-consumption-oriented colonial products, which themselves came to be mass-produced: above all sugar, Asian cotton textiles (calicoes and muslins), tobacco, tea, coffee, codfish, lumber. That colonial reexport trade rose from just 4 percent of total export values in 1640 to 31 percent in 1700, thereby reducing the dependence on woolen cloth exports from 92 percent in 1640 to 48 percent in 1700.[84] Throughout the eighteenth century, the colonial reexport trades consistently accounted for about a third of total export values.[85] Ralph Davis called that transformation a Commercial Revolution, while Eric Hobsbawm called it New Colonialism, demonstrating that it was vastly more profitable and more conducive to economic growth than was the so-called Old Colonialism (based, in his view, on the seemingly profitable lure of spices and precious metals).[86] It is also, of course, known as the Age of Mercantilism, whose significance for this topic may lie in the ways that state-supported economic nationalism, with the twin goal of increasing national wealth and national power, fostered and fortified the rent-seeking goals of many English entrepreneurs, especially in commerce and finance (Viner 1948; Wilson 1949, 1958).

Limitations of the Early-Modern Joint-Stock Companies

The joint-stock company was not, however, destined to become the predominant form of business enterprise, and certainly not the major vehicle for capital formation in mining and manufacturing in the Industrial Revolution itself. Its inherent weakness, at least for those joint-stock companies operating within the local domestic economy, was its legal status. For English law regarded joint-stock companies as nothing more than large partnerships. Under long-standing commercial law throughout western Europe, from Roman times, a simple partnership (*societas, compagnia*) was subject to unlimited liability for all its partners—and thus for all shareholders in unchartered joint-stock companies. Typically, and usually, partners bore liability for losses in proportion to their capital investments in the firm; but in fact, under customary and common law, all were collectively and severally responsible for all of the debts, losses, and other liabilities of the firm. This sword of Damocles, this prospect of unlimited debt, undoubtedly discouraged those who did not enjoy asymmetric information, with an intimate knowledge of the company's business, from buying shares in such companies (see, in general, Scott 1912, 1:1–14, 150–65, 439–72).

The joint-stock companies discussed previously, those in foreign trade and those that were the most important in the early-modern English economy, enjoyed a major benefit and advantage over most others: possession of a charter of incorporation. Such charters were derived from the constitutions of medieval English guilds and civic corporations, which made them, as a *corpus*, a separate body and legal entity that could sue and be sued in their own corporate name, without financially or otherwise legally obligating or involving in any way the individual status or the fortunes of its members. For a joint-stock corporation, that meant in particular limited liability: that is, the liability of each individual shareholder was limited to the amount that he or she had agreed to pay in buying the shares, usually on margin.

Curiously enough, the English never availed themselves of a compromise form of business organization that the French government (and then other European governments) had sanctioned from about 1670: the *société en commandite*. It provided limited liability to all those shareholders (or silent partners) who took no active role in the operations of the company, reserving complete, unlimited liability only for those shareholders who did take an active entrepreneurial role. Of course, the whole issue of limited liability is really one of risk allocation and moral hazard: to the extent that shareholders, that is, those with equity in the firm, are protected by limited liability, the firm's creditors (lenders, bond or debenture holders), are thus subject to increased risk of loss in the event of the firm's failure. In compensation for such increased risks, these creditors may have demanded higher interest rates (Heywood 1992; Price 1981).

The other significant limitation, and one that applied to virtually all joint-stock companies from the mid-sixteenth to very late seventeenth century, was the absence of an organized and effective stock market; that is, a secondary market in securities. For obviously most investors would have been reluctant to buy shares in a joint-stock company without the opportunity to recover their capital investment by the resale of the shares to other parties. Indeed, one strong incentive to buy such shares was to realize a capital gain through their subsequent sale, even if, of course, purchasers also bore a risk of capital losses. While the wealthier, more prominent, and influential businessmen did have some prospect of finding individual brokers to handle such secondary stock sales (and purchases, for those who wished to acquire new or more shares), most potential investors did not.

In 1695, however, England did gain its own London Stock Exchange (or Royal Exchange): beginning with the regularly scheduled meetings of stockbrokers or "jobbers" in London coffeehouses in or near Lombard Street, near the location of the new Bank of England, so recently established, in 1694. By that time, England already possessed 137 joint-stock companies, for domestic and foreign enterprises; and the creation of the London Stock Exchange soon encouraged the formation of many more new, and generally unchartered and unincorporated, joint-stock companies (Scott 1912, 1:326–87; Michie 1999). That in turn eventually spawned a speculative boom, especially in the years from 1711, from the formation of the South Sea Company (with a royal charter) to the infamous South Sea Bubble of 1720–21—a speculative era much akin to that of the 1920s.[87]

That story is far too complex to discuss here. Suffice it to say that the South Sea Company was formed ostensibly to acquire a monopoly on British trade in the Pacific, a dubious proposition, since that trade was firmly controlled by Spain—a nation then very hostile to Great Britain. But its real purpose was to acquire most of the outstanding national debt, which had ballooned during the costly War of the Spanish Succession, from 1701 to 1714: that is, the national debt not then held by the Bank of England and the East India companies. This amounted to £31,490,800 sterling, or 63.2 percent of the total permanent national debt. In essence, the company proposed to buy up or exchange that debt, much of it short term, for perpetual South Sea stock, paying 5 percent, and readily marketable on the London Stock Exchange.

In the final stage of this remarkable enterprise, in 1720, when the company had to raise new capital—that is, by selling new stock issues—its directors unwisely sought to curb the competition from other joint-stock companies in the capital market by having Parliament enact statute 6 George I cap. 18—thereafter known as the Bubble Act. It forbade the sale of any shares on the stock exchange issued by any joint-stock company that did not already possess a charter of incorporation, or one that possessed a charter issued for some other purpose. In August, the South Sea Company sought to enforce the act by securing writs of *scire facias* against some unchartered companies and companies with dubious charters. At the same time, the company directors were engaged in illegal activities—as later revealed—to inflate the prices of South Sea Company stock in order to exchange fewer shares for outstanding government debt issues, thus feeding the now expanding "bubble."

They failed miserably to anticipate the consequences. As the stock market prices of the affected companies fell sharply, and as prices of other stocks fell in the ensuing panic, those who had bought stocks "on margin," usually with a 10 percent down payment, with "call loans" for the balance, received a demand from their creditors to pay the full amount owing immediately. The same was true for many merchants who had used stock as collateral for other loans. That meant the forced sale of not only the affected stocks, but also of perfectly good stocks, in order to raise sufficient funds to pay creditors. It was the stock market equivalent of Gresham's Law.

The obvious political consequence of the ensuing horrendous stock market crash was a Parliamentary inquiry, begun in December 1720. Among the major discoveries was indisputable evidence that South Sea Company officials had bribed government ministers, other members of Parliament, and royal officials; and also, as indicated earlier, evidence of illegalities in inflating share prices.[88] According to many historians, so traumatic were both the financial losses from the Bubble and the stench of corruption that henceforth the government and Parliament interpreted the Bubble Act in highly restrictive terms. In particular, Parliament made incorporation extremely difficult: it now required, in all instances, a costly private act of Parliament, which in turn generally required that all or most of the subscribed capital be placed on deposit with the Bank of England until that incorporation act was formally approved. Very few if any small companies, especially those just starting operations, could have then afforded to pay for such acts and acquire the required charters of incorporation.

In the 105 years of the Bubble era that followed, until its repeal in 1825, the only notable exceptions, that is, the only joint-stock corporations that did acquire such charters, were the canal companies in the 1780s and 1790s. Why they were exceptions is obvious: they needed large capital investments and clearly served the general public good, for such transportation improvements were desperately needed for the expanding market of the Industrial Revolution. Obviously canal companies could not have raised the required capitals except by joint-stock financing. In any event, the authorization for the creation of a canal company, with monopoly rights and with necessary public expropriations (eminent domain), also required private acts of Parliament.

The chief response to the view that the Bubble Act impeded capital formation in British industry, and thus implicitly impeded industrialization itself, is the obvious fact that the Industrial Revolution nevertheless did take place during this very era of the Bubble restriction. Phyllis Deane and others have argued in particular that neither the technological needs of the Industrial Revolution nor the scale of enterprise, in turn a function of commercial scales, required large initial amounts of capital, citing in particular the growth of the cotton industry (Deane 1965, 203–6; see also Ashton 1955, 118–21). But when one considers the vastly larger scale required for the new coke-fueled and steam-powered iron industry—in mining, smelting, and refining—one may contend that had chartered and incorporated joint-stock financing been available, without the legal and financial encumbrances just outlined, the British Industrial Revolution might have progressed faster and earlier, with better-financed and larger-scale industrial enterprises. At the same time, we should also consider, in terms of the previously discussed Weber-Tawney thesis, that the virtual absence of joint-stock financing made entrepreneurial profit reinvestment (or profit retention) all the more important for industrial capital formation during that early, pre-1825 phase, of the Industrial Revolution.

Some Conclusions on Entrepreneurship in Early Modern England

As was stressed in the introduction to this current study, Richard Tawney's lifelong pursuit of the origins of a distinctly new and "modern" form of capitalism—so different from its medieval forms—implicitly involved seeking out the origins of modern capitalist entrepreneurship, and thus the origins of the modern Industrial Revolution, that is, from the second half of the eighteenth century. The thesis of this study is that those origins are to be found, not in Tawney's century (1540–1640), but rather in the ensuing century, 1640–1740, that is, from the Civil War era, and the era of Puritan ascendancy, to the eve of the Industrial Revolution. The corollary and ancillary thesis is that such new forms of entrepreneurship, if not entirely explaining how the modern Industrial Revolution came about, certainly constituted the most vital force in producing it—and in its true homeland of Great Britain (England, Scotland, Wales). While some economic historians dispute the reality of the Industrial Revolution, pointing out the continued low levels of economic growth until, say, the 1830s or 1840s,[89] the very idea that there had been no Industrial Revolution is hardly worthy of serious debate. For the ensuing and completely unprecedented rates of sustained aggregate economic growth, demographic growth, and growth in per capita incomes, from the 1840s until World War I, could not have taken place without a prior industrial revolution: that is, without a truly revolutionary transformation of virtually all sectors of the economy, with backward and forward linkages to industry. How could England and Wales have more than tripled their populations in the century from 1811 to 1911—from 10.563 million to 36.136 million—while not only fully feeding that far higher population (from imports) but also experiencing a 2.76-fold rise in the real wage index (for building craftsmen, from 49 to 135), and a 43.4 percent decline in mortality rates (from 25.6/1,000 in 1811 to 14.5/1,000 in 1911)? That truly marks a fundamental watershed in human history, for never before had all such forms of economic growth ever been so combined and sustained (providing a virtual escape from the Malthusian Trap).[90]

If, surely, it is impossible to refute or otherwise negate the significant roles that entrepreneurs did play, not only in creating and fashioning that Industrial Revolution, but also in laying its foundations in that crucial century of 1640–1740, then we must conclude that early-modern England (then Great Britain) was blessed with a very substantial number of practically innovative, highly productive and successful, profit-maximizing entrepreneurs, arguably more so than any other region—except possibly Holland and the northern American colonies (which were then virtually an extension of England). As documented in some detail in this study, the very considerable number of both institutional and technological innovations that did take place in this crucial century—not just in industry, but also in agriculture, overseas trade, and finance—illustrate how successful British entrepreneurs were in implementing and ensuring their success. Who would doubt their vital importance for the ensuing Industrial Revolution, and for Britain's economic growth, up to World War I?

Of course, we must always be careful—as stressed earlier—to distinguish between inventions, which may or may not have any real impact on economic growth, and innovations that so often do have such an impact. We must also recognize that many entrepreneurs, in a market economy, proved to be failures, in that sense—and one thinks of those involved in trying but failing to create and use coke fuels, before Abraham Darby (e.g., Dud Dudley). Most economic historians are instinctively inclined to study successes rather than failures; and also to do so without having the relevant data to measure those successes, except for some general indications of long-term results. We do not, therefore, usually possess any mechanism to measure the actual financial rewards that accrued to the individual entrepreneurs who initiated the productive and profitable innovations. Furthermore, in view of the prior discussion of both the Protestant Ethic and of institutional restrictions (the Bubble Act) their financial rewards may have been chiefly in the growth of their enterprises (including amalgamations, as the winners took over the assets of the losers).

We should also qualify the term *profit-maximizing*. It should be used only in the context of the ethos of so many of these entrepreneurs, for reasons examined in that initial and core section of this study: on the relationship between religion (Dissenters), social and political institutions, and entrepreneurship in the crucial century 1640–1760. In particular, this study has focused on those political and institutional changes that flowed from, or at least ensued from, the Glorious Revolution of 1688, including in particular, the Financial Revolution, culminating with Pelham's Conversion of 1749–57. That also included the remarkable success of so many new joint-stock companies in this era, though we must also note that for many their successes dated from the earlier, post-Restoration period (i.e., from 1660). As argued earlier in that section of this study, those political, social, and institutional changes were a very major factor in promoting and ensuring the economic success of so many entrepreneurs.

That brings us to the important issue of the social status of entrepreneurs in early-modern, or post-1640, England. This study has, quite obviously, solidly endorsed the Weber-Tawney thesis, in particular the view that, if entrepreneurial success came to be viewed—certainly by the mid-seventeenth century (and just as certainly not in the mid-sixteenth century)—as a positive sign of Election, that is, to enjoy Paradise with God in the hereafter, then that change in both religious and social *mentalité* itself proved to be a socioeconomic revolution in making highly individualistic and intensely competitive capitalist entrepreneurship, successful entrepreneurship, not just socially acceptable, but socially meritorious.

That was in stark contrast to prevalent views of medieval society that had stressed the overall primacy of the entire community—especially urban communities—over the individual, and that so often viewed business success as a threat to social harmony, while also reflecting common religious views that scorned not just usury but profit-seeking avarice.[91] A very common belief in medieval society (indeed to the early seventeenth century) was the oft-quoted biblical statement of Jesus (Matthew 19:24): that "it is easier for a camel to go through the eye of a needle than for a rich man to enter into the kingdom of God." So many in medieval society had assumed that those who did become rich had done so only at the direct expense of the rest of society—and not from a creative, innovative, productive entrepreneurship that brought about economic growth, and rising real incomes, to the benefit of most of society. To be sure, as stressed earlier, Calvinism (or Protestantism in general) in its first century, to the 1640s, was as hostile to usury, and perhaps to capitalism in general, as the Catholics were and had been. But from the Civil War era such hostilities virtually vanished (in Holland as well as in England), to permit and promote a revolutionary change in general social attitudes about competitive capitalist entrepreneurship and to business enterprises in general.

At the same time, the peculiar success of so many (but not all, obviously) English Dissenters and Scottish Presbyterians in the conjoined worlds of science and business during the later seventeenth and eighteenth centuries also reflected the impact of the post-Restoration religious, political, and social restrictions imposed on them by Parliament's Corporation and Test Acts. For those restrictions were only partially removed by the 1689 Toleration Act, following the Glorious Revolution. As argued earlier, however, the ensuing state of quasi-toleration, ensuring a distinctive minority status for Dissenters, may, if only in part, help to explain their entrepreneurial successes. A specifically important attribute of that legislated minority status were the Academies, which the Dissenters were thus forced to establish, since they had been denied entry into traditional educational institutions. For certainly these new academies had fostered in a very material sense those entrepreneurial successes. In other words, some institutional limitations that appear to have been harmful may in fact prove to have been the key spurs to successful entrepreneurial innovations and, in more general terms, to economic growth itself, in early-modern England.

There remains, finally, one presumed institutional impediment to business organization, and thus possibly to entrepreneurial success to be considered: the Bubble Act, enduring from 1720 to 1825; or more correctly the ways in which Parliament interpreted that act to prevent the formation of joint-stock companies during this era. Whether or not business enterprises and their leading entrepreneurs would have enjoyed a very different and perhaps more profitable existence during the ensuing Industrial Revolution without the Bubble Act, is an exercise in counterfactual economic history that does not now seem worthwhile exploring.

Notes

[1] These were chiefly Calvinist-oriented Protestants who had refused to swear an oath to accept the Thirty-nine Articles of the established Church of England. As correctly stated in the online Answers.com: "The Thirty-Nine Articles of Religion were established in 1563...and are those finally agreed by the convocation of the Church of England in 1571. They comprise a set of doctrinal statements which were intended to define the position of the reformed Church of England. Printed as an appendix to the 1662 Book of Common Prayer, their declared purpose is 'for the avoiding of diversities of opinions and for the establishing of consent touching true religion.' They steer a careful—and sometimes ambiguous—path between Catholic and reformed doctrines. Subscription to them is still required of the clergy, but since 1865 only a general affirmation is required."

[2] The most important study is Merton 1970, especially chap. 4: "Puritanism and Cultural Values," 55–79; and chap. 6: "Puritanism, Pietism, and Science," 112–36. See also Merton 1938, 1957; Thorner 1952; Mason 1953; Hill 1964a, 1964b, 1964c, 1965a; Kearney 1964, 1965; Rabb 1965; Hill 1965b, providing comments on both Kearney and Rabb; Rabb 1966, a note in reply to Hill; Musson and Robinson 1960, 1969; Musson 1972, his collected essays; Calder 1953. On this point see also Landes 1998, 176–77.

[3] See Davis 1973a, 310: "Dissent was strongest in northern and Midland England, where industry was growing most rapidly, and an extraordinarily high proportion of known inventors, innovators, and successful entrepreneurs of the later eighteenth century have been shown to be Dissenters." See also Ashton 1948, 17–21. He also observes that "the growth of industry was connected historically with the rise of groups which dissented from the Church."

[4] Richard Tawney taught at the London School of Economics from 1917 to 1949 (serving as professor of economic history from 1931). See Fisher 1961, 1-14; Wright 1987; Terrill 1974.

[5] See also Weber 1961, part 4, "The Origins of Modern Capitalism," 207–70 (and especially chapter 20: "The Evolution of the Capitalist Spirit," pp. 258–70). See also the following note.

[6] John Calvin (1509–1564) published his seminal *Institutes of the Christian Religion* in 1536 (Calvin 1960, 1961 1960). See, inter alia, Harkness 1958; Bainton 1952; Biéler 1959.

[7] For the following, see sources cited in nn. 5 and 6 above, and n. 10 below.

[8] See the sources in nn. 5–7 above, and n. 11 below.

[9] From Answers.com: "Riches, avarice, and worldly gain personified as a false god in the New Testament. Middle English, from Late Latin *mammon*, from Greek *mamōnās*, from Aramaic *māmonā*, riches, probably from Mishnaic Hebrew *māmôn*."

[10] For an important overview, very favorable to the Weber-Tawney thesis, see Landes 2003; and even more so, Landes 1998, 174–81, and 516 (see n. 2 above). Needless to say, I fully endorse his views, even though, as Landes notes (177), "most historians today would look upon the Weber thesis as implausible and unacceptable." For other views, see in particular Lehmann and Roth 1985; Turner 2000: in particular Elster 2000, Hamilton 2000, Engerman 2000; Besnard 1970; Munro 1973, a review article based on Besnard; Mitzman 1970; Schumpeter 1991; Fischoff 1944; Hill 1961; Luthy 1963, 1964; Eisenstadt 1968; Van Stuivenberg 1975; Burrell 1964; Kitch 1967. For the chief critics, see also Robertson 1933; Fanfani 1935; and especially Samuelsson 1961.

[11] For some of the literature on the relationship between Protestantism and a new "capitalism" in Tawney's century, to 1640, in both England and Scotland, see the sources in n. 10, and also Jones 1997; George and George 1958; Burrell 1960; Hill 1964b; Ashton 1965, a critique of Christopher Hill's writings on this theme; Trevor Roper 1967; Little 1969; Marshall 1980; Durston and Eales 1996. But, for another valuable perspective, see O'Connell 1976. For the usury question, see nn. 24–29 and accompanying text.

[12] See, inter alia: Heal and O'Day 1977; O'Day 1986; Cliffe 1984, 1988; Durston and Eales 1996; Wedgwood 1966, 1970a, 1970b.

[13.] The Corporation Act, 1661: statute 13 Car. II c. 1 was the initial stage of the Earl of Clarendon's program to reassert Anglican supremacy after the Restoration: it required anyone holding municipal office to qualify by taking communion with the Church of England. The Test Act, 1673: 25 Car. II c. 2 required all officeholders under the Crown, including members of Parliament, to receive communion according to the rites of the Church of England (Thirty-nine Articles) at least once a year, and to make a declaration against the Catholic doctrine of transubstantiation. Neither was repealed until 1828, which repeal was followed by the Catholic Emancipation Act of 1829.

[14] The Unitarians, who denied the divinity of Christ, owed their origins to the sixteenth-century Italian theologian Lelio Sozzini (1525–62), whose followers, principally in Poland (to which Sozzini had fled), were called Socinians. The Methodists were founded by John and Charles Wesley, at Oxford's Holy Club, in 1729 (nicknamed "Methodists" by critics).

[15] More, formally, the Act of Toleration, enacted on May 24, 1689, as statute 1 William & Mary, c. 18, was entitled: "An Act for Exempting their Majestyes Protestant Subjects dissenting from the Church of England from the Penalties of certaine Lawes." It included all non-Conformists except Unitarians. See also Mijers 2007; Troost 2005; Claydon 2002. William III's rule and the victory of the Glorious Revolution was not ensured, however, until his victory over James II and his Irish armies, at the Battle of the Boyne, in 1690. See the intriguing essay by Goldstone (2002).

[16] Ashton 1948, 19, noting that "this view is supported by a consideration of the part played...by the stream of energy that poured into England from Presbyterian Scotland after (though not immediately after) the Union of 1707." See Herman 2001, especially chap. 12: "Scots in Science and Industry," 320–44. See also West 1975, especially chap. 6, "Scottish Elementary Education," 59–73; and also O'Day 1982.

[17] Cardinal Richelieu, responding to the Catholic clergy's bitter hatred of the Edict of Nantes, had in fact annulled the political clauses in 1629; but the far greater damage was done by Louis XIV in 1685. See also the comments of Ralph Davis, in referring again to the English Dissenters: "Their peculiar social position had no French counterpart, and France was economically the worse for this" (1973a, 310), and, "Although the need for innovation was as strong in France as in England, French society offered a less congenial climate to innovation than did English society" (1973a, 313).

[18] Landes 2006, 8: "That means family, continuity, good marriages, dynastic succession." As he also comments (10): "Within this [English] business world, banking held top rank, and international and large-scale commerce generally enjoyed greater respect than industrial endeavours." Similar arguments for the international importance of family connections, in foreign "diasporas," have been advanced for both French Huguenot and Jewish banking and commercial firms, in the eighteenth and nineteenth centuries.

[19] See in particular: Jonassen 1947; McClelland 1953, 1975; McClelland, Winter, and Winter 1969. See also n. 10 above.

[20] See Thompson 1967. For a corresponding French view on this confessional difference between Catholics and Protestants, see Camus 1981; and McBride 1992.

[21] North and Weingast 1989. See also North 1984, 1985.

[22] See Tracy 1985; Hart, Jonker, and van Zanden 1997; Hart 1991; Fritschy 2003.

[23] See in particular: Dickson 1967; and also Roseveare 1991; and O'Brien 1988, 2002; O'Brien and Hunt 1993; Brewer 1990.

[24] 13 Elizabeth I, c. 8 (1571): in Great Britain, Record Commission, *Statutes of the Realm*, ed. T. E. Tomlins, J. Raithby, et al., 6 vols. (London, 1810–22), 4:1, 542.

[25] Statute 37 Henrici VIII, c. 9 (1545) and Statute 5–6 Edwardi VI c. 20, in *Statutes of the Realm*, 3:996; 4:1, 155.

[26] See Bainton 1952, 247–50, noting few differences between Luther and Calvin on this issue. See n. 6 above.

[27] Harkness 1958, 201–10. See n. 6 above.

[28] Cited in Tawney 1926, 94; see also pp. 61–115.

[29] Coquillette 1993, 94–99, citing also a similar statement from John Blaxton, *The English Usurer* (1634).

[30] Richards 1929, 19–20; and statute 17–18 Victoria c. 90 (1854).

[31] See n. 23 above, and Dickson 1967, table 7, p. 80. Note that in 1711 and 1712, the English Exchequer had sold redeemable debentures with an interest rate of 6.0 percent. But thereafter all annuities were issued at 5.0 percent or less.

[32] See n. 23. Sir Henry Pelham, both chancellor of the exchequer and prime minister (1743–d. 1754), undertook the conversion of the national debt from 1749 to 1752: first, into 3.5 percent consols (Consolidated Stock of the Nation: perpetual redeemable and negotiable annuities); and then from 1757 (by his successor), into 3.0 percent consols, which endured unchanged until 1888, when Chancellor of the Exchequer George Goschen converted them into 2.75 percent annuities, with the provision that they be converted into 2.5 percent annuities in 1903, the rate that prevails to this day for consols sold on the London Stock Exchange. On June 9, 2009, the market price of 2.5 percent consols on the London Stock Exchange was £53.04, to provide a yield of 4.71 percent (i.e., 2.5/53.04). See Dickson 1967, 486–520; Harley 1967, 101–6.

[33] For several different perspectives, but more for the subsequent era, see Williamson 1984; Crafts and Harley 1992; Heim and Mirowski 1987; Mokyr 1987; Black and Gilmore 1990; Heim and Mirowski 1991; Clark 2001, 403–36.

[34] On the English gentry, and its relationships with the peerage or titled aristocracy, the most important study is Mingay 1976. See also for the literature of the debate on the Tawney thesis: Stone 1948; Trevor-Roper 1951, a vigorous (indeed heartless) attack on Stone; Stone 1952; Trevor-Roper 1953; Stone 1956; Kerridge 1969, more concerned with the question of enclosure than with the gentry debate per se; Simpson 1961; Cornwall 1965, 1988; Batho 1967; Aston and Philpin 1987, which reprints Brenner 1982 and Cooper 1978; Cooper 1956; Coss 1995, 2003.

[35] For a contemporary definition of the Tudor gentry, see Smith 1906, chap. 20, pp. 39–40: "Whosoever studieth the lawes of the realme, who studieth in the universities, who professeth liberal sciences, and to be shorte, who can live idly and without manuall labour, and will beare the port, charge and countenance of a gentleman, . . . he shall be taken for a gentleman."

[36] Habakkuk 1958. The proximate cause of Henry's break with Rome was Pope Clement VII's refusal (1529) to grant Henry's divorce from Catherine of Aragon, who had produced only a daughter (Mary, in 1516), when Henry was desperate to have a male heir to ensure the survival of his Tudor dynasty.

[37] For the literature on the Price Revolution, and my own views on inflation, see Munro 2003c, 2004, 2008b. These publications also discuss the now enormous literature on this subject. Tawney did not, in fact, have a good understanding of the Price Revolution, or of inflation in general.

[38] See Phelps Brown and Hopkins 1981, with price indexes for subgroups not in the original publication (1956). Their basket of consumables price index, as calculated in quinquennial means, with a base of 1451–75 = 100, rises from 108.60 in 1511–15 to a peak of 733.20 in 1646–50. My recalculation (unpublished) of their price index, from their own working papers in the Archives of the British Library of Political and Economic Science, and using a different methodology (based on actual prices) rises from a quinquennial mean of 106.04 in 1511–15 to one of 646.40 in 1646–50 (peaking in the same quinquennium).

[39] For both the evidence and analysis, see Tawney 1941 and nn. 34 above and 40 below.

[40] For Tudor-Stuart era enclosures the literature is again vast. See in particular: Thirsk 1967a, esp. Thirsk 1967b; Thirsk 1984, 1985a; Overton 1996a; McCloskey 1975a, 1975b; Yelling 1977; Kussmaul 1990; Allen 1992; Mingay 1968; Brewer 1972; Wordie 1983.

[41] See in particular Habakkuk 1940. See also the sources cited in n. 40 above and n. 44 below.

[42] See the literature on this debate in n. 34 above. The most trenchant (and often unfair) critics of the Tawney thesis were Eric Kerridge, Hugh Trevor-Roper (Lord Dacre), and J. P. Cooper.

[43] Bettey 2003; Delorme 1989; Bowie 1987; Martins and Williamson 1994; Kerridge 1973, chap. 4, "The Great Inventions," 103–29; Kerridge 1967; Overton 1996a, esp. chap. 3, "Agricultural Output and Productivity, 1500–1800," 63–132.

[44] See the sources cited in nn. 40, 43 above; and also the following: Thirsk 1967c, 1985b; Jones 1967; Mingay 1977; Broad 1980; Overton 1984; Outhwaite 1986; Clay 1984, vol. 1, chap. 3, "Rural Society," 53–101, and chap. 4, "The Progress of Agriculture," 102–41; Campbell and Overton 1991, especially the studies by Overton, Allen, Shiel, and Clark; Campbell and Overton 1993; Overton 1996b; Allen 1999; Wrigley 2006. The most recent study is Allen 2008.

[45] On the importance of mortgaging enclosed lands to furnish capital, see Hudson 2004.

[46] Schumpeter 1949. See also Schumpeter 1961, 1987, 1989, 1997; Backhaus 2003.

[47] See sources cited in nn. 40, 43–44.

[48] See Hamilton 1928, 1929a, 1929b, 1934, 1936, 1942, 1947, 1952; and Munro 2007a.

[49] Keynes 1930, 2:152–63, esp. 154–55: "It is the teaching of this Treatise that the wealth of nations is enriched, not during Income Inflations, but during Profit Inflations—at times, that is to say, when prices are running away from costs"; and on p. 163: "The intervening Profit Inflation which created the modern world was surely worth while if we take a long view."

[50] See the Phelps Brown "basket of consumables" composite price index, in n. 38 above.

[51] Van der Wee 1963, vol. 1, appendix 45/2, pp. 525–27. The outbreak of the Revolt of the Low Countries in 1568 renders subsequent data, when available, useless, in this context. The real interest rate is the nominal rate less (minus) the rate of inflation.

[52] See the following: Nef 1923, in particular, vol. 1, part 2, "Coal and Industrialism," 133–264 (chap. 2 of this section is entitled "An Early Industrial Revolution," 165–89); Nef 1934, 1936, 1937; Nef 1950, part 1 (1494–1640), chap. 4, "Progress of Capitalist Industry," 65–88.

[53] See Wrigley et al. 1997, appendix 9, pp. 613–16. See also Wrigley and Schofield 1980, 528–29.

[54] See in particular: Coleman 1956; 1975b, 35–49; 1975a, chap. 5, "Occupations and Industries, 1450–1650," 69–90, chap. 9, "Industrial Change, 1650–1750," 151–72; Rackham 1976, 1980; Zell 1993. For an overview, see Hatcher 1993, 31–55. In effect, while acknowledging the many faults in Nef's research and analyses, he lends support to the Nef thesis, as does Brinley Thomas in two articles (1985, 1986). See also nn. 55, 64 below.

[55] See figure 5.1. The charcoal prices are taken from college and institutional accounts in Cambridge, Eton (Berkshire, near Windsor), and Westminster (London); the coal prices are similarly from these three same sources, plus (later) Greenwich, which I took from the Phelps Brown and Beveridge price data in the Archives of the British Library of Political and Economic Science (at the London School of Economics). The timber prices are from Cambridge alone, taken from Bowden 1967, table 6, pp. 846–50. I have converted his original base, 1450–99 = 100 (7.99s for 100 faggots) to the PBH base of 1451–75. Unfortunately, we do not possess any usable coal price series that may be compared with charcoal prices, until 1584—with the exception of coal prices alone at Hull (1471–1700): Hatcher 1993, table B.4, pp. 577–78. The statistical table on which this figure has been based has been published in Munro 2008a, table 8, p. 57.

[56] Hatcher has correctly observed that, at Westminster, "by the close of the 1630s charcoal was virtually twice as expensive as coal [in terms of heat produced)" (1993, 39). An even greater difference can be found at Cambridge, if we also take account of a second factor: that a ton of charcoal and a ton of coal have almost identical calorific values, a comparison disguised in measuring charcoal prices in loads (about one ton) and coal prices in chaldrons (36 heaped bushels = 28 cwt. = 3,135 lb. or 1.568 tons). In the 1630s, a ton of charcoal at Cambridge cost (on average) 27.38 shillings, but a ton of coal cost only 10.70 shillings (Rogers 1866–1902, 4:385–87, 5:398–402). But in terms of just relative prices, with a base 1580–89 = 100, the charcoal price index had risen to 140.3 in 1630–39, while the coal price index had risen to 126.9. For calorific values, see Hatcher 1993, 39.

[57] From Answers.com. The best example is Dud Dudley (1599–1684). The illegitimate son of Edward Sutton, the Ninth Baron of Dudley, he was given the task of managing the family's ironworks in Staffordshire. He was the first to experiment with smelting iron ore in a coal-fired furnace. Dudley patented his innovation in 1621, but the poor quality of his metal limited its sale. Dudley's work culminated in Abraham Darby's coke-fired furnace in 1709. See n. 64 below.

[58] Mokyr 1990. See also see the sources cited in nn. 53, 55, above.

[59] Glassmaking is good example of an industry that had to adopt the new furnace technology, because it obviously could not have transported its delicate products from forest sites along bad roads to urban

markets; and indeed it had to locate as closely as possible to those markets. See Crossley 1972; Hatcher 1993, 422–58; Mokyr 1990, 62 (also for the date).

[60] See n. 53 above.

[61] For the evidence on rising real incomes in this era, at least in the English building trades, see Phelps Brown and Hopkins 1956; Allen 2001; and Munro 2002.

[62] In 1640, when textiles still accounted for almost all of English exports, 92.3 percent by value, the woolens of the Old Draperies still exceeded the value of the products of the New Draperies (bays, says, serges, perpetuanas, etc.), but not by much: 48.9 percent for the former vs. 43.3 percent, for the latter (Clay 1984, vol. 2, table 13, p. 144; see also Van der Wee 2003).

[63] *Columbia Encyclopedia:* "Coke is a solid carbonaceous residue derived from low-ash, low-sulfur bituminous coal. The volatile constituents of the coal (including water, coal-gas and coal-tar) are driven off by baking [the coal] in an *airless* oven at temperatures as high as 1,000 degrees Celsius, so that the fixed carbon and residual ash are fused together. Since the smoke-producing constituents are driven off during the coking of the coal, coke forms a desirable fuel."

[64] See the sources cited in n. 54 above; and also Ashton 1924, 1–23; Ashton and Sykes 1964; Schubert 1957; Hammersley 1957, 1973, 1976; Flinn 1958, 1959, 1978, 1984, esp. 23–35, 286–328; Jack 1977, esp. chap. 2, pp. 66–121; Riden 1977; Hyde 1973, 1977, esp. chap. 1, pp. 7–22, also chap. 3, pp. 42–52; Pollard 1980; Harris 1988. See also Mokyr 1990, 93, 160, who cites Flinn (1958, 1978) to dispute the "scarcity of wood" thesis, stating that Flinn's "evidence on prices does not confirm this view." But Flinn provides no statistics on prices in these publications; and the evidence on wood, charcoal, and coal prices in my figure 5.1 contradicts Flinn's views, though, as noted above, only from the 1640s. No comparative prices are provided in Flinn 1984; but see table 9.4, pp. 303–4, for an index of coal prices, 1700–1830. The quinquennial mean index (base 1770–79 = 100) falls from 90.94 in 1701–5 to 80.22 in 1726–30, and thereafter rises slowly into the early era of the Industrial Revolution, reaching 95.60 in 1771–75; over the same period, the Phelps Brown–Hopkins composite price index (adjusted to this same base) rises from 70.85 in 1701–5 to 103.45 in 1771–75: i.e., rising more than the coal price index.

[65] Wrigley 1988, 54. See also Wrigley 2000; Hatcher 1993, 555–56 (also citing a figure of 15 millions tonnes for 1800), stating that "the major turning point for the British coal industry occurred in the second half of the eighteenth century"); Pollard 1980.

[66] Flinn 1984, table 1.2, p. 26, providing an estimate aggregate coal production of 3.033 million tonnes. Hatcher's subsequently published coal statistics differ for 1700, as noted: 2.640 million tonnes. See Hatcher 1993 and n. 64 above. 1 metric tonne = 1000 kilograms = 2,205 lb. = 1.1025 short ton.

[67] Wrigley 1988, 54–55, also stating (n. 52) that "the heat output of combustion of bone-dry wood is 4,200 kcal/kg compared with 8,000 kcal/kg for bituminous coal." For a very similar estimate, see Hatcher 1993, 39.

[68] A recent, iconoclastic dissenting view can be found in Clark and Jacks 2007. I must note that their data set is very different from and—in my view—less complete than what I have produced in figure 5.1 (see n. 55, above) ; and their comparisons of fuel prices are very different as well.

[69] See nn. 65–67 above.

[70] See Unger 1980, 1981, 1987; Cipolla 1965; Boxer 1969; Elbl 1985, 1994; Lewis and Runyan 1985.

[71] Gould 1970; Challis 1967, 1971, 1978; Van der Wee 2003. See n. 62 above.

[72] After 1552, cloth export statistics are available only for London, which, however, then accounted for over 90 percent of total exports, and virtually all of its exports were sent to the Antwerp market. Statistics extracted from Carus-Wilson and Coleman 1963; Bridbury 1982, appendix F, pp. 118–22; Gould 1970, 136; and Fisher 1940. A standard and fully finished broadcloth measured 24 yards in length and 1.75 yds in width.

[73] Its original title was the "Mysterie and Companie of the Marchants Adventurers for the discoverie of regions, dominions, islands and place unknown." In 1556, by an act of Parliament, its name was shortened to the Fellowship of English Merchants for discovery of New Trades. See the following note.

[74] The classic study is and remains Scott 1912. Similar joint-stock companies were set up in the Dutch Republic, or Republic of the United Provinces (fundamentally established by the Union of Utrecht, in January 1579); and they may have existed earlier in the former county of Holland—known as *rederij* in maritime shipping and commerce.

[75] Scott 1912, 1:18–21, 2:36–69, carrying the history of the company to its effective end in 1699, when it lost its monopoly in the Russian-Persian trade. The company was not dissolved, however, until as late as 1917. See also Willan 1956, 1968, 1973.

[76] Scott 1912, 1:8–12. See also Carus-Wilson 1933; Van Houtte 1940, 1961; Van der Wee 1963, vol. 2, part 1, chaps. 2–5; Davis 1976.

[77] See Scott 1912, 1:18. He speculates that the Russia Company's first governor, Sebastian Cabot (ca. 1476–1557), son of the ill-fated John Cabot (whose last naval expedition disappeared at sea, in 1498, without a trace), may have learned about joint-stock organization from his native Italy.

[78] One major new trading enterprise not mentioned here, because it was not undertaken by a joint-stock company, was the Eastland Company, established in 1579, by members of its parent organization, the Merchants Adventurers, with the objective of marketing English woolens in Prussia and Livonia, in the eastern Baltic. Marking England's first reentry into the Baltic trades in more than a century, the Eastland Company faced an overwhelming Dutch supremacy in these trades, and was thus doomed to failure, especially with inadequate capitalization. On Dutch trade and Baltic commerce, see in particular Israel 1989; De Vries and Van der Woude 1995; Unger 1997.

[79] Technically, the first successful English maritime venture was the arrival of the *Swallow* in the harbor of Livorno (Leghorn) on June 23, 1573; and Livorno would continue to be very important for English trade in the Mediterranean. See Pagano de Divitiis 1997, 5. See also Scott 1912, 2:83–88; Cawston and Keane 1968, 67–85.

[80] See Munro 2007b. As Ralph Davis has commented, "When the cold gales of autumn blew from the uplands of Asia Minor and the Balkans, the prosperous Turk or Persian counted himself lucky to be wrapped in the thickest and heaviest of English woollens" (1961, 122–23).

[81] See Davis 1961, 126–37; 1962, 1–57, 228–56; 1973b, 20–31; Pagano di Divitiis 1997, 41–55, especially table 2.1, p. 43.

[82] In the decade 1710–20, the decennial mean fine silver exports of the English East India Company were 41,133.6 kilograms, compared to 37,108.1 kilograms by the Dutch Company. Gaastra 1983; Chaudhuri 1968, table 1, pp. 497–98.

[83] For the English East India Company, see Scott 1912, 2:89–206; Cawston and Keane 1968, 86–153; Chaudhuri 1965, 1968, 1978; Bowen, Lincoln, and Rigby 2002; Bowen 2006.

[84] Sources: Fisher 1950; Davis 1954, 1973a, tables 1–5, pp. 52–57; Clay 1984, 2:103–202, esp. tables 10, p. 125; 11–15, pp. 142–46; 16–20, pp. 155–60; 21, p. 180.

[85] Statistics extracted or calculated from Mitchell and Deane 1962, 274–337; and Mathias 1983, 87–88.

[86] Davis 1973b, 250–87; 1973a, 26–40; Hobsbawm 1954. See also Parker and Smith 1978; Rabb 1976, 3–34; De Vries 1976, 1–29.

[87] For the following, and also for the complex, most detailed story, see Scott 1912, 1:387–438, 3:287–360. See also Dickson 1967; and Neal 1990.

[88] See sources cited in the preceding note.

[89] See n. 33 above.

[90] Scotland is not included because of inadequate data to make these comparisons. See Phelps Brown and Hopkins 1956, 30–31; and Wrigley et al. 1997, 613–16. See also Komlos 2000; Thomas 1985. For a different perspective, see Clark 2007.

[91] See Tawney 1926 and other studies discussed in nn. 2–29 above and accompanying text.

References

Allen, Robert C. 1992. *Enclosure and the Yeoman: The Agricultural Development of the South Midlands, 1450–1850.* Oxford: Clarendon Press.

———. 1999. "Tracking the Agricultural Revolution in England." *Economic History Review*, 2nd ser., 52:209–35.

———. 2001. "The Great Divergence in European Wages and Prices from the Middle Ages to the First World War." *Explorations in Economic History* 38(4): 411–47.

———. 2008. "The Nitrogen Hypothesis and the English Agricultural Revolution: A Biological Analysis." *The Journal of Economic History* 68(1): 182–210

Ashton, Robert. 1965. "Puritanism and Progress. " *Economic History Review*, 2nd ser., 17:579–87.

Ashton, T. S. 1924. *Iron and Steel in the Industrial Revolution.* Manchester: Manchester University Press, reprinted 1951.

———. 1948. *The Industrial Revolution, 1760–1830*. New York: Oxford University Press.

———. 1955. *An Economic History of England: The 18th Century*. London: Methuen

Ashton, T. S., and Joseph Sykes. 1964. *The Coal Industry of the Eighteenth Century.* 2nd ed. Manchester: Manchester University Press.

Aston, T. H., and C.H.E. Philpin, eds. 1987. *The Brenner Debate: Agrarian Class Structure and Economic Development in Pre-industrial Europe*. Cambridge: Cambridge University Press.

Backhaus, Jürgen. 2003. *Joseph Alois Schumpeter: Entrepreneurship, Style, and Vision*. New York: Kluwer Academic Publishers.

Bainton, Roland. 1952. *The Reformation of the Sixteenth Century.* Boston: Beacon Press.

Batho, Gordon. 1967. "Noblemen, Gentlemen, and Yeomen." In *The Agrarian History of England and Wales*, vol. 4, *1500–1640*, ed. Joan Thirsk, 276–306. Cambridge: Cambridge University Press.

Besnard, Philippe, ed. 1970. *Protestantisme et capitalisme: La controverse post-Weberienne*. Paris: A. Colin.

Bettey, Joseph. 2003. "The Development of Water Meadows on the Salisbury Avon, 1665–1690." *Agricultural History Review* 51:163–72.

Biéler, André. 1959. *La pensée économique et sociale de Calvin*. Geneva: Librairie de l'université.

Black, Robert, and Claire Gilmore. 1990. "Crowding Out during Britain's Industrial Revolution." *Journal of Economic History* 50, no. 1: 109–31.

Bodin, Jean. 1946. *The Response of Jean Bodin to the Paradoxes of Malestroit and The Paradoxes, translated from the French Second Edition, Paris 1578*. Trans. George A. Moore. Washington, DC: Country Dollar Press.

Bowden, Peter. 1967. "Agricultural Prices, Farm Profits, and Rents." In *The Agrarian History of England and Wales*, vol. 4, *1500–1640*, ed. Joan Thirsk. Cambridge: Cambridge University Press.

Bowen, H. V. 2006. *The Business of Empire: The East India Company and Imperial Britain, 1756–1833*. Cambridge: Cambridge University Press.

Bowen, H. V., Margarette Lincoln, and Nigel Rigby, eds. 2002. *The Worlds of the East India Company*. Woodbridge, Suffolk: Boydell Press.

Bowie, G. G. 1987. "Watermeadows in Wessex: A Re-evaluation for the Period 1640–1850." *Agricultural History Review* 35:151–58.

Boxer, C. R. 1969. *The Portuguese Seaborne Empire, 1415–1825*. London: Hutchinson.

Brenner, Robert. 1982. "The Agrarian Roots of European Capitalism." *Past and Present* 97:16–113.

Brewer, J. G. 1972. *Enclosures and the Open Fields: A Bibliography*. London: British Agricultural History Society.

Brewer, John. 1990. *The Sinews of Powers: War, Money, and the English State, 1688–1783*. Cambridge: Harvard University Press.

Bridbury, A. R. 1982. *Medieval English Clothmaking: An Economic Survey*. London: Heinemann Educational, Pasold Research Fund.

Broad, John. 1980. "Alternate Husbandry and Permanent Pasture in the Midlands, 1650–1800." *Agricultural History Review* 28:77–89.

Burrell, Sidney A. 1960. "Calvinism, Capitalism, and the Middle Classes: Some Afterthoughts on an Old Problem." *Journal of Modern History* 32:129–41.

———, ed. 1964. *The Role of Religion in Modern European History*. New York: Macmillan.

Calder, Ritchie. 1953. *Profile of Science*. London: Allen and Unwin

Calvin, Jean, 1960. *Calvin: Institutes of the Christian Religion*. 2 vols. London: Westminster Press.

———. 1961. *Institution de la religion chrestienne*. 4 vols. Paris: Société d'Édition "Les Belles Lettres."

Campbell, Bruce M. S., and Mark Overton, eds. 1991. *Land, Labour, and Livestock: Historical Studies in European Agricultural Productivity*. Manchester: Manchester University Press.

———. 1993. "A New Perspective on Medieval and Early Modern Agriculture: Six Centuries of Norfolk Farming, c.1250–c.1850." *Past and Present* 141:38–105.

Camus, Albert. 1981. *Correspondance, 1932–1960*. Paris: Gallimard.

Carus-Wilson, Eleanora M. 1933. "The Origins and Early Development of the Merchant Adventurers' Organization in London as Shown in Their Own Medieval Records." *Economic History Review*, 1st ser., 4:147–76. Reprinted in Eleanora M. Carus-Wilson, *Medieval Merchant Venturers: Collected Studies* (London: Methuen, 1954), 143–82.

Carus-Wilson, Eleanora M., and Olive Coleman. 1963. *England's Export Trade, 1275–1547*. Oxford: Oxford University Press.

Cawston, George, and A. H. Keane. 1968. *The Early Chartered Companies, A.D. 1296–1858*. 1896; New York: B. Franklin.

Challis, Christopher E. 1967. "The Debasement of the Coinage, 1542–1551." *Economic History Review*, 2nd ser., 20:441–66.

———. 1971. "The Circulating Medium and the Movement of Prices in Mid-Tudor England." In *The Price Revolution in Sixteenth-Century England*, ed. Peter Ramsey, 117–46. London: Methuen.

———. 1978. *The Tudor Coinage*. Manchester: Manchester University Press; New York: Barnes and Noble.

Chapman, Stanley. 1992. *Merchant Enterprise in Britain from the Industrial Revolution to World War I*. Cambridge: Cambridge University Press.

Chaudhuri, K. N. 1965. *The English East India Company: The Study of an Early Joint Stock Company, 1600–1640*. London: F. Cass.

———. 1968. "Treasure and Trade Balances: The East India Company's Export Trade, 1660–1720." *Economic History Review*, 2nd ser., 21:480–502.

———. 1978. *The Trading World of Asia and the English East India Company, 1669–1760*. Cambridge: Cambridge University Press.

Cipolla, Carlo. 1965. *Guns, Sails, and Empires: Technological Innovation and the Early Phases of European Expansion 1400–1700*. New York: Pantheon.

Clark, Gregory. 2001. "Debts, Deficits, and Crowding Out: England, 1727–1840." *European Review of Economic History* 5:403–36.

———. 2007. *A Farewell to Alms: A Brief Economic History of the World*. Princeton: Princeton University Press.

Clark, Gregory, and David Jacks. 2007. "Coal and the Industrial Revolution, 1700–1869." *European Review of Economic History* 11:39–72.

Clay, Christopher. 1984. *Economic Expansion and Social Change: England, 1500–1700*. 2 vols. Cambridge: Cambridge University Press.

Claydon, Tony. 2002. *William III*. London: Longman.

Cliffe, J. T. 1984. *The Puritan Gentry: The Great Puritan Families of Early Stuart England*. London: Routledge.

———. 1988. *Puritans in Conflict: The Puritan Gentry during and after the Civil Wars*. London: Routledge.

Coleman, Donald C. 1956. "Industrial Growth and Industrial Revolutions." *Economica* n.s. 23:1–22. Reprinted in *Essays in Economic History*, ed. Eleanora M. Carus-Wilson (London: E. Arnold, 1962), 3:334–52.

———. 1975a. *The Economy of England, 1450–1750*. London: Oxford University Press.

———. 1975b. *Industry in Tudor and Stuart England*. London: Macmillan.

Cooper, J. P. 1956. "The Counting of Manors." *Economic History Review*, 2nd ser., 8:377–86.

———. 1967. "The Social Distribution of Land and Men in England, 1436–1700." *Economic History Review*, 2nd ser., 20:419–40.

———. August 1978. "In Search of Agrarian Capitalism." *Past and Present* 80:20–65.

Coquillette, Daniel. 1993. "The Mystery of the New Fashioned Goldsmiths: From Usury to the Bank of England (1622–1694)." In *The Growth of the Bank as Institution and the Development of Money-Business Law*, ed. Vito Piergiovanni, 94–99. Berlin: Duncker & Humblot.

Cornwall, Julian. 1965. "The Early Tudor Gentry." *Economic History Review*, 2nd ser., 17:456–71.

———. 1988. *Wealth and Society in Early Sixteenth-Century England*. London: Routledge and Kegan Paul.

Coss, Peter R. 1995. "The Formation of the English Gentry." *Past and Present* 147:38–64.

———. 2003. *The Origins of the English Gentry*. Cambridge: Cambridge University Press.

Crafts, N.F.R., and C. K. Harley. 1992. "Output Growth and the British Industrial Revolution: A Restatement of the Crafts-Harley View." *Economic History Review*, 2nd ser., 45:703–30.

Crossley, D. W. 1972. "The Performance of the Glass Industry in Sixteenth-Century England." *Economic History Review*, 2nd ser., 25:421–33.

Crouzet, François. 1991. "The Huguenots and the English Financial Revolution." In *Favorites of Fortune: Technology, Growth, and Economic Development since the Industrial Revolution*, ed. Patrice Higonnet, David Landes, and Henry Rosovsky, 221–66. Cambridge: Harvard University Press.

Davis, Ralph. 1954. "English Foreign Trade, 1660–1700." *Economic History Review*, 2nd ser., 7:150–66.

———. 1961. "England and the Mediterranean, 1570–1670." In *Essays in the Economic and Social History of Tudor and Stuart England, in Honour of R. H. Tawney*, ed. F. J. Fisher, 117–26. Cambridge: Cambridge University Press.

———. 1962. *The Rise of the English Shipping Industry in the Seventeenth and Eighteenth Centuries*. London: Macmillan.

———. 1973a. *English Overseas Trade, 1500–1700*. London: Macmillan.

———. 1973b. *Rise of the Atlantic Economies*. Ithaca, NY: Cornell University Press.

———. 1976. "The Rise of Antwerp and Its English Connection." In *Trade, Government, and Economy in Pre-industrial England: Essays Presented to F. J. Fisher*, ed. Donald C. Coleman and A. H. John, 2–20. London: Weidenfeld and Nicholson.

De Vries, Jan. 1976. *The Economy of Europe in an Age of Crisis, 1600–1750*. Cambridge: Cambridge University Press.

De Vries, Jan, and Ad Van der Woude. 1995. *Nederland 1500–1815: De eerste ronde van moderne economische groei*. Amsterdam: Balans. Translated as *The First Modern Economy: Success, Failure, and Perseverance of the Dutch Economy, 1500–1815* (Cambridge: Cambridge University Press, 1997).

Deane, Phyllis. 1965. *The First Industrial Revolution*. Cambridge: Cambridge University Press.

Delorme, Mary. 1989. "A Watery Paradise: Roland Vaughan and Hereford's 'Golden Vale.'" *History Today* 39:38–43.

Dickson, Peter G. M. 1967. *The Financial Revolution in England: A Study in the Development of Public Credit, 1688–1756*. London: Macmillan; New York: St. Martin's Press.

Durston, Christopher, and Jacqueline Eales, eds. 1996. *The Culture of English Puritanism, 1560–1700*. London: Macmillan.

Eisenstadt, S. N., ed. 1968. *The Protestant Ethic and Modernization: A Comparative View*. New York: Basic Books.

Elbl, Martin. 1985. "The Portuguese Caravel and European Shipbuilding: Phases of Development and Diversity." *Revista da Universidade de Coimbra* 33:543–72.

———. 1994. "The Caravel and the Galleon." In *Cogs, Caravels, and Galleons: The Sailing Ship, 1000–1650*, ed. Robert Gardiner, 91–98. London: Conway Maritime Press.

Elster, Jon. 2000. "Rationality, Economy, and Society." In *The Cambridge Companion to Weber*, ed. Stephen P. Turner, 21–41. Cambridge: Cambridge University Press.

Engerman, Stanley. 2000. "Max Weber as Economist and Economic Historian." In *The Cambridge Companion to Weber*, ed. Stephen P. Turner, 256–71. Cambridge: Cambridge University Press.

Fanfani, Amintore. 1935. *Catholicism, Protestantism, and Capitalism*. London: Sheed & Ward.

Fischoff, Ephraim. 1944. "The Protestant Ethic and the Spirit of Capitalism: The History of a Controversy." *Social Research* 11:61–77.

Fisher, F. J. 1940. "Commercial Trends and Policy in Sixteenth-Century England." *Economic History Review*, 1st ser., 10:95–117.

———. 1950. "London's Export Trade in the Early Seventeenth Century." *Economic History Review*, 2nd ser., 3:151–61.

———. 1961. "Tawney's Century." In *Essays in the Economic and Social History of Tudor and Stuart England, in Honour of R. H. Tawney*, ed. F. J. Fisher, 1–14. Cambridge: Cambridge University Press.

Flinn, Michael. 1958. "Revisions in Economic History: XVII: The Growth of the English Iron Industry, 1660–1760." *Economic History Review*, 2nd ser., 11:144–53.

———. 1959. "Timber and the Advance of Technology: A Reconsideration." *Annals of Science* 15:109–20.

———. 1978. "Technical Change as an Escape from Resource Scarcity: England in the Seventeenth and Eighteenth Centuries. In *Natural Resources in European History: A Conference Report*, ed. Antoni Mączak and William N. Parker, 139–59. Washington, DC: Resources for the Future.

———. 1984. *The History of the British Coal Industry*. Vol. 2, *1700–1830: The Industrial Revolution*. Oxford: Clarendon Press.

Fritschy, Wantje. 2003. "A 'Financial Revolution' Revisited: Public Finance in Holland During the Dutch Revolt, 1568–1648." *Economic History Review*, 2nd ser., 56:57–89.

Gaastra, F. S. 1983. "The Exports of Precious Metal from Europe to Asia by the Dutch East India Company, 1602–1795 A.D." In *Precious Metals in the Medieval and Early Modern Worlds*, ed. John F. Richards, 447–76. Durham, NC: Carolina Academic Press.

George, C., and K. George. 1958. "Protestantism and Capitalism in Pre-Revolutionary England." *Church History* 27:351–71.

Goldstone, Jack A. 2002. "Europe's Peculiar Path: Would the World Be 'Modern' if William III's Invasion of England in 1688 Had Failed?" In *Unmaking the West; What-If Scenarios That Rewrite World History*, ed. Philip E. Tetlock, Ned Lebow, and Geoffrey Parker, 168–196. Ann Arbor: University of Michigan Press.

Gould, John D. 1964. "The Price Revolution Reconsidered." *Economic History Review*, 2nd ser., 17:249–66. Reprinted in *The Price Revolution in Sixteenth-Century England*, ed. Peter H. Ramsey (London: Methuen, 1971), 91–116.

———. 1970. *The Great Debasement: Currency and the Economy in Mid-Tudor England*. Oxford: Oxford University Press.

Habakkuk, H. J. 1940. "English Land Ownership, 1680–1740." *Economic History Review*, 1st ser., 10:2–17.

———. 1958. "The Market for Monastic Property, 1539–1603." *Economic History Review*, 2nd ser., 10:362–80.

Hamilton, Alastair. 2000. "Max Weber's *Protestant Ethic and the Spirit of Capitalism*." In *The Cambridge Companion to Weber*, ed. Stephen P. Turner, 151–71. Cambridge: Cambridge University Press.

Hamilton, Earl J. 1928. "American Treasure and Andalusian Prices, 1503–1660: A Study in the Spanish Price Revolution." *Journal of Economic and Business History* 1:1–35. Reprinted in *The Price Revolution in Sixteenth-Century England*, ed. Peter H. Ramsey (London: Methuen, 1971), 147–81.

———. 1929a. "American Treasure and the Rise of Capitalism, 1500–1700." *Economica* 27:38–57.

———. 1929b. "Imports of American Gold and Silver into Spain, 1503–1660." *Quarterly Journal of Economics* 43:436–72.

———. 1934. *American Treasure and the Price Revolution in Spain, 1501–1650*. Cambridge: Harvard University Press.

———. 1936. *Money, Prices, and Wages in Valencia, Aragon, and Navarre, 1351–1500*. Cambridge: Harvard University Press.

———. 1942. "Profit Inflation and the Industrial Revolution, 1751–1800." *Quarterly Journal of Economics* 56:256–73. Reprinted in *Enterprise and Secular Change: Readings in Economic History*, ed. Frederic C. Lane and Jelle C. Riemersma (London: George Allen and Unwin, 1953), 322–49.

———. 1947. *War and Prices in Spain, 1651–1800*. Cambridge: Harvard University Press.

———. 1952. "Prices as a Factor in Business Growth: Prices and Progress." *Journal of Economic History* 12:325–49.

Hammersley, George. 1957. "The Crown Woods and Their Exploitation in the Sixteenth and Seventeenth Centuries." *Bulletin of the Institute of Historical Research, University of London* 30:154–59.

———. 1973. "The Charcoal Iron Industry and Its Fuel, 1540–1750." *Economic History Review*, 2nd ser., 26:593–613.

———. 1976. "The State and the English Iron Industry in the Sixteenth and Seventeenth Centuries." In *Trade, Government, and Economy in Pre-Industrial England: Essays Presented to F. J. Fisher*, ed. Donald Coleman and A. H. John, 166–86. London: Weidenfeld and Nicholson.

Harkness, Georgia. 1958. *John Calvin: The Man and His Ethics*. New York: H. Holt.

Harley, C. Knick. 1967. "Goschen's Conversion of the National Debt and the Yield on Consols." *Economic History Review*, 2nd ser., 29:101–6.

Harris, John R. 1988. *The British Iron Industry, 1700–1850*. London: Macmillan.

Hart, Marjolein 't. 1991. " 'The Devil or the Dutch': Holland's Impact on the Financial Revolution in England, 1643–1694." *Parliaments, Estates and Representatives* 11, no. 1: 39–52.

Hart, Marjolein 't, Joost Jonker, and Jan Luiten van Zanden, eds. 1997. *Financial History of the Netherlands*. Cambridge: Cambridge University Press.

Hatcher, John. 1993. *The History of the British Coal Industry*. Vol. 1, *Before 1700: Towards the Age of Coal*. Oxford: Clarendon Press.

Heal, Felicity, and Felicity O'Day, eds. 1977. *Church and Society in England: Henry VIII to James I*. London: Macmillan.

Heim, Carol E., and Philip Mirowski. 1987. "Interest Rates and Crowding-Out during Britain's Industrial Revolution." *Journal of Economic History* 47:117–39.

———. 1991. "Crowding Out: A Response to Black and Gilmore." *Journal of Economic History* 51:701–6.

Herman, Arthur. 2001. *How the Scots Invented the Modern World*. New York: Three Rivers Press.

Heywood, Colin. 1992. *The Development of the French Economy, 1750–1914*. Basingstoke: Macmillan.

Hill, Christopher. 1961. "Protestantism and the Rise of Capitalism." In *Essays in the Economic and Social History of Tudor and Stuart England, in Honour of R. H. Tawney*, ed. F. J. Fisher, 15–39. Cambridge: Cambridge University Press.

———. 1964a. "Puritanism, Capitalism, and the Scientific Revolution." *Past and Present* 29:88–97.

———. 1964b. *Society and Puritanism in Pre-Revolutionary England*. London: Secker & Warburg.

———. April 1964c. "William Harvey and the Idea of Monarchy." *Past and Present* 27: 54–57.

———. 1965a. *The Intellectual Origins of the English Revolution*. Oxford: Oxford University Press.

———. 1965b. "Science, Religion and Society in the Sixteenth and Seventeenth Centuries." *Past and Present* 32:110–12.

Hobsbawm, Eric. 1954. "The Crisis of the Seventeenth Century." *Past and Present* 5:33–53 and 6:44–65. Reprinted in *Crisis in Europe, 1560–1660: Essays from Past and Present*, ed. Trevor Aston (London: Routledge and Kegan Paul, 1965), 5–58, 97–112.

Hudson, Patricia. 2004. "Land Markets, Credit and Proto-Industrialization in Britain and Europe." In *Il mercato della terra, seccoli XIII–XVIII*, ed. Simonetta Cavaciocchi, 721–42. Florence: Le Monnier.

Hyde, Charles K. 1973. "The Adoption of Coke-Smelting by the British Iron Industry, 1709–1790." *Explorations in Economic History* 10:397–418.

———. 1977. *Technological Change and the British Iron Industry, 1700–1870*. Princeton: Princeton University Press.

Israel, Jonathan I. 1989. *Dutch Primacy in World Trade, 1585–1740*. Oxford: Clarendon Press.

Jack, Sybil. 1977. *Trade and Industry in Tudor and Stuart England*. London: Allen and Unwin.

Jonassen, Christen T. 1947. "The Protestant Ethic and the Spirit of Capitalism in Norway." *American Sociological Review* 12:676–86.

Jones, E. L., ed. 1967. *Agriculture and Economic Growth in England, 1650–1815*. London: Methuen; New York: Barnes and Noble.

———. 1997. "Capitalism: One Origin or Two?" *Journal of Early Modern History: Contacts, Comparisons, Contrasts* 1, no. 1: 71–76.

Kearney, H. F. 1964. "Puritanism, Capitalism, and the Scientific Revolution." *Past and Present* 28:81–101.

———. 1965. "Puritanism and Science: Problems of Definition." *Past and Present* 31: 104–10.

Kerridge, Eric. 1967. *The Agricultural Revolution*. London: Allen and Unwin.

———. 1969. *Agrarian Problems in the Sixteenth Century and After*. London: Allen and Unwin; New York: Barnes and Noble.

———. 1973. *The Farmers of Old England*. London: Allen and Unwin.

Keynes, John Maynard. 1930. *A Treatise on Money*. 2 vols. London: Macmillan.

Kitch, M. J., ed. 1967. *Capitalism and the Reformation*. London: Longmans.

Komlos, John. 2000. "The Industrial Revolution as the Escape from the Malthusian Trap." *Journal of European Economic History* 29:307–31.

Kussmaul, Ann. 1990. *A General View of the Rural Economy of England, 1538–1840*. Cambridge: Cambridge University Press.

Landes, David. 1998. *The Wealth and Poverty of Nations: Why Some Are So Rich and Some So Poor*. New York: Norton

———. 2003. *The Unbound Prometheus: Technological Change and Industrial Development in Western Europe from 1750 to the Present*. 2nd ed. Cambridge: Cambridge University Press.

———. 2006. *Dynasties: Fortunes and Misfortunes of the World's Great Family Businesses*. New York: Viking.

Lehmann, Hartmut, and Guenther Roth, eds. 1985. *Weber's Protestant Ethic: Origins, Evidence, Contexts*. Cambridge: Cambridge University Press.

Lewis, Archibald, and Timothy Runyan. 1985. *European Naval and Maritime History, 300–1500*. Bloomington: Indiana University Press.

Little, David. 1969. *Religion, Order, and Law: A Study in Pre-Revolutionary England*. New York: Harper and Row.

Luthy, Hubert. 1963. "Calvinisme et capitalisme: Après soixante ans de débat." *Cahiers Vilfredo Pareto* 2:5–35. Republished in Hubert Luthy, *Le passé present: Combats d'idées de Calvin à Rousseau* (Monaco: Éditions du Rocher, 1965).

———. 1964. "Once Again: Calvinism and Capitalism." *Encounter* 22, no. 1: 26–38.

Marshall, Gordon. 1980. *Presbyteries and Profits: Calvinism and the Development of Capitalism in Scotland, 1560–1707*. Oxford: Clarendon Press.

Martins, Susanna Wade, and Tom Williamson. 1994. "Floated Water-Meadows in Norfolk: A Misplaced Innovation." *Agricultural History Review* 421:20–37.

Mason, S. F. 1953. "Science and Religion in Seventeenth-Century England." *Past and Present* 3:28–44.

Mathias, Peter. 1983. *The First Industrial Nation: An Economic History of Britain, 1700–1914*. 2nd ed. London: Methuen.

McBride, Joseph. 1992. *Albert Camus: Philosopher and Littérateur*. London: St. Martin's Press.

McClelland, David C. 1953. *The Achievement Motive*. New York: Appleton-Century-Crofts.

———. 1975. *The Achieving Society: With a New Introduction*. New York: Irvington, distributed by Halstead Press.

McClelland, David C., David G. Winter, and Sara K. Winter. 1969. *Motivating Economic Achievement*. New York: Free Press.

McCloskey, Donald N. 1975a. "The Economics of Enclosure: A Market Analysis." In *European Peasants and Their Markets: Essays in Agrarian Economic History*, ed. W. N. Parker and E. L. Jones, 123–60. Princeton: Princeton University Press.

———. 1975b. "The Persistence of English Common Fields." In *European Peasants and Their Markets: Essays in Agrarian Economic History*, ed. W. N. Parker and E. L. Jones, 92–120. Princeton: Princeton University Press.

Merton, Robert K. 1938. "Science, Technology, and Society in Seventeenth-Century England." *Osiris* 4:360–78.

———. 1957. "Puritanism, Pietism, and Science." In *Social Theory and Social Structure*, 575–606. Rev. ed. Glencoe, IL, Free Press.

———. 1970. *Science, Technology, and Society in Seventeenth-Century England*. New York: H. Fertig.

Michie, Ranald. 1999. *The London Stock Exchange: A History*. Oxford: Oxford University Press.

Mijers, Esther. 2007. *Redefining William III: The Impact of the King-Stadholder in International Context*. Aldershot: Ashgate.

Mingay, George E. 1968. *Enclosure and the Small Farmer in the Age of the Industrial Revolution*, Studies in Economic History series. London: Macmillan.

———. 1976. *The Gentry: The Rise and Fall of a Ruling Class*. London.

———, ed. 1977. *The Agricultural Revolution: Changes in Agriculture, 1650–1880*. London: Longman.

Mitchell, B. R., and Phyllis Deane. 1962. *Abstract of British Historical Statistics*. Cambridge: Cambridge University Press.

Mitzman, A. 1970. *The Iron Cage: An Historical Interpretation of Max Weber*. New York.

Mokyr, Joel, 1987. "Has the Industrial Revolution Been Crowded Out? Some Reflections on Crafts and Williamson." *Explorations in Economic History*, 24(3): 293–319.

———. 1990. *The Lever of Riches: Technological Creativity and Economic Progress* p. 62. Oxford and New York: Oxford University Press, 1990.

Munro, John. 1973. "The Weber Thesis Revisited—and Revindicated?" *Revue belge de philologie et d'histoire* 51:381–91.

———. 1988. "Textile Technology." in Joseph R. Strayer, et al., eds., *Dictionary of the Middle Ages*, 13 vols. (New York: Charles Scribner's Sons/MacMillan, 1982–88), Vol. 11, pp. 693–711.

———. 1994. "Patterns of Trade, Money, and Credit." In *Handbook of European History in the Later Middle Ages, Renaissance, and Reformation, 1400–1600*, ed. James Tracy, Thomas Brady Jr., and Heiko Oberman, vol. 1, *Structures and Assertions*, 147–95. Leiden: E. J. Brill.

———. 1999. "The Symbiosis of Towns and Textiles: Urban Institutions and the Changing Fortunes of Cloth Manufacturing in the Low Countries and England, 1270–1570." *Journal of Early Modern History: Contacts, Comparisons, Contrasts* 3, no. 1: 1–74.

———. 2002. "Prices, Wages, and Prospects for 'Profit Inflation' in England, Brabant, and Spain, 1501–1670: A Comparative Analysis." Working paper, Department of Economics, University of Toronto. http://www.economics.utoronto.ca/index.php/index/research/workingPaperDetails/141.

———. 2003a. "The Medieval Origins of the Financial Revolution: Usury, *Rentes*, and Negotiablity." *International History Review* 25:505–62.

———. 2003b. "Medieval Woollens: Textiles, Textile Technology, and Industrial Organisation, c. 800–1500." In *The Cambridge History of Western Textiles*, ed. David Jenkins, 1:181–227. Cambridge: Cambridge University Press.

———. 2003c. "The Monetary Origins of the 'Price Revolution': South German Silver Mining, Merchant-Banking, and Venetian Commerce, 1470–1540." In *Global Connections and Monetary History, 1470–1800*, ed. Dennis Flynn, Arturo Giráldez, and Richard von Glahn, 1–34. Aldershot: Ashgate.

———. 2004. "Inflation." In *Europe, 1450–1789: Encyclopedia of the Early Modern World*, ed. Jonathan Dewald et al., 3:262–65. New York: Charles Scribner's Sons, Gale Group.

———. 2007a. "Classic Reviews in Economic History:" Earl Hamilton, *American Treasure and the Price Revolution in Spain, 1501–1650*. EH.NET Book Review, January 15. http://eh.net/bookreviews/library/munro.

———. 2007b. "South German Silver, European Textiles, and Venetian Trade with the Levant and Ottoman Empire, c. 1370 to c. 1720: A Non-mercantilist Approach to the Balance of Payments Problem." In *Relazione economiche tra Europa e mondo islamico, seccoli XIII–XVIII*, ed. Simonetta Cavaciocchi, 907–62. Florence: Le Monnier.

———. 2008a. "Money, Prices, Wages, and 'Profit Inflation' in Spain, the Southern Netherlands, and England during the Price Revolution Era: ca. 1520–ca. 1650." *História e Economia: Revista Interdisciplinar* 4:13–71.

———. 2008b. "The Price Revolution." In *The New Palgrave Dictionary of Economics*, ed. Steven N. Durlauf and Lawrence E. Blume, no. 1339. 2nd ed. 6 vols., London: Palgrave Macmillan.

———. 2008c. "The Usury Doctrine and Urban Public Finances in Late-Medieval Flanders (1220–1550): Rentes (Annuities), Excise Taxes, and Income Transfers from the Poor to the Rich." In *La fiscalità nell'economia Europea, secc. XIII–XVIII / Fiscal Systems in the European Economy from the 13th to the 18th Centuries*, ed. Simonetta Cavaciocchi, 973–1026. Florence: Firenze University Press.

Musson, Albert E. 1972. *Science, Technology, and Economic Growth in the Eighteenth Century*. London: Methuen.

Musson, Albert E., and Eric Robinson. 1960. "Science and Industry in the Late Eighteenth Century." *Economic History Review*, 2nd ser., 13:222–45.

———. 1969. *Science and Technology in the Industrial Revolution*. Toronto: University of Toronto Press.

Neal, Larry. 1990. *The Rise of Financial Capitalism: International Capital Markets in the Age of Reason*. Cambridge: Cambridge University Press.

Nef, John U. 1923. *The Rise of the British Coal Industry*. 2 vols. London: G. Routledge. Reprinted London: F. Cass, 1966.

———. 1934. "The Progress of Technology and the Growth of Large Scale Industry in Great Britain, 1540–1640." *Economic History Review*, 1st ser., 5:3–24. Reprinted in John U. Nef, *Conquest of the Material World* (Chicago: University of Chicago Press, 1964), 121–43.

———. 1936. "A Comparison of Industrial Growth in France and England, 1540–1640." *Journal of Political Economy* 44:643-66. Reprinted in John U. Nef, *Conquest of the Material World* (Chicago: University of Chicago Press, 1964), 144–212.

———. 1937. "Prices and Industrial Capitalism in France and England, 1540–1640." *Economic History Review*, 1st. ser., 7:155–85. Reprinted in *Enterprise and Secular Change: Readings in Economic History*, ed. Frederic C. Lane and Jelle C. Riemersma (London: George Allen and Unwin, 1953), 292–321.

———. 1950. *War and Human Progress: An Essay on the Rise of Industrial Civilization*. Cambridge: Harvard University Press. Reprinted New York: Russell & Russell, 1968.

Noonan, John T. 1957. *The Scholastic Analysis of Usury*. Cambridge: Harvard University Press

North, Douglass. 1984. "Government and the Cost of Exchange in History." *Journal of Economic History* 44:255–64.

North, Douglass. 1985. "Transaction Costs in History." *Journal of European Economic History* 14:557–76.

North, Douglass, and Barry Weingast. 1989. "Constitutions and Commitment: The Evolution of Institutions Governing Public Choice in Seventeenth-Century Britain." *Journal of Economic History* 49:803–32.

O'Brien, Patrick. 1988. "The Political Economy of British Taxation." *Economic History Review* 2nd ser., 41:1–32.

———. 2002. "Fiscal Exceptionalism: Great Britain and Its European Rivals—from Civil War to Triumph at Trafalgar and Waterloo." In *The Political Economy of British Historical Experience, 1688–1914*, ed. Patrick O'Brien and Donald Winch, 245–65. Oxford: Oxford University Press.

O'Brien, Patrick, and P. Hunt. 1993. "The Rise of a Fiscal State in England, 1485–1815." *Historical Research* 66:129–76.

O'Connell, Laura. 1976. "Anti-entrepreneurial Attitudes in Elizabethan Sermons and Popular Literature." *Journal of British Studies* 15:1–20.

O'Day, Rosemary. 1982. *Education and Society, 1500–1800: The Social Foundations of Education in Early Modern Britain*. London: Longman.

———. 1986. *The Debate on the English Reformation*. London: Methuen.

Outhwaite, R. B. 1986. "Progress and Backwardness in English Agriculture, 1500–1650." *Economic History Review*, 2nd ser., 39:1–18.

Overton, Mark. 1984. "Agricultural Revolution? Development of the Agrarian Economy in Early-Modern England." In *Explorations in Historical Geography: Interpretative Essays*, ed. A.R.H. Baker and D. J. Gregory, 118–39. Cambridge: Cambridge University Press.

———. 1996a. *Agricultural Revolution in England: The Transformation of the Agrarian Economy, 1500–1800*. Cambridge: Cambridge University Press.

———. 1996b. "Re-establishing the English Agricultural Revolution." *Agricultural History Review* 44:1–20.

Pagano de Divitiis, Giglioa. 1997. *English Merchants in Seventeenth-Century Italy*. Trans. Stephen Parkin. Cambridge: Cambridge University Press. Originally published as *Mercanti inglesi nell'Italia del Seicento: Navi, traffici, egemonie* (Venice: Marsilio Editore, 1990).

Parker, Geoffrey. 1974. "The Emergence of Modern Finance in Europe, 1500–1750." In *The Fontana Economic History of Europe*, vol. 2, *Sixteenth and Seventeenth Centuries*, ed. Carlo Cipolla, 527–94. Glasgow: Collins/Fontana.

Parker, Geoffrey, and L. M. Smith, eds. 1978. *The General Crisis of the Seventeenth Century*. London: Routledge and Kegan Paul.

Pettegree, Andrew, Alastair Duke, and Gillian Lewis, eds. 1994. *Calvinism in Europe, 1540–1620*. Cambridge: Cambridge University Press.

Phelps Brown, E. H., and Sheila V. Hopkins. 1956. "Seven Centuries of the Prices of Consumables, Compared with Builders' Wage Rates." *Economica* 23:296–314. Reprinted in E. H. Phelps Brown and Sheila V. Hopkins, *A Perspective of Wages and Prices* (London: Methuen, 1981), 13–39.

Pollard, Sidney. 1980. "A New Estimate of British Coal Production, 1750–1850." *Economic History Review*, 2nd ser., 33:212–35.

Price, Roger. 1981. *An Economic History of Modern France, 1730–1914*. Rev. ed. London: Macmillan.

Rabb, Theodore K. July 1965. "Religion and the Rise of Modern Science." *Past and Present* 31:111–26.

———. 1966. "Science, Religion and Society in the Sixteenth and Seventeenth Centuries." *Past and Present* 33:148.

———. 1976. *The Struggle for Stability in Early Modern Europe*. Oxford: Oxford University Press.

Rackham, Oliver. 1976. *Trees and Woodland in the British Landscape*. London: J. M. Dent.

———. 1980. *Ancient Woodland: Its History, Vegetation, and Uses in England*. London: Edward Arnold.

Richards, R. D. 1929. *The Early History of Banking in England*. London: P. S. King & Son.

Riden, Philip. 1977. "The Output of the British Iron Industry before 1870." *Economic History Review*, 2nd ser., 30:442–59.

Riemersma, Jelle C. 1967. *Religious Factors in Early Dutch Capitalism, 1550–1650*. The Hague: Mouton,

Robertson, H. M. 1933. *Aspects of the Rise of Economic Individualism: A Criticism of Max Weber and His School*. Cambridge: Cambridge University Press.

Rogers, James E. Thorold. 1866–1902. *History of Agriculture and Prices in England*. 7 vols. Oxford: Clarendon Press.

Roseveare, Henry. 1991. *The Financial Revolution, 1660–1760*. London: Longman.

Samuelsson, Kurt. 1961. *Religion and Economic Action*. London: Heinemann.

Schubert, H. R. 1957. *The History of the British Iron and Steel Industry from ca. 450 B.C. to A.D. 1775*. London: Routledge and Kegan Paul.

Schumpeter, Joseph A. 1949. "Economic Theory and Entrepreneurial History." In *Change and the Entrepreneur: Postulates and Patterns for Entrepreneurial History*, ed. Research Center in Entrepreneurial History, Harvard University, 63–84. Cambridge: Harvard University Press. Republished in *Essays of J. A. Schumpeter*, ed. Richard Clemence (Cambridge, Addison-Wesley, 1951), 248–66.

———. 1961. *The Theory of Economic Development: An Inquiry into Profits, Capital, Credit, Interest, and the Business Cycle*. Trans. Redvers Opie. 1934; New York: Oxford University Press.

———. 1987. *Capitalism, Socialism, and Democracy*. London. Unwin Paperbacks.

———. 1989. *Business Cycles: A Theoretical, Historical, and Statistical Analysis of the Capitalist Process*. 1964; New York: Porcupine Press.

———. 1991. "Max Weber's Work." In *The Economics and Sociology of Capitalism*. Ed. Richard Swedberg. Princeton: Princeton University Press.

———. 1997. *Essays: On Entrepreneurs, Innovations, Business Cycles, and the Evolution of Capitalism*. New York: Transaction.

Scott, William Robert. 1912. *The Constitution and Finance of English, Scottish, and Irish Joint-Stock Companies to 1720*. 3 vols. Cambridge: Cambridge University Press.

Simpson, Alan. 1961. *The Wealth of the Gentry, 1540–1660*. Chicago: University of Chicago Press.

Smith, Sir Thomas. 1906. *De Republica Anglorum: A Discourse on the Commonwealth of England*. 1583. Ed. L. Alston. Cambridge: Cambridge University Press.

Stasavage, David. 2003. *Public Debt and the Birth of the Democratic State: France and Great Britain, 1688–1789*. Cambridge: Cambridge University Press

———. 2007. "Partisan Politics and Public Debt: The Importance of the 'Whig Supremacy' for Britain's Financial Revolution." *European Review of Economic History* 11:123–53.

Stone, Lawrence. 1948. "The Anatomy of the Elizabethan Aristocracy." *Economic History Review*, 1st ser., 18:1–53.

———. 1952. "The Elizabethan Aristocracy: A Restatement." *Economic History Review*, 2nd ser., 4:302–21.

———. 1956. *The Crisis of the Aristocracy, 1558–1641*. Oxford: Oxford University Press.

Sussman, Nathan, and Yafeh, Yishay. 2006. "Institutional Reforms, Financial Development and Sovereign Debt: Britain, 1690–1790." *Journal of Economic History* 66:882–905.

Tann, Jennifer. 1973. "Fuel Saving in the Process Industries during the Industrial Revolution: A Study in Technological Diffusion." *Business History* 15:149–59.

Tawney, Richard H. 1912. *The Agrarian Problem in the Sixteenth Century*. London: Longmans, Green. Reissued with an introduction by Lawrence Stone (London: Harper and Row, 1967).

———. 1926. *Religion and the Rise of Capitalism: A Historical Study*. London: J. Murrary. Reissued London: Penguin, 1990.

———. 1941. "The Rise of the Gentry, 1558–1640." *Economic History Review*, 1st ser., 11:1–38. Reprinted with a postscript in *Essays in Economic History*, ed. Eleanora M. Carus-Wilson (London: E. Arnold, 1954), 1:173–214.

Terrill, Ross. 1974. *R.H. Tawney and His Times: Socialism as Fellowship*. London: Deutsch.

Thirsk, Joan, ed. 1967a. *The Agrarian History of England and Wales*. Vol. 4, *1500–1640*. Cambridge: Cambridge University Press.

———. 1967b. "Engrossing and Enclosing." In *The Agrarian History of England and Wales*, ed. Joan Thirsk, vol. 4, *1500–1640*, 200–256. Cambridge: Cambridge University Press.

———. 1967c. "Farming Techniques." In *The Agrarian History of England and Wales*, ed. Joan Thirsk, vol. 4, *1500–1640*, 161–99. Cambridge: Cambridge University Press

———. 1984. *The Agrarian History of England and Wales*. Vol. 5, *1640–1750*. Part 1, *Regional Farming Systems*. Cambridge: Cambridge University Press.

———. 1985a. *The Agrarian History of England and Wales*. Vol. 5, *1640–1750*. Part 2, *Agrarian Change*. Cambridge: Cambridge University Press.

———. 1985b. "Agricultural Innovations and their Diffusion." In *Agrarian History of England*, vol. 5, ed. Joan Thirsk, part 2, *Agrarian Change*, 533–89. Cambridge: Cambridge University Press.

Thomas, Brinley. 1985. "Escaping from Constraints: The Industrial Revolution in a Malthusian Context." *Journal of Interdisciplinary History* 15:729–54.

———. 1986. "Was There an Energy Crisis in Great Britain in the 17th Century?" *Explorations in Economic History* 23:124–52.

Thompson, E. P. 1967. "Time, Work-Discipline, and Industrial Capitalism." *Past and Present* 38:56–97.

Thompson, F.M.L. 1966. "The Social Distribution of Landed Property in England since the Sixteenth Century." *Economic History Review*, 2nd ser., 19:505–17.

Thorner, Isidor. 1952. "Ascetic Protestantism and the Development of Science and Technology." *American Journal of Sociology* 58:25–33.

Tracy, James D. 1985. *A Financial Revolution in the Habsburg Netherlands: Renten and Renteniers in the County of Holland, 1515–1565*. Berkeley and Los Angeles: University of California Press.

———. 1995. "Taxation and State Debt." In *Handbook of European History, 1500–1600: Late Middle Ages, Renaissance, and Reformation*, ed. Thomas Brady, Heiko Oberman, and James Tracy, vol. 1, *Structures and Assertions*, 563–88. Leiden, E. J. Brill.

———. 2003. "On the Dual Origins of Long-Term Urban Debt in Medieval Europe." In *Urban Public Debts: Urban Government and the Market for Annuities in Western Europe, 14th–18th Centuries,* ed. Karel Davids, Marc Boone, and V. Janssens, 13–26. Turnout: Brepols

Trevor-Roper, Hugh R. 1951. "The Elizabethan Aristocracy: An Anatomy Anatomized." *Economic History Review*, 2nd ser., 3:279–98.

———. 1953. *The Gentry, 1540–1640. Economic History Review*, supplement no. 1. Cambridge: Cambridge University Press

———. 1963. *Religion, the Reformation, and Social Change.* London: Bowes & Bowes.

Troost, Wouter. 2005. *William III the Stadholder-King: A Political Biography.* Aldershot: Ashgate

Turner, Stephen P., ed. 2000. *The Cambridge Companion to Weber.* Cambridge: Cambridge University Press.

Unger, Richard W. 1980. *The Ship in the Medieval Economy, 600–1600.* London: Croom Helm.

———. 1981. "Warships and Cargo Ships in Medieval Europe." *Technology and Culture* 22:233–52.

———. 1987. "Portuguese Shipbuilding and the Early Voyages to the Guinea Coast." In *Vice-Almirante Avelino Teixeira da Mota, In Memoriam*, ed. Academia Portuguesa da História, 1:229–49. Lisbon: Academia de Marinha / Instituto de Investigacao Cientifica Tropical.

———. 1997. *Ships and Shipping in the North Sea and Atlantic, 1400–1800.* Aldershot: Ashgate.

Van der Wee, Herman. 1963. *The Growth of the Antwerp Market and the European Economy, 14th–16th Centuries.* 3 vols. The Hague: Martinus Nijhoff.

Van der Wee, Herman (in collaboration with John Munro). 2003. "The Western European Woollen Industries, 1500–1750." In *The Cambridge History of Western Textiles*, ed. David Jenkins, 2:397–472. Cambridge: Cambridge University Press.

Van Houtte, Jan A. 1940. "La genèse du grande marché international d'Anvers à la fin du moyen âge." *Revue belge de philologie et d'histoire* 19:87–126.

———. 1961. "Anvers aux XVe et XVIe siècle." *Annales: Economies, Sociétés, Civilisations* 16:248–78.

Van Stuivenberg, J. H. 1975. "The Weber Thesis: Attempt at Interpretation." *Acta Historiae Neerlandicae* 8:50–66.

Viner, Jacob. 1948. "Power vs. Plenty as Objectives of Foreign Policy in the Seventeenth and Eighteenth Centuries." *World Politics* 1:1–29. Republished in *Revisions in Mercantilism*, ed. Donald C. Coleman (London: Methuen, 1969), 61–91.

Weber, Max. 1904–5. *Die Protestantische Ethik und der Geist des Kapitalismus.* Berlin. Trans. Talcott Parsons as *The Protestant Ethic and the Spirit of Capitalism* (New York: Charles Scribner's Sons, 1930).

———. 1961. *General Economic History.* Trans. Frank H. Knight. New York: Collier Books

Wedgwood, Cicely V. 1966. *The King's War, 1641–1647.* London: Collins.

———. 1970a. *The King's Peace, 1637–1641: The Great Rebellion.* London: Collins Fontana.

———. 1970b. *Oliver Cromwell and the Elizabethan Inheritance.* London: J. Cape

West, E. G. 1975. *Education and the Industrial Revolution.* London: B. T. Batsford.

Wiebe, Georg, 1895. *Zur Geschichte der Preisrevolution des XVI. und XVII. Jahrhunderts.* Leipzig: Duncker & Humblot.

Williamson, Jeffrey. 1984. "Why Was British Growth So Slow during the Industrial Revolution?" *Journal of Economic History* 44:687–712.

Willan, Thomas S. 1956. *The Early History of the Russia Company, 1553–1603.* Manchester: Manchester University Press.

————. 1973. *The Muscovy Merchants of 1555*. New York: A. M. Kelly.

————. 1968. *Studies in Elizabethan Foreign Trade*. New York: A. M. Kelly.

Wilson, Charles. 1949. "Treasure and Trade Balances: The Mercantilist Problem." *Economic History Review*, 2nd ser., 2:152–61.

————. 1958. *Mercantilism*. Historical Association Pamphlet No. 37. London: Historical Association.

Wilson, Thomas. 1925. *A Discourse Upon Usury By Way of Dialogue and Orations*. With a historical introduction by R. H. Tawney. London: G. Bell.

Wordie, S. R. 1983. "The Chronology of English Enclosure, 1500–1914." *Economic History Review*, 2nd ser., 36:483–505.

Wright, Anthony. 1987. *R. H. Tawney*. Manchester: Manchester University Press.

Wrigley, E. Anthony. 1988. *Continuity, Chance, and Change: The Character of the Industrial Revolution in England*. Cambridge: Cambridge University Press.

————. 2000. "The Divergence of England: The Growth of the English Economy in the Seventeenth and Eighteenth Centuries." *Transactions of the Royal Society*, 6th ser., 10:117–41.

————. 2006. "The Transition to an Advanced Organic Economy: Half a Millennium of English Agriculture." *Economic History Review*, 2nd ser., 59:425–80.

Wrigley, E. Anthony, R. S. Davies, J. E. Oeppen, and R. S. Schofield. 1997. *English Population History from Family Reconstitution, 1580–1837*. Cambridge: Cambridge University Press.

Wrigley, E. Anthony, and, R. S. Schofield. 1980. *The Population History of England, 1541–1871: A Reconstruction*. Cambridge: Cambridge University Press.

Yelling, J. A. 1977. *Common Field and Enclosure in England, 1450–1850*. London: Macmillan.

Zell, Michael. 1993. *Industry in the Countryside: Wealden Society in the Sixteenth Century*. Cambridge: Cambridge University Press.

Chapter 6 ⸺⸺⸺⸺⸺⸺⸺⸺⸺⸺⸺⸺⸺⸺

The Golden Age of the Dutch Republic

Oscar Gelderblom

THE DUTCH GOLDEN AGE is an icon of premodern economic growth. The revolt against Philip II and his successors in the late sixteenth and early seventeenth centuries coincided with an unprecedented economic boom and cultural flowering. Between 1580 and 1650 the Dutch became the dominant player in European trade—an achievement based on their large-scale commercial agriculture and fisheries, market-oriented manufacturing, and low-cost shipping services. In addition, a combined military and commercial effort allowed the Dutch colonial companies, VOC (Verenigde Oost-Indische Compagnie) and WIC (West-Indische Compagnie), to establish a dense network of trading posts in Asia, Africa, and the Americas.

The Dutch Republic was a country of entrepreneurs, a society in which the livelihood of a considerable number of men and women depended on their judgmental decisions about the buying and selling of goods and services.[1] These entrepreneurs included not just merchants involved in long-distance trade, but also shipmasters, fishermen, millwrights, farmers, artisans, and shopkeepers. Except for the directors of colonial joint-stock companies and the managers of a few large farm estates and manufacturing firms—men who received a fixed reward for their judgmental decisions—the income of these entrepreneurs depended on the profits or losses they made in the marketplace.

The origins of this entrepreneurial class predate the Golden Age by at least two centuries. From the late fourteenth century the Dutch were involved in commercial dairy farming, the importation of bread grains, and the export of herring, beer, and textiles. In the first half of the sixteenth century the commercialization of agriculture continued with the development of stockbreeding and peat digging, while merchants and shipmasters in the coastal provinces established a regular trade with Flanders and Brabant, the Baltic Area, England, and the Atlantic coasts of France and Spain. In short, the entrepreneurial success of the Golden Age was to a large extent the realization of an already existing potential.

Even so, important changes did occur after the independence of the United Provinces. The removal of thousands of laborers and artisans from the southern provinces in the 1580s and 1590s stimulated the manufacturing of textiles, refined sugar, weaponry, paintings, books, maps, and myriad other luxury wares. The fall of Antwerp in 1585 and the emigration of at least a fifth of its merchant community added considerably to the scale and scope of the Amsterdam market. Finally, without the independence from the Habsburg Empire, the establishment of direct trading links between the Low Countries and Africa, America, and Asia would have been inconceivable.

This chapter analyzes the contribution entrepreneurs in agriculture, industry, and trade made to the Dutch Golden Age. Were these men and women with outstanding personal qualities, either in terms of human, social, or financial capital? Or was it a favorable set of legal, political, and economic institutions—either inherited from an earlier period or copied from more advanced economies—that allowed more men and women than elsewhere in Europe to set up their private businesses, market goods and services, and manage the risks entailed by their reliance on market exchange? Or was there nothing special about either entrepreneurs or institutions, with the Dutch simply taking advantage of economic opportunities foregone by potential competitors caught up in economic crises and continuous warfare elsewhere in Europe?

A Country of Entrepreneurs?

In most accounts of the Dutch Golden Age the contribution of entrepreneurs revolves around the economic achievements of a relatively small group of highly successful merchants and manufacturers.[2] The usual suspects include the rich and well-connected Flemish and Portuguese merchants who settled in Amsterdam at the turn of the seventeenth century; the skilled instrument makers, cartographers, schoolmasters, book printers, sugar refiners, painters, and silk weavers from Flanders and Brabant who followed in their wake; and, in the later seventeenth century, the experienced Huguenot silk weavers from France.[3] Very few historians of entrepreneurship have considered the many other men and women who made judgmental decisions about the buying and selling of goods and services.[4] And yet their number must have been in the tens of thousands.

A very crude measure for the number of active entrepreneurs would be the urbanization ratio of the Dutch Republic. By the mid-seventeenth century some 40 percent of the total population lived in towns, albeit with strong regional differences. Urbanization in Holland reached an impressive peak of 60 percent while it did not exceed 25 percent in several of the inland provinces (De Vries and Van der Woude 1997). Such a high level of urbanization would have been unthinkable without entrepreneurs. First there were the numerous commercial farmers, wholesalers, retailers, and shipmasters responsible for the food supply of the town populations.[5] Then there was a group of self-employed artisans and shopkeepers who supplied households with all kinds of consumer durables (Posthumus 1908, 269–70, 274). Finally, the Dutch economy thrived on the imports and exports of agricultural produce, manufactures, and colonial wares—activities that further stimulated entrepreneurship in town and countryside.[6]

Yet to claim that the Dutch Republic was a country of entrepreneurs requires more persuasive reasoning. We need to estimate their numbers. An appropriate starting point would be the countryside of the coastal provinces Holland, Friesland, and Zeeland in the late fourteenth and fifteenth centuries, when soil compaction dramatically changed the economic outlook of the rural population.[7] Peasants who had previously grown bread grains shifted their production to dairy, meat, and industrial crops such as hemp and madder that were subsequently marketed in the Dutch beyond. At the same time they took on by-employment as peat diggers, brickworkers, fishermen, and shipmasters, the result of which was a surprisingly modern-looking rural economy with at least part of the peasant households earning their living with a combination of wage labor and entrepreneurial activities (Van Bavel 2003, 2004).

A first approximation of the number of rural entrepreneurs in the countryside can be obtained by looking at the number of households involved in dairy farming—perhaps the single most important agricultural sector. The Italian chronicler Lodovico Guicciardini wrote in 1567 that the annual production of cheese and butter in Holland equaled the value of Portuguese spice imports (Guicciardini et al. 1567). Preliminary calculations, taking into account the small size of landholdings, and the limited number of cows per household, suggest that around 1500 between one-half and two-thirds of the total number of households in Holland were involved in commercial dairy farming. Most of these farms were productive enough to secure full employment for the family and in some cases even additional maids or farmhands (Van Bavel and Gelderblom 2010). The total number of rural entrepreneurs in Holland was higher still. For one thing, the peasant households relied on wholesalers and retail traders in villages or small towns to supply their food, clothing, and farm supplies such as dung, hay, fodder, equipment, and breeding stock.[8] For another, there were hundreds of herring fishers and shipmasters, as well as a small but thriving contingent of entrepreneurs who ran paper and sawmills, salt refineries, madder kilns, brick- and tileworks, and shipyards on the banks of the major rivers and lakes (Van der Woude 1972; Van Bavel and Van Zanden 2004).

But how many were these entrepreneurs? A detailed reconstruction of the wealth and principal occupation of heads of households in the small town of Edam, north of Amsterdam, allows a tentative estimate.[9] In 1462 Edam, with a population of 2,400, counted at least 200 fishermen, shipmasters, wholesalers, shipwrights, and well-to-do peasants (with five cows or more). That is not including bakers, butchers, fishmongers, and the like. If we assume that the total workforce made up two-thirds of the population, the share of this class of entrepreneurs in this early period was 12.5 percent. In 1560 the number of town dwellers had grown to 3,750, but now there were fewer (160), rather than more, entrepreneurs with a comparable economic status—a development that might be explained by the decline of the number of town dwellers that owned large farm holdings, a greater scale of operations in industry, and perhaps a stronger hold of Amsterdam merchants and shipmasters over shipping and trade.

Now the highly commercialized countryside of Holland was a world apart, even in the Dutch Republic.[10] Only parts of the coastal provinces of Friesland and Zeeland went through a similar process of agricultural specialization early on.[11] The inland provinces retained large areas where agriculture was dominated by subsistence farming, and where urban entrepreneurs offered only a limited set of goods and services (Brusse 1999). Still, even here one finds highly productive agricultural regions dominated by small numbers of wealthy farmers. In the Guelders river area, for example, the early development of term leases, the obligation of landowners (noblemen, religious institutions, and town dwellers) to fund repairs, waterworks, and physical infrastructure, made for high reinvestment ratios (Van Bavel 2001). This stimulated the growth of a small group of large tenants who used their high in-

TABLE 6.1
Estimated Number of Entrepreneurs Working in Various Sectors in Amsterdam, circa 1620

Entrepreneurs	Number	% population 15–64 years
Retail trade	2,600	3.7%
Manufacturing	2,300	3.3%
Wholesale trade	1,350	1.9%
Transportation	1,250	1.8%
Other services	1,100	1.6%
Total	8,600	12.2%

Sources: See chapter appendix.

comes from farming to fund short-term investments in livestock, seeds, implements, and labor. Using local labor surpluses created by the ever more skewed distribution of landownership and leases, they were able to step up production for the market in the course of the sixteenth century.

Still, the most obvious place to look for entrepreneurial activity is in the major ports and manufacturing centers that were actively involved in domestic and international trade. These included Leiden, Haarlem, Rotterdam, Middelburg, several smaller ports in Holland and Friesland, and of course the city of Amsterdam. The very rich historiography of the latter port allows us to estimate the number of entrepreneurs that worked here in the first quarter of the seventeenth century (table 6.1).

The largest group of entrepreneurs in Amsterdam were its 2,600 shopkeepers. These were the butchers, bakers, grocers, cobblers, and traders in wine, fish, and fruit who sustained an urban population of 120,000 in 1620. There were about as many manufacturers, part of whom also catered to the needs of the local people. However, besides the master artisans that produced clothes, shoes, pots and pans, and other household items, there were shipwrights, gold- and silversmiths, painters, and printers, working for local and foreign customers alike. Amsterdam's leading role in international trade is reflected in the large number of merchants and shipmasters, as well as the brokers, hostellers, and notaries that supported the commercial sector. Together, the various groups of entrepreneurs made up an estimated 12.5 percent of Amsterdam's working population. If this relative share is in any way representative for other towns in the Dutch Republic, already in 1600 the total number of urban entrepreneurs may have been as high as 45,000, rising to over 60,000 in 1650.[12]

Entrepreneurs and Innovation

The high rate of self-employed men and women in towns and villages was a salient feature of the early modern Dutch economy. But were these all entrepreneurs in the sense of Joseph Schumpeter's theory about creative destruction? Surely, the majority would have responded to new economic opportunities rather than created them. Indeed, classic accounts of how entrepreneurs may have spurred economic change in preindustrial Europe all favor a more restrictive definition, as they focus on the specific qualities of a few individuals, including their management skills, technical capabilities, commercial networks, financial capital, or even a capitalistic spirit.[13]

This interest in the personal attributes of a few exceptional entrepreneurs is echoed in the Dutch historiography of the Golden Age. Notably the Flemish merchants and artisans immigrating from the southern provinces after 1585 have often been described as more highly skilled, richer, better connected, and more daring than their Dutch counterparts—a reputation they share with the much smaller group of Portuguese Jews arriving in the same period.[14] A case in point are the Antwerp merchants Isaac Lemaire and Dirck van Os, both of whom figured prominently in the expansion of trade with Russia, Spain, and Italy; the spice trade with the East Indies; and the huge land reclamations north of Amsterdam. The fact that Lemaire's investments in the VOC led to multiple lawsuits, bankruptcy, and ultimately his departure from the city has only added to his reputation.[15]

It seems probable enough that a country catapulted into a position of economic and technological leadership achieved this status through a massive mobilization of innovative entrepreneurs. One example would be Cornelis Cornelisz. van Uitgeest, a farmer and millwright in a village near Amsterdam who built the first wind-driven sawmill in 1594 (De Vries and Van der Woude 1997, 345–49; Bonke et al. 2002). The name of Willem Usselincx is inextricably linked to the exploration of new markets in the Americas after 1600 (Den Heijer 2005). In the first decade of the sixteenth century Lambert van Tweenhuysen initiated whaling expeditions in the northern seas.[16] In 1618 Louis de Geer and Elias Trip started to set up extensive ironworks in Sweden. But even if these men all had exceptional business acumen, their endeavors fall short in explaining the exceptional growth of the Dutch economy.

In many sectors of the economy important technological and organizational changes occurred long before the Golden Age. This is true for improvements in the design of vessels used in the herring fisheries and ocean shipping (Unger 1978); the processing of foodstuffs such as butter, beer, and herring;[17] the opening up of new markets in Scandinavia, Poland, France, and the Iberian Peninsula (Van Tielhof 2002; Posthumus 1971; Lesger 2006); water management in the polders of Holland (Van Tielhof and Van Dam 2007; Greefs and Hart 2006); the introduction of peat as an energy source in manufacturing (Van Tielhof 2005); and finally the development of rural industries such as the processing of red dyes from madder, salt refining, and brick making.[18] It is important to note that very few of these innovations are linked to particular engineers or entrepreneurs. Even very famous attributions, like that of herring-gutting to Flemish fisherman Willem Beukelszoon, are currently disputed (Doorman 1956).

This lack of names linked to innovations before the Golden Age is not just an artifact of an incomplete historical record. It also reflects the incremental nature of technological change.[19] This is visible, for example, in the increasingly competitive production of butter and cheese in Holland and Friesland. The growing quantity and gradually improving quality of dairy in the fifteenth and sixteenth centuries was the result of changes in the keeping, feeding, and breeding of the cattle that led to higher milk yields per cow, and concomitant adaptation of the interiors of farm buildings, the utensils for churning and cheese-making, and the actual preparation of butter and cheese. As a result, not a single peasant, or his wife, has been credited with this achievement. In fact, even the cattle-driven churn mill that took over much of their handwork in the seventeenth century remains without a known inventor (Boekel 1929, 42n).

Meanwhile, the technological advance of the Dutch Republic was driven by a constant interaction between economic sectors (Davids 1995, 2008). One such web of innovation can be spun around the Dutch windmill (Davids 1998). After a first adaptation of grain mills to the needs of water management in the fifteenth century, windmill technology spread further to industrial mills for oil, paper, and timber during the Golden Age. Saw milling in turn stimulated the growth of Dutch shipbuilding, with all its improvements in ship design. The Dutch competitiveness in shipping and trade in turn was related to improvements in navigational instruments and maps, and the introduction of the *partenrederij*, a limited liability contract first used in shipping but eventually also in paper and sawmills (see infra, "Property and Contract Law").

The exchange of goods and services between regions also contributed to the advance of individual sectors. This is most apparent from the growing interaction between the northern and southern provinces of the Low Countries in the course of the sixteenth century. In exchange for the import of high-value manufactures and capital from the southern provinces, Holland exported large quantities of cheese, herring, and peat, and they organized a transit trade in grain, hides, salt, and wine from the Baltic area and the Atlantic coast of France. The result was a process of ongoing economic specialization (Lesger 2006; Gelderblom 2003a).

Most innovations in products, markets, and production processes in the Golden Age cannot be traced to individual entrepreneurs either. But there are a few exceptions, most notably in the first few decades after the fall of Antwerp in 1585. These include the first merchants trading with Italy, Russia, and West Africa, the initiators of the trade with Asia and America, the shipwright who built the first *fluytschip*, the printers of better maps, the inventor of the ribbon loom (Vogel 1986), and the first producers of luxury items such as glass, tulips, and ivory combs. Sometimes one can discern a small group of men responsible for the introduction of new products and techniques, like the Flemish schoolmasters who taught double entry bookkeeping in the principal ports of Holland and Zeeland, the owners of the earliest sugar refineries, or the first jewelry merchants in Amsterdam (Davids 2008).[20]

This string of innovations in industry, shipping, and trade at the turn of the seventeenth century was at least partially due to the political turmoil of the time. The disruption of the economy of the Low Countries in the early decades of the Dutch Revolt was such that deficient supply of goods and services raised prices, inflated profits, and reduced risks for the beginning entrepreneurs that most of the immigrants from the southern provinces were. At the same time, the entrepreneurs identified with the introduction of new markets, products, and technologies benefited from the knowledge and skills of migrant workers. For example, the Flemish and Portuguese jewelry merchants who settled in Amsterdam after 1595 put out their production to highly skilled goldsmiths and diamond cutters from Antwerp. The owners of the first sugar refineries hired experienced German and Flemish masters to supervise production while limiting their own role to the purchase of raw materials, and the sales of sugar. Similar combinations of skilled workers and wealthy merchants existed in the production of textiles, leather, salt, madder, and tobacco.[21]

The organization of these urban industries also bears out the importance of the institutional framework that shaped manufacturing. The craft guilds in Dutch towns allowed merchants to pay master artisans a wage for the production of luxury items, and thus appropriate a considerable part of their value added. Urban craftsmen accepted these arrangements, at least in the early phases of economic expansion, because their retained earnings were high enough for some of them to rise through the ranks and become merchants themselves. This is borne out by several artisans who started as goldsmiths in Amsterdam in the late sixteenth century, to become wealthy jewelry merchants by the end of their careers.[22]

Urban magistrates also tried to lure beginning entrepreneurs to their towns, especially in the boom years between 1580 and 1620. Silk weavers, glassmakers, sugar refiners, and various other manufacturers benefited from tax exemptions, cheap (child) labor, favorable loans, guaranteed sales, or even entire production facilities.[23] The main interest of the municipalities was in import substitution, employment for the unskilled or urban poor, and the support of ailing industries. The effect of their policies is hard to measure in an environment where many industries prospered anyway. On the other hand, several entrepreneurs left their host town within a few years, or even failed spectacularly, as with the attempts to grow mulberry trees to substitute for Asian silk imports (Eerenbeemt 1983, 1985, 1993).

A far more targeted stimulus for entrepreneurial activity was the patenting system introduced by the States of Holland in the late sixteenth century (Davids 1995; De Vries and Van der Woude 1997). In textiles, milling, shipping, and several other sectors, this system allowed the producers of new knowledge to secure a share of the profits that issued from the application of their insights. Especially between 1580 and 1650 patents gave hundreds of talented craftsmen and engineers the possibility of reaping the fruits of their ingenuity. Another instrument used by the government to stimulate innovation was the granting of monopolies for the entry into new markets or the sale of new goods. These rights to exclusive purchases and sales—appropriately termed *octrooien*, just like the patents for technical novelties—created similar financial rewards for innovators (Davids 1995). The best-known examples are the joint-stock companies trading with Asia and America, but monopoly rights were also granted to the whalers who worked near Greenland (Hacquebord 1994), to Flemish drapers in Leiden (Posthumus 1939), and to the producers and traders of such an ephemeral product as civet, a smelly substance used for the making of perfume that was "harvested" from African cats (Prins 1936). With the exception of the colonial companies none of these monopolies survived after 1650, but in later years Dutch entrepreneurs did obtain similar rights from foreign rulers who tried to stimulate their own economies (Eeghen 1961).

The exclusion of competitors through cartels and monopolies is ill-reputed because the rents that are created are believed to exceed the profits necessary for the remuneration of labor and capital. However, the practical use of the Dutch *octrooien* was in fact in these rents: an income that entrepreneurs could use to cover their start-up costs, and some of the risks involved in the new activities.[24] This financial rationale mirrors Joseph Schumpeter's understanding of entrepreneurship and points to a final and perhaps most important explanation for the wide application of new knowledge during the Dutch Golden Age: the greater ability of entrepreneurs to mobilize capital for investments in agriculture, industry, and services.

Riches

Particularly puzzling about the Dutch Golden Age is the almost complete absence, as late as 1580, of entrepreneurs wealthy enough to finance large investments in agriculture, industry, and trade. Before the Dutch Revolt brewers, textile manufacturers, and merchants in the northern part of the Low Countries seldom owned more than a few thousand guilders (e.g., Brünner 1924). For example, in 1498 only five drapers in Leiden—at the time the principal producer of woolen cloth in Holland—were worth more than 5,000 guilders (Posthumus 1908, 278). Similarly modest was the capital of the merchants and manufacturers operating in mid-sixteenth century Holland and Zeeland. Habsburg tax receivers in 1543 estimated the capital invested by entrepreneurs from Amsterdam, Delft, Middelburg. Flushing, and Veere at 6,000 guilders or less.[25] These estimates pale into insignificance compared with the tens of thousands of guilders, and sometimes considerably more, owned by the richest foreign and local merchants in Antwerp at that time.

It thus comes as no surprise that many historians have argued that economic expansion only truly began once wealthy merchants from the southern provinces fled to the north. Their capital would have allowed the rapid expansion of trade within Europe, the foundation of the colonial companies VOC (1602) and WIC (1621), and the large turnover realized from the very moment the Bank of Amsterdam was established in 1609. However, a closer look at the wealth of these immigrants shows that the vast majority came to Amsterdam with little or no money. Even the largest investors in the VOC started with modest capital of only several thousands of guilders (Gelderblom 2000; see also Gelderblom 2003a). The limited data available on the wealth of other immigrant merchants, notably Germans, Portuguese Jews, and Englishmen, show a similar picture.

This is not to say that these entrepreneurs made no contribution to the growth of the Amsterdam market. Quite the contrary. In Amsterdam the immigrants from the southern provinces and their children made up a third of the merchant community between 1580 and 1630. Their personal wealth was in keeping with this share, and hence their arrival raised the capital available for investment by some 50 percent. However, if these were small capitals to begin with, how can one explain the explosive growth of the Dutch economy between, roughly, 1590 and 1620?

One explanation could be that the closure of the Scheldt, and the warfare that occupied the Habsburg Empire, France, and England created windfall profits for merchants in the United Provinces willing to take the risks and trade with the Iberian Peninsula, Italy, and the Levant. However, in all these markets the Dutch had to compete with English and French traders. At the same time, returns on investment in the highly competitive Baltic run—the traditional Dutch stronghold—were never higher than 5 or 10 percent either (Van Tielhof 2002; Gelderblom 2000).

A far more important lever of riches was the trade with the East Indies. By 1608 the cumulative returns of the early companies sailing from Amsterdam between 1595 and 1602 amounted to 15 million guilders, against cumulative investments of 9 million—including a 3.6 million investment in the local chamber of the VOC in 1602. The Dutch East India Company proved at least as lucrative in the following decades. In 1631, thirty years after its establishment, total dividend payments stood at 11 million guilders. In other words, Amsterdam's investors in the East India trade accumulated seventeen (6 plus 11) million guilders in less than forty years. To put this figure into perspective: the assessment for a 0.5 percent wealth tax in 1631 yielded an estimated wealth for the entire population of 66 million guilders—35 of which can be traced to the city's merchant community. Now even if this tax did not include movable goods and taxpayers played down their wealth, the contribution of the East India trade to Amsterdam's wealth was formidable. But still, how did merchants with modest means manage to fund such huge investments to begin with?

Property and Contract Law

An entrepreneur with only limited financial means has to rely on others to fund his business. In preindustrial Europe the preferred means to acquire additional capital was to rely on relatives. It was no different in Dutch agriculture, industry, shipping, and trade. On the one hand, fathers, brothers, uncles, and cousins worked together in partnerships. On the other, relatives with money to spare who did not want the exposure to commercial risks could deposit their funds with enterprising family members in exchange for a fixed return on their loans. Through marriage and long-standing friendship it was often possible to widen this circle of trusted partners and creditors further.

The financial challenge for entrepreneurs in the Dutch Republic at the beginning of the Golden Age was that the wealth of their relatives and friends was limited, while potentially profitable investment projects abounded. The only possible way for them to take advantage of these opportunities was to find outside investors— partners with whom to share profits and losses, or lenders willing to part with their money in return for a fixed reward. However, without personal relations to rely on, it was more difficult for these outsiders to establish beforehand the trustworthiness of potential associates or debtors, as it was to secure their compliance after a contract was signed. This put a premium on the development of debt and equity contracts that allowed the transfer of funds between strangers.

A first solution was the adaptation of the general partnership through the writing of company contracts.[26] The specification of the duration and purpose of a joint venture limited the liability of the partners to transactions that fell within the terms of their agreement. Notarial deeds that survive for Amsterdam show that these company contracts were used in a variety of economic sectors. However, the spread of this very basic limitation of liability may have been much wider, because by the end of the sixteenth century it sufficed for partners to record such agreements in private (e.g., Moree 1990). What company contracts could not do was limit the liability for debts partners incurred within the boundaries of their agreement. In other words, a creditor of a firm could always claim an outstanding debt from any single partner of the company—leaving it to this particular partner to share the burden with the others. This is why even company contracts were often written between entrepreneurs with social ties between them.

A way out of this situation was found with the creation of the *partenrederij*—a contractual arrangement for the joint ownership of vessels either for fishing, transportation, or trade (Riemersma 1952; Posthumus 1953; Broeze 1976–78). In what seems to have been an adaptation of the generally accepted limitation of losses at sea to the total value of a shipping enterprise, the *partenrederij* limited the liability of each of the shareholders to the value of his investment. It was not uncommon for the ownership to be divided into eight, sixteen, thirty-two, or even more shares, thus giving even owners of the smallest wealth the opportunity to participate. In addition, the contract allowed for the delegation of the management of the company to one or two owners, and thus it could potentially serve a much larger crowd of investors. It remains unclear when and where this contractual form was first introduced, but certainly by 1450 it was common practice in the fisheries and shipping in the Low Countries and northern Germany.

In the Golden Age the *partenrederij* spread to several other sectors with high capital requirements, including paper mills, sawmills, peat exploitations, and most important, the first ventures to West Africa and Asia.[27] All of the early colonial companies that sailed from Amsterdam, Rotterdam, Middelburg, and a few other ports in the 1590s were owned by dozens of shareholders, several of whom resold part of their investments to others. Indeed, the financial organization of the VOC closely resembled that of the *partenrederijen*, albeit with one crucial difference: investments in the VOC were understood to be used for more than a single voyage. Indeed, the first company charter stipulated a ten years' term for repayment of the initial shares, and this term was then prolonged several times to create a permanent joint-stock company effectively.

By 1650 equity finance with limited liability was common practice in Dutch ocean shipping, the herring fisheries, whaling, colonial trade, and a few capital-intensive manufactures, but not in other parts of the economy (De Vries and Van der Woude 1997). In agriculture, wholesale trade, retailing, and craft production entrepreneurs continued to work with their own funds or in small partnerships. A further extension of their working capital, if needed, was achieved through medium- or long-term loans, mostly deposits from relatives, but also funds from outsiders. However, in order for entrepreneurs to obtain credit from strangers, they had to pledge some kind of collateral to assure the creditor that he would get his money back.

Interestingly, one of the oldest forms of such collateral was still based on personal relations: namely the use of guarantors who had both sufficient knowledge of the financial position of the debtor, and a credible reputation known by the creditor. Provided the guarantor could easily be found by the creditor in case of default, the guarantee was a great help in securing repayment.[28] How much credit was backed by personal guarantors is impossible to say, but notarial deeds suggest it was widely used in Dutch trade, industry, and agriculture before and during the Golden Age.

Entrepreneurs who could not, or did not want to, rely on the creditworthiness of relatives and close friends could use their own property as collateral instead. One obvious possibility was use of their own products to secure loans. This is, of course, the principle underlying the postponed payment of goods, but it was also used for longer-term credit operations. Peasants in Holland and Zeeland, for example, signed forward contracts for their grain, madder, and butter. Urban craftsmen and retailers left their property with pawnbrokers and *banken van lening* to obtain ready money.[29] However, the use of merchandise as collateral had serious limitations. Creditors had to assess the exact quality of the goods, and they had to store them in a safe place in order to prevent material deterioration, damage, theft, or embezzlement by the borrower (Gelderblom and Jonker 2005). Especially the latter requirement made it difficult to sell goods on short notice. Furthermore, leaving goods in the hands of a lender was of little use to entrepreneurs who wanted to be able to sell them at short notice.[30]

A more appropriate means to obtain long-term funding was to sell annuities secured by real estate. This instrument was first used in the Low Countries in the thirteenth century, and its importance increased considerably over the next centuries (Zuijderduijn 2009). Entrepreneurs who needed funds sold the right to an annual income (*rente*), in return for which they received a principal sum. For savers with excess funds who wanted to secure a future stream of rents, but were unwilling to bear high risks, annuities were an attractive proposition. For one thing, the *rente* was not considered usurious. For another, the value of the underlying real estate was rather stable, especially once a growing number of houses were built in brick instead of timber. Furthermore, legislation by Charles V in the early sixteenth century gave creditors who wanted to liquidate their claims the right to sell them to a third party (Van der Wee 1967; Gelderblom and Jonker 2004). Finally, all real estate transactions and related credit operations had to be registered by the magistrates of towns and villages.[31] This measure was taken for fiscal purposes, but the registers obviously contained all the information *renten* buyers needed to establish the creditworthiness of their debtors—information that could be used in court in case of default.

Evidence from various parts of the Low Countries suggests that annuities were an important means for small entrepreneurs to expand their operations. In Holland and Brabant urban registers of private debt have survived from the late fifteenth century onward.[32] A case study of the jewelry trade shows that in Antwerp between 1530 and 1565 goldsmiths and diamond cutters from Flanders, Brabant, and Holland sold annuities to establish themselves as independent jewelry merchants.[33] A preliminary analysis of the annuities registered by the town magistrate of Leiden in 1620 and 1660 reveals a similar pattern (table 6.2).

In 1620 some 170 small entrepreneurs in Leiden sold term annuities with a total value of 77,000 guilders. Half of these men worked in the textile and building industries, while another third were craftsmen, retailers, shipmasters, and fishermen. At 450 guilders the average value of all the annuities was rather low, especially when compared to the few that were sold by wholesale traders (at 1,800 guilders on average). Forty years later the number of entrepreneurs who used this credit instrument had not grown much, but the value of their separate claims had almost tripled. Builders, textile producers, and other craftsmen still dominated the body of lenders.

Annuities, however, had their limitations when it came to funding businesses. Besides mandatory registration, interest rates were fixed at 6.25 percent, which was a competitive rate in the sixteenth century but less and less so in the seventeenth century (Gelderblom and Jonker 2004). This problem was eventually resolved by a lowering of the statutory rate, but there were other difficulties. Most important, one could only fix so many *renten* on a particular piece of real estate—a limitation that would be felt in the later seventeenth and the eighteenth century when the towns no longer expanded, and rental values stabilized or even declined. Thus, in addition to annuities entrepreneurs had a real need for other medium- or long-term loans that did not depend on their ownership of real estate. But what could they pledge as collateral?

In the mid-sixteenth century merchants on the Antwerp money market began to sell promissory notes, also known as bills obligatory or IOUs. These credit instruments, which were also used in other countries, were transferable, interest-

TABLE 6.2
Number and Total Value of Term Annuities Registered by Aldermen of Leiden
in 1620 and 1660

Economic sector	1620 Number	1620 Value	1660 Number	1660 Value
Building	47	26,732	25	34,300
Textile industry	41	12,144	12	8,100
Food and beverages	14	7,613	9	9,300
Fishing and shipping	15	6,936	1	800
Various crafts	15	5,639	9	7,950
Wholesale trade	2	3,600	3	12,000
Handling of goods	4	650	3	3,100
Schoolmasters	1	500	2	4,500
Public officials			1	800
Widows	10	2,738	11	8,550
Unknown	*20*	*10,628*	*104*	*118,431*
Total	**169**	**77,179**	**180**	**207,832**

Source: City Archives Leiden, Rentenboeken, Inv. No. 71, numbers P, Q, LL, MM, NN, OO.

bearing loans with a standardized maturity of three, six, or twelve months (Ehrenberg 1896, 25; Van der Wee 1967, 1080–81; Van der Wee 1977). After 1585 the large-scale emigration of Antwerp merchants brought the bill obligatory to Amsterdam. The advantage of bills obligatory over both annuities and family deposits was that creditors could determine in advance when they wanted to get their money back. For borrowers this was not a problem, for they could contract with a variety of lenders and differentiate the dates at which their loans matured.[34] What is more, in practice many bills were rolled over on expiry, effectively creating a long-term credit instrument (Gelderblom and Jonker 2004).

The only remaining problem, at least for the lenders, concerned the collateral. Borrowers simply pledged their persons and goods without any further specification. Even if individual bills represented only small amounts of money—often no more than 1,000 or 1,500 guilders—liquidation of a bad debt might be problematic with such general collateral. The transferability of IOUs, firmly established by an imperial ordinance, did not really solve this problem because only merchants familiar with a debtor's financial position would be willing to take over a debt. Hence Charles V's additional ordinance of 1543 that limited the use of the IOUs to the merchants active on the Antwerp Exchange (Gelderblom and Jonker 2004).

It was the foundation of the Dutch East India Company in 1602 that eventually created the ideal collateral for loans: the VOC share.[35] Merchants in Amsterdam, who had begun using Antwerp-style IOUs to attract external funds for their businesses in the 1590s, almost immediately recognized the potential of the share, as "a

TABLE 6.3
Obligations Recorded by Notaries, and Term Annuities Recorded by Notaries
and Town Magistrates in Gouda in 1650

Sector	Notarial IOUs		Term annuities	
	Number	Value	Number	Value
Food and beverages	18	13,424	5	2,900
Various crafts	15	6,155	32	11,336
Services	6	6,724	3	3,500
Building	12	6,260	6	2,500
Fishing and shipping	18	4,321	2	200
Wholesale trade	6	3,745	1	200
Professionals	3	2,300		
Public officials	3	725		
Textile industry	3	612	10	2190
Unknown	*140*	*75,843*	*29*	*10,450*
Total	**224**	**120,109**	**88**	**33,276**

Sources: Gouda City Archives, Oud Rechterlijk Archief, Inv. no. 477 Rentenboek no. VII, 1649–55; Notarial archives 1650.

claim on a company known to all; very liquid, so easy to sell in case of default; with daily price quotations for quick valuation; and with ownership easily ascertained" (Gelderblom and Jonker 2004, 660). Borrowing on the security of shares—even today a widely used financial technique—allowed merchants with no personal ties to engage in credit operations, for the lender could always attach and liquidate the share. It did not take long for this technique to take root among the merchant community at large.

But how could smaller entrepreneurs who did not own VOC shares secure additional funding for their businesses? This question is at the heart of current research on the evolution of financial markets in the Dutch Republic. One very tentative answer based on data collected for *one* town in *one* year points to the role notaries may have played in matching supply and demand for funds. The protocols that have survived of notaries in Gouda in 1650 show their writing of 220 obligations for a varied crowd of artisans, shipmasters, retailers, and other small businessmen. A comparison with the total value of term annuities sold in the same year (mostly registered by the town magistrate, but sometimes also by notaries) suggests notarial credit may have filled a void, as it is known to have done in early modern France.[36] But frankly this remains speculation, given the sparse data now available.

Risks

Making judgmental decisions about the marketing of goods and services implies risk—and not just unexpected price fluctuations due to adverse market conditions.

Dutch entrepreneurs were also confronted with natural disaster, warfare, crime, and dishonest behavior of partners and employees (Van Leeuwen 2000). Farmers regularly suffered from extreme weather, diseases, and warfare. Merchants, shipmasters, and fishermen encountered shipwreck and privateering raids. Wholesalers, retailers, and manufacturers had to deal with thieves, nonpaying clients, and suppliers tampering with the quality of their wares. Dutch entrepreneurs, like anyone else, wanted to prevent such misfortune, or at least to secure compensation for losses that did occur.[37]

Local and central authorities in the United Provinces played a crucial role in the prevention of opportunism, violence, and, one might even argue, natural disaster (Gelderblom 2003). Obviously Dutch rulers realized they could not stand in God's way, but nevertheless determined attempts were made to try to limit the damage of nature's single biggest threat: water. With the creation of water boards in the late Middle Ages, the Dutch created an efficient administrative apparatus to prevent inundation of the continuously subsiding lowlands of the coastal provinces. Landowners and tenants were initially forced to contribute their labor and later on mostly their money to build and maintain canals, dikes, sluices, and windmills. Even if neighboring water boards sometimes wrangled about each other's lack of effort, the system by and large succeeded in stabilizing the quality of the soil (Van Tielhof 2009).

The prevention of violent assaults on entrepreneurs in the Dutch Republic also depended on government intervention. Already in the late Middle Ages towns had secured a local monopoly on violence that allowed them to clamp down on robbers, thieves, and other criminals. Through persuasion and relatively mild repression the town magistrates in Holland also managed to nip in the bud the dozens of food and tax riots that broke out in the seventeenth and eighteenth centuries (Dekker 1982). At the same time the Dutch managed to push the theater of their war of independence to the fringes of their territory, thus securing the undisturbed exchange of goods and services in the heartland, that is, Holland (Tracy 2004). Finally, the Dutch Republic was one of the first European states to command a standing navy that was used, among other things, to protect the merchant fleet (Bruijn 1993).

Furthermore, local and central rulers contributed to the prevention of cheating and slacking by trading partners, employees, and other agents. Even if Dutch businessmen displayed a persistent preference for trading with relatives and friends, their dependence on the market made business transactions with strangers inevitable (Gelderblom 2003b). Town magistrates made it easier to find honest agents through the creation of a market infrastructure and the regulation of financial and commercial intermediation. Local courts facilitated the speedy settlement of the widest possible range of business conflicts, while leaving open the possibility of appeal to a higher court (Gelderblom 2005).

A major improvement in the settlement of disputes in the Dutch Golden Age emerged from a combined effort of magistrates and entrepreneurs. On the one hand, courts began to accept account books as legal proof for disputed transactions. On the other, businessmen increasingly kept detailed accounts of their commercial and financial transactions.[38] It will come as no surprise that long-distance traders in the major ports of the Dutch Republic were trained to use double entry bookkeeping. However, the habit of keeping a paper track of one's money and goods spread much wider. Farmers, textile manufacturers, and retailers also kept detailed accounts of their operations. Indeed, women were trained to do so, witness several surviving account books from the seventeenth century (Sterck 1916; Boot 1974, 32–33; Vrugt

1996). With the acceptance of these accounts in court, what was initially a monitoring device now doubled as a means to enforce contracts.

Finally, the government's role in mitigating the detrimental effect of price fluctuations differed strongly among sectors. While no entry barriers affected European trade, the two big colonial companies were given full monopolies upon their creation. In agriculture, all peasants and farmers were free to produce whatever they wanted, but urban magistrates did not shirk from regulating the supply of grain, bread, and other necessities of life, if doing so could prevent dearth. In manufacturing, some guilds used their corporate powers to exclude competitors and secure a steady income for the members, while others allowed subcontracting or production by outsiders (Prak 1994; Davids 1995; Posthumus 1908, 118–29, 275). The latter freedom certainly existed in the unincorporated industries for the processing of colonial wares, such as sugar and diamonds.

All these efforts notwithstanding, natural disaster, violence, opportunism, and price fluctuations did occur (Klein and Veluwenkamp 1993, 27–53). So entrepreneurs had to think of measures to manage these risks. One basic, though not necessarily wise, solution was to limit their exposure to the market. This was common enough in the early phases of commercialization of Dutch agriculture. While they began to produce butter, cheese, and hemp for the market, peasant households in Holland continued to provide at least part of their own food supply, while at the same time seeking additional employment in peat digging, fishing, shipping, and all kinds of menial work on bigger farms (Van Bavel 2003; Baars 1975, 28). Urban craftsmen could also combine work on their own account with wage labor for others. One example is the goldsmiths and diamond cutters of Amsterdam, who in the early seventeenth century received wages for jewelry they wrought for local merchants. To date the extent of this phenomenon of urban putting-out has not been investigated, however.

And yet the Dutch economy stands out for the relatively large number of entrepreneurs whose income did entirely depend on profits and losses made in the market. For men and women with only modest means—which certainly includes the majority of peasants, craftsmen, and retailers—the maintenance of a stable clientele could secure a steady income. Entrepreneurs with more financial scope could also try to diversify their business. This was the typical strategy for the merchants who worked in Amsterdam in the opening decades of the Golden Age. They traded on several European markets, in several products, and at the same time invested in shipping, whaling, industry, and even land reclamation. Especially shipping share companies (*partenrederijen*) allowed merchants with even modest means to combine investments. A similar preference for diversification can be found in agriculture, where dairy farmers used some of their land for growing hemp, and grain farmers began to produce tobacco.

Mixed husbandry was not always possible, however. In Zeeland, for example, the farmers' basic choice was between grain and madder, both of which were crops that tied up capital for a considerable time period, with sales concentrated in the harvest season and, hence, a great sensitivity to adverse market conditions. For the production of madder a solution was found in the transfer of financial risks to urban financiers. Merchants from Rotterdam bought the madder while it was still in the field, and then, after it had been processed, sold the various qualities of red dyes to textile finishers around Holland, and abroad (Priester 1998; Baars 1975, 22, 52).

The most extensive forward trading in the Golden Age occurred in Amsterdam. Here merchants began to write contracts for the future delivery of grain in the mid-1550s. Their purchases in anticipation of expected shortages led to a public outcry, but despite government measures to prevent further transactions, forward trade continued, and in later years spread to other bulk commodities such as herring and sugar, as well as to VOC shares and tulips. Still, it took a sufficiently large group of wealthy merchants to bear and share the financial risks involved in this trade, and hence it remained but a marginal solution for the risks implied in long-distance traffic.

A far less controversial means to transfer risks to a third party was through maritime insurance. First introduced in Italy in the fourteenth century, this instrument was regularly used by merchants in Antwerp in the sixteenth century. It was probably in the 1590s that the first policies were written for voyages on the war-ridden trading routes to southern Europe. By 1650 merchants in Amsterdam could take out insurance for shipments to markets around Europe, while smaller markets had emerged in secondary ports such as Middelburg and Rotterdam.

Conclusion

Increasingly poor soil conditions in the late Middle Ages created comparative advantages for peasants in Holland who specialized in dairy farming, shipping, fishing, peat digging, and weaving. This rural stronghold, combined with the proximity of regions with very different opportunity structures, the easy access to the northern seas, and the multitude of navigable rivers and lakes, led to a precocious growth of interior and ocean shipping and domestic and foreign trade after 1400. In the sixteenth century the Dutch economy developed a complementary relationship with that of the southern provinces. Luxury manufactures and capital began to flow to the north, while various foodstuffs, raw materials, and shipping services were sold in the south.

This early interdependence of the two regions is one explanation for the immigration of so many merchants and artisans from Flanders and Brabant in the years following the Dutch Revolt. The subsequent boom in trade, shipping, craft production, and agriculture has led historians to insist on the personal wealth, social networks, commercial and technical skills, or even the capitalist spirit of these immigrants. Besides the numerous Flemish newcomers, and the much smaller group of Portuguese Jews, there was an even larger community of local entrepreneurs who were equally successful in the introduction of new products or the exploration of new markets. Ocean shipping, textile manufacturing, milling, the fisheries, colonial trade, food processing—each of these sectors witnessed important innovations between 1580 and 1650.

More important than the particular skills of a limited number of innovative entrepreneurs was the institutional framework that allowed a much larger number of men (and women) of relatively modest means to set up their own businesses for the marketing of goods and services. On the one hand, towns and villages created commodity markets with the appropriate physical infrastructure, payment system, contracting rules, and a legal system to protect merchants and their goods from violence and opportunism. On the other hand the Dutch Republic boasted efficient factor markets that allowed entrepreneurs to hire laborers, rent land, and obtain capital to invest in their business operations. Commodity and capital markets contributed further by allowing a better management of the risks involved in judgmental decisions about the marketing of goods and services.

The benefits for Dutch entrepreneurs were impressive. From the 1580s onward merchants and manufacturers accumulated large amounts of capital. Colonial trade, commercial farming, urban manufactures, and the exchange of goods within Europe all helped to built large fortunes (Soltow and Van Zanden 1998). Reinvestment of the money earned continued until at least the middle of the seventeenth century. By then, the Dutch Republic boasted a middle class consisting of tens of thousands of self-employed men (and women) who led comfortable lives in the highly urbanized Dutch society (De Vries and Van der Woude 1997, 507–606). A very small group of regents and public officeholders lived more comfortably still, but the large majority of the Dutch population had to make do with only modest wages, or less (Prak 2005, 122–34).

Dutch entrepreneurs did so well in the Golden Age that it seems difficult to explain why the economy lost much of its luster in the late seventeenth and the eighteenth century. The population stopped growing; the pace of technological change slackened; foreign trade and manufacturing stagnated. It has been argued that this is a classical case of entrepreneurial failure.[39] The creation of monopolies and cartels increased risk averseness, or even conspicuous consumption may have stifled growth. It is a tempting proposition, given the image of the eighteenth-century Republic as one of regents and *renteniers*. Few families remained in business for more than three generations, the country's wealth was increasingly concentrated in a few hands; and the most prominent capitalists invested in government bonds and foreign loans rather than business enterprise.

And yet it would be wrong to attribute economic stagnation to entrepreneurial failure. There are several examples of towns adapting the organization of craft production to changing circumstances (Lesger and Noordegraaf 1999b). In Amsterdam commercial and financial innovation continued after 1670. Foreign merchants settled to build up their extensive commission trade, financial entrepreneurs created the first mutual funds and unit trusts, and the largest merchant houses set up as bankers to foreign rulers (Jonker and Sluyterman 2000). Meanwhile, the institutional framework for finance and trade created in the sixteenth and seventeenth centuries was so efficient that it was copied in surrounding countries. Dutch craftsmen and engineers continued to be sought after by foreign rulers who wanted to improve water management, construction works, and manufacturing in their own territories (Davids 1998). To some extent, the Dutch might be considered victims of their own technological success, for the high quality of the existing infrastructure, transportation system, and energy supplies greatly reduced the expected return from any further improvement (Davids 1995).

If anything, entrepreneurs in the later seventeenth and eighteenth centuries displayed a rational attitude toward the political and economic constraints of the time. From the 1670s onward England and France shielded their domestic markets from products from the United Provinces. Investments were redirected and sectors untouched by protectionism continued to have a comparative advantage and consequently remained highly competitive until the late eighteenth century.[40] Particularly noteworthy was the strengthening of Amsterdam's economy, with its growing imports from Asia and America, and the financial services it offered to international traders and foreign rulers. The one weak spot exposed by this rebound of the Amsterdam market was the sacrifice of the interests of industrial entrepreneurs in the inland provinces in favor of long-distance trade.[41]

Appendix: An Estimate of the Number of Entrepreneurs in Amsterdam around 1620

The basic source for the calculation of figures on the number of entrepreneurs in Amsterdam is an official count, instigated by the town magistrate, of the number of active guild members in 1688 (Oldewelt 1942). All but seven guilds responded and reported the size of their membership. To arrive at an estimate for 1620 I calculated the share of these different professional groups in the population of 1680, and then multiplied their relative share by the population of 1622.[42] This led to crude estimates for the number of entrepreneurs in manufacturing (2,638), transportation (950), retail trade (1,688), and professional services (i.e., surgeons, notaries, and lawyers, 199).

Obviously, this guild survey only provides us with a rough estimate at best. One of the possible distortions is that entrepreneurs might be a member of more than one guild (Van Tielhof 2002). Furthermore, we merely follow the mainstream view of the massive body of literature on Dutch guilds to argue that, as a rule, the membership of the guilds was limited to the masters, not the journeymen and apprentices (Prak et al. 2006). Although there is evidence to suggest (for example for shipwrights) that some of these masters were employed by others, and worked for wages, it seems reasonable to suggest that the vast majority of guild members were entrepreneurs in the sense that they made judgmental decisions about the employment of labor and capital.

It is fortunate for the present purpose that four of the seven guilds that did not reply to the magistrate's request in 1688 united porters and other handlers of goods—laborers who were the exception to the rule that guilds consisted of entrepreneurs. Of the other three only the Groote Kramers (great retailers) are a problem. For the brokers and lightermen alternative estimates are available. Meanwhile, for various professional groups our estimates are corroborated by other evidence. For example, the total number of mills (including copper- and paper mills, and the like) in Amsterdam in the eighteenth century is estimated at 135, against 94 members of the corn- and timbermillers' guild in 1688 (Honig 1930).

Finally, a host of primary and secondary sources allows amendment and further refinement of our estimates, as described next:

1. There are two ways to estimate the total number of *wholesale traders* in Amsterdam. One is to use the number of accountholders in the Exchange Bank in 1620 (1,202) as a proxy (Van Dillen 1925, 2:985). Another is to rely on the very detailed estimate of the number of merchants from the southern Netherlands (400) active in Amsterdam in 1620, and their estimated 30 percent in the city's total merchant community (Gelderblom 2000). This yields a slightly higher estimate of 1,333 merchants. Given that the clientele of the Wisselbank was still expanding at the time (reaching 1,348 accountholders in 1631), I follow the second estimate and set the number of wholesale traders in 1620 at 1,350.

2. Only one important group of *retail traders* is missing from the guild survey: the Groote Kramers, who specialized in the retail sale of all kinds of textiles. I estimate that their

number was similar to that of the Kleine Kramers (about 400), which brings our estimate of the total number of retailers in Amsterdam to 2,600.

3. *Transportation*. All but two of the major groups of shipmasters in Amsterdam appeared in the guild survey of 1688.

a. The guild of the *lightermen*, the shipmasters carrying mainly grain from the oceangoing vessels to shore, was asked but did not give information on its membership. However, a by-law issued in 1624 to reduce their number to 225 suggests their number must have been at least 250 in 1620 (Van Tielhof 2002).

b. We also lack information on the number of oceangoing shipmasters residing in Amsterdam in 1620. If we combine the estimated size of the Dutch fleet in the 1630s (1,750) with information on the residence of shipmasters from samples of freight contracts to the Baltic Sea (3 to 6 percent), Norway (0 to 5 percent) and the Iberian Peninsula (17 percent) between 1595 and 1650, a high estimate would be that 150 (i.e., 8.5 percent) shipmasters lived in Amsterdam.[43]

4. *Manufacturing*

a. First, I have included entrepreneurs in industries that were not organized in guilds (Van Dillen 1929). I estimate the number of sugar refiners at twenty-five, soap boilers at thirteen to seventeen, and breweries at fifteen to twenty (Poelwijk 2003). To be sure, several of these installations were owned by two or more proprietors, but these were typically merchants, which implies they are already counted with the merchants. Based on the incidence of the professions *distilleerder* and *brandewijnbrander* mentioned in contemporary sources (ninety distillers against 125 *brewers* between 1580 and 1630; these are both workers and bosses), I estimate the number of (brandy) distillers, in keeping with the number of brewers, at fifteen. We also know that in the early seventeenth century the city counted one or two glass producers, a few copper mills, perhaps a salt refinery, and a vinegar boiling house. All in all, an estimate of a total of 150 entrepreneurs, active in unincorporated industries in Amsterdam in 1620, seems reasonable.

b. Diamond cutters are not counted separately, for an analysis of this sector in the period 1590–1610 suggests that in the first decades of the seventeenth century the cutting of stones was largely a putting-out business organized by merchants (Gelderblom 2003b, 2008).

5. The last category, *other services*, comprises the following professional groups: brokers, hostellers, surgeons, lawyers, and notaries.

a. Oldewelt (1942) mentions 175 as the number of notaries and solicitors in 1688, which, following our estimation strategy would boil down to 84 of them in 1620. This estimate seems reasonable considering the 16 notaries for whom protocols survive in Amsterdam's city archive.

b. Oldewelt (1942) finds 241 surgeons in 1688. I estimate their number at 115 in 1620.

c. The number of brokers in 1618 is known from the membership register of the guild: 438. As for the hostellers, older historians have estimated that the city may have had as many as 500 in the early seventeenth century (Stuart 1879; Visser 1997). This may seem rather high but between 1578 and 1606 alone over 100 hostellers bought the freedom of the city (Amsterdam City Archives, *poorterboeken*); if we accept that besides inns, Amsterdam also had its fair share of taverns, the 500 seems a number good enough to go by.

The size of the adult population is that of the total population in 1622, adjusted for the share of 15–64 year olds in 1680 (32.8 percent) as estimated by van Leeuwen and Oeppen (1993).

Notes

The author would like to thank William Baumol, Joel Mokyr, Maarten Prak, and Timur Kuran for comments on an earlier version of this chapter and Heleen Kole and Jaco Zuijderduijn for excellent research assistance.

[1] The definition of entrepreneurship follows (Casson 2003).

[2] Klein 1965. Cf. also Israel 1989; Lesger 2006. Even scholars playing down the contribution of entrepreneurship implicitly consider a small group of innovative businessmen (De Vries and Van der Woude 1997; Prak 2005).

[3] On Flemish immigrants: Gelderblom 2003a, with references to the extensive Dutch literature on the topic. See also Lesger 2006. On the Huguenots: Frijhoff 2003; on the Portuguese Jews: Israel 2002 with references to older studies, including his own.

[4] The obvious exception is the vast Dutch-language literature on craft guilds, which has always focused on the artisans in individual workshops (Prak et al. 2006). For a reappraisal of the role of female entrepreneurs in the Dutch Republic, see Van den Heuvel 2007.

[5] De Vries and Van der Woude 1997, 61. More detailed case studies of the supply of towns include Lesger 1990 and Boschma-Aarnoudse 2003.

[6] The most comprehensive English-language overviews of early modern Dutch entrepreneurship are two edited volumes: Lesger and Noordegraaf 1995, 1999. The older literature is summarized in Klein and Veluwenkamp 1993..

[7] Van Zanden 1993; De Vries and Van der Woude 1997; see also the various contributions in Hoppenbrouwers and Van Zanden 2001.

[8] De Vries and Van der Woude 1997, 204–5. See Lesger and Noordegraaf 1999, 27–29, and literature cited there on the creation of local commercial infrastructures.

[9] The following is based on Boschma-Aarnoudse 2003, 423–26, 453–57.

[10] De Vries 1974; For a comparative approach: De Vries and Van der Woude 1997, 507–21.

[11] The best general overview is Bieleman 1992. For a detailed case study of one such area: Van Cruyningen 2000.

[12] Estimate based on (a) the low and high population estimates of De Vries and Van der Woude (1997, 50–52) for 1600 (1.4 and 1.6 million) and 1650 (1.85 and 1.9 million); (b) two-thirds of this population aged between fifteen and sixty-five; (c) 40 percent of the population living in towns.

[13] See, for example, Ehrenberg 1896; Jeannin 1957. Fernand Braudel (1979) explicitly distinguished capitalist entrepreneurs in the major commercial centers of early modern Europe, and self-employed men and women in other areas.

[14] Recent Dutch studies on the Flemish immigrant entrepreneurs: De Jong 2005; Wijnroks 2003; Gelderblom 2000; Enthoven 1996; on the Portuguese merchants see Vlessing 1995; Lesger 2006; and Israel 1990.

[15] The histories of Lemaire and Van Os are recounted in Gelderblom 2000. See also Van Dillen 1930.

[16] The first voyages of Tweenhuysen are detailed in Hart 1957. See also the even older Muller 1874.

[17] On beer: Yntema 1992, Unger 2001. On dairy production: Boekel 1929; Van Bavel and Gelderblom 2010.

[18] On brickworks: Kloot-Meyburg 1925; on madder: Priester 1998, 324–65; on salt refining: Van Dam 2006.

[19] My interpretation of technological change builds on Davids 1995. See also Davids 2008.

[20] On the exploration of new markets: Israel 1989; on bookkeeping: Davinds 2004.

[21] On sugar refiners see, for example, Poelwijk 2003; on leather production, Gelderblom 2003b; on tobacco manufacturing, Roessingh 1976.

[22] The example is based on Gelderblom 2003b.

[23] Davids 1995; On glass manufacturers: Mentink 1981; for silk: Colenbrander 1992.

[24] The greater efficiency that could be achieved with such measures, provided the government carefully weighed opposing economic interests, has been argued by Lesger 1999, 33–35, 39–40.

[25] Meilink 1922. In 1542 the Habsburg rulers demanded a 10 percent levy on the profits from trade. After fierce protests the levy was replaced by a tax on a fictional 6 percent return on the capital of merchants, shipmasters, herring fishers, and exporting beer brewers.

[26] The following is based on Gelderblom, forthcoming.

[27] The following is based on Gelderblom and Jonker 2004.

[28] For the guarantor to be credible required him to pledge his own person and goods as surety. Since he did not have to do anything but assert this pledge, only merchants whose wealth was relatively well-known to the other party would be accepted as surety. This reliance on familiarity would make it more problematic for itinerant merchants, hence presumably the initial rule—implicit in the privileges of the German Hansa—that any group member could be held responsible.

[29] Maassen 2005. Pawning had been a common procedure in the Low Countries since at least the twelfth century: Godding 1987, 256–57.

[30] As a result the only commodities widely used as collateral for loans other than postponed payments were jewelry, gold and silver plate, and precious stones. In Amsterdam, notarial deeds testify to the use of precious stones and jewelry as collateral: In 1627 the Amsterdam merchant "nam tot zich" jewels and paintings to compensate for an obligation of 1,029 guilders (including interest) that had not been repaid (GAA NA Card Index, NA 392/82, August 2, 1627). In 1630 an Amsterdam merchant held a jewel to secure money lent by him to a fellow merchant (GAA NA Card Index, NA 847/141, April 6, 1630); for other examples: NA 646b 1035–36 (October 22, 1624); NA 700 A 235–37 (June 21, 1625); NA 307/blz. 196–97 (November 26, 1632); NA 642/344 (February 24, 1637); NA 676/68–69 (September 24, 637).

[31] For the introduction of these rules in the late medieval period: Zuijderduijn 2009. In 1622 the Dutch Republic required the registration, by the local court, or a notary—in the case of Amsterdam—of transfers of ships of four lasts (eight tons) and bigger in case of sale or pledging as collateral. Dutch customary law did not allow creditors of loans with ships as collateral to repossess the ship to get their money back (Lichtenauer 1934, 53–56).

[32] Hugo Soly (1977, 81) was the first to draw attention to the use of annuities for the funding of small businessmen. His analysis of the sellers of these *renten* in Antwerp in 1545 and 1555 bears out the importance of the instrument for merchants, cloth finishers, masons, carpenters, and various other artisans.

[33] For a detailed analysis of loans by goldsmiths: Gelderblom 2008.

[34] Following the rules set by Charles V in the 1540s, creditors who wanted to liquidate a claim prematurely could do so by selling the obligation to a third party.

[35] The following is based on Gelderblom and Jonker 2004.

[36] See Hoffman et al. 2000 for the role of notaries in Parisian credit markets after 1660.

[37] One could also argue that the success of Dutch entrepreneurs in the Golden Age resulted from their great willingness to take these risks. This is one of two arguments Roessingh put forward to explain the willingness of Dutch peasants to grow tobacco plants for the national and international market in the seventeenth century (Roessingh 1976, 278–79). However, he does not provide solid evidence for this thesis.

[38] The point is further developed in Gelderblom, forthcoming.

[39] For a historiography of the debate on entrepreneurial failure: Lucassen 1991.

[40] For new initiatives in tobacco manufacturing: Roessingh 1976, 408–24; Verduijn 1998; Mayer-Hirsch 1999. For a successful start-up, see, for example, the Utrecht wine seller Barend Blomsaet, who started his career with a few hundred guilders, a capital that grew within two decades to 15,000 guilders (Tigelaar 1998, 23–24).

[41] Lesger and Noordegraaf's (1999) interpretation: urban and provincial particularism (a medieval legacy) brought Holland on top of the rest of the Republic. It fostered its growth but damaged the economic interests of other provinces.

[42] Town population from Lourens and Lucassen 1997.

[43] Jonker and Sluyterman 2000; Knoppers 1977; Winkelman 1983; Schreiner 1933; Christensen 1941, 264–65.

References

Baars, C. 1975. "Boekhoudingen van landbouwbedrijven in de Hoeksewaard uit de zeventiende en achttiende eeuw." *A.A.G. Bijdragen* 19:3–136.

Bieleman, Jan. 1992. *Geschiedenis van de landbouw in Nederland, 1500–1950: Veranderingen en verscheidenheid*. Meppel: Boom.

Boekel, Pieter N. 1929. *De zuivelexport van Nederland tot 1813*. Utrecht: Drukkerij Fa. Schotanus & Jens.

Bonke, A.J.J.M., W. Dobber, et al. 2002. *Cornelis Corneliszoon van Uitgeest: Uitvinder aan de basis van de Gouden Eeuw*. Zutphen: Walburg Pers.

Boot, J. A. 1974. "De markt voor Twents-Achterhoekse weefsels in de tweede helft van de 18de eeuw." *Textielhistorische Bijdragen Jaarverslag* 16:21–68.

Boschma-Aarnoudse, C. 2003. *Tot verbeteringe van de neeringe deser stede*. Hilversum: Verloren.

Braudel, Fernand. 1979. *Civilisation Matérielle, économie et capitalisme, XVe–XVIIIe siècles*. Paris: Colin.

Broeze, F.J.A. 1976–78. "Rederij." In *Maritieme geschiedenis der Nederlanden*, ed. F.J.A. Broeze, J. R. Bruijn, and F. S. Gaastra, vol. 3. Bussum: Unieboek.

Bruijn, Jaap R. 1993. *The Dutch Navy of the Seventeenth and Eighteenth Centuries*. Columbia: University of South Carolina Press.

Brünner, Eduard C. G. 1924. "Een Hoornsch koopmansboek uit de tweede helft der 15e eeuw." *Economisch-Historisch Jaarboek* 10:3–79.

Brusse, Paul. 1999. *Overleven door ondernemen: De agrarische geschiedenis van de Over-Betuwe 1650–1850*. Wageningen: Afdeling Agrarische Geschiedenis Landbouwuniversiteit.

Casson, Mark C. 2003. "Entrepreneurship." In *Oxford Encyclopaedia of Economic History*, ed. Joel Mokyr, 2:210–15. Oxford: Oxford University Press.

Christensen, Aksel E. 1941. *Dutch Trade to the Baltic about 1600: Studies in the Sound Toll Register and Dutch Shipping Records*. Copenhagen: E. Munksgaard.

Colenbrander, S. 1992. "Zolang de weefkonst bloeijt in 't machtig Amsterdam. Zijdelakenfabrikeurs in Amsterdam in de 17de en 18de eeuw." *Textielhistorische Bijdragen Jaarverslag* 32:27–44.

Davids, Karel. 1995. "Beginning Entrepreneurs and Municipal Governments in Holland at the Time of the Republic." In *Entrepreneurs and Entrepreneurship in Early Modern Times: Merchants and Industrialists within the Orbit of the Dutch Staple Market*, ed. Clé M. Lesger and Leo Noordegraaf, 167–83. The Hague: Stichting Hollandse Historische Reeks.

———. 1995. "Shifts of Technological Leadership in Early Modern Europe." In *A Miracle Mirrored: The Dutch Republic in European Perspective*, ed. K. Davids and J. Lucassen, 338–66. Cambridge: Cambridge University Press.

———. 1998. "Successful and Failed Transitions: A Comparison of Innovations in Windmill Technology in Britain and the Netherlands in the Early Modern Period." *History and Technology* 14:225–47.

———. 2004. "The Bookkeeper's Tale: Learning Merchant Skills in the Northern Netherlands in the Sixteenth Century." In *Education and Learning in the Netherlands, 1400–1600: Essays in Honour of Hilde de Ridder-Symoens*, ed. K. Goudriaan, J. v. Moolenbroek, and A. Tervoort, 235–51. Leiden: Brill.

———. 2008. The Rise and Decline of Dutch Technological Leadership. Technology, Economy and Culture in the Netherlands, 1350-1800. 2 vols. Leiden/Boston: Brill.

Den Heijer, H. J. 2005. *De geoctrooieerde compagnie: De VOC en de WIC als voorlopers van de naamloze vennootschap*. Deventer: Kluwer.

De Vries, Jan. 1974. *The Dutch Rural Economy in the Golden Age, 1500–1700*. New Haven: Yale University Press.

De Vries, Jan, and Ad Van der Woude. 1997. *The First Modern Economy: Success, Failure, and Perseverance of the Dutch Economy, 1500–1815*. Cambridge: Cambridge University Press.

Dekker, Rudolf. 1982. *Holland in beroering. Oproeren in de 17de en de 18de eeuw*. Baarn.

Doorman, G. i. 1956. "Het haringkaken en Willem Beukels." *Tijdschrift voor Geschiedenis* 69:371–86.

Eeghen, I.H.v. 1961. "Buitenlandse monopolies voor de Amsterdamse kooplieden in de tweede helft der zeventiende eeuw." *Jaarboek van het Genootschap Amstelodamum* 53:176–84.

Eerenbeemt, H.F.J.M van den. 1983. "Zijdeteelt in Nederland in de 17e en eerste helft 18e eeuw." *Nederlands Economisch Historisch Archief—Jaarboek* 46:142–53.

———. 1985. "Zijdeteelt in de tweede helft van de 18e eeuw." *Nederlands Economisch Historisch Archief—Jaarboek* 48:130–49.

———. 1993. *Op zoek naar het zachte goud. Pogingen tot innovatie via een zijdeteelt in Nederland 17e–20e eeuw*. Tilburg: Gianotten.

Ehrenberg, Richard. 1896. *Das Zeitalter der Fugger, Geldkapital und Creditverkehr im 16. Jahrhundert*. Vol. 2, *Die Weltbörsen und Finanzkrisen des 16. Jahrhunderts*. Jena: Fischer.

Enthoven, Victor. 1996. "Zeeland en de opkomst van de Republiek. Handel en strijd in de Scheldedelta c. 1550–1621." Ph.D. diss., Rijksuniversiteit Leiden.

Frijhoff, Willem. 2003. "Uncertain Brotherhood: The Huguenots in the Dutch Republic." In *Memory and Identity: The Huguenots in France and the Atlantic Diaspora*, ed. Bertrand Van Ruymbeke and Randy J. Sparks, 128–71. Columbia: University of South Carolina Press.

Gelderblom, Oscar. 2000. *Zuid-Nederlandse kooplieden en de opkomst van de Amsterdamse stapelmarkt (1578–1630)*. Hilversum: Verloren.

———. 2003a. "From Antwerp to Amsterdam: The Contribution of Merchants from the Southern Netherlands to the Commercial Expansion of Amsterdam (c. 1540–1609)." *Review: A Journal of the Fernand Braudel Center* 26, no. 3: 247–83.

———. 2003b. "The Governance of Early Modern Trade: The Case of Hans Thijs (1556–1611)." *Enterprise and Society* 4:606–39.

———. 2005. "The Resolution of Commercial Conflicts in Bruges, Antwerp, and Amsterdam, 1250–1650." http://www.lowcountries.nl/2005-2_gelderblom.pdf.

———. 2008. "Het juweliersbedrijf in de Lage Landen," *unpublished working paper* Utrecht University.

———. Forthcoming. *Violence, Opportunism, and the Growth of Long-Distance Trade in the Low Countries (1250–1650)*.

Gelderblom, Oscar, and Joost Jonker. 2004. "Completing a Financial Revolution: The Finance of the Dutch East India Trade and the Rise of the Amsterdam Capital Market, 1595–1612." *Journal of Economic History* 64, no. 3: 641–72.

———. 2005. "Amsterdam as the Cradle of Modern Futures Trading and Options Trading, 1550–1650." In *The Origins of Value: The Financial Innovations That Created Modern Capital Markets*, ed. William N. Goetzmann and K. Geert Rouwenhorst, 189–205. Oxford: Oxford University Press.

Godding, Philippe. 1987. *Le droit privé dans les Pays-Bas méridionaux, du 12e au 18e siècle*. Brussels: Académie royale de Belgique.

Greefs, Hilde, and Marjolein 't Hart, eds. 2006. *Water Management, Communities, and Environment: The Low Countries in Comparative Perspective, c. 1000—c. 1800*. Hilversum: Verloren.

Guicciardini, L., G. Silvius, et al. 1567. *Descrittione di M. Lodouico Guicciardini patritio Fiorentino, di tutti i Paesi Bassi, altrimenti detti Germania inferiore: Con piu carte di geographia del paese, & col ritratto naturale di piu terre principali*. In Anuersa: Apresso Guglielmo Siluio stampatore regio.

Hacquebord, L. 1994. "Van Noordse Compagnie tot Maatschappij voor de Walvisvaart. Honderd jaar onderzoek naar de geschiedenis van de Nederlandse walvisvaart." *Tijdschrift voor Zeegeschiedenis* 13:19–40.

Hart, Simon. 1957. "De eerste Nederlandse tochten ter walvisvaart." *Jaarboek van het Genootschap Amstelodamum* 49:27–64.

Hoffman, Philip T., Gilles Postel-Vinay, and Jean-Laurent Rosenthal. 2000. *Priceless Markets: The Political Economy of Credit in Paris, 1660–1870*. Chicago: University of Chicago Press.

Honig, Gerrit J. 1930. "De Molens van Amsterdam (De invloed van de molens op het Indus- trieele leven in de Gouden Eeuw)." *Amstelodamum. Jaarboek van het genootschap Amste- lodamum* 27:79–159.

Hoppenbrouwers, Peter C. M., and Jan Luiten Van Zanden, eds. 2001. *Peasants into Farmers? The Transformation of Rural Economy and Society in the Low Countries (Middle Ages–19th Century) in Light of the Brenner Debate*. CORN Publication Series 4. Turnhout: Brepols.

Israel, Jonathan I. 1989. *Dutch Primacy in World Trade, 1585–1740*. Oxford: Clarendon Press; New York: Oxford University Press.

———. 1990. *Empires and Entrepots: The Dutch, the Spanish Monarchy, and the Jews, 1585–1713*. London: Hambledon Press.

———. 2002. *Diasporas within a Diaspora: Jews, Crypto-Jews, and the World Maritime Empires (1540–1740)*. Leiden: Brill.

Jeannin, Pierre. 1957. *Les marchands au XVIe siecle*. Paris: Editions du Seuil.

Jong, Michiel de. 2005. *"Staat van oorlog." Wapenbedrijf en militaire hervorming in de Re- publiek der Verenigde Nederlanden, 1585–1621*. Hilversum: Verloren.

Jonker, Joost, and Keetie E. Sluyterman. 2000. *At Home on the World Markets: Dutch International Trading Companies from the 16th Century until the Present*. The Hague: Sdu Uitgevers.

Klein, P. W. 1965. *De Trippen in de 17e eeuw: Een studie over het ondernemersgedrag op de Hollandse stapelmarkt*. Assen: Van Gorcum.

Klein, P. W., and Jan-Willem Veluwenkamp. 1993. "The Role of the Entrepreneur in the Economic Expansion of the Dutch Republic." In *The Dutch Economy in the Golden Age: Nine Studies*, ed. Karel Davids and Leo Noordegraaf, 27–53. Amsterdam: Nederlandsch Economisch-Historisch Archief.

Kloot-Meyburg, B.W.v.d. 1925. "Eenige gegevens over de Hollandsche steenindustrie in de 17e eeuw." *Nederlands Economisch Historisch Archief—Jaarboek* 10:79–160.

Knoppers, J.V.T. 1977. "De vaart in Europa." In *Maritieme geschiedenis der Nederlanden*, ed. F.J.A. Broeze, J. R. Bruijn and F. S. Gaastra, 226–61. Bussum: Unieboek.

Lesger, Clé M. 1990. *Hoorn als stedelijk knooppunt: Stedensystemen tijdens de late middel- eeuwen en vroegmoderne tijd*. Hilversum: Verloren.

———. 2006. *The Rise of the Amsterdam Market and Information Exchange: Merchants, Commercial Expansion, and Change in the Spatial Economy of the Low Countries, c. 1550–1630*. Trans. J. C. Grayson. Burlington, VT: Ashgate.

Lesger, Clé M., and Leo Noordegraaf, eds. 1995. *Entrepreneurs and Entrepreneurship in Early Modern Times: Merchants and Industrialists within the Orbit of the Dutch Staple Market*. The Hague: Stichting Hollandse Historische Reeks.

———. 1999a. Introduction. *Ondernemers & bestuurders: Economie en politiek in de Noor- delijke Nederlanden in de late Middeleeuwen en vroegmoderne tijd*, ed. Clé M. Lesger and Leo Noordegraaf, 11–60. Amsterdam: Nederlandsch Economisch-Historisch Archief.

Lesger, Clé M., and Leo Noordegraaf, eds. 1999b. *Ondernemers & bestuurders: Economie en politiek in de Noordelijke Nederlanden in de late Middeleeuwen en vroegmoderne tijd*. Amsterdam: Nederlandsch Economisch-Historisch Archief.

Lichtenauer, W. F. 1934. "De ontwikkeling van het Nederlandsche Zeerecht onder den invloed van wetenschap en handelspraktijk met bijzondere inachtneming van de Rotterdamsche in- vloeden." *Themis. Verzameling van bijdragen tot de kennis van het publiek en privaatrecht* 95:48–80, 115–70.

Lourens, Piet, and Jan Lucassen. 1997. *Inwonertallen van Nederlandse steden ca. 1300–1800*. Amsterdam: Nederlandsch Economisch-Historisch Archief.

Lucassen, Jan. 1991. *Jan, Jan Salie en diens kinderen. Vergelijkend onderzoek naar continu- iteit en discontinuiteit*. Amsterdam: Stichting beheer IISG.

Maassen, H.A.J. 2005. *Tussen commercieel en sociaal krediet. De ontwikkeling van de Bank van Lening in Nederland van Lombard tot Gemeentelijke Kredietbank 1260–1940*. Hilver- sum: Verloren.

Mayer-Hirsch, S.B.N. 1999. "Benjamin Cohen (1725–1800) tabaksplanter, koopman, bankier." In *Utrechtse biografieën. Het Eemland. Levensbeschrijvingen van bekende en onbekende mensen uit het Eemland*, ed. Y. M. van den Akker et al, 2:51–57. Utrecht: SPOU.

Meilink, P. A. 1922. "Gegevens aangaande bedrijfskapitalen in den Hollandschen en Zeeuwschen handel in 1543." *Economisch-Historisch Jaarboek* 8:254–77.

Mentink, G. J. 1981. "Fabricage van 'klein-geweer' te Culemborg in de periode 1759–1812." *Nederlands Economisch Historisch Archief—Jaarboek* 44:22–30.

Moree, M. 1990. "Echten tot Echten, Roelof van (1592–1643)." In *Drentse biografieën. Levensbeschrijvingen van bekende en onbekende Drenten*, ed. Paul Brood, Willem Foorthuis, and Jan Bos, 2:44–48. Meppel: Boom.

Muller, Samuel. 1874. *Geschiedenis der Noordsche Compagnie*. Utrecht: Provinciaal Utrechts Genootschap van Kunsten en Wetenschappen.

Oldewelt, W.F.H. 1942. "Een beroepstelling uit den jare 1688." In *Amsterdamsche Archiefvondsten*, ed. W.F.H. Oldewelt, 172–76. Amsterdam: J. H. de Bussy.

Poelwijk, Arjan. 2003. *"In dienste vant suyckerbacken": De Amsterdamse suikernijverheid en haar ondernemers, 1580–1630*. Hilversum: Verloren.

Posthumus, N. W. 1908. *De geschiedenis van de Leidsche lakenindustrie*. Vol. 1, *De Middeleeuwen (veertiende tot zestiende eeuw)*. The Hague: Martinus Nijhoff.

———. 1939. *De geschiedenis van de Leidsche Lakenindustrie*. Vol. 2, *De Nieuwe tijd (zestiende tot achttiende eeuw) de lakenindustrie en verwante industrieën (eerste deel)*. The Hague: Martinus Nijhoff.

———. 1953. *De Oosterse handel te Amsterdam: Het oudst bewaarde koopmansboek van een Amsterdamsche vennootschap betreffende de handel op de Oostzee, 1485–1490*. Leiden.

———. 1971. *De uitvoer van Amsterdam, 1543–1545*. Leiden: Brill Archive.

Prak, Maarten. 1994. "Ambachtsgilden vroeger en nu." *Nederlands Economisch Historisch Archief—Jaarboek* 57:10–33.

———. 2005. *The Dutch Republic in the Seventeenth Century: The Golden Age*. Cambridge: Cambridge University Press

Prak, Maarten, Catharina Lis, Jan Lucassen, and Hugo Soly, eds. 2006. *Craft Guilds in the Early Modern Low Countries: Work, Power, and Representation*. Aldershot, UK: Ashgate.

Priester, Peter R. 1998. *Geschiedenis van de Zeeuwse landbouw. ca. 1600–1910*. 't Goy-Houten: Hes Uitgevers.

Prins, I. 1936. "Gegevens betreffende de 'Oprechte Hollansche Civet' (17e–18e eeuw)." *Economisch-Historisch Jaarboek* 20:1–211.

Riemersma, Jelle C. 1952. "Trading and Shipping Associations in 16th Century Holland." *Tijdschrift voor Geschiedenis* 65:330–38.

Roessingh, H. K. 1976. *Inlandse tabak: Expansie en contractie van een handelsgewas in de 17e en 18e eeuw in Nederland*. Zutphen: Walburg Pers.

Schreiner, Johan. 1933. *Nederland og Norge, 1625–1650: Trelastutførsel og handelspolitikk*. Oslo: Dybwad.

Soltow, Lee, and Jan Luiten Van Zanden. 1998. *Income and Wealth Inequality in the Netherlands, 16th–20th Century*. Amsterdam: Het Spinhuis.

Soly, Hugo. 1977. *Urbanisme en kapitalisme te Antwerpen in de 16de eeuw: De stedebouwkundige en industriële ondernemingen van Gilbert van Schoonbeke*. [Brussels]: Gemeentekrediet van België.

Sterck, J.F.M. 1916. "Een Amsterdamsche Zijdewinkel in de Warmoesstraat 1634–1637." *Jaarboek Amstelodamum* 14:145–83.

Stuart, T. 1879. *De Amsterdamse makelaardij. Bijdrage tot de geschiedenis onzer handelswetgeving*. Amsterdam.

Tigelaar, H. 1998. "Barend Blomsaet (1669–1730), Wijnkoopman, ter dood veroordeeld wegens sodomie." In *Utrechtse biografieen. Levensbeschrijvingen van bekende en onbekende Utrechters*, ed. W.v.d. Broeke et al., 5:23–28. Amsterdam: Boom.

Tracy, James D. 2004. *For Holland`s Garden: The War Aims of the States of Holland, 1572–1588*. Amsterdam: Amsterdams centrum voor de studie van de Gouden Eeuw, Universiteit van Amsterdam.

Unger, Richard W. 1978. *Dutch Shipbuilding before 1800*. Assen: Van Gorcum.

———. 2001. *A History of Brewing in Holland, 900–1900: Economy, Technology, and the State*. Leiden: Brill.

Van Bavel, Bas J. P. 2001. "Land, Lease and Agriculture: The Transition of the Rural Economy in the Dutch River Area from the Fourteenth to the Sixteenth Century." *Past and Present* 172:3–43.

———. 2003. "Early Proto-industrialization in the Low Countries? The Importance and Nature of Market-Oriented Non-agricultural Activities in the Countryside in Flanders and Holland, c. 1250–1570." *Revue Belge de Philologie et d'Histoire* 81:1109–63.

Van Bavel, Bas J. P., and Oscar Gelderblom. 2010. "A Land of Milk and Butter: The Economic Origins of Cleanliness in the Dutch Golden Age." *Past and Present*, forthcomimg.

Van Bavel, Bas J. P., and Jan Luiten Van Zanden. 2004. "The Jump-Start of the Holland Economy during the Late-Medieval Crisis, c. 1350–c.1550." *Economic History Review* 57:503–32.

Van Cruyningen, P. J. 2000. *Behoudend maar buigzaam. Boeren in West-Zeeuws Vlaanderen 1650–1850*. Wagening: Afd. Agrarische Geschiedenis, Wageningen universiteit.

Van Dam, Petra. 2006. "Middeleeuwse bedrijven in zout en zel in Zuidwest-Nederland. Een analyse op basis van de moerneringsrekening van Puttermoer van 1386 in vergelijkend perspectief." *Jaarboek voor Middeleeuwse Geschiedenis* 9:85–115.

Van den Heuvel, Danielle. 2007. *Women and Entrepreneurship: Female Traders in the Northern Netherlands c. 1580–1815*. Amsterdam: Aksant Academic Publishers.

Van der Wee, Herman. 1967. "Anvers et les innovations de la technique financière aux XVIe et XVIIe siècles." *Annales ESC* 22:1067–89.

———. 1977. "Monetary, Credit and Banking Systems." In *The Cambridge Economic History of Europe*, vol. 5, *The Economic Organization of Early Modern Europe*, ed. E. E. Rich and C. H. Wilson, 290–392. Cambridge: Cambridge University Press.

Van der Woude, Adrianus Maria. 1972. *Het Noorderkwartier. Een regionaal historisch onderzoek in de demografische en economische geschiedenis van westelijk Nederland van de late Middeleeuwen tot het begin van de 19e eeuw*. Wageningen: H. Veenman & Zonen.

Van Dillen, J. G. 1925. *Bronnen tot de geschiedenis der Wisselbanken. (Amsterdam, Middelburg, Delft, Rotterdam*. Rijks geschiedkundige publicatien, 59. The Hague: Nijhoff.

———, ed. 1929. *Bronnen tot de geschiedenis van het bedrijfsleven en het gildewezen van Amsterdam*. Vol. 2, *1612–1635*. Rijks geschiedkundige publicatiën. Grote serie 78. The Hague: Nijhoff.

———. 1930. "Isaac le Maire en de handel in actiën der Oost-Indische compagnie." *Economisch-Historisch Jaarboek* 16:1–165.

Van Leeuwen, Marco H. D. 2000. *De rijke Republiek. Gilden, assuradeurs en armenzorg, 1500–1800*. Amsterdam: Verbond van verzekeraars / Nederlandsch Economisch-Historisch Archief.

Van Leeuwen, Marco H. D., and James E. Oeppen. 1993. "Reconstructing the Demographic Regime of Amsterdam 1681–1920." *Economic and Social History in the Netherlands* 5:61–102.

Van Tielhof, Milja. 2002. *The "Mother of All Trades": The Baltic Grain Trade in Amsterdam from the Late 16th to the Early 19th Century*. Leiden: Brill.

———. 2005. "Turfwinning en proletarisering in Rijnland 1530–1670." *Tijdschrift voor Sociale en Economische Geschiedenis* 4:95–121.

———. 2009. "Financing Water Management in Rijnland,1500-1800." In *The Political Economy of the Dutch Republic*, ed. Oscar Gelderblom, 197–222. Aldershot: Ashgate.

Van Tielhof, Milja, and Petra Van Dam. 2007. *Waterstaat in stedenland. Het hoogheemraadschap van Rijnland voor 1857*. Utrecht: Matrijs.

Van Zanden, Jan Luiten. 1993. *The Rise and Decline of Holland's Economy: Merchant Capitalism and the Labour Market.* Manchester: Manchester University Press.

Verduin, J. 1998. "Jan Agges Scholten (1690–1772). Tabaksteler en heer van Asschat." In *Utrechtse biografieën. Het Eemland. Levensbeschrijvingen van bekende en onbekende mensen uit het Eemland,* ed. Y. M. v. d. Akker et al., 1:180–85. Utrecht: SPOU.

Visser, N. 1997. "Adriaentgen Adriaens (±1590–1648), Herbergierster." In *Utrechtse biografieën. Levensbeschrijvingen van bekende en onbekende Utrechters,* ed. W.v.d. Broeke et al., 4:11–17. Amsterdam: Boom.

Vlessing, O. 1995. "The Portuguese-Jewish Mercantile Community in Seventeenth-Century Amsterdam." In *Entrepreneurs and Entrepreneurship in the Orbit of the Dutch Staple Market,* ed. Clé M. Lesger and Leo Noordegraaf, 223–43. The Hague: Stichting Hollandse Historische Reeks.

Vogel, J. 1986. "De zijdelintindustrie te Haarlem, 1663–1780." *Jaarboek voor de Geschiedenis van Bedrijf en Techniek* 3:76–91.

Vrugt, M.v.d. 1996. "Johanna de Milan-del Corne (?–1674)." In *Utrechtse biografieën,* ed. J. Aalbers et al., 3:131–35. Amsterdam: Boom.

Wijnroks, Eric H. 2003. *Handel tussen Rusland en de Nederlanden, 1560–1640: Een netwerkanalyse van de Antwerpse en Amsterdamse kooplieden, handelend op Rusland.* Hilversum: Verloren.

Winkelman, P. H. 1971–83. *Bronnen voor de geschiedenis van de Nederlandse Oostzeehandel in de zeventiende eeuw.* The Hague: Nijhoff.

Yntema, Richard J. 1992. "The Brewing Industry in Holland, 1300–1800: A Study in Industrial Development." Ph.D. diss., University of Chicago.

Zuijderduijn, C. J. 2009. *Medieval Capital Markets: Markets for Renten, State Formation, and Private Investment in Holland (1300–1550).* Leiden: Brill.

Chapter 7

Entrepreneurship and the Industrial Revolution in Britain

JOEL MOKYR

THE "NEW ECONOMIC HISTORY" has had little patience with entrepreneurial explanations of major economic developments. Ever since the emergence of a cliometric literature on the economic history of modern Britain in the 1970s, economic historians trained in economics have debunked the view that Britain's late-nineteenth-century decline could be explained in some way by social factors that led to "entrepreneurial failure."[1] In this chapter I will look at entrepreneurship in an earlier period, the decades of the Industrial Revolution. This subject is at least not nearly as controversial as the "Victorian decline." The Industrial Revolution has remained a staple of the literature (despite ill-conceived attempts to banish it).[2] On the Victorian decline, there are now serious doubts that it ever happened at all and that we need a theory of failure in this case.

The fundamental intellectual dilemma in explaining the relationship between the Industrial Revolution and entrepreneurship is well understood. It is, at base, an identification problem. Does entrepreneurial behavior engender economic progress and technological change, or do potential entrepreneurs naturally respond to opportunities emerging from new techniques, emerging markets, or changing prices, and is it explaining the latter that really counts? It is not a debate that can be decided with an econometric breakthrough, and the answer "both" is not likely to be very satisfying either. Yet something can be learned from the conversation even if no conclusive evidence can be produced.

In the past decade the overall attitude toward institutional and cultural factors in the economics profession has changed. Once regarded as "soft" and "not amenable to measurement," institutions have more recently been recognized as important elements in explaining differences in economic attainment.[3] In his pathbreaking work on the medieval commercial revolution, Greif has shown the importance of "cultural beliefs" (1994; see also Greif 2005). Economists have shown remarkable ingenuity in measuring cultural factors and successfully relating them to economic development (see esp. Guiso, Sapienza, and Zingales 2006; Tabellini 2008). Economic historians have turned around and have begun to rethink the meaning of culture in changing economies, and to criticize the work of economists as well as other social scientists on culture (Jones 2006).

The renewed interest in culture and institutions in economic change cannot but have an effect on our thinking about entrepreneurship.[4] If economics is going to bring culture back into arguments about the sources of economic growth, it will have to return to entrepreneurship as well. Andrew Godley (2001, 13) has stated quite appropriately that "culture might be of particular importance when it comes to explaining variations in the supply of entrepreneurship." The debate between those who believed that the supply of entrepreneurship was exogenous, much like a cultural endowment, and those who argued that entrepreneurship responds to incentives and opportunities and is thus endogenous to other factors can be advanced by the new insights from neoinstitutional analysis. Institutions create the incentives and the relative payoffs faced by potential entrepreneurs. These incentives are one of the upshots of the modern interpretation of the impact of institutions on economic development. At one time, the research on institutions in economic history mostly focused on issues such as secure property rights and "law and order." It is now realized that institutions did and do much more: they channel and direct the efforts of the most creative and resourceful citizens toward their highest payoff, wherever these are (Murphy, Shleifer, and Vishny 1991; Baumol 2002). Institutions favorable to growth induce them to apply their efforts in the most remunerative and socially productive ways. In other words, institutions determine whether those efforts will result in the *creation* of wealth or primarily in its *redistribution*. Rent-seeking societies do not necessarily have fewer "entrepreneurial types" than more liberal market-oriented ones. However, the entrepreneurs in the former will apply themselves to activities that seek to create income by redistribution: exclusions and special privileges, through lawsuits and tax-exemptions, and through the manipulation of the political machinery to attain these objectives (Baumol 1993, 2002). A highly destructive form of such activities after predatory raids and other violent crime is the resistance to innovation exerted by incumbent vested interests, trying to protect the value of physical or human capital threatened by innovation with obsolescence.[5] If successful, resistance will clearly channel entrepreneurs away from innovative activities, as it reduces the expected payoff to an already risky activity.

The argument I will make below is that in eighteenth-century Britain, perhaps more than anywhere else, institutions were becoming more favorably disposed toward *technologically* innovative entrepreneurship. In the past, these kinds of changes have been associated with formal institutions such as the rule of law, intellectual property rights, and government legislation favorable to industrialists (North 1990). Yet scholars are increasingly recognizing the importance of *in*formal institutions, which take the form of accepted codes of behavior, patterns of beliefs, trust relations, and similar social patterns. It is simply not plausible that third-party enforcement was the main institution on which economic progress relied during the Industrial Revolution (Mokyr 2008). Formal law enforcement in eighteenth-century Britain left a great deal to be desired, and if a large number of economic agents had decided to renege on contracts and engage in blatantly opportunistic behavior, it is highly doubtful that the courts and law-enforcement agencies, such as they were, would have been able to dissuade them. These formal institutions did not have to, however.

Institutions that channel creativity into productive activities are the taproot of entrepreneurial success. But this argument seems just to push the explanation one step back: why do some nations have institutions more suitable to creative entrepreneurship than others? This is not the place to present a full theory of institutions, but four points seem relevant to the issue of entrepreneurship. First, institutions display a great deal of persistence in history. Societies exist with a certain institutional structure, and in most cases these structures change but slowly, much like culture. Far from arguing that History is Destiny, however, modern approaches to institutions stress that they follow normally an evolutionary process in which the present is constrained by the heritage of the past and can make at best local changes in the short run. In the long run these small differences can result in rather striking differences between economic performance. Second, as noted, informal norms and codes of behavior are as important as the formal rule of law. It is critical for agents to be somehow persuaded by concerns about morality or reputation to play cooperatively in games of exchange or production and to eschew opportunistic behavior. Third, institutions can change more easily and at lower cost when there is a *meta*-institution that has by general consensus the legitimacy to change other institutions and have its decisions accepted even by losers. Britain was almost unique in Europe in having developed such an institution after 1650. Indeed, by 1714 Parliament had acquired a position of legitimacy and power and, at least in retrospect, was gaining more and more in unassailability. Fourth, institutions are intimately related to elite ideology. Societies will set up institutions that are the outcome of both interests and beliefs. Any simple-minded theory that attributes institutions to material factors alone or to beliefs alone cannot explain the changes in British institutions between 1688 and 1850. Institutions need to reflect not only what serves people's interests but also what those with political power believe is "right" and "just." Here, more than anywhere else, we need to allow for the influence and eventual triumph of Enlightenment beliefs (see Mokyr 2006a, 2006b). As British policymakers were slowly persuaded that exclusionary arrangements, monopolies, restrictions, privileges, tariffs, bounties, and controls on free markets were harmful, these institutions were reformed and eventually abolished. To be sure, the process was not complete until the mid-nineteenth century, but it occurred without violence and within the existing political framework.

Thus the institutional developments in Britain in the eighteenth century were, on the whole, more conducive to entrepreneurship than elsewhere. This is not to say that British institutions were, by some standard, optimal or even very good. However, by the standards of the time Britain was clearly ahead of the competition. Britain provided opportunities for successful entrepreneurs to have a better chance at reaching financial and social success than elsewhere, and was able to attract a number of highly creative and successful entrepreneurs from abroad to complement the supply of local talent.[6] The institutional environment was sufficiently superior to provide Britain with a lead in the process of technological progress over other European economies in which institutional change was slower and less smooth.

For more than a century before the "start" of the Industrial Revolution, barriers to entry and exclusionary arrangements in the British manufacturing and service sectors had been breaking down or were being eroded by noncompliance. While Adam Smith may still have been complaining about the economic harm caused by Laws of Settlement or the guilds in 1776, the fact remains that in eighteenth-century Britain there were fewer formal or informal barriers to the entry of young lads into a branch they felt they could prosper in than two centuries earlier.[7] True, the Statute of Apprentices still formally barred people from exercising many trades without a formal apprenticeship, but long before its repeal in 1809 this statute was enforced very spottily. Every branch of economic activity was contestable. Barriers to entry into commerce were either ignored or circumvented. Only careers in the military, the civil service, and politics were still by and large reserved to members of the privileged Anglican landowning classes. This division, with some exceptions, served the economy well.

The other institutional advantage in Britain was that it was a society in which reliable information and credible commitments allowed exchanges between people who may not have known one another very well and whose interests were not harmonious. The successful entrepreneur in the Industrial Revolution, as I shall argue, was not necessarily a many-sided person who could do it all, as maintained by Charles Wilson (1963, 175). What he represented was one side of the business (either technical or managerial), having the ability to identify a need or an opportunity, then cooperate with others who possessed a different comparative advantage to take advantage of it. Such cooperation often took the form of partnerships or market transactions at arm's length, although a personal element was rarely missing altogether. In other cases, it involved hiring an expert, a manager, an overseeing engineer, who could be trusted. Sidney Pollard (1968) has shown that the finding of such personnel was an important skill in and of itself and often a test of successful entrepreneurship. At times, such employees eventually became successful entrepreneurs themselves, Robert Owen being the best-known example. In other cases, such as Boulton and Watt's star engineer, William Murdoch, they remained in the shadow of their masters. Entrepreneurial success was based on such successful transactions, not necessarily on a multitalented genius who could do it all. Even at the level of the firm, the classical principles of division of labor and comparative advantage held. Successful institutions were the ones that reduced transaction costs for entrepreneurs.

Entrepreneurship and Institutions

The Industrial Revolution is often viewed by economists as the beginning of modern economic growth in Europe. All the same it bears repetition that the Industrial Revolution was in its first stages a local phenomenon, confined to a fairly limited number of successful industries in a few corners of the kingdom. Sustained economic growth proper did not start until the second quarter of the nineteenth century. The true discontinuity was not so much the successful mechanization of these industries but the unprecedented event that technological progress did not lose momentum when the first round of technological opportunities was exhausted. Instead, progress gathered more and more thrust as time went on. In Britain, more than anywhere else, technological innovation was mostly confined to the private sector, with the state remaining more in the background than elsewhere in Europe, though at times it intervened. The pivotal individuals who facilitated this process were the entrepreneurs. Much has been written about the social origins of entrepreneurship, and its implication for social mobility, but less about the incentives and motives that induced them to do what they did.[8]

It would be easy to maintain simply that the payoff to effort and ingenuity increased in the eighteenth century. But as Murphy, Shleifer, and Vishny (1993) and Baumol (2002) have stressed, such effort and ingenuity can be directed toward lobbying government for exclusionary privileges or subsidies, or be aimed at military careers, privateering, and other wasteful efforts. Alternative avenues to wealth had very different implications for economic outcomes, because redistributions through political lobbying were a "leaky bucket" transfer. Resources were wasted in the process itself. In continental countries, especially France and Prussia, the market was less of an attraction to talent than the enticements of the court, government service, and especially the military. If this was so during the ancien régime, it was true *a fortiori* after 1789. Britain's institutions represent something of a paradox. While Britain was one of the most heavily taxed nations in Europe (far more heavily than France or Prussia), the heavy hand of government regulation and continental *dirigisme* was felt less and less. The eighteenth-century British Civil Service was minuscule, justice was administered by mostly unpaid part-timers or volunteers, and police and other services were essentially nonexistent. Many of the institutions we associate with public goods, such as roads, schools, and public safety, were farmed out to the private sector. Britain was still far from a pure laissez-faire economy, but it was getting closer. The only big government expenditure was defense, that is, wars and the navies and armies to fight them, and the interest payments on debts incurred in past wars (see esp. O'Brien 1994, 2002, 2006).[9] This effort included some obstreperous parts of Britain itself, such as Ireland. On the whole, however, an ambitious and talented young person in Britain would be far more inclined to seek his fortune in commerce, industry, or finance than he would be elsewhere in Europe.

The result was, above all, the growth of a small but significant economic elite that carried the Industrial Revolution. This elite consisted of a number of subgroups, not all of which can be described as entrepreneurs sensu stricto. Entrepreneurship and hardware were complementary inputs, and a country that was good at producing hardware (and the people who could use it) provided unique opportunities to those who could take advantage of them. Boulton found his Watt, Clegg his Murdoch, Marshall his Murray, and Cooke his Wheatstone. The couplings of individuals with technical skill and those with commercial acumen personalize the great advantage that Britain enjoyed in this dimension, namely the complementarity of human capital and favorable institutions. Beside the "heroic inventors" whom Samuel Smiles and other Victorians loved to praise and who are immortalized in high school textbooks, the Industrial Revolution could rely on a much larger army of less famous highly skilled craftsmen and instrument makers who could turn original ideas into a physical reality and actually build the machines that their clever colleagues designed, not just once but over and over again. These mostly anonymous craftsmen and mechanics were the unsung foot soldiers of the Industrial Revolution. These were men of dexterity and experience, who possessed a technical savoir faire taught in no school, but whose workmanship constituted the difference between an idea and a product. In Britain, the high quality of workmanship available to support grand ideas, both local and imported, helped create the Industrial Revolution.[10]

The complementarity was symmetric: those with technical ability, whether creative or supportive, needed people who could run a business, understood markets, knew about the recruitment and management of workers and foremen, had access to credit and other technical consultants, and above all, were ready to accept the uncertainties of innovation. Economists understand that such people exist in every society, but that their talents are directed in different directions depending on the incentives set by the institutional framework of society. Successful careers as leaders of mercenary bands or religious organizations required similar talents but did not produce economic growth.

Norms, Gentlemen, and Entrepreneurs

As noted, the supply of these entrepreneurs was in part determined by the payoffs to various alternative activities. In this regard, what is significant in the decades before the Industrial Revolution is the growth of a set of social norms that, beyond the formal "rule of law" and explicit penalties for opportunistic behavior, made entrepreneurial activities in Britain more attractive. The Industrial Revolution in the final analysis was propelled by technological progress, but to succeed its propagators (entrepreneurs, engineers, merchants, financiers, and technical consultants) needed contracts, credit, and credible commitments. Given that third-party (state) contract enforcement was rudimentary at best, what was the source of the cement that held British economic society together? The answer is that besides the formal mechanisms of the state, invoked only as a last resort, there was a set of social norms that supported entrepreneurial activity to a point not fully recognized. These norms may be called the culture of the gentleman-entrepreneur.

The cultural importance of the concept of a "gentleman" has been the subject of much literature, but its economic importance as a constraint on opportunistic behavior and thus a support for functioning markets has only been stressed by a few perceptive scholars such as Cain and Hopkins (1993, 22–42; see also Daunton 1989; Casson and Godley, this volume). The difficulty is that the word *gentleman* has taken on two rather inconsistent meanings. One of them is a member of the landowning gentry, a person of leisure and civic duties, with no mercenary interests, without an occupation, and therefore honorable and believable. By that definition a "gentleman of business was an absurdity," as McCloskey notes (2006, 471). It used to be thought that a "gentleman's mentality" was antientrepreneurial, that economic activities were looked at with disdain and discouraged, that nouveaux riches were a butt of derision by the real aristocrats.[11] However, while such views were surely held, they were not the chief impact of gentility on economic life. This is not just because the aristocratic lifestyle needed money, but also and perhaps more so because there was more to this culture than just snobbishness and a high predilection for leisure. The origins of the cultural idea of a gentleman go back to feudalism and the medieval landowning aristocracy.

The other meaning of the word at first blush means the reverse. By 1700, the concept of gentility was becoming less one of class than one of wealth, acquired by commercial and industrial means as much as from landownership. Defoe famously wrote that "wealth, however got, in England makes lords of mechanics, gentlemen of rakes; Antiquity and birth are needless here; 'Tis impudence and money makes a peer." Dr. Johnson, in the same spirit, noted that "an English tradesman is a new species of gentleman" if he prospered sufficiently.[12] Some brewers, papermakers, potters, and ironmasters became barons, earls, MPs, and castle dwellers.[13] Many more hoped to be. But the connection was historically important. What matters here is that if everyone could think of himself potentially as *noblesse*, everyone was *obligé* by a gentlemanly code of behavior. As Mason (1982) notes similarly, the word *gentleman* had acquired a double meaning: first, implying a person with some degree of distinction, quite disjoint from the lowest rung of society, and, second, "always suggesting certain standards of behavior." In the search for norms of behavior, Mason comments, Christianity, as a prescription for a code of conduct, was too demanding, yet some standard was necessary, and "behaving like a gentleman" became that standard. A gentleman must behave with consistency and integrity, and above all "must fulfill his obligations to those who have obligations to him" (Mason 1982, 16–17).

In eighteenth-century Britain, a businessman's most important asset was perhaps his reputation as a gentleman even if he was not a gentleman. Landowning parasitic drones were no more "gentlemen" than sword-wielding medieval thugs were "chivalrous." The ideal and the reality were increasingly divorced. There were certain things that a gentleman did and others he did not; and while such norms were of course no more perfectly followed than formal laws, breaking the rules of gentlemanly conduct was costly.[14] By the middle of the eighteenth century, before the Industrial Revolution, the idea of a gentleman implies certain behavioral codes that signaled that a person was trustworthy. It was, above all, important not to come across as greedy and rapacious.[15]

The economics of the culture of gentleman-entrepreneurs has in the past decade been made considerably clearer by the attempts to formalize ideas associated by some with "social capital." A good summary is provided by Posner (2000), who points out that cooperation between two mutually trusting agents produces not only a private good, but also an externality or network effect for the entire population. The key to being part of a community of trustworthy people is to send out a costly signal so as to make it credible. For British gentlemen these signals included dress codes, table manners, speaking styles, and personal behavior. It also included membership in organizations that helped transmit and filter signals about the trustworthiness of individuals (Sunderland 2007).

Formalizing such social networks is not hard. One such idea (e.g., Spagnolo 1999) links two types of games, one a social game that lasts for a long time and the other a one-shot economic game. If two agents face one another in both spheres, the punishment in one game may be used to induce cooperation in the other. Such cooperation is not always welfare-improving, since the trust and cooperation can be used to support socially detrimental organizations and networks. However, in Britain during the Industrial Revolution, with an increasing emphasis on honesty and truthfulness, it supported cooperative equilibria that allowed commercial and credit transactions to be consummated without excessive concern for opportunistic behavior. Gentlemen (or those who aspired to become gentlemen) moved in similar circles and faced one another in a variety of linked contexts. These models point to the likelihood that trust can be transferred from a social relation into an economic relation and thus sustain cooperative outcomes in which exchange is sustained and disputes are resolved even without the strict third-party enforcement of contracts by a powerful system of impartial courts or arbiters. It is this kind of environment that created the possibility of voluntary cooperation even when standard behavior in finite games would suggest that defection and dishonest behavior might have been a dominant strategy.

How should we assess the impact of the culture of gentility on the nature of entrepreneurship? Some entrepreneurs were obsessed with the ideal of becoming country gentlemen by getting rich. Adam Smith still was thinking about merchants when he wrote that their ambition was to become country gentlemen (1976, 432). This became equally true for many industrialists. To be sure, the famous examples of wealthy cotton masters Richard Arkwright, Jedediah Strutt, John Horrocks, linen manufacturer John Marshall, engineer John Braithwaite, and a few others notwithstanding, relatively few of the entrepreneurs of the Industrial Revolution achieved this ideal. Yet we cannot be sure that there is no reverse causality at work, in the sense that British culture was not constant but itself adapting to changes in the economic opportunities of society in the eighteenth century to create a growing respect for non-landed wealth so as to make it possible for markets and new technology to work as well as possible (Jones 2006).

In some sense, belief that by being successful and virtuous a businessman could buy himself into the elite and become a gentleman was a positive thing, creating an incentive for merchants and manufacturers to succeed, since money would buy not just material goods but also social advancement (Perkin 1969).[16] At the same time, by the late seventeenth century, at least some members of the landed aristocracy increasingly swallowed their putative disdain for moneymaking activities and came to embrace the ideals of a market economy, if mainly through intermediaries such as estate agents. "Improvement" may have meant "increased rent," and the large landlords—with some notable exceptions—did not normally get deeply involved in agricultural improvements (Mingay 1963, 172). But the movement of rents clearly shows that those who charged them knew what the markets could bear. The polite culture of the landowning gentry and the acquisitive culture of the merchant merged and created a blend that turned out to be suitable to the kind of economy Britain became in the late eighteenth century. The great legal scholar William Blackstone referred to Britain as a "Polite and Commercial People."[17] Politeness was widely equated with law-abiding behavior, and it was intuitively sensed that commercial success depended a great deal on politeness.

As Cain and Hopkins put it, "Gentlemanly ideals...provided a shared code, based on honor and obligation, which acted as a blueprint for conduct in occupations whose primary function was to manage men rather than machines" (1993, 26). I should add, however, that the typical entrepreneur during the Industrial Revolution had to manage both machines and men, as well as to manage the men who ran the machines. These shared codes, transmitted through families, were a matter of education and other mechanisms through which culture disseminates, and they correlated with certain forms of etiquette such as clothing, accent, and more generally politeness.

What mattered for the development of the economy was that people who felt constrained by the gentlemanly code of behavior behaved honorably, kept their word, and did not renege on promises. They did not blindly maximize profits. A gentleman, Asa Briggs (1959, 411) noted, was someone who accepted the notion of progress but was always suspicious of the religion of gold. In other words, someone who did not play necessarily "defect" in prisoner's dilemma situations even if that might have been in his immediate interest. In other words, gentlemanly capitalism made opportunistic behavior sufficiently taboo so that only in a few cases was it necessary to use the formal institutions to punish deviants. It created the kind of cultural beliefs in which two persons expected the other person to behave honorably. These beliefs created the environment in which complementarities between the entrepreneurs and their technological partners became possible.

True gentlemen, noted Samuel Smiles writing in 1859, looked each other in the eye and knew each other instinctively (cited by Briggs 1959, 411). For Smiles and his contemporaries, the ideal of integrity was to the tradesman, the merchant, and the manufacturer what honor was to the soldier. The standard was set by gentlemanly ideals: the gentleman's "standard of probity is high...his law is rectitude...above all a gentleman is truthful" (Smiles 1863, chap. 8, p. 36, chap. 13, pp. 28–29).[18] Shorn of their Victorian sanctimony, these ideas did set a norm, and Smiles's success demonstrates that his work struck a sensitive note. These codes of behavior, if observed by enough people, made it possible to trade with strangers and deal with people with whom there might not be repeated transactions at arm's length, without trying to take a short-term advantage from the situation. Gentlemanly enterprise, argue Cain and Hopkins, was strongly personal and held together by a social network (1993, 36). In short, gentlemanly enterprise was an informal institution, but one that supported the integrated and soon-to-be national market in Britain. That market may not have created the Industrial Revolution, perhaps, but it was an essential complement to it.[19]

To support the emergence of a set of behavioral codes that made it possible to overcome free riding and opportunistic behavior, a mechanism that supported these norms had to emerge. What some choose to call "social capital" grew at an astonishing rate in the age of Enlightenment. Britain witnessed an unprecedented blossoming of voluntary organizations, from scientific academies to drinking clubs, that created networks that supported market activity. These organizations created the ideal conditions for the linkages that, as we saw, helped bring about cooperative behavior. Social networks of this kind were essential if markets were to exist and contracts to be honored. British Masonic lodges and friendly societies provided mutual insurance and widows' pensions, but they also cemented commercial relations. Many societies that brought together artisans from different trades introduced rules that only one person per occupation could be a member with the understanding that fellow members would get priority in any commercial transaction, thus explicitly linking the commercial business-to-business vertical relations with a social connection (Brewer 1982, 222). Membership selection of many of these clubs was neither by religious nor political affiliation, but by codes of behavior and common economic interests that enhanced cooperative outcomes. By creating the kind of linkages that made selfish economic agents overcome their opportunistic instincts (and penalizing the few who did not), these social norms could become a pivotal institution that contributed a great deal to economic development. Networks were an essential underpinning of British entrepreneurship in this period of transition, because by disseminating information, they made reputation mechanisms work. Reputational mechanisms were essential if the kind of contractual environment necessary for entrepreneurs to operate was to be sustained. Many of these clubs were purely social, eating and drinking clubs, or devoted to common interests and hobbies, but they clearly functioned as clearinghouses for information as well.[20]

A prime example of the operation of gentlemanly codes was eighteenth-century credit markets. An exchange economy depended on a means of exchange. In Britain, like anywhere else, transactions were paid for by some combination of credit and cash. As contemporaries were fully aware, credit was of considerable importance to this economy, especially because the monetary system was, by wide consensus, inadequate. Contemporaries believed that credit financed the majority of transactions in Britain, and that it was more important than money for that purpose. Charles Davenant wrote in 1695 that "nothing is more fantastical and nice than Credit," and many eighteenth-century writers felt that it was the "Jewel of Trade." However, credit must eventually be settled, and therefore it depended to a great extent on beliefs and trust. Credit markets, much like the markets for ideas, depended above all on a set of self-enforcing codes framed by the norms of gentlemanly conduct. Even with the possibility of imprisonment for debt, seventeenth-century credit market transactions were enforced primarily by reputational mechanisms (Muldrew 1998, 148–72).[21] The importance of reputation was especially marked in the securities trade. In 1734, Barnard's Act outlawed time bargains in future assets (options), and the securities market had to rely on an internally enforced code of conduct because the market was formally extralegal and could not rely on third-party enforcement, based on reputation and the fear of being excluded from trade if violations occurred (Michie 2001, 31).

Connections and networks mattered a great deal in entrepreneurial success, as is increasingly recognized for other economies as well (Laird 2006). For one thing, it reduced risk. Trust made it possible to use partners and borrow from local country banks, in an age when incorporation was still not an option. Access to short-term credit, essential for working capital, was still the biggest source of demand for capital. Furthermore, it facilitated interindustry flows of funds. In a recent important paper, Pearson and Richardson (2001) have shown that the typical entrepreneur in the Industrial Revolution was heavily diversified. Rather than describing the entrepreneur as a single-minded owner-manager who spent his entire life on one business, they show the extent to which early entrepreneurs were involved in noncore ventures. Cotton masters and other textile producers in Manchester, Leeds, and Liverpool, for example, could be found as directors of insurance companies, canal and turnpike companies, gas companies, banks, and firms in other sectors.[22]

The arguments made by Pearson and Richardson about the networked nature of British entrepreneurs in this era cast an interesting light on the informal institutions of the time. Businessmen of different religious backgrounds and political convictions were working together in the boardrooms. They had no problem cooperating in developing local infrastructures, and contributed to charitable works, cultural patronage and voluntary subscriptions (Pearson and Richardson 2001, 672). On the local level, of course, reputation was everything, but the shared norms that transcended their differences helped to settle disputes and minimize opportunistic behavior. A reputation for solidity, respectability, and probity was a key to success. The informal institutions, in other words, allowed the society to operate far more efficiently than if every player had played pure Nash strategies (opportunistically). That the country was not altogether devoid of Uriah Heep types is quite obvious, but as long as opportunistic behavior remained a minority phenomenon and was dealt with mercilessly, the cultural norms of gentility prevailed. Far from being a "neoclassical" profit-maximizing egotist, the British entrepreneur during the Industrial Revolution was very much part of a shared value system that economists have only recently come to appreciate is essential in underpinning a sophisticated market economy (McCloskey 2006).

Gentlemanly codes thus engendered trust. Trust was an essential component of effective markets and a critical ingredient of the environment that created British entrepreneurship. But it was telling that it was not confined to that sphere. It was equally important in the development of British science. In a highly original contribution, Steven Shapin (1994) argued that in scientific progress (much as in commerce), trust was indispensable, and that the hallmark of a gentleman was that he could be trusted, that he spoke the truth. When a scientist reported a set of experiments or observations to a public, his status as a gentleman meant that he could be believed. A set of behavioral codes were held up as the standard that conditioned interactions between strangers and made civil society possible. Such informal codes were widespread in British society, and they were precisely the kind of institution that set up the payoff structures so favorable to entrepreneurial success.

Can we know for sure that higher levels of trust in Britain's commercial and artisanal classes led to an improved supply of entrepreneurship? Given that we have no way of measuring the levels of trust in the past, inferences here must remain indirect and speculative. Anecdotal data from travelers seems consistent with the observation.[23] Modern data, based on surveys in which people were asked directly about trust (either whether they trusted others or whether they felt that they themselves were trustworthy—the two tend to be correlated) can be used to measure this dimension of social capital. The finding is striking: Guiso, Sapienza and Zingales (2006, 34–36) find not only that the level of trust is strongly correlated with the chance of becoming an entrepreneur (approximated by whether one is self-employed), but also that a comparison of their estimates suggests that trust affects the tendency to become an entrepreneur not just through the authors' chosen instruments to serve as proxies for trust (religious affiliation and ethnic background) but also through other channels, not fully understood. In other words, modern economic research has concluded tentatively that "better cultural values have a large economic payoff" (45). It would be imprudent to dismiss such findings for an earlier period such as the British Industrial Revolution; indeed it might be argued that the conclusions should hold *a fortiori* for an earlier period (Sunderland 2007).

More generally, coupling "law and order" neglects the fact that the moral codes of polite society were a main mechanism through which a market economy could operate. Order could exist without law, that is, third-party enforcement, as it does today (Ellickson 1991). Day-to-day security depended more on social conventions and self-enforcing modes of behavior than on the administration of justice by an impartial judiciary. Commercial disputes rarely came to court and were often settled through arbitration. Voluntary compliance and respect for property and rank as social norms may have been as important as formal property rights in making the wheels of the British economy turn. Charles Davenant (1699, 55) put it well: "Nowadays Laws are not much observed, which do not in a manner execute themselves." Civil suits declined in the eighteenth century, and special arbitration tribunals emerged (Brooks 1989).

Although the Industrial Revolution changed the economic game a great deal, gentlemanly ideals did not disappear and indeed seem to have flourished during the Victorian era. Yet the informal codes of honor became less effective in large urban areas with rising rates of personal mobility, in which it became increasingly difficult to distinguish true gentlemen from opportunists and swindlers (Robb 1992). As the nineteenth century progressed, formal law and third-party enforcement slowly but certainly replaced reputation mechanisms and gentlemanly codes of behavior. It was the price of progress. The new industrialists needed to deal with an ever-growing number of people at arm's length in a market context: suppliers, creditors, subcontractors, employees, customers, and consultants. Access to useful knowledge and best-practice technology became increasingly important, and contracts became more and more complex. Despite the fact that industrialists found themselves less and less aligned with the original "gentlemen," their behavior remained anchored in the (largely imaginary) standards of decency and honorableness believed to have prevailed in an earlier age.

In the equilibrium that emerged from these standards we find a high payoff to individual initiative, to innovation, to quick and decisive perception of opportunities, and all the activities we associate with successful entrepreneurship. Such outcomes are, however, ex ante. One question of considerable interest is whether entrepreneurship actually paid ex post, that is, were perceived payoffs to entrepreneurial activity in alignment with reality. It is to this question I now turn.

Luck, Uncertainty, and the Industrial Revolution

Institutions, formal and informal, supported entrepreneurship in the Industrial Revolution by setting incentives. Yet it is a hard question whether entrepreneurship *actually* paid off for the actors themselves. If it did not, this does not necessarily mean that the incentives did not work. We know, of course, that the entrepreneurs of the Industrial Revolution, together with the engineers, the skilled craftsmen, and the inventors, created a modern sector in which technological progress thrived and which eventually turned into the modern economy. The general belief is that entrepreneurs had a high tolerance for uncertainty or for uninsurable risk in the Knightian sense, a strong ability to cope with ambiguity, and a lack of the kind of regret and the paralyzing fear of making the wrong decision that afflicts others.[24] Risk taking, of course, was a scarce resource, but the incidence of risk could be mitigated by diversification. The tightly knit network of elites was able to create what Pearson (1991) has called *collective diversification*, allowing British cotton-masters to spread their investments over a substantial number of projects with low cross-correlations, such as insurance, canals, railroads, utilities, and banks. In this way, the trust generated by the social capital of the British middle-class elites allowed them to weather the rigors and shocks of the first half-century of the mechanized cotton industry.

Whatever else, the entrepreneurs of the British Industrial Revolution were hard workers, technically and (usually) commercially adept, courageous and perseverant, who devoted themselves to their work and rarely engaged much in the frivolous leisure activities that occupied much of Britain's privileged classes. But did they themselves necessarily gain? Were entrepreneurs on average actually rewarded for the risks they took and the efforts they invested? To be sure, for incentives to work what mattered was what they expected ex ante, not what they received ex post. But if the two differed a great deal, the system was out of equilibrium, and eventually, economic theory suggests, expectations would have adjusted and the entire momentum of the Industrial Revolution would have slowed down.

The question of the rate of return to entrepreneurial activity is not easy to settle empirically. There is a substantive view that maintains that the only reason entrepreneurs can function is that they systematically overestimate their own ability. This view was most forcefully expressed by John Nye in a pathbreaking paper, in which he argued that the entrepreneur is a "somewhat overoptimistic fellow who has systematically overestimated the returns to a given innovation or research project (or underestimated the risk)" (1991, 134). Adam Smith in a famous passage thought this was a more general property of people, and while he did not make the inference that this kind of behavior can explain innovative and entrepreneurial behavior, he noted that this bias led people to gamble despite the odds and to underpurchase insurance.[25] Yet, as both Nye (1991) and Kamien (2005) stress, entrepreneurial activity has the element of a lottery ticket, with the odds against you (see also Baumol 2005). Equilibrium analysis suggests that if entrepreneurs were in a high-risk occupation, their earnings should be *higher* to compensate them for the higher riskiness. Such a finding, however, assumes that everyone assesses the risk to be the same, which evidently is not the case.

The empirical problem for the historian, as will be readily apparent, is one of truncation. We do not observe the tail of the distribution of would-be entrepreneurs whose failure was so immediate or so complete that the historical record contains no crumb of evidence pointing to their existence. Indeed, we do not know for sure that this population only constitutes a *tail* of the distribution; it may well be that *most* of the people who by some definition qualify as entrepreneurs failed and never made it to the history books. Nye suggests provocatively that the rate of return to entrepreneurship, corrected for this kind of truncation, may well have been negative. For entrepreneurship to have been a positive factor in economic development in a social welfare sense, he submits, there must have been significant externalities, that is, positive social value created by such people that they themselves did not capture. For modern data, it has been shown that the percentage captured by the inventor is shockingly low: Nordhaus (2004) has estimated that in modern America only 2.2 percent of the surplus of an invention is captured by the inventor himself. Were things looking better for inventors in the eighteenth century?

The anecdotal evidence of the business failures during the Industrial Revolution seems to indicate that in the more spectacular cases, such spillovers could be very large indeed. Some of the better-known cases are those of great inventors who, unlike James Watt, tried their hand at both the business side and the technological side of the Industrial Revolution. Thus the Scottish chemist and inventor John Roebuck, the founder of the Carron Ironworks near Falkirk and famous for his invention of lead chambers to manufacture sulphuric acid, went into business with two of the pivotal figures of the Industrial Revolution, Samuel Garbett and James Watt, but neither of these two ventures was a success. Richard Trevithick, the inventor of the high-pressure steam engine, and Richard Roberts, possibly the greatest mechanical genius of the early nineteenth century, were both failed entrepreneurs who died essentially penniless. These people, and others like them, created huge externalities in the sense that others were able to capture the fruits of their efforts even if they were not. At times, these efforts were rewarded by the authorities, tacitly recognizing the gap between social and private returns.[26]

Yet the somewhat pessimistic view of Nye needs to be qualified in a number of ways. First, the costs of "failure" here are somewhat ill-defined, and hence the size of the survival bias in the historical record in underestimating the cost of failed entrepreneurship is uncertain. There surely must have been a considerable number of people who invested heavily in entrepreneurial careers that did not pan out, and who therefore found themselves in the truncated portion of the distribution of returns on entrepreneurship on whom we have no information (which presumably is largely in the negative quadrant). However, the exact opportunity costs of these efforts are far from clear. How many of these "failures" really wasted their entire careers and invested their assets in an unsuccessful business is hard to know. Many bankrupt businessmen, presumably, fell back on their next-best alternative and found employment or other careers as managers or consultants, and while their failure surely was a disappointment, the magnitude of the net costs to themselves, let alone to society, is not obvious.[27] Some of the more notable entrepreneurial figures who failed tried again and again and in the end landed on their feet.[28] While we cannot be sure how often this was the case, indirect support for this view comes from Crouzet's findings that most industrialists and successful entrepreneurs came from a class of people that were already involved in some fashion with some industrial pursuit. About half of all "founders" were either merchant-traders or involved in manufacturing as a manager, craftsman, skilled worker, or manager. Such men, if they failed to strike it rich as self-employed entrepreneurs, could return to employment and have a decent middle-class life even if they did not get rich.[29] Finally, it bears stressing that by any definition of entrepreneurs, only a small minority of the entire population of entrepreneurs in Britain at the time of the Industrial Revolution were actually at the technological frontier. The others, businessmen, contractors, manufacturers, financiers, and merchants in traditional goods, may have been producing a great deal of social value and done so under conditions of heavy risk. But they were not the ones that propelled the Industrial Revolution. The latter comprised the small minority of technological pioneers on whose shoulders the rapidly growing economy of the second half of the nineteenth century stood, but they may have been self-selected and not representative of the population of entrepreneurs.

These entrepreneurs, moreover, were driven not only by the profit motive. As Schumpeter (1934, 93) noted, they were also driven by the joy of creating, by the satisfaction of a job well done, and by the triumph of getting a problem solved. Greed, of course, played an important role in the incentives of the British entrepreneurial class in this age, but for many others ambition and the need to impress one's peers may have been just as important.[30] In a world of commerce and finance, in which entrepreneurial activity had largely the character of arbitrage, nonpecuniary motives may not have been of great significance. But in the Industrial Revolution, the entrepreneurs at the technological cutting edge of the Industrial Revolution were building a new world, and they became increasingly aware of it.[31] Many of the best mechanical talents and practical skills tried their hand at entrepreneurship in one form or another, but their interests lay primarily elsewhere.[32] Baumol (2005) attributes the willingness of entrepreneurs to be consistently underpaid to general overoptimism as well as the "psychic benefits" of being an entrepreneur, although the question whether these benefits extend to the entrepreneurs who are unambiguous financial failures remains.[33] Moreover, there was no contradiction between the ideal of following a gentlemanly culture and experimentation. Although not many of the industrialists in Britain came from the landowning ranks, there were clearly enough gentlemen among the cutting edge of science and technology to demonstrate that it was no longer frowned upon to be excited by innovation.[34]

On the whole, being such an entrepreneur in Britain at this time shared some elements with buying a ticket in a lottery; part of the reason why people buy such tickets despite the odds against them is Smith's explanation that they misjudge their own abilities or luck. The thrill of playing and the dream of winning, moreover, must also have played a role. However, Nye is correct in pointing out that entrepreneurship is not wholly like playing the lottery because the probability of success is not predetermined but rather is conditional on what the person does. In that sense, the comparison between an entrepreneur and the buyer of a lottery ticket is misleading.

The amount of uncertainty was certainly compounded by the fact that a set of new technologies came on line after 1760, with which people had no experience and little sense of how to produce and market. This was obviously true for cotton goods and railroads, but equally for gas lighting, machine tools and instruments, food preservation, papermaking, bleaching, glass and pottery manufacturing, printing, and other industries in which radically new technologies were introduced. When experience provides little information about how likely a new idea is to work, the potential innovator has little to go by and thus only a vague idea about the distribution of the payoffs. As noted, this could be an advantage, since it could create an exaggerated sense of optimism, but there is little doubt that it was costly in terms of disappointment and wasted effort.[35] All the same, entrepreneurs were not fools, and many of the more successful ones diversified in other branches, thus reducing the chances of failure.

Entrepreneurial Failure and Entrepreneurial Success in the Industrial Revolution

The Nye hypothesis—that the average rate of return on entrepreneurship for the entire population of entrepreneurs may well have been negative in the economists' sense, that is, less than they could have earned if they had chosen other available occupations, cannot be tested directly because the historical record only mentions the more spectacular failures, or failures by those who became known in another context. Needless to say, a lot depends on the exact definition of the population. If we take, as do Barton Hamilton (2000) or Gelderblom (this volume), the population of entrepreneurs to be the population of all self-employed workers whose income was derived from market activities, we would obtain very different results than if we defined entrepreneurs as leaders, innovators, and people whose economic activity affected a substantial number of others. After all, by the wider definition many of the domestic industrialists who were part of the *Kaufsystem*—that is, sold their own wares rather than worked for a putting-out merchant-manufacturer—would be counted as entrepreneurs, and clearly for these people the Industrial Revolution was a disastrous era.

Turning to the more conventional definition, examples of highly successful entrepreneurs and of spectacular failures can be found without too much difficulty, but how to add them up in a meaningful way is problematic. All the same, something can be learned by taking a closer look at the historical records of the dramatis personae, keeping in mind that survival bias is only one problem in making this judgment. For instance, we need to ask who, exactly, should count as a failure in this case. Does a person who spends six months trying to start a business, gives up, and returns to his old job count as a failed entrepreneur? Is a person who makes a fortune and then loses it again in bankruptcy a failed entrepreneur? Formally speaking, we should compute the returns to entrepreneurship by comparing the net wealth accumulated over a lifetime of entrepreneurial activity with the opportunity costs of that activity, but in practice it is impossible to measure this ratio with any accuracy.

Much of the literature on the economics of entrepreneurship in the British Industrial Revolution has dealt with the question of origins. Were they Dissenters or members of the Church of England? What were the advantages of belonging to minority groups? Were they of middle-class origins, well connected with merchants?[36] But the answers to these questions at the end of the day shed little light on the all-important issue of incentives, and whether socially productive entrepreneurship also paid substantial private benefits. One imperfect measure of success is wealth at death. This information is quite frequently provided in the *Dictionary of National Biography*, which is now accessible online. In principle, this value should be compared to wealth at birth, which in some cases can be guessed, at least approximately, from the occupation and socioeconomic status of the parents. By this measure, at least, there were some spectacular successes. John Marshall, the Leeds flax spinner, left at his death in 1845 about £2,000,000; he inherited from his father exactly £9,000 (a tidy sum, to be sure). The only manufacturer who left a known sum larger than that was William Crawshay, the ironmaster, but he was of course born into a successful business. In cotton, besides the textbook example of Arkwright, we know of the successful Jedediah Strutt, his erstwhile partner and son of a "small farmer and maltser," who left £160,000 in 1797. John Horrocks (whose father was "a small quarrymaster" [Crouzet 1985, 131]) left £150,000, and quite a few lesser-known spinners left estates valued at £40,000 or more.

Even those who died insolvent, as I argued above, should not necessarily be written off as failures. Some obvious candidates for "failure" in the cotton industry can, of course, be found. One was William Radcliffe, a Derbyshire "improver of cotton machinery," who bought Samuel Oldknow's mill after the latter's bankruptcy, and apparently died poor after a roller-coaster career. Another was Samuel Hall, a cotton-spinner and engineer who died in "very reduced circumstances." The cotton merchant Thomas Walker had to live his final years from a bequest. Perhaps the most spectacular example of a failed entrepreneur was the highly eccentric Archibald Cochrane, Earl of Dundonald, who spent his family's fortune on an ill-fated chemical business. More than anything else, however, Cochrane was unlucky.[37] Somewhat comparable was the case of Henry Fourdrinier, a well-to-do London stationer who gambled on the main innovation in papermaking of his age, Robert's continuous papermaking machine. He spent £60,000 on the business and failed in 1810. Both Dundonald and Fourdrinier are thus examples of a significant negative private return on entrepreneurship, hardscrabble lives ending in poverty that might have given the entrepreneurial career a bad name. But how typical were they?

What makes the idea of "failure" ambiguous, however, is that many of the cases that would qualify as entrepreneurial failures during the Industrial Revolution were engineers, businessmen, and manufacturers who had started from the bottom, then worked their way up enough to earn entries in the *DNB* or in any of the other sources on which Crouzet relied, but eventually died in modest or even penurious circumstances. Some of the most famous figures in the Industrial Revolution fall in that category: the inventors Richard Roberts, Richard Trevithick, and Henry Cort, the wool manufacturer William Hirst, and the ironmaster David Tanner. As noted, it is hard to place an exact social cost on these failures; some of these men appear to have had little interest in enriching themselves; while others were simply too absorbed by their technical work to pay much attention to the financial side of things; still others simply were unlucky or naive. It is not altogether certain whether such people ought to be regarded as entrepreneurial "failures." Would they have been better off if they had lived their *entire* lives in obscurity and poverty? The answer is almost surely no; if we ask whether the economy would have been better off in that case, we can be sure of it.

To produce a more systematic picture of the returns to entrepreneurship during the Industrial Revolution, I have created a database of 1,249 personalities active in Britain at this time who could be regarded as entrepreneurs or innovators (including architects, engineers, inventors, instrument makers, and similar occupations). Rather than focus on the origins of these people, I simply asked: how well off were they at the end of their lives? Apart from the *DNB*, I tracked the names and information that appeared in Crouzet (1985) and Honeyman (1983) and followed many of their sources. The people selected were those described as businessmen, merchants, bankers, industrialists, as well as inventors, architects, engineers, publishers, and mechanics. For intellectuals to be included in the population checked, they had to have some economic or business venture, so pure academic scientists were excluded. Thus a few individuals who made their fame in some other activity were still included because of some activity that could be regarded as entrepreneurial.[38]

The data in this database are in some ways quite incomplete. Only for a subsample do we actually know from probate records the wealth of the person at death. Even here there are ambiguities: the probate records, on which the *DNB* evidently relied, listed "personal property" and excluded real estate wealth (Rubinstein 1981, 35, 59). Large settlements made to family members may have exceeded the total assets, as was the case with the Glasgow tobacco merchant and cotton spinner John Glassford. Yet he left unentailed assets valued at £40,000, so while his finances may have been chaotic, he surely was not destitute. For many others, no data exist to document their exact wealth at death, but some statement by their biographers indicates their situation. William James, a railway developer and land agent at his death in 1837 left "his family unprovided for." The Butterley ironmaster Benjamin Outram left his affairs even more chaotic when he passed away in 1805. "His wife and family...were reduced to near poverty when the rashness of some of his actions became clear after his death." The data problem is amplified by the ambiguity in assigning occupations: no fewer than 75 of the 706 individuals declared two (or more) professions, and it became ambiguous how to classify them. The lines between merchants, bankers, and industrialists were fluid, and as we noted above, many individuals diversified their activities. This ambiguity underlies the difference between parts A and B of table 7.1.

To create some order in these biographies, we divided all entries of would-be entrepreneurs born between 1700 and 1799 in the *DNB* and other sources into three categories. First, for those who actually left a probated estate specified in money terms, we counted as unsuccessful ($W = 1$) those who left estates under £1,000, as successful ($W = 2$) those who left estates between £1,000 and £10,000, and as highly successful ($W = 3$) those who left estates over £10,000. For those who left estates that were not specified in monetary value but whose biographers left us a clue to how well-off they were we followed more subjective rules. On the whole this turned out to be feasible. Many entrepreneurs were described as "destitute" or "living in reduced circumstances," which earned them a $W = 1$. Those who were described as Wealth unknown, but bequeathed an apparently profitable business at death, were awarded a $W = 2$. Examples are the St. Helens chemical manufacturer Josias Gamble, who left his firm to his son David, or the Cornish merchant and industrial entrepreneur Robert Were Fox, who before 1810 consolidated his company's position in the rich Gwennap copper mines in Cornwall, or the West Bromwich hardware maker Archibald Kenrick, who left a business to his children that at the time of his death employed 200–300 workers. Finally, entrepreneurs such as the brewer William Worthington, who "left his sons and widow substantial property in Burton, farms at Hartshorne and Gresley, and a considerable fortune" were awarded a $W = 3$. That this kind of scoring is somewhat subjective and that a few ambiguous cases may have been misclassified goes without saying. All the same, it is the first systematic attempt to look at the wealth left by the individuals who made enough of a mark to be included in the *DNB*. Beside the 706 persons who could be classified by their wealth-at-death status, the sample yielded 543 people about whom no definite judgment could be made.

Despite the truncation bias (caused by the omission of those who remained obscure) inherent in this kind of analysis, it is quite astonishing how successful entrepreneurs were in leaving substantial wealth at death. On the whole, the mean value of W for the entire sample is somewhere around 2.4, though the standard deviation is quite high (about 0.7). At the same time, the data show that the pivotal people in the Industrial Revolution (industrialists and architects/engineers) were doing somewhat worse than merchants and financiers.

Tables 7.1 through 7.3 summarize the data on British entrepreneurship in the eighteenth century. Beside the overall high level of W for the entire sample, a weaker version of the Nye hypothesis is corroborated by the fact that industrialists left sig-

TABLE 7.1
Wealth at Death, by Occupation

	Average value of W	SD	n
A. Those reporting one occupation			
Merchant	2.48	0.71	105
Industrialist	2.33	0.76	266
Banker/financier	2.65	0.64	69
Engineer/architect	2.28	0.79	180
Physician/chemist	2.50	0.65	14
All	**2.38**	**0.75**	**634**
B. Those reporting multiple occupations included in all			
Merchant	2.44	0.75	144
Industrialist	2.32	0.77	311
Banker/financier	2.55	0.71	110
Engineer/architect	2.27	0.79	194
Physician/chemist	2.55	0.67	22
All	**2.37**	**0.76**	**781**[a]

[a] Total affected by double-counting those declaring multiple occupations; actual number of observations equals 706.

TABLE 7.2
Wealth at Death by Subperiod and Occupation

	Before 1800	1800–1825	1826–1850	1851+
Merchant	2.35 (0.81), 34	2.24 (0.79), 33	2.41 (0.78), 29	2.67 (0.59), 49
Industrialist	2.16 (0.78), 64	2.22 (0.72), 59	2.20 (0.83), 66	2.52 (0.73),124
Banker/financier	2.38 (0.81), 16	2.50 (0.75), 28	2.50 (0.71), 26	2.70 (0.65), 40
Engineer/architect	2.08 (0.78), 24	2.32 (0.77), 28	2.18 (0.80), 38	2.33 (0.79), 104
Physician/chemist	3.00 (—), 2	2.83 (0.41), 6	2.00 (0.82), 4	2.50 (0.71), 10
All[a]	2.23 (0.78), 123	2.30 (0.75), 135	2.27 (0.80), 149	2.51 (0.72), 302

Note: Numbers in cells are mean (SD), *n*.

[a] In this row, individual components add up to more than total because multiple occupations have been counted in both categories.

TABLE 7.3
Average Specific Financial Bequests, by Subperiod and Occupation (in £)

	Before 1800	1800–1825	1826–1850	1851+	Total
Merchant	182, 405 (292,322, 16)	176,214 (360,326, 17)	193,801 (221,761, 20)	378,339 (856,345, 43)	271,445 (625,283, 96)
Industrialist	121,726 (236,193, 26)	141,587 (313,672, 27)	93,311 (336,339, 44)	148,346 (336,671, 109)	132,445 (321,269, 206)
Banker/financier	4,000 (65,803, 5)	174,952 (246,674, 18)	267,998 (551,537, 19)	511,508 (972,354, 38)	344,138 (740,763, 80)
Engineer/architect	21,275 (48,913, 13)	25,067 (36,354, 19)	41,879 (70,484, 23)	60,019 (131,081, 90)	49,088 (109,417, 145)
Physician/chemist	25,000 (na, 1)	98,643 (131,537, 3)	n/a	22,369 (23,190, 10)	38,902 (63,897, 14)
All	89,966 (194,065, 49)	105,785 (236,883, 68)	126,865 (357,693, 96)	197,319 (551,926, 256)	157,275 (444,826, 491)

Note: Standard deviations and cell sizes are given in parentheses.

nificantly ($t = 1.79$) *less* wealth than merchants for the period as a whole (table 7.1a) and mildly significant ($t = 1.62$) for the sample in table 7.1b. The difference between engineers and bankers/financiers is larger and significant in both tables ($t = 3.82$ and 3.24 respectively). Thus, it seems that the more industrial occupations yielded lower average rates of return and, to judge from the standard deviations, higher risks. This seems consistent with the intuitively appealing hypothesis that entrepreneurs in the modern sector suffered a higher failure rate, but when they struck it big, they did so on a larger scale. It is also consistent with Rubinstein's view that "the wealthy in Britain have disproportionately earned their fortunes in commerce and finance…rather than in manufacturing and industry" (1981, 61). Note, however, that this difference declines over time and becomes small after 1850. It is also striking that there is little improvement in the wealth at death either in table 7.2 or table 7.3 over time, with the notable exception of those who lived beyond 1850. Again, this is consistent with

Rubinstein's findings, although his approach to the data is quite different (1981, 35–37). This must in part reflect the fact that the economic payoff to the efforts made during the Industrial Revolution accrued mostly to the people living in the second half of the nineteenth century, though part of it also reflects the fact that some of these people ended up living to an older age.

Conclusions

Three important conclusions emerge. One is that the topic of entrepreneurship needs to be studied as part of the modern approach to the phenomenon of economic growth by looking at cultural and institutional factors that made more sophisticated economies possible. This approach will shed light on the question "why Britain led" perhaps more than "why an Industrial Revolution happened at all." The environment that made British entrepreneurship so effective during the Industrial Revolution consisted of institutions that created the right incentives, and the complementarities created by human capital, natural resources, and a more effective polity (Mokyr 2007). If their role is cast in those terms, it may well be time for entrepreneurs to resume their rightful place in the economic history literature as agents of economic progress right next to inventors, scientists, and enlightened politicians.

Second, I have shown that contrary to what is sometimes believed, entrepreneurs in the Industrial Revolution on the whole probably were not "lucky fools" but committed individuals who had a fair chance of doing well, even if they did not all strike gold. In a competitive environment, this is perhaps to be expected. But many more acquired the respect of their peers, some measure of economic security, and enjoyed what they did. In other words, the British entrepreneur could reasonably expect to be rewarded for his contribution, even if the reward bore no proportion to the social surplus it helped create. That contribution, it turns out, depended not only on the classic characteristics of entrepreneurs, but also on their ability to cooperate with others and establish relations based on trust without depending on third-party enforcement.

Third, the British institutional environment was an important element in British early leadership in the Industrial Revolution (Mokyr 2008). In the eighteenth century, rent-seeking and other leaky-bucket policies slowly fell out of favor, in part because the new industrial classes objected to them on purely selfish grounds. Thus, the struggle over restrictions on the adoption of new technology was unequivocally decided in favor of the entrepreneurs and the innovators. But in part rent seeking fell out of favor also because a new enlightenment ideology was being absorbed by the landed and commercial elites. This ideology persuaded them that the economic game was not zero-sum and that a free-market environment of open access, competition, and unrestrained innovation was the patriotic and virtuous thing to do. As it turns out, it was also the profitable thing to do.

Notes

The loyal and competent research assistance of Marianne Hinds is acknowledged. Michael Silver helped edit the manuscript. The comments and suggestions of William Baumol, Louis Cain, Andrew Godley, and Deirdre McCloskey have helped improve an earlier draft. Prepared for the "Entrepreneurship in History" conference, New York, October 20–21, 2006.

[1] The *opus classicus* remains McCloskey 1971. More recent works such as Dormois and Dintenfass 1999 have treaded gingerly the topic of entrepreneurial factors in the putative decline of the British economy. One prominent book, Wiener 1981, has returned to the theme of entrepreneurial failure driven by cultural factors, but his work has not persuaded the cliometricians, to say the least. For some second thoughts, however, see McCloskey (1998; 2006), who now believes that "to explain how markets live, where technology and taste originate…we need culture" (McCloskey 1998, 300).

[2] For a catalog of economic explanations of the Industrial Revolution, see Mokyr 1998, 2002; and more recently Floud and Johnson 2004, chapters 1 and 5.

[3] See especially Acemoglu, Johnson, and Robinson 2005; Rodrik, Subramanian, and Trebbi 2004; Dam 2005. For a critique, see Glaeser et al. 2004. The standard works applying institutional analysis to economic history are North 1990, 2005; and Greif 2005.

[4] I will define here institutions in the Northian way, including the socially determined "rules" by which the economic game is played and which are given exogenously to each individual, both formal and informal. Culture is simply a set of shared beliefs, attitudes, and preferences that are passed on from generation to generation through *nongenetic* (i.e., soft-wired) mechanisms.

[5] On the political economy of resistance to technological progress see Mokyr 2002.

[6] Among the best known are the Swiss Aimé Argand, whose revolutionary lamp failed to interest Parisians and who went to Britain in the 1780s, where commercial success eluded him despite the success of his invention. More successful was the Walloon inventor John-Joseph Merlin, whose many patents included roller skates, musical instruments, a rotisserie, and a wheelchair, and who was the technical genius behind James Cox's "Mechanical Museum" that opened in 1772 in Spring Gardens near Charing Cross, displaying various wondrous inventions. Successful Germans included Friedrich Koenig, a printer who complained in 1806, "There is on the Continent no sort of encouragement for an enterprise of this description…after having lost in Germany and Russia upward of two years in fruitless applications, I at last resorted to England" (cited by Smiles 1884, chap. 6). His steam-driven printing press was the first to use cylindrical impression and inking, and the first edition of the *Times* was printed on a steam-driven press in 1814. Frederic Winsor (né Winzer) played an important role in the exploitation and commercialization of gas lighting. John Jacob Holtzapffel, born in Alsace, settled in London in 1787 and built a successful business making and selling lathes. The great Swedish engineer and inventor John Ericsson came to Britain in 1826 and stayed until 1839 before leaving for the United States. The most important imports from France were the Brunels, a father and son dynasty: Marc Isambard, the father, escaped France in 1793 (he had royalist sympathies and an English wife) and settled in London in 1799. While he found the freedom and opportunities to engage in a large number of innovative projects and became quite eminent, he did not become rich, and depended for income on his wife and later his son Isambard Kingdom, arguably the leading civil engineer of his age.

[7] The career of Josiah Mason (1795–1881) is a good example. The son of a carpet weaver, he worked as a shoemaker, a carpenter, a blacksmith, and a housepainter, before becoming manager of a hardware manufactory in Birmingham. In 1829 he entered the steel-pen business in which he made his fortune, though at a later stage he also entered the electroplating industry.

[8] The best systematic work on the origins of British entrepreneurs in the Industrial Revolution, definitive in many respects, is Crouzet 1985. More limited is Honeyman 1982.

[9] See especially O'Brien 1994, 2002, 2006

[10] British (and especially Scottish) millwrights, to cite one more example, were highly sophisticated: the engineer John Fairbairn, a millwright himself, noted that eighteenth-century British millwrights were "men of superior attainments and intellectual power," and that the typical millwright would have been "a fair arithmetician, knew something of geometry, levelling and mensuration and possessed a very competent knowledge of practical mechanics" (cited in Musson and Robinson 1969, 73). John Rennie (1761–1821), who introduced the sliding hatch to the water wheel and built some of London's greatest bridges, began his career as a millwright, as did his apprentice Peter Ewart (1767–1842), who worked for Boulton and Watt and later for the cotton spinner Samuel Oldknow, and who ended his career as chief engineer in His Majesty's dockyards. Britain was thus fortunate to possess a class of able and skilled people that were hard to find in the same degree elsewhere. The difference was not only in the level or prevalence of mechanical skills but in their nature as well. Among them were mathematically sophisticated instrument makers such as the optician John Dollond (1707–61), who started off as a silk weaver and amateur optician, and ended up winning the Copley medal (1761) for his work on achromatic lenses; Jesse Ramsden, a top-notch instrument maker who designed surveying and measuring instruments of unprecedented accuracy and user-friendliness; John Hadley (1682–1744), a mathematician who built a new and more accurate navigational instrument named Hadley's quadrant (or octant); and Edward Troughton (1753–1835),

who became the best instrument maker in London after Ramsden's death. There were the mechanics Joseph Bramah and his gifted apprentice Henry Maudslay, the fathers of British machine tool industry. Bryan Donkin, famous for his improvements to the basic machine that mechanized papermaking, was also the inventor of the tachometer, a steel nib pen, and the metal tin for canned food. Equally impressive were clockmakers like John Kay (not to be confused with his namesake who invented the flying shuttle), who assisted Richard Arkwright, and John Whitehurst, a member of the Lunar Society and later the keeper of stamps and weights in London.

[11] As Daunton (1989, 125) summarizes the traditional argument, "The more an occupation or a source of income allowed for a life style which was similar to that of the landed classes, the higher the prestige it carried and the greater the power it conferred. The gentleman-capitalist did not despise the market economy but he did hold production in low regard and avoided full-time work."

[12] Defoe 1703, 19; Johnson cited by Porter 1990, 50. Men of business could, through money, "advance in rank and contend with the landlords in the enjoyments of leisure, as well as luxuries," as Malthus (1820, 470) put it.

[13] Local studies confirm the importance of wealth as a determinant of status. Urdank, in his study of Gloucestershire, found that "between 1780 and 1850 wealth had become a more obvious criterion for defining status than in the past, so much so that men with the humblest occupations might call themselves 'gentlemen' if the size of their personal estates seemed to warrant the title" (1990, 52).

[14] McCloskey (2006, 294–96) traces the transformation of the word *honor* from its aristocratic sense ("reputation") to its more capitalist sense of "honesty" (reliability, truth-telling) at the time when the importance of these concepts began to increase in the eighteenth century.

[15] The Shropshire Freemason Wellins Calcott in the 1750s described what he meant by a "man of honour": someone who not only "executes the relative duties of life with Justice and Honour" but does so with the "decorations, embellishments and graces that flow from a fine taste." A figure drawn from Sallust is "the loyal subject...the merciful landlord, the compassionate master, the generous patron, the unwearied advocate for the poor...in a word, the compleat *fine Gentleman*" (1759, 155, 59).

[16] Perkin pointed out perceptively that British society in the century following the Civil War increasingly established a link between wealth and status. Status here means not only political influence and indirect control over the lives of others but also the houses to which one was invited, the partners who were eligible for one's children to marry, the rank one could attain (that is, purchase) in the army, where one lived, and how one's children were educated. In Perkin's view, the quality of life was determined not just by "consumption," as usually defined by economists, but by the relative standing of the individual in the social hierarchy.

[17] "People are apt to be angry at the want of simplicity in our laws: they mistake variety for confusion, and complicated cases for contradictory. They bring us the examples of arbitrary governments, of Denmark, Muscovy, and Prussia; of wild and uncultivated nations, the savages of Africa and America; or of narrow domestic republics, in antient Greece and modern Switzerland; and unreasonably require the same paucity of laws, the same conciseness of practice, in a nation of freemen, a polite and commercial people, and a populous extent of territory" (Blackstone 1765–69, book 3, chap. 22).

[18] Foreign visitors, even the most sophisticated ones, noticed the same thing. Hippolyte Taine, the great historian, who visited Britain in the 1850s, commented in his *Notes sur l'Angleterre* that "'gentleman' expresses all the distinctive features of the English upper class...a truly noble man, worthy to command, a disinterested man of integrity" (1958, 145).

[19] Langford (1989, 71) points to the ambiguities of the term *politeness*, which refers to material possessions, as well as to intellectual and aesthetic taste, but above all was that "*je ne sais quoi* that distinguished the innate gentleman's understanding of what made for civilized conduct, but did not inhibit others from seeking more artificial means of acquiring it."

[20] The extent of the spreading of these clubs is reflected by the founding of the Sublime Club of Beefsteaks" devoted to carnivory in 1735. The total membership of friendly societies in 1800 is estimated at 600,000 (Porter 1990, 156–57). See especially Clark 2000.

[21] Daniel Defoe, perceptive as ever, noted that "credit is a consequence, not a cause...it is produced and grows insensibly from fair and upright dealing, punctual compliance...the Off-spring of universal probity" (1710, 9). Elsewhere he noted how essential trade credit was to a merchant: "It is the choicest ware he deals in...'tis current money in his cash chest; it accepts all his bills, 'tis the life and soul of his trade." Reputation was everything here, and "a tradesman's credit and a maid's virtue ought to be equally sacred from evil tongues" (1738, 1:195–214).

[22] The cotton merchant Benjamin Braidley calculated in his diary that he spent over thirty-six hours each week "on matters totally unconnected with my own business" (cited by Pearson 1991, 388).

23 The French traveler Pierre Jean Grosley noted the "politeness, civility and officiousness" of citizens and shopkeepers "whether great or little" (1772, 1:89, 92). The eighteenth-century Italian writer and philosopher Alessandro Verri believed that London merchants were far more trustworthy than those in Paris (cited by Langford 2000, 124). One French visitor to early nineteenth-century London noted the *probité* and good faith of British shopkeepers, and that a child could shop as confidently as the most streetwise market shopper. He thought that these habits had been copied by the merchant class from the Quakers (Nougaret, 1816, 12). Charles Dupin (1825, xi–xii) went as far as to attribute Britain's economic successes to the "wisdom, the economy and above all the probity" of its citizens. Reputation was critical. Prosper Mérimée, commenting on the open access policies in the British Museum Library in 1857, observed that "The English have the habit of showing the greatest confidence in everyone possessing character, that is, recommended by a gentleman...whoever obtains one is careful not to lose it, for he cannot regain it once lost" (1930, 153–54).

24 To paraphrase F. Scott Fitzgerald, the hallmark of a good entrepreneur is the ability to hold two opposing ideas in one's mind and yet retain the capability to function (cited by Kamien 2005, 2).

25 The famous quote is "Their absurd presumption of their own good fortune is...still more universal [than people's overestimating their own abilities] ...the chance of gain is by every man more or less overvalued, and the chance of loss...Under-valued" (Smith 1996, 120). For a modern view, see Brunnermeier and Parker 2005.

26 Both Samuel Crompton, the inventor of the mule, and Edmund Cartwright, the inventor of the power loom, were rewarded by Parliament with considerable sums, though they captured but a minute fraction of the social surplus that their inventions eventually created. A petition for the estate of Henry Cort was denied by Parliament, but the fact that other ironmasters entered a subscription for the benefit of Cort's widow demonstrates that contemporaries sensed significant spillovers here. The pioneers of the papermaking machines, Henry and Sealy Fourdrinier, too, were awarded a grant of £20,000 by a Parliamentary committee (after many manufacturers testified that the continuous paper machines had been of huge benefit to their respective branches), though this amount was later reduced to £7,000 and paid in 1840, when Henry was already in his seventies. Edward Jenner was voted a grant of £30,000 in 1815. The scientist William Sturgeon, one of the pioneers of electrical technology in the 1830s, fell on hard times toward the end of his life, and was awarded a one-off payment of £200 plus a small pension by Lord John Russell's government. In all these cases, and many others, there was an explicit recognition that these people had added to the well-being of the realm; in other words, they had produced positive externalities.

27 John Roebuck, as we have seen, failed in 1773 in a classic case of failed backward integration: in trying to supply his ironworks in Carron with coal, he bought a coal mine, which turned out to be beyond his technical capacities, and he was forced to declare bankruptcy. Yet he remained manager of his works and lived the life of a Scottish gentleman of some means, though at his death his widow was left penniless. Samuel Clegg, one of the pioneers of gas lighting in the early nineteenth century joined an ill-fated Liverpool engineering firm and "lost everything he possessed," yet had a good career as a consulting engineer afterward and served, among other capacities, as a consultant to the Portuguese government, and as one of the surveying officers for conducting preliminary inquiries on applications for new gas bills. Samuel Oldknow, the weaver of muslins, as is well known, died insolvent after his business empire collapsed in 1792, owing Arkwright over £200,000. But would that have made him a "failed entrepreneur?" After his bankruptcy in 1792, he became a successful farmer in Derbyshire during the Napoleonic Wars, high sheriff of his county, and chairman of its Agricultural Society.

28 The Scottish chemist and industrialist James Keir at age forty-five had failed in his attempts to add a chemical side to Boulton and Watt and to market his own patented alloy, "Keir's metal" (an alloy of nonferrous metals). Yet he persisted, and his alkali factory near the Birmingham canal, to which he applied his practical knowledge of chemistry, became a success, and he died worth £250,000.

29 One interesting case is that of Birmingham ironmaster Samuel Garbett, who declared bankruptcy in 1782, and then became the chief lobbyist for British manufacturers in Parliament, as head of the General Chamber of Manufacturers founded by himself and the potter Josiah Wedgwood. Garbett left £12,000 at his death, so clearly he was not destitute and his career as a businessman was still the source of income through the experience and connections he had acquired. See Norris 1958.

30 The famous passage in Smith's *Theory of Moral Sentiments* is worth citing again: "To what purpose is all the toil and bustle of the world...the pursuit of wealth, of power, and preeminence? Is it to supply the necessities of nature? The wages of the meanest labourer can supply them.... What then is the cause of our aversion to his situation?... Do the rich imagine that their stomach is better, or their sleep sounder in a palace than in a cottage? The contrary has so often been observed.... What are the advantages [then] by that great purpose of human life which we call bettering our condition?... It is the vanity, not the ease of the pleasure, which interests us. But vanity is always founded upon our belief of our being the object

of attention and approbation. The rich man glories in his riches, because he feels that they naturally draw upon him the attention of the world.... Everybody is eager to look at him.... His actions are the objects of the public care. Scarce a word, scarce a gesture can fall from him that is altogether neglected. In a great assembly he is the person upon whom all direct their eyes.... It is this, which...renders greatness the object of envy and compensates...all that toil, all that anxiety, all those mortifications which must be undergone in the pursuit of it" (1759, 50–51).

[31] Josiah Wedgwood, the very epitome of an enlightened entrepreneur, wrote in 1767 to his friend, the merchant and later partner Thomas Bentley, that a "revolution was at hand" and urged him to "assist in, proffitt by it" (1973, 1:164–65). Robert Owen (1927, 120, 121) added that "the general diffusion of manufactures throughout a country generates a new character in its inhabitants.... This change has been owing chiefly to the mechanical inventions which introduced the cotton trade into this country...the immediate effects of this manufacturing phenomenon were a rapid increase in the wealth, industry, population, and political influence of the British Empire." It was an exciting time to be alive, and of course pure bliss if one also got rich in the process.

[32] For example, Francis Hauksbee of London, a maker of optical instruments, balances, and pumps, and much active as a scientific lecturer, was also engaged in a substantial number of business ventures, some of them unrelated to his mechanical skills (such as the sale of a new therapy for venereal disease).

[33] Interestingly, research on contemporary data (Hamilton 2000) has equally concluded that the median income of entrepreneurs is about a third less than that of equally qualified and experienced workers, which he interprets as a compensating differential for the nonpecuniary benefits of being an entrepreneur. His definition of an "entrepreneur" is quite different from the one employed here: it consists basically of self-employed workers. This kind of definition will, of course, not do for the period of the Industrial Revolution. It is interesting to note that despite the care with which Hamilton analyzes his data, he does not test for the possibility that part of the explanation may be that "entrepreneurs" systematically overestimate their chances of doing well ex ante. Yet his results imply that this may be the case, because the *mean* income of the self-employed is quite high because of the presence of a few superstars who win the "lottery."

[34] One thinks of the popularity of Coke of Holkham's annual sheepshearing ceremony and Lord Kames's writings on agricultural technology, to say nothing of the admittedly eccentric Earl of Dundonald or Henry Cavendish.

[35] Payne (1978, 191) has argued that the technological riskiness of new techniques has been exaggerated by historians because the technological frontier was limited so that the points at which improvements could be made were fairly obvious. He fails to realize that the risks were compounded because new equipment and materials embodied the new techniques, and if they malfunctioned, repair and adjustments were themselves a costly source of trial and error. Complementary inputs of human capital that could maintain and fix new and unfamiliar equipment and work with new substances were scarce, and any downtime was obviously a significant cost. Moreover, the new technology required novel and unfamiliar forms of organization, above all the "factory system," whatever is precisely meant by that. New technology, by its very nature, created uncertainty not only on the demand side but also on the management and equipment end, and even microinventions could introduce serious risks of disruptions and shocks in steady production.

[36] The conclusion reached by Crouzet (1985) is that the bulk of the entrepreneurs came from the lower middle class of small merchants and artisans. The importance of dissenting religions in the Industrial Revolution in supplying a much larger than proportional number of captains of industry is beyond question, though it is hard to disentangle purely ideological causes from the exclusion of Dissenters from careers in the public sector before 1829.

[37] His coal tar, intended as a sealant for ship bottoms, was rejected by the admiralty. On the whole, however, coal tar was to prove, as Dundonald had foreseen, a valuable raw material.

[38] Thus I included in the sample the physicist George Green (1793–1841) because he was also a miller, and the engraver John Oldham (1779–1840) because he was also the inventor of a machine for individually numbering banknotes to prevent forgery as well as a system of propelling ships by means of steam-driven paddles.

References

Acemoglu, Daron, Simon Johnson, and James Robinson. 2005. "Institutions as a Fundamental Cause of Long-Run Growth." In *Handbook of Economic Growth*, ed. Philippe Aghion and Steven N. Durlauf, 1A:385–472. Amsterdam: Elsevier.

Baumol, William J. 1993. *Entrepreneurship, Management, and the Structure of Payoffs.* Cambridge: MIT Press.

———. 2002. *The Free-Market Innovation Machine: Analyzing the Growth Miracle of Capitalism.* Princeton: Princeton University Press.

———. 2005. "The Return of the Invisible Men: The Microeconomic Value of Inventors and Entrepreneurs." Presented at the meetings of the American Economic Association, Boston.

Blackstone, William. 1765–69. *Commentaries on the Laws of England.* Oxford: Clarendon Press. http://www.yale.edu/lawweb/avalon/blackstone/blacksto.htm.

Brewer, John. 1982. "Commercialization and Politics." In *The Birth of a Consumer Society: The Commercialization of Eighteenth Century England*, ed. Neil McKendrick et al., 197–262. Bloomington: Indiana University Press.

Briggs, Asa. 1959. *The Age of Improvement.* London: Longman.

Brooks, C. W. 1989. "Interpersonal Conflict and Social Tension: Civil Litigation in England, 1640–1830." In *The First Modern Society: Essays in English History in Honor of Lawrence Stone*, ed. A. L. Beier. Cambridge: Cambridge University Press.

Brunnermeier, Markus K., and Jonathan A. Parker. 2005. "Optimal Expectations." *American Economic Review* 95, no. 4: 1092–118.

Cain, Peter, and Anthony G. Hopkins. 1993. *British Imperialism: Innovation and Expansion.* Harlow, Essex: Longman.

Calcott, Wellins. 1759. *Thoughts moral and divine; collected and intended for the better instruction and conduct of life.* 3rd ed. Coventry: Printed by T. Luckman.

Clark, Peter. 2000. *British Clubs and Societies, 1580–1800: The Origins of an Associational World.* Oxford: Clarendon Press.

Crouzet, François. 1985. *The First Industrialists: The Problems of Origins.* Cambridge: Cambridge University Press.

Dam, Kenneth W. 2005. *The Law-Growth Nexus: The Rule of Law and Economic Development.* Washington, DC: Brookings Institution Press.

Daunton, Martin J. 1989. "Gentlemanly Capitalism and British Industry 1820–1914." *Past and Present* 122:119–58.

Davenant, Charles. 1699. *Essay upon the probably methods of making a people gainers in the balance of trade... By the author of the Essay on ways and means.* London: printed for J. Knapton. Reprinted in *The political and commercial works of that celebrated writer Charles D'avenant, LL.D.*, collected and revised by Charles Whitworth (London, 1771), 2: 168–382.

Defoe, Daniel. 1703. *A collection of the writings of the author of The true-born English-man.* London: n.p.

———. 1710. *An Essay upon Publick Credit.* London: Printed and sold by the Booksellers.

———. 1738. *The Complete English Tradesman.* 4th ed. 2 vols. London: C. Rivington.

Dormois, Jean-Pierre, and Michael Dinterfass. 1999. *The British Industrial Decline.* London: Routledge.

Dupin, Charles. 1825. *The Commercial Power of Great Britain: Exhibiting a complete view of the public works of this country.* 2 vols. London: Printed for C. Knight.

Ellickson, Robert C. 1991. *Order without Law: How Neighbors Settle Disputes.* Cambridge: Harvard University Press.

Floud, Roderick, and Paul Johnson, eds. 2004. *The Cambridge Economic History of Modern Britain.* Vol. 1, *Industrialization, 1700–1860.* Cambridge: Cambridge University Press.

Glaeser, Edward L., Rafael La Porta, Florencio Lopez-de-Silanes, and Andrei Shleifer. 2004. "Do Institutions Cause Growth?" *Journal of Economic Growth* 9:271–303.

Godley, Andrew. 2001. *Jewish Immigrant Entrepreneurship in New York and London, 1880–1914.* Houndsmills, Basingstoke: Palgrave.

Greif, Avner. 1994. "Cultural Beliefs and the Organization of Society: A Historical and Theoretical Reflection on Collectivist and Individualist Societies." *Journal of Political Economy* 102:912–41.

———. 2005. *Institutions and the Path to the Modern Economy: Lessons from Medieval Trade*. Cambridge: Cambridge University Press.

Grosley, Pierre Jean. 1772. *A Tour to London; or, New observations on England, and its Inhabitants*. Trans. Thomas Nugent. London: Printed for Lockyer Davis.

Guiso, Luigi, Paola Sapienza, and Luigi Zingales. 2006. "Does Culture Affect Economic Outcomes?" *Journal of Economic Perspectives* 20, no. 2: 23–48.

Hamilton, Barton H. 2000. "Does Entrepreneurship Pay? An Empirical Analysis of the Returns to Self Employment." *Journal of Political Economy* 108:604–31.

Honeyman, Katrina. 1983. *Origins of Enterprise: Business Leadership in the Industrial Revolution*. New York: St. Martin's Press.

Jones, Eric L. 2006. *Cultures Merging: A Historical and Economic Critique of Culture*. Princeton: Princeton University Press.

Kamien, Morton I. 2005. "Entrepreneurship by the Books." Kellogg Graduate School of Management.

Laird, Pamela Walker. 2006. *Pull: Networking and Success since Benjamin Franklin*. Cambridge: Harvard University Press.

Langford, Paul. 1989. *A Polite and Commercial People: England, 1727–1783*. Oxford: Oxford University Press.

———. 2002. "The Uses of Eighteenth-Century Politeness." *Transactions of the Royal Historical Society* 12:311–31.

Maitland, Frederic. 1911. *The Constitutional History of England*. Cambridge: At the University Press.

Malthus, Thomas R. 1820. *Principles of Political Economy*. London: J. Murray.

Mason, Philip. 1982. *The English Gentleman: The Rise and Fall of an Ideal*. New York: William Morrow.

McCloskey, Deirdre N., ed. 1971. *Essays on a Mature Economy: Britain after 1840*. London: Methuen.

———. 1998. "Bourgeois Virtues and the History of P & S." *Journal of Economic History* 58:297–317.

———. 2006. *The Bourgeois Virtues: Ethics for an Age of Commerce*. Chicago: University of Chicago Press.

Merimée, Prosper. 1930. "Études Anglo-Americaines." In *Oevres Complètes*, ed. Pierre Trahard and Édouard Champion, vol. 8. Paris: Librairie Ancienne Honoré Champion.

Mingay, George E. 1963. *English Landed Society in the Eighteenth Century*. London: Routledge and Kegan Paul.

Michie, Ranald. 2001. *The London Stock Exchange: A History*. Oxford: Oxford University Press.

Mokyr, Joel. 1998. "Editor's Introduction: The New Economic History and the Industrial Revolution." In *The British Industrial Revolution: An Economic Perspective*, ed. Joel Mokyr, 1–127. Boulder, CO: Westview Press.

———. 2002. *The Gifts of Athena: Historical Origins of the Knowledge Economy*. Princeton: Princeton University Press.

———. 2006a. "The Great Synergy: The European Enlightenment as a Factor in Modern Economic Growth." In *Understanding the Dynamics of a Knowledge Economy*, ed. Wilfred Dolfsma and Luc Soete, 7–41. Cheltenham: Edward Elgar.

———. 2006b. "Mercantilism, the Enlightenment, and the Industrial Revolution." In *Eli F. Heckscher (1879–1952): A Celebratory Symposium*, ed. Ronald Findlay, Rolf Henriksson, Håkan Lindgren, and Mats Lundahl, 269–303. Cambridge: MIT Press.

———. 2008. "The Institutional Origins of the Industrial Revolution." In *Institutions and Economic Performance*, ed. Elhanan Helpman, 64–119. Cambridge: Harvard University Press.

Muldrew, Craig. 1998. *The Economy of Obligation*. New York: St. Martin's Press.

Murphy, Kevin, Andrei Shleifer, and Robert Vishny. 1991. "The Allocation of Talent: Implications for Growth." *Quarterly Journal of Economics* 106:503–30.

Musson, A. E., and Eric Robinson. 1969. *Science and Technology in the Industrial Revolution*. Manchester: Manchester University Press.

Nordhaus, William D. 2004. "Schumpeterian Profits in the American Economy: Theory and Measurement." Cowles Foundation Discussion Paper No. 1457, April.

Norris, J. M. 1958. "Samuel Garbett and the Early Development of Industrial Lobbying in Great Britain." *Economic History Review* 10:450–60.

North, Douglass C. 1990. *Institutions, Institutional Change, and Economic Performance*. Cambridge: Cambridge University Press.

———. 2006. *Understanding the Process of Economic Change*. Princeton: Princeton University Press.

Nougaret, Pierre J-B. 1816. *Londres: La Cour et Les provinces d'Angleterre*. 2 vols. Paris: Chez Briand.

Nye, John Vincent. 1991. "Lucky Fools and Cautious Businessmen: On Entrepreneurship and the Measurement of Entrepreneurial Failure." In "The Vital One: Essays in Honor of Jonathan R. T. Hughes," ed. Joel Mokyr, *Research in Economic History*, suppl. 6:131–52.

O'Brien, Patrick K. 1994. "Central Government and the Economy." In *The Economic History of Britain since 1700*, 2nd ed., ed. Roderick Floud and Deirdre N. McCloskey, 1:203–41. Cambridge: Cambridge University Press.

———. 2002. "Fiscal Exceptionalism: Great Britain and Its European Rivals from Civil War to Triumph at Trafalgar and Waterloo." In *The Political Economy of the British Historical Experience, 1688–1914*, ed. Donald Winch and Patrick O'Brien, 245–65. Oxford: Oxford University Press.

———. 2006. "The Hanoverian State and the Defeat of the Continental System: A Conversation with Eli Heckscher." In *Eli Heckscher, International Trade, and Economic History*, ed. Ronald Findlay, Rolf G. H. Henriksson, Håkan Lindgren, and Mats Lundahl, 373–405. Cambridge: MIT Press.

Owen, Robert. 1927. "Observations on the Effects of the Manufacturing System." In *A New View of Society and Other Writings*, ed. G.D.H. Cole. London: Everyman's Library.

Payne, Peter. 1978. "Industrial Entrepreneurship and Management in Great Britain." In *The Cambridge Economic History of Europe*, ed. Peter Mathias and M. M. Postan, 3.1: 193–210. Cambridge: Cambridge University Press.

Pearson, Robin. 1991. "Collective Diversification: Manchester Cotton Merchants and the Insurance Business in the Early Nineteenth Century." *Business History Review* 65:379–414.

Pearson, Robin, and David Richardson. 2001. "Business Networking in the Industrial Revolution." *Economic History Review* 54:657–79.

Perkin, Harold J. 1969. *The Origins of Modern English Society, 1780–1880*. London: Routledge and Kegan Paul.

Pollard, Sidney. 1968. *The Genesis of Modern Management*. London: Penguin.

Porter, Roy. 1990. *English Society in the 18th Century*. Rev. ed. London: Penguin.

Posner, Eric. 2000. *Law and Social Norms*. Cambridge: Harvard University Press.

Robb, George. 1992. *White-Collar Crime in Modern England: Financial Fraud and Business Morality, 1845–1929*. Cambridge: Cambridge University Press.

Rodrik, Dani, Arvind Subramanian, and Francesco Trebbi. 2004. "Institutions Rule: The Primacy of Institutions over Geography and Integration in Economic Development." *Journal of Economic Growth* 9:131–65.

Rubinstein, William D. 1981. *Men of Property: The Very Wealthy in Britain since the Industrial Revolution*. London: Croom Helm.

Schumpeter, Joseph A. 1934, *The Theory of Economic Development*. Oxford: Oxford University Press.

Shapin, Steven. 1994. *A Social History of Truth*. Chicago: University of Chicago Press.

Smiles, Samuel. 1863. *Self-Help: With Illustration of Character and Conduct.* Boston: Ticknor and Fields.

———. 1884. *Men of Invention and Industry.* London: J. Murray.

Smith, Adam. 1759. *The Theory of Moral Sentiments.* London: A. Millar.

———. 1976. *The Wealth of Nations.* Ed. Edwin Cannan. Chicago: University of Chicago Press.

Spagnolo, Giancarlo. 1999. "Social Relations and Cooperations in Organizations." *Journal of Economic Behavior and Organizations* 38:1–25.

Sunderland, David. 2007. *Social Capital, Trust and the Industrial Revolution, 1780–1880.* London and New York: Routledge.

Tabellini, Guido. 2008. "Institutions and Culture (Presidential Address)." *Journal of the European Economic Association* 6, nos. 2–3: 255–94.

Taine, Hippolyte. 1958. *Notes on England.* Trans. Edward Hyams. Fair Lawn, NJ: Essential Books.

Urdank, Albion. 1990. *Religion and Society in a Cotswold Vale.* Berkeley and Los Angeles: University of California Press.

Wedgwood, Josiah, 1973. *Letters of Josiah Wedgwood.* Ed. Katherine Euphemia, Lady Farrer. Manchester: E. J. Morten [for] the Trustees of the Wedgwood Museum.

Wiener, Martin J. 1981. *English Culture and the Decline of the Industrial Spirit, 1850–1980.* Cambridge: Cambridge University Press.

Wilson, Charles. 1963. "The Entrepreneur in the Industrial Revolution in Britain." In *The Experience of Economic Growth,* ed. Barry Supple, 171–78. New York: Random House.

Chapter 8 ————————————————————————

Entrepreneurship in Britain, 1830–1900

Mark Casson and Andrew Godley

This chapter examines the role of entrepreneurship in the growth of the Victorian economy over a seventy-year period, beginning at a time when the Industrial Revolution was approaching maturity (see the previous chapter) and ending when the overseas British Empire was approaching its zenith (see the following chapter).

While the factory system was the major technological innovation of the Industrial Revolution (1760–1830), the introduction of railways, and the switch from sail to steam in oceangoing shipping, were the major technological innovations of the Victorian period (1830–1900). It was not so much in manufacturing, but rather in infrastructure, and most particularly in transport and communications systems, that Victorian Britons made their mark.

It is therefore a mistake to suppose that technological innovation in the manufacturing sector was the driving force in the Victorian British economy. There was certainly a good deal of incremental innovation in manufacturing, concerned with the fine-tuning of product design, but relatively little radical innovation. Steam power was the principal moving force at the end of the Victorian period, just as it was at the beginning, and horses still provided the major motive power on the roads. Although the principles of electromagnetism were discovered in Britain before the Victorian period, it was only after the end of the period that large-scale urban electrification—let alone rural electrification—got under way. Apart from the electric tram, little systematic use was made of electrical power until the very end of the nineteenth century.

It was not only technological innovation that was important in the Victorian era, however: institutional innovations were important too. Entrepreneurial attitudes were not confined to the private business sector; they were also evident in farsighted political leadership, and in the rapidly growing professional civil service too.

The Victorians were immensely proud of Britain's (unwritten) political constitution. They created an empire that exported British institutions to many parts of the world—most notably the Indian subcontinent and the large settler economies of Canada and Australia. Having "learned their lesson" from the American Revolution of 1776, when their principal colonial foundation declared independence, successive British governments administered their empire in a relatively decentralized manner. Although external access to imperial markets was restricted, trade within the empire was largely based on the principles of free trade enunciated by Adam Smith. The empire therefore constituted an enormous captive export market for British manufacturing firms, which they accessed through the transport linkages provided by rail and sea. The steady growth of the imperial population, through both natural increase and territorial expansion, coupled with rising incomes in the settler economies, encouraged product innovations. By the end of the Victorian period, British firms exported an enormous range of trademarked products, especially in sectors such as steam-powered machinery and metal household goods.

Private entrepreneurs did not enjoy particularly high status in Victorian Britain. Indeed, the owners of small firms were often classed as "tradesmen" and looked down upon by middle-class professionals and those with inherited wealth. On the other hand, setting up a business was easy, as regulations were few. A partnership between a wealthy investor and an enterprising artisan became a widely accepted and very successful business model. But other avenues of wealth accumulation were possible too. The ever-shifting imperial frontier provided potentially rich pickings for soldiers and bounty hunters. Furthermore, many young men of great ability chose to enter the church in search of spiritual rather than material rewards, with the risk-takers opting for missionary work overseas.

The principle of partnership was extended during the Victorian period through a series of reforms to company law that made it much easier for large businesses to be incorporated as joint-stock companies with limited liability for their shareholders. This in turn increased liquidity in stock markets by making it easier for ordinary people to buy and sell shares in small denominations. This in turn facilitated the growth of large firms.

However, little trust was placed in the law as a means of resolving business disputes. The law had a bad reputation for being slow, complex, and extremely expensive. Many businesses, including quite large businesses, therefore relied on local people to subscribe capital. The family was an important unit of business organization: it was not only the moral bedrock of Victorian society, but also a device for building trust between partners in a business. Many large businesses remained under the control of family dynasties, and "marrying the boss's daughter" was a reliable way of securing promotion in many firms. This illustrates the general point that Victorians invested heavily not only in political institutions, but in social and moral institutions too.

While the Victorian economy is, in many respects, a success story, it certainly had its failures. Its failure to develop the economic potential of new technologies such as electricity has already been noted. While electricity was widely used to facilitate imperial communications through the electric telegraph, mundane applications such as household lighting and power supply were relatively neglected. Similar criticisms can be made in terms of Britain's failure to capitalize on chemical discoveries such as synthetic dyes, which allowed Germany to gain a major technological lead in the chemical and pharmaceutical industries. Britain was also slow to exploit the potential of the internal combustion engine. Engineers were more concerned to perfect the working of the steam engine. Their decision to ignore the new technology was reinforced by the large supply of cheap coal available in Britain, the poor state of the roads, and highway regulations that protected the interests of pedestrians and horse traffic.

The evidence on Victorian entrepreneurship is compatible with general theories of entrepreneurship that emphasize the role of entrepreneurs in making sound decisions regarding risky innovations. Victorian Britons generally made good judgments regarding infrastructure investments and their use in building an empire of free trade, but their judgments were much weaker in the manufacturing sector. Entrepreneurs appear to have been aware of their own strengths and weaknesses, and to have concentrated on investing in those areas in which their judgments were likely to prove successful. However, if entrepreneurship is understood exclusively in terms of small business formation and growth, initiated by the self-employed, then the theory does not work so well in explaining the facts of the Victorian period. The large infrastructure projects, such as railways, at which the Victorians excelled were not run by the self-employed, but by boards of directors of joint-stock companies: boards that comprised professional experts such as engineers, bankers, and lawyers, together with leading merchants and manufacturers who had already built large businesses of their own. The distinguishing feature of successful Victorian entrepreneurship was that it was based on extensive partnerships between wealthy investors and professional specialists, rather than on the efforts of thousands of small-scale self-employed businessmen. While there were many such small businessmen, most successful small businesses seem to have thrived mainly because of the large size of the imperial market to which they had access. This market was not the product of technological innovation by small private enterprises, but of political initiatives backed up by large infrastructure projects, endorsed by politicians and civil servants and implemented by large joint-stock firms.

Background: Key Features of British Economic and Social Development, 1830–1900

The period 1830–1900 was a time of considerable political and social change. The period began badly. Following the end of the Napoleonic Wars in 1815, the economy had entered a serious depression. There were riots in Manchester and other cities. The Duke of Wellington, the hero of Waterloo, soon became a most unpopular prime minister.

The political situation improved after 1832, when the Reform Act extended the franchise and removed some of the "rotten boroughs." But new problems emerged. In Ireland the mismanagement of the famine stimulated calls for Home Rule. Population grew rapidly (see figure 8.1), and rural poverty was rife. The great industrial cities were insanitary, as a result; and health became a major Victorian obsession. Millions left the land and emigrated to Australia, New Zealand, North America, and elsewhere.

Nevertheless, in comparison with other European countries, the UK remained remarkably stable. The Victorian notion of paternalism encouraged local elites to be responsive to local needs, and many successful businessmen became social reformers. Religion was very important to the Victorians. It provided a bond between members of different social and economic classes, particularly in the Nonconformist churches, where artisans and small businessmen could take on responsible roles as pastors. Although there was conflict between different denominations, the Christian ethic was a potent unifying force, promoting high standards of behavior in both public and private life.

The performance of the economy was steady, if unspectacular, by modern standards. But compared to the relative stasis of medieval and early modern times,

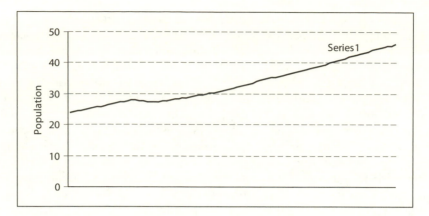

Figure 8.1. Population of the United Kingdom (in millions), 1830–1914.
(Source: Officer 2005.)

growth appears to have been remarkably high. Gross domestic product per head rose from £1,672 in 1830 to £3,911 in 1900 (at 2003 market prices), an average compound percentage growth of just over 1.2 percent per year (figure 8.2). Prices were steady throughout the period, apart from cyclical changes caused by periodic booms and slumps (figure 8.3). The stability of prices helped to sustain relatively low rates of interest. Long-term interest rates were rarely above 3.5 percent, and in the 1890s fell to below 2.5 percent (figure 8.4), although short-term rates were far more volatile, particularly at times of financial crisis, such as 1846 and 1866.

The combination of low inflation and low interest rates encouraged long-term investment. The Victorians were great builders—in almost every sense of the word. They built grand public buildings, which were symbolic of national pride, such as the new Houses of Parliament and, at a local level, they built numerous town halls, and clock towers too. They built institutions—reforming local government and creating numerous local charities; they built an empire, on which they believed that "the sun would never set," and—most importantly for this book—they built a massive infrastructure of ports, railways, urban gas and water systems, and so on. This infrastructure supported the evolution of major agglomerations of factories—the specialized industrial districts later described by Alfred Marshall (1923). Thus, despite the apparently modest levels of growth in national income they attained, the Victorians left a valuable and impressive legacy. Although much of this legacy was squandered in the twentieth century in fighting two world wars and defending the empire overseas, the Victorians built so well that a significant amount of their infrastructure—both social and physical—has survived to this day.

The Victorian period in Britain has always been controversial. No sooner had Queen Victoria died in 1901 that Edwardian intellectuals began to criticize her legacy, and the debates have continued on various fronts ever since. This chapter begins by looking at the controversies over entrepreneurship in Victorian Britain that began in the 1960s and still continue today. It shows that a bewildering variety of factors have been used to explain the performance of the Victorian economy. Although several writers have identified entrepreneurship as an explanatory factor, their ex-

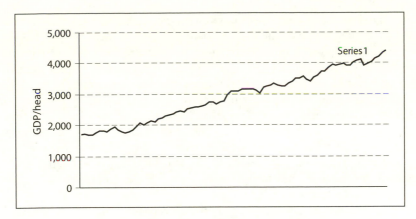

Figure 8.2. Gross Domestic Product per Head in the United Kingdom, 1830–1914. (Source: Officer 2005.)

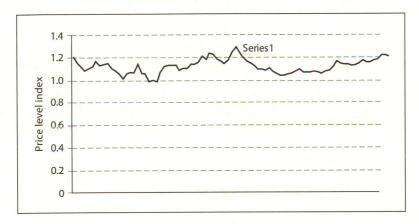

Figure 8.3. Price level in the United Kingdom, 1830–1914 (1851 = 100). (Source: Officer 2005.)

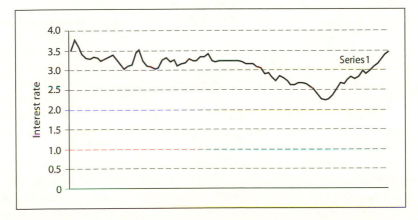

Figure 8.4. Long-Term Interest Rates in the United Kingdom, 1830–1914. (Source: Officer 2005.)

planations have not been developed in a systematic way. They rely too heavily on a simplistic social stereotype of the entrepreneur.

This chapter employs a more systematic approach to the study of entrepreneur. This approach was anticipated in the previous chapter and is further developed in the following one. It is argued that the entrepreneur is someone who specializes in taking very risky decisions about major investments. These investments involve irreversible commitments; people cannot easily get their money back if an entrepreneurial project fails. Good judgment is crucial to success under these conditions. Entrepreneurs come forward to take these decisions because they believe that their judgment is better than that of other people. If other people share that judgment, then they will lend their money to the entrepreneur. The entrepreneur will control an enterprise funded by other people's money.

If he puts his own money at risk, then the entrepreneur is a risk-bearer, whereas if he mainly risks other people's money, he is more of a risk-manager instead. The quality of his judgment in assessing the risks is put to the market test in the project that he undertakes; if his judgment is good his investors will be rewarded by handsome profits, and if he makes a mistake then they will be punished with losses. If the entrepreneur is a pure risk-manager, then it is his reputation rather than his wealth that is put at risk. Victorian society placed considerable weight on personal reputation, and so loss of reputation was a potentially serious penalty for a risk manager to incur.

As emphasized in the other chapters, if profitable projects are socially beneficial, then society benefits from the intervention of the entrepreneur, but if the entrepreneur, through political lobbying or underhand practices, profits at the expense of the public, then society will be worse off instead.

The Victorians, we shall argue, were basically successful entrepreneurs operating under good incentives that rewarded socially beneficial enterprise. They were not good at everything, however. As the Victorian era progressed, entrepreneurs increasingly focused their efforts on promoting large infrastructure projects. This was because factory production became less profitable and infrastructure projects more profitable.

In the late eighteenth century, at the start of the Industrial Revolution, infrastructure projects were often undertaken mainly as an adjunct to factory-building. Entrepreneurship was focused on the innovation of the water-powered (and later steam-powered) factory. The building of canals, and the conversion of roads into turnpikes, was useful to entrepreneurs because it reduced transport costs and thereby widened the market for their mass-produced factory goods. Many factory masters therefore invested in canal projects, for example (Pearson and Richardson 2001). By the start of the Victorian period, however, the first major wave of factory-building had come to an end. After the final defeat of Napoleon in 1815, Britain was the master of the seas, and there were major opportunities to extend maritime trade. This encouraged investments in ports and harbors instead.

To realize their full potential, however, ports needed to be connected to the great industrial centers, and canals were proving inadequate for this purpose; they dried up in summer and iced up in winter. Railways were the answer. But it soon turned out that railways could do much more than carry freight; they could carry mail and passengers at unbelievably high speed as well. New opportunities for tourism, commuting, and the development of a national system of banking were opened up. Infrastructure projects acquired a life of their own. Cities began to develop as information hubs as well as industrial centers—a function that they had always performed but could perform more easily once long-distance communication had been speeded up.

The social tensions alluded to earlier led to difficult industrial relations in many factory-based industries. British workers valued autonomy—a status very much associated with the skilled artisan—and resented the military-style discipline of the factory. If labor had been cheap, then factory owners could simply have ignored the wishes of their workers, but their workers had alternatives to factory employment; not only emigration, but employment in service industries such as transport, retailing, and banking. Factory production became steadily less economic as a result.

Infrastructure, on the other hand, prospered. The British Empire was growing fast, and everywhere there were new opportunities for development. Ports, railways, telegraphs, and urban investments were the key. It was not so much the factory as the engineering workshop that became the hub of British manufacturing. While the factory remained dominant in the textile trades, engineering workshops and "yards" were responsible for producing most of the sophisticated machinery that was exported overseas; in particular, ships and steam locomotives, and the prefabricated bridges and pipework that were exported for use in overseas projects. By the end of the century the Victorian economy was economically driven by—and dependent upon—the project of imperialism.

When the age of imperialism came to an abrupt end in 1914, so did much of British entrepreneurship (as described in the following chapter). A whole generation of budding entrepreneurs was wiped out in the trenches of World War I. Furthermore, the international political instability created by the postwar settlement at Versailles undermined the system of international trade on which the empire was built. It was not the fault of individual British entrepreneurs that they became locked in to such a vulnerable imperial system. If there was a failure, it was an overoptimistic belief, encouraged by Britain's political leaders, that the project of empire would continue indefinitely without disruption.

The Rise and Decline of Entrepreneurship in Victorian Britain: The Debate

The historical literature on Victorian entrepreneurship has focused on a rather limited range of issues. Two of these issues are briefly considered here. The first is the role of free trade policies and laissez-faire in encouraging entrepreneurship, and the second is the apparent decline of entrepreneurship in late-Victorian Britain.

Laissez-Faire

Modern political writers have looked back to early Victorian Britain in an attempt to discover the roots of modern economic growth. It is often suggested that Victorian Britain was committed to a policy of laissez-faire. According to this view, there was a popular belief that the pursuit of profit, constrained only by free competition, would lead to benefits for all; consequently, state interference was rejected as meddlesome. Under this regime of laissez-faire, entrepreneurship thrived; the fetters of government regulation were discarded, and the economy "took off." But then trades unions appeared, the story goes, and they began to monopolize the supply of labor. Using the political power of the Independent Labour Party, they crushed the spirit of enterprise. The Victorian British economy went into decline, and the responsibility carrying the torch of free enterprise passed to the United States.

There are a number of difficulties with this story. The first involves a question of dates. For a significant period prior to 1830 Britain was at war with Napoleonic France. During this period, government had an active role in stimulating demand for both textiles (e.g., military uniforms) and engineering products (e.g., guns and armor), and when this demand ceased at the end of the war a serious recession ensued. Indeed, some military historians turn the argument around, and maintain that military procurement, by setting challenging targets for entrepreneurs, stimulated investment and innovation in precision-made factory products.

Furthermore, free trade was not official government policy until the repeal of the Corn Laws in 1846, and the prime minister, Robert Peel, who pushed through this reform, split his political party in the process. Although Richard Cobden, John Bright, and other members of the "Manchester School" had been vociferous lobbyists for free trade, it was neither their free market ideology nor the prospective benefit to industry that finally swayed Peel and his followers, but the benefits to the workers themselves. Peel was concerned that the benefit to workers of any reduction in the price of corn would be neutralized by lower wages, and it was only when he was persuaded that wages would remain high because of buoyant product demand that he agreed to the reform (Prest 2004).

Another reason for government involvement in the economy was that many of the major industrial projects in Victorian Britain involved the compulsory acquisition of land, as explained below. Far from defending individual property rights unequivocally, government presided over a system in which large amounts of private land were acquired, subject to arbitration, on the authority of the state. It is a mistake to assume that, as in the United States, land could simply be acquired by pushing forward the frontier of settlement. By 1830 Britain was already a relatively mature and densely populated country, and government regularly authorized the subordination of private property rights to the public interest.

While it is true that Adam Smith had set out in the *Wealth of Nations*, as early as 1776, the benefits of a deregulated market economy, his ideas did not have the immediate impact on policy that is sometimes alleged. As an intellectual product of the Enlightenment, Smith was interested in the roots of progress. His major contribution was to identify the division of labor and the growth of trade as the main drivers of progress. His major criticism of the British government was that it had given a monopoly of the country's foreign trade to the chartered trading companies such as the East India Company. The profits of these companies were essentially a tax on trade, and Smith proposed to remove this tax by taking away the privileges of these companies and promoting competition instead. While Smith believed that competition was part of the natural order, and should be employed to good effect, he did not state that competition should be given completely free reign, as suggested by the later doctrine of laissez-faire (Nicholson 1909).

If there was a governing principle in early Victorian society, it was that advances in technology created the potential for sustained improvement in the standard of living. Unlocking this potential required good institutions, and since not all institutions were fully rational, institutional reform was required. The liberalization of markets emphasized by Smith was only one of the reforms required. It was also important to ensure that the benefits of improvement were fairly distributed between different members of society. Political reform in support of a more just distribution of the benefits of progress was an important aspect of legislation from 1830 to 1850.

There was disagreement, however, about how radical the reforms should be. Some people argued that existing institutions must already be rational, in the pragmatic sense that they had stood the test of time. Others argued that they were irrational legacies from the medieval period. Radical populists such as Marx and Engels (both of whom lived in England in the 1840s) argued that technological improvements, by liberating workers from the backbreaking toil of agricultural labor, should allow them to spend more time in rewarding and creative craft production. But factory work was anything but creative and rewarding, they observed—it was repetitive, highly disciplined, and alienating. Having escaped from the tyranny of the local squire, the worker was now tyrannized by the local industrial capitalist instead. Marx and Engels predicted a worker's revolution, but in practice the Chartist Revolution of 1848 quickly fizzled out.

In the 1870s democratic socialists promoted trade unions. The idea was that the trade union would neutralize the power of the capitalist by exercise a countervailing monopoly power through control of the labor supply. The trade union movement gained considerable support after 1880—initially among skilled workers, and later among the unskilled as well. By 1900 several industries had become dominated by large and powerful trades unions, some of whose leaders sought to use strike action not only to improve wages and conditions of employment, but also to challenge the traditional rights of employers over their workers. In manufacturing, mining, and transport, wage rates rose, basic hours of work fell, and productivity growth stagnated (Broadberry 1997, 2006).

Labor disputes began to polarize political opinion. Some employers turned to confrontation, locking workers out before a strike could take effect, and hiring strikebreakers, while others agreed to conciliation. Some embraced novel forms of profit-sharing and part-ownership with employees, while others emphatically asserted their absolute rights as employers. Government began to legislate over worker's rights and trade union representation, leading to high-profile court cases that resolved the immediate issues but often left more ill-feeling between the parties than there had been before.

By 1900 many aspects of economic life were tightly regulated, and an increasing number of activities, such as education and local transport, were coming under local government control. If there was a period of laissez-faire in Britain, then it was certainly a very short one—say between 1850 and 1880—and even then the economic freedom prevailing in Britain was nowhere as great as the freedoms that existed at this time in the United States.

The Onset of Decline

The zenith of Britain's technological leadership is commonly said to be 1851—the year of the Great Exhibition in Hyde Park, London. The key innovators, it is said, were artisan entrepreneurs who, from the late eighteenth century, had pioneered the mechanized factory system (Deane 1979; Mokyr 2004). International exhibitions became popular attractions in the nineteenth century, attended by increasing numbers of the general public, and after 1851 the success of British entrepreneurs in winning prizes went into decline, while that of U.S. and continental European entrepreneurs rose.

Not everyone agrees that the decline of Victorian entrepreneurship can be conveniently dated to some time in midcentury, however. An emphasis on economic performance rather than the pace of technological innovation suggests dating decline to the end of the mid-Victorian boom and the onset of the great depression in 1873 (Church 1975; Saul 1969).

Crafts (1985) has taken a more radical view. He argues that the impact of the "industrial revolution" on British productivity growth in the first half of the nineteenth century has been exaggerated. Mass production was mainly confined to the textile industries of the north: cottons in Lancashire and woolens in Yorkshire. More generally, Pollard (1997) has argued that throughout European history innovations in manufacturing have been concentrated in marginal agricultural areas such as the north of England, where local families combined mixed farming with protoindustrial pursuits. Crafts's view suggests that there was greater continuity between the two halves of the nineteenth century than the traditional view suggests, with a modest rate of productivity growth being sustained throughout.

It is possible that while entrepreneurship was sustained for longer than previously thought, its direction shifted. As suggested in the introduction to this chapter, there was a major shift from developing the resources of the domestic economy into imperial development. Around midcentury growing numbers of the "middling sort" who aspired to fame and fortune emigrated to the settler economies within the empire, such as Australia and New Zealand, while the more highly educated joined the growing colonial civil service. On this view, the dynamism of the late-Victorian economy shifted to the frontier of empire. Some aristocratic families made a smooth transition into merchant banking, helping to fund the growth of imperial trade and investment from its London hub. The rapid growth of financial services, together with artisan emigration, drew resources away from manufacturing industry. Overcrowding and insanitary conditions in the industrial cities reduced the quality of the manufacturing labor force, fueled labor discontent, and accelerated the spread of trade unionism to unskilled workers. As a result, the rapid industrialization of the United States, Germany, and other continental European countries exposed the weaknesses caused by low manufacturing productivity growth in Britain.

Schumpeter's (1939) analysis of long waves in the world economy leads to similar conclusions regarding structural change, but by a different route. According to Schumpeter, Britain pioneered not one but two major innovations: first the factory system and then the railroads. Since the diffusion of the railroad system was a feature of the second half of the nineteenth century rather than the first, this suggests that Britain may have continued to be entrepreneurial, but switched its focus from manufacturing to transport infrastructure and utilities (Broadberry 2006). While early transport investments focused on the domestic economy, later investments were mainly concerned with supporting international trade. Railroad technology pioneered in Britain was exported to the colonial frontier. Overseas railroad investments were supported by investments in shipping lines, whereby steam-powered vessels provided regular communications with harbors served by local railroads. The growing influence of infrastructure investment, and its international orientation, is reflected in the growth of British coal exports to overseas bunkering stations, and the declining proportion of coal output supplied to domestic heavy industry (Church 1986).

Chandler (1990) suggests a different perspective on British decline, however, derived from different sources—business histories rather than national income accounts and business cycle data (as described in detail in the following chapter). According to Chandler, British entrepreneurs were slow to make the three-pronged investments in marketing, professional management, and organized research that he considers necessary for an economy to make the transition from artisan production to mass production. A conservative attachment to the institution of the family firm, and a cult of amateurism in management, made British firms unable to respond to U.S. and German competition in high-technology industries in the late nineteenth century.

An alternative view, however, would suggest that British entrepreneurs neglected investment in mass production manufacturing industry because they perceived more profitable opportunities elsewhere. Economies of mass production, as exemplified by the Chicago meatpacking industry, benefited from cheap unskilled immigrant labor and abundant land—both factors that were missing from Britain, where land was scarce, towns were congested, and most workers aspired to artisan status. Because the territorial area of the UK is so much smaller than that of the United States, British entrepreneurs were more concerned to expand internationally. They needed to invest overseas in a range of relatively small colonial markets. As a result, they evolved more flexible managerial forms than the hierarchical Chandlerian enterprise. A good example of a flexible form is the "free-standing firm," whose operations were based wholly overseas—often in a single country—and which were controlled from a small head office, usually in London (Wilkins 1986; Wilkins and Schroter 1998). A constellation of several free-standing firms provided greater flexibility than would a single hierarchical firm on the U.S. model, managing overseas operations through national subsidiaries. By incorporating each major project as a separate company, financial transparency was increased, allowing shareholders rather than salaried managers to decide whether profits should be reinvested in new schemes.

Olson (1982) offers yet another perspective on the subject. He argues for the institutionalization of collusion as a general cause of economic decline in nations, and he uses Britain as an exemplary case. His focus is on two types of horizontal combination: combinations of workers—namely trades unions—and combinations of firms—namely trade associations and cartels. These combinations are designed to raise wages and prices by eliminating competition; in other words, they are generated by rent-seeking rather than efficiency-seeking behavior (Baumol 1994).

To discourage the entry of new competitors, a combination can obtain privileges from the state—such as immunity for strikers in the case of unions, and official recognition as lobbyists in case of trade associations. In addition, unions and employers can join forces to lobby for protective tariffs. This is what happened in Britain at the end of the nineteenth century, according to Olson. Lengthy apprenticeship schemes and restrictive practices reduced occupational mobility. The labor market became segmented into distinctive crafts, with particular types of job reserved for members of particular unions. A social hierarchy of crafts developed, analogous to an Indian caste system. So far as firms were concerned, the protection of domestic and colonial markets became increasingly important as the international competitiveness of British labor declined.

One of the difficulties with the Olson thesis is that the types of combination that impeded growth in Britain have been credited with accelerating growth in continental economies. It is said that in Germany, for example, cartels facilitated the rationalization of industry, leading to efficiency gains from the exploitation of economies of scale, while labor unions supported the diffusion of technical knowledge through industrial training schemes.

Indeed, Olson's own theory indicates that horizontal combinations can generate productivity gains as well as losses. Local trade associations not only fix prices: they can organize the provision of public goods, such as harbor improvements, which improve productivity in industrial districts. Indeed, shareholders in joint-stock firms combine horizontally to finance indivisible investments; without such combinations, large firms could not evolve to compete in international markets. Horizontal combination is therefore not intrinsically collusive in nature.

To interpret the traditional view of nineteenth-century Britain in terms of the Olson thesis it is necessary to suppose that efficiency-seeking combinations, geared to the diffusion of knowledge and the provision of public goods, dominated in the first half of the century, and that rent-seeking trades unions and cartels dominated in the second half. Part of the explanation may lie in the shakeout of the less productive firms that seems to have occurred in a number of manufacturing industries as they matured through the Victorian period. In an infant industry composed mainly of dynamic small firms, such as the early textile industry described in the previous chapter, there can be a problem in providing industry-specific public goods; since individual firms are too small to have much political influence, they must organize the provision of these goods among themselves, perhaps by forming a trade association for this purpose. As the industry matures, however, and price competition intensifies, reducing costs through economies of scale can promote industrial concentration, with small firms joining forces through merger or takeover, or simply closing down and quitting the industry. The few remaining large firms now have more political clout, and can easily dominate the trade association and use it as a front for lobbying government for subsidies or for protection from foreign competition. On this view the maturing of the manufacturing industries that were established at the time of the Industrial Revolution could account for much of the sclerosis that seemed to afflict British manufacturing industry in the late Victorian period. Government failed to respond to the policy challenges of regulating mature manufacturing industries in which firms had switched from efficiency-seeking to rent-seeking activities.

Cultural Explanations of Entrepreneurial Decline

Decline is popularly attributed to premature gentrification. In the second half of the nineteenth century, it is claimed, the social gulf between artisans and aristocrats widened. Self-employed artisans and the owners of small family firms could no longer aspire to the fame and fortune that had motivated earlier generations. Wealthy industrialists no longer challenged the aristocracy for political power, but bought into it by investing in country estates.

Wiener (1981) claims that from about 1850 Victorians became increasingly concerned about the adverse moral and social consequences of rapid industrialization. Talented young men preferred to make a career in church or state rather than trade—religious zeal and social reform provided them with greater emotional satisfactions than what was perceived as the venal pursuit of personal profit. The most prestigious schools and universities in England taught classical studies rather than science and technology, because a knowledge of the Greek and Roman empires was considered to be more relevant for careers in the army, church, or colonial service. As private enterprise was drained of talent, entrepreneurship declined, the rate of profit diminished, and investment was reduced.

McCloskey and others have challenged the notion of entrepreneurial decline in Britain by arguing that British entrepreneurs' decisions not to invest in new technologies—for example, ring spindles in the cotton textile industry—were a fully rational response to local conditions (McCloskey 1971; Leunig 2001). McCloskey's criticisms were directed at Aldcroft (1964) and others who blamed economic decline on the poor quality of British management. Like Wiener, these writers linked poor management to cultural failings.

McCloskey argues for the irrelevance of a cultural approach, claiming that entrepreneurs continued to make rational decisions; if the cumulative effect of individual entrepreneurial decisions was, say, the decline of the textile industry, then it was because entrepreneurs were pursuing an enlightened long-term "exit strategy" in response to the decline of British comparative advantage, as reflected in shifts in the international terms of trade.

Economic rationality does not have to be construed in the narrow way adopted by McCloskey, however. Rational individuals may pursue nonpecuniary advantage at the expense of pecuniary advantage, and so quit industries and trades that do not fulfill their social aspirations. Entrepreneurs from other countries, who have different preferences, and place greater weight on pecuniary rewards, may take their place in world markets. Rational action may also be contingent on the mental model used by an entrepreneur, with entrepreneurs in different cultures perceiving similar constraints in different ways. One mental model may identify only a narrow range of options, such as a narrow range of scientific techniques, while another mental model may reveal a wider range. The entrepreneurs who choose from a wider range of options are likely to make better decisions. Godley (2001) has argued that east European Jewish immigrants migrating to London embraced a local culture that was preoccupied with achieving social status through a professional career, whereas their counterparts who settled in New York embraced the local culture of the independent small businessman instead; in this way local culture can perpetuate itself through the process of assimilation even at times when quite high rates of migration occur.

This emphasis on rational action within culturally contingent mental models is a useful framework in which to evaluate the Cain and Hopkins thesis. Cain and Hopkins (2002) argue that "gentlemanly capitalism" is a continuing, though evolving, theme in British trade and investment from the seventeenth to the twentieth century. They emphasize that the moral and social aspirations that govern gentlemanly behavior impinge not only on the desirability of a career in trade, but in the way that trade itself is conducted. The gentleman trader likes to trade with people who come from the same social class—who were educated at the same school, served in the same regiment, and whose families are related, if only distantly. A gentleman can enlarge his social circle by being introduced to other gentlemen by a reputable third party. This third party acts as a bridge between the two social circles to which the respective gentlemen belong. High-status women are well qualified to act as "bridgers," as they have both the opportunity to cultivate social networks and the capacity to offer hospitality on a large scale.

There is a minimum amount of wealth (or credit) that is required to sustain a gentlemanly lifestyle, and marriage to a wealthy heiress—such as the daughter of successful gentleman trader—can augment capital within the business community. Bridgers can therefore play a useful role as marriage brokers.

Gentlemanly capitalism is related to, though not identical with, what Chandler (1990) calls "personal capitalism." But while Chandler emphasizes the negative aspects of personal capitalism, Cain and Hopkins emphasize the positive features of gentlemanly capitalism. Investment in social networks, they suggest, reduces transaction costs. Gentlemanly capitalism was particularly well adapted to the conduct of maritime trade, because merchants required a network of trusted agents in all the major ports with which they were connected. While some cultures were forced to rely on kinship ties to sustain trust, gentlemanly capitalists could rely on regimental loyalty and "the old school tie" instead (Jones 1998, 2000). Overseas agents could be recruited not just from the extended family but from the wider expatriate community. The honesty of local agents was reinforced by peer-group monitoring within the expatriate community, based around "the club."

Gentlemanly capitalism had its political uses too. The values of the gentleman were useful in ensuring integrity in colonial administration. A gentleman had obligations to his social inferiors, which meant that gentlemanly administrators were more likely to pay attention to local needs than officials who saw themselves simply as bureaucrats employed by a colonial power. These values of self-restraint in the exercise of power assisted the growth of empire, allowing it to be extended (to some degree) through agreements with native leaders rather than by military conquest. The importance of empire as a link between the economic, political and cultural aspects of Victorian Britain is a theme to which we return at the end of this chapter.

The Concept of the Entrepreneur

Although the term *entrepreneur* is widely used in histories of Victorian Britain, there is no consistency in the way that it is employed. Most writers treat the entrepreneur as a Weberian ideal type. This ideal type is, in turn, often drawn from literature rather than life. Charles Dickens's description of horse traders at Howden fair, in East Yorkshire, is a case in point. With breath smelling of beer and stale tobacco, they talk among themselves in a private language, clinching deals with a shake of the hand. Every horse has it price; Dickens jokes that if the Queen arrived at the horse-fair in a "coach and four," the dealers would not be shy to offer her a price for her horses.

Dickens, as a social critic, did not portray Victorian entrepreneurs in flattering terms. Perhaps the most influential contemporary was Karl Marx, who equated the entrepreneur to a capitalist. To Marx, the fundamental feature of early Victorian capitalism was the alienation of the worker from the means of production. The artisan no longer owned his own tools, and his work had been deskilled. Under the factory system, his tools had been replaced by large-scale machinery, operated by teams of workers subject to military-style discipline. The expense of the machinery meant that the ownership of the means of production, and hence the control of the worker, had fallen into the hands of a specialized capitalist class.

While Marx identified the capitalist entrepreneur with large-scale production, he also recognized the role of the petit bourgeoisie—such as the traders described by Dickens. Modern labor economists also emphasize the petit bourgeoisie in their discussion of entrepreneurship. They typically define entrepreneurship in terms of self-employment (Casson et al. 2006). This definition is too narrow to be of much use in analyzing the Victorian economy, however. In the early nineteenth century a high proportion of the population was either wholly or partially self-employed. Even women and children, gleaning in the fields after harvest, were often self-employed. The factory revolution actually reduced self-employment, rather than increased it, by turning self-employed outworkers into wage workers, and the subsequent growth of major transport and utility industries sustained this trend. Self-employed entrepreneurship remained vibrant in the retail trades, as "the nation of shopkeepers" prospered, but only a small proportion of shopkeepers demonstrated significant entrepreneurial ability by introducing new retail concepts—such as the high-street chain and the department store. To identify Victorian entrepreneurship with self-employment is therefore misleading, as entrepreneurship reduced self-employment rather than increased it, and those who were self-employed were not particularly notable for their entrepreneurship.

This highlights the fact that there is much more to being an entrepreneur than being self-employed. One of the main reasons why entrepreneurship is valued, and usually commands respect in successful economies, is that entrepreneurship is a scarce ability. The value of this scarce ability is reflected in the above-average profits earned by firms controlled by successful entrepreneurs. Entrepreneurs can appropriate their personal rewards either through ownership of a firm, or as managers whose success is recognized by promotion, bonuses, stock options, or other forms of performance-related pay. Many small firms are, in fact, unsuccessful according to the profit criterion, as the average rate of profit for small firms is often lower than for larger ones; this is because some founders of small businesses may deliberately set out to discover by trial and error whether they have good judgment or not, while others may be content to accept a low rate of profit because they value the independence that self-employment confers. This underlines the fact that many small firms that are "entrepreneurial" in the sense of being run by self-employed owner-managers may not be entrepreneurial in the sense described here, because their owner-managers lack ability; they have poor judgment that leads to a below-average rate of profit.

What kind of decisions do entrepreneurs take using this scarce ability? According to Schumpeter (1939), entrepreneurs commit to making an innovation. Without the entrepreneur, the rate of innovation would be lower, productivity growth would be smaller, and the economy would fail to develop as it should (Baumol 2002). But why is the ability to innovate so scarce? According to Schumpeter, innovation requires vision and commitment—vision to imagine an alternative world in which the innovation has taken place, and commitment to mobilize resources to realize the vision rather than to just to sit back and fantasize about it. Only a few people with heroic temperament have these qualities, according to Schumpeter.

Kirzner (1973, 1979) takes a different approach: he argues that entrepreneurs discover opportunities that could easily be missed. In a volatile economy, markets are always in disequilibrium, and people who are alert can always find opportunities to buy cheap and sell dear. Entrepreneurs are people who recognize an opportunity, and commit to arbitrage in order to exploit it. Unlike Schumpeter, Kirzner believes that almost everyone has the potential to be an entrepreneur. While Schumpeter emphasizes intermittent major innovations made by heroic individuals, Kirzner highlights continuous minor profit-making deals made by ordinary people. In this respect, the two approaches complement each other quite nicely. Schumpeter's approach explains radical innovations in factories and railroads, while Kirzner's approach explains the vitality of small manufacturing businesses and the retail sector.

Not all opportunities are what they seem, however. Some may be traps for the unwary. Knight (1921) emphasizes the risks that are taken by the entrepreneur. No one can be certain that an opportunity will turn out well. Risks are subjective, so that different people perceive different degrees of risk in the same opportunity (Casson 1982). This subjectivity highlights the difference between being an entrepreneur and being a successful entrepreneur. An entrepreneur innovates and takes risks, but a successful entrepreneur discriminates between good risks and bad risks. He does not need to discriminate perfectly. He simply needs to do it better than his competitors in the same industry.

The decisions of entrepreneurs, when taken collectively, affect the aggregate performance of the economy. It is sometimes supposed that from a social perspective, more entrepreneurship is always desirable, but this depends upon how entrepreneurship is defined. If entrepreneurship is defined as innovation, then it is certainly possible to "have too much of a good thing." Excessive innovation can artificially reduce the supply of traditional products, and subject working lives to unnecessary change. It is obviously possible to have too much risk. While some risk is unavoidable in any innovation, a successful entrepreneur does not incur avoidable risks however bold and charismatic he may appear as a result.

The one thing that it is impossible to have too much of is good judgment (Casson 2000). Judgment is a capacity to take successful decisions under unprecedented conditions where there is no agreed procedure, or a lack of objective evidence. Good judgment trades off the risks of missing good opportunities through failure to innovate against the risk of making mistakes by making the wrong sort of innovation. A successful entrepreneur with good judgment takes only the opportunities that are really profitable. Provided that social incentives are properly aligned by a competitive market system, private profit will be associated with enhanced social welfare and higher performance. The market for corporate control allocates the best entrepreneurs to the most responsible jobs, by recruiting the most reputable entrepreneurs to run the biggest firms in each industry. Badly performing entrepreneurs who have lost reputation are replaced; if the board of directors does not dismiss them, then the firm will be taken over as shareholders sell out to the highest bidder.

This focus on judgment is well adapted to the study of entrepreneurship in Victorian Britain. The framework of company law within which entrepreneurs operated changed significantly over the Victorian period, so that any definition of entrepreneurship in terms of the ownership or management of firms suffers from the problem that the legal nature of the firm was undergoing significant change at this time. On the other hand, the function of exercising judgment in high-risk innovative sectors remained a constant requirement.

In early Victorian Britain firms could obtain joint-stock status and limited liability only by an act of Parliament, following the precedents set by the early chartered trading companies. All canal and railway promoters, for example, had to apply to Parliament if they required these privileges (see below). These companies were typically incorporated with a large authorized capital, because additional capital could only be raised by a further act. Thus most large firms were "born large"—they did not grow from small beginnings, as happened later. Most small firms were started as partnerships or family businesses, and although they could grow by increasing the number of partners, or extending the family through marriage, and so on, there were limits to how far and how fast they could grow. By the end of the century, however, companies could incorporate as joint-stock limited liability companies through a simple act of registration. This allowed small firms to grow into large industrial enterprises without a major reconstruction of their capital.

Nevertheless, as Chandler has pointed out, many family firms remained suspicious of diluting ownership by flotation on a stock exchange. They were also reluctant to delegate entrepreneurial decisions to professional employees, especially, it would seem, when the professional specialists were better qualified than the family members themselves. The predominance of close-held family firms impeded the operation of the market in corporate control alluded to above. The owners of many family firms adopted a dynastic view—treating the firm as they treated their land; as an asset to be maintained under family ownership and control as held in trust for future generations. The eldest son had a customary right to run the business, and an obligation to exercise this right, irrespective of his inclination or his competence. This created an endemic "succession" problem (Rose 1993), made famous as the "Buddenbrooks syndrome" of "rags to rags in three generations." However, focusing heavily on the limitations of small family firms, as Chandler is inclined to do, distorts the picture of Victorian entrepreneurship, because the most important field for entrepreneurial judgment at that time was not in small manufacturing firms but in the growing number of large joint-stock companies.

A Project-Based View of the Economy

To appreciate fully the significance of innovation and risk-management, and the impact of good judgment on economic performance, it is useful to adopt a project-centered view of the economy. According to this view, the economy is not a collection of activities—as portrayed in a standard economics textbook—but a collection of projects instead. Projects are much more heterogeneous than activities—as Knight emphasized, no two projects are ever alike; for example, the outputs cater to different market niches, while the availability of inputs reflects the location of facilities, and so on. Projects have substantial setup costs, which activities do not. Projects have finite lives, with a distinct life-cycle of start-up, consolidation, maturity, and decline. Projects are risky, because the setup costs cannot be recovered if a project fails. Risks cannot be diversified away. Projects have a minimum efficient scale, so that risks cannot be spread over a large number of tiny projects. While individuals may be able to diversify risks using share portfolios, society is still exposed to systemic risk if a major project fails.

The view of the economy as a collection of projects is extremely appropriate where the Victorian British economy is concerned. Throughout the nineteenth century the projects undertaken by British entrepreneurs became increasingly ambitious—especially in scale. Even the early railway schemes had impressive titles, such as "Great Western Railway" and "Grand Junction Railway," and architectural allusions to the Roman Empire and the Egyptian pharaohs were exceedingly common. While the pace of technological progress in Britain may have diminished as the century progressed, the diversity of the projects, and the locations in which they were based, increased dramatically as the empire expanded. Entrepreneurship became increasingly focused on managing and financing a range of projects in infrastructure, urban development, shipping, and financial services. These projects involved the use, not only of British resources, but the resources of colonies, dominions, protectorates, mandates, and independent countries under British influence, all around the world.

These imperial projects were based on domestic blueprints. Transport, communications, utilities, and public services developed in Britain were transferred abroad, being adapted incrementally to foreign conditions. Although these overseas projects sometimes foundered because local conditions were unexpectedly different from those in Britain, the performance of overseas projects often surpassed that achieved in Britain because lessons had been learned from mistakes made in the domestic environment. The Indian railway system, for example, was developed along lines designed to avoid the problems created in Britain by the railway mania, and the defective system of government regulation at that time.

Table 8.1 reports the number of acts of Parliament authorizing large projects over the period 1800–1910. It shows that number of relevant acts—so-called "Local and Personal Acts"—classified by type of project. The data presented consist of ten-year averages; the evidence is summarized using a bar chart in figure 8.5. The table provides an approximate measure of the level and direction of project-centered entrepreneurial activity. No entrepreneur could compulsorily acquire land, or otherwise interfere with property rights, without such an act. Not all applications for acts were successful, as opposition from landowners, and the promoters of rival schemes, was often acute. The numbers should be doubled, at very least, to allow for the number of unsuccessful applications. Nor were all the authorized projects successfully completed—many failed, or were scaled down, because of lack of capital.

The table indicates the flow of new projects rather than the stock of existing projects. However, since it also includes authorized amendments to schemes in progress, and changes to the capital stock of existing schemes, the flow at any one time reflects to some extent the accumulated stock. This in turn reflects the fact that entrepreneurship becomes a continuing activity when projects run into difficulties, because judgment must continue to be applied in order to rescue the project from failure.

Prior to 1830, large projects focused on the enclosure of commons and the extension of agricultural estates, together with road improvements effected by turnpike trusts and the building of canals. These reforms improved the productivity of the land, and the local transport infrastructure, providing increased traffic that could

TABLE 8.1
Number of Local and Personal Acts of Parliament, 1800–1910, by Type of Project,
Ten-Year Averages

	(a) Projects relating to inland transport						
	Railway	Tramway	Road	Canal	River	Drain	Bridge
1800–1809	1.2	0	48.9	5.9	2.9	3.4	3.1
1810–19	1.5	0.1	50.6	5.3	1.9	3.5	4.8
1820–29	5.2	0	63.7	3.7	2.8	1.6	6.8
1830–39	18.4	0	41.4	3.0	2.6	2.5	5.9
1840–49	82.0	0	13.4	3.8	3.2	3.0	2.3
1850–59	73.1	0.2	18.8	1.3	4.0	2.7	2.7
1860–69	144.6	1.0	11.7	1.4	2.9	4.0	5.0
1870–79	81.7	11.7	1.2	1.8	3.4	5.9	4.2
1880–89	70.4	17.9	1.8	1.2	3.2	5.3	4.0
1890–99	64.1	13.4	0.6	4.1	3.7	3.2	2.7
1900–1909	40.4	20.9	0.1	1.4	2.2	3.4	1.4
1910–14	21.8	7.6	2.2	1.4	2.6	5.6	1.0

	(b) Projects relating to external trade, urban infrastructure, and social improvement						
	Harbor	Water	Gas	Electricity	Towns	Social	Other
1800–1809	6.4	1.6	0.1	0	9.7	6.3	52.2
1810–19	5.3	2.3	2.2	0	15.4	8.6	55.8
1820–29	5.6	3.1	8.0	0	16.6	5.0	11.1
1830–39	8.5	4.4	3.8	0	12.1	3.9	14.2
1840–49	13.7	7.4	7.8	0	18.4	4.7	14.0
1850–59	10.3	14.7	12.0	0	17.5	2.2	10.6
1860–69	13.5	19.3	19.8	0	16.3	3.9	10.7
1870–79	15	19.6	22.5	0.1	21.6	12.6	18.5
1880–89	13.5	18.5	12.5	2.4	23.6	15.2	28.6
1890–99	15	25.0	17.5	11.3	32.6	13.0	32.0
1900–1909	11.5	20.9	27.2	15.0	41.3	11.2	30.5
1910–14	10.6	16.0	24.8	9.2	34.4	8.4	29.8

Source: Compiled from UK Law Commission and Scottish Law Commission 1996.

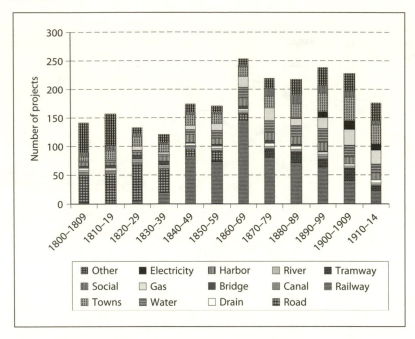

Figure 8.5. Promotion of Large Projects Requiring Statutory Authorization in the United Kingdom, 1800–1914.

be fed into, or distributed by, the railway system. Town improvements—such as new slaughterhouses and cattle markets—also helped.

Railway projects "take off" in the 1830s, with a peak in the 1860s. The first railway mania occurred in the period 1844–46. The railways promoted during this period were authorized with a one-year lag in the period 1845–47. There were 119 railway Acts in 1845, 263 in 1846, and 187 in 1847. Many small investors lost their life savings in the speculation that surrounded the Mania. It was a long time before the public regained its confidence in railway investment, but when it did, a second—less virulent—Mania developed. It began in 1861, when 160 railway schemes were authorized. The number rose to 251 in 1865, falling slightly to 199 in 1866. The Mania ended with the collapse of Overend Gurney bankers in 1866—an apparently respectable firm that had been heavily involved in railway finance.

During the Second Mania, many of the schemes that had failed in the First Mania were relaunched under new names and new management. Some of the schemes were supported by towns that had missed out on the railway altogether, while other towns encouraged new schemes in the interests of greater competition, which they believed would lead to lower fares and freight rates.

New canal projects were still in progress at the time that the first interurban railway—the Liverpool & Manchester—was completed in 1830. This explains the intensity of opposition from canal interests in the early years of railway development. By 1840, however, most schemes were either for merger and rationalization, or for the conversion of canals into railways. Canal building revived at the end of the century with the construction of the Manchester Ship Canal.

From the seventeenth century onward, river navigations have made a significant contribution to freight transport in Britain, by allowing river traffic to penetrate further inland, thereby connecting the industrial heartlands to the coast. In East Anglia river navigations also assisted the drainage of the fens. The importance of maritime trade to an island such as Britain is underlined by the significant number of port and harbor improvement schemes that were promoted throughout the nineteenth century. The statistics for harbors also include piers built to develop tourism at seaside resorts.

The different transport schemes were complementary to each other. Roads fed traffic to the railways, and the railways fed traffic to the ports. The rapid extension of maritime trade in the age of "high imperialism" after 1870 allowed parts of the railway system to act as a land-bridge for traffic between the North Sea ports on the east coast, the Channel ports on the south coast, and the Atlantic ports on the west coast. Even the canals, which competed most directly with the railways, could take slow-moving heavy traffic off the railway and free up the capacity for higher-value loads.

The social problems of rapid urbanization had become acute by midcentury, not just in the industrial Midlands and north, but in London too. Victorian moral revulsion, particularly at child poverty and the incidence of disease, was translated into practical action in the form of water schemes for the piping of fresh water into city centers. These were often allied to river and drainage schemes to carry sewage out to the coast. Control of crime was aided by street lighting. A ready supply of coal, facilitated by the railways, encouraged lighting by gas, both in the streets and in the home. Electrical power was slow to develop, although the switch from horse power to electric power made the tram an important competitor to the railways so far as suburban transport was concerned.

The concept of "town improvement" had been a well-established concept in Britain since Norman times (Chalklin 1998). In the eighteenth century spa towns like Bath and Cheltenham, and fashionable resorts like Weymouth, were improved by large-scale property development in the Georgian style. In the early part of the nineteenth century, the provision for the poor, the sick, and the elderly, through the construction of workhouses and infirmaries, became a priority. Early railway stations were often on the margins of towns, on low-value marshland, for example, close to cattle markets, gasworks, asylums, and jails. As stations penetrated further into the heart of cities, they became agents of slum clearance (Kellett 1969). Some of the workers expelled from the slums were relocated to new working-class suburbs from which they commuted in special workmen's trains. Municipal socialism, which began to flourish in the 1870s, gave an added impetus to town improvement. New urban facilities that had previously been promoted by individual Parliamentary acts were increasingly promoted with the framework of local government acts, as statutory orders approved by Parliament. Towns and cities extended their administrative boundaries, and often took the initiative for promoting projects away from private enterprise. Many of these towns and cities were controlled by business elites, who used their influence to extend the boundaries of their town and applied the local rates to investments in public facilities that would improve the competitiveness of their town relative to its rivals.

Part B of table 8.1 contains a diverse and changing mixture of schemes. In the first half of the nineteenth century financial institutions—particularly mutual assurance societies—predominate, while in the second half investment trusts and large industrial enterprises—including several steam shipping lines—come to the fore. Industrial patents and educational institutions are the subject of some acts. The growing amount of local government legislation described above is also included in this category when it cannot be attributed to any single sector mentioned elsewhere in the table.

The local and personal acts are mainly concerned with projects based wholly in Britain. Projects concerned with colonial development were authorized by the colonial governments, or the Colonial Office, and are not included except in special cases. The substantial growth of overseas projects owned and managed from Britain can be readily documented from other sources. Wilkins (1989), for example, offers a comprehensive account of British enterprise in the nineteenth-century United States. The global spread of UK-based entrepreneurship can be assessed from other sources. Thus Bradshaw's Railway Manual indicates that by 1912 no fewer than 109 large overseas railway systems in twenty-nine countries were owned and managed from Britain; 32 were in the empire, and 65 in Latin America (Bassett 1913, parts 2–4; a somewhat higher figure is given by Corley 1994). Many of these companies made huge investments, although, because they often acquired control through state concession, they did not always enjoy ownership in perpetuity, as with conventional manufacturing investments.

The Role of Entrepreneurs in the Promotion of Large Projects: The Case of the Railway System

The railway industry makes an excellent case study in the finance and management of large projects by British entrepreneurs. Railways were developed through visionary foresight. The vision was implemented by entrepreneurs who showed considerable perseverance under difficult conditions.

It is possible to distinguish five main visions of the railway system in early Victorian Britain.

- The notion of an integrated national network organized around a central north-south spine was set out by the artisan philosopher Thomas Gray (1825) in the 1820s. The proposed technology was not very futuristic, however, being based on the existing mineral railways of the time.
- George Stephenson—the "father of the railways"—discovered the key combination of components that made possible the modern railway: straight routes on easy gradients, steam locomotive power, and double tracks of iron rails. As a colliery engineer, however, Stephenson always attached considerable weight to the carriage of freight rather than passengers, and the carriage of coal in particular. It was said that Stephenson always looked out for signs of coal deposits when surveying a new line of railway. His vision for the British railway system was once unkindly described as a glorified coal distribution system.
- Brunel, the author of this remark, provided the grandest vision of the railway system: a high-speed luxury transport system for the social elite (Rolt 1957). The elite would travel over land by rail, and overseas by steam-powered iron-built liner ships, which would connect with the trains at the ports.
- Robert Stephenson, George Stephenson's son, believed that every part of the country should have access to a railway. He was interested in the railway as an agent of rural devel-

opment, and not just as a means of serving industry and commerce (Bailey 2003; Addyman and Haworth 2005). Stephenson's approach was very influential in other countries, but in Britain many of his regional projects achieved only limited success.

• Finally, there was a political vision of a United Kingdom bound together by rails. Railways were seen as important in allowing Scottish and Irish members of Parliament to take up their places in Westminster, and to carry the policies enacted there back to their provincial constituencies. Government therefore intervened to ensure that London was well connected by rail to Dublin via ferry and Edinburgh.

Before 1830 the typical railway project involved a short line of wooden rails from a coal mine or quarry to a neighboring port, river quay, or canal dock, where the cargo would be transferred to water (Lewis 1970). In 1830 the world's first interurban high-speed railway opened, carrying both passengers and freight on scheduled services. The success of this line, both in generating new traffic, and diverting existing traffic from road and canal, led directly to the railway mania of 1845. The financial collapse that destroyed many of the schemes promoted at the time of the mania provided a continuing agenda that lasted until 1914: namely to revive the failed mania schemes and so complete the national network that had been envisaged in 1845.

Between 1830 and 1860 the promotion of a railway was usually undertaken by a small group of local citizens, anxious to connect their town to a local port or industrial city, or to connect their port or city to London (Casson 2009). They would obtain advice on the route from a reputable engineer, and consult a local solicitor about the purchase of land. They would organize a public meeting, chaired by a local dignitary, at which a motion supporting the railway scheme would be proposed. Opponents, such as local landowners, canal proprietors, turnpike trustees, or the promoters of rival canal schemes, would often turn up and attempt to disrupt the meeting. In this case the outcome could well hinge on a timely intervention from the engineer—a role in which showmen such as Brunel excelled.

A provisional committee would be formed with a mandate to secure an act of Parliament, until which time the committee would act as a "shadow" board of directors. The 10 percent deposit paid by shareholders provided them with salable scrip—a tradable option. Because options were so much cheaper than shares, even household servants and laborers could afford to invest their meager savings in speculative railway stock. Once the first trunk lines to London had opened by 1840, it was clear that towns that were bypassed by a railway were destined to decline. Railway promotion now became a civic duty, and towns vied with each other to get themselves "on the railway map."

Although the social elites in many towns were split along religious and party lines—for example, Church of England and Nonconformist, Whigs and Tories—civic pride and collective self-interest were sufficiently strong to unite them. Most of the competition was between towns rather than within towns; where competition arose within towns it was usually because of speculators moving in from outside, as in the case of the London-to-Brighton line. After 1850, however, interfirm competition became more common, with large regional companies, such as the London & North Western Railway and the Great Western Railway, seeking to invade each other's territory.

Parliament took the view that public benefit was the only reason for interfering with landowners' private property. A railway project afforded a potential "improvement," and there was a long-standing tradition, derived from earlier forms of improvement, such as land enclosures and canal projects, that the benefits of an improvement should be distributed fairly between the different groups involved. No one should lose out; thus if a loss were sustained, the person concerned should be compensated. The benefits should be shared by the shareholders who financed the railway and bore the commercial risks, and the local communities whose members used the railway.

In presenting a bill to Parliament, the promoters had to prove that the prospective benefits were substantial. Promoters made traffic surveys along roads and canals to establish the existence of demand, and proposed schedules of maximum fares and freight rates to ensure that much of the benefit of the railway would accrue to the public. At the same time they had to show that their construction costs were reasonable, and their estimates robust. If their scheme was financially unsound, then the countryside might be dug up for nothing.

With so many lawyers sitting in Parliament as MPs or Lords it is not surprising that cross-examination by hired advocates was the preferred way of presenting evidence to a Parliamentary committee (Kostal 1994). To ensure compliance with standing orders, Parliamentary agents were hired. Many technical "knockouts" were achieved, and often the knockouts were mutual, so that both schemes failed. When a scheme failed, the engineers, solicitors, and Parliamentary agents would submit their claims for fees, using up all the deposits and leaving nothing for the shareholders. If the scheme succeeded, then the newly established board would issue calls on the shares so that construction could begin. Contracts for separate sections of line would be put out to tender. Although the process was nominally competitive, some contractors might have friends on the board. In common with many construction projects, initial estimates were often too low, and so the project would either have to be scaled down, and part of the route abandoned, or additional capital would have to be raised. This could require further application to Parliament, as an act limited both the amount of capital and the time in which it could be raised.

Once a line was opened, competition for traffic would begin (Reed 1957). In many cases, the strongest rivalry came from an alternative railway route. As the network developed, so the number of alternative routes between any two places increased (Turnock 1998). Mergers provided an obvious solution, but from the mid-1850s Parliament became increasingly concerned about their monopolistic tendencies, and only approved them in exceptional cases. In the 1840s and early 1850s, however, major speculative gains could be made from the promotion of mergers. The "Railway King," George Hudson, a draper from York, made his name by engineering the merger that created the Midland Railway (Arnold and McCartney 2004). He eliminated competition between Derby and London, and between Leeds and Hull. The tradition of "railway politics" was continued by the "Second Railway King," Sir Edward Watkin, who coordinated the management of different companies through an interlocking chairmanship (Hodgkins 2001). His grand design was for a through line from Manchester to Paris via a Channel Tunnel. He was successful in gaining financial support from shareholders and political support from government, but engineering problems and the costs they created defeated him in the end.

Popular mythology recognizes the railway engineers—men such as George and Robert Stephenson (father and son), Joseph Locke and Isambard Kingdom Brunel—as the true entrepreneurs of the railway system. Samuel Smiles's (1862) hagiography portrays Victorian engineers not only as technocrats, but as the strategic thinkers behind the new industries that they helped to create. Detailed evidence on company promotion, such as Brunel's letterbooks (1836), suggests that this assessment is correct. It was not so much the owners of the railways as their consultant engineers who masterminded strategy in the early years. The reason is quite straightforward: the principles of railway strategy were specific to railways—a new type of network industry with a very costly infrastructure—but common across all locations. While shareholders were often endowed with good local knowledge, they had limited experience of the railway system as a whole. Consulting engineers, however, would have experience of several schemes, from which they could identify specific patterns.

Consulting engineers also socialized with each other. They met as peers at meetings of the Institutional of Civil Engineers and other professional associations, and as adversaries before Parliamentary committees on railway bills. Although Brunel and Robert Stephenson could not even agree on the best gauge for a railway—Brunel favoring the broad gauge and Stephenson the modern standard gauge—they remained the best of friends. They fought an intense battle in Parliament over lines in the West Midlands, which Brunel won; yet they dined together, and even died at about the same time! Both men advised their respective companies on strategy—the Great Western and London & North Western—planning routes that would block rival lines, devising trunk line routes to maximize the potential for profitable branch line traffic, and helping to monopolize key ports.

By midcentury it was the company secretary who was becoming the major strategic thinker in the railway sector, together with the company chairman. In the second half of the nineteenth century the most successful railway entrepreneurs seem to have been those who combined practical experience of the industry with a wide range of general interests—such as Samuel Laing, the chairman of the London Brighton and South Coast Railway, who was a former official with the railway department of the Board of Trade and who became a popular writer on philosophical issues.

Mining as a Project-Based Industry

Not all projects require Parliamentary authorization, of course. There are many projects that can be undertaken as soon as customers have revealed a demand, and a business opportunity has been recognized. This is particularly true of the mining industry.

The British Isles are rich in minerals. The Romans mined gold and lead in Wales when they occupied the country. Coal was mined as a substitute for charcoal in medieval times—albeit on a small scale (Hatcher 1993). The ironmasters of the early Industrial Revolution generated a huge demand for coal and coke, and this stimulated mining on an industrial scale. Many of the earliest mines were driven horizontally into hillsides, making it easy to bring out the minerals. Indeed, some of the key components of railway technology originated in the mining industry, where wooden tramways were used to transport minerals out of the mine and down to a river or coastal port.

Even before the Industrial Revolution, coal shipped from Newcastle, in the North East, had been widely used for brewing ale and heating the home—especially by wealthy Londoners (Nef 1932). The discovery of iron ore nearby gave a huge boost to this industry. The Staffordshire coalfield developed as the Midlands town of Birmingham expanded its specialty metals trades.

Once mineral deposits near the surface had been exhausted, it was necessary to go further down. Shafts were sunk, and winding gear installed. Pumps were necessary once the mine went down beneath the water table. The stationary steam engine was ideal for providing power to a mine—especially in a coal mine, because the mineral extracted could be used directly as the fuel. Mounting a stationary steam engine on a colliery wagon was one of the earliest inspirations for the railway locomotive.

The aristocratic owners of large estates asserted rights to the minerals underneath their land. During the eighteenth and early nineteenth centuries the aristocracy began to exploit their mineral reserves in a highly organized way (Ashton and Sykes 1929). Increasingly, the sinking of a coal mine became a major project. A large tract of land would be required, with not only mineral rights but also surface rights to facilitate access to the mine, to accommodate spoil heaps, and to provide washing and processing facilities for the coal. A large amount of expensive machinery would have to be installed. In remote locations, workers' housing and village facilities would have to be provided too.

There was no guarantee that the mine would be a success. In the early nineteenth century the science of geology was in its infancy, and so the volume of the deposits, as determined by the dimensions of the seams, could not be known in advance. Unexpected geological faults could always emerge, causing the mine to flood or the tunnel passages to cave in.

The mineral industry therefore required project-centered entrepreneurship of a high order. The scale of the investment required meant that coal mining was not an industry for the "self-made man" operating on a small scale (Mitchell 1984). Only a wealthy aristocrat could afford to "go it alone"—and even such persons would find their personal resources stretched. For this reason wealthy people often formed partnerships—sometimes with family members, creating a dynastic ownership structure. In other cases they made alliances with other families.

Since no single person could possess all the technical expertise required to operate a large mine, it was the usual practice for the owners to hire professional managers—the colliery viewers. Viewers were often self-taught, had plenty of practical experience, and needed entrepreneurial qualities. A successful viewer was someone who could improvise effective solutions to unexpected problems. Because they were so versatile, colliery viewers often moved around the country, helping to start up mines in new areas. They also transferred their skills to other industries too—thus several viewers from the North East transferred their skills to the railway industry. The most prominent example was George Stephenson. He took with him not only his familiarity with steam technology but also his ability to recognize the mineral potential of any district in which he worked. One of the skills that commended Stephenson to railway promoters was his ability to assess the mineral potential of the district through which a railway was intended to pass.

As steamships replaced sailing ships on the main ocean shipping routes, a demand was created for a network of bunkering stations around the world. Ships, like railway locomotives, needed top-quality steam coal, which was only available from a limited number of sources. South Wales was the main source of steam coal. Initially coal was mined in Wales to support the iron industry (centered on Merthyr Tydfil), but as iron ore deposits became exhausted, the coal was increasingly exported to bunkering stations instead. It was this development that led to the enormous expansion of Cardiff (and later Barry) as a port (Church 1986).

In the latter part of the nineteenth century important coal deposits were identified in south Yorkshire, near the railway town of Doncaster (Buxton 1978). A huge amount of investment went into this coalfield, including the building of several new railway lines. At a time when British manufacturing industry was losing its global market share, Britain was becoming increasingly specialized in the coal export trade. It is, to some extent, indicative of the relative decline of British manufacturing in the late Victorian period that so little of the newly discovered coal was consumed by domestic industry, and so much of it was exported instead. Because coal of different grades is found in different parts of the world, there is no economic objection to a country exporting coal of one grade and importing coal of another. At the end of the nineteenth century, however, British coal was following British capital in leaving the country. Rather than being channeled into domestic manufacturing, it was employed to support the country's imperial linkages instead.

Entrepreneurship and the Culture of Improvement: Some Reflections on the Victorian Experience

Examining Victorian enterprise from the perspective of infrastructure investment provides a fresh perspective on some of the historical controversies discussed above. Investment in railways was just the contemporary manifestation of a more general concern with "improvement" that took hold of British society in the eighteenth century. This concern with improvement was underpinned by a changing mind-set in which natural phenomena were increasingly interpreted as the outcome of hidden processes driven by universal physical laws. The created order was fundamentally rational, it was believed, and could therefore be comprehended by rational human beings. The cultivation of rationality required education, which in turn depended on the spread of literacy and numeracy. In Victorian Britain this demand for education and literacy was fed by the growth of schooling and local newspapers. Schooling was provided initially by "dame schools," private grammar schools and the so-called public schools, but from 1870, it was provided increasingly by churches and the state.

If the entire created order was rational, then society too must be based on rational principles, it would seem. For many intellectuals this had radical policy implications. Inherited aristocratic landholdings, and the privileges of monarchy, should be swept away as anachronistic in a modern rational society. The leaders of the French Revolution pursued this line of argument to its logical conclusion—and beyond.

The lessons of the bloody French Revolution were not lost on Victorian Britons. Populist political leaders in command of a mob were infinitely more dangerous than a traditional monarchy. Absolutist states posed a military threat to their neighbors, and absolute political power of any kind should therefore be avoided.

The British already had a parliamentary system that addressed this issue—at least partially. The system was not completely democratic; only male property-owners had the vote before 1832. The monarch was not, strictly speaking, accountable to the people, but rather to the representatives of local elites—the MPs. The essence of British government was that it was local rather than national, and this was reflected in Parliamentary behavior toward the railways, as explained above.

Improvement was not just a question of raising the material standard of living, although alleviating poverty was certainly a major concern (as demonstrated by the Poor Law Report of 1834). Improvement was a moral phenomenon (Searle 1998). Material improvement was merely an instrument for alleviating the constraints on the moral improvement of the individual, and hence the moral improvement of society.

The importance of morality is exemplified in the career of William Gladstone, who was prime minister on no fewer than four occasions in the Victorian period (Matthew 2004). While Gladstone's responsibilities involved economic regulation and national budgeting, he spent most of his time reading theology (on which he amassed an enormous library that can still be consulted today). His political speeches focused on the application of moral principles to contentious issues, and eschewed the type of propaganda about wealth-creation so familiar today.

Gladstone and his many supporters perceived no conflict between acting morally and acting rationally. Revealed religion promised rewards for moral behavior in the afterlife. No rational individual would risk eternal damnation for the sake of a short-term gain. So promoting morals and promoting reason were essentially the same thing.

The passions were the main threat to rational action. The need to resist the most dangerous passions was emphasized by the Ten Commandments, which were liberally displayed on either side of the altar in the churches that the Victorians built or restored.

Self-discipline and self-control were therefore the hallmarks of a rational person. The greater a person's wealth or power, the greater their need to exercise self-control. Positions of great responsibility therefore needed to be filled by people with great self-control. Team games were deemed to provide useful exercise in self-control. Team players put the performance of their team ahead of their own interests; it was commitment and effort that counted, and not just ability.

Wealth posed a moral danger, because of the temptation to use it selfishly. Wealth must be used responsibly, by putting poor people to work, and supporting charitable causes. Personal reputation was not acquired by wealth alone, but by the proper use of wealth. Able people could be in particular moral danger unless they found a moral challenge that was matched to their level of ability. Not everyone might have the ability to take on a major challenge, but everyone could aspire to modest respectability.

Despite the success of the Victorian economy, and the prominent role of entrepreneurship within it, Victorian society did not have an "enterprise culture" as that term is commonly understood today. The Victorians were supremely confident in their abilities to make improvements, and did not feel the need for government to promote an enterprise culture in order to foster change. In modern Western countries it was the economic failures of 1970s—associated with large and bureaucratic "national champion" firms and their inability to handle Asian competition—that led to a preoccupation with enterprise culture in the 1980s and 1990s. This switched the emphasis in Western countries from championing large firms to championing small ones instead. The Victorians experienced no such failures, and therefore saw no need to compensate for them. In the Victorian economy the direction of industrial change was the opposite to that of the modern West: the Victorians were involved in creating large firms like the major textile and engineering firms and—preeminently—the railway companies. If there is a lesson for entrepreneurship from the Victorian economy, it is not that laissez-faire promotes prosperity, but rather that a sincere concern for moral and social improvement widely shared by all groups in society will generate material improvements too. John Stuart Mill observed, in his *Autobiography*, that happiness cannot be achieved by aiming for happiness, and the Victorian experience suggests that the same might be said about economic success—it is not achieved by aiming for economic success, but by aiming for something more fundamental that brings success in its wake.

Conclusion

The importance of the railways—and infrastructure in general—to the Victorian economy illustrates the danger of placing undue emphasis on manufacturing industry when evaluating entrepreneurship in Victorian Britain. Railway promotion was a highly entrepreneurial activity. A general approach to entrepreneurship, based on innovation, risk-management, and judgmental decision-making, captures the full significance of the Schumpeterian railway revolution in a way that other approaches do not.

Railway companies were born large. Sales growth occurred mainly through long-term traffic growth fueled by the gradual expansion of the economy, rather than by bidding traffic away from other companies. Growth of the capital stock occurred largely through merger and acquisition. Subsequent concentration of power was achieved by interlocking chairmanships and directorships. Shareholders took most of the risks, but specialist entrepreneurs took the strategic decisions: initially the consulting engineers, and later the company secretaries and chairmen.

At the time of their construction, most railway lines were projected as civic enterprises, representing a single town, or a coalition of towns along the route. Civic enterprise was particularly notable in some of the old county towns, like Chester, Lincoln, York, and Shrewsbury, which sought to renew themselves as railway hubs. The most spectacular example of a coalition of towns creating a new trunk railway was the Great Northern Railway—one of the most successful of the mania schemes. This was a merger of rival schemes, based upon a common interest in serving country towns in Bedfordshire, Huntingdonshire, and Lincolnshire. Because of its length, it connected London directly to York and Edinburgh, by a junction near Doncaster, and because of its breadth, achieved by a loop line, it was able to serve the agricultural districts of Lincolnshire too. The merger was organized by Edmund Dennison, MP for Doncaster. He used his political influence to serve his constituents by insisting that the railway terminate near Doncaster, thereby transforming a declining gentrified horse-racing town into a prosperous railway hub.

The railways system was just one of the many innovations exported from Britain to the empire in the age of high imperialism. Professional governance, which had evolved steadily since the Norman age, was exported through systems of colonial administration. This provided a framework of law and order within which various types of large project could be exported too. While many of these projects were first developed in Britain, others—such as river navigation, drainage, and water supply systems—involved refinements of technologies developed elsewhere.

Overseas projects involved the export, not only of British technology and management, but British capital and labor too. Much of the labor was highly skilled. Many of the civil engineers who left Britain for the colonies in the second half of the nineteenth century never returned to Britain. There were so many opportunities for engineers on the colonial frontier that there was little incentive for them to return. It was mainly the senior professionals, who ran consulting practices from London, who remained in Britain. Many of these consultants became involved in high finance and political negotiation, as foreign monarchs and ministers came to Britain to negotiate for railway schemes. The engineer Sir John Fowler, for example, received his knighthood not for his engineering expertise, but for the political assistance he rendered to the British government during the war in Sudan.

One of the key aspects of entrepreneurship is that it facilitates structural change. It is mistake to infer that entrepreneurship declined in late-Victorian Britain just because Britain failed to maintain its industrial lead over Germany and the United States. British entrepreneurs may well have been slow to recognize the magnitude of scale economies in heavy industries, and to appreciate the commercial benefits of organized industrial research in well-equipped laboratories. But in a small and increasingly crowded country, this was not where national comparative advantage lay.

The late-Victorian economy is an example of what is now called the knowledge-based economy. Its comparative advantage lay increasingly in the export of knowledge-intensive services, such as public administration, trade, shipping, finance, and engineering consultancy. These services were mainly delivered in packages relating to major projects for colonial and overseas development. Each project required inputs of several of these knowledge-based services for its successful completion. The whole process depended on specialized institutions such as the London Stock Exchange, an agglomeration of scientific and professional institutions, and the "free-standing" overseas company.

The twentieth century saw enormous geopolitical changes, most of which disadvantaged British entrepreneurship. War, followed by the collapse of international trade and global demand, more war and then the loss of empire, all reduced the scope for large, complex, project-based entrepreneurship coordinated through traditional British institutions such as the London stock market. The notion of an empire based on trade in agricultural products and knowledge-intensive services was replaced by the notion of an empire based on large-scale high-technology manufacturing industry. Economic logic now favored the hierarchical multinational firm rather than the free-standing firm. It is a mistake to suppose, however, that the loss of empire, and twentieth -entury economic failure, can be blamed on the deficiencies of the Victorian British entrepreneur. Entrepreneurship was a vibrant force in Britain throughout the nineteenth century. This chapter has shown that once an appropriate concept of entrepreneurship is used as an analytical template, the persistence of entrepreneurship in Britain to the end of the century can be discerned clearly.

References

Addyman, John, and Victoria Haworth. 2005. *Robert Stephenson: Railway Engineer*. Stretford, Manchester: North Eastern Railway Association.

Aldcroft, Derek H. 1964. "The Entrepreneur and the British Economy, 1870–1914." *Economic History Review* 17:113–34.

Arnold, A. J., and Sean McCartney. 2004. *George Hudson: The Rise and Fall of the Railway King. A Study in Victorian Entrepreneurship*. London: Hambledon and London.

Ashton, Thomas S., and Joseph Sykes. 1929. *The Coal Industry of the Eighteenth Century*. Manchester: Manchester University Press.

Bailey, Michael R., ed. 2003. *Robert Stephenson: The Eminent Engineer*. Aldershot: Ashgate.

Bassett, Herbert H., ed. 1913. *Bradshaw's Railway Manual, Shareholders' Guide, and Official Directory*. London: Henry Blacklock.

Baumol, William J. 1994. *Entrepreneurship, Management, and the Structure of Pay-offs*. Cambridge: MIT Press.

———. 2002. *The Free-Market Innovation Machine*. Princeton: Princeton University Press.

Broadberry, Stephen. 1997. *The Productivity Race: British Manufacturing in International Perspective, 1850–1990*. Cambridge: Cambridge University Press.

———. 2006. *Market Services and the Productivity Race, 1850–2000*. Cambridge: Cambridge University Press.

Brunel, Isambard K. 1836. Letterbooks. University of Bristol Library, Special Collections, DM1306.

Cain, P. J., and A. G. Hopkins. 2002. *British Imperialism, 1688–2000*. 2nd ed. London: Longman.

Casson, Mark. 1982. *The Entrepreneur: An Economic Theory*. Oxford: Martin Robertson.

———. 2000. *Enterprise and Leadership*. Cheltenham: Edward Elgar.

———. 2009. *The World's First Railway System: Enterprise, Competition, and Regulation on the Railway Network in Victorian Britain*. Oxford: Oxford University Press.

Casson, Mark, Bernard Yeung, Anuradha Basu, and Bernard Yeung, eds. 2006. *Oxford Handbook of Entrepreneurship*. Oxford: Oxford University Press.

Chalklin, Christopher W. 1998. *English Counties and Public Building, 1650–1830*. London: Hambledon Press.

Chandler, Alfred D., Jr., ed. 1965. *Railroads: The Nation's First Big Business*. New York: Harcourt, Brace and World.

Chandler, Alfred D., Jr., with Takashi Hikino. 1990. *Scale and Scope: The Dynamics of Industrial Capitalism*. Cambridge: Harvard University Press.

Church, Roy A. 1975. *The Great Victorian Boom, 1850–1873*. London: Macmillan.

———. 1986. *History of the British Coal Industry*. Vol. 3, *1830–1913, Victorian Pre-eminence*. Oxford: Clarendon Press.

Corley, Tony A. B. 1994. "Britain's Overseas Investments in 1914 Revisited." *Business History* 36:71–88.

Crafts, Nicholas F. R. 1985. *British Industrial Growth during the Industrial Revolution*. Oxford: Oxford University Press.

Deane, Phyllis. 1979. *The First Industrial Nation*. Cambridge: Cambridge University Press.

Godley, Andrew. 2001. *Jewish Immigrant Entrepreneurship in New York and London, 1880–1914*. London: Palgrave.

Gourvish, Terence R. 1980. *Railways and the British Economy, 1830–1914*. London: Macmillan.

Hatcher, John. 1993. *The History of the British Coal Industry*. Vol. 1, *Before 1700: Towards the Age of Coal*. Oxford: Clarendon Press.

Hodgkins, David. 2001. *The Second Railway King: The Life and Times of Sir Edward Watkin, 1819–1901*. Whitchurch, Cardiff: Merton Priory Press.

Jones, Geoffrey G., ed. 1998. *The Multinational Traders*. London: Routledge.

———. 2000. *From Merchants to Multinationals*. Oxford: Oxford University Press.

Kihlstrom, R. E., and J. J. Laffont. 1979. "A General Equilibrium Entrepreneurial Theory of Firm Formation Based on Risk Aversion." *Journal of Political Economy* 87:719–48.

Kirzner, Israel M. 1973. *Competition and Entrepreneurship*. Chicago: University of Chicago Press.

———. 1979. *Perception, Opportunity, and Profit*. Chicago: University of Chicago Press.

Knight, Frank H. 1921. *Risk, Uncertainty, and Profit*. Boston: Houghton Mifflin.

Kostal, Rande W. 1994. *Law and English Railway Capitalism, 1825–1875*. Oxford: Clarendon Press.

Leunig, Tim. 2001. "New Answers to Old Questions: Explaining the Slow Adoption of Ring Spinning in Lancashire, 1880–1913." *Journal of Economic History* 61:439–66.

Lewis, M.J.T. 1970. *Early Wooden Railways*. London: Routledge.

Matthew, H.C.G. 2004. "Gladstone, William Ewart (1809–1898)." *Oxford Dictionary of National Biography*. Oxford: Oxford University Press.

McCloskey, Donald N., ed. 1971. *Essays on a Mature Economy: Britain after 1840*. Princeton: Princeton University Press.

Milward, Robert. 1991. "Emergence of Gas and Water Monopolies in Nineteenth-Century Britain: Contested Markets and Public Control." In *New Perspectives on the Late Victorian Economy*, ed. James Foreman-Peck, 96–124. Cambridge: Cambridge University Press.

Mitchell, Brian R. 1984. *Economic Development of the British Coal Industry*. Cambridge: Cambridge University Press.

Mokyr, Joel. 2004. *The Gifts of Athena: Historical Origins of the Knowledge Economy*. Princeton: Princeton University Press.

Nef, John U. 1932. *The Rise of the British Coal Industry*. 2 vols. London: Routledge.

Nicholson, J. Shield. 1909. *A Project of Empire: A Critical Study of the Economics of Imperialism, with Special Reference to the Ideas of Adam Smith*. London: Macmillan.

Officer, Lawrence H. 2005. "The Annual Real and Nominal GDP for the United Kingdom, 1086–2005." Economic History Services, http://eh.net/hmit/ukgdp.

Olson, Mancur. 1982. *The Rise and Decline of Nations*. New Haven: Yale University Press.

Payne, Peter L. 1988. *British Entrepreneurship in the Nineteenth Century*. 2nd ed. London: Macmillan.

Pollard, Sidney. 1997. *Marginal Europe: The Contribution of Marginal Lands since the Middle Ages*. Oxford: Clarendon Press.

Prest, John. 2004. "Peel, Sir Robert, Second Baronet, (1788–1850)." *Oxford Dictionary of National Biography*. Oxford: Oxford University Press.

Reed, M. C., ed. *Railways and the Victorian Economy*. Newton Abbot: David & Charles.

Rolt, L.T.C. 1957. *Isambard Kingdom Brunel: A Biography*. London: Longman.

Rose, Mary B. 1993. "Beyond Buddenbrooks: The Management of Family Business Succession." In *Entrepreneurship, Networks, and Modern Business*, ed. Jonathan Brown and Mary B. Rose, 127–43. Manchester: Manchester University Press.

Saul, S. B. 1969. *The Myth of the Great Depression, 1873–1896*. London: Macmillan.

Schumpeter, Joseph A. 1939. *Business Cycles*. New York: McGraw-Hill.

Searle, Geoffrey R. 1998. *Morality and the Market in Victorian Britain*. Oxford: Clarendon Press.

Smiles, Samuel. 1862. *Lives of the Engineers*. London: John Murray.

Turnock, David. 1998. *An Historical Geography of Railways in Great Britain and Ireland*. Aldershot: Ashgate.

UK Law Commission and Scottish Law Commission. 1996. *Chronological Table of Local Legislation: Local and Personal Acts, 1797–1994*. 4 vols. London: HMSO.

Wiener, Martin. 1981. *English Culture and the Decline of the Industrial Spirit*. Cambridge: Cambridge University Press.

Wilkins, Mira. 1986. "The Free-Standing Company, 1870–1914: An Important Type of British Foreign Direct Investment." *Economic History Review*, 2nd ser., 41:259–82.

———. 1989. *The History of Foreign Investment in the United States to 1914*. Cambridge: Harvard University Press.

Wilkins, Mira, and Harm Schroter, eds. 1998. *The Free-Standing Company in the World Economy, 1830–1996*. Oxford: Oxford University Press.

Chapter 9

History of Entrepreneurship: Britain, 1900–2000

ANDREW GODLEY AND MARK CASSON

Features of British Economic Development in the Twentieth Century

In 1900 Britain was at the apogee of confidence in the justness and might of its role as world leader. Its rise to mastery through the Victorian Age had been squarely based on economic success. And this had emerged through its early dominance of world textiles markets—cotton and woolens—and then the iron and steel industry, coal, shipbuilding, and other pre-mass-production forms of mechanical engineering—the so-called staple industries. In 1900 British firms enjoyed a 35 percent share of the global trade in manufactured products, when Britain had less than 2 percent of the world's population (Matthews et al. 1982, 435). Economic success was the foundation of global political power, and the British Empire was, it is easy to forget, "the nearest thing there has ever been to a world government" (Ferguson 2003, xxvi). And that success had been created by British entrepreneurs.

Power, of course, brought rewards for Britons in the early twentieth century; most obviously among the entrepreneurial and capitalist classes. In 1913 the richest 0.1 percent of Britons received over 12 percent of the nation's income (Atkinson 2002). It permitted a lavish lifestyle, as the economist John Maynard Keynes wistfully recollected in 1919.

> For...the middle and upper classes...life offered, at a low cost and with the least trouble, conveniences, comforts and amenities beyond the compass of the richest and most powerful monarchs of other ages. The inhabitant of London could order by telephone, sipping his morning tea in bed, the various products of the whole earth in such quantity as he might see fit, and reasonably expect their early delivery upon his doorstep; he could at the same moment and by the same means adventure his wealth in the natural resources and new enterprises of any quarter of the world, and share, without exertion or even trouble, in their prospective fruits and advantages. (Cited in Ferguson 2003, 324)

But the benefits also trickled down to the ordinary British working-class families too, albeit at a much reduced level. Only in the resource-abundant and labor-scarce United States, Canada, Australia, and New Zealand were wages for unskilled workers higher (Williamson 1995).

There was also an important second string to Britain's economic bow of around 1900 according to Keynes's aphorism. British overseas investment had attained wholly unprecedented levels by World War I. Never before nor since has any major nation committed such a large part of its economic resources to activities overseas (Edelstein 1982). And in Keynes's mind the link between domestic consumption and overseas investment was abundantly clear, for it was such prodigious levels of British investment in foreign economies that led to the creation of transport networks and infrastructure necessary for integrating far-flung places into the world trading system, enabling the world's resources to be productively deployed. It was investment in railways, ports, and harbors, in tramways and electric utilities, in plantations of tea, coffee, cotton, rubber, and cocoa, in mines and oil wells, all around the world, within the empire and without, that created the supply lines, the institutional framework for market exchange, as well as the principal economic activities themselves that led to a level of global economic integration that has only very recently been recaptured (Jones 2005, chap. 2).

The conventional wisdom is that the British economy faltered in the twentieth century and that this was to some considerable extent the fault of its entrepreneurs, who, as the previous chapter has shown, were alleged to have been reluctant to embrace the new technologies of the second industrial revolution—transport using the oil-based internal combustion engine, the new electrical engineering, and modern chemicals—and the new business techniques—like mass production—to manage them. It is a conventional wisdom that needs qualifying with a better understanding of the changing economic context facing British entrepreneurs in the twentieth century, and a wider appreciation of the degree of specialization in the staple industries and in overseas investments that had already taken place.

The combined sum of British overseas investments represented the equivalent of one-third of net national wealth in 1913 (Edelstein 2004), or the equivalent of 57 percent of British GDP (Houston and Dunning 1976, 12). This was a level of commitment that attracted some controversy, as critics bemoaned its corollary: the relative lack of investment in Britain's domestic industry. It was a pertinent criticism. In 1913 British industry remained especially focused on the traditional staple industries, its legacy from the era of the Industrial Revolution (see Mokyr in this volume); 60 percent of British exports still came from the cotton and woolen textiles, coal, iron and steel, and machinery sectors (Magee 2004, table 4.9). But these were all sectors that depended upon a high labor content of production. They were all sectors that were vulnerable therefore to either cheaper labor or substitution through mechanization.

Moreover, the sectors that were growing in prominence in the world economy were sectors that relied both on a much higher scientific content of production and far more sophisticated managerial practices—most obviously in electrical engineering, in chemicals, and in advanced mechanical engineering sectors. The world's leading producers of electric power generation equipment, of synthetic dyestuffs, and automobiles depended upon a qualitatively superior level of engineering knowledge in product and process design. Compared with Britain's leading firms in the staples, the technological content of production at Siemens's vast factory site in Berlin, or the move to systematic research and development at Du Pont, or Bayer or BASF in the chemical industry, or the intensity of the flow of production at Ford's Highland Park manufacturing plant, revealed a level of inferiority that shocked British commentators of the day. Britain's share of exports from vehicles and electrical goods was barely 1 percent in 1913. And while British chemicals output and export share was higher, British chemicals firms were largely focused on increasingly outdated products and processes (Lindert and Trace 1971). In these technologically advanced sectors first movers pursued vertical integration strategies and developed strong managerial capabilities in order to compensate for the absence of specialist market-making intermediaries in what were novel markets. With their specialization in older, more labor-intensive industries, it is unsurprising that overall British labor productivity had been overtaken by both the new technological leaders of United States and Germany by 1913 (Broadberry 1998). But it was also the case that with intermediaries already established in these sectors, British entrepreneurs were not forced to develop managerial capabilities in the same way as U.S. and German technologically advanced firms were. And so, according to the conventional wisdom, the prevailing theme of British twentieth-century economic history was set. As other nations specialized in the more technologically intensive sectors of the second industrial revolution, British firms and entrepreneurs appeared unable to make the transition from their specialization in the lower-productivity staples into the higher-productivity new sectors. Where British entrepreneurs emerged in these sectors, they typically were only able to enjoy success when protected from the full force of competition. As protection began to disappear in the 1970s and 1980s, so British weaknesses here were exposed and these firms mostly failed.

By 2000 Britain enjoyed only a 6 percent share of world trade in manufactures, barely one-sixth the share at the century's beginning (Economist 2005). With the disappearance of the staple industries, Britain, the country of the world's first industrial revolution and the global superpower of 1900, had been relegated to the second division of national economies. In what was seen as a great indignity in the UK, Italians celebrated *Il Sorpasso* in 1990, as the GDP of Italy overtook that of the UK for the first time since the days of the Medici. The 1992 ejection from the European Exchange Rate Mechanism seemed to be the culmination of almost a century of economic weakening. Of course, British households were many times richer than they had been at the century's beginning, but such was the deterioration of Britain's rank in the world order, that the overwhelming consensus was that the country had somehow failed during the twentieth century.

Influential commentators penned titles like *The British Disease* (Allen 1976), "How British is the British Sickness" (Brittan 1978), and "The Slide of Britain" (Porter 1990, 482ff.). But then in the final few years of the century an economic renaissance appeared to take place, as British economic growth accelerated. Suddenly the entire framework for interpreting Britain's twentieth-century economic experience was transformed. What was it all about, after all, if not a story of decline? While its determinants still remain subject to some considerable debate, this very recent transformation in British economic fortunes therefore demands that economic historians begin to reinvestigate the traditional interpretation of relatively poor British twentieth-century performance and the alleged failure of its entrepreneurs.

So, free from having to account for the now reversed inexorable relative economic failure and its inferred entrepreneurial deficiencies, this survey will depart from the conventional treatments of the topic. Instead, we begin with a widely accepted theory of entrepreneurship and then proceed by surveying the areas of significant entrepreneurial activity in a more or less chronological fashion. We discover that British entrepreneurship was less of a failure and that entrepreneurs were themselves less culpable than previous summaries have suggested.

Entrepreneurship, Status, and Culture

Entrepreneurs were an obvious and early target for commentators wanting to understand British industrial lethargy; but not exclusively so.

> The list of explanations which have been advanced during the past forty years to explain Britain's failure to match her competitors is truly vast. It includes a divisive class system, an innate cultural hostility to industrialisation, the domination of government and industry by the financial interests of the City of London, lack of venture capital, excessive taxation, too much government spending, too little planning, insufficient expenditure on education and training, an adversarial two-party electoral system, restrictive labour practices and over-manning, incompetent managers and obstructive trade unions. (Feinstein 1994, 116)

The net effect is that the British entrepreneur is one of the best-studied sociological classes of the twentieth century, but paradoxically also one of the least well understood: the scholarly context has, after all, always been to try to explain a "failure," an axiom that very recent economic history suggests is only partial at the very least.

Over the course of the century the focus of blame has moved from a fairly general concern with poor leadership in the emerging industries of the second industrial revolution (Clapham 1938; Orsagh 1961), to specific criticisms of apparent failure by entrepreneurs to invest in new technology (Aldcroft 1964), or to adopt improved management techniques (Chandler 1990; Hannah 1983). Explanations of why British entrepreneurs failed to invest in new equipment, techniques, or organization (and so apparently to forego profits so willingly) often revolved around allegedly antientrepreneurial qualities in British culture. David Landes famously quipped that British enterprise reflected a

> combination of amateurism and complacency.... The British manufacturer was notorious for his indifference to style, his conservatism in the face of new techniques, his reluctance to abandon the individuality of tradition for the conformity implicit in mass production. (Landes 1969, 337)

Despite fierce criticism from scholarly historians, Martin Wiener's claim that Britain possessed an "anti-industrial spirit" (1981) resonated with politicians and public alike and has had a powerful impact on public policy, providing the moral underpinning for twenty-five years of the promotion of the "enterprise culture." In fact, and despite the criticism of the cultural declinists, much evidence has emerged to support one or other of the culturalists' hypotheses. Although, sadly for Wiener, his elegant pitch for the influential but effete elite as the principal retardant has been exposed as somewhat shallow (Collins and Robbins 1990).

It is important not to overstress the differences between British and other nations' entrepreneurs. Recent comparative studies mostly highlight similarities; or at least variations from the traditional theme. Cassis (1997) and Wardley (1999) warn against judgments of inferiority among British big business, for instance. Berghoff discovered that the entrepreneurs in British provincial towns closely matched German entrepreneurs across a range of parameters (Berghoff and Möller 1994; Berghoff 1995). While Nicholas (1999), Rose (1986), and others have debated the relative merits of the persistence of family control, it was only in the United States that family control ever stopped being the norm, and even then only very recently and by less than commonly thought (Anderson and Reeb 2003). And of course the opportunity set facing entrepreneurs in Britain's relatively mature economy was different from that facing those in faster-growing, less developed economies elsewhere. British entrepreneurs remained prisoners of their constraints (McCloskey and Sandberg 1971).

But in one sense there was a difference, certainly when compared with the United States. British society had matured and stabilized by 1900, with powerful social rigidities set in place. There were fundamental barriers to the supply of entrepreneurs able to bring about "creative destruction." As Kindleberger noted (1964), by 1900 the supply of outsider entrepreneurs had diminished. A wave of European immigrants during the early and middle decades of the nineteenth century had contributed many important figures to the Industrial Revolution. They were succeeded by a far larger population of immigrants from 1880 to 1914, but this one dominated by east Europeans, lacking both skills and capital to make any immediate impact on the British economy—although, as explained below, their role was to be profound indeed by midcentury. From 1914 the borders remained essentially closed until the 1950s.

Moreover, in the early decades of the century, there were relatively few self-made entrepreneurs in Britain. To be sure, there weren't many anywhere else. Even in the United States the Horatio Alger ideal was exposed as a myth (Sarachek 1978). Senior executives and the leading business owners were disproportionately drawn from the elite (Temin 1999). But the sheer extent of the rigidity between the main social classes has been a feature of successive studies of social mobility in Britain (Miles 1999; Goldthorpe 1980). Not only did such immobility retard competitive entry from below, but without any credible prospect for social ascent, it influenced expectations and values among the dispossessed. This was to influence persistently low educational attainment among the working classes, which later became important in explaining low levels of labor productivity growth. But Godley's (2001) comparison of east European Jews in both the United States and in Britain showed that as Jewish immigrants assimilated host country cultural values, their preference for entrepreneurship altered. Those in Britain began increasingly to opt for craft employment rather than business careers for any given wage and profit level. With almost no options for self-advancement, British working-class culture reinforced its strong and conservative craft values, erecting an additional barrier to pursuing entrepreneurship. And so with fewer competitive challenges from either immigrants or from aspirant men from below, incumbents remained unthreatened and in place. Such relative frigidity among the entrepreneurial class was underpinned by the move to protectionism from the Import Duties Act of 1932 onward. Cultural and regulatory protection allowed the incumbent business-owning families to serve much of the British market however they wished and with relative impunity for the middle decades of the century.

The relationship between culture and entrepreneurship has been fraught with scholarly contention for over forty years. But the mechanism between entrepreneurship and cultural values can be better understood once the economic function of entrepreneurship is clarified. Entrepreneurship's environment is when transactions occur under conditions of uncertainty. Entrepreneurship is the exercise of judgment (Casson 1982). And judgment has to be involved whenever a decision is made without access to any generally agreed rule derived from publicly available, validated information about how to proceed (Casson and Godley 2007).

Consider what happens when information is cheaply available. Then firms are able to establish reliable algorithms showing how to manage a set of functions, and the business activity represents the classic small firm in perfectly competitive markets. But should some exogenous event cause turbulence in the economy, information may no longer be either cheap or easily available. Any transaction then becomes risky, but the entrepreneur minimizes risk both by developing a framework to interpret the impact of the turbulence, and by investing in gaining additional, relevant information. Superior frameworks lead to superior outcomes for any given investment. But developing such a judgment-intensive framework depends also on efficient information acquisition, and on testing the entrepreneur's self-perception of complex and inchoate commercial situations. Both the need to acquire specialist information and the need to refine interpretative frameworks lead entrepreneurs to seek out the opinions of other information-gathering specialists, and so provide the incentives for one of the most striking features of entrepreneurial behavior, which is the strength and persistence of entrepreneurial networks. These specialized groups, expert in particular fields, with access to privileged sources of information, and, no doubt like all social groups, with distinct cultural values, are also more likely to find that they can command privileged access to funding, as investors follow their trails. As has been emphasized in both the previous chapters, the importance of entrepreneurial networks making allocative decisions is a persistent feature of British economic activity from the Industrial Revolution to the present.

Entrepreneurship then, certainly in a larger historical context, is about far more than firm formation and venture capital funding (the two features so beloved of management scholars today) and can be most frequently located in those environments that call for the greatest intensity of judgment. Judgment is of course not an observable variable. But given the reasonable assumption that entrepreneurs need other entrepreneurs for privileged access to information, for testing and validating their interpretative frameworks, as well as for specialized sources of venture financing, the presence of entrepreneurial networks is likely to be positively correlated with entrepreneurial judgment. And over historical time and space, these networks are observable.

For this summary of British entrepreneurship in the twentieth century, and in particular in an attempt to fashion an explanation for its apparent long-term secular decline and then sudden reemergence at century's end, these conceptual clarifications are important. Posing the entrepreneurial function as a series of investments in information acquisition and developing a level of expertise at interpreting complex commercial situations suggests that entrepreneurs and entrepreneurial networks have high sunk costs. It would be rare for an expertise developed in one sector to be relevant when transferred to another. Such lack of relevance may be construed as an entrepreneurial "failure," but only in the sense that distinguished physicists, say, might be castigated for being flawed violinists. The extent to which British entrepreneurial networks were able to diversify their expertise bases into higher value areas also depended on external circumstances. And as we shall see, British entrepreneurs throughout the first three-quarters of the twentieth century found themselves facing situations where the value of the stock of their entrepreneurial expertise suddenly depreciated because of a series of exogenous events. The rest of this chapter traces the development of British entrepreneurship over the twentieth century. The period from 1900 to 1929 saw the zenith of British entrepreneurs' global influence yet the increase in domestic difficulties that had begun to emerge in the late Victorian period. The middle years from 1930 to 1975 saw entrepreneurship suffer from a combination of an ever more challenging international environment coupled with a retreat from the market domestically. Finally in the latter years from 1975 to 2000, there has been something of a renaissance in British entrepreneurship.

Entrepreneurial Activities, 1900–1929: Rival Avenues to Wealth

When Royal Dutch-Shell acquired Weetman Pearson's oil major, Mexican Eagle, in 1919, the Shell Group had engineered control of Britain's most valuable company (Bud-Frierman, Godley, and Wale 2010; and table 9.1 in this chapter). Along with Churchill's capture of Anglo-Persian for His Majesty's Government in 1914, it was the most dramatic corporate event in the new century. It also highlights where so much British entrepreneurial activity was located.

British entrepreneurship has largely been criticized because of the relatively poor performance of the British domestic economy, especially during the 1960s and 1970s, when other economies began to overtake the British with great regularity. But at the outset of the period perhaps the greatest concentration of entrepreneurial activity was not to be found in the domestic economy at all, but rather overseas. This was not simply the exploitation of privileged access to the empire, although of course British firms were actively engaged in imperial markets (Hannah 1980, 61–63), but rather the concentration on ever more sophisticated business operations throughout the entire globe. Unlike their German and American counterparts, British entrepreneurs had a rival avenue to wealth creation, bound up with the imperial project (Baumol 1990).

Of course Britain's entrepreneurs, like their American and German equivalents, were active and successfully so in the domestic economy as well. Broadberry's study of comparative productivity reveals that British firms held comparative advantages in several staple industries, most notably in cotton textiles in 1913 (Broadberry 1998). As already noted, these sectors tended to be more labor intensive than the newer industries. But with British labor comparatively expensive, and with mechanization reducing the advantages of skill, British comparative advantage leached away; to Germany in coal mining already by 1911, for example. Other countries found their natural resource endowments lent themselves for more efficient use. In iron and steel, for example, it was apparent by 1900 that British ores were located in relatively expensive areas. In a world of scarce entrepreneurial talent, British home-based entrepreneurs were concentrated in what were, at the time, sunset industries. Their routes to increasing profitability were not always obvious or sustainable.

In the past economic historians have criticized what was comparatively poor investment by British entrepreneurs in the newer industries, the industries of the second industrial revolution like electricals and automobiles (Alford 1988). But from the perspective of the entrepreneurs themselves it is easier to understand why there was reluctance to embark on wholly new ventures in such sectors, where their existing stock of expertise carried little value and where their traditional networks of information gathering carried little relevance.

Rather, as the previous chapter has emphasized, by the final decades of the nineteenth century much entrepreneurial activity in Britain was focused in highly complex infrastructure developments, most notably in railways and then increasingly in tramways and utilities. Given such high sunk costs by entrepreneurs in information acquisition, the costs associated with embarking on ventures in the newer industries like electricals and automobiles may have seemed prohibitive. This is particularly the case when, in the face of declining profits at home, British entrepreneurs were faced with a very obvious alternative of investing in more profitable opportunities overseas, opportunities directly related to the specific expertise available in the British entrepreneurial networks in the development of highly complex infrastructure projects.

It has long been a commonplace of twentieth-century economic history that Britain was financially committed to overseas investment. Indeed such a commitment has mostly been criticized as an additional reason for the relatively slow growth of the newer capital-intensive industries in Britain (Kennedy 1987). But what has until recently largely been ignored is that a very large minority, almost half, of this flow of overseas investment was direct investment by firms and entrepreneurs in acquiring productive assets and businesses overseas, over which they had direct managerial control and from which they received a profit.

In 1905 the total value of British-owned overseas assets was almost one-third the country's net national wealth (Edelstein 2004, 193). By 1913 overseas investment had grown by significantly more than the domestic economy (Matthews et al. 1982), and the share of income from overseas assets to GDP edged higher (Jones 1994). Never before nor since has any major economy so systematically transferred so high a proportion of its resources overseas. And while much of this ownership of overseas assets was the result of portfolio investment, much was not.

According to John Dunning, 40 percent of the value of British overseas investment in 1913 was direct. In a more recent estimate Tony Corley (1994) has placed the share even higher, at 45 percent. These estimates are inevitably partial, but Corley's thorough reworking of all the available data suggests that British entrepreneurs were active all around the world, with around half of all British foreign direct investment going to imperial destinations (South Africa being the largest single recipient during the early years of the century), but around half going to destinations outside the empire. Around 10 percent went to the United States, and perhaps up to a third to Latin America (Corley 1994, table 3).

This commitment to foreign direct investment is obvious among the largest of British companies in table 9.1. The table shows the twelve largest British companies in 1919, headed by Weetman Pearson's Mexican oil business, and where their assets were principally held. If data were available for some other very large overseas-based but wholly private British firms that might figure in this ranking—like Werner Beit, De Beers, Rio Tinto and others—the extent of British business's dependence on global trading and investment links would be even more glaring (Cassis 1997, 23).

But in fact British outward foreign direct investment is wholly underrepresented by focusing on the biggest firms. For these British entrepreneurial activities were overwhelmingly wrapped in a particular institutional form that for a long time was not well understood by historians. Mira Wilkins (1986) summarized these entrepre-

TABLE 9.1
Britain's Largest Firms, 1919

	Market capitalization (£ millions)	Sector	Principal geographic area
Pearson Group	79.1	Oil and contracting	Mexico
Burmah Oil	62.8	Oil	Burma, India
J & P Coats	45.0	Cotton thread	US, world
Anglo-Persian Oil	29.1	Oil	Middle East
Lever Brothers	24.3	Soap and fats	Africa, World
Imperial Tobacco	22.8	Cigarettes	Asia, World
Vickers	19.5	Transportation equipment	UK
Guinness	19.0	Beer	UK, Empire
Brunner, Mond	18.7	Chemicals	UK
Shell Transport & Trading	18.2	Oil	SE Asia, world
Nobel Explosives	16.3	Chemicals	UK, Russia
Courtaulds	16.0	Textiles	UK, US

Source: Bud-Frierman, Godley, and Wale 2010; Hannah 1980.

neurial multinational enterprises as *free-standing companies*. There were thousands of British free-standing companies, and they were usually firms that were created to invest in and develop a specific activity—tin mining in Malaya, or hardwood cultivation in Burma, or electric power plants in Latin America, for example. Because of their focus on a specific project or opportunity, it was normal for the investment to be sold off and for the firm to be wound up after completion: once the power plant was built, or the mahogany plantation or the tin mine operational.

By 1914 the range of industries British entrepreneurs were investing in around the globe had increased markedly. Late-nineteenth-century foreign direct investment was very much concentrated in railways, landownership, and mining. While these three sectors still loomed large by 1914, other sectors had together increased their share of British foreign direct investment markedly. Corley's sectoral breakdown of British overseas firms shows that oil companies represented over 5 percent of the total by 1914. Overseas banking and insurance companies were 4 percent of the total. Various utilities companies, from tramways and electric power station builders, to gas- and waterworks producers, together accounted for nearly one-tenth of the total. These newer sectors were together at least as significant as the more traditional entrepreneurial ventures by then.

Collectively this role of overseas entrepreneurship was enormously important. The stock of British foreign direct investment was 45 percent of total global foreign direct investment in 1913. Overseas investments in the manner of free-standing companies were, in other words, the key entrepreneurial route for integrating resources into the global economy at the time, not the world's emerging giants in automobiles, chemicals, and electricals.

Free-standing companies, as described in the previous chapter, were typically loosely organized around a group of key individuals. These brought all the necessary skills and knowledge required for the particular entrepreneurial venture, and so the entrepreneurial function was concentrated into a team composed of promoters, financiers, solicitors and accountants, trading companies, merchant banks, surveyors, and a whole host of associated professionals required for the specific projects: mining engineers for mining projects, electrical engineers for electricity ventures, oil surveyors for oil wells, agricultural specialists for plantations, and so on (Jones and Wale 1999; Jones 2005, 23–24). These entrepreneurial teams would therefore move from one venture to the next, reconstituting themselves as appropriate, bringing in new experts, dropping those whose expertise was now less relevant. During the early

TABLE 9.2
Sectoral Distribution of Quoted British Overseas Companies, 1907–1938 (%)

Sector	1907	1914	1938
Resource-based			
Mining	25.1	24.9	19
Oil	1.4	5.2	12
Plantations (tea, coffee, rubber)	2.6	23.3	11
Total	29.1	53.5	42
Market-based			
Food (esp. brewing)	1.7	3.3	1
Metals and manufacturing		4.1	1
Other	7.6	4.5	15
Total	9.3	11.9	17
Infrastructure, utilities, and services			
Electric, gas, and water	3.0	4.2	8
Tramways	3.5	1.4	4
Telegraphs	3.4	1.3	3
Shipping, docks, etc.	0.6	1.6	1
Land and other	18.4	12.4	12
Railways	27.4	10.3	8
Banking and insurance	5.3	3.5	6
Total	61.6	34.7	42
	100.0	100.0	100

Source: Adapted from Corley 1994, table 2; and Corley 1997, table 4.

decades of the twentieth century they became ever more global in focus, not only in the regions of the world they operated in, but also in the individuals brought in, with American and European specialists recruited into the teams where necessary. So much of this overseas activity was property-based entrepreneurship, and much required high sunk costs in location-specific, indivisible assets. These were typically large, complex projects that required specialist expertise and access to sophisticated sources of venture capital.

As a new opportunity emerged, an entrepreneurial team formed and then sought second-tier financing by selling equity stakes on the London Stock Exchange. Despite the obvious high risk associated with placing new ventures, investors were evidently more than happy to supply capital. Companies would then return to the market for any subsequent round of financing. The conventional understanding of British entre-preneurship has tended to emphasize the geographic and institutional gaps between the City and the manufacturing centers in the Midlands and the north, gaps that allegedly led to insufficient finance being channeled into new investment in British industrial plants and equipment. Yet such allegations appear difficult to sustain once the evidence of the sheer scale of the London Stock Exchange funding of free-standing companies is understood. Indeed when compared with what is overwhelmingly a private market for venture capital today, the City's provision of venture capital for these free-standing companies in the early decades of the twentieth century appears to have been both more sophisticated and transparent as well as successful in raising what were very large amounts (Corley 1994).

These entrepreneurial networks of (mostly) British businessmen remained highly active during and after World War I right through to the 1970s (Jones 2000). As the world economy developed, so British foreign direct investment switched increas-ingly from older ventures (building and managing overseas railways, for example) to new (Corley 1997). Investors drew on the cultural traditions of "gentlemanly capi-talism," traditions that, as the earlier chapters have made clear, gained legitimacy many decades before. And they proved to be an optimal organizational response to the worldwide demand for complex project management skills exercised over long distances in an era when relatively poor communications meant that corporate head offices were unable to monitor such investments.

But the free-standing companies' flexibility and their loose and efficient organi-zational structures depended on a relatively stable institutional structure for their vi-ability. They were knowledge-transferring, market-creating organizations. But once projects were up-and-running, dedicated operators and specialist intermediaries took control of the resulting revenue flows. The geographically dispersed resources easily became integrated into the existing world economy and its institutions sup-porting international trade. And so free-standing companies, unlike the larger, "clas-sic" multinationals, rarely needed to develop large central office support structures. They remained dependent on what was a sophisticated institutional structure sup-porting contractual rights. But when the disaster of World War I was followed by the turbulence of the 1930s global crisis, they were unable to internalize markets. As transaction costs became too high, they were forced to withdraw.

Initially, in fact, the British response was to relocate as market activity was fore-closed. From 1917 to 1922 first Russia, then the Ottoman Empire, and Mexico all plunged into civil war, and conditions for international trade deteriorated. British entrepreneurs responded by moving to newer regions of the globe and emerging opportunities. They were responsible for much of the development of the eastern seaboard of China during the second and third decades of the century, and the rapid economic growth in the short-lived boom in the Middle East in the 1920s, for example (Plüss 2004; Jones 2000). But during the 1930s profits plummeted. While income from British foreign direct investment remained broadly stable in real terms between 1907 and 1927, it fell from then to 1938 (Corley 1997, table 3). After the World War II large swathes of the globe put up the shutters again. Postwar governments in Southeast Asia, China, Africa, and the Middle East all declared their own *intifadas* against the previously ubiquitous British entrepreneur.

Focusing on overseas investments and free-standing companies suggests, in other words, that there was no failure in British entrepreneurship during the twentieth century. Rather there was something of a bifurcation in activities. Previously successful areas like the staple industries found the competitive environment increasingly harsh and increasingly sought government protection (Bamberg 1988). But rival opportunities for entrepreneurial wealth creation increased overseas. British entrepreneurs with long histories and vast accumulated expertise (notably of course through developing global markets for the staple industries) developed a key institutional structure for their entrepreneurial ventures overseas, based around the free-standing company and the London Stock Exchange. Their great contribution to the world economy was not especially in the realm of new technology, but in drawing together skills and finance to initiate and complete complex projects far away from the centers of financial power. They were novel solutions to the dilemmas posed by the risks of such long-distance trades suffering from opportunistic behavior by agents in far-flung places. The long-standing criticism of the British entrepreneurs in the twentieth century, that they failed to invest in the new industries of automobiles, chemicals, and electricals, is, in other words, a simple misinterpretation of the situation. Why should they have ventured into areas where they were particularly at a disadvantage compared with American and German technological leaders and when British entrepreneurial networks were enjoying such striking success at developing and exploiting overseas ventures?

Entrepreneurial Activities, 1930–1975: Institutional Impediments to Innovation and the Retreat from the Market toward Protectionism

1920s Prelude

Traditional economic histories of Britain typically treat the interwar period as a single epoch in British industrial development, an era that saw the continued stagnation of the staple industries and the eventual emergence of domestically focused newer industries, in automobiles, chemicals, and electricals (Aldcroft 1964). And in one sense a similar periodization for any treatment of British entrepreneurship makes perfect sense.

During the restocking boom of 1919–20, it appeared that *Pax Britannica* had been restored. Not everywhere of course. Only blind optimists believed that Bolshevik Russia would return to the fold. But it was possible to imagine that the world economy would continue into the 1920s much as it had in the years up to 1914. But whether through managerial inadequacies or increased union resistance to mechanization, Britain had lost its comparative advantage in many staple industries, and for British producers the only real hope was for the value of the pound to fall to a level that restored competitiveness. Yet in order to preserve global economic stability, the British Government pursued the opposite policy. Interest rates rose and sterling appreciated back to its prewar parity, prompting export sales to collapse. What began as a necessary restructuring of the British economy was spiked with an added monetary twist in the 1920s.

Mergers often followed this loss of export competitiveness, with the cotton and woolen textiles, iron and steel, coal, and chemicals industries all experiencing major restructuring (Bamberg 1988; Hannah 1983). But the underlying impetus was now mostly defensive, to retreat from competitive markets. Concern was for protection either through official government controls or industry cartels. The 1926 General Strike simply reinforced the view of needing to protect society from the vicissitudes of the world economy. Successive Governments promoted horizontal integration, and the cartelization of British domestic industry accelerated in the 1920s. So incentives for innovative entrepreneurship diminished, noncompetitive behavior was rewarded, and the potential productivity advantages of increasing scale were largely squandered (Westall 1994). To be sure, the domestic crisis of the interwar period was perceived in terms of the need to protect jobs and money wages. But the net effect was for Governments and business leaders to conspire against both consumer welfare and long-term industrial competitiveness by institutionalizing noncompetitive behavior. The domestic British economy suffered the results.

1930s–1950s: Institutional Impediments to Innovation: Protectionism and Public Sector Encroachment

As far as the wider picture of the British entrepreneurship is concerned, the epoch-making events occurred elsewhere. The global economic crisis of the 1930s and the subsequent war and decolonization meant that British outward direct investment was threatened. Overseas assets were sold, often at a loss, and funds repatriated into a stagnant British economy. The Pearson Group, for example, switched focus from being one of the world's most entrepreneurial oil majors, to becoming a London-based investment trust. No doubt directors' lunches improved, but Pearson's entrepreneurial dynamism fizzled out (Bud-Frierman, Godley, and Wale 2010). Other overseas groups with fewer opportunities to cash out also mutated. Some trading companies looked for opportunities for investing at home. The trading company Booker lost much of its value by reversing into poorly performing retailers, for instance. Others, by contrast, shifted their center of gravity even further away from Britain, moving their corporate headquarters to their Asian markets, for example (Jones 2000).

The twin strike on British entrepreneurship of an uncompetitive currency and then the global economic crisis simply undermined the ability of entrepreneurs to act in the two core areas of comparative advantage: the traditional staple industries and the overseas focused free-standing companies. The expertise so carefully acquired by the key entrepreneurs and their networks over so many years had suddenly lost its value. New entrepreneurs and new networks needed to emerge, and in what was an unprecedentedly difficult international environment during the 1930s, those new networks began to prosper at home. For after the passing of the 1932 Import Duties Act, Britain had become a highly protected market.

The conventional treatment of the 1930s in economic history textbooks is to emphasize the emergence of important new firms and sectors in the British economy. Unemployment still reached almost 30 percent at the worst moments in the early 1930s. But with entrepreneurs like Morris and Austin in the automobile industry, the successful merger of the Nobel and Brunner, Mond chemicals firms to form ICI (in 1926), the British economy seemed to weather the 1930s crisis better than elsewhere. But while this reflects important shifts in economic activity, we should be cautious in embracing such an interpretation wholeheartedly. By 1939 the staple industries still dominated British output and exports, and the combined output of the much vaunted new British motor car and electrical engineering industries amounted to less than 5 percent of total manufacturing output. The new infant industries remained protected but relatively insignificant. What can be stated is that the impact of rising real wages created new consumer demands, and many British entrepreneurs were not slow in meeting them.

This rise in living standards continued a long trend. Earlier innovations in branded consumer goods saw the rise of the powerful British tobacco industry, in particular the Wills' Imperial Tobacco (Alford 1973; Hannah 2006). Other companies developed strong brands in foodstuffs and confectionery, beverages, and branded medicines in the first half of the twentieth century. Rank, Huntley and Palmers, Horlicks, Colman, Cadburys, and Rowntree in foodstuffs, Guinness in beverages, and Beecham in household products all embraced novel marketing campaigns and built up strong brands. But, perhaps tellingly, all of these family firms were managed by second, third, or even later generations already by the first decades of the twentieth century.

Rising living standards meant a growing demand for new services also. And here the trend was for genuine new entrants—in catering and retailing, in transport and in entertainment. Nevertheless the genuine entrepreneurial entrants in these sectors, like their counterparts in automobiles, electricals, and chemicals, were unable to build firms and industries with significant productivity advantages over German and American rivals (Broadberry 1998, 2006). During the protected 1930s, 1940s, and 1950s this largely did not matter. The British market had become a largely domestic concern, and British entrepreneurs were able to enjoy success in meeting domestic needs. But as tariff barriers began to fall from the 1960s and international competition reemerged, British frailties in the tradable sectors were exposed.

New entrants of any genuine significance in the 1930s through to the 1950s can largely be grouped together under two headings: they were either British subsidiaries of American multinationals, which brought their technologically intensive manufacturing processes with them, or they were immigrant entrepreneurs who clustered in the new services or related products. In retrospect, they were of great significance because had Britain been a less open society, had U.S. multinationals been refused entry, had the Jewish immigrants been persecuted—both of which were very real alternative scenarios elsewhere in Europe—the level of entrepreneurial activity in Britain during these troubled decades would have sunk to a very low ebb indeed.

American multinational entrants, like Gillette and Hoover (building on the earlier example of Singer) were not, of course, examples of British entrepreneurship, but their demonstration effect was important to some British businesses (Jones and

Bostock 1996; Godley 1999, 2006). In fact, some U.S. subsidiaries were quickly acquired by British entrepreneurs. Woolworths, for instance, entered the British retailing market in 1909 and quickly expanded its coverage during the 1920s and went on to become Britain's largest retailer by the 1950s. But its entrepreneurial managing director, William Lawrence Stephenson, was a Yorkshireman hired by Frank Woolworth to run the British subsidiary (Godley 2008; Shaw 2004). After it was spun out on the London stock market in 1931, Stephenson acquired a major stake and went on to become one of Britain's richest men (Rubinstein 2006). Among others, Singer and Ford of Britain also acquired autonomy during this time.

But the real entrepreneurial outsiders were immigrants. Some were already established in business before they arrived, especially those from the Dominions, but the majority had been brought over by their parents in the wave of east European Jewish immigration. These mostly second-generation Polish and Lithuanian Jews collectively transformed much of the British economy during the long retreat from global competition from the 1930s through to the 1970s (Godley 2001).

The east European Jews built on the entrepreneurial success of an earlier generation of German Jewish immigrants. Joe Lyons created his eponymous restaurant chain in the 1900s, while Oscar Deutsch transformed the cinema sector in the 1920s, themselves building on German Jewish success in the City during a previous generation. But the truly significant entrepreneurs during this middle third of the twentieth century in Britain were east European Jewish immigrants and largely concentrated in retailing. Both Montague Burton (in men's clothing) and Simon Marks (Marks and Spencer's variety chain stores and women's clothing) experienced very rapid growth from very small bases during the 1920s and 1930s. They spawned several successful imitators, also largely drawn from the Jewish immigrant community, which collectively transformed the distribution of clothing, and, through their impact on supply chains, its manufacture. Similarly Drage's in furniture, along with their ultimate nemesis Isaac Wolfson's Great Universal Stores, experienced dramatic growth and transformed their sector. In food retailing Jack Cohen's Tesco had emerged by the end of the 1930s as perhaps the largest regional grocer.

While productivity in British retailing overall remained significantly below American (but not German) levels, these innovative entrants were quick to acquire market share. Such entrepreneurial growth was wholly exceptional in British retailing at this time. Limited consumer mobility and only a very modest level of urban change gave incumbents much greater market power to deter new entrants from acquiring precious High Street sites. But the Jewish retailers were able to overcome such barriers through first exploiting two novel financial instruments, and second, through being very close to the emerging commercial property market.

The two novel innovations in financial instruments were, first, the development of sale and leaseback finance by Burton (and later used by Jack Cohen) to fund rapid store growth and, second, the capitalization of consumer debt by the furniture retailers Drage's and Great Universal, enabling them to borrow on the strength of hundreds of thousands of weekly installment commitments (Scott 1994, 2009).[1] Singer, the creator of mass installment sales, had never seen its consumer debt as a leverageable asset, for instance (Godley 2006).

The modern commercial property sector also emerged in the 1920s as the beginning of suburbanization, especially in London, led to new High Street developments. Many second-generation Jewish immigrants became attracted to the sector, knowing as they did the particular streets and settings so well. Charles Clore left his father's clothing factory and, after a short interlude as a cinema owner and impresario, moved into property development. Jack Rose's ascent began when leaving the East End and working as an office boy for a West End surveyor. The changing commercial property market in the 1930s enabled new entrants to muscle their way through new developments into an otherwise conservative retailing sector. But it was also these second-generation Jewish immigrant property entrepreneurs who went on to become central to the most impressive manifestation of British entrepreneurship in the postwar era through to the early 1970s.

1950 to 1975: The Growth of the Public Sector and the Era of Replicative Entrepreneurship

The outbreak of war in September 1939 heralded necessary encroachment of government control over ever greater swaths of the British economy. Along with the entire private sector, entrepreneurship was squeezed. The postwar period began in Britain with a leitmotif that was antipathetic to free market activity. The continuing problems of coal and steel prompted the Labour Government to nationalize the industries, and, it was thought, so protect remaining jobs and improve management. Similarly, the continually underperforming railway companies were forced to come under Government ownership. With the creation of the welfare state, very much higher marginal tax rates, far greater powers for unions, and the adverse effect on planning from the volatile demand management policies,[2] the postwar environment for entrepreneurs was very different. Resources were increasingly transferred away from private sector entrepreneurship and either toward the public sector or toward powerful rent-seeking groups in the private sector, like the union barons and powerful incumbent businesses (Bacon and Eltis 1976). Industrial policy concentrated on investing in national champions, like British Leyland in the automobile sector, with near universal disappointment at the eventual outcome. Unsurprisingly, room for entrepreneurial start-ups in the British economy was squeezed. Britain experienced the lowest rate of new firm formation in the world in the 1960s and 1970s (Bolton Report 1971; Wilson Report 1979).

Other economies in Europe also pursued the model of extensive state involvement in the economy but, by contrast, largely experienced successful growth records. The French most notably enjoyed the *trentes glorieuse* from the late 1950s as state-led restructuring brought managerial advantages and additional investment to its preferred sectors. But while the British economy grew at an unprecedented rate during the late 1950s and early 1960s, the British experiment with central planning was nevertheless far from a success. The golden age, characterized by big government, big business and big unions, began to sour in the British economy during the 1960s and 1970s.

Yet within this standard treatment of faltering postwar economic maturity, entrepreneurial inertia, and a relative decline in living standards, there remained an active hinterland of entrepreneurial dynamism. Indeed, with annual economic growth at 3–4 percent, such was the rate of change that opportunities inevitably emerged. Gerald Ronson, one of Britain's leading property entrepreneurs since the 1960s, suggested it was an easy time to be an entrepreneur because there was so little competition: "You could make money falling out of bed."[3]

As a young man Ronson had recognized the potential in the property business, persuaded his father to sell his family furniture factory in London's East End and invest in a rising market. He was one of seventy to eighty Jewish property millionaires identified by Oliver Marriott (1967), who collectively transformed much of the British commercial property landscape during the 1950s through to the 1970s. They were the most dynamic entrepreneurial presence in an otherwise sluggish private sector. The most spectacularly successful of all was Charles Clore, whose search for new property deals brought him to realize that traditional and conservatively managed retail chains were sitting on enormously undervalued property portfolios and were reluctant to allow their asset base to be realized. Clore decided that they should be forced to and so pioneered competitive takeovers in Britain with his hostile acquisition of the large, integrated shoe company J. Sears.

Sears in 1953 could be described as a stereotype of the conservatively managed, third- or fourth-generation British family firm; its entrepreneurial phase had finished several decades before (Jefferys 1954). It was one of Britain's largest firms and dominated shoe manufacturing, with the largest shoe factory in Britain. Its undervalued property portfolio of 920 shoe stores in every High Street in the land was the attraction to Clore (Clutterbuck and Devine 1987, 64). The 1948 Companies Act provided the legal structure for transfers of share ownership, but until Clore no one had tested the legitimacy of contested takeovers. The culture and tradition of the City was that if the target company's board did not agree to the takeover, minority shareholders would not accept an offer. By appealing directly to shareholders and offering them an attractive price, Clore introduced the market for corporate control in Britain. He went on to repeat the trick several times and so indirectly became Britain's leading retailer during the 1960s. More important, however, the demonstration effect prompted others to hunt for publicly listed firms, where management seemed chronically unable to generate any reasonable profit from their asset bases. Clore's reward was popular infamy, comforted no doubt by an enormous personal fortune. By the early 1970s apart from pop stars and football players, the property entrepreneurs appeared to be the only group in society with the Midas touch. But unlike Ringo Starr or Georgie Best, the reputation of entrepreneurship plumbed new depths.

The linkages between the property sector and retailing had been established during the 1920s and 1930s, and they continued through into the 1950s and 1960s. Jack Cohen's expansion strategy at Tesco was predicated on profits from property investment subsidizing retail expansion, for example. Cohen was one of three or four particularly active entrepreneurs in food retailing responsible for introducing self-service techniques. But Alan Sainsbury was the key figure here, as Sainsbury's quickly moved from being one of a dozen or so large regional grocers to the largest food retailer in Britain.

The Sainsbury's example is noteworthy because the company appears to have been an entrepreneurial exception to the rule in British business, with the third (Alan Sainsbury) and fourth (John Sainsbury) generations more innovative than the founder. The successful introduction of self-service was the key to this company's success from the late 1950s, but their model was wholly novel.

Self-service had been developed in the United States in the 1930s and its raison d'être was to cut costs in a highly price competitive market. Goods were stacked on shelves for consumers to self-select, so reducing labor inputs. Sites were chosen away

TABLE 9.3
British Grocery Market Share, 1960–1975

	Total store numbers, 1960		Market share		
	All	Self-service	1971	1975	Acquired by
Sainsbury's	254	24	6.7%	9.0%	
Tesco	278	60	6.4%	8.0%	
Allied Suppliers	3,800	548	5.3%	5.5%	Cavenham Foods 1972
Fine Fare	43	43	5.5%	4.8%	
Asda	0	0	1.9%	4.3%	
International Group	550	63	2.8%	3.8%	BAT 1972
Safeway	0	0	1.0%	2.0%	
Waitrose	17	0	1.0%	2.0%	

Source: Godley and Williams 2009a, 2009b.

from congested town centers, so reducing rents. In the 1930s United States, shoppers demonstrated highly price elastic behavior, paving the way for this innovative format to spread. The model was tried in Britain by several pioneers in the 1950s, notably several co-operatives, Tesco, and Garfield Weston's Canadian import Fine Fare. But this insertion of American practice invariably met with disappointing results. British consumers apparently preferred their traditional counter service format, and when prices of all branded groceries were controlled by their manufacturers under the regime of resale price maintenance, consumers had little incentive to opt for what was a reduced service at the fledgling supermarkets.

But Sainsbury's held two major advantages over rivals. First, their long-standing strategy of selling their own-brand products enabled them to undercut rivals bound by resale price maintenance without losing product quality. This was made possible because of their long-term relationships with favored suppliers, which meant that once the decision to turn to American methods had been made, they were able to draw on the experience and knowledge of the wide and supportive network of their supply chain as they searched to find a successful self-service model. Second, their historic emphasis on carrying a larger range of produce than competitors had prompted them to invest heavily in refrigeration. This meant that, unlike rival supermarket chains, Sainsbury's were able to cater for a full range of meat products and frozen goods, especially the remarkably fast-growing demand for poultry (Godley and Williams 2009a, 2009b). The net result was a model of self-service that emphasized both a very much greater scale of capital investment than rivals were able to pursue, but at the same time no reduction in labor content, with a high-quality service maintained. It was an expensive expansion strategy, but it was this, the Sainsbury model, that won out and has since become the industry standard (since extended by Tesco and exported around the world). By 1975 Sainsbury's was the undisputed king of British food retailers and one of several entrepreneurial newcomers to the list of Britain's largest retailers.

Table 9.4 indicates the transformation of one of the few sectors characterized by significant entrepreneurial endeavors during the period from 1930 to 1975. The prominence of east European Jewish immigrants (first and second generation) is striking—yet still understated—in the table. Clore also owned the Lewis' department store chain in addition to Sears, for example. Montague Burton's untimely death in 1952 meant that his longtime competitor, Henry Price's Fifty Shilling Tailors (which became United Drapery Stores) overtook the earlier leader in the 1950s and 1960s. But Bernard Lyons was a second-generation east European Jewish immigrant as well. In this sector the role of outsider entrepreneurs had transformed British business. In addition to Clore, Burton, and Lyons, Wolfson, Cohen, Marks, and Sieff were all second-generation East European Jews as well. Moreover, each was surrounded by a cluster of allies and supporters; several of the Jewish retailers vied jealously for intra-communal influence. Stephenson, by contrast, was no immigrant, but was an outsider and was given an opportunity to fast-track to top management as Frank Woolworth's protégé that would surely never have happened had he stayed in a British firm.

In fact the only entrepreneurial second-generation (or later) leaders to attain success in retailing were John Campbell Boot, who developed his father's eponymous

TABLE 9.4

Britain's Ten Largest Retailers in 1975 (by employment) and Key Entrepreneurial Figures during the Period 1930–1975

Firm	Sector	Employees	Entrepreneur
F. W. Woolworth	Variety (toys and confectionery)	81,669	William Lawrence Stephenson (1923–48)
Boots	Chemists	68,846	John Campbell Boot, 2nd Lord Trent (1920–56)
Sears Holdings	Shoes	65,000	Charles Clore (1953–)
GUS	Furniture	47,615	Isaac Wolfson (1930–)
Cavenham Foods	Food	40,300	Former giant Allied Suppliers. Acquired by corporate raider James Goldsmith in 1972.
Tesco Stores	Food	40,245	Jack Cohen (1919–)
Marks & Spencer	Variety (women swear and food)	39,480	Simon Marks (1916–64)
United Drapery Stores	Menswear	37,000	Joseph Collier (1944–) and Bernard Lyons (1957–). Formerly Montague Burton.
Debenhams	Department store	33,000	Large old-fashioned department store group partially reorganised by John Bedford (1949–71)
J. Sainsbury	Food	31,000	Alan (1933–67) and John Sainsbury (1958–92)

Sources: Adapted from Jeremy 1998, table 9.12; Aris 1970, 102–10; Chapman 1974; Shaw 2004a, 2004b; and Godley 2008.

chemist's chain, and the Sainsburys (Chapman 1974). Both had been successful in grafting American retailing methods into their otherwise traditional British retailing organizations (Boot through losing family control of the firm to the American druggist king, Louis Liggett, during the 1920s, who then imported American management methods).

As can be seen in table 9.3, Allied Suppliers had long been the largest retailer in Britain, but decades of conservative management meant its fortunes were overtaken by others. Like Debenhams, Allied retained a high rank because of the legacy of past success, although it became increasingly vulnerable and was acquired by the corporate raider, James Goldsmith's Cavenham Foods, in 1972.

Apart from the several clusters of Jewish immigrant entrepreneurial networks, the second prominent outsider influence on British entrepreneurship during the period was from U.S. multinationals. Already important before the war, as noted above, U.S. firms began to establish British subsidiaries with alacrity from 1950, having an important impact on the productivity growth in the wider British economy (Jones and Bostock 1996). Their impact was inevitably directly felt by inferior British competitors, but equally in some sectors U.S. foreign direct investment actually stimulated British entrepreneurship and innovation, and in at least one very prominent case the wholly unanticipated spillover effect was to create an entirely new industry.

With tariff barriers too high for direct exports, U.S. firms continued to open branch plants to serve the British and European markets. These inward investments were concentrated in the mechanical engineering sector (including extending earlier investments in American automobile subsidiaries), pharmaceuticals, and electrical engineering (Bostock and Jones 1994; Jones and Bostock 1996; Godley 1999).

The consequence for the British automobile and mechanical engineering and electrical sectors, where British firms came face to face with superior U.S. technology was for their market position to deteriorate, first in Europe, and then increasingly in the domestic market as well. In these industries the consequence of the "American invasion" appeared grim (Servan-Schreiber 1967). The Americanization of the pharmaceutical sector, by contrast, appeared to initiate very different results. It wasn't that British firms held a technological advantage. In pharmaceuticals, as elsewhere, U.S. firms were far more likely to hold patents and invest in research (Slinn 2006). The atomistic American health care market, where prescribing authority was vested in physicians, gave pharmaceutical companies there a tremendous incentive to pursue direct marketing strategies (Greene 2005). With the National Health Service monopsony, Britain presented a very different market environment, yet one where the international reputation of medical researchers and the British School of Physiology was such that a successful collaboration represented an important commercial endorsement for any pharmaceutical company (Quirke 2005).

British pharmaceutical companies already carried their strong links with leading researchers from the 1930s and, especially, during the war. And while they had been less able to commercialize some of the results (Pfizer won the race to mass-produce penicillin, and Merck gained the lion's share of the world market through its international licensing strategy), the research networks were cemented in place (Athreye and Godley 2009). It was these networks and public-private partnerships that U.S. entrants sought to break into. Merck, Pfizer, American Cyanamid, and others therefore all opened major new research centers during the 1950s and 1960s to collaborate with British scientists and British pharmaceutical companies.

The spillover gain for the British firms was that they were then able to observe at close quarters just how important an effective marketing strategy was for this most research intensive of all industries. Glaxo in particular benefited from a strong relationship with Merck (Quirke 2005). And while Wellcome had already developed very strong American links with its U.S. subsidiary, Burroughs Wellcome, as the British firms responded, the competitive positions of Beecham, Glaxo, ICI, and Wellcome all improved. For a while in the 1980s these four British firms were among the world's leading dozen pharmaceutical firms. Uniquely among advanced economies, Britain's share of world exports in pharmaceuticals remained stable from 1938 onward at 12 percent in what was an incomparably more valuable market by the 1990s. By contrast German exports fell from 39 percent to 9 percent, and the American share from 34 percent in 1955 to 9 percent in 1995 (Broadberry 2004, table 3.8).

Elsewhere British entrepreneurship gained from the American invasion through a wholly unanticipated manner. The creation of the Eurobond market was the catalyst that enabled London to recapture its position as the world's leading center of international finance, and the role of American multinational subsidiaries was crucial. Siegmund Warburg had pioneered the concept of firms issuing dollar-denoted bonds as an innovative use of the pool of offshore dollars. But President Kennedy's interest equalization tax (1963) along with the Foreign Direct Investment Program (1968) required U.S. corporations to finance overseas investment by overseas borrowings. Eurobond issues rose dramatically in consequence from $348 million in 1963 to £5,508 million in 1972 (Roberts 2001, table 1).

The City of London had stagnated in the years since 1930. Investment banking had diminished in importance and British positions in international trade had deteriorated. There was relatively little to do. Banking had become heavily regulated. Where innovation was occurring, with Burton's and Clore's property-related activities, or with Warburg's creation of the Eurobond market, participation was restricted to a small group of insiders—the entrepreneurial networks. The London Stock Exchange, formerly the locus of so much dynamic venture capital funding for overseas investments, had sacrificed competitive behavior for comfort. Overseas ventures had collapsed. Michie's (1999) chapter covering the 1950s is entitled "Drifting towards Oblivion"! The Eurodollar and Eurobond markets lifted the City out of its torpor.

This was too late for British entrepreneurship to benefit from any of the technology bubbles in the American stock markets during the 1950s and 1960s. Without any equivalent of the active U.S. over-the-counter securities trading market, there were almost no initial public offerings in electricals in Britain during the late 1950s and early 1960s. New issues to young electrical companies in the United States peaked at $135 million and $140 million in 1959 and 1960 respectively (O'Sullivan 2006). In Britain there were successful diversifications by the dominant and long-established electrical companies into consumer appliances (AEI developed the successful Hotpoint brand, for instance), but entrepreneurial start-ups met with only short-lived success. A. J. Flatley gained some prominence for novel clothes-drying machines; John Bloom some notoriety for his electric washing machines. But neither entrepreneur could match the market power of the large incumbents and so withdrew in 1962 and 1964 respectively (Corley 1966, 55–61). The dead hand of antientrepreneurial regulation in the market for investment finance short-circuited competitive entry, and there was simply no equivalent of the American electronics revolution that ultimately led to the modern computer industry there.

The single initial public offering in Britain of the 1960s that enabled an entrepreneurial start-up to grow into a large, successful firm was Stanley Kalms's Dixons. This small camera retailer, with just sixteen branches and a busy mail order business, went public in 1963, in the midst of the American photography bubble—Polaroid was trading on a price-earnings ratio of over 100 in New York![4] Even so, Kalms later reflected that so onerous were the demands of the London Stock Exchange that he wished he had remained private.[5] The sole bright spot in the entire venture capital landscape in Britain was a Government agency, the ICFC, the forerunner of 3i, but compared with the sheer scale of venture financing that had been available to finance British overseas ventures through the London Stock Exchange before 1930, its impact was minimal (Michie 1999, 258–59, 281–82; Coopey and Clarke 1995, appendix).

Outside the stultifying effect of government control, entrepreneurs remained active in the postwar "golden age," most spectacularly in property, but also in transforming British retailing and pharmaceuticals. Entrepreneurs in Britain's traditional overseas' markets struggled against the forces of decolonization and nationalist economic policies. One who kicked against this trend was Tiny Rowland, who built up Lonrho, but so aggressive was his approach in sub-Saharan Africa that in 1973 Prime Minister Edward Heath described him as the "unacceptable face of capitalism" and was widely lauded for doing so. No doubt Rowland deserved vilification. But the reputation of entrepreneurship was at low ebb. As the economic fortunes of most began to stagnate, the politics of envy dictated that the successful few were vilified. There was no one to champion the entrepreneurs' cause. That such a high proportion of the successful few at this time were second- or third-generation Jewish immigrants prompted them to adopt low profiles. In obituaries in the British press, Jewish magnates were described principally for their philanthropic work! Even then antientrepreneurialism meant Britain lost out. These Jewish tycoons endowed more university chairs in Israel than Britain. Elsewhere the dynamic, innovative few left in the "Brain Drain," especially for the former dominions, the United States and increasingly mainland Europe. Emigration's corollary was the unprecedented rate of immigration, especially of Asians from the Indian subcontinent, many of whom would become important British entrepreneurs by the century's end.

From Pessimism to Renaissance? Innovative Entrepreneurship *Redevivus* from 1975 to 2000

The transformation of the British economy during the final quarter of the twentieth century and the rejection of protectionist policies is mostly associated with Margaret Thatcher's regime (1979–90), although several events before 1979 paved the way. Perhaps the most notable was the rejection of incomes policy by the Labour chancellor, Denis Healey, in 1975. A gale of competitive destruction howled through British industry as inefficient working practices, weak managerial control, tardy marketing techniques, and inept financing structures were exposed during the 1980s and 1990s. Much wailing and gnashing of teeth ensued. It was the peak of pessimism. A conveyor belt of "declinist" literature flowed, with even scholarly tomes adopting lurid titles like *Why Are the British Bad at Manufacturing?* (Williams, Williams, and Thomas 1983).

The list of disasters was long. British Leyland and Jaguar, the rump of the much vaunted British motor car industry, went bankrupt and had to be rescued by the Government in 1974. After an accounting fiasco, Rolls Royce followed that same year. Unemployment began to rise and Government authority was challenged by powerful unions with major strikes in 1978–79, and again in 1984–85. Fellow European Governments embarking on the giant European Community project simply could not fathom the extent of Britain's domestic economic problems. Self-employment in Britain in the mid-1980s was mostly understood as a strategy by the newly unemployed to seek refuge from the strictures of the labor market (Storey 1994). Successive surveys revealed that the status of entrepreneurship in British popular culture reached its nadir at the end of the 1970s and into the 1980s (Farnie 1998). Even in the pharmaceuticals sector, the one bright spot in the British industrial landscape at the time, the entrepreneurial CEOs of Glaxo and (the newly merged) SmithKline-Beecham were American citizens. When Britain was summarily ejected from the European Exchange Rate Mechanism in 1992, it appeared as if the nation's entire industrial future might be as a heritage park to world tourism.

In the midst of such pessimism about the nation's entrepreneurial attributes, however, fundamental changes were taking place. The Employment Acts of the 1980s had engendered a brisker approach to recruitment—unemployment fell. The deregulation of the financial services sector in 1984 transformed the equity market and the nature of competition in the City of London. And the privatization program represented the "biggest transfer of resources since the dissolution of the monasteries" (Middleton 2006). This brought gains mostly to British taxpayers and consumers, but only a mixed outcome to British entrepreneurs, as control of most utilities passed to European firms (Kitson 2004). The most impressive case for the renaissance of British entrepreneurship, however, is to be seen in the privatized telecoms business, where four of the world's leading telecoms firms are based in Britain: Vodafone (the former wireless arm of the British Ministry of Defence), Orange (now French owned), BT (the rump of the original state telecoms monopoly), and O2 (the spun-out mobile division of BT, now Spanish owned).

Perhaps even more important to the British economy has been the impact of the resumption of globalization in the 1980s and 1990s. As the Southeast Asian "tiger" economies and then China have become more fully integrated into the world economy, many British businesses found themselves unable to compete. As the floor on world unskilled wages fell, so British clothing manufacturing virtually ceased, for example. But British entrepreneurs were quick to spot the opportunities of managing long-distance trading relationships with the low-cost producers in these low-wage economies. Indeed, as China has grown to become the factory of the world, the value-adding activity is in the market-making, not the manufacturing. Suddenly the long dormant British business skills of international negotiation and managing cross-cultural relationships flourished, as did the much diminished but never extinguished networks of expertise. The continued British presence in Hong Kong provided an important bridge for business links into China and long-standing connections with India have powered the "offshoring" move there.

Formation of firms continued to rise throughout the 1990s. But in contrast to the 1980s, entrepreneurship was increasingly seen as a desirable option. As so often in the past, it was outsiders who represented the driving force, with many Asian immigrants (especially those expelled from East Africa after 1972) creating successful businesses. But it was only at the century's end, in the heady days of the dot-com bubble, that entrepreneurship became seen by many as an attractive career route. Here the gamine figure of Martha Lane Fox almost at a stroke transformed British ambivalence to entrepreneurship, creating the online retailer Lastminute.com in 1998 and seeing it soar to a valuation of £733 million on flotation in March 2000, and yet being instantly recognizable to all as an entirely normal, petite, and articulate middle-class woman. A survey of international opinion found 45 percent of Britons aspired to be entrepreneurs in 2001—a remarkable transformation in attitudes from just one generation before (Blanchflower et al. 2001).

Conclusion

The conventional survey of British economic performance over the twentieth century has prompted considerable gloom and, in consequence, a persistent search for scapegoats. Entrepreneurs have been a favorite target. The traditional conclusion would be that, perhaps because of some aspect of British culture, perhaps because of the increasing encroachment of the state into the economic arena, perhaps because of the diminution of competitive forces, entrepreneurs became less innovative and less influential in Britain over the course of the twentieth century. Yes, the critics have claimed, they had been successful in the traditional staple industries of cotton, iron and steel, and coal during the Industrial Revolution (as described in the previous two chapters). But then they failed to move into the manufacturing sectors of the second industrial revolution, the chemical, electrical, and, above all, automobile industries; they failed to innovate and to exploit these new technologies.

But the apparent renaissance in entrepreneurial skills at the century's end demands a reexamination of such an interpretation of long-term entrepreneurial failure in Britain. This chapter has therefore first given due emphasis to Britain's role as provider of entrepreneurial services to the world in the first third of the twentieth century, and then second emphasized more continuity in British entrepreneurship in the twentieth century than would most traditional surveys. To be sure British entrepreneurs in the twentieth century were not at the forefront of introducing new technologies. Rather, the specialization in transferring knowledge-intensive project management skills into complex infrastructure or resource-focused investments all around the world was the striking contribution. It has been neglected by historians for too long. It needs to be realized that it was this transference that powered global economic integration from the 1880s through to the 1920s, not the firms of the second industrial revolution.

While Weetman Pearson was the most famous, and most successful, there was in truth a large number of highly innovative British entrepreneurs. Together they developed specialized skills, specific institutional structures, and sophisticated entrepreneurial networks—notably centered on finance—to engage in these activities throughout the world economy. It is important to emphasize that the role of these overseas-facing British entrepreneurs was not confined to the British Empire; indeed Latin America and the United States were major regions for British foreign direct investment. They were not simply reliant on markets where they may have enjoyed some political protection or privilege. Rather these finance- and knowledge-intensive entrepreneurial networks had a genuinely global perspective. And as the profitability of the staple industries at home began to slacken, it was naturally toward these overseas opportunities that British entrepreneurs increasingly gravitated, not to electricals and automobiles.

Yet fortune was not on their side. The international crisis of the 1930s, World War II, slow postwar restructuring, and then the traumas of decolonization reduced the value of much of the stock of painfully acquired entrepreneurial expertise and ruined much of the institutional structure that had supported entrepreneurs' previous activities. As the political and institutional conditions around the world changed, so the traditional role for the British overseas entrepreneur diminished. New national governments promoted economic policies that discriminated against British firms. Without much use, these entrepreneurial networks slowly dispersed, or entered sectors where their knowledge and expertise carried little favor. Their rewards diminished accordingly. Only with the resumption of rapid global economic integration in the 1980s and, especially, the 1990s did British comparative advantage in managing complex, long-distance international transactions reassert itself. Outward foreign direct investment soared, and British entrepreneurs once again facilitated the development of new industries around the globe.

At home the competitive environment deteriorated from 1930 onward, partly because of direct effects of government policy in promoting protectionism, encouraging the cartelization of British business, and increasing the power of unions, but also because of earlier restrictions on immigration and the long acceptance of grave social divides in British culture. Increasingly free from competitive rivalry, the incumbent business-owning families responded predictably and settled for a comfortable life. The inability to introduce mass production techniques in the British automobile industry shows that new inventions in product and process technologies disseminated only slowly from the 1950s to the 1970s. British relative productivity fell alarmingly. Innovative, entrepreneurial types emigrated in droves, mostly to the dominion economies of Australasia and Canada, but also to the United States and Europe. There were, of course, entrepreneurial opportunities in the 1950s and 1960s but, the prevailing institutional structure actively discouraged entrepreneurship. Entrepreneurs' social status fell to its lowest ever ebb during the 1970s and 1980s, and the pool of innovative entrepreneurs diminished.

In fact the most significant new group of entrepreneurs to emerge in the middle decades of the century were a group of outsiders. The east European Jewish immigrants and their children largely enjoyed their career success through exploiting the property market. This was closely bound up with retailing, and many proved to be exceptional retailers as well. Their rise to prominence also came through the creation and exploitation of several innovative financial instruments, and their private financial rewards were great. But their impact on British productivity growth overall appears to have been only slight. The diffusion of novel technologies during this period was largely through the large corporations, not these outsider entrepreneurs. Moreover, this exceptional success of a few Jewish entrepreneurs failed to prompt a groundswell of popular support for a more entrepreneurial society; indeed the contrast between the largely Jewish entrepreneurs and the antipathy toward entrepreneurship among British society at large prompted many of these tycoons to disguise their financial success, scarred as they were by the recent experience of prejudice across much of Europe.

As the reversal of protectionism continued from the 1980s onward, so entrepreneurship began to renew itself in Britain: first, in overseas trading and multinational investments, and then, finally, in the embrace of new technology. From the vantage point of a century-long perspective, the events at the very end of the century appear to indicate the beginnings of a truly significant change. For here Martha Lane Fox, the daughter of an Oxford historian, became a cultural icon at the peak of the dot-com bubble because she represented what, in the context of the twentieth century, was a striking shift in attitudes among the British mainstream during the 1990s. Her example became a tipping point, legitimizing the entrepreneurial aspirations of millions of others.

At the century's end, entrepreneurs have reacquired a social status that had been lost in British culture for two or three generations. The prospect of great financial rewards from both the technological revolution of the 1980s and 1990s, and from the relocation of many economic activities with the rapid integration of China and India into the world economy, may well have acted as a powerful demonstration to many potential entrepreneurs. And with the political reforms of the 1980s making the British economy one where it became easier to act entrepreneurially, entrepreneurship has become a pastime for the masses, rather than one merely for the financial elite, as at the beginning of the century.

The circularity in the reemergence of entrepreneurship in British society is surprising, prompting historians to reexamine traditional surveys of British entrepreneurship in the twentieth century. Perhaps the relative decline in the influence of entrepreneurs in the economy has been overemphasized; perhaps there was more continuity than previous surveys have suggested. Nevertheless the overall contours remain clear. Britain had a substantial and highly active population of overseas-facing entrepreneurs that was disproportionately responsible for the global dissemination of essential expertise in a host of important development projects. As the global trading economy contracted and then fissured into much smaller blocs, many actively discriminating against British interests, so British entrepreneurship inevitably suffered. Despite the important role of the Jewish immigrant entrepreneurs during the middle decades, it was not until the final two decades of the twentieth century that global economic integration enabled British entrepreneurship to reemerge.

Notes

[1] In fact the mostly anonymous Joseph Littman was the architect of sale and leaseback. Littman collaborated with Burton during the 1920s and 1930s. He died in 1953 (aged only fifty-five), and while he had amassed a considerable fortune—Rubinstein (2006, 286–89) ranks his estate as the fourth largest of all those dying between 1950 and 1954—had he lived to old age, his achievements would have undoubtedly brought much greater recognition.

[2] Under the regime of fixed exchange rates, economies like Britain that suffered from persistent balance-of-payment deficits had to constrain domestic demand to reduce imports. Only when the external account was in balance could governments stimulate domestic demand.

[3] Gerald Ronson, interview by Andrew Godley, London, September 3, 2002.

[4] *Statist*, November 6, 1964, 371.

[5] Stanley Kalms, interview by Andrew Godley, London, August 12, 2003.

References

Aldcroft, Derek. 1964. "The Entrepreneur and the British Economy, 1870–1914." *Economic History Review* 17:113–34.

Alford, B.W.E. 1973. *W.D. & H.O. Wills and the Development of the U.K. Tobacco Industry, 1786–1965*. London: Methuen.

———. 1988. *British Economic Performance, 1945–1975*. Basingstoke: Macmillan.

Allen, G. C. 1976. *The British Disease: A Short Essay on the Nature and Causes of the Nation's Lagging Wealth*. [London]: Institute of Economic Affairs.

Anderson, Ronald C., and David M. Reeb. 2003. "Founding-Family Ownership and Firm Performance." *Journal of Finance* 58:1301–28.

Aris, Stephen. 1970. *The Jews in Business*. London: Jonathan Cape.

Athreye, Suma, and Andrew Godley. 2009. "Internationalisation to Create Firm Specific Advantages: U.S. Pharmaceutical Firms in the 1930s and 1940s and Indian Pharmaceutical Firms in the 1990s and 2000s." *Industrial and Corporate Change* 18:295–323.

Atkinson, A. B. 2002. "Top Incomes in the United Kingdom over the Twentieth Century." University of Oxford Discussion Papers in Economic and Social History No. 43.

Bacon, Robert, and Walter Eltis. 1976. *Britain's Economic Problem: Too Few Producers*. Basingstoke: Macmillan.

Bamberg, James. 1988. "The Rationalization of the British Cotton Industry in the Inter-war Years." *Textile History* 19:83–102.

Baumol, William J. 1990. "Entrepreneurship: Productive, Unproductive and Destructive." *Journal of Political Economy* 98:893–921.

Berghoff, Hartmut. 1995. "Regional Variations in Provincial Business Biography: The Case of Birmingham, Bristol and Manchester, 1870–1914." *Business History* 37:64–85.

Berghoff, Hartmut, and R. Möller. 1994. "Tired Pioneers and Dynamic Newcomers? A Comparative Essay on English and German Entrepreneurial History, 1870–1914." *Economic History Review* 47:262–87.

Blanchflower, David G., Andrew J. Oswald, and Alois Stutzer. 2001. "Latent Entrepreneurship across Nations." *European Economic Review* 45:680–91.

Bolton, J. E. 1971. *Report of the Committee of Inquiry on Small Firms*. London: HMSO.

Bostock, Frances, and Geoffrey Jones. 1994. "Foreign Multinationals in British Manufacturing, 1850–1962." *Business History* 36:89–126.

Brittan, Samuel. 1978. "How British Is the British Sickness?" *Journal of Law and Economics* 21:245–68.

Broadberry, S. 1998. *The Productivity Race: British Manufacturing in International Perspective, 1850–1990*. Cambridge: Cambridge University Press.

———. 2006. *Market Services and the Productivity Race, 1850–2000: Britain in International Perspective*. Cambridge: Cambridge University Press.

Bud-Frierman, Lisa, Andrew Godley, and Judith Wale. 2010. "Weetman Pearson in Mexico and the Emergence of a British Oil Major, 1901–1919." *Business History Review* 84, no. 2, forthcoming.

Cassis, Youssef. 1997. *Big Business: The European Experience in the Twentieth Century*. Oxford: Oxford University Press.

Casson, Mark. 1982. *The Entrepreneur: An Economic Theory*. Oxford: Martin Robertson.

———. 1992. *The Economics of Business Culture*. Oxford: Clarendon Press.

Casson, Mark, and Andrew Godley. 2007. "Revisiting the Emergence of the Modern Business Enterprise: Entrepreneurship and the Singer Global Distribution System." *Journal of Management Studies* 44:1064–77.

Chandler, Alfred D., Jr., with Takashi Hikino. 1990. *Scale and Scope: The Dynamics of Industrial Capitalism*. Cambridge: Harvard University Press.

Chapman, Stanley D. 1974. *Jesse Boot of Boots the Chemists*. London: Hodder & Stoughton.

Clapham, John H. 1938. *An Economic History of Modern Britain*. Vol. 3. Cambridge: Cambridge University Press.

Clutterbuck, David, and Marion Devine. 1987. *Clore: The Man and His Millions*. London: Weidenfeld and Nicolson.

Collins, Bruce, and Keith Robbins, eds. 1990. *British Culture and Economic Decline*. London: Palgrave Macmillan.

Coopey, Richard, and Donald Clarke. 1995. *3i: Fifty Years of Investing in Industry*. Oxford: Oxford University Press.

Corley, T.A.B. 1966. *Domestic Electrical Appliances*. London: Cape.

———. 1994. "Britain's Overseas Investments in 1914 Revisited." *Business History* 36:71–88.

———. 1997. "Competitive Advantage and Foreign Direct Investment: Britain, 1913–1938." *Business and Economic History* 26:599–608.

Economist. 2005. *The World in 2005*.

Edelstein, Michael. 1982. *Overseas Investment in the Age of High Imperialism: The United Kingdom, 1850–1914*. London: Methuen.

———. 2004. "Foreign Investment, Accumulation and Empire, 1860–1914." In *The Cambridge Economic History of Modern Britain*, ed. Roderick Floud and Paul Johnson, 2:190–226. Cambridge: Cambridge University Press.

Farnie, David A. 1998. "The Wiener Thesis Vindicated: The Onslaught of 1994 upon the Reputation of John Rylands of Manchester." In *Religion, Business, and Wealth in Modern Britain*, ed. David Jeremy, 86–107. London: Routledge.

Feinstein, C. 1994. "Success and Failure: British Economic Growth since 1948." In *The Economic History of Britain since 1700*, ed. Roderick Floud and Donald N. McCloskey, 3:95–122. Cambridge: Cambridge University Press.

Ferguson, Niall. 2003. *Empire: How Britain Made the Modern World*. London: Penguin.

Godley, Andrew. 1999. "Pioneering Foreign Direct Investment in British Manufacturing." *Business History Review* 73:394–429.

———. 2001. *Jewish Immigrant Entrepreneurship in New York and London, 1880–1914: Enterprise and Culture*. Basingstoke: Palgrave.

———. 2003. "Foreign Multinationals and Innovation in British Retailing: 1850–1962." *Business History* 45:80–100.

———. 2006. "Selling the Sewing Machine around the World: Singer's International Marketing Strategies, 1850–1920." *Enterprise and Society* 7:266–314.

———. 2008. "American Multinationals in British Retailing." In *American Firms in Europe: Strategy, Identity, Performance, and Reception*, ed. Hubert Bonin and Ferry de Goey, 261–82. Geneva: Droz.

Godley, Andrew, and Bridget Williams. 2009a. "The Invention of the 'Technological Chicken' and the Emergence of the Modern Poultry Industry in Britain." *Business History Review* 83, no. 2, forthcoming.

Godley, Andrew, and Bridget Williams. 2009b. "The Chicken, the Factory Farm, and the Supermarket: The Emergence of the Modern Poultry Industry in Britain." In *Food Chains: From Farmyard to Shopping Cart*, ed. Roger Horowitz and Warren Belasco, 47–61. Philadelphia: University of Pennsylvania Press.

Goldthorpe, John H. 1980. *Social Mobility and Class Structure in Modern Britain*. Oxford: Oxford University Press.

Greene, Jeremy. 2005. "Releasing the Flood Waters: Diuril and the Reshaping of Hypertension." *Bulletin of the History of Medicine* 79:749–94.

Hannah, Leslie. 1980. "Visible and Invisible Hands in Great Britain." In *Managerial Hierarchies: Comparative Perspectives on the Rise of the Modern Industrial Enterprise*, ed. Alfred D. Chandler Jr. and Herman Daems, 41–76. Cambridge: Harvard University Press.

———. 1983. *The Rise of the Corporate Economy*. 2nd ed. London: Methuen.

———. 2006. "The Whig Fable of American Tobacco." *Journal of Economic History* 66: 42–73.

Houston, Tom, and John H. Dunning. 1976. *UK Industry Abroad*. London: Financial Times.

Jefferys, James B. 1954. *Retail Trading in Britain, 1850–1950: A Study of Trends in Retailing with Special Reference to the Development of Cooperative, Multiple Shop, and Department Store Methods of Trading*. Cambridge: Cambridge University Press.

Jeremy, David J. 1998. *Business History of Britain, 1900–1990s*. Oxford: Oxford University Press.

Jones, Geoffrey. 1994. "British Multinationals and British Business since 1850." In *Business Enterprise in Modern Britain: From the Eighteenth to the Twentieth Century*, ed. M. W. Kirby and Mary B. Rose, 172–206. London: Routledge.

———. 2000. *Merchants to Multinationals: British Trading Companies in the Nineteenth and Twentieth Centuries*. Oxford: Oxford University Press.

———. 2005. *Multinationals and Global Capitalism from the Nineteenth to the Twenty-first Century*. Oxford: Oxford University Press.

Jones, Geoffrey, and Frances Bostock. 1996. "US Multinationals in British Manufacturing before 1962." *Business History Review* 70:207–56.

Jones, Geoffrey, and Judith Wale. 1999. "Diversification Strategies of British Trading Companies: Harrisons & Crosfield, c.1900–c.1980." *Business History* 41:69–101.

Kennedy, William P. 1987. *Industrial Structure: Capital Markets, and the Origins of British Economic Decline*. Cambridge: Cambridge University Press.

Kindleberger, Charles P. 1964. *Economic Growth in France and Britain, 1851–1950*. Oxford: Oxford University Press.

Kitson, Michael. 2004. "Failure Followed by Success or Success Followed by Failure? A Re-examination of British Economic Growth since 1949." In *The Cambridge Economic History of Modern Britain*, ed. Roderick Floud and Paul Johnson, 3:27–56. Cambridge: Cambridge University Press.

Landes, David S. 1969. *Unbound Prometheus: Technological Change and Industrial Development in Western Europe from 1750 to the Present*. Cambridge: Cambridge University Press.

Lindert, Peter H. and Keith Trace. 1971. "Yardsticks for Victorian Entrepreneurs." In *Essays on a Mature Economy: Britain after 1840*, ed. Donald N. McCloskey, 239–74. London: Methuen; Princeton: Princeton University Press.

McCloskey, Donald N. and L. Sandberg. 1971. "From Damnation to Redemption: Judgements on the Late Victorian Entrepreneur." *Explorations in Economic History* 9:89–108.

Magee, Gary B. 2004. "Manufacturing and Technological Change." In *The Cambridge Economic History of Modern Britain*, ed. Roderick Floud and Paul Johnson, 2:74–98. Cambridge: Cambridge University Press.

Marriott, Oliver. 1967. *The Property Boom*. London: Hamish Hamilton.

Matthews, R.C.O., C. H. Feinstein, and J. C. Odling-Smee. 1982. *British Economic Growth, 1856–1973*. Oxford: Oxford University Press.

Michie, Ranald. 1999. *The London Stock Exchange: A History*. Oxford: Oxford University Press.

Middleton, Roger. 2006. "The Mother of New Labour. Review of Ewen Green, *Thatcher*." *Times Higher Education Supplement*, September 1.

Miles, Andrew. 1999. *Social Mobility in Britain, 1837–1914*. Basingstoke: Palgrave-Macmillan.

Nicholas, Tom. 1999. "Clogs to Clogs in Three Generations? Explaining Entrepreneurial Performance in Britain since 1850." *Journal of Economic History* 59:688–713.

———. 2004. "Enterprise and Management." In *The Cambridge Economic History of Modern Britain*, ed. Roderick Floud and Paul Johnson, 2:227–52. Cambridge: Cambridge University Press.

Orsagh, T. 1961. "Progress in Iron and Steel, 1870–1913." *Comparative Studies in Society and History* 3:216–30.

O'Sullivan, Mary A. 2006. "Riding the Wave: The US Financial Markets and the Postwar Electronics Boom." Paper presented to the Business History Conference, Toronto, June 8–10.

Porter, Michael E. 1990. *The Competitive Advantage of Nations*. Basingstoke: Macmillan.

Plüss, Caroline. 2004. "Globalizing Ethnicity with Multi-local Identifications: The Parsee, Indian Muslim and Sephardic Trade Diasporas in Hong Kong." In *Diaspora Entrepreneurial*

Networks, ed. Ina Baghdiantz McCabe, Gelena Harlaftis, and Ioanna Pepelasis Minoglou, 245–68. Oxford: Berg.

Quirke, Viviane. 2005. "Making British Cortisone: Glaxo and the Development of Cortico-steroids in Britain in the 1950–1960s." *Studies in History and Philosophy of Biological and Biomedical Sciences* 36:645–74.

Roberts, Richard. 2001. *Take Your Partners: Orion, the Consortium Banks, and the Transformation of the Euromarkets*. London: Palgrave Macmillan.

Rose, Mary B. 1986. *The Gregs of Quarry Bank Mill: The Rise and Decline of a Family Firm*. Cambridge: Cambridge University Press.

Rubinstein, William D. 1993. *Capitalism, Culture, and Decline in Britain, 1750–1990*. London: Routledge.

———. 2006. *Men of Property: The Very Wealthy in Britain since the Industrial Revolution*. 2nd ed. London: Social Affairs Unit.

Sarachek, Berenard. 1978. "American Entrepreneurs and the Horatio Alger Myth." *Journal of Economic History* 38:439–56.

Scott, Peter. 1994. "Learning to Multiply: The Property Market and the Growth of Multiple Retailing in Britain, 1919–39," *Business History* 36:1–28.

———. 2009. "Mr Drage, Mr Everyman, and the Creation of a Mass Market for Domestic Furniture in Interwar Britain." *Economic History Review*, forthcoming.

Servan-Schreiber, Jean-Jacques. 1967. *Le défi américain*. Paris: Denoel.

Shaw, Gareth. 2004a. "Stephenson, William Lawrence. 1880–1963." *Oxford Dictionary of National Biography*. Oxford: Oxford University Press. http://www.oxforddnb.com/view/article/42154, accessed October 6, 2006.

———. 2004b. "Bedford, John. 1903–1980." *Oxford Dictionary of National Biography*. Oxford: Oxford University Press. http://www.oxforddnb.com/view/article/46613, accessed October 10, 2006.

Slinn, Judy. 2006. "'A Cascade of Medicines': The Marketing and Consumption of Prescription Drugs in the UK, 1948–2000." In *From Physick to Pharmacology: Five Hundred Years of British Drug Retailing*, ed. Louise Hill Curth, 143–69. London: Ashgate.

Storey, David. 1994. *Understanding the Small Business Sector*. London: Routledge.

Temin, Peter. 1999. "The American Business Elite in Historical Perspective." In *Elites, Minorities, and Economic Growth*, ed. Elise S. Brezis and Peter Temin, 19–39. Amsterdam: Elsevier.

Wardley, Peter. 1999. "The Emergence of Big Business: The Largest Corporate Employers of Labour in the United Kingdom, Germany and the United States c. 1907." *Business History* 41:88–116.

Westall, Oliver M. 1994. "The Competitive Environment of British Business, 1850–1914." In *Business Enterprise in Modern Britain: From the Eighteenth to the Twentieth Century*, ed. M. W. Kirby and Mary B. Rose, 207–35. London: Routledge.

Wiener, Martin. 1981. *English Culture and the Decline of the Industrial Spirit*. Cambridge: Cambridge University Press

Wilkins, Mira. 1988. "The Free-Standing Company, 1870–1914: An Important Type of British Foreign Direct Investment." *Economic History Review* 41:259–85.

Williams, Karel, John Williams, and Dennis Thomas. 1983. *Why Are the British Bad at Manufacturing?* London: Routledge and Kegan Paul.

Williamson, Jeffrey G. 1995. "The Evolution of Global Labor Markets since 1830: Background Evidence and Hypotheses." *Explorations in Economic History* 32:141–96.

Wilson Committee. 1979. *The Financing of Small Firms*. London: HMSO.

Chapter 10

History of Entrepreneurship
Germany after 1815

ULRICH WENGENROTH

THE HISTORY OF ENTREPRENEURSHIP in Germany is as tortured as the history the country inflicted on its neighbors and on itself. For much of the nineteenth and twentieth centuries, entrepreneurs in Germany were confronted by the consequences of political upheaval, shifting borders, major institutional rearrangements in the wake of regime changes, and all the limitations and temptations that went with frequent redefinitions of the rules of the game. With six political systems—two of them side by side for the second half of the twentieth century—two controversial political unifications, two aggressively fought world wars, and continually changing borders, Germany after 1815 was a taxing environment for such planning as building a firm. It is no wonder, therefore, that the two spells of prolonged political stability, from first unification in 1871 until World War I and the post–World War II period in West Germany, were those when most big enterprise was formed and when innovativeness, though very different in style, was a pertinent characteristic of German enterprise.

Schumpeterian entrepreneurs are particularly capable of responding to incentives and opportunities in their environment and of dodging its limitations. Their great contribution to the economy as a whole resides in their ability to put the potentials within their reach to more profitable use than they would receive under established routines and practices. If they are motors of change and productive unrest, innovative entrepreneurs themselves seem to thrive under conditions of institutional predictability amid favorable resource endowments. To assess better the preconditions for innovative entrepreneurship through the history of the Germany economy, I turn to a brief outline of its natural and its human resources as well as its institutional framework.

The German Economy, 1815–2006

Geography, Borders, and Natural Resources

The German Confederation, created in 1815, was a loose formation of thirty-nine sovereign states where German was the dominating if not always the exclusive language. The two major states, Prussia and the Habsburg Empire, had territories

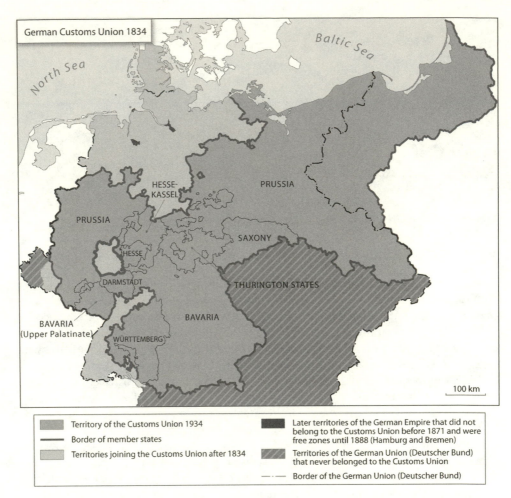

Figure 10.1. The German Confederation and the German Customs Union in 1834. (Source: http://www.ieg-maps.uni-mainz.de/mapsp/mapz834d.htm, accessed October 10, 2007.)

within and outside the German Confederation. Against a reluctant Austria, Prussia took the initiative of facilitating trade among the German states and eventually, in 1834, was successful in creating the German Customs Union, which, most significantly, excluded Austria. In the middle of the nineteenth century, the German Confederation was economically divided between Austria and a Prussian-dominated area largely within the borders of what was to become the German Empire in 1871. By 1834, entrepreneurs in the German Customs Union were already operating in a nascent common market long before there was political unification. Economically, the Prussian-dominated German Customs Union developed more quickly than the Habsburg Empire. Politically, however, the situation was anything but stable and predictable. With a revolution in 1848–49 and three "wars of unification" that drove Austria out of Germany and brought the other sovereign German states under Prussian dominance, the political and institutional environment did everything but inspire confidence. Stability did exist, however, within Prussia, which comprised about

Figure 10.2. The Federal Republic and the GDR 1957. (Source: http://www.ieg-maps.uni-mainz.de/mapsp/mapp957d.htm, accessed October 10, 2007.)

two-thirds of the later German Empire. In Prussia we find the most vigorous economic development, spreading from there to the other partners in the Customs Union.

Prussia, which had absorbed many territories in the west after the defeat of Napoleon and the dismantling of ecclesiastical territories, was also in a privileged position when it came to natural resources. Germany's main hard coal, lignite, and iron ore deposits were all in Prussian territory. The most valuable asset was an enormous hard coal deposit in the Ruhr district close to the river Rhine. This area became the powerhouse of the German economy well into the twentieth century. It was not coal mining, though, that kicked off industrialization in Germany but railway construction (Fremdling 1985; Holtfrerich 1973). In the absence of suitable waterways—the main rivers run from south to north while the potential domestic market stretched from west to east—railways were to become the integrating infrastructure of the nascent industrial economy. Railway construction, mostly private, but backed by some state guarantees in Prussia, was a great opportunity for the financial sector as well as for iron-making and machine-building. Once the railways were in place, they supported the division of labor within the economy and transport of cheap fuel to places outside the mining areas. Only heavy coal consumers like the chemical industry (Hoechst, BASF) would go for locations along the navigable parts of the river Rhine but closer to consumers in traditionally more urbanized southern Germany. Berlin, the Prussian and later German capital, became a center for modern mechanical and electrical industries, which had to rely on state support in their formative years (von Weiher 1987). A more traditional center of mechanical engineering was Saxony, a semisovereign kingdom south of Berlin. A second coal basin was in Prussian Upper Silesia, in southeast Germany, about the same distance from Berlin as the Ruhr district. The east-west orientation of the German economy as well as the dominance of coal-based industries persisted until the end of World War II.

With the east-west division of Germany after World War II and the loss of the eastern coal basin and agricultural surplus regions to Poland, however, the economic geography of both German postwar states was fundamentally transformed. Geographically and hence economically, post–World War II Germany is a country very different from the former "Reich." Together with this geographical reorientation, hard coal lost its competitiveness in the late 1950s, leaving only lignite in both German states as a domestic if largely insufficient source of energy and the very last natural resource that could be exploited profitably (Abelshauser 1984). While Germany started with comparatively good resource endowments in the nineteenth century, today only ecologically highly controversial lignite is left for some electricity generation. According to an often evoked self-perception in postwar Germany, its only natural resource is the gray matter in German brains.

Human Capital Formation

Human capital formation was an early success story in Germany. Primary education was fairly advanced in Prussia. Vocational training had traditionally been a stronghold of the guilds and trades. Higher education was very much helped by political fragmentation of Germany in the nineteenth century and by federalism in the twentieth. Since every prince believed he must have a university, a polytechnic, and trade schools of his own, Germany was comparatively oversupplied with these institutions. This was also true of Prussia, as the newly incorporated and rather unenthusiastic territories that had put Prussia on an equal footing with Austria had to have the full array of institutions of higher education not to feel treated as second-class provinces. This fortunate diversity and plurality very much helped the creation of a great number of polytechnics along the model of the French École Polytechnique in the middle decades of the nineteenth century before German unification. The alumni of these polytechnics—there were no formal degrees until 1899—in the majority did not go to industry but became state officials with little if any beneficial effect upon Schumpeterian entrepreneurs' success (Lundgren 1990, 44). The same is true for science graduates from universities. Nevertheless this oversupply of highly qualified scientists and engineers turned to Germany's advantage when the first science-based industries emerged at the end of the nineteenth century. Institutes of technology and science departments in universities were well developed and among the most attractive in the world. Around the turn of the century German was the privileged language of science. German companies could draw from the most productive pool of scientists and engineers and cooperate with the most advanced university departments (Wengenroth 2003, 246–52).

This fortuitous setting was brought down by Nazi politics after Hitler's rise to power early in 1933, in a two-pronged attack on German universities. First, student enrollment was more than halved by the Nazis in the six years up to World War II, out of fear of an academic proletariat. In 1939 Germany had no more students than in 1900 (Berg and Hammerstein 1989, 210). Second, from spring 1934 all state employees who were defined as Jewish by the Nazis were expelled from their positions. The same law applied in all annexed territories beginning with Austria in 1938. Along with much greater tragedy, this led to an enormous loss of scientific elite, with 20 Nobel laureates among them (Titze 1989, 219). The two policies together came close to a self-decapitation of the German innovation system. A second and a third wave of emigration of scientific and engineering talent followed in the years after the war. First, a great number of top scientists left right after the war, either because they feared to be taken to justice for war crimes such as abuse of concentration camp inmates, or because they were hired (in the case of the USSR also abducted) by the victorious allies, and often for both reasons. The third wave occurred in the decade after the war when Germany was banned from developing a number of cutting-edge technologies. Young scientists who wanted to work at the research frontier and have a career in cutting-edge technologies had to leave the country, preferably toward America. In sum, these three waves of elite loss substantially contributed to the fundamental transformation of the German innovation system in the middle decades of the twentieth century from a high-tech pioneer to a fast follower with an uneven product portfolio (Wengenroth 2002). The loss of the leading position in Nobel

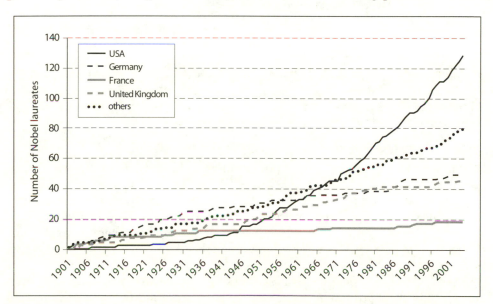

Figure 10.3. Cumulated number of Nobel laureates in physics and chemistry. (Source: nobelprize.org.)

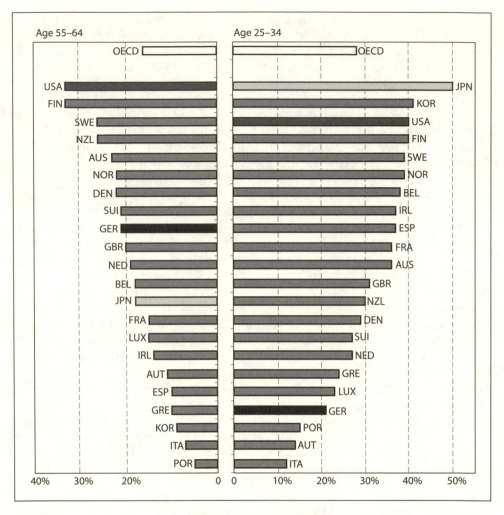

Figure 10.4. Population with a tertiary education as a percentage by selected age groups, 2002. (Source: Federal Ministry of Education and Research, 2005 Report on Germany's Technological Performance—Main statements from the federal government's point of view, 4.)

laureates in physics and chemistry is just one of many illustrations of this transformation, to which of course the stunning success of American science is the other side.

Today, Germany has barely an average share of population with a university or equivalent degree, compared with other advanced OECD (Organization for Economic Cooperation and Development) countries. The times when entrepreneurs could draw on an overabundant supply of excellently educated young people are behind us.

As the OECD compilation in figure 10.4 shows, Germany in 2002 had a respectable if not brilliant position in the age group 55–64, but has failed to keep up with its competitors in the younger age group 25–34. It seems to be a characteristic of the German educational system that it continues to lose steam. The OECD's PISA report came to the same conclusion. And the most recent 2007 OECD report "Higher Education and Regions" confirms this negative trend. Germany is among the underperformers in an OECD-wide comparison of higher education in key sectors like engineering, biotechnology, science, and agriculture.

For German entrepreneurs this means that their home base is no longer privileged to the extent it once was when it comes to recruiting the kind of academic excellence that is usually understood to be the backbone of innovativeness in business. Major companies, therefore, have undertaken to increase their share of foreign employees in R & D in recent years. The inhospitable policy of the German government vis-à-vis foreign labor, however, makes Germany an unattractive destination for the most ambitious and best-educated professionals, who increasingly bypass Germany for more promising careers in other west European countries. Indicative of this somewhat worrisome trend is Germany's position in Richard Florida's Euro-Creativity-Index. While Germany in this comparison of fourteen European societies and the United States still ranked a reassuring third in the overall innovation index and a respectable sixth in the high-tech innovation index, it is only eleventh in the creative class index (Florida and Tinagli 2004, 32). Here again, we have the picture of a downward slide from bustling top performer to struggling second-rater. It is still difficult for a substantial number of politicians to accept that there is no easy way back to the modernist, highly creative, and scientifically stimulating Germany of the early twentieth century when talented students all over the world learned German to visit and participate in a then highly creative milieu. Today, for a bright east European scientist from one of the new member states of the European Union, the UK or the Netherlands is a more promising place to go.

The Institutional Framework

The trade policy of the nineteenth-century Customs Union was based on the principle of "educational tariffs," that is, tariffs that were adopted to protect infant industries until they could withstand international competition. Customs duties were gradually reduced up to the first years of the German Empire, opening the German market to ever more industrial products and—very important—coal from Britain for places like Hamburg or Berlin that had water access. This trend toward free trade came to a halt and was eventually reversed in the 1870s in the wake of a major international financial and trade crisis triggered by the collapse of the American railway boom. By 1878 the tide had turned and Germany had a protectionist policy, one way or another, until after World War II.

Dependent on tariff protection, a second and even more important anticompetitive arrangement was the enormous spread and, eventually, even enforceability of cartels. Cartels mushroomed after the protectionist reversal of the 1870s. They were defended as freedom of contract, and the highest court of the empire in 1897 decided that cartel agreements were not only legal but binding on all partners and could be enforced (Wengenroth 1985). To Alfred Chandler, Jr., this was a watershed setting Germany firmly on the path of cooperative rather than competitive capitalism (Chandler 1990, 393–95). By 1897, however, big industry in Germany had already twenty years of intensive cartelization behind it. The climax of cartelization came with the Nazis and their *Zwangskartellgesetz* of 1933, which made cartels mandatory in the interest of Nazi economic planning. After World War II, under pressure from the United States, the cartelization of German industry was largely made illegal if not completely abolished. It was a second watershed when in 1957, after almost a decade of debates and preparations, anticartel legislation reversed the rules of the game after sixty years of formal and almost a century of informal dominance of co-operative capitalism. With integration in the European Economic Union and falling tariffs in a number of GATT agreements the main pillar of cartelization, the protection of the domestic market was finally eroded. This did not spell the end of collusive action, especially since the EEU established its own fabric of market regulation that often came close to cartels, but it greatly reduced its reach and made it an awkward and clandestine refuge rather than a legitimate and legally protected policy.

Intellectual property rights were hardly protected before 1877 when the German patent law was passed. Before that year, governments of German states, and particularly of Prussia, were reluctant to grant patent protection in an effort to ease transfer of knowledge from abroad. There were famous cases of patent denial like both the Bessemer and the open-hearth processes of mass steel production, both of which had successfully been patented in Great Britain. All this changed when Prussia believed that German industry had successfully caught up and was in a position to turn from imitator to bona-fide innovator. The German patent law protected the process rather than the product, thus stimulating research for alternative ways to turn out the same product. This proved to have a highly stimulating effect on corporate research and development (Seckelmann 2006).

The Overindustrialized Economy

The German economy has mostly been identified with its industrial prowess. Services are not a hallmark of its reputation. In comparison with its nearest competitors and certainly in comparison with the United States, the German economy was over-industrialized all through the twentieth century. This strength of German industry came at some opportunity costs that are currently creating major problems in the transition to markets dominated by immaterial products or the immaterial aspect of "things." Since productivity per hour worked was not higher in Germany than among its neighbors and often lower, the focus on industrial rather than service production didn't necessarily constitute an advantage. The high share of employment in the industrial sector did, however, strongly influence self-perception and eventually what might be called innovation culture. Germans were confident about their industry, a view that was reaffirmed by many foreign observers, and believed in the competitive advantage of German industrial production. That this advantage might have been more an effect of the size of the effort that went into industry than of productivity did not occur to the public nor to the authors of much of the literature on German economic history.

Comparing the German situation with that of the United States, by all means the most productive economy in the twentieth century, which in the mid-1920s and the mid-1950s turned out about 45 percent of the world's industrial products, makes evident the importance of the fact that in productivity calculations the labor force is the denominator. International productivity comparisons by Baumol and others show the modest productivity of the German economy (Baumol et al. 1989, 92; Maddison 2001, 353).

Germany's great reliance on industry was also reflected and continues to be reflected in its science and technology policy. The federal ministry of education and

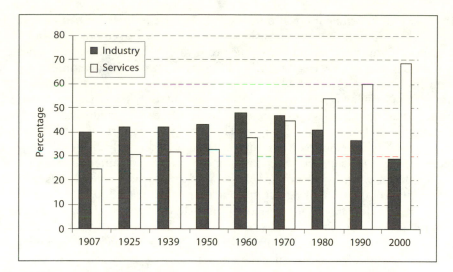

Figure 10.5. Employment in Services and Industry, Germany. (Data source: 1950–2000: http://www.destatis.de/jetspeed/portal/cms/Sites/destatis/Internet/DE/Content/Statistiken/Zeitreihen/LangeReihen/Arbeitsmarkt/Content75/lrerw 13a,templateId=renderPrint.psml (accessed: October 14, 2007); 1907–39: Geißler and Meyer 1996, 29.)

research favors the promotion of industrial technologies and hardly supports the development of services—including knowledge-intensive services—at all. Over the years 2007–2011 a mere €70 million will be devoted to research in services while billions will go to technologies.[1] The lag in transforming the German economy into something like a knowledge and information society has crystallized into a

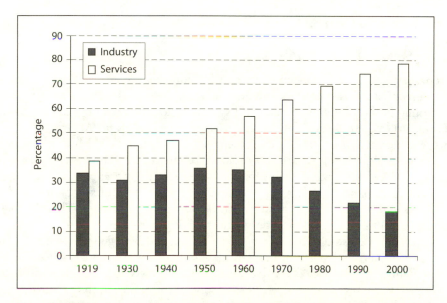

Figure 10.6. Employment in Services and Industry, United States. (Data source: U.S. Census Bureau, Historical Statistics of the United States, Colonial Times to 1970, Series D 1-25, Statistical Abstract of the United States: 2003, HS 29-30.)

cultural lag of the whole innovation system. It seems extremely difficult for the political system as well as for the business community to overcome the industrial-technological imprint acquired during the protectionist decades from late nineteenth to mid-twentieth century. Reading official German statistics is sometimes remindful of Marxist terminology, when what is called "industry" or "manufacturing" in other countries in Germany is *produzierendes Gewerbe*, literally translated as "producing trades," while no other sector of the economy qualifies as "producing," suggesting that everything else is "unproductive." The latter view is certainly still very much in the mind of many engineers, who unsurprisingly find it difficult to appreciate the services let alone the semiotic character of most modern consumer goods.

This disrespect notwithstanding, labor in cutting-edge services in Germany is more productive than in cutting-edge technologies (Götzfried 2005, 4). On the other hand, Germany does have a lower than average share of employment in knowledge-intensive services than its neighbors in the European Union of fifteen. Productivity in knowledge-intensive services among Germany's western neighbors is significantly higher (Felix 2006, 3). Here again, the opportunity costs of sticking to traditional strengths in industrial production seem substantial. Because of the overindustrialized structure of the German economy, as much as the overindustrialized mentality in society, we find more entrepreneurial innovativeness in industry than in services. Moreover, of the one hundred largest industrial corporations of 1913, eighty-seven produced raw materials, intermediates, and investment goods, while only thirteen belonged to the consumption good sector, whereas in America and Great Britain the two sectors of industry held about equal shares (Dornseifer 1995, n. 7; Chandler 1990, appendices). While a balanced history of the German economy after 1815 would focus on the service sector at least as much as on industry, a history of innovative entrepreneurship inevitably favors the latter.

Entrepreneurs in German Society

Entrepreneurs in Early Industrialization

Entrepreneurs were newcomers to the elites of nineteenth-century German society. They were mostly close to the reform movements of European liberalism. Those who were young in the 1840s often had great sympathy for the revolutionary parliament in Frankfurt. When the revolution was crushed by Prussia and Austria, many students, among them many future entrepreneurs, left the country. More liberal Switzerland and its splendid Zurich Polytechnic, founded in 1856, were to become a temporary haven for young engineers and scientists. Entrepreneurs in the western provinces of Prussia moved freely among Belgium, France, Luxembourg, and the Rhineland and felt limited solidarity with the new rulers in Berlin. This skepticism was largely mutual and took decades to subside. Railway entrepreneurs of early industrialization were said to have displayed a "profound bourgeois closeness" (Then 1997, 258). There has been an ongoing debate over the extent to which German entrepreneurs after the failed revolution of 1848–49 moved to the right politically or whether they stuck to their republican convictions. This problem is even more complicated by the fact that the more left-leaning democratic faction was both corporatist and protectionist, while more conservative "big business" and landowners favored deregulation. It seems that entrepreneurs with trading interests and in manufacturing industries continued to lean toward liberalism (in the European sense), while those whose business was rooted in domestic raw materials moved to the conservative and protectionist right (Wehler 1995; Biggeleben 2006).

Anti-Semitism

Excluded from such public recognition of respect by the traditional elites were Jewish entrepreneurs. Anti-Semitism was pervasive in the empire (Mosse and Pohl 1992). And in spite of continuous progress toward emancipation, Jews remained sidelined in imperial Germany. Under the Weimar Republic this seemed to change for the better. Although entrepreneurs were not known to appreciate the new democracy, as they favored an authoritarian regime that had made life for them so predictable through the decades of the German Empire of 1871, anti-Semitism was not felt to be on the increase. Even many Jewish entrepreneurs didn't take the anti-Semitic aggressions of the rising Nazi party too seriously, believing it to be more propaganda than policy (Feldman 1998).

Even in the early 1930s, hardly anybody among the Jewish business elites was prepared for the catastrophe to come. With hindsight, this complacency about the Nazis' plans seems very naive. The political scientist Karl W. Deutsch has characterized the 1930s in Germany as a time of "cognitive catastrophes," when much of the German public and entrepreneurs among them failed to realize the murderous implications of official anti-Semitism (Deutsch in Broszat 1983, 324). The dominant attitude among business elites, including many Jewish entrepreneurs, was the desire for some form of authoritarian regime to reign in socialism and bring back the stability of the late empire that had been glorified retrospectively. To many, Nazi rule was an unpleasant if preferable alternative to, as it was seen, divisive democracy. When outright persecution of the Jewish population set in, however, it became clear that humanitarian values were not a priority to the vast majority of German entrepreneurs. Only very few of them hesitated to enrich themselves on the spoils of "Aryanization."

It seems true that in their majority entrepreneurs were not ardent Nazis. Nor had German business "paid Hitler." Support, including support by Jewish entrepreneurs, went rather to other authoritarian parties of the Weimar Republic, which eventually paved the way for Hitler, whom they erroneously had believed to be their puppet (Turner 1985; Neebe 1981; Weisbrod 1978). In the end it was the total absence of morality and compassion that struck their victims as much as most observers from abroad. To German entrepreneurs the company came first, and it was their standard excuse after the war that they had to shepherd the company "through difficult times" (Erker and Pierenkemper 1999). Well into the postwar years it didn't occur to them that moral indifference vis-à-vis a murderous regime constituted a catastrophic failure on their side. As Paul Erker observed, summing up research on the continuity of business elites and their mind-set from the Nazi years to the early Federal Republic, there was "no rethinking and hardly any meditation" (Erker in Erker and Pierenkemper 1999, 16).

Nonmonetary Rewards for Entrepreneurs

While profit is the ultimate yardstick of entrepreneurial success, it is certainly not the only source of respect. Entrepreneurs, like anyone else, aspired to nonmonetary rewards to gain status. Schumpeterian qualities, however, were not a consideration, although they could come into play indirectly. During the nineteenth century and until the end of World War I, nonmonetary rewards most sought after were titles bestowed upon by the monarch. This could range from the *Kommerzienrat* (councilor of commerce) to nobility. The Kommerzienrat or the more prestigious version, the *Geheimer Kommerzienrat*, which meant that he had access to the court, was mostly earned for some substantial charitable endowment. The Kommerzienrat was so widespread among entrepreneurs that it didn't carry much prestige. It was more an embellishment of the person's salutatory address and proof that he could afford to be generous. And, equally important, it was not a political commitment to the monarchy.

This was different from nobility. While craving for nobility was notorious among bureaucrats and officers and turned into an inflationary process during World War I, it was not a matter of course that successful entrepreneurs would by all means at their disposal strive for a prestigious *von* in front of their name. In fact, German entrepreneurs were much less likely to be ennobled than their British counterparts. Some of the most prominent and highly successful entrepreneurs in the German Empire kept their distance from feudal values. Krupp, both Alfred and his son Friedrich Alfred, and August Thyssen, the most successful steel barons of the German Empire, turned down the offer, while Werner Siemens, who began his career in the Prussian army, gladly accepted the distinction. Such was the steel barons' pride in their own name that their children, when they married into the nobility, kept their common name in front of the noble family name.[2] In their eyes an industrial empire was obviously already more of an achievement than noble descent. Pride in and respect for entrepreneurial success began to eclipse hereditary status at the turn of the century (Berghoff 1994).

At the same time a new source of respect and status emerged. Kaiser Wilhelm, himself a great admirer of science and engineering, very much against the opposition of the traditional universities created the title of "doctor engineer" for the *Technische Hochschulen* (institutes of technology). This opened new opportunities for ambitious engineers to gain the kind of respect and recognition that had been the privilege of the humanistic elites of the traditional worlds of learning (König 1999). And it was a watershed; academic titles in engineering and science soon displaced the Kommerzienrat and the Geheimer Kommerzienrat, while the *Honorarprofessor* (honorary professor), which in everyday life often was stripped of its somewhat depreciating prefix *Honorar* to sound like a bona-fide professorship, carried the status of nobility. Whatever the dubiousness of some honorary degrees, the currency of status and vanity had changed. More prestigious universities would look more closely at the validity of reasons to confer academic distinction. The Honorarprofessor, even if a CEO, would have to teach students and often was interested in fostering common research programs in his company and his university. The academization of entrepreneurial prestige through the twentieth century was as much an expression as a strengthening of a knowledge-based approach to managing product development. Moreover, empirical studies show that honorary titles toward the end of the twentieth century tended to be given more to distinguished people in the field than to industrialists of the nearby region (Fraunholz and Schramm, forthcoming).

Internationalization of German Entrepreneurs

Even if German nationalism comes first to mind, German enterprise for most of its history had a strong international dimension. In early industrialization we find

Belgian entrepreneurs who, by following markets and raw materials, crossed the border into the western parts of Prussia. They were among the most innovative iron- and steelmakers, bringing modern British steel technology to Germany and using their German companies as a launching pad for direct investment in tsarist Russia, taking talented German managers with them (Troitzsch 1972; Wengenroth 1988). The longtime president of the most influential lobbying organization of the west German iron and coal industries in the early years of the empire was William Thomas Mulvany from Dublin, Ireland. With the annexation of Alsace and Lorraine in 1871, a great number of French entrepreneurs, very much to their dismay, found themselves in Germany. At the same time, German-owned companies would recruit top managers in Great Britain. One example is Krupp, who had recruited Alfred Longsdon from the Dowlais Iron company in South Wales as one of his directors (Wengenroth 1994a, 74–91). Longsdon was personified technology transfer and a driving force behind converting Krupp into one of Europe's first mass steel producers. Together with Dowlais and another British steelmaker, Krupp acquired Europe's richest iron ore deposits for high-quality steelmaking in northern Spain in the 1870s, setting up a Spanish company registered in London that turned out to be a backbone of Krupp's profitability until World War I. Thyssen, who had been too late for the Spanish bonanza, created a number of raw material suppliers from France to Sweden, carefully tiptoeing around national sensibilities (Wengenroth 1987). Well into the twentieth century the Netherlands was both the most important channel of trade and a preferred smokescreen of the German steel industry's international operations. The German electrical industry preferred Belgium and Switzerland for their financial operations worldwide (Liefmann 1913). In the decades up to World War I, a number of major German companies made nationality part of their strategy. At the last AEG shareholders meeting before the war, Emil Rathenau was confident that "political unrest and wars in Europe" would do only little harm to the company's business since "a substantial part of our customers is spread all over the globe" (AEG 1956, 189).

The two wars Germany fought against its neighbors and America in the first half of the twentieth century, as well as intensified protectionism, turned earlier international integration into isolation. By losing many of their foreign subsidiaries and much international goodwill, German companies became more German, and German entrepreneurs were increasingly confined to the homeland. If there were still substantial exports, they were no longer accompanied by the extensive networks of foreign direct investment that had helped German entrepreneurs feel at home in the world. The world had turned more into an outside. It took decades of reconstruction and reintegration into world trade after World War II before German entrepreneurs again moved as easily on the international scene as they had before 1914. A German accent wasn't really a recommendation, and German was no longer a lingua franca among European business, especially after the iron curtain had cut off Germany's privileged markets in east and central Europe. Like the Federal Republic in general, German entrepreneurs had to turn west exclusively. Americanization is the catchword in the discussion about German business culture in the second half of the twentieth century (Berghahn 1986). While there is disagreement about how far this went, there is no doubt that massive American investment in Germany as well as German investment first in western Europe and then overseas very much contributed to English becoming the second working language in most major companies. Since the late 1990s even the minutes of the board of directors of big companies like Deutsche Bank or DaimlerChrysler have been kept in English exclusively.[3] Moreover, English was quickly established as the working language in European cooperations from SMEs (small and medium enterprises) to Airbus.

Learning Democracy

The widespread antidemocratic attitude among business elites from imperial to Nazi Germany persisted even through World War II, when German entrepreneurs expected Allied and especially American administrations to provide another stable authoritarian framework for business as usual. It was "a painful learning process" for the German business elite to see in democracy more than just an expedient form of governance to ride out international pressure after two lost wars (Henke 1995, 511). Only slowly and very much helped by a change of generations did German entrepreneurs embrace democratic culture as their authentic self-conception rather than a smart implement of American control. From the late 1950s, ideas of democratization and Americanization went hand in hand (Berghahn 1986). An unquestioned democratic culture was not dominant among big German enterprise before the 1960s. There is agreement in the literature that the sixties and not the end of the war was the watershed in the mentalities of German business. Americanization eventually gave way to a more pluralistic approach, incorporating management models from Japan, intensifying cooperation with business in neighboring countries, and developing a European rather than just a German home base (Kleinschmidt 2002, 395–403; Wengenroth 2007).

Entrepreneurs and Entrepreneurship in the German Innovation System, 1815–2006

Innovativeness is always related to its environment. "The national innovation systems approach stresses that the flows of technology and information among people, enterprises and institutions are key to the innovative process," in which the key actors are "enterprises, universities and government research institutes" (OECD 1997, 4). What did innovative entrepreneurs in Germany make of the setting in which they found themselves? How did they utilize the institutional and intellectual resources available to them, and how did they cope with the changing rules of the game? And the rules of the game did change. In a first approach one can distinguish three phases after 1815. There was a long first phase of expansion of the German economy and its innovative potential until World War I, during which entrepreneurs in Germany were confronted with predictable forms of change. A second, much shorter, violent, and disruptive phase embraced the two closely related and aggressively fought world wars and their aftermaths, which completely disrupted the earlier, seemingly stable trajectory. In a third phase, a reconstructed and closely monitored market economy in a much smaller West Germany had to find its place on a world market where America had become the undisputable benchmark and technology leader.

Expansion (1815–1914)

EARLY INDUSTRIALIZATION

After the defeat by the Napoleonic armies, Prussia set out on a course of reform to strengthen the country's economy and unleash the productive potential of its trade and infant industries. To promote industry, a new institution, the Preußische Gewerbeförderung, the Prussian institution for the advancement of trades and crafts, was created in 1821. This institution engaged in importing machines and especially machine tools from England, much of it clandestinely and by way of smuggling and industrial espionage. Promising craftsmen could study British machinery or might even get state-sponsored machine tools to copy and learn from. A particularly successful investment of that kind was young August Borsig, who, about three decades after he had received his stipend and fifteen yeas after the beginning of the railway boom, turned out his 500th locomotive. Machine building in Prussia and—not much different in its early state support—in Saxony started by copying and adapting to the requirements of the German market. Machine tools were the most crucial element in this technology transfer from Britain, since unlike any other machine, machine tools were the seed of replication. This, after all, was the reason why their export from Britain, unlike that of steam engines and textile machinery, had been banned into the early 1840s. Local mechanics, like August Borsig, and especially clockmakers of heavy tower clocks were well equipped to turn their expertise in metal casting and metal cutting via the new array of industrial machinery (Paulinyi 1982). Innovativeness came with improving design, setting an early example of German incrementalism. By 1850, ten years after the opening of the first significant railway line in Germany, the German machine industry was capable of turning out all rolling stock for the then most dynamic sector of the economy.

As a number of quantitative studies have conclusively shown, railways and railway construction were the leading sector of German industrialization in the decades after 1840. Railways literally pulled all other industries along, first, by helping to create a financial sector that was capable of turning short-term deposits into long-term investment. State guarantees of minimum interest rates on railway stocks had been instrumental in overcoming the hesitation of investors, and very soon railways were more profitable than other stock. State investment itself was insignificant. Second, railway construction and operation created sufficient domestic demand to allow expanding business in machine building, coal mining, and iron and steel production. Third, railways quickly and significantly brought transport costs down in a country that for geographical reasons could not rely on water transport. By 1900 transport costs on the railways were about a quarter of what they had been half a century earlier (Fremdling 1985; Aubin and Zorn 1976, 563).

The banks had looked at the French Credit Mobilier. The machine builders, as a model, as we have seen via the example of the Prussian Gewerbeförderung, had looked to England. Coal mining was developed using as models mostly Belgian companies that had been working the same deposits further to the west, and iron and steelmaking equally looked to industries in Belgium and in England. The innovativeness of all these partners in the railway business did not reside in their creating something fundamentally new but in doing it in a new environment. In not protecting intellectual property rights—or doing so only reluctantly—and by engaging actively in espionage and illegal imports of high technology of the day, the Prussian government went out of its way to promote technology transfer to the nascent domestic industry. This does not mean that German companies could rely solely on imitation. In the case of the iron industry, iron-makers had to find ways to turn German coal, which was chemically different from English or Belgian coal, into coke, had to learn how to use German ores that had a different set of accompanying minerals, and so forth. Plenty of new knowledge and new skills were generated in that way.

HEAVY INDUSTRIES: INNOVATION IN NEGOTIATED MARKETS

With domestic railway construction peaking in the 1870s, the iron industry, which had entered mass steel production by that time, using the two unprotected steel-making processes mentioned above, had to look for new outlets for its production. "Overproduction" was the scare of the time and it led to a completely new complex of cartelization, tariff protection, and innovativeness that was to become typical for German heavy industries until the interwar years. Overproduction had mostly arisen from rapidly developing economies of scale in the mass production of steel. Domestic cartels were created and very much supported by creditor banks to protect the majority of companies from going bankrupt (Wengenroth 1994a, 124–26). This did not lead, however, to bank control of the iron and steel industry (Wellhöhner 1989). It was a mutual interest in cartels and tariff protection at a time of crisis, not a policy to promote *Finanzkapital* in sense of Hilferding, a Marxist economist who eventually became minister of finance in the Weimar Republic. The tariff, meant to protect the home market, was developed into an instrument to protect differential pricing on domestic and export markets. Export dumping was the means to buy peace at home while simultaneously creating an opportunity for the most dynamic entrepreneurs. They ran their plant to full capacity, matching American "hard driving," and by this means effectively reduced production costs. The surplus above the domestic cartel share was dumped at very low prices—prices well below average production costs—on export markets, driving British companies out of the market (Wengenroth 1994a, chap. 4).

Innovativeness in this setting focused almost completely on cost reduction. With prices and quantities fixed on the domestic market, costs became the one variable that was open to innovative design. Without price competition, companies had to resort to cost competition. Production quantities that were needed to achieve the most effective economies of scale could be guaranteed by exports at dumping prices, around which there was plenty of room for maneuver thanks to cartel provisions. There were two main strategies for cost reduction. One, as already mentioned, was to drive the plant at optimum speed. The second was to enter into vertical integration to circumvent high cartel prices of domestic raw materials, especially coal. Eventually, the most successful German steel barons, like Krupp and Thyssen, would have fully integrated works, from coal and ore mining at the bottom to all lines of finished steel at the top. Their plant, especially that of Thyssen, the most dynamic steel manufacturer in imperial Germany, were models of energy efficiency and by-product recovery. Internally they were examples of successive decentralization, with a number of "modules" (Fear 2005, 40) operating rather independently from each other. These works would not only be self-sufficient in energy but also sell on the market gas and electricity, both by-products of blast furnace and coke oven operations. They were islands of an extensive, privately planned industrial economy.

By integrating as many steps of production as possible, the interface to the market was minimized while internal technical and organizational complexity grew. These vertically integrated companies, with their heat- and gas-exchange systems covering little "counties," were dreams of engineering control, largely shut off from disturbing environments. They worked fine under tariff protection, which was the convenient if always a bit precarious arrangement to enable lesser competitors to survive. It did not, however, withstand the storm of a real depression. In the mid-1920s, with demand very low after the stabilization of the mark and concurrent inflation of the French franc, which closed many export markets and blocked the dumping mechanism, most of Germany's big steel producers—a total of about one-half of production capacity—ran for cover in a merger of desperation, the Vereinigte Stahlwerke (VSt—United Steelworks). The first strategy of VSt was to lay idle as much capacity as possible and to run the remainder at optimum speed. This scheme, however, quickly ran into limits, as the intricate gas- and heat-exchanges broke down, driving costs up (Reckendrees 2000).

The engineering marvel of "total integration" failed miserably when output could no longer be negotiated. It had no flexibility; it was not made for the vicissitudes of real markets. Eventually, almost in a state of absent-mindedness, the German state took the majority of the stock of VSt, effectively if not intentionally nationalizing the company and with it most of German steel. More than any American reeducation toward competition and free markets, the disaster of VSt was a lesson learned by German entrepreneurs. They would begin to plan for individual competitive companies long before World War II was over. The innovative path toward a technological world of market-avoidance had produced great technologies and singular skills in physically connecting many different production lines, but it would only work in an economically stable environment with steady, moderate growth rates, as had been the case in the pre-1914 years (Wengenroth 1994b).

MECHANICAL INDUSTRIES

For the mechanical industries, American manufacture with interchangeable parts had become a model at about the same time that the leading steel manufacturers took to American "hard driving" of their plant. Especially the display of American machine tools at the Paris exhibition of 1867 and the news about mass production of guns and rifles during the Civil War had generated great interest among the more enterprising manufacturers. The great chance for a decisive leap forward came after the Franco-Prussian War of 1871. The Prussian military was absolutely determined both to equip its infantry with better guns and to acquire modern American gun factories as a backbone of future armament. These factories, bought ready to operate from Pratt & Whitney, making them this company's biggest single contract in its history, were the technological seed opening a new era of German manufacturing. Automatic and semiautomatic machine tools, together with innumerable jigs and gauges costing as much as the machines themselves, were models and blueprints for the modernization of a number of army contractors—very much like the imports of the Gewerbeförderung earlier in the century. The idea was to create a dual-use industry that could quickly turn from sewing-machines to guns. And it worked.

The most successful army contractor was the Berlin company Loewe, which, after a short detour into mass-producing sewing machines, replicated American automatic and semiautomatic machine tools, and adapted their design to both the European market and European iron and steel qualities. At the same time, Loewe continued to perfect its plant for gun production. In the 1880s, Loewe, to give just one example, was turning out Smith & Wesson revolvers for the Russian army. And Loewe now was in a position to do for Europe what Pratt & Whitney had done for the Prussian state: offering turn-key workshops for the mass production of small iron and steel components that were widely used for bicycles, sewing-machines, typewriters, and so on (Wengenroth 1996).

THE RISE OF SCIENCE-BASED INDUSTRIES

Chemical Industry

The showcase of German science-based industry was undoubtedly organic chemistry. From the 1880s until well after World War II German companies held a commanding position in most products based on carbon hydrates, especially when it came to high-value products like pharmaceuticals. The success story began with synthetic dyestuffs in the 1880s. Although the first synthetic dyestuffs were created in France and England, the latter in a laboratory set up by a student of the German chemist Liebig, it was German firms, supported by academic chemists from universities and engineers from the polytechnics, that turned synthetic dyestuffs into an industry with a highly methodical and scientific approach. The main strategy was always the same: analyze a natural product and then find ways to synthesize it cheaply from the tar derivatives the heavy industries and gasworks would abundantly supply. The overabundant supply of first-rate human capital for industrial research, plus the additional incentive of not having access to natural resources from colonies, created a situation that proved to be immensely fortunate (Reinhardt 1997). Only the Swiss chemical industry, also with a good supply of academically trained scientists and no colonies, could match the progress of German organic chemistry. It was one of the first examples after the Industrial Revolution when the absence of natural resources proved to be beneficial. Apart from the availability of highly qualified human capital, the German dyestuffs industry benefited from having hit a treasure trove of potential products, and the most innovative entrepreneurs were smart enough to see and fully utilize that potential.

Serendipity had it that hydrocarbons are at the root of three major product families: dyestuffs, synthetic materials, and pharmaceuticals. In looking for one, chemists would inevitably find the others. They just had to find out what the properties of the respective stuff were they had hit upon. This was done by massive testing on a hitherto unprecedented scale by hundreds of professionals in the laboratories of the big three (Hoechst, Bayer, BASF) of the German chemical industry. In the words of Carl Duisberg, head of Bayer, there was "nowhere any trace of a flash of genius" in the labs, just academic toil and screening (van den Belt and Rip 1987, 154). Eventually his company found more than 10,000 synthetic dyestuffs before the eve of World War I, 2,000 of which were marketed. At the same time they had hit on dyestuffs that wouldn't dye but could cure ills. Many twentieth-century drugs are "failed dyes," Valium being just the most profitable among them. Next to drugs a host of synthetic materials was found "on the way" and gave rise to ever more scrutiny when laboratories were testing newly synthesized chemicals.

Charts of tar-based products show a wide spectrum from explosives to anesthesia, Bakelite, and a number of synthetic dyestuffs and their intermediaries. In protecting processes rather than products the German patent law further stimulated the research drive into ever more fields. It took the German chemical industry's competitors decades and the scrapping of all property rights in the wake of wars slowly to erode the position it had built by the turn of the century. Only with two paradigm shifts in the industry, from coal to oil and from chemical synthesis to biotechnology, did foreign—mostly American—companies draw even with and eventually surpass the "big three," only two of which are still German with BASF being number one globally, while Hoechst has become part of the French Aventis (Wengenroth 2007).

Electrical Industry

An industry that was almost as successful in making the most of the great pool of talent at the many polytechnics was electrical engineering. This industry was governed by two very different titans of German enterprise, Werner Siemens, who had introduced the telegraph to Germany, and Emil Rathenau, the founder of AEG (Allgemeine Elektrizitätsgesellschaft = General Electric Company). Rathenau had been a restless innovator in his early years. He began his career as a designer and director of a company specialized in small, fairly standardized, and cheaply produced steam engines. This is how he met Siemens, who was looking for small mobile steam engines to drive field generators for army telegraphs. Rathenau sold his stake in the steam engine company just before it went bankrupt in the crisis of the 1870s. Looking for new opportunities and with good reason not to be seen for a while by his erstwhile shareholders, Rathenau, like Loewe whom he knew well, went several times to America to look for new products. From his first journey he returned with automatic machine tools—they were to become the business of Loewe. The next trip brought the Bell telephone and, again, cooperation with Siemens, who would manufacture it. To the dismay of Rathenau, the postmaster general decided that the telephone would fall under the same royal privilege as the telegraph and would run as a state company. Eventually Rathenau was lucky. The next business idea imported from America worked: Edison's electric light. Again, Siemens was the partner to do the manufacturing in the jointly owned "German Edison Company." The partnership with Siemens proved uneasy, however. Rathenau eventually took most of the business out of this partnership and created AEG (Wengenroth 1990).

In a major crisis soon after the turn of the century, most electric manufacturers went bankrupt when the gap between investment costs and returns from municipalities widened. The outcome on the German market was a duopoly of AEG and Siemens and remained that until the decline of AEG in the 1980s. Here again, basic innovations did not originate in Germany, but German entrepreneurs found ways to accommodate the new technology not only to the German market but to a great number of similar markets in smaller countries and overseas. Through these adaptations and modifications of Edison's electric light system, as through the adaptations of machine tools in the earlier example, it was the German companies that benefited most on export markets from what had been American technology. The solid background of a great number of competitive polytechnics provided the human capital and the research input that was needed to support this aggressive policy. Although it has been debated whether electrical manufacturing was a science-based industry or an industry-based science in Germany, there is agreement that the close and extensive cooperation of manufacturers and polytechnics greatly helped to solve innumerable problems occurring on the way to innovations that eventually created the high reputation for equipment "made in Germany" (König 1996).

UNTERNEHMERGESCHÄFT

With AEG, Rathenau was free to run a more enterprising course, the early pillar of which was the Unternehmergeschäft (entrepreneur business). In the Unternehmergeschäft, AEG would finance the erection of its own electric power systems and eventually sell the plant and the installations to the municipalities. This proved to be immensely successful, since many European municipalities could not or would not finance a major electric power plant. They would, however, grant a concession to AEG or other manufacturers to build the plant and operate it for a number of years, provided it would then fall to the city. The same deal applied to electric streetcars. Wary of privately owned infrastructure, European city councils were more easily convinced to go electric that way. To finance the Unternehmergeschäft, Rathenau and the many followers he had in the electric industry created banks and holding companies in Switzerland and Belgium, countries with a very liberal attitude to such institutions (Liefmann 1913). Soon the Unternehmergeschäft branched out to many overseas countries, with a particular stronghold in South America (Jacob-Wendler 1982). The electric manufacturers thereby created their own market. Not all were as clever as Rathenau and Siemens in keeping control over their huge investments on borrowed money.

NATIONAL NORMS

Ludwig Loewe, like so many other German entrepreneurs and engineers, had made it a routine to go to America frequently to scout the works and exhibitions for new ideas and to invite American engineers to his company in Berlin, which was famously credited in the *American Machinist* as the "finest American workshop" in Europe. Eventually it was Loewe who saw the great potential of a heavy Norton grinding machine that at the turn of the century had failed to convince American manufacturers. Loewe rested on the strength of his environment. He let one of his directors, the twenty-five-year-old Walter Schlesinger, go to the Berlin polytechnic to conduct research in metal cutting using heavy grinding machines. For the highly gifted young Jewish engineer, an academic distinction was one of the few pathways to be respected in the title-minded imperial society (Ebert and Hausen 1979). The result was the first ever German dissertation in mechanical engineering, the establishment of a "norm factory" on the premises of Loewe, and the beginning of what was to become the greatest export success of German mechanical industry ever, the DIN (Deutsche Industrie Normen)—German industrial norms used by countries around the world, among them more recently the Peoples Republic of China. In creating norms for fits, Schlesinger and his comrades-in-arms—literally, because most breakthroughs happened through World War I—established national norms rather than proprietary factory norms. With national norms, all German industry could participate in decentralized mass production. Products and components designed meeting these norms would always fit together. The test run was arms production in World War I, when a highly decentralized German industry had to turn out components for uniform mass products (Santz 1919; Garbotz 1920). It was another American observer who had quickly identified the synergies between the strength of academic training and systematic approaches to "normalization": „One meets with some undoubted improvement over American designs, due to characteristic Teutonic thoroughness in reducing all calculations to mathematical certainty" (Tupper 1911, 1481–82).

For smaller economies like those all over Europe, these national norms were a much better solution than proprietary norms. And as Germany moved ahead in creating a system of norms, other countries did not bother to invent something new but adopted DIN norms and later also their electrical counterpart, VDE norms (VDE = German Association of Electrical Manufacturers). There were very few innovations, if any, that helped German industry better to conquer export markets for mechanical and electrical products. Schlesinger and Loewe together had established this path, and others were quick to follow, seeing that agreeing on a common norm helped German business more than going proprietary. It is no surprise that German industry's tradition of collective action and cooperation was further strengthened by that strategy.

MIDDLE RANGE TECHNOLOGIES

A related strategy of German mechanical engineering was combining the versatility of universal machine tools with features of specialized one-purpose machines, as was developed in the American system of manufacture. While the American original, which was much copied ever since it had been imported after the Franco-German war, was tailor-made for large batch production, the German adaptation was a variety of single-purpose add-ons to a universal machine. This didn't give the same low unit-costs an American workshop turning out thousands of identical parts would provide. But it helped small and medium sized enterprise that was so typical for developing industries and for highly differentiated European markets to benefit to some extent from American principles of mass production without having to undertake an investment in single-purpose machinery that would never pay off (Dornseifer 1995; 1993b, 73-4). This innovation strategy, focusing not so much on fundamental breakthroughs as on adaptation of known principles to specific markets, achieved two things at the same time. It brought cutting-edge technology at competitive costs into the reach of small and medium enterprise (Magnus 1936). And, together with the protection of investment offered by the German industrial norms, this portfolio of highly flexible and adaptable machinery gave German industry a strong position in the many markets where entrepreneurs would import rather than manufacture their production technology. In the 1920s this branch of medium-sized firms supplied a fifth of the world machine exports and had more people employed than the iron and steel industry (Nolan 1994, 149–50). German mechanical industry turned into an opportunity the backwardness vis-à-vis the American system of manufacture that German manufacturing industry shared with so many other countries.

PUBLIC ENTERPRISE

An important group of entrepreneurs in Germany were state servants. While imperial Germany and most of its states had favored private enterprise during industrialization, there were some notable exceptions. In the case of postal services it was a royal prerogative that had been quite unceremoniously inflicted on the Princely Mail of Thurn and Taxis, a Frankfurt-based private mail service operating in Germany and its European neighbors. Thurn and Taxis were pro-Austrian, and when Prussian troops occupied Frankfurt at the end of the Austro-Prussian war of 1866–67 the company had to abandon its business to Prussia and its allies. Ever since, until privatization in 1995, postal services, including telegraph and telephone, were state-run in Germany. With the foundation of the German Empire in 1871 the Reichspost (Imperial Post) was created. Heinrich von Stephan, postmaster general until his death in 1897, was an entrepreneur rather than just an administrator. Son of a tailor and with nine siblings, Stephan was a good example of both upward mobility and nonmonetary rewards. Working his way up the career ladder of the Prussian post, he received an honorary doctorate from the prestigious University of Halle for his scientific publications in 1873, was eventually ennobled in 1885, became a member of the Prussian House of Lords, and was canon secular in the city of Merseburg.[4] It had been his memoir to the Prussian court that suggested the forcible takeover of the Princely Mail of Thurn and Taxis as soon as this was militarily feasible.

The growth rate of his business, which eventually included simple banking and savings services, was about ten times the growth rate of the economy. In the 1890s its annual budget was about $100 million and continued to grow. But the Reichspost was never meant to make large profits. Very much to the chagrin of Parliament and with strong support by imperial government, Stephan, a system builder par excellence, plowed back profits and subsidized peripheral regions of the empire through a system of standard rates. Among his many institutional innovations was the General Postal Union created in Switzerland in 1874, which very much simplified international mail services. Only three years after the Franco-Prussian War, Stephan had no qualms about agreeing on French as the working language of the Postal Union (Wengenroth 2000, 104–5).

Another important nationalization of private enterprise took place between 1879 and 1885 when the Prussian state nationalized most of its private railways after Bavaria and Saxony had already consolidated their state railways by acquiring the remaining private companies on their territory. There had been many complaints from trade and industry in the 1870s over widespread corruption, cartels for railway tariffs, and mismanagement among private railways, which were seen to be obstacles to industrial growth. At the end of the nineteenth century about 90 percent of German railways were state-run and highly profitable. Unlike the Reichspost, the Prussian railways, like the other state railways, were major contributors to state revenue. While the postmaster general delivered less than $20 million in 1913, the railways contributed more than $160 million to the state budget. In many years the Prussian railways generated more state revenue than all state taxes combined. Nobody doubted that they were more efficient than their private predecessors, and they were certainly a large improvement in safety and reliability. What on the eve of World War I was the largest single enterprise in the world ruthlessly exploited its monopoly (Wengenroth 2000, 106–7). In contrast to the Reichspost, the Prussian railways had a decentralized structure: at the top was the Prussian ministry of trade, while entrepreneurial activity was mostly concentrated in the regional railway directorates.

Both post and railways continued to be successful enterprises after World War I, although the railways had had a disastrous start when they lost 5,000 locomotives and 150,000 carriages to the Allies. This disaster was turned into an opportunity, however, in that the Reichsbahn, now a single national enterprise instead of a number of state railways, thoroughly modernized and standardized its rolling stock, turning the freshly established national system of norms to its advantage. Between 1924 and 1932 the Reichsbahn could contribute about $1 billion to the reparations account. The combined turnover of both, Reichspost and Reichsbahn, in 1929 peaked at $1.8 billion with a favorable balance of $260 million, which was about equal to the annual dividends of all German joint-stock companies in that year (Wengenroth 2000, 111).

Violence and Stagnation (1914–1955)

WARS AND AUTARCHY

The investment strategy developed in the late nineteenth century by the heavily cartelized and protected heavy industries to build tightly coupled, vertically integrated plants to avoid integration via the market as much as possible, was intensified through wars and autarchy. Germany, which was in no position to safeguard its raw material supplies from a vastly superior British navy, during conflict and in preparing for war turned to processing poor raw materials from its own territory and producing *Ersatz* to overcome supply shortages by second-rate material. Enormous ingeniousness and innovativeness were invested in autarchy technologies that were dead-ends on free markets and steered much effort away from future competitiveness (Wengenroth 2002).

The strength of the German chemical industry in synthesizing chemical compounds that were found in nature or compounds close to them was greatly in demand when the country went into World War I. Just before the war, Fritz Haber had created a process to synthesize ammonia, by this being able to produce nitrogen, which had mostly been imported from South America before the war and, more important, before the blockade by the British navy. Nitrogen was indispensable for both ammunition and fertilizers. Without Haber's invention, the war would have been over in summer 1915, since Germany would have run out of ammunition. Haber's ammonia synthesis was a classical case of industry-university cooperation. Haber, an entrepreneurial scientist par excellence, designed the process at the university and then went to BASF, taking his process with him. Another product Haber developed was weaponized gas. He himself led the first gas attack of World War I. Since Haber was Jewish, he only had the rank of a *Vizewachtmeister* (vice-constable). The Prussian army's officer corps had been one of the strongholds of anti-Semitism. All these complications of rank and order notwithstanding, it was Vizewachtmeister Haber who effectively ran the first gas attack and not the colonel officially in charge. Only after the "successful" attack was Haber promoted to the rank of a captain (Szöllösi-Janze 1998, 327–30).

More on the autarchy line like ammonia synthesis were developments of coal hydrogenation that were begun during World War I and completed with the advent of World War II to produce both gasoline and rubber from domestic coal. The R & D strategy was not so different from chemical synthesis in the prewar years, but it steered away from international markets and considerations of competitiveness of the new production lines. What was quite rational, given the resource poverty of Germany and its inability to break a British naval blockade, slowly turned into a new paradigm of a self-sufficient Germany that would not have to negotiate its way on international markets but could retreat into some self-designed cage. While before World War I chemical synthesis was a way to beat prices and quality of products based on natural resources, after the war and very much in the Nazi years it became a gospel of independence for conducting wars (Petzina 1968). A great share of innovative capacity was thus diverted toward a long-term economic cul-de-sac.

The German chemical industry—and to some extent also the steel industry, which was forced to process poor domestic ore—became world leaders for products and processes nobody else wanted. Scientific and technological excellence focused on products without markets and without a known future. Talent was wasted on, or rather sacrificed to, unaccomplishable political ambition. Add to this the self-decapitation of the German innovation system through the Nazis' policies and its aftereffects as described earlier and you get a picture of self-destruction on a grand scale. This is not to argue that Germany could still be something like the world's science and technology leader. Given the size of the economies and their respective productivities it was inevitable that the United States would sooner or later assume that position. But German politics in and between the world wars, in particular anti-Semitism, contributed substantially to hasten that transition. Unabated innovativeness in these years too often followed a disastrous track that took German industry away from international competitiveness. Without a sustainable political perspective, which given the size and geopolitical situation of Germany could only have been peaceful, innovation following military short-term objectives, in the long run neutralized much of the country's economic and technological potential.

STIFLED MARKETING INNOVATIONS

While innovation in industry suffered from being directed toward autarchy and *Ersatz*, especially during the Nazi years, innovation in marketing and retailing was stifled from the beginning. Because of its focus on investment and intermediary goods, German enterprise had been in a comparatively weak position in marketing in the early twentieth century. In 1907 only twenty-one of the 100 largest German industrial corporations had a bona-fide marketing organization, while forty-nine of the top-100 corporations sold their product exclusively via cartel syndicates (Dornseifer 1993b, 75). This tradition was turned into an aggressive policy and ideology by the Nazis, who, before their rise to power, had promised to expropriate big department stores, which were reviled as manifestations of Jewish and plutocratic exploitation of both German workers and German shopkeepers. While expropriation did not occur—with the important exception of "aryanization" of Jewish property—the Nazis did place a ban on further retail outlets and controlled concessions for retailing a few weeks after Hitler's rise to power. And as they had introduced mandatory cartels in industry, they also introduced enforceable resale price maintenance and thereby effectively abolished price competition. This rule was in effect until January 1974 and kept productivity in retailing low (Wengenroth 1999, 122). It was large, family-owned mail-order firms with good access to nonbranded imported goods that managed to bypass this stifling situation in the fifties and sixties, eventually putting protected retailing under such pressure that price regulation was abandoned. Ironically, the large mail-order companies were among the first to suffer from price deregulation when their price-quality ratio was matched by department stores and specialized dealers. Only a few general mail-order firms managed to survive, but the leader in the field, Otto-Group, which includes a small tourism segment and financial services for consumers with a turnover of more than €15 billion, is today the largest mail-order company in the world (Geschäftsbericht Otto-Group 2006–7). With no limit on the number of retail outlets, retail chains at long last began to flourish in Germany. It is telling of the innovative potential of German retailing that once it was freed from anticompetitive regulations, Germany is the only major market where Wal-Mart failed. After almost a decade of heavy losses amounting to more than €3 billion, Wal-Mart wound up its German business in 2006 and sold most of its 85 shopping centers to a German competitor. At the same time, the owners of the leading German retailer Aldi have been quite successful with their Trader Joe's chain in America.[5]

Finding Its Place (1955–2007)

RECONSTRUCTION LEGACY: LEADING INCREMENTALISTS

After the autarchic interlude of the years between the world wars, German business in the West—that in the East was quickly nationalized—had to adapt to yet another set of rules, opportunities, and limitations. Autarchy was definitely out. Imported oil replaced domestic coal as the main source of energy and as the main raw material for the chemical industry. World markets were accessible for both imports and exports. Cartels were banned as of 1957. European integration already began in the early 1950s with the formation of the European Community for Steel and Coal. Because of wartime destruction, the capital stock was comparatively young. Reconstruction demand was enormous. On the downside were Allied restrictions on a number of cutting-edge technologies until 1955, which made Germany fall further behind in research for knowledge-intensive products, although they had little effect on industrial production proper since industry was still busy reconstructing (Neebe 1989, 51–52; Abelshauser 2004, 229).

In this situation German companies quite rationally focused on perfecting existing technologies for the purpose of reconstruction at home and supplying export markets with the wide range of not-so-high-tech products like cars, multipurpose machine tools, standard chemical products, and so on. Werner Abelshauser has forcefully argued that reconstruction has been the dominating mode of the German economy in the twentieth century: reconstruction after World War I, extensive reconstruction after World War II, and reconstruction of the ex-GDR after unification in 1990 (Abelshauser 2001). Reconstruction is not technologically daring, since the technologies are all in place and well known. The great opportunity of this reconstruction mode is, however, to become a superior debugger of new technology, the best incremental innovator around. Looking at Germany's export portfolio, it becomes clear that this is very much what happened. Germany is excellent in technology-intensive products that are not cutting-edge, with automobiles being the current top-runner, while German information technology is in a rather modest position (Abelshauser 2003, 185; BMBF 2005, 48–54). Biotechnology is another example. At the first glance German companies are doing quite respectably, but their strength is in so-called platform technologies, that is, the toolbox or machine tools of biotech. When it comes to substances that go into clinical testing, Germany is far behind Switzerland.

Reconstruction has conditioned German industries by creating many opportunities and, most important, career patterns for its scientific and technological elite. The great export success that came out of reconstruction kept German business in industry and prolonged the dominance of industrial employment in comparison to other European countries and certainly in comparison to the United States. There is great concern among leaders in government and business that Germany may fall behind and fail to command new technologies. As the most recent data on Germany's competitiveness shows, however, there is little reason to be worried in the overall picture. In comparison with its main competitors, Germany's balance of trade in R & D–intensive goods is very good.

The strength of Germany's position lies overwhelmingly in advanced technologies, not so much in cutting-edge technologies. This comparison confirms the cultural imprint in the German innovation system of reconstruction and incremental innovations—a trait it shares with Japan. But even when it comes to cutting-edge technologies, Germany's balance of trade is still positive, illustrating that the fast follower

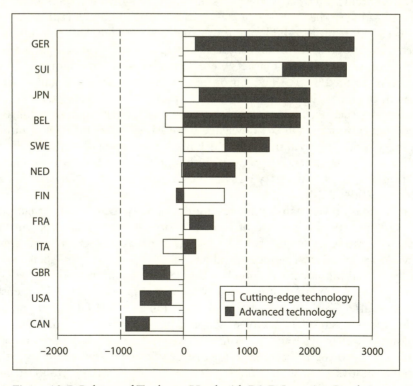

Figure 10.7. Balance of Trade per Head with R&D-Intensive Goods in 2004 (in US$). (Source: Federal Ministry of Education and Research, 2007 Report on the Technological Performance of Germany, Summary, 9.)

strategy is working, not in fields like information and communication technology, but certainly on average over all branches of industry. The backbone of Germany's great export successes in Schumpeterian goods is not the heroic entrepreneur who is ushering a new basic innovation to the world but the shrewd manager of continuous novelty that keeps his company in business. Perpetual incremental innovations and close market observation are the foundations for the strong position of German manufacturers on world markets.

BUYING INNOVATIVENESS

An expedient way to benefit from innovations elsewhere is to buy them. This is standard practice and is hardly worth mentioning in the context of an industrializing country like Germany in the nineteenth and early twentieth centuries. The introduction of mass production of interchangeable parts by importing American machinery after the Franco-German war was one example mentioned earlier. More noticeable, however, is a policy of buying rather than developing in a mature economy of the twentieth century. Reasons for this policy in Germany may be manifold. In the Nazi years the spectacular cases were the consequence of bitter conflict over industrial strategy between the party and tycoons of industry. When the German steel industry was reluctant to embark on autarchy by processing poor domestic ores, the Nazi party hired the American Brassert company to erect the "Hermann-Göring-Werke," which were intended to become the largest iron- and steelworks in the world (Riedel 1973; Meyer 1986). Brassert had developed a blast furnace process specifically suited to the Nazi autarchy in steel. He left the work unfinished at the outbreak of World War II. The process never worked satisfactorily and was soon abandoned. Next to the Hermann-Göring-Werke, Ford engineers from America built the Volkswagen-Werk, very much along Fordist principles of uniform mass-production after the German car industry had rejected Porsche's design of the "beetle" (Mommsen and Grieger 1996, 250–52). This venture proved to be a great success.

In the postwar years German industry bought a number of technologies, mostly from America, to catch up and to compensate for ill-conceived earlier innovation policies. Petrochemistry, which quickly replaced the autarchy-based coal chemistry, is a striking example (Stokes 1994). Biotechnology is another. The German chemical industry had become so complacent over its many successes in chemical synthesis that it allowed Germany to lose its earlier formidable position in fermentation technology and other biotechnical processes (Marschall 2000). Plant for penicillin production had to be imported. And when biotechnological processes proved vastly superior to the traditional German approach of chemical synthesis, the German pharmaceutical industry did not join the effort of the Federal ministry of research to build up domestic research capacities but went to America, to buy its way into new technologies. Hoechst, one of the big three of German chemistry and pharmaceuticals, in a spectacular deal in 1981 contracted for research at Massachusetts General Hospital and in this led the way for other German pharmaceutical companies to buy innovative potential abroad—mostly in America—rather then develop it from scratch at home (Wengenroth 2007).

A similar pattern can be found in computing. Here, again, the federal government funded research and development with a view to creating a German counterpart to the dominating American companies; the foremost, IBM, had its own very successful subsidiary in Germany. But not much came of this effort. Eventually Siemens, which had pioneered the world's first fully transistorized computer and had benefited from massive financial support by the federal government, abandoned all efforts to go it alone or with German partners and in the late 1970s approached Fujitsu, whose IBM-compatible computers were more advanced. From 1981 Siemens would sell Fujitsu Computers (Janisch 1988, 134–37, 152). This was a blow to German industrial policy similar to the Hoechst-MGH deal of the same year. Both cases demonstrated that even the best-equipped German firms were in no position to match the pace of international development in their respective fields. And while the companies quickly understood what their place on the world market realistically could be, the government and the public still took a while to accept that there was no return to German scientific and technological leadership that the country had enjoyed before the disaster of the Nazi years. Entrepreneurial rationality was no longer to dream of leading technological development, but to design a strategy of fast follower that would bring the German strength in incremental innovation and perfection, rather than first creation of cutting-edge technology products, into play.

SMALL CHAMPIONS

A particular strength of innovativeness in German industry is found in small and medium enterprise. Many improvements and quite a number of breakthroughs, mostly of engineering products, can be traced back to small independent suppliers. Their regional stronghold is the southwest of Germany, but they are all over the country. Gary Herrigel, whose work is central to understanding the importance of small enterprise for the high quality and sophistication of many German engineering products, called the networks of large and small enterprise "a new hybrid mass-production strategy" where small-scale industry was used "as external sources of manufacturing capacity" (1996, 155). The history of small-scale industries went from victims of industrialization in the nineteenth century, when great concern over their fate was the topic of inquiry, to appreciating them as a backbone of German competitiveness.

A theoretical problem for appreciation of the success of small-scale enterprise is that it doesn't grow, or if it does it is no longer small scale. There are, however, markets that by their nature are of limited size and don't allow the kind of growth we see in the showcases of big industry. In view of the stunning resilience and continuing success of small industry in Germany, there was a renewed interest in that group in the 1990s when the German economy was trailing behind its European neighbors. Some of the small champions, as the SMEs have been affectionately called, turned out to be very innovative world market leaders in highly specialized market niches. There was, for example, Baader, a company that held 90 percent of the world market of fish-filleting machinery; or Söring with a staff of twenty and a world market share of 36 percent in ultrasonic dissectors (Simon 1996, 26, 55). These small and medium high-tech companies were both a source of continuous innovation, or "continuous novelty" as Phil Scranton (1997) called the somewhat larger American equivalents, and a formative springboard for managerial and entrepreneurial talent.

"SERVICE DESERT GERMANY"

While federal science and technology policy is concentrating on supporting cutting-edge technologies, the market has long moved on to knowledge-intensive services. In the EU-15, Germany's most important market, there are three times as many people employed in cutting-edge knowledge-intensive services as in cutting-edge technologies. In Germany and Switzerland, with their very strong position in the second tier of industrial Schumpeter goods, there are still twice as many in cutting-edge services as in cutting-edge technologies (Felix 2006). Productivity in such services is higher than in such technologies all over the EU-15. In Germany this difference is less striking than among its neighbors, though. The reason is not above-average productivity in technologies but below-average productivity in services (Götzfried 2005, 4). The concentration of German innovative entrepreneurs on technologies, which have always been understood as the stronghold of the German economy, has begun to turn into a disadvantage. The phrase "service desert Germany" was coined in the mid-1990s to alert both policymakers and managers to that problem. The opportunity costs of favoring material over immaterial production have been rising for a number of years. It remains to be seen whether German innovative entrepreneurs wake up to that change and manage what comes close to a minor cultural revolution, moving the focus of innovative activity from industry to services.

Schumpeterian Entrepreneurs in Germany

Schumpeterian entrepreneurs in Germany were confronted with very different environments over the two centuries after 1815. For most of the nineteenth century, replicative strategies, that is, adoption of what had been invented elsewhere to the natural and institutional conditions of Germany, was all they needed to thrive through industrialization. Seeds of future inefficiencies were, however, planted by a revival of protectionism and judicially supported cartelization. Toward the end of the nineteenth century and in the early decades of the twentieth century German entrepreneurs, very much helped by the unique creativity of the German system of higher education, reached a position that enabled them to embark on fundamentally new technologies. Science-based industries like organic chemistry and electric engineering flourished in Germany and made the late empire's industry a world leader in many product lines. Entrepreneurs in the chemical and electrical industries were shrewd enough to benefit from this extraordinary endowment of human capital and to develop industrial research, marketing, and foreign direct investment to their advantage.

After World War I this momentum was lost. The few years of favorable business conditions in the second half of the 1920s were not enough to reinvigorate the innovative potential of German industry. With the Nazis' rise to power, autarchy and preparation for war ruled the agenda, both of which were detrimental to the competitiveness of industry in the long run. Moreover, ruthless anti-Semitism and downsizing of student enrollment led Germany on an unparalleled path of intellectual self-decapitation. At the same time, mass marketing and large-scale retailing were both reviled and obstructed, stifling potential innovations and permitting only copying and adapting in the ever more important service sector of the economy. This disastrous development kept up until well after World War II. Important institutional reforms such as the banning of cartels, lifting retail price regulations, and abandonment of protectionism slowly redirected Germany's business culture toward more competitive and open-market ideals.

With reconstruction being the dominating and least troubling business for decades, German entrepreneurs excelled in incremental innovations. When a dominant position in cutting-edge technologies that had seemed to come within reach before World War I was no longer a realistic option in the second half of the twentieth century, a very successful culture of improving and debugging existing technologies developed. Ironically, the consequences of a disastrous history were turned into a comparative advantage. While biotechnology and computing continue to be precarious industries, even struggling to be fast followers, highly refined automobiles are doing extremely well. Even business fields like retailing that had been discriminated against by both politics and popular values show some notable successes in employing known strategies to their advantage. German entrepreneurs are unlikely to be the first to seize a fundamentally new opportunity, but they seem well equipped to be successful second movers.

Notes

[1] http://www.bmbf.de/press/1761.php, accessed October 14, 2008.
[2] The new family names were "Krupp von Bohlen und Halbach" and "Thyssen-Bornemisza de Kászon."
[3] Personal communication by the head archivists of the two companies.
[4] *Allgemeine Deutsche Biographie* 54:477–501.
[5] *Handelsblatt* online, July 28, 2006.

References

Abelshauser, Werner. 2001. "Umbruch und Persistenz: Das deutsche Produktionsregime in historischer Perspektive." *Geschichte und Gesellschaft* 27:503–23.

Abelshauser, Werner, ed. 2004. *German Industry and Global Enterprise: BASF. The History of a Company*. Cambridge: Cambridge University Press.

Arundel, Anthony, Gert van de Paal, and Maastricht Economic Research Institute on Innovation and Technology. 1995. *Innovation Strategies of Europe's Largest Industrial Firms: Results of the Survey for Information Sources, Public Research, Protection of Innovations and Government Programmes; Final Report, PACE Report*. Maastricht: MERIT.

Berg, Christa, and Notker Hammerstein, eds. 1989. *Handbuch der deutschen Bildungsgeschichte*. Vol. 5. Munich: C. H. Beck.

Berghahn, Volker R. 1986. *The Americanisation of West German Industry, 1945–1973*. Leamington Spa: Berg.

Biggeleben, Christof. 2006. *Das "Bollwerk des Bürgertums": Die Berliner Kaufmannschaft (1870–1920)*. Munich: C. H. Beck.

Broszat, Martin, and Internationale Konferenz zur nationalsozialistischen Machtübernahme. 1983. *Deutschlands Weg in die Diktatur: Internationale Konferenz zur nationalsozialistischen Machtübernahme im Reichstagsgebäude zu Berlin; Referate und Diskussionen; ein Protokoll*. Berlin: Siedler.

Bundesministerium für Bildung und Forschung (BMBF). 2004. *Bundesbericht Forschung 2004*. Berlin: BMBF.

———. 2005. *2005 Report on Germany's Technological Performance*. Berlin: BMBF.

Chandler, Alfred D., Jr., and Takashi Hikino. 1990. *Scale and Scope: The Dynamics of Industrial Capitalism*. Cambridge: Belknap Press of Harvard University Press.

Erker, Paul, and Toni Pierenkemper, eds. 1999. *Deutsche Unternehmer zwischen Kriegswirtschaft und Wiederaufbau Studien zur Erfahrungsbildung von Industrie-Eliten.* Munich: Oldenbourg.

Fear, Jeffrey Robert. 2005. *Organizing Control: August Thyssen and the Construction of German Corporate Management.* Cambridge: Harvard University Press.

Feldman, Gerald Donald. 1984. *Vom Weltkrieg zur Weltwirtschaftskrise: Studien zur dt. Wirtschafts- und Sozialgeschichte 1914–1932.* Göttingen: Vandenhoeck & Ruprecht.

Feldman, Gerald D. 1998. "Politische Kultur und Wirtschaft in der Weimarer Zeit: Unternehmer auf dem Weg in die Katastrophe." *Zeitschrift für Unternehmensgeschichte* 43, no. 1: 3–18.

Felix, Bernard. 2006. "Beschäftigung im Spitzentechnologiebereich." *Eurostat: Statistik kurz gefasst. Wissenschaft und Technologie* 1:1–7.

Fremdling, Rainer. 1985. *Eisenbahnen und deutsches Wirtschaftswachstum 1840–1879: Ein Beitr. zur Entwicklungstheorie u. zur Theorie d. Infrastruktur.* 2nd ed. Dortmund: Gesellschaft für Westfälische Wirtschaftsgeschichte.

Geißler, Rainer, and Thomas Meyer. 1996. *Die Sozialstruktur Deutschlands zur gesellschaftlichen Entwicklung mit einer Zwischenbilanz zur Vereinigung.* Opladen: Westdeutscher Verlag.

Götzfried, August. 2005. "Spitzentechnologie: Unternehmen und Handel." *Statistik kurz gefasst: Wissenschaft und Technologie* 9:1–6.

Hayes, Peter. 1987. *Industry and Ideology: IG Farben in the Nazi Era.* Cambridge: Cambridge University Press.

———. 2005. *From Cooperation to Complicity: Degussa in the Third Reich.* Cambridge: Cambridge University Press.

Henke, Klaus-Dietmar. 1995. *Die amerikanische Besetzung Deutschlands.* Munich: Oldenbourg.

Kleinschmidt, Christian. 2002. *Der produktive Blick: Wahrnehmung amerikanischer und japanischer Management- und Produktionsmethoden durch deutsche Unternehmer 1950–1985.* Berlin: Akademie Verlag.

König, Wolfgang. 1996. "Science-Based Industry or Industry-Based Science: Electrical Engineering in Germany before World War I." *Technology and Culture* 37, no. 1: 70–101.

Lindner, Stephan H. 2005. *Hoechst. Ein I.G. Farben Werk im Dritten Reich.* Munich: Beck.

Lundgreen, Peter. 1990. "Engineerig Education in Europe and the U.S.A., 1750–1930: The Rise to Dominance of School Culture and the Engineering Professions." *Annales of Science* 47, no. 1: 33–75.

Marschall, Luitgard. 2000. *Im Schatten der chemischen Synthese: Industrielle Biotechnologie in Deutschland (1900–1970).* Frankfurt am Main: Campus-Verlag.

Mosse, Werner Eugen, and Hans Pohl. 1992. *Jüdische Unternehmer in Deutschland im 19. und 20.* Stuttgart: Steiner.

Neebe, Reinhard, Paul Silverberg, and Reichsverband der Deutschen Industrie in der Krise der Weimarer Republik. 1981. *Großindustrie, Staat und NSDAP, 1930–1933: Paul Silverberg und der Reichsverband der Deutschen Industrie in der Krise der Weimarer Republik.* Göttingen: Vandenhoeck & Ruprecht.

Paulinyi, Akos. 1982. "Der Technologietransfer für die Metallbearbeitung und die preußische Gewerbeförderung (1820–1850)." *Schriften des Vereins für Socialpolitik, Gesellschaft für Wirtschafts- und Sozialwissenschaften,* n.s., 125:99–141.

Porter, Michael Eugene. 1990. *The Competitive Advantage of Nations.* London: Macmillan.

Reckendrees, Alfred. 2000. *Das Stahltrust-Projekt. Die Gründung der Vereinigte Stahlwerke A.G. und ihre Unternehmensentwicklung 1926–1933/34.* Munich: Beck.

Reinhardt, Carsten. 1997. *Forschung in der chemischen Industrie: Die Entwicklung synthetischer Farbstoffe bei BASF und Hoechst, 1863 bis 1914.* Freiberg: Technische Universität Bergakad.

Troitzsch, Ulrich, and Wolfhard Weber. 1982. *Die Technik: Von den Anfängen bis zur Gegenwart.* Braunschweig: Westermann.

Turner, Henry Ashby. 1985. *German Big Business and the Rise of Hitler*. New York: Oxford University Press.

Weisbrod, Bernd. 1978. *Schwerindustrie in der Weimarer Republik: Interessenpolitik zwischen Stabilisierung und Krise*. Wuppertal: Hammer.

Wellhöner, Volker. 1989. *Großbanken und Großindustrie im Kaiserreich*. Göttingen: Vandenhoeck & Ruprecht.

Wengenroth, Ulrich. 1985. "Die Entwicklung der Kartellbewegung bis 1914." In *Kartelle und Kartellgesetzgebung in Praxis und Rechtsprechung vom 19. Jahrhundert bis zur Gegenwart*, ed. H. Pohl, 14–27. Wiesbaden: Franz Steiner.

———. 1988. "Hoffnungen auf Mitteleuropa. Absatzstrategien und Interessenpolitik der deutschen Schwerindustrie im Reichsgründungsjahrzehnt." In *Deutschland und Europa in der Neuzeit*, edited by Ulrich Wengenroth, Ralph Melville, and C. Scharf, 2:537–53. Stuttgart: Franz Steiner.

———. 1990. "Emil Rathenau." In *Berlinische Lebensbilder-Techniker*, ed. W. Treue and W. König, 193–209. Berlin: Colloquium-Verlag.

———. 1991. "Iron and Steel." In *International Banking, 1870–1914*, ed Rondo Cameron and V. I. Bovykin, 485–98. Oxford: Oxford University Press.

———, ed. 1993. *Technische Universität München. Annäherungen an ihre Geschichte*. Munich: TUM.

———. 1994a. *Enterprise and Technology: The German and British Steel Industries, 1865–1895*. Cambridge: Cambridge University Press.

———. 1994b. "The Steel Industries of Western Europe Compared, 1870–1914." In *Economics of Technology*, ed. Ove Granstrand, 375–96. Amsterdam: Elsevier.

———. 1996. "Industry and Warfare in Prussia." In *On the Road to Total War: The American Civil War and the German Wars of Unification, 1861–1871*, ed. Stig Förster and Jörg Nagler, 249–62. New York: Cambridge University Press.

———. 1997a. "Deutsche Wirtschafts- und Technikgeschichte seit dem 16. Jahrhundert." In *Deutsche Geschichte. Von den Anfängen bis zur Gegenwart*, ed. M. Vogt, 297–396. Stuttgart: J. B. Metzlersche Verlagsbuchhandlung.

———. 1997b. "Germany: Competition Abroad—Cooperation at Home, 1870–1990." In *Big Business and the Wealth of Nations*, ed. Alfred D. Chandler Jr., Franco Amatori, and Takashi Hikino, 139–75. New York: Cambridge University Press.

———. 1998. "Innovations in Mature Industries: Steel and Beyond." In *The Steel Industry in the New Millennium*, vol. 1, *Technology and the Market*, ed. Ruggero Ranieri and Jonathan Aylen, 187–194. London: Institute of Metals.

———. 2002. "Die Flucht in den Käfig: Wissenschafts- und Innovationskultur in Deutschland 1900–1960." In *Wissenschaften und Wissenschaftspolitik. Bestandsaufnahme zu Formationen, Brüchen und Kontinuitäten im Deutschland des 20. Jahrhunderts*, ed. Brigitte Kaderas and Rüdiger vom Bruch, 52–59. Stuttgart: Franz Steiner.

———. 2003. "Science, Technology, and Industry." In *From Natural Philosophy to the Sciences: Writing the History of Nineteenth-Century Science*, ed. David Cahan, 231–53. Chicago: University of Chicago Press.

———. 2006. "Innovationskultur in Deutschland. Rahmenbedingungen der Wissenschafts- und Technologiepolitik." Research report for the Federal Ministry for Education and Research.

———. 2007. "The German Chemical Industry after World War II." In *The Global Chemical Industry in the Age of the Petrochemical Revolution*, ed. Louis Galambos, Takashi Hikino and Vera Zamagni, 141–67. New York: Cambridge University Press.

Zorn, Wolfgang, Knut Borchardt, and Hermann Aubin, eds. 1976. *Das 19. und 20. Jahrhundert, Handbuch der deutschen Wirtschafts- und Sozialgeschichte*. Vol. 2. Stuttgart: Klett.

Chapter 11

Entrepreneurship in France

MICHEL HAU

FOR DECADES, THERE HAVE BEEN two schools of thought about the business development of France in the nineteenth and twentieth centuries: the pessimists' and the optimists'. The pessimists emphasize that British GNP grew faster than the French during the nineteenth century and exceeded the French by 50 percent at the beginning of the twentieth century. The optimists focus attention on the performance of French small-scale output in the secondary sector and assert that although the French path to economic modernity was different, it was no less efficient. Perhaps both are right: French national data hide large regional variations. In some places the Industrial Revolution was fast and was led by dynamic employers, whereas in others it was slow and incomplete. The behavior of local employers constituted, independently of the cost of raw materials or of the availability of labor, a comparative advantage for the industrial development of some French regions. On the national level, the state made efforts to stimulate industrialization, beginning in the epoch of Louis XIV and his finance minister, Colbert. But a tradition of free enterprise also existed in France in each period and flourishes now, in a time of international competition.

The First Rise of French Industry (1815–1870)

The Industrial Revolution began in France after that of the United Kingdom. It was delayed by the disorders of the French Revolution and the Napoleonic Wars. But the Revolution abolished all guild restrictions, and the Code of Commerce, promulgated in 1807 under Napoleon, created favorable conditions to entrepreneurship. State institutions, such as engineering schools, the Académie des Sciences, and the Conservatoire National des Arts et Métiers, helped the dissemination of technological innovations. In 1815, with the return of peace, the process of industrialization accelerated and, at the time of the conclusion of the Anglo-French free trade treaty of 1860, French industrial output amounted to 40 percent of that of Britain. In 1865, the engine builder Eugene Schneider could proudly announce to the French Parliament that he had succeeded in selling fifteen locomotives to England and said that it was the "greatest joy" of his life. At that time, at the end of the 1860s, French industrial output was also exceeded by those of Germany and the United States, but remained fourth in the world until about 1930.

The Scarcity of Large Companies

French industrialization took place in a context of costly coal and high protectionism. Coal was rare, except for the small basins of the Massif Central and the north. A law voted in 1816 protected by prohibitions or very high customs duties the textile and iron industries. The persecutions of Protestants by Louis XIV (Lüthy 1955–61) and then the troubles under the Revolution (Perrot 1982; Bonin 1985; Crouzet 1989; Aerts and Crouzet 1990) had more or less durably weakened entrepreneurship in many parts of France.

The old techniques (cast iron made with charcoal, manual weaving, hydraulic mills), less greedy in energy and capital, coexisted until about 1860 with the most modern modes of production. Big factories, like the glass producer Saint-Gobain, were rare. Only the mines, the waterways, the large iron and steel firms, and the railroads were financed by limited-liability companies, whose creation was subject to authorization until 1867. The capital of industrial firms was generally provided by the founder's family, later by self-financing (Lévy-Leboyer 1974, 1985; Marseille 2000). The passage from the small workshop consuming little energy and still using largely craft-based techniques toward the large company using the steam engine and the latest techniques occurred slowly and at very unequal rates that varied among areas. French producers made an effort to compensate for their weakness in mechanization by the aesthetic quality of their product. They specialized in printed cottons, silk textiles, and luxury handicraft products (*articles de Paris*). Engineering colleges gave artistic drawing an important place in their curriculum.

The geographical distribution of the dynamic centers is instructive. During the nineteenth century, the southwest of France was industrially inactive and remained anchored in an agricultural and craft-based economy (Armengaud 1960; Crouzet 1959; Poussou 2000). The Atlantic and Mediterranean coasts (in particular the ports of Nantes and Bordeaux, on the Atlantic Ocean) suffered much from the British maritime blockade. But after the war, from 1815, their tendency to deindustrialization did not stop (Poussou 1989; Butel 1991; Armengaud 1960). Industrial employers put their money in land and real estate with poor but less dubious profits. In contrast, factory development was remarkably dynamic in Paris, at Lyons, and, from the beginning of the nineteenth century, in the peripheral zones of northern and eastern France. Machine cotton spinning developed quickly in the north (Lille, Roubaix, Tourcoing) and in Alsace (Toulemonde 1966; Barbier 1989; Pouchain 1998; Daumas 2004b; Hau 1987; Stoskopf 1994; Hau and Stoskopf 2005). After the end of Napoleonic Wars, Nicolas Koechlin and Daniel Dollfus-Mieg, whose factories employed thousands, exported printed fabrics from Mulhouse to all the world. Nicolas Schlumberger introduced in 1817 in Guebwiller the British technique for fine yarn and the production of mule jennies. In 1826 Marc Seguin built the railway line Lyons-Saint-Etienne and, three years later, launched the production of a new type of locomotive, with tubular boilers, in Lyons.

Barriers to Diffusion of Entrepreneurship in France at the Beginning of the Nineteenth Century

At the beginning of nineteenth century, several factors exerted a negative influence on the development of the entrepreneurship: the political power of the landowners, the attraction of gentry status or of high public office for the elites, the conflict between the Catholic Church and the Revolution, and finally, increasingly radical protests coming from the intellectual and artistic elites.

THE POLITICAL WEIGHT OF THE LANDOWNERS

The Revolution released the peasants from seigneurial charges, but it did not call into question the urban middle-class ownership of arable land. Around Paris and the cities of southern France, many middle-class men placed their fortune in the ground. Indicator of social rank, symbol of safety, landownership remained, at least into the last quarter of the nineteenth century, a major competitor to industrial investment. The majority of the members of Parliament and senior officials were landowners, more aware of and sensitive to agricultural problems than the prospects opened by industrialization. The debates in Parliament revealed blockages about railroad construction: long-term concessions and loan guarantees were refused by the deputies. Liberalization of the creation of limited companies had to wait until 1867. The administrative and political elites were anxious about the risks of speculation or financial domination by big business. Thus, the political community was reticent about the development of large-scale industry and the growth of vast worker concentrations. The British example was, for many of them, something to be avoided, rather than a model to be followed. But after 1852, the regime of Napoleon III made bolder moves and pushed reluctant political circles toward modernization (Landes 1967; Gille 1959, 1968).

THE PRESTIGE OF THE GENTRY AND OF THE HIGH CIVIL SERVICE

A part of the entrepreneurial elite conceived enterprise as a way to gain a fortune, to buy land, and to enter into the gentry. The most famous example is that of Auguste-Thomas Pouyer-Quertier. He developed a large cotton-spinning factory in Normandy. In 1857 he was elected deputy to the French Parliament and, in 1871, became minister of finance. From this time, he neglected his firm, which declined, and he married his two daughters to noblemen. This behavior was widespread in Normandy, where industrial dynasties rarely lasted more than two generations (Barjot 1991).

There was also in bourgeois families a strong pull to the civil service. The French monarchy developed a centralized, general-purpose, and hierarchical administration. The senior civil servants were recruited after the Revolution by selective contest, and this system put into competition the best graduates of the secondary schools. The bourgeois families of Paris and the provinces made it a point of honor to enter high public office, which before the Revolution had conferred ennoblement. This attraction of talent for the service of the state diverted part of the elite from the world of enterprise. The schools of engineers created by the Monarchy at the end of the eighteenth century and later by the Republic had initially the function of providing the administration and the army with scientific and technical competences. Thereafter, things began to change; with the growth of the number of engineers in business companies, the various schools of engineering, in particular the Ecole Polytechnique, provided more and more for the needs of industry.

THE CONFLICT BETWEEN THE CATHOLIC CHURCH AND MODERNITY

France was primarily a country of Roman Catholic religion. However, the rationalist movement and then the Revolution revealed the difficulty of the Catholic Church in adapting to modernity. Among many Catholics, there occurred, starting at the end of the eighteenth century, a brutal rupture with the religious tradition: they had to choose between their traditional faith and the ideals of the Enlightenment. Part of the Catholic middle class felt obliged to give up its ancestral faith and to break with a number of traditional attitudes in order to open its mind to science and industry (Groethuysen 1927, xi, xii). In contrast, Protestants and Jews preserved their religious spirit intact throughout the nineteenth century. For the Protestant or the Jew, to make a company thrive seemed a moral duty, whereas for the agnostic, it was only a right related to ownership. The difference here was less between Catholicism and Jewish or Protestant religion than between unbelief and faith.

THE PROTESTS EMANATING FROM THE INTELLECTUAL AND ARTISTIC ELITES

After the Revolution had abolished the privileges of the aristocracy, the wealth and the social status of the entrepreneurs put them on the first rank in the French society. The most successful of these entrepreneurs could soon accumulate wealth surpassing those of the biggest landowners. After 1830, bankers and industrialists such as Jacques Laffitte or Casimir Périer under Louis-Philippe or Jean Dollfus under Napoleon III played an important role in the government. But, in removing the aristocracy, the French Revolution had invented two new rival elites: on the one hand, that of artists and intellectuals (writers, painters, musicians, etc.); on the other, that of entrepreneurs. The first despised the second, which it reproached for being deaf to passions, blind to art, and insensitive to the misery of their workforce (Heinrich 2006).

Progressively, at the end of the nineteenth century, as industrial development proceeded, the positions of some writers were radicalized; thus Emile Zola left us a particularly sinister description of large-scale industry and the coal mines. The influence of the writers on public opinion was particularly important in France. It hampered, to a degree impossible to determine, the vocation of entrepreneurs.

Local Backgrounds Favorable to Entrepreneurship

FAST INDUSTRIAL GROWTH IN THE NORTH AND EAST OF FRANCE

The north of France, Alsace, Lorraine, Franche-Comté, and the region of Lyons saw industrial output grow vigorously in the nineteenth century, along with continuity of powerful entrepreneurial dynasties. The two phenomena are correlated: because industry benefited from the presence of a middle class durably committed to the technological and commercial adventure, it was able to resist successive crises. The capacity of regional employers to pass their companies from one generation to the next was one of the hidden faces of French economic performance.

Entrepreneurship does not only lie in creating new enterprises. It lies also in developing inherited enterprise and in maintaining and using the family fortune effectively. Employers' dynasties that reached or exceeded four generations are not distributed in a random way on the map of France. One finds them only at some very special locations. Thus, the principal employers' dynasties of northern and eastern France were at the origin of companies of world notoriety. Families like Motte, Danel, Schlumberger, Dollfus-Mieg, de Dietrich, Peugeot, or de Wendel originated in a surprisingly small number of localities: Lille, Roubaix, Tourcoing in the north; Guebwiller, Mulhouse, Strasbourg in Alsace; Montbéliard in the Franche-Comté; or

Lyons. The majority of these enterprises under the Second Empire belonged to families that had maintained their industrial activity over at least four successive generations (Stoskopf 1994, 32), in contrast to Normandy. The old Alsatian industrial dynasty de Dietrich had ruled its family enterprise since 1685 and is today at its tenth generation of entrepreneurs. The Koechlin family displays thirteen entrepreneurs of the sixth or seventh generation, the Schlumberger family, ten; the Dollfus family, two (Hau and Stoskopf 2005, 525–45).

In the matter of religion, one will note that entrepreneurship was especially developed in minority groups tardily integrated into French society: the Protestants and the Jews. Such families as Hottinguer, Mallet, Vernes, and Odier were Protestants from Switzerland, often of Huguenot origin. Jews of Rhenish origin, such as the families Worms and Rothschild, were among the most important in Paris. From the end of the eighteenth century, they constituted the *haute banque* and played an essential role in the development of railroads and large-scale industry. This "outside" contribution confirms the inhibiting aspect of official power and political centralization already observed on the geographical level.

THE TRADITION OF URBAN AUTONOMY IN THE RECENTLY INTEGRATED PROVINCES

The map of the most dynamic French industrial centers shows that the entrepreneurship was more active in the provinces of the north and the east, that is, the communities most tardily integrated into the French nation. They had not belonged before to a great centralized state and had maintained longer than elsewhere the medieval tradition of urban autonomy.

The north of France, which was attached to the Duchy of Burgundy at the end of the Middle Ages, formed part of the Rhenish area, where European technological innovation mainly developed. Industrial employers were drawn primarily from the patriciates of these cities. These territories were incorporated by Louis XIV into France: Artois in 1659 and Lille in 1668. The "capitulations" then authorized by the king made it possible for the cities of the area to preserve some autonomy. At the end of the eighteenth century, metallurgy and cotton spinning developed there in large manufactures.

The same applies to the east of France. The employer's dynasties of Alsace and Franche-Comté started as lines of municipal notables, sometimes two centuries before they created industrial companies. Strasbourg, free city of the empire, had negotiated its absorption by the Kingdom of France in 1681 by safeguarding multiple religious, institutional, and linguistic freedoms. Lorraine was attached to France only in 1766. Mulhouse, a small republic allied with the Swiss cantons, had waited until 1798 before being incorporated in the French Republic. Montbéliard, principality attached to Wurtemberg, was integrated into France only with the treaty of Lunéville, in 1801. Like all the Rhenish populations, these bourgeoisies had never benefited from the protection of a great centralized state and were accustomed to count, above all, on themselves.

FAMILY STRUCTURES INFLUENCED BY THE MODEL OF THE STEM FAMILY

As we have seen, a very clear opposition existed between the behavior of the Norman businessmen on the one hand, and those of northern and eastern France on the other. At the beginning of the nineteenth century, Normandy was the leading French industrial area. But Norman employers were not much inclined to remain in industry.

Their companies changed hands, and the fortunes made in industry were thereafter invested in land and buildings. The scarcity of industrial dynasties in Normandy can be related to the prevalence of looser family structures, those of the nuclear family. At their majority, children felt themselves less bound by obligations to their parents and their family heritages.

In contrast, the principal force of the employers of the north and east lay in the cohesion and extent of the family bonds. Emmanuel Todd puts the north and east of France in the "stem family" areas (1990, 62). This type of family emphasizes parental authority, which prevails even after the children reach adulthood. The consequence was the success of companies, often called "houses," over several generations. There was clear identification between family and company. This almost always took the form of a partnership, combining a limited number of shareholders bound by the closest family ties: father and son, brothers, father and son-in-law, and so on. The transformation of these firms into limited companies occurred only after 1870, when and if funds were available; or in Alsace, to allow those of the heirs who did not want to assume German nationality to resell their share to those relatives who remained. But the shift to limited liability long remained a matter of form and masked continued family control, often for decades. These families were often large: in 30 percent of the cases, in the north, the households of entrepreneurs counted six or more children (Barbier 1989, 14). These big families wove among them multiple matrimonial bonds that made it possible to limit the wasting of fortunes and decline of training. Companies resting on less prolific families had to find external collaborators, and these could leave much to be desired, especially in matters of loyalty and remuneration.

THE INFLUENCE OF RELIGION ON ECONOMIC PERFORMANCE

In Normandy, many entrepreneurs experienced a weakening of Catholic faith toward the end of the eighteenth century. This change was often accompanied by liberation from rules of conduct now perceived as unnecessarily constraining. Only one-tenth of Norman entrepreneurs engaged in religious activities (Barjot 1991, 234). Compare the north, which remained under the influence of a rigorous Catholicism (Barbier 1989, 6; Darnton 1983, 195), and the east, faithful to Protestantism or Judaism.

Politically, the businessmen of the north were conservative, even reactionary, and few engaged in scientific studies: the influence of Catholicism worked against the Enlightenment. The major figures financed Catholic charities, and some of the children entered the clergy. The case of the banker Auguste Scalbert is typical: two of his six sons entered the clergy and three banking (Barbier 1989, 30; Hirsch 1991). What is more, the Catholicism of the north was significantly different from that of most of France. The towns of Roubaix and Tourcoing were strongly influenced in the eighteenth century by Jansenism, a belief system that stressed individual ethics and behavior more than sacramental practices (Delsalle 1987, 149–56). The same can be said about the Catholic families of silk merchants of Lyon: the family Berliet belonged to the "Petite Eglise" (Little Church), which did not accept the concordat of 1801 between the pope and Napoleon (Angleraud and Pellissier 2003, 161). The strength of these employers lay in their ethic of work and saving.

In Alsace and Franche-Comté, the largest and most durable dynasties were Protestant (Schlumberger, Koechlin, Dollfus, Peugeot) or Jewish (Dreyfus, Bloch, Blin). These minority entrepreneurs developed prosperous firms in cotton or wool spinning and mastered the printing of all kinds of textiles. They also created an industry for building machines. In Alsace, neither Protestantism nor Judaism had any problem with rationalist thought. The Reformation, because it shook the authority of tradition, encouraged more favorable attitudes to scientific advances. Hence the scientific leaning of Mulhousian bourgeois. The Koechlin and Dollfus families were descended from the famous mathematician Johann Bernouilli, and their dynasties would go on to marry with such scientific families as the Curies and the Friedels. Some of these entrepreneurs were also seen as first-rate scientists as, for example, Daniel Dollfus-Ausset and his cousin Daniel Koechlin (Mieg 1948, 32; Hau 1987, 476–80; Hau and Stoskopf 2005, 479–92). The Mulhousian manufacturers founded in 1826 the Société industrielle de Mulhouse, which promoted technological progress in Alsace by the way of conferences and publications. Science also drew in some of the Protestant metallurgists. Thus Philippe-Frédéric de Dietrich was known at the end of the eighteenth century for his works on mineralogy and metallurgy.

The same can be said about the Jewish entrepreneurs. Judaism had always insisted on the obligation, for each believer, to study the holy scriptures and the Law, which meant a duty to read and remember. This led to a community attentive to and respectful of science. This parallelism of attitudes between Jews and Protestants owed much to the mutual esteem of the two communions, particularly at Mulhouse.

As one might expect, the values that Max Weber described as favorable to the growth of capitalism, namely work and thrift, were those most honored by the employers of eastern France (Weber 1905). Among Alsatian entrepreneurs, work was seen as an absolute virtue; wealth did not exempt one from the duty to work. Many Alsatian businessmen stayed at the head of their firms until death; or they retired to do research. The same for frugal living. Thus, Normandy was much more corrupted by Parisian values than Alsace (Chaline 1988, 200). Mulhousians kept the memory of the sumptuary laws that had ruled their city before its absorption into France. Frugality in turn fostered the accumulation of considerable financial resources (Hau 1987, 348–54.).

DISCIPLES OF SAINT-SIMON AND THE BELIEF IN SCIENTIFIC AND TECHNOLOGICAL PROGRESS

On the national level, an influential group, the disciples of the comte de Saint-Simon (died 1825), promoted entrepreneurship and industrialization. The Comte had a strong faith in science. He thought that economic development would eliminate poverty and that the world of the future should be governed by scientists and engineers. The best way to do this would be to transfer wealth from the unproductive aristocracy to the productive class, the employers. His ideas were very popular among the students of French engineering schools and among Parisian bankers. His disciples, engineers like Paulin Talabot and businessmen like the brothers Emile and Isaac Pereire, tirelessly promoted his ideas in journal articles. Whereas some economists stressed the need to preserve the craft system in order to maintain France's competitive advantage in the luxury trades, the Saint-Simonians argued that France's long-term prosperity depended on following Britain into mechanized factory production.

Large Companies in Railroads, Banking, and Trade after 1850

During the years 1850–75, France effected a dual revolution in transport and banking that made possible the full maturation of merchant and finance capitalism, and the flowering of industrial capitalism.

Railroads were the work of private companies because the French government would not take a responsibility for building railroads similar to the responsibility it had taken for roads or canals. The Alsatian industrialist Nicolas Koechlin devoted all his wealth to building a line in 1844 from Strasbourg to Basel. A company dominated by James de Rothschild built in 1846 the line from Paris to Lille. Some Parisian bankers (the *haute banque*) joined with young promoters to found other railway companies. In the 1840s, only 12 percent of the railway shares being offered were actually subscribed: the government refused to guarantee a minimum return on their bonds. In January 1848, France had only 1,860 km of rail line as against 5,900 in Great Britain. But after the election of Louis Napoleon Bonaparte as president of the Second Republic, the government reconceived the legal basis for railroad construction. The extension of concessions to ninety-nine years gave more time to recoup investments, and the French state now guaranteed interest on railroad bonds. In less than twenty years, France built a world-class network. Capitalized at 400 million francs and operating 4,010 km of line, the Paris-Lyons-Marseilles (PLM) company, under the direction of Paulin Talabot, was the largest corporation in France.

After 1850, a cohort of Saint-Simonian bankers founded a new kind of joint-stock investment bank, which transformed France's financial landscape (Stoskopf 2002, 44–48). The Saint-Simonians had concluded that the most efficient way to mobilize capital was to set up limited-liability joint-stock companies that could issue shares or bonds in denominations small enough to draw the savings of the middle class. Under the French commercial code, in effect since 1808, such a company required the approval of the Conseil d'Etat. But Louis Napoleon favored such companies, and in 1867 their creation became totally free.

The decisive step toward transforming the banking system was the foundation of the Crédit Mobilier in 1852. This bank, under the brothers Emile and Isaac Pereire (from the Jewish community of Bordeaux), mobilized unprecedented amounts of capital to launch an array of subsidiaries in France: railroads (the PLM among others), steamship lines, insurance companies, engineering and construction firms, industrial enterprises, and so on. It also led to the creation of a whole phalanx of new joint-stock banks. These promoted industrialization not only in France but in all continental Europe. In the financial downturn of 1866–67, the brothers Pereire took heavy losses and were obliged to shrink their company considerably.

In the meantime, however, other joint-stock banks had won official approval: The first was the Comptoir d'Escompte de Paris, founded in 1848 with semipublic status and converted in 1854 into a conventional joint-stock institution specializing in overseas trade (Bonin 1991). The second, Crédit Industriel et Commercial, was created in 1859 to finance the daily movement of goods by discounting bills of exchange and warehouse warrants. It then moved into financing overseas trade, especially in Asia, which led to the founding in 1875, in collaboration with the Comptoir d'Escompte, of the Banque d'Indochine (Meuleau 1990). A third, destined to be even more important than the others, was the Crédit Lyonnais, the only one of these originating outside of Paris, founded by silk merchants and local bankers from Lyons and Geneva. Its Paris branch soon overshadowed the home office and became in 1882 the bank's headquarters. A fourth, the Société Générale, was founded in 1864. Once launched, it moved beyond investment banking into deposit banking, leading to a large network of branches in Paris and throughout the country. Finally we have the Banque de Paris et des Pays-Bas, founded in 1872 by the merger of two Paris firms. This bank did not aim at the larger public, but rather at a select clientele of investment bankers, moving them from family capitalism into a corporate age. It was in effect France's first *banque d'affaires* (investment bank).

In 1860 the French government, following the advice of the Alsatian industrialist Jean Dollfus, felt France strong enough to sign a free-trade treaty with Great Britain. This constituted a major change from generations of high protection. This treaty was followed by others with European neighbors. France was the second exporter of manufactures in the world behind Great Britain. Most of these were silk and woolen textiles and the so called *articles de Paris*: jewels, perfumes, fashions, furniture, and other luxury articles.

The Employers of the Second Industrialization (1870–1940)

Economic Deceleration, 1870–1880

French industry suffered much from the great depression of the end of the nineteenth century, yielding a hecatomb of small companies using the traditional techniques. Some of these firms were using methods that went back to the time of proto-industrialization. Normandy and Picardy saw decline accelerate (Cailly 1993; Barjot 1991; Chaline 1982; Leménorel 1988; Armengaud 1960; Terrier 1996; Johnson 1995). In addition, until the nineties, the government was financing important military expenses and covering its budget deficit by loans that diverted French savings from business. The Paris joint-stock banks were more and more operating abroad (in eastern Europe, the Mediterranean countries, South America, and so on) and seemed to be losing interest in French enterprise. Yet, as Maurice Lévy-Leboyer (1977a) has shown, the resources invested abroad were in the long run smaller than the incomes they earned. The most important factor of this period is labor hoarding by agriculture (some 40 percent of the French workforce before World War I and yet more than a third before World War II). This was only partly made up by foreign immigration. Even so, modernization of French capitalism continued.

Modernization of French Capitalism

After 1890, the state issued fewer bonds, leaving more room for business investment. Except for the wartime years, the period from 1890 to 1930 was one of rapid growth for French capitalism. The banks financed the industrial firms more and more (Bussière 1995). The failure of the Paris joint-stock banks to support home industry was offset by the activities of a new generation of investment and regional banks.[1] But industrial growth met new obstacles: a tougher, more contentious labor movement; and growing criticism by intellectuals.

THE GROWTH OF LARGE INDUSTRIAL FIRMS

Entrepreneurship was dynamic in a few regions. In Lorraine and the north, the iron industry was growing fast. In the Franche-Comté, industry moved to clocks and automobiles (Daumas 2004a; Olivier 2004; Lamard 1988, 1996). Around Paris we find a diversity of manufactures (autos, chemicals, electrical engineering). The same for Lyons: autos, chemicals, photography. Ports like Marseilles (Raveux 1998; Chastagnaret and Mioche 1998), Le Havre, and Nantes (Pétré-Grenouilleau 2003) processed raw materials.

And so in the late nineteenth century, France built up a roster of large corporate enterprises that would dominate the home economy and project France's influence throughout the world. Many of these companies were founded after 1890, especially in such new industries as autos, electrical engineering, and chemicals. For autos, we have Berliet at Lyons, Peugeot near Montbéliard, Citroen and Renault in Paris (Fridenson 1998; Schweitzer 1992; Fridenson 2001; Moine 1989; Baudant 1980). They had their own funds and good bank credit. They also found eager customers. There was a great incentive to use this new invention in France, because the good quality of the main roads made it possible to drive fast. In February 1899, the brothers Marcel and Fernand Renault created their auto company. In 1905, the firm received an order for 250 taxis, the beginning of mass production. In 1919, the company reorganized on the American model and limited subcontracting to a minimum. And in 1937, the brothers opened a large plant in Boulogne-Billancourt, a suburb of Paris (Fridenson 1998; Loubet 1990, 1999, 2001; Gueslin 1993). French autos proved popular abroad as well as at home: until 1929 France was the biggest car exporter in the world. France was a leader in other industries as well. At Lyons, the brothers Auguste and Louis Lumiere invented the cinematograph in 1895. To develop and exploit this invention, they helped to found the Pathé cinematograph company which made movies for the general public. In 1904, they founded their first foreign subsidiary, Lumiere North America. Other big firms were Air Liquide (Jemain 2002), Fougerolle and Eiffel (civil engineering) (Barjot 1989, 1992, 1993, 2003), Gillet (artificial silk), the Bon Marché and other big retail stores. Gustave Eiffel and Maurice Koechlin finished their Paris tower in time to commemorate the first centenary of the Revolution. The relatively high price of coal in France gave an incentive to develop the technologies of hydroelectricity. Péchiney became an important firm in electrometallurgy (Barjot, Morsel, and Coeuré 2001; Vuillermot 2001; Joly et al. 2002; Le Roux 1998; Torres 1992; Smith 2001).

Although French capitalism was planting itself in eastern Europe, Africa, and Asia (Bonin 1987), French firms were still smaller than American, British, or German ones. The biggest French company, Saint-Gobain (glass and chemicals) amounted to a twentieth of U.S. Steel. Schneider, which made arms and weapons, equaled a fifth of Krupp; Thomson-Houston a sixth of Siemens (Verley 1994, 194).

The French big businesses called more and more on outsider engineers and managers to direct the enterprise (Meuleau 1995). After World War I, more than half of the managers of big enterprises were graduates of engineering schools (Lévy-Leboyer 1979, 152; Thépot 1985; Belhoste 1995). The high level of the new techniques and the cooperation between government and the private sector during the war accelerated this tendency in the 1920s.

GROWTH AND SPECIALIZATION IN BANKING

The banking sector offered an ever-wider array of services to their expanding clientele. Before World War I, the Crédit Lyonnais had become the biggest bank in Europe (Cassis 1997, 240–47). The Paris joint-stock banks were operating increasingly outside the country. They financed foreign governments and serviced French business abroad. They were the strongest banks in eastern Europe, the Mediterranean, and South America. But they were weak in the biggest and most expansive market, the United States. A long-standing criticism is that, after 1873, they deprived the home economy of resources by putting money in unproductive foreign loans. But historians are now inclined to see this as a response to declining home demand for railroads and other public installations and have shown that between 1873 and 1914, the yield on external investments widely surpassed the total of foreign investments (Lévy-Leboyer 1977b). Besides, this failure of Paris banks to support home industry after 1870 was offset by a new generation of investment banks such as the Banque Suisse et Francaise (which later became the Crédit Commercial de France) and by regional banks (Lescure and Plessis 2004).

MODERNIZATION IN THE COMMERCIAL SECTOR

Wholesale trade was largely transformed by the rise of specialized commodity traders in staples and industrial raw materials, and of middlemen trading in manufactures. Paris and big provincial cities saw the installation of department and chain stores. The most famous was Le Bon Marché, founded in 1872 by Aristide Boucicaut, established in the world's largest commercial structure. Costs were cut by sending buyers directly to manufacturers. In some cases (ready-made clothing), the *grands magasins* became their own manufacturers and suppliers.

New Obstacles to the Entrepreneurship in France after 1870

THE NEW REPUBLICAN POLITICAL LEADERSHIP

During the Second Empire, the high bourgeoisie was very active politically, and some entrepreneurs sat in the Parliament. Under the Third Republic, representatives of the liberal professions and public officials took their place. Ignorant of the needs imposed by international competition and afraid of fast industrialization, they led the French electorate to fear big business. The *parti radical*, which became the leading political party at the start of the twentieth century, made it its goal protection and preservation of small producers. It became a force for economic conservatism, but it also promoted the creation of many small firms. Before World War I, France, a nation of small farms, knew millions of these tiny industrial units, many of them individual entrepreneurs. In 1906, 71 percent of the plants in the craft and industrial sector were individual enterprises, employing 21 percent of the industrial workforce. The domestic system continued to dominate industries like clothing. In 1935, the French government protected small shops by discouraging the creation of supermarkets. In this way, France remained a nation of small independent producers—not efficient perhaps, but socially egalitarian.

A Rightist Anticapitalism: Anti-Semitism

The great industrial families were resented by the reactionary elements of French society. The big employers were often members of religious minorities, Protestant or Jewish. Their attempts to enter the social elite, for example the corps of army officers, met with resentment and hostility. This was the making of the infamous Dreyfus affair, in which a French officer from a Jewish entrepreneurial family was unjustly accused and convicted of spying for Germany. The French found it hard to understand the quick enrichment of Protestant and Jewish families, just as they found it hard to comprehend the fast rise of German power, or of the Anglo-Saxon countries. French reactionaries were quick to blame France's loss of power and position on the supposed defects of republican government. Anti-Semitism gave force to this attitude by blaming failings on the Jews.

Anarchism and Marxism

French trade unionism was invested in the 1880s by revolutionaries, often of anarchistic inspiration. They thought industrial disputes should aim less at limited improvement than at major confrontations with the bourgeoisie. This attitude substantially radicalized labor relations. In those areas where workers lived—harbors, mining basins, city suburbs—labor relations grew embittered. Strikes and violence reached a peak in 1906. But the strikes of 1936 proved more costly to employers because the workers occupied the factories and mills and the government (the Front Populaire) did not intervene against these occupations.

Anticapitalism of the left also spread in intellectual circles. From the 1890s teachers at the Ecole Normale Supérieure, who set the tone among French intellectual elites, spread a climate of hostility to businessmen, especially the richest of them, called by the Left *les 200 familles*, and accused of them of undermining the French currency as a way of discrediting the leftist government.

A Withdrawal into the Home Market

The second industrialization of France proceeded in a difficult social and economic context. Growth had slowed after 1860, owing to decline of the birthrate, the narrowness of the home market, and the swollen, unproductive agricultural sector. After World War I, mass production suffered from inadequate demand. The standard of living was half the American, and 70 percent of the population lived in small towns and villages of less than 20,000 inhabitants (Lévy-Leboyer 1996, 18).

After 1871, industry also suffered from the loss of Alsace and its enterprising businessmen. Some of these re-created industrial firms in the Vosges or in Normandy, but most of them were lost to Germany. Some left for other countries—thus Koechlin to Switzerland and Schlumberger to France and America. But the defeat of 1871 diverted many brave children of these families to military careers. With the Alsatians gone, the most conservative elements of the French *patronat* regained their influence. The free-trade treaties of the 1860s were called into question by employers' associations (Lambert-Dansette 2000, 136). The spirit of protection returned. But the big companies remained, open to the larger world. The biggest handicap for industrial exporters came from agricultural protectionism. Thus concern for grape growers blocked industrial agreements with the countries of eastern and southern Europe and left the field to German exporters (Poidevin 1995).

The Golden Age of Dirigisme (1940–1983)

Bases of French Neo-Colbertism

From the 1930s French industrial investment shrank sharply. Capacities for modernization were much reduced. Meanwhile the new dictatorships in Nazi Germany, fascistic Italy, and Soviet Russia boasted of real or alleged achievements. Would-be French "modernizers" denounced the real or supposed routine of family capitalism, calling for an alliance of big business and the state and even a recourse to economic planning. The defeat of 1940 gave these modernizers access to power. Many served the Vichy regime and only later joined the Resistance (if they ever did), so that the Liberation regime was on many points continuing actions and programs begun under Vichy.

The Liberation regime was the product of a compromise between the two greatest Resistance forces, the Gaullists and the Communists. The latter gave up their arms in exchange for a wide program of business nationalization and control of major public-sector trade unions. This public sector, in turn, controlled such areas as scientific research, education, coal mining, the press, output of electricity, rail transports, seaports, and postal and telephone services.

Coal, electricity, gas, nuclear energy, oil, railroads, aeronautics, most of the big Parisian banks and the Renault auto plants were nationalized. This pleased the "modernizers," who thought that only the state could promote modernization (Andrieu and Van-Lemesle 1987; Kuisel 1984; Picard, Beltran, and Bungener 1985; Jeanneney 1959; Desjardins et al. 2002). At the head of the nationalized companies, the government placed graduates of the engineering schools, new young elites, aspirants to social progress.

A four-year plan (after 1966, five-year plans) made it possible for French businessmen to pursue their goals for development. And after the fifth plan (1966–70), the growing importance of international trade freed French firms from dependence on the plan, whose aims concerned above all domestic demand.

Constraints on Private Firms

From 1945, taxes weighed heavily on private firms, which largely paid the cost of the new social security: family allowances, accident insurance, health and old age coverage, contributions to transport and housing costs; plus, after 1958, unemployment insurance and, after 1971, contribution to employee training.

The government now held a wide range of financial instruments for intervening in the economy. Price controls were instituted from 1939, with opportunities for dialogue between businesspeople and the administration. Credit control was also introduced with the nationalization of the Banque de France, of the four big deposit banks, and of the major insurance companies. Note also that the state controlled other financial establishments: the Caisse des Dépots et Consignations, which manages the deposits of notaries and savings banks (Aglan, Margairaz, and Verheyde

2003); the Crédit National (created in 1919 for reconstruction); the Crédit Foncier de France; and the Crédit Agricole. Finally, in 1948, the state created the Fonds de Modernisation et d'Equipement to allocate Marshall Plan aid. This fund was supplemented after 1955 by the state-financed Fonds de Développement Economique et Social. In this way, the Ministry of Finances, heart of the French administrative elite, was able to direct much of the country's investment (Quennouëlle-Corre 2000). Railways, electricity, and coal mines received huge, state-of-the-art equipment. French trains became some of the fastest in the world and the power stations of Electricité de France some of the most productive.

By comparison, private financing was weak. Price control hurt, and in contrast with the 1920s, the stock exchange did little. French companies had little recourse to new shares or bonds because of monetary depreciation and the competition of government loans. So only bank financing was left. After 1945, the preferred choice was medium-term (five years) credit. French companies were financially fragile.

The socialist nationalizations of 1981 moved more capital into government hands. The state share of the industrial labor force went from 6 percent to 19 percent, and it controlled 90 percent of bank deposits. Now the state controlled thirteen of the twenty biggest companies in the country. The state increased the capital of these companies and subsidized those in difficulty: Bull, Rhone-Poulenc, Thomson, Pechiney, and so forth. At its maximum in 1985, government share of the capital of the French companies was 10 percent.

French Entrepreneurship, 1940–1983

French employers were not afraid of decolonization (Marseille 2004; Eck 2003; Fridenson 1994). But they were worried about lower customs duties and the elimination of import quotas, which left them in naked competition with a German industry paying lower social contributions and taxes. As in 1860, a goodly share of French employers, above all the heads of small firms, were opposed to lower protection. When in 1959, General de Gaulle, in fulfillment of treaty obligations, instituted free currency convertibility, an end to import quotas, and a first fall in the customs dues, he made a lot of people unhappy.

Big business continued to be tied to the state, where it found its top executives (some thousands of individuals) (Bauer and Bertin-Mourot 1997) recruited from the top engineering schools.[2] This was the French ruling class. It had known defeat in 1940 and shared the point of view of the historian Marc Bloch: "What was defeated is our dear small town" (Bloch 1995, 182; Daumard 1987, 380). France had not been enough industrialized to face successfully the new German army. Now it was time to catch up with other advanced countries, to make up for lost time. Georges Pompidou, prime minister from 1962 to 1968 and president of the Republic from 1969 to 1974, then Valéry Giscard d'Estaing, president from 1974 to 1981, were part of this meritocratic, ambitious world, because they resulted quite from the same meritocracy (Ecole Normale Supérieure was Pompidou's school and Polytechnique was that of Giscard d'Estaing) (Fridenson 1997, 219). None saw any reason for economic growth to slow. In a revival of Saint-Simonian spirit, Pierre Massé, *commissaire au Plan* (chief of the Planning Commission), optimistically anticipated: "The mean standard of living can double in twenty years and perhaps even faster if our mastery of technology and economics continues to grow" (Massé 1965, 89).

During World War II, French industrial technology seriously lagged. From 1948, French engineers and entrepreneurs made organized five-week trips to the United States to learn new production and management techniques (Barjot 2002). During the 1950s, 267 such productivity missions comprised some 2,600 participants. After 1960, the continuing flow of American investment entailed transfer of American economic and technical methods to France.

Indeed, the years of the Pompidou government and presidency saw France's most brilliant economic performance ever. Between 1962, when France rid itself of the burden of war in Algeria, and 1974, when it ran into its first oil crisis, gross domestic product grew 5.2 percent in annual average. Many left agriculture for industry: during the 1970s, the agricultural sector fell to under 10 percent of the workforce. Engineers confidently made plans, with the confidence that the state would help carry them out. State and elites had grand visions. The generations formed just before the war or during the German occupation were reacting against the narrow vision of their predecessors. So France in 1969 saw the launching of the Airbus, the first flight of the supersonic Anglo-French Concorde, and the first two experimental cars of the high-speed train (TGV) (Lachaume 1986). In 1971, the first entirely digitalized phone exchange began operation in the Breton town of Perros-Guirec. And 1973 saw the start of the European space launcher Ariane.

That same year, a European agreement led to creation in France of a factory for uranium enrichment for civil reactors. This was followed by construction of nuclear power stations, to the point where France was getting three-quarters of its electrical supply from this source—more than any other country. The French firm Framatome (later renamed Areva) became a rival of Westinghouse on the international market. That was France's answer to oil crisis (Beltran 1985).

The Policy of Creating "National Champions"

Meanwhile the French government encouraged mergers to build larger companies, "national champions" of European (continental) size. The aim was to defend French firms against foreign penetration, and the result was the formation of diversified conglomerates. In oil, the merger of several state-owned firms led to the creation of Elf. In banking, the fusion between the Banque Nationale pour le Commerce et l'Industrie and the Comptoir d'Escompte de Paris gave the Banque Nationale de Paris; at the same time the big Parisian banks took over most of the regional banks. In chemicals, the Office National de l'Azote joined with the Potasses d'Alsace to create the Entreprise Miniere et Chimique. In the same way, at the beginning of 1968, a score of small insurance companies created three big groups of European dimensions. The iron and steel industry was soon gathered into two units, Sacilor in the east and Usinor in the north. In electrical engineering, one had the Cie Générale d'Electricité; in telecommunications Alcatel; in electronics Thomson; in aeronautics Aérospatiale (Fridenson 2006b). But these national champions built primarily on size. They paid less attention to competitive choice of investments.

Meanwhile organizational and regulatory innovations (introduction of leasing, creation of a mortgage market, suppression of the exchange control) helped the French financial system make up for lost time. The innovator here was Michel Debré, minister of finance from 1966 to 1968. When France abolished the distinction between deposit and investment banks, it put its financial sector on a better basis

TABLE 11.1
Annual Mean of Creations of Companies

	General partnerships	Limited liability companies	Limited companies
1929–38	1,314	6,223	1,917
1945–54	1,551	17,576	923
1955–64	1,087	8,231	3,726

Source: Caron 1981, 215.

than those of its neighbors, except for that of the United Kingdom. Yet the money market remained stodgy: too much of it rested on bond issues—some 70 percent in 1970. For all this period, the money market generated only 10 percent of company finance.

This pattern of state-controlled development did well until 1974. In that year, output per man-hour was higher in France than in Federal Republic Germany or in Great Britain. No wonder French elites stuck to these arrangements (Maddison 2006, 353). Besides, they liked the power and place state control gave to them as elites.

The Rise of a Capitalism Independent of the State

Is this to say there was no autonomous capitalism in those years? No. A private sector emerged in the manufacture and sale of consumer goods. Thus, with bank support, we have a new agribusiness in the agricultural and food sector (Bonin 2005). The Danone group was originally created by Gervais and then bought up by the glass group Boussois-Souchon-Neuvesel. Similar new groups were to be found in building and public works, chemicals, and beauty products. An example is L'Oréal, which began by making scented soaps. Moulinex and SEB specialized successfully in small household electrical devices (Seb 2003; Gaston-Breton and Defever-Kapferer 1999; *Pernod-Ricard* 1999). In autos, Peugeot repurchased Citroen to form the PSA group. All of these companies had extensive recourse to advertising. Such performances call into question the negative appraisal of French small and medium-size companies.

In retail trade, the restrictive legislation protecting small shops was gradually annulled after 1959. Big supermarkets, like Leclerc and Carrefour, appeared. And then the latter invented the biggest form of commercial organization: the hypermarket.

With these new trade giants came a decline in general partnerships and growing recourse to limited liability. The vitality of this capitalism showed in the boom of small enterprises in the years 1945–54, and the boom in limited companies after 1955.

Back to Liberalism (from 1983 to Today)

The Withdrawal of the State

After 1981, the socialist government of François Mitterrand intervened in the economy more than ever. It nationalized the last independent private banks and most of the big industrial firms. But the nationalized firms did not make money and needed more and more state support (Cohen 1989). The debts of the national railways (SNCF) and power supply system (Electricité de France) kept going up, in spite of public subsidies. These nationalized firms created few jobs, and their managements made big mistakes. The worst was the Crédit Lyonnais, which lost a fortune and had to pay a record fine of one billion dollars because of failure to observe American regulations. All of this sounded the knell of Socialist industrial policy.

The turning was March 1983, with the socialists still in power. Faced with rising deficits and a disastrous fall in the exchange value of the franc, the government abandoned its active economic interventionism. The effects were gradual, but the French economy now lined up with those of the liberal economies of western Europe. In 1984 financial circuits were freed up, and wages were no longer indexed on prices. The share of value-added going to wages reached a maximum of 68 percent in 1983, then fell fast to less than 60 percent. In 1984, the metallurgical group Creusot-Loire had huge losses. This was the largest French group in fine steel and machinery and employed 23,000 workers. After much hesitation, the government decided to abandon support, and the group failed financially in 1984.

The elections of 1986 brought the Right back to power. It decided on full price freedom and took the state out of thirteen big financial and industrial firms, including all the banks nationalized in 1945. Carmaker Renault was privatized in 1994. The public financial sector was now limited to the Caisse des Dépots et Consignations, still powerful, and the Post Office. With the launch of the euro in January 1999, France entered European financial circuits.

Even so, the state tried to create two business groups: one composed of the Banque Nationale de Paris, Elf, Saint-Gobain, Pechiney, Suez, and the Union des Assurances de Paris, the other of the Assurances Générales de France, Alcatel, Havas, Paribas, Rhone-Poulenc, the Société Générale, and Total. But this system based on cross participations immobilized large sums and led to undercapitalization of these firms, preventing further mergers and growth. Things broke down in the midnineties. Once again shareholders broke away.

Foreign investors now moved in. By the end of 1999, a little more than half the authorized capital of the largest French firms was held by foreigners (Morin and Rigamonti 2002). Selecting privatization had aimed at protecting French firms from outside takeovers, but it had the opposite effect: it had weakened their capitalization and made them targets. Today France is one of the countries most open to foreign capital. Between 30 and 50 percent of such firms as the Banque Nationale de Paris, the Societé Générale, Alcatel, Axa or Vivendi were in foreign hands in 2005. In 2006 the French government had no way to prevent the Anglo-Indian businessman Mittal from controlling Arcelor, the biggest European steelmaker, built by a merger of firms from France, Luxembourg, and Spain.

Triumph of the Financial Markets

Helped by international economic circumstances, French stock exchange prices were multiplied by four from 1981 to 1987. This was followed by another rise in the 1990s. The stock exchange, which accounted for only 27 percent of the financing of the French economy in the 1980s, accounted for 80 percent in 1997. France was not ready for this revolution. Savings accounted for 15 percent of GDP, but the state diverted them to debt finance. This left the field free to foreign institutional investors. Meanwhile, French institutional investors, like insurance companies, preferred government loans.

Thanks to greater financial freedom, French companies could reduce debt, reinforce capital, and engage in self-financing. Big firms adapted well and began to play a role on world markets. French owners could move freely, globalize, and develop subsidiaries around the world. In 2005, 40 French multinationals were among the first 500 in the world. Among the leaders: LVMH (luxuries) L'Oréal (cosmetics), Danone (dairy products), Vinci (civil engineering), Vivendi (film, music, publishing), Veolia (water treatment), Air France, Areva (nuclear), Air Liquide (industrial gas) or Essilor (eyeglasses). The French did well in publishing, data processing (Marseille and Eveno 2002; Gaston-Breton 1997), hotel trade (Luc 1998), luxury articles (Bergeron 1998; Marseille 1999; Ferrière 1995; Dalle 2001; Dubois 1988), energy engineering, transportation (Barjot 1992, 1993, 2003), or large-scale distribution (Villermet 1991; Chadeau 1995; Petit, Grislain, and Le Blan 1985). American and British investment funds set the example, and French firms were quick to react to market signals in the field of finance. One saw a new type of entrepreneurs, from elsewhere in the world, open to the world. An example is Carlos Ghosn, chairman of Renault. Of Lebanese origin, born in 1954 in Brazil, student at Polytechnique in Paris, he succeeded in 1999 in merging Renault with Nissan and in 2005 became president of the joint company.

The enormous power of the chairmen, characteristic of the French model, was now free of government constraints but responsive to the increasing influence of shareholders. Financial logic in the short run displaced industrial logic in the long run (Trumbull 2004; Fridenson 2006a).

The Persistence of Family Capitalism

The risk of strikes and the load of administrative constraints (such as the thirty-five-hour week, the complexity of the fair labor standards act, corporation taxes, social contributions) continue to discourage company formation in France. France is the European country where creation of companies is seen as most difficult. That is why so many French are now living and working abroad. For example, 200,000 or more live today in London.

During these last years, administrative difficulties have much diminished. Formalities have been regrouped, social security taxes reduced. French companies have moved toward the Anglo-Saxon model and there is more private shareholding. In 2003, 7.2 million French held company shares (one household on four), more than the number of trade unionists. The west of France (Bretagne, the Vendée, Mayenne) is experiencing an economic revival, with much cooperation among medium and small enterprises (Lescure 2002).

Conclusion

France has inherited two traditions: On the one hand, that of a controlled economy led by a monarchical state or later by socialist ideology; on the other, that of market capitalism, especially strong in regions (north and east) and among religious groups (Protestants and Jews) tardily integrated into the larger society.

The administrative and political power of the strongly centralized French state never prevented a substantial group of innovative entrepreneurs from promoting industrialization and technical progress in France. State institutions founded by the Monarchy at the end of the eighteenth century or by the Revolution helped the dissemination of inventions among French manufacturers. But the initiatives came above all from the entrepreneurs. Northern and eastern France as well as Paris were the regions or places where entrepreneurs were the most innovative. It seems that traditions of urban self-government and independence from the centralized state stimulated entrepreneurship.

The role of innovating entrepreneurs was essential in the process of industrialization. Many of the inventors were also industrialists developing each innovation and making it practical for the end-user. For instance, the French locomotive-constructors made engines more coal-sparing than the British, adapting their models to the conditions of a country with expensive coal. Another example is that of the brothers Lumiere: they invented the cinematograph and they helped to found a company to make movies for the general public.

After the Revolution, at the beginning of the nineteenth century, entrepreneurs reached the first rank in the French society. The wealth of the richest entrepreneurs surpassed soon that of the biggest landowners and, after 1830, they were influential at the highest level of the state. But their social climbing was criticized by other elites such as the old aristocracy, and the new intellectual and artistic elites. The process of industrialization itself was disapproved of by a part of public opinion. Until to World War II, many deputies in the French Parliament were reticent about the development of large-scale industry and the growth of vast worker concentrations. The impediments against the diffusion of entrepreneurship in France came above all from right- or left-wing extremists. During the nineteenth century, a part of the elites preferred to pursue a career in public office or in the army rather than enter private industry. But increasingly, things began to change. During the twentieth century, high civil service officers and entrepreneurs, belonging to the same meritocracy, coming from the same engineering schools, merged in a unique ruling class. This trend accelerated after World War II: the French state played an important role in order to promote new technologies, financing huge investments in energy and transports.

Between 1940 and the middle of the 1980s, the political and administrative elites chose the model of a state-controlled economy and tried to develop large national firms. This tendency was reinforced during the first years of socialist government under the presidency of François Mitterrand, from 1981 to 1983. But, after 1983, the French government decided to abandon interventionist policy and returned slowly to liberal rules.

Today it would seem that entrepreneurship in France enters in a new era: entrepreneurs have greatly gained in power. In twenty years, the country has passed from state capitalism to market capitalism. The postwar legacy of "national champions" sees French multinationals working like foreign multinationals. New enterprises have now appeared and are growing. Their biggest task is to grow fast enough not to remain small.

Notes

1 Banque de l'Union Parisienne, Banque Suisse et Française (later renamed Crédit Commercial de France), Banque Internationale de Paris (later renamed Banque française pour le Commerce et l'Industrie), etc.
2 Jean Meynaud estimated their number at 5,000–6,000 (1964, 165).

References

Aerts, Erik, and François Crouzet, eds. 1990. *Economic Effects of the French Revolutionary and Napoleonic Wars: Proceedings of the Tenth International Economic History Congress.* Leuven: Leuven University Press.

Aglan Alya, Michel Margairaz, and Philippe Verheyde, eds. 2003. *La Caisse des Dépôts et Consignations: La Seconde Guerre mondiale et le XXe siècle.* Paris: Albin Michel.

Albert, Michel. 1991. *Capitalisme contre capitalisme.* Paris: Le Seuil.

Amable, Bruno. 2005. *Les Cinq capitalismes: Diversité des systèmes économiques et sociaux dans la mondialisation.* Paris: Le Seuil.

Andrieu, Claire, and Le Van-Lemesle Lucette, eds. 1987. *Les nationalisations de la Libération: De l'utopie au compromis.* Paris: Presses de la Fondation nationale des Sciences politiques.

Angleraud, Bernadette, and Catherine Pélissier. 2003. *Les dynasties lyonnaises.* Paris: Perrin.

Armengaud, André. 1960. "A propos des origines du sous-développement industriel dans le Sud-Ouest." *Annales du Midi* 1:75–81.

Asselain, Jean-Charles. 1984. *Histoire économique de la France du XVIIIe siècle à nos jours.* 2 vols. Paris: Le Seuil.

Barbier, Frédéric, ed. 1989. *Le patronat du Nord sous le Second Empire. Une approche prosopographique.* Geneva: Droz-Champion.

Barjot, Dominique. 1989. *La grande entreprise française de travaux publics, 1883–1974.* Lille: A.N.R.T, Université de Lille III.

———, ed. 1991. *Les patrons du Second Empire. Anjou, Normandie, Maine.* Paris: Picard.

———. 1992. *Fougerolle. Deux siècles de savoir-faire.* Caen: Editions du Lys.

———. 1993. *Travaux publics de France. Un siècle d'entrepreneurs et d'entreprises.* Paris: Presses de l'Ecole des Ponts-et-Chaussées.

———, ed. 2002. *L'americanisation de l'Europe occidentale au XXe siècle: Mythe et réalité.* Paris: Presses de l'Université de Paris–Sorbonne.

———. 2003. *La trace des bâtisseurs. Histoire du groupe Vinci.* Vinci: Rueil-Malmaison.

Barjot, Dominique, Eric Anceau, Isabelle Lescent-Gilles, and Bruno Marnot, eds. 2003. *Les entrepreneurs du Second Empire.* Paris: Presses de l'Université de Paris–Sorbonne.

Barjot, Dominique, Henri Morsel, and Sophie Coeuré. 2001. *Les compagnies électriques et leurs patrons. Stratégies, gestion, management, 1895–1945.* Paris: Fondation Electricité de France.

Baudant, Alain. 1980. *Pont-à-Mousson (1918–1939): Stratégies industrielles d'une dynastie lorraine.* Paris: Publications de la Sorbonne.

Bauer, Michel, and Bénédicte Bertin-Mourot. 1987. *Les 200. Comment devient-on un grand patron?* Paris: Seuil.

———. 1997. *L'ENA est-elle une business school?* Paris: L'Harmattan.

Belhoste, Bruno, ed. 1995. *La France des X, deux siècles d'histoire.* Paris: Economica.

Beltran, Alain. 1985. *Histoire de l'EDF. Comment se sont prises les décisions de 1946 à nos jours.* Paris: Dunod.

Beltran, Alain, Jean-Pierre Daviet, and Michèle Ruffat. 1995. *L'histoire d'entreprise en France. Essai bibliographique.* Paris: Institut d'histoire du temps présent.

Bergeron, Louis. 1998. *Les industries du luxe en France.* Paris: Odile Jacob.

Bloch, Marc. 1995. *L'étrange défaite.* Paris: Folio Histoire.

Bonin, Hubert. 1985. "La Révolution a-t-elle brisé l'esprit d'entreprise?" *L'Information historique* 5:193–204.

———. 1987a. *CFAO (Compagnie française de l'Afrique occidentale). Cent ans de compétition (1887–1987)*. Paris: Economica.

———. 1987b. *Suez. Du canal à la finance (1858–1987)*. Paris: Economica.

———. 1991. "Le Comptoir d'Escompte de Paris: Une banque impériale, 1848–1940." *Revue Française d'Histoire d'Outre-Mer* 78:477–97.

———. 1992. *Une grande entreprise bancaire: Le Comptoir national d'escompte de Paris dans l'entre-deux-guerres*. Paris: Comité pour l'Histoire économique et financière.

———. 1995. *Les groupes financiers français*. Paris: Presses universitaires de France.

———. 1999. *Les patrons du Second Empire. Bordeaux et la Gironde*. Paris: Picard.

———. 2001. *La Banque de l'Union Parisienne. Histoire de la deuxième banque d'affaires française (1874/1904–1974)*. Paris: P.L.A.G.E.

———. 2005. *Les coopératives laitières du grand Sud-Ouest (1893–2005)*. Paris: P.L.A.G.E.

Breton, Yves, Albert Broder, and Michel Lutfalla, eds. 1997. *La longue stagnation en France. L'autre grande dépression, 1873–1897*. Paris: Economica.

Bussière, Eric. 1992. *Paribas, l'Europe et le monde, 1872–1992*. Anvers: Fonds Mercator.

———. 1995. "Paribas and the Rationalization of the French Electricity Industy, 1900–1930." In *Management and Business in Britain and France: The Age of the Corporate Economy*, ed. Youssef Cassis, François Crouzet, and Terry Gourvish, 204–13. Oxford: Clarendon Press.

Butel, Paul. 1991. *Les dynasties bordelaises, de Colbert à Chaban*. Paris: Perrin.

Cailly, Claude. 1993. *Mutations d'un espace proto-industriel: Le Perche aux XVIIIe–XIXe siècles*. Lille: A.N.R.T, Université de Lille III.

Cameron, Rondo. 1971. "L'esprit d'entreprise." In *La France et le développement économique de l'Europe, 1800–1914*. Paris: Le Seuil.

Carlier, Claude. 1992. *Marcel Dassault: La légende du siècle*. Paris: Perrin.

———. 2003. *Matra, la volonté d'entreprendre. De Matra à EADS*. Paris: Editions du Chêne-Hachette.

Caron, François. 1981. *Histoire économique de la France XIXe–XXe siecles*. Paris: Armand Colin.

———, ed. 1983. *Entreprises et entrepreneurs XIXe–XXe siècles*. Paris: Presses de l'Université Paris–Sorbonne.

———. 1995. *Histoire économique de la France, XIXe–XXe siècles*. 2nd ed. Paris: Armand Colin.

Carter, Edward C., ed. 1976. *Enterprise and Entrepreneurs in Nineteenth- and Twentieth-Century France*. Baltimore: John Hopkins University Press.

Cassis, Youssef. 1997. *Big Business: The European Experience in the Twentieth Century*. Oxford: Oxford University Press.

Cassis, Youssef, François Crouzet, and Terry Gourvish, eds. 1995. *Management and Business in Britain and France: The Age of the Corporate Economy*. Oxford: Clarendon Press.

Caty, Roland, Eliane Richard, and Pierre Echinard. 1999. *Les patrons du Second Empire. Marseille*. Paris: Picard.

Cayez, Pierre. 1988. *Rhône-Poulenc, 1895–1975. Contribution à l'étude d'un groupe industriel*. Paris: Armand Colin-Masson.

Cazes, Bernard, and Philippe Mioche. 1990. *Modernisation ou décadence. Contribution à l'histoire du Plan Monnet et de la planification en France*. Aix-Marseille: Publications de l'Université de Provence.

Chadeau, Emmanuel. 1987. *L'industrie aéronautique en France, 1900–1950*. Paris: Fayard.

———. *L'économie du risque*. 1988. *Les entrepreneurs de 1850 à 1980*. Paris: Olivier Orban.

———. 1995. "Mass Retailing: A Last Chance for the Family Firm in France, 1945–1990?" In *Management and Business in Britain and France: The Age of the Corporate Economy*, ed. Youssef Cassis, François Crouzet, and Terry Gourvish, 52–71. Oxford: Clarendon Press.

Chaline, Jean-Pierre. 1982. *Les bourgeois de Rouen: Une élite urbaine au XIXe siècle*. Paris: Presses de la FNSP.

———. 1988. "Idéologie et mode de vie du monde patronal haut-normand sous le Second Empire." *Annales de Normandie*, May–July.

Chassagne, Serge. 1991. *Le coton et ses patrons en France, 1760–1840*. Paris: EHESS.

Chastagnaret, Gérard, and Philippe Mioche, eds. 1998. *Histoire industrielle de la Provence*. Aix-Marseille: Publications de l'Université de Provence.

Cohen, Elie.1989. *L'Etat brancardier. Politiques du déclin industriel (1974–1984)*. Paris: Calmann-Lévy.

Cohen, Elie, and Michel Bauer. 1985. *Les grandes manoeuvres industrielles*. Paris: Belfond.

Crouzet, François. 1959. "Les origines du sous-développement economique du Sud-Ouest." *Annales du Midi* 1:1–79.

———. 1989. "Les conséquences économiques de la Révolution française. Réflexions sur un débat." In "Révolution de 1789, guerres et croissance économique," ed. Jean-Charles Asselain. *Revue économique* 40:1189–1203.

Dalle, Francois. 2001. *L'aventure L'Oréal*. Paris: Odile Jacob.

Darnton, Robert. 1983. *Boheme littéraire et Revolution: Le monde des livres au XVIIIe siècle*. Paris: Gallimard.

Daumard, Adeline. 1987. *Les bourgeois et la bourgeoisie en France depuis 1815*. Paris: Aubier.

Daumas, Jean-Claude, ed. 2004a. *Les systèmes productifs dans l'Arc jurassien. Acteurs, pratiques et territoires (XIXe–XXe siècles)*. Besançon: Presses Universitaires de Franche-Comté.

———. 2004b. *Les Territoires de la laine. Histoire de l'industrie lainière en France au XIXe siècle*. Villeneuve d'Ascq: Presses Universitaires du Septentrion.

Daviet, Jean-Pierre. 1989. *Une multinationale à la française. Histoire de Saint-Gobain, 1665–1989*. Paris: Fayard.

Delsalle, Paul. 1987. *Tourcoing sous l'Ancien Régime*. Lille: Impr. du Siècle.

Desjardins, Bernard, Michel Lescure, Roger Nougaret, Alain Plessis, and André Straus. 2002. *Le Crédit lyonnais, 1863–1986. Etudes historiques*. Geneva: Droz.

Dubois, Paul. 1988. *L'industrie de l'habillement. L'innovation face à la crise*. Paris: La Documentation française.

Eck, Jean-François. 2003. *Les entreprises françaises face à l'Allemagne de 1945 à la fin des années 1960*. Paris: Comité pour l'Histoire économique et financière de la France.

Ferrière, Marc de. 1995. *Christofle: Deux siècles d'aventure industrielle, 1793–1993*. Paris: Le Monde Editions.

Fridenson, Patrick. 1994. "Les patronats allemands et français au XXe siècle. Essai de comparaison." In *Eliten in Deutschland und Frankreich im 19. und 20. Jahrhundert. Strukturen und Beziehungen*, ed. Rainer Hudemann and Georges-Henri Soutou, 153–67. Munich: Oldenburg Verlag.

———. 1997. "France: The Relatively Slow Development of Big Business in the Twentieth Century." In *Big Business and the Wealth of Nations*, ed. Alfred D. Chandler Jr., Franco Amatori, and Takashi Hikino, 207–45. Cambridge: Cambridge University Press.

———. 1998. *Histoire des usines Renault. Naissance de la grande entreprise 1898–1939*. 2nd ed. Paris: Le Seuil.

———, ed. 2001. *Mémoires industrielles II. Berliet, le camion français est né à Lyon*. Paris: Editions de la Maison des Sciences de l'Homme-Syrinx.

———. 2006a. "The Main Changes in the Behavior of French Companies in the Past 25 Years." *Bulletin de la Société franco-japonaise de gestion*, May, 15–25.

———. 2006b. "La multinationalisation des entreprises françaises publiques et privées de 1945 à 1981." In *L'économie française dans la compétition internationale au 20e siècle*, ed. Maurice Lévy-Leboyer, 311–35. Paris: Comité pour l'histoire économique et financière de la France.

Fridenson, Patrick, and André Straus, eds. 1987. *Le capitalisme français XIXe et XXe siècles. Blocages et dynamismes d'une croissance*. Paris: Fayard.

Gaston-Breton, Tristan. 1997. *De Sogeti à Cap Gemini, 1967–1997. 30 ans d'histoire*. Paris: CGS.

———. 1998. *Lesieur. Une marque dans l'histoire, 1908–1998*. Paris: Perrin.

Gaston-Breton, Tristan, and Patricia Defever-Kapferer. 1999. *La magie Moulinex*. Paris: Le Cherche-Midi.

Gille, Bertrand. 1959. *Recherches sur la formation de la grande entreprise capitaliste, 1815–1848*. Paris: SEVPEN.

———. 1968. *La banque et le crédit en France de 1815 à 1848*. Geneva: Droz.

Goyer, Michel. 2003. "Corporate Governance, Employees, and the Focus on Core Competencies in France and Germany." In *Global Markets, Domestic Institutions: Corporate Law and Governance in a New Era of Cross-Border Deals*, ed. Curtis J. Milhaupt, 183–213. New York: Columbia University Press.

———. 2006. "La transformation du gouvernement d'entreprise." In *La France en mutation 1980–2005*, ed. Pepper D. Culpepper, Peter A. Hall, and Bruno Palier, 71–108. Paris: Presses de Sciences Po.

Groethuysen, Bernard. 1927. *Les origines de l'esprit bourgeois en France*. Vol. 1, *L'Eglise et la bourgeoisie*. Paris.

Gueslin, André, ed. 1993. *Michelin, les hommes du pneu, 1889–1940*. Paris: Les Editions de l'Atelier.

Hall, Peter A. 1986. *Governing the Economy: The Politics of State Intervention in Britain and France*. Oxford: Oxford University Press.

Hall, Peter A., and David Soskice. 2001. "An Introduction to Varieties of Capitalism." In *Varieties of Capitalism: The Institutional Foundations of Comparative Advantage*, ed. Peter A. Hall and David Soskice. Oxford: Oxford University Press.

Hancké, Bob. 2002. *Large Firms and Institutional Change: Industrial Renewal and Economic Restructuring in France*. Oxford: Oxford University Press.

Hau, Michel. 1987. *L'industrialisation de l'Alsace (1803–1939)*. Strasbourg: Presses Universitaires de Strasbourg.

Hau, Michel, and Nicolas Stoskopf. 2005. *Les dynasties alsaciennes*. Paris: Perrin.

Heinrich, Nathalie. 2006. *L'élite artiste. Excellence et singularité en régime démocratique*. Paris: Gallimard.

Hirsch, Jean-Pierre. 1991. *Les deux rêves du commerce. Entreprise et institution dans la région lilloise (1780–1860)*. Paris: Editions de l'Ecole des Hautes Etudes en Sciences Sociales.

Holworth, Jolyon, and Philip Cerny, eds. 1981. *Elites in France: Origins, Reproduction, and Power*. London: Frances Pinter, for the Association for the Study of Modern and Contemporary France.

Hudemann, Rainer, and Georges-Henri Soutou, eds. 1994. *Eliten in Deutschland und Frankreich im 19. Und 20. Jahrhundert. Strukturen und Beziehungen*. Munich: Oldenburg Verlag.

Jeanneney, Jean-Marcel. 1959. *Forces et faiblesses de l'économie française*. Paris: Fondation nationale des Sciences politiques.

Jemain, Alain. 2002. *Les conquérants de l'invisible. Air liquide, 100 ans d'histoire*. Paris: Fayard.

Johnson, Christopher. 1995. *The Life and Death of Industrial Languedoc, 1700–1920*. Oxford: Oxford University Press.

Joly, Hervé Alexandre Giandou, Muriel Le Roux, Anne Dalmasso, and Ludovic Cailluet, eds. 2002. *Des barrages, des usines et des hommes. L'industrialisation des Alpes du Nord entre ressources locales et apports extérieurs*. Grenoble: Presses Universitaires de Grenoble.

Kuisel, Richard. 1984. *Le capitalisme et l'Etat en France. Modernisation et dirigisme au XXe siècle*. Paris: Gallimard.

Lachaume, P. 1986. "De l'hélice à l'aviation à réaction (moteurs civils)." In *Colloque de l'aéronautique et de l'espace, quarante années de développement aérospatial français, 1945–1985*, 195–202. Paris: Institut d'histoire des conflits contemporains, Centre d'histoire de l'aéronautique et de l'espace.

Lambert-Dansette, Jean. 1992. *La Vie des chefs d'entreprise en France (1830–1880)*. Paris: Hachette.

Lamard, Pierre. 1988. *Histoire d'un capital familial au XIXe siècle: Le capital Japy (1777–1910)*. Belfort: Société Belfortaine d'Emulation.

———. 1996. *De la forge à la société holding, Viellard-Migeon et Cie, 1796–1996*. Paris: Polytechnica.

Lambert-Dansette, Jean. 2000. *Histoire de l'entreprise et des chefs d'entreprise en France*. Vol. 1. Paris: L'Harmattan.

Landes, David S. 1951. "French Business and the Businessman: A Social and Cultural Analysis." In *Modern France: Problems of the Third and Fourth Republics*, ed. M. Earle, 334–53. Princeton: Princeton University Press.

———. 1967. *The Unbound Prometheus: Technological Change and Industrial Development in Western Europe from 1750 to the Present*. London: Cambridge University Press.

———.1999. *The Wealth and Poverty of Nations: Why Some Are So Rich and Some Are So Poor*. New York: Norton.

———. 2006. *Dynasties, Fortunes, and Misfortunes of the World's Great Family Businesses*. New York: Viking.

Lanthier, Pierre. 1988. "Les constructions électriques en France. Financement et stratégies de six groupes industriels internationaux." Thesis, Université de Paris X–Nanterre.

Le Roux. Muriel. 1998. *L'entreprise et la recherche: Un siècle de recherche industrielle à Péchiney*. Paris: Editions Rive droite.

Leménorel, Alain. 1988. *L'impossible révolution industrielle? Économie et sociologie minière en Basse-Normandie*. Caen: Annales de Normandie.

Lescure, Michel. 1996. *PME et croissance économique. L'expérience française des années 1920*. Paris: Economica.

———. 2002. "Entre ville et campagne: L'organisation bancaire des districts industriels. L'exemple du Choletais (1900–1950)." In *Villes et districts industriels en Europe occidentale, XVIIe–XXe siècles*, ed. Jean-François Eck and Michel Lescure, 81–102. Tours: Presses de l'Université de Tours.

Lescure, Michel, and Alain Plessis, eds. 2004. *Banques locales et banques régionales en Europe au XXe siècle*. Paris: Albin Michel.

Levy, Jonah D. 1999. *Tocqueville's Revenge: State, Society, and Economy in Contemporary France*. Cambridge: Harvard University Press.

Lévy-Leboyer, Maurice. 1974. "Le patronat français a-t-il été malthusien?" *Le Mouvement social* 88 (July–September): 3–49.

———. 1977a. "La balance des paiements et l'exportation des capitaux français." In *La position internationale de la France. Aspects économiques et financiers, 19e–20e siècles*, ed. Maurice Lévy-Leboyer, 71–92. Paris: Editions de l'Ecole des Hautes Etudes en Sciences Sociales.

———, ed. 1977b. *La position internationale de la France. Aspects économiques et financiers, 19e–20e siècles*. Paris: Editions de l'Ecole des Hautes etudes en sciences sociales.

———. 1979. "Le patronat francais 1912–1973." In *Le patronat de la seconde industrialisation*, ed. Maurice Lévy-Leboyer, 137–88. Paris: Cahiers du Mouvement Social.

———. 1980. "The Large Corporation in Modern France." In *Managerial Hierarchies: Comparative Perspectives on the Modern Industrial Enterprise*, ed. Alfred D. Chandler Jr. and Herman Daems, 117–60. Cambridge: Harvard University Press.

———. 1985. "Le patronat français a-t-il échappé à la loi des trois générations?" *Le Mouvement social* 132 (July–September): 3–7.

———. 1996, "La continuité française." In *Histoire de la France industrielle*, ed. Maurice Lévy-Leboyer, 15-19. Paris: Larousse.

Lévy-Leboyer, Maurice, and François Bourguignon. 1985 *L'économie française au XIXe siècle. Analyse macro-économique*. Paris: Economica.

Lévy-Leboyer, Maurice, and Jean-Claude Casanova. 1991. *Entre l'Etat et le marché, l'économie française des années 1880 à nos jours*. Paris: Gallimard.

Loubet, Jean-Louis. 1990. *Automobiles Peugeot. Une réussite industrielle, 1945–1974*. Paris: Economica.

———. 1999 *Citroën, Peugeot, Renault. Histoire de stratégies d'entreprises*. Boulogne: ETAI.

———. 2001. *Histoire de l'automobile française*. Paris: Le Seuil.

Luc, Virginie. 1998. *Impossible n'est pas français. L'histoire inconnue d'Accor, leader mondial de l'hôtellerie*. Paris: Albin Michel.

Lüthy, Herbert.1955–61. *La banque protestante en France de la révocation de l'Édit de Nantes à la Révolution*. 2 vols. Paris: SEVPEN.

Maddison, Angus. 2006. *The World Economy: A Millennial Perspective*. Paris: OECD.

Marseille, Jacques. 2000. *Créateurs et création d'entreprises de la révolution industrielle à nos jours*. Paris: Association pour le Développement de l'Histoire économique.

———. 2004. *Empire colonial et capitalisme français, Histoire d'un divorce*. 1984; Paris: Albin Michel.

———, ed. 1992. *Alcatel-Alsthom. Histoire de la Compagnie générale d'électricité*. Paris: Larousse.

———, ed. 1999. *Le luxe en France du siècle des Lumières à nos jours*. Paris: Association pour le Développement de l'Histoire économique.

———. 2000 *Créateurs et création d'entreprises de la révolution industrielle à nos jours*. Paris: Association pour le Développement de l'Histoire économique.

Marseille, Jacques, and Patrick Eveno, eds. 2002. *Histoire des industries culturelles en France, XIXe–XXe siècles*. Paris: Association pour le Développement de l'Histoire économique.

Massé, Pierre. 1965. "Allocution inaugurale des Journées d'Études de Lyon, 4 juin 1959." In *Le plan ou l'anti-hasard*. Paris: Gallimard.

Mayaud, Jean-Luc. 1991. *Les patrons du Second Empire. La Franche-Comté*. Paris: Picard.

Meuleau, Marc. 1990. *Des pionniers en Extrême-Orient: Histoire de la Banque de l'Indochine 1875–1975*. Paris: Fayard.

———. 1995. "From Inheritors to Managers: The Ecole des Hautes Etudes commerciales and Business Firms." In *Management and Business in Britain and France: The Age of the Corporate Economy*, ed. Youssef Cassis, François Crouzet, and Terry Gourvish, 128–46. Oxford: Clarendon Press.

Meynaud, Jean. 1964. *La technocratie, mythe ou réalité?* Paris: Payot.

Mieg, Philippe. 1948. "L'apport des Mulhousiens dans les domaines de la Science et de la Technique." *Bulletin de la Société Industrielle de Mulhouse* 24–26.

Moine, Jean-Marie. 1989. *Les barons du fer. Les maîtres de forges en Lorraine*. Nancy: Editions Serpenoise–Presses Universitaires de Nancy.

Morin, Francois, and Eric Rigamonti. 2002. "Evolution et structure de l'actionnariat en France." *Revue française de gestion* 141:155–81.

Olivier, Jean-Marc. 2004. *Des clous, des horloges et des lunettes. Les campagnards moréziens en industrie (1780–1914)*. Paris: Editions du CTHS.

Pernod-Ricard. D'un siècle à l'autre en 25 marques. 1999. Paris: Textuel.

Perrot, Jean-Claude, ed. 1982. *Voies nouvelles pour l'histoire économique de la Révolution. Annales historiques de la Révolution française*, special issue. Paris.

Petit, Francis Jacqueline Grislain, and Martine Le Blan. 1985. *Aux fils du temps. La Redoute*. Paris: Robert Laffont.

Pétré-Grenouilleau, Olivier 2003 "Un port pour horizon. L'économie nantaise à l'heure de l'ère industrielle." In *Nantes. Histoire et géographie contemporaine*. Nantes: Editions Palantines.

Picard, Jean-François, Alain Beltran, and Martine Bungener. 1985. *Histoire de l'EDF. Comment se sont prises les décisions de 1946 à nos jours*. Paris: Bordas.

Poidevin, Raymond. 1995. *Péripéties franco-allemandes du milieu du XIXe siècle aux années 1950*. Berne: Peter Lang.

Pouchain, Pierre. 1998. *Les maîtres du Nord du XIXe siècle à nos jours*. Paris: Perrin.

Poussou, Jean-Pierre. 1989. "Les activités urbaines en France pendant la Révolution." *Revue Economique* 40:1061–78.

———. 2000. "Le Sud-Ouest de la France est-il au XIXe siècle une région sous-industrialisée et sous-développée?" In *L'économie française du XVIIIe siecle au XIXe siecle. Perspectives nationales et internationales*, ed. Jean-Pierre Poussou, 643–70. Paris: Presses de l'Université de Paris–Sorbonne.

Quennouëlle-Corre, Laure. 2000. *La direction du Trésor, 1947–1967. L'État-banquier et la croissance*. Paris: Comité pour l'Histoire économique et financière de la France.

Raveux, Olivier. 1998. *Marseille, ville des métaux et de la vapeur au XIXe siècle*. Paris: CNRS Editions.

Schmidt, Vivien. 1996. *From State to Market? The Transformation of French Business and Government*. Cambridge: Cambridge University Press.

Schweitzer, Sylvie. 1992. *André Citroën, 1878–1936: Le risque et le défi*. Paris: Fayard.

Seb. 2003. *1953–2003. La cocotte traverse le temps*. Paris: Textuel.

Smith, Michael Stephen. 2005. *The Emergence of Modern Business Enterprise in France, 1800–1930*: Cambridge: Harvard University Press.

Smith, Robert. 2001. *The Boucayers of Grenoble and French Industrial Enterprise, 1850–1970*. Baltimore: John Hopkins University Press.

Stoskopf, Nicolas. 1994. *Les patrons du Second Empire. Alsace*. Paris: Picard.

———. 2002. *Les patrons du Second Empire. Banquiers et financiers parisiens*. Paris: Picard.

Terrier, Didier. 1996. *Les deux âges de la proto-industrie. Les tisserands du Cambrésis et du Saint-Quentinois, 1730–1880*. Paris: EHESS.

Thépot, André, ed. 1985. *L'ingénieur dans la société française*. Paris: Les éditions ouvrières.

Todd, Emmanuel. 1990. *L'invention de l'Europe*. Paris: Le Seuil.

Torres, Félix. 1992. *Une histoire pour l'avenir, Merlin-Gérin, 1920–1992*. Paris: Albin-Michel.

Toulemonde, Jacques. 1966. *Naissance d'une métropole. Histoire économique et sociale de Roubaix-Tourcoing au XIXème siècle*. Tourcoing: Georges Frère.

Trumbull, J. Gunnar. 2004. *Silicon and the State: French Innovation Policy in the Internet Age*. Washington DC: Brookings Institution Press.

Verley, Patrick. 1994. *Entreprises et entrepreneurs du 18e siècle au début du 20e siècle*. Paris: Hachette.

Villermet, Jean-Marc. 1991. *Naissance de l'hypermarché*. Paris: Armand Colin.

Vuillermot, Catherine. 2001. *Pierre-Marie Durand et l'Energie industrielle. Histoire d'un groupe électrique, 1906–1945*. Paris: CNRS Editions.

Weber, Max. 1905. *Die protestantische Ethik und der Geist des Kapitalismus*. Berlin.

Woronoff, Denis. 1994. *Histoire de l'industrie en France du XVIe siècle à nos jours*. Paris: Le Seuil.

Chapter 12

Entrepreneurship in the Antebellum United States

LOUIS P. CAIN

A General Description

WHAT BECAME THE UNITED STATES OF AMERICA was born of entrepreneurship. When independence was gained, American disposable incomes were among the highest in the world, but, early in the colonial period, entrepreneurial failure was as likely as success (Hughes and Cain 2007, 51). Indeed, Jamestown, the first permanent colony, an entrepreneurial venture of the Virginia Company of London, became the first government bailout of a private North American business when it was converted to a crown colony. By independence, agriculture and trade were well established, but manufacturing was still in its infancy.

If, as Schumpeter (1934) thought, entrepreneurs seek to upset equilibrium, it is a fair question whether the colonial economy was ever in equilibrium. The story seems more consistent with Kirzner's (1973) notion that entrepreneurs recognize the profit opportunities in existing disequilibria, thereby moving the economy toward new equilibria. It also requires a broad definition of entrepreneurship such as that provided by Landes:

> The entrepreneurs, that is, the decision-makers of the economy, include not only the traditional owner-operators and the newer class of pure managers, but a growing number of government bureaucrats and technicians. (1969, 325–26)

This study of American entrepreneurship begins with American independence, when the former colonies constituted one of the most developed countries in the world. It grew to such status under English rules, but, as a newly independent country, it could write its own.[1]

As a new nation, the United States had to define an institutional environment in which creative activity could flourish. Entrepreneurial activity requires the conjoining of the creative and the banal; it is often a team effort. The first three sections discuss the innovations made in the law, in finance, and in transportation-communication. All three bring government into the picture to some degree. The first deals with the rules. There was general agreement among the new country's leaders that the national government was not functioning efficiently under the Articles of Confederation, so a constitutional federal system was introduced relatively quickly. It has remained in place ever since and is heralded as one of the underlying causes of the country's growth and development. The second section deals with the financial rules that also date back to the formation of the new nation, though they changed more often over the years. The third section discusses the improvements in transportation and communication that created a market which, before the Civil War, stretched from the Atlantic well past the Mississippi, and reached the Pacific in 1869. The roles of the attorney, banker, and teamster were complementary to that of the entrepreneur. The cost reductions in moving both goods and information enabled entrepreneurs to increase the size of their firms and realize economies of scale.

The final section investigates the goods that dominated antebellum markets and the reasons for their dominance. Where the government remains in the picture, it is in the background. Agricultural goods were the most important exports, and three implements (the cotton gin, the plow, and the reaper) plus the evolving transportation network were responsible for the ability of cotton plantation owners in Texas and grain farmers in Iowa to sell their output in European markets. Manufactured goods were slower to develop, but cotton production in the South contributed to the development of a cotton textile industry in the North. Over time, there was a flowering of industrial production that reached adolescence, if not maturity, in the decade before the Civil War. Europeans called it "the American system." It performed remarkably well before the Civil War and created a dominant industrial nation thereafter. The roots of that dominance can be found early in the life of the nation. It would not be divided like Europe; the American states were a "common market." Antebellum American entrepreneurs had to compete on an ever-expanding stage.

Law: A Pertinent Institution Defining the Rules

Entrepreneurs respond to incentives, and the law is one of the first places to look for such incentives. As James Willard Hurst observed, "The 19th century was prepared to treat law as an instrument to be used wherever it looked as if it would be useful." Further, "What business wanted from law was the provision for ordinary use of an organization through which entrepreneurs could better mobilize and release economic energy" (1978, 111–14). The initial "law of the land" was the Articles of Confederation and Perpetual Union, which loosely tied the thirteen colonies. However, the Confederation proved too weak a foundation for an effective national government. In particular, the power to tax remained the responsibility of the individual states; the national government had to requisition funds from the states. Consequently, because the states could free-ride on this arrangement, "The United States in Congress Assembled" was left in debt following the Revolution.

The Continental Congress had proclaimed that the "common law of England" was the right of all Americans. Several state constitutions explicitly laid claim to the same set of inherited rules. The common law proved workable at the state and local level, but something new was needed at the top. Kenneth Dam (2006) argues that public law, constitutional development, has been as important as private law in promoting economic development and creating an environment in which entrepreneurship can thrive.[2]

Constitutional law. In 1786, only five years after the Articles were ratified, delegates from six states met at Annapolis, Maryland, and issued a call for a Constitutional Convention. The meeting at Philadelphia the following spring addressed the question whether a strengthened central government would be based on a federal system with considerable state sovereignty or a national system with limited or no state sovereignty. In September 1787, the delegates proposed that the states ratify a document based on a federal system, and, by June 1788, that was accomplished. In March of the following year, Congress declared the Constitution to be in effect. The Beard tradition (1913) characterizes the intent of this exercise as rent-seeking, but it should not be surprising that a democratic republic of entrepreneurs created favorable rules (see also McGuire 2003).

The Constitution introduced sweeping changes that required restrictions on state sovereignty. The representatives of the individual states conscientiously guarded their power and, in Article I, Section 8, relinquished to the federal government only those rights they believed were essential. Article I, Section 10 restricts individual state's dealings with foreign powers and prohibits the creation of state paper money. It includes the famed contract clause that establishes the sanctity of contract, the deliberate protection of property rights, and the equally famed commerce clause that prohibits restrictions on interstate commerce. With this, the United States was ensured of an internal common market; local entrepreneurial ventures could grow to serve a national market with few impediments.

Patent law. While the Articles of Confederation were still in effect, several states passed copyright laws and at least one passed a combined copyright-patent law, but it was recognized that federal legislation would prove necessary. The Constitution gave Congress the power "to promote the progress of science and useful arts by securing for limited times to authors and inventors the exclusive right to their respective writings and discoveries" (Article II, Section 8, paragraph 8). The first patent law was enacted in 1790. Applications were to be reviewed by the attorney general, secretary of state, and secretary of war and, following the common law, were to be awarded based on careful examinations for both novelty and usefulness. By 1793, the large number of applications and the time pressure on cabinet officers caused the procedure to become essentially one of registration.[3] By the 1830s, litigation over rights led to reform.[4] The 1836 law sought to compromise the interests of inventors, of those who purchased patent rights or to whom patent rights were assigned, and of the consumers of patented goods. It put in place the main features of today's patent system in which a staff of technical experts examine applications for novelty and utility. As Steven Lubar has argued, "Nineteenth-century patent law embodied a delicate balance of monopoly, to encourage invention; the dissemination of new ideas, to encourage the increase of knowledge; and ease of use of patents, to encourage innovation" (1991, 934). Numerous scholars who have used patent data credit this reform with accelerating the rate of change. At the outset, a large number of talented "amateur" inventors, including clergymen and women, received patents. As time passed, invention became a more specialized endeavor.

Land law. The new United States was largely a nation of farmers, and that was likely to continue as the population migrated to the west. However, there were overlapping claims to the western lands that the colonists received from the British in 1783. The Articles of Confederation contained a clause to the effect that the national government should not take this land from the states. Land speculators favored the opposite policy, as did some statesmen with purer motives who also wanted the new government to be endowed with public lands. New York, one state whose claims were part of the confusion, offered to relinquish those claims to the national government in 1781, and later that year, when Virginia offered to contribute its enormous claim, the creation of a public domain was assured (see Treat 1962).

The next task was to sell the land to private owners, and it was they who cut the western lands into millions of pieces. The Land Ordinances of 1785 and 1787 created the rules under which public land would be sold, what rights the buyers of that land would have, and how new states would be admitted to the union. The foundation of future American entrepreneurship, private ownership and control of productive resources (even when those resources were on public land), was in place at an early date (Gates 1968; Hughes 1987; Cain 1991).

Business law. Classical economic theory as applied in the United States was based on the principle that the state best encouraged economic growth and development by leaving entrepreneurs alone (Hovenkamp 1988, 1991). The state's primary responsibility was to assure unobstructed investment arteries so that capital would flow toward profitable investments. The acceptance of this policy in the first decades of the nineteenth century dramatically changed the concept of the corporation. Previously, corporations were unique entities created by government for a special purpose. As such, they enjoyed a privileged relationship with the state. The very act of incorporation presumed state involvement. If a business was dependent exclusively on the market, there was no reason to incorporate. As the classical corporation evolved, two propositions remained fundamental. First, the corporate form was not a special privilege; it was one of several alternative ways of organizing a firm. Second, the special feature of the corporate form, the one the law should encourage, was the ability to raise capital more efficiently than the alternative forms.[5]

Initially, the Supreme Court deemed special franchise corporations to be grants of monopoly, but, with the acceptance of classical economic theory, the Court overturned the ancient conception that a special-franchise charter *implied* a grant of monopoly. In *Charles River Bridge v. Warren Bridge*, Chief Justice Taney wrote, "in grants by the public, nothing passes by implication."[6]

By 1790, there were forty American corporations. The numbers increased each decade thereafter. In general, each charter was a special act of a state legislature. However, beginning in 1811, the state of New York allowed general rules of incorporation for manufacturing concerns that did not require special legislative charters, but generalized incorporation did not become common until the 1870s.[7] Usually, corporate charters stated the nature of the business venture, its purpose, its location, and the amount of capital it could employ, limitations that seemed reasonable at the time.

Since corporations were groups of people who commingled their capital, the law treated a corporation as a legal person.[8] The concept of personhood was the Supreme Court's guarantee that the owners of corporately held property received the same constitutional protections as the owners of personal property. This was a vitally important development. The corporation evolved into an entity with the rights of a person, but with limited liability and perpetual life. As Arthur Selwyn Miller describes corporations, they are "feudal entities within the body politic" (1972, 14).

In sum, what can be said generally of the antebellum period is that the law aided the evolution of the main ideas and institutions of developing American capitalism—economic growth based mainly upon private decision-making regarding the exploitation of privately owned productive resources. Behind these developments was the assumption that most economic life was a private matter—government aided and supported entrepreneurship and relied upon entrepreneurs to produce economic growth.

Finance: A Pertinent Institution Lubricating the System

Since the Continental Congress lacked the authority to levy taxes, and since there was no systematic way to raise money from the states, financing the American Revolution was a "near thing." As a result, between 1776 and 1780, Congress paid its bills by printing paper money. Too much was printed, and it depreciated badly. Between 1776 and 1782, Congress borrowed about $7.7 million domestically (measured in specie); between 1780 and 1783, it borrowed $7.8 million more internationally, mostly from the French. Beginning in 1783, the Confederation government's fiscal affairs deteriorated badly; it could not tax, and it was forced to borrow from Dutch bankers to stay afloat.

Hamilton's policies. All this changed with the ratification of the Constitution in 1789. Secretary of the Treasury Alexander Hamilton innovated a financial system that gave the new nation and its entrepreneurs the means for managing risk.[9] The Constitution established federal finance on a completely different basis, giving Congress the authority to levy taxes, to borrow, to issue money and "regulate" its value, and it implemented these constitutional powers with vigorous policies.[10]

Richard Sylla (1998) argues that Hamilton's policies, by the standard of their time, gave the United States a "world class" financial system; they ushered in a "financial revolution." Whether or not one agrees, the development of good financial systems is an important entrepreneurial achievement. In particular, the financial system is an important component of an entrepreneur's ability to accept risk.[11] As Sylla notes, "Good finance helped to institutionalize entrepreneurship" (456). He argues there are six important components to a successful financial system: stable public finance and debt management; stable money; a functioning banking system; an effective central bank; active securities markets; and a growing number of businesses, including financial institutions.[12] Before Hamilton's tenure, the United States had none; by 1795, it had all six. Though some of the states were doing well, as John Steele Gordon noted, "In the 1780s the United States had been a financial basket case. By 1794 it had the highest credit rating in Europe, and some of its bonds were selling at 10 percent over par" (1997, 38–39).

Stable public finance and debt management. In his first "Report on Public Credit," sent to Congress in January 1790, Hamilton's proposed three policies that contributed to the evolution of financial stability: the establishment of tariffs and other taxes for federal revenue; the complete refunding (with arrangements for redemption) of the wartime debts of the Continental Congress; and the assumption by the federal government of the states' wartime debts.[13] Beginning with the tariff law of 1789, Hamilton's immediate designs were partially realized. The tariff yielded nearly all the federal government's revenues.

Hamilton estimated that the national debt in 1790 was about $54 million, and that the outstanding state war debts totaled about $25 million.[14] In 1790 and 1795, provisions were made to refund all this debt with various new issues and ultimately to retire it by setting money aside in a sinking fund. Although the debt was never completely retired, Hamilton's system placed the federal government and the balance of the states on a sound financial basis.

Stable money. The Mint Act of 1792 provided for a Philadelphia mint and specified two monetary metals, gold and silver. Such bimetallic systems are often troublesome because the two metals constantly fluctuate in price against each other.[15] Hamilton's currency system, first sent to Congress in 1791, called for a ten-dollar gold coin (the Eagle), a silver dollar, and fractional coins. Until the mid-1830s, little American metallic coin was in circulation.[16] It made little difference, however, because the new state banks discussed below provided what people used as a medium of exchange—paper. Although the new Constitution forbade the states to issue their own paper money, state-chartered banks supplied the needed amounts.[17]

A functioning banking system. In 1781, Robert Morris and his colleagues founded the Bank of Pennsylvania to help finance the Revolution; it performed its duties well. Consequently, Morris persuaded Congress to charter the Bank of North America in 1784, a limited-liability corporation that handled the government's finances. In most respects, it did the chores of a central bank, and it has been argued that this bank is the first real U.S. central bank, an appellation usually reserved for the First Bank of the United States (Studenski and Krooss 1952, 31). Two additional banks were chartered in 1784, Hamilton's Bank of New York and the Massachusetts Bank. In 1787 the Bank of North America received a charter from Pennsylvania and became a state bank.

These early banks were part of the development of a system of financial intermediation peculiar to the nation's needs and laws. Before 1838, state-chartered banks were special-franchise corporations whose owners engaged in obvious rent-seeking behavior, though they did mobilize capital. Many early New England banks were credit banks whose main business was to discount commercial paper. Naomi Lamoreaux (1994) argues that these banks were extensions of a system of family capitalism, a mix of banking and entrepreneurial ventures. Such banks marketed their shares to outsiders as a way of generating funds to lend to insiders, what Lamoreaux calls "investment clubs." Robert Wright's (1999) study of New York and Pennsylvania banks finds that banks in those states were more widely owned than Lamoreaux's New England banks. They had a large capitalization that forced their lending practices to be less concentrated; they lent to a wide variety of borrowers including small business and farmers.[18]

An effective central bank. A great deal has been written about the two "central" banks chartered by Congress in 1791 and in 1816 for twenty-year periods (Holdsworth and Dewey 1910; Catterall 1903; Schlesinger 1945; and Hammond 1947, 1957). There is no question that the Bank of England was the model for both. In his "Report on a National Bank," Hamilton called for a public-private partnership, an entrepreneurial venture, in which the U.S. Treasury would own one-fifth of the stock and private persons the rest. Like the Bank of England, both the First and Second Banks of the United States were in direct competition with private commercial banks and were expected to turn a profit.[19] As a consequence of this competition, the rest of the banking community generally was opposed to them. The idea of joint public-private ownership, embodied in both the First and the Second Bank charters, was entirely suitable to democratic ideas about the partnership between government and business. But, in both cases, the sale of bank stock to foreigners raised hostility to the banks.

The First Bank performed its functions well, but the Jeffersonians simply allowed its charter to expire. The Second Bank also performed well, especially during the presidencies of Langdon Cheves and Nicholas Biddle. Yet, the attempt to recharter the Second Bank was killed in 1832 when Andrew Jackson vetoed the enabling legislation and subsequently withdrew federal funds. Jackson's veto message emphasized that it was a privileged monopoly, its stock largely owned by foreigners and the "rich" (Taylor 1949; see also Schlesinger 1945). Both banks were huge compared to state banks. By using drafts on its branches as money, they were, in fact, creating a uniform currency, a practice much feared by the private bankers.[20] Today we believe central banks ought to have a money monopoly, but such was not true in the 1830s.

By 1860, the United States had gone without a central bank for almost three decades. Much has been written about the system during the era of "wildcat banking," but entrepreneurs may have benefited from an absence of central bank regulation.

Active securities markets. State banks were commercial banks, operating as intermediaries in the world of business and as instruments of commerce. Peter Rousseau and Sylla (2005) attribute much of the growth in securities markets to the First Bank of the United States. To borrow long-term monies and sell equities (shares of ownership), businesses and governments needed organized capital markets. The entrepreneurs behind the new transportation companies and, increasingly, the rising manufacturing firms required a forum.

The New York Stock Exchange Board was formally organized in 1817 after twenty years of less formal existence (Banner 1998; see also Davis and Gallman 2000). It slowly forged ahead of securities markets established in other cities to become the center of the nation's capital markets—just as New York City itself took the lead in commerce and growth. By the 1850s, the major financial centers were linked by telegraph, with the focus on the New York exchange. From the beginning, common stocks (usually those of transportation companies) were sold, as were the bonds of municipal, state, and federal governmental bodies. During the 1830s, preferred shares (with a preferred claim to dividends) appeared, and, later, industrialists followed the lead of governments and began issuing long-term bonds for subscription in the public capital markets.

Other intermediaries also appeared. Mutual savings banks, carefully governed depositories for the savings of the poor, appeared early on the American scene. The first was organized in Philadelphia in 1816 based on an idea imported from England. Emphasis was on the safety of the loans, even if earnings were deliberately low. Life and fire insurance companies were formed in the early nineteenth century, along with burial societies and building societies. All were techniques for mobilizing the funds of a group against disasters that struck individual families. Experimentation was necessary as new needs developed, and the American economy before 1860 was alive with such experiments.[21]

Before 1860, a special element in the U.S. financial system played an important role in antebellum Southern economic expansion. An intricate system of cotton finance evolved, comprised of agents of British banks, discount houses, and cotton importers located throughout the cotton-growing and cotton-shipping South. The historical tendrils from cotton finance eventually were a primary origin of American investment banking. George Peabody, a Yankee financier, had a long and successful career in London. His firm, Peabody & Company, was an "American house" that, for the most part, dealt in cotton finance. In 1854, he invited a new partner to London, Junius Spencer Morgan, whose son, J. Pierpont, joined his father in London in time to observe the Bank of England's dramatic actions during the panic of 1857. After an apprenticeship in London, J. P. Morgan went to New Orleans in the fall of 1859 to learn the American side of cotton finance. During the Civil War, he moved to New York City, where he became the primary founder of modern American investment banking (Hughes 1986, chap. 9).

Once all the parts were assembled and allowed to grow, what can be said of the U.S. financial system of the antebellum period? The tariff was long the mainstay of federal finance, but Hamilton's internal taxes were less successful. The assumption of Revolutionary debt by the federal government did establish the federal credit. Securities markets became "much deeper and more active," in spite of the absence of a strong central bank in the years immediately before the Civil War (Snowden 1998, 102). Most importantly, as Sylla argues, "They [the six components of a successful financial system] are at the very core of entrepreneurship and economic development" (2003, 457).

Transportation and Communication: Entrepreneurial Infrastructure That Broadens and Deepens the Market

Throughout the antebellum period, transportation and communication costs declined, broadening the market and raising productivity. Initially, water provided the most efficient mode of transport, but that would change as the nation vigorously pursued transportation improvements. In England, canals and railroads were built by private capitalism almost without government participation. In the United States, canals and railroads were mixed enterprises—part private and part governmental. Carter Goodrich (1960) believed that, given the vast area of the United States, the sheer size of the investment required for improvements like canals and railroads was beyond the capability of private entrepreneurs acting alone.[22] The possibility of government involvement, of subsidization, meant that rent-seeking themes were often part of entrepreneurial overtures.

Would-be entrepreneurs and those who would benefit from lower transportation costs hoped their new federal government would play a major role in promoting economic development. By 1806 work was under way to build a national road from Cumberland, Maryland, westward to Illinois. Also by 1806, some members of Congress were proposing federal aid for canal building with the thought that the revenue from the sale of public lands could be used to fund such projects. In 1807, the Senate asked Secretary of the Treasury Albert Gallatin to prepare "a plan for the application of such means as are within the power of Congress, to the purposes of opening roads and making canals" (Goodrich 1960, 27). Gallatin's plan, submitted in April 1808, emphasized "the extent of territory compared to the population" and the lack of sufficient private capital to exploit potential opportunities. In addition to the east-west National Road, he proposed north-south "tidewater inland navigation" from Massachusetts to Georgia; major east-west links such as one between the Hudson River and Lake Champlain; and connecting road links such as one between the Monongahela and Potomac Rivers. Gallatin estimated his plan would cost the federal government $20 million ($2 million per year for ten years). Once the projects generated sufficient revenues, they could be sold to private companies and the proceeds used to promote further internal improvements.

Presidents Madison and Monroe favored federal participation in internal improvement projects such as turnpikes, but they believed that federal action within a state was unconstitutional.[23] When President Jackson vetoed the Maysville Road bill in 1830, federal financing faded. Nevertheless, between 1824 and 1828, about $2 million of federal funds was spent on canals, and another $7 million was spent on the National Road (Hughes 1991, 68–76). As Goodrich notes, in the absence of substantial federal support, states and private entrepreneurs ultimately completed most of the Gallatin Plan (1960, 34–35).

Roads. The first major improvements were turnpikes, intercity toll roads. Intracity roads were adequate, but intercity roads appeared to benefit others more than the residents of specific cities. By offering more dependable road surfaces that enabled greater speed, private entrepreneurs as well as state governments hoped to attract sufficient long- and middle-distance traffic to make a turnpike viable. In the first decades of the nineteenth century, more than $25 million of private capital was invested by several hundred turnpike companies.[24] These companies were often special-franchise corporations that tied entrepreneurs to state governments. Since tolls were regulated, and since the charters restricted the company's activities to road operations, profits were disappointing.[25] By the 1830s, most turnpikes had been overtaken by canals, then by railroads, and were subsequently abandoned.

Steamboats. Robert Fulton's steam-powered paddlewheel freed the bottleneck of traveling upriver; flatboats and keelboats had given farmers a way to move their crops downriver. The introduction of the steamboat, however, depended on both Fulton and his partner, Robert Livingston. Fulton went to England in 1787 to study portraiture, but he also studied canal construction before moving to Paris in mid-1797. Livingston, Jefferson's minister to France, who arrived in the summer of 1802, held exclusive rights to operate steamboats in New York, but he lacked a steamboat. The partnership was formed in October 1802. Fulton proffered his engineering talent as a way to improve upon what others had tried.[26] In 1804, in the midst of the Napoleonic War, Fulton left Paris for England in the hope of obtaining a Boulton and Watt steam engine, a good whose export was prohibited, especially to France.

Fulton returned to the United States in December 1806 with such a steam engine, and, in August 1807, his *North River Steam Boat* (later referred to as the *Clermont*) made a successful trial run between New York City and Albany.[27] A second boat was added in 1809 and soon the Fulton-Livingston partnership was at the center of a network of companies operating steam vessels on the Hudson, Delaware, Potomac, James, Ohio, and Mississippi Rivers, in Chesapeake Bay, and in New York harbor. The partnership's success created challenges to the monopolies that they had been granted in the states of New York and Louisiana.[28] Since one of the challengers was Livingston's brother-in-law, Fulton hesitated to obtain a patent, but ultimately did so to safeguard the monopoly and to hinder the competition. His 1809 and 1811 applications claim that his "scientific principles" and "mathematical proportions" were original, as was the use of side waterwheels. After the patents were granted, opposition to the partnership, which included the superintendent of the Patent Office, was energized. In the 1824 case of *Gibbons v. Ogden*, it was determined the state monopolies granted to the partnership, and to others, were unconstitutional. Thus, Fulton is remembered both for introducing steam navigation to the world and, albeit unwittingly, for removing a barrier to entrepreneurial competition. Livingston's equally important role has been forgotten, but in this case, as in others, the entrepreneurs were a team. The desire to exploit a monopoly position played an important role in steamboat development.

The steamboat had its greatest impact on the western river system (e.g., the Ohio, Missouri, and Mississippi rivers) that drains half of the country. Between 1815 and 1860, Mak and Walton argue, the steamboat transformed this area into an agricultural heartland (1972, 620). The boats were not cheap; the capital embedded in the least expensive vessel was equal to the price of an average farm and greater than what was invested in 85 percent of manufacturing firms (Atack 1999, 5). Before 1860 the average working life of a river steamboat was only about 5.5 years. There were numerous accidents, including a high risk that an engine would explode (Haites and Mak 1973, 28). The financial risk was not the only one these entrepreneurs accepted.

By the end of the 1850s roughly 800 steamboats serviced the interior rivers of the United States. Transit and turnaround times fell dramatically. Freight rates fell by 90 percent in real terms between 1815 and 1860 for the upstream trip and by nearly 40 percent downstream. Steamboats, and the technology associated with them, drastically cut transit and turnaround times.[29]

Canals. The American canal-building era arrived with the end of the War of 1812 and departed in the wake of the Panic of 1837. Although canal construction continued in the west after the Panic, completing canals previously begun, attention turned to railroads. As noted, like turnpikes before and railroads after them, canals were mixed enterprises.[30] Although there were a few private canals (e.g., South Carolina's Santee Canal and Massachusetts's Middlesex Canal), it was New York's Erie Canal (publicly financed and completed by the state in 1825) that pointed to a promising future. The person whose entrepreneurial energy was most responsible for seeing the canal through to completion was Governor DeWitt Clinton. It was he who convinced the New York legislature to pass the laws necessary for building the 363-mile long canal after President Madison vetoed an 1817 bill that would have provided $1.5 million of federal money. As Landes suggested, some entrepreneurs operated in the public sector, and Clinton was one who made a difference. When the canal was completed, the cost of shipping a ton of wheat from Buffalo to New York City fell from $100 per ton to $10. Shipping times fell to one-third of what they had been. The canal shifted settlement in the Northwest Territory north from the Ohio and Mississippi Rivers to the Great Lakes. New York became the nation's largest city.

One of the first post-Revolution graduates of Columbia University, Clinton was appointed a U.S. senator in 1802. He resigned the following year to become mayor of New York City, a position he held for most of the next twelve years. Unlike many members of the (National) Republican party, Clinton favored canal construction. He became a canal commissioner in 1810, and the major canal bill passed the legislature in 1817, his first year as governor. In 1825, at the official opening in New York City, Clinton poured water from Lake Erie into the Atlantic Ocean (the "Wedding of the Waters") to symbolize connecting the two bodies. The completed canal cost $7 million; the bill was paid with a combination of earmarked taxes, borrowing on state credit, and toll collection as sections of the canal opened. Citizens of New York purchased the initial issues of Erie bonds, but, once the success of the canal became evident, large investors and foreign buyers entered the market.[31]

The canal produced two significant externalities that could have justified federal involvement. First, as symbolized by Clinton's pouring of the water, it tied together parts of the country that effectively had been separated by the Appalachian Mountains. As early as 1775, George Washington worried about losing the land west of the mountains to France or Canada unless the mountain barrier could be overcome.[32] Second, the canal trained a large number of engineers who ultimately would help to build the nation's canals, railroads, and sanitation systems.

The three engineers assigned responsibility for constructing the Erie Canal were all surveyors.[33] Benjamin Wright was hired in 1816. He was in his mid-twenties when he learned surveying (and the law) from an uncle. In 1808, following his election to the New York legislature, he introduced a bill jointly with Joshua Forman calling for a survey of a canal route between the Hudson River and Lake Erie.[34] James Geddes's surveying and engineering skills were a result of learning by doing. Following his election to the New York legislature, Geddes was asked by Simeon De Witt, surveyor general of New York, to conduct the survey required in the 1808 Forman-Wright bill. Geddes conducted the survey successfully without the benefit of technical training. His report was the first to argue that a continuous canal from Lake Erie to the Hudson River was feasible (Bernstein 2005, 136).

The contributions of Geddes's surveying assistant, Canvass White, proved crucial. White became friendly with DeWitt Clinton, and it was Clinton who urged White to travel to England to learn about modern canal construction. White's detailed knowledge and drawings, and the modern surveying equipment he purchased in England, led to his promotion to Wright's primary assistant. It was White who was responsible for the design and construction of the locks and of the first canal boat. And it was White who was responsible for the development of an improved hydraulic cement, which he patented in 1820, that is estimated to have reduced the Erie's cost by about 10 percent.[35]

John Jervis is the final notable member of the Erie engineering corps. He began as Wright's apprentice, but became a resident engineer within a few years.[36] As chief engineer for the Delaware & Hudson Canal Company in 1827, Jervis designed the railway that carried coal to the canal. In 1829, he introduced America to the railway locomotive, the "Stourbridge Lion" imported from England.[37] When that engine proved too heavy for American track, Jervis designed his own locomotive (the 4-2-0 type better known as the Jervis type) that proved an immediate success. In 1836, he was appointed the chief engineer of the Croton Dam and Aqueduct project to supply New York City with water. Jervis is the embodiment of the transition in American engineering from the talented amateurs responsible for the Erie Canal to the professional engineers that, by midcentury, were responsible for the nation's public works (Larkin 1990).

The success of the Erie Canal brought expansion and emulation; it brought competition among the entrepreneurial merchants in the port cities. In 1826 the Pennsylvania legislature voted to build the 359-mile long Main Line Canal with state funds.[38] It would prove a complicated project involving transfers of cargo to surface transport (later to rail links) at several points because of the Appalachian Mountains' height and width. It was completed in 1835 and cost approximately $12 million. While it was a technological marvel, it was a financial disaster; the Erie always maintained a competitive advantage.[39] In the mid-Atlantic and Midwest, where natural waterways offered the opportunity for canals, states actively became involved in canal building. While these canals fostered a manufacturing sector serving agriculture, a major portion of this manufacturing was the processing of agricultural output for export out of the regions served by the new canals (Ransom 1964; Niemi 1970, 1972; Ransom 1971). None had the impact of the Erie Canal.

Railroads. In the popular imagination, railroads symbolize the spirit of the antebellum period. They further reduced transportation costs and opened the country. As Alfred Chandler (1965) emphasized, the railroads were the nation's first giant enterprises. Their management problems and methods proved instructive to all U.S. industrial entrepreneurs. Their securities dominated commodity trading in the growing U.S. capital markets for some time.[40]

Robert Fogel (1964) and Albert Fishlow (1965) attempted to assess the contribution of the railroads by asking the counterfactual question of how the United States might have developed had there been no railroads.[41] They argued the contribution of the railroad can be determined by what was termed the *social saving*, the difference between how much it would have cost to haul an equivalent amount of freight on the least expensive, alternative transportation route and the actual cost of using the railroads. With respect to freight, rates by water were lower than rates by rail, but the advantage was lost when all costs were included (e.g., additional wagon hauling, transshipment, cargo lost in transit, a reduced season of navigation, and the need to carry additional inventory because deliveries were slower). With respect to passengers, the calculation emphasized the time saved by taking the railroad. Both Fishlow and Fogel found that the railroad's social saving was on the order of 4–5 percent of GNP. This is a large percentage for a single industry; no single industry in this country today accounts for anything like that proportion of total output. However, the crucial conclusion was that the railroad was not indispensable; no single innovation created American economic growth.

The railroad is an important example of technology transfer. The first U.S. railroad, the Baltimore and Ohio, began operations in 1830, five years after the Stockton and Darlington began operating in England. American entrepreneurs adapted British technology to local conditions, initially building railroads as spokes out of a city.[42] By the Civil War, U.S. mileage exceeded that of railroads in the United Kingdom, France, and the German states combined. Total investment in railroads then was more than $1 billion.[43] Nevertheless, the value of output of railroad equipment in 1859 was only a quarter of the market value of all transportation equipment produced; railroads accounted for a mere 6 percent of machinery output.

The encroachment railroads made on river and canal traffic was based upon the savings in transport costs for shippers. Railroads offered year-round service, while the main canals faced ice-bound conditions during the weeks of hard winter. In addition, railroads offered more contact points for producers, cutting down the costs of wagon haulage, unloading, and reloading. They tended to be built along river routes where the terrain was flat, so that, to a large extent, they ran parallel to water routes. By the Civil War, waterways, including coastal shipping, still carried far more freight than did the new railroads, but the handwriting was on the wall.

In 1850 the federal government, at the urging of Illinois's Senator Stephen Douglas, made a huge, 3.75 million-acre land grant to Illinois, Alabama, and Mississippi to finance the building of the Illinois Central Railroad.[44] The road initially was projected to follow the eastern bank of the Mississippi River the length of Illinois. Douglas advocated extending the road south to New Orleans and building a branch to Chicago. This was not the first land grant for internal improvements, but it was by far the largest to date and a harbinger of things to come. Land grants helped sub-sidize construction of transportation improvements that increased the value of the land, including the alternate sections the government retained. They also created an incentive to engage in rent-seeking behavior that afflicted several roads. Shortly after his election, Douglas moved to Chicago and became active in real estate.

The first president of the Union Pacific Railroad, William Ogden, is representa-tive of many entrepreneurs associated with railroads and canals whose business and political interests were conjoined, but who generally avoided conflicts of interest. His entrepreneurial skills were tapped for the first time in 1821 when, at age sixteen, he was forced to forego his studies to take charge of his father's business affairs.[45] In 1834, still in his twenties, he was elected to the New York legislature. In a speech to the legislature advocating the construction of the New York & Erie Railroad, Og-den envisioned "continuous railways from New York to Lake Erie...through Ohio, Indiana, and Illinois, to the waters of the Mississippi, and connecting with railroads running to Cincinnati and Louisville in Kentucky, and Nashville in Tennessee, and to New Orleans." It would be, he argued, "the most splendid system of internal communication ever yet devised by man" (quoted in Downard 1982, 50). Ogden believed the position New York occupied as a result of the Erie Canal would be threatened if it did not embrace the newer technology. While this might be construed as replicative rather than innovative, Ogden's entrepreneurial vision encompassed more than the railroad.

In 1835, Ogden's brother-in-law and associates acting as the American Land Company paid $100,000 for 182 acres on Chicago's north side that had been pur-chased the previous year for $20,000. Ogden was sent to manage the property. The plot was covered with oak and brush and was muddy from a recent rain; it was not clear to him why it was worth the purchase price. Nevertheless, Ogden established a loan and trust agency just as government land sales brought Easterners to the Midwest. Ogden held an auction at which he sold roughly a third of the property for more than $100,000. After wintering in the East, Ogden moved to Chicago in 1836. He became an advocate of the Illinois & Michigan Canal and helped promote its construction at the same time that he was promoting Chicago's first railroad, the Galena & Chicago Union. The canal was completed in 1848, the same year the first trip was made on a completed section of the railroad.

Ogden's vision extended well beyond transportation; he had a model of urban development that he actively pursued. He recognized the need for additional entre-preneurs to develop business in the city. Thus, in 1847, at Ogden's urging, Cyrus McCormick moved his reaper works to Chicago to take advantage of Chicago's location and transportation relative to the emerging wheat-growing region. Another reason was the presence of people such as Ogden who had foreseen the value of McCormick's firm to the city and offered to help finance the move (Cain 1998). Al-though the term wasn't fashionable at the time, Ogden was Chicago's first "venture capitalist."

Ogden also recognized the need for other forms of urban infrastructure. He was the first mayor of Chicago and later served in the state legislature. He was the first president of Rush Medical College, president of the Chicago Branch of the State Bank of Illinois, president of Chicago's board of sewerage commissioners, and president of the board of trustees of the (first) University of Chicago. And that is just a small sampling of his involvement (Andreas 1884, 617). Colleagues such as

J. Young Scammon, the financial manager behind many of Ogden's enterprises, were also actively immersed in the city's development. Scammon was president of both the Chicago Marine & Fire Insurance Company and the Marine Bank, founder of the *Inter-Ocean* newspaper, and chair of the director's committee of the Galena & Chicago Union Railroad. Ogden and his associates saw from the first that the city's institutional and transportation infrastructure was a necessary complement to entrepreneurship.

With the driving of the golden spike, the railroads traversed the continent, and William Ogden was part of each step of that evolution. His speech to the New York legislature was about a road that would connect New York and the west. His Galena & Chicago Union Railroad reached westward from Chicago, while, as president of the Union Pacific Railroad, he helped complete coast-to-coast connections. His adopted city, Chicago, grew in part because it became the western terminus of many important eastern railroads and the eastern terminus of many important western railroads. The railroads made it possible for passengers and goods to reach all corners of the common American market, promoted urbanization, and enabled firms capable of serving a national market to realize scale economies.

Communication. The handwritten letter remained the common form of business communication throughout the antebellum period. The Post Office Act of 1792 set relatively high rates in an attempt to make the service self-supporting. By 1840, that approach had changed; rates were lowered and the number of post offices increased. From 75 post offices in 1790, the number grew to almost 13,500 in 1840; the population served per post office declined from over 43,000 in 1790 to just over 1,000 in 1840.[46] Further, as the new modes of transport reduced travel times, delivery times fell commensurately. In addition, as Richard John (1995) notes, the lower rates encouraged the growth of the press. Thanks in part to postal subsidization, the number of newspapers grew from 100 in 1790 to over 1,400 in 1840. A specialized business press evolved that provided more timely information, facilitating transactions, and, therefore, an increase in trade.

The most dramatic fall in communication time came as a result of Samuel Morse's telegraph (see Hindle 1981). Morse, a Yale graduate, initially pursued a career in art, but, following a series of frustrations, turned to other pursuits. In 1834 while working as an unpaid art professor at what would become New York University, Morse began working seriously on the telegraph. His first telegraph could send messages only a few feet, but, by 1837, with the help of chemistry professor Leonard Gale, Morse increased the distance to ten miles. He considered this to be practical because, at ten-mile intervals, relay switches could convey sequences of short (dots) and long (dashes) pulses over as long a distance as needed. In early January 1838, Morse completed a dictionary of words translated in dots and dashes for trials. By late January, the dots and dashes had become individual letters, and, in 1844 the letter system was altered to become the familiar Morse code.

In May 1844, the message "What hath God wrought" traveled the forty miles from Washington to Baltimore and back. Entrepreneurs such as Amos Kendall and Ezra Cornell helped Morse establish a New York–Washington line whose success firmly established the telegraph. Morse retreated from day-to-day operations, content to collect his portion of the fees for licensing the use of his patent. By 1860, the telegraph network stretched over 60,000 miles, and it reached the West Coast the following year. The vast majority of telegraph messages were commercial messages.

News of interest rate movements, news that goods were shipped, moved across telegraph lines, usually constructed adjacent to rail lines, as fast as the operators could push the key (Bodenhorn and Rockoff 1992).

Thus, by the end of the antebellum period transportation and communication facilities had expanded to create a national market. The cost of reaching that market had fallen substantially, and would continue to fall. Entrepreneurs who once served local markets could now serve a national one.

Manufactured Goods: The Gestation of Industrialization

When the first census was taken in 1790, 95 percent of the population was involved in agricultural production. Farmers had occupied the land and brought it into production. By 1850, farmers were still almost 60 percent of the labor force and were responsible for a good deal of nonagricultural production as well. In his "Report on Manufactures," Alexander Hamilton estimated that between two-thirds and four-fifths of the population's clothing was homemade. Towns contained artisans who made tools, shoes, hats, pots, and pans by hand. Lumber mills on the edges of rivers like the Merrimac resembled small factories, as did the Du Pont powder works on the Brandywine.

Throughout the antebellum period, in spite of an abundance of land, farmers applied scientific principles to agriculture, particularly in the search for improved plants and livestock. They widely adopted crop rotation, improved fertilizers, and techniques to minimize soil erosion. Agricultural societies disseminated information about these changes through fairs and a growing body of agricultural publications. By the 1850s, several states opened agricultural schools and colleges. Congress passed the Morrill Act (the land-grant college act) in 1862 providing land grants to each state still in the union to establish agricultural colleges. However, the most impressive improvements took place in farm machinery and tools. As a result of these improvements, family farms in the North could thrive without a dependence upon a large supply of hired labor; on average, each farm had an estimated one-half hired male worker. Southern farmers also quickly innovated and adopted productivity-enhancing machinery. By the end of the antebellum period, industrialization had proceeded to where the industries producing these machines purchased inputs from a separate machine-tool industry.

In the early years of the period, American manufacturers found it difficult to compete with the British. Although significant domestic production began in the years just prior to the War of 1812, the vast majority of American establishments were relatively small scale (less than ten employees; a relatively large firm had between thirty-five and forty employees) and used time-honored processes; the textile industry was the notable exception. Such firms could be replicated quickly when trade with Britain was suspended. Many of these firms could be traced back to merchants who, over time, became increasingly specialized with respect to function, products, and geographical areas. As late as 1820, the vast majority of manufacturing was concentrated in the Northeast. Using the surviving patent records, Kenneth Sokoloff finds there were some scale economies in the expansion of shop size from the "artisan" enterprise to a prefactory specialized workshop employing ten to fifteen workers: "These new types of firms were frequently marked by a minute division of labor that reduced the share of the work force with general skills, greater supervision and attention to maintaining an intense work regime, and a concern for standardization of product" (1984, 357).

According to Sokoloff, before the Civil War, technological change in manufacturing advanced in two phases. The first phase, which occupied most of the period, was characterized by the spread of factories from textiles to other industries. The second phase, which began around 1850, was defined by the adoption of inanimate power sources. Sokoloff and Zorina Khan (1990) stress the increased importance of investment in "invention-generating capital." The initial expansion of markets broadened the number and type of people who participated in the process; for example, housewives and clergymen held patents. Over time, however, specialization developed in inventing, as in other economic activities. The move toward specialization in inventive activity is evident in their data. So, too, is the move toward cities where more resources were available.

The Industrial Revolution began in England, and the United States materially benefited from British out-migration. The brothers Schofield, who arrived in the early 1790s from Yorkshire, built wool-carding machinery driven by waterpower; among their American apprentices was Paul Moody, who would play a major role in the development of the American textile industry. The Scots engineer Henry Burden, who was responsible for crucial innovations in that "cradle of American technology" the Springfield (Massachusetts) Armory, followed a policy of bringing over immigrant mechanics to work there. David Thomas, a Welsh immigrant, first introduced anthracite iron smelting into the Pennsylvania iron industry in 1840.

The primary conduit of technology transfer was the Yankee merchant. Never wanting to allow money to sit idle, he invested his profits in a variety of pursuits. Nathan Trotter, a Philadelphia merchant, was the driving force behind the Lancaster Turnpike. Stephen Girard used funds generated in trade with China and the West Indies to open a bank. Many were involved in importing industrialization from Britain, and it was they who created America's textile industry. On the other hand, much of the work done to improve agricultural implements was homegrown, as was the work in many other industries. In what follows, the focus is on a few of the many entrepreneurs active in the American economy during the antebellum years.

Agricultural Implements

In conjunction with their farming operations, farmers and plantation owners might operate sawmills, tanneries, blacksmiths' shops, flour mills, and dairies. A closer look at three critical agricultural implements helps capture the period's dynamism.

The cotton gin. After the American Revolution, cotton textile production expanded first in old England, then in New England, leading to an increased demand for cotton. The key to the growth and geographic expansion of American cotton production was Eli Whitney's "invention" of 1793, the cotton gin.[47] Devices that separated cottonseeds from fiber were in existence for centuries before Whitney's, and their evolution didn't end with him.

After graduating from Yale, Whitney moved to Georgia, where he had accepted a tutor position, a position secured for him by Phineas Miller. On the way, he stopped in Savannah to see Miller, who was managing the cotton plantation of Catherine Greene, widow of General Nathanael Greene. When it appeared that Whitney's tutoring job offer was not firm, as Hughes comments, "Whitney took the easy, and the more intelligent, way out. He lingered a year or so with Catherine Greene and her gay companions—by invitation" (1986, 129).

It was Mrs. Greene who inspired Whitney to design a machine to clean the tight-clinging green seeds from short-staple cotton. Within a few days, Whitney's gin came into being. It used wire teeth embedded in a wooden roller to pull fibers through a grate mesh that was too fine for the seeds to pass. The idea was incredibly simple; Whitney's gin was easy to build and to operate. Anyone who saw it could quickly copy it, and Hughes notes that Mrs. Greene showed it to "virtually all of her aficionados" (1986, 130).

Whitney returned to New Haven to build works to manufacture gins and to apply for a patent, which was granted in March 1794. The initial business plan was that planters would bring their cotton to a gin site; Whitney and Miller would return one pound of clean cotton to the planter for every five pounds of raw cotton delivered to their gins; roughly two-thirds of a pound of clean cotton would be kept as their fee. When it became clear the New Haven plant would be unable to produce sufficient gins quickly enough for their proposed strategy to work, a new plan was adopted—production of gins would be licensed, a common way to disseminate technology, as will become clear. Then, in 1795, the New Haven works burned to the ground. Two years after the fire, Hughes estimates, there were 300 illegal copies of Whitney's gin, and 'improved' models in operation (132). Whitney turned to the courts for redress, but the patent law was worded in such a way that such suits were not possible. This changed in 1800, and Whitney ultimately received some relief on a state-by-state basis.[48]

The cotton gin was aimed at the bottleneck of cotton production, harvesting the crop. By resolving that bottleneck, it increased labor productivity. As McClelland (1997) notes, much of the productivity differential between North and South at the time of the Civil War is attributable to the fact that no implement shaped northern agriculture as the cotton gin had southern agriculture. The gin itself was a tremendous success; cotton became king.

The plow. The creation of a new family farm required clearing land and constructing fences and buildings.[49] In the five to ten years it took to build a modest frontier farm, the ratio of investment to total activity was extraordinarily high. Once improved farm machinery appeared, such family farms began to grow in both number and size, albeit slowly. The plow was one such implement, and the soils found as the frontier moved westward created problems for the plows used in the East.

Holland Thompson argued that "Roman ploughs were probably superior to those in general use in America eighteen centuries later" (1921, 111). A common plow in use at the time of the Revolution (and in Illinois until the War of 1812) was essentially a small tree limb with a crooked end on which a piece of iron was attached with rawhide. Such plows could do little more than scratch the ground. Country blacksmiths made to order heavier plows that could turn a furrow, a small tree trunk shaped with a hatchet to which a wrought-iron plowshare was attached. If the ground were soft, perhaps one man and two oxen could use such a plow, but harder ground required more men and more oxen.

The first practicable plow is attributed to Charles Newbold, a New Jersey blacksmith, who patented a cast-iron plow in June 1797. He spent an estimated $30,000, a large sum for the day, developing his plow.[50] Farmers were reluctant to use it; they believed the iron "poisoned the soil," but that fear abated as competition forced farmers to adopt the superior technology. A bigger problem was that, when rust inevitably claimed one part, the entire plow had to be replaced. Among the many other cast-iron plow patents, the one issued in 1807 to David Peacock, also of New Jersey, was for a plow with separate parts; broken parts could be replaced.[51] However, the person most associated with a standardized three-piece plow with replaceable parts was Jethro Wood of New York who received patents in 1814 and 1819. Wood's design improved upon others by allowing the parts most exposed to wear to be replaced in the field. This plow proved popular, in part because of Wood's marketing ability. When a steel tip was added to the share, the plow cut Eastern soils more easily and required less sharpening than its cast-iron competitors.[52]

In the Midwest, prairie sod rendered a wooden plow with a wrought-iron share useless. At first, Midwestern pioneers stayed away from the prairies, preferring lands in or near stands of timber because they acquired building materials and fuel as natural by-products of clearing. Farmers who settled on the prairies typically used a breaking plow (prairie breaker), a metal plow with a moldboard that weighed as much as 125 pounds.[53] Steel appeared to be the answer, and, some time around 1833, John Lane, an Illinois blacksmith, plated a wooden moldboard with steel strips he took from an old saw. The Lane plow performed better on prairie soil than any other, but steel was expensive before the Bessemer process lowered its cost. Nevertheless, others followed up on Lane's success, the most important being John Deere of Illinois, who first produced an all-steel plow in 1837.

Deere developed an excellent reputation as a blacksmith in his native Vermont.[54] He later moved to Grand Detour, Illinois, a community established by fellow Vermonters that was in need of a blacksmith. It was there he designed a plow with a polished steel moldboard that successfully "scoured" itself as it moved through the soil. It would become "the plow that broke the plains." R. Douglas Hurt notes, "If Deere's plow was an overnight success from a design standpoint, as a businessman he faced an uphill battle" (1994, 138). Given the price of steel, it did not make economic sense until the mid-1850s to produce all-steel plows in volume. Initially, just the plowshare would be made from steel. After moving to Moline, Illinois, in 1848 to take advantage of a Mississippi River location, Deere manufactured a great variety of plows, many under license from others—a practice that Newbold, Wood, and Peacock among others had used to increase the production of their inventions (Danhof 1972, 88).

From the outset, Deere was a more aggressive marketer than his competitors, and this was critical to his firm's success. Marketing the plows was not easy; most sales had to be on credit, given the primitive nature of the area's banking system and the scarcity of currency. Through his "travelers," Deere developed a network of wholesalers and retailers throughout North America. To help advertise his wares, he bought print advertising, entered his plows in plowing contests, and displayed at fairs throughout the country. The reputation for excellence the Deere Company earned and retained is based on more than just production.

The reaper. In 1833, Obed Hussey of Maryland patented a reaper and began selling it immediately, although it remained unimproved and never worked as well as intended. One year later, Cyrus Hall McCormick of Virginia patented his reaper; however, he did little with it for several years.[55] It was not until 1840 that McCormick believed his reaper was sufficiently improved to offer for sale. Hussey's design proved far better for mowing grass than reaping grain; McCormick's was just the opposite.

In 1845, McCormick moved from Virginia to a production facility in Cincinnati because he realized that the demand for his reapers would be much greater in the west than in Virginia. Two years later, he responded to the incentives offered by William Ogden and moved his operations to Chicago.[56] The move would benefit the city, the McCormick firm, and Ogden's railroad. Hussey remained in the east.

The McCormick firm adopted a number of business practices that make it appear more like a modern firm than many other nineteenth-century firms. For example, the firm established agency relationships with local businessmen whose job it was to promote the use of reapers. It was one of the first manufacturing enterprises to offer a written guarantee on every machine, and it offered a free trial period during which dissatisfied customers could get a refund of the stated purchase price. In contrast to the normal selling procedure in which the seller and buyer haggled over price, McCormick widely advertised the price in farm journals, newspapers, and other print media. A typical ad, which was intended to be "educational" in nature, included a picture, testimonials, the terms of sale (including credit), and an order blank (see Cronon 1991, 313–18; Miller 1996, 103–6). It can be argued that, as was true of Deere, it was McCormick's ability to mass-produce and market his machines, not just his skills as an inventor, that underlay his success.

By 1860, there were perhaps 100 companies selling reapers, but McCormick was by far the largest. The explanation for this rapid growth seems to be that mechanical reaping was more efficient where the terrain was flat, and it was adopted as Midwestern agriculture was brought into production (David 1975, 89). The reaper removed a major bottleneck to production. Given grain's perishability, a family farm could only plant as much as the family could harvest. The reaper made it possible to do in one day what previously had occupied the harvest season.

Many agricultural implements, particularly the reaper, were shared, rented, jointly owned, or otherwise acquired. This was especially true as the cash outlay for implements increased. The rapidly growing number of implements allowed a family to farm more acres and thus to expand output. Adoption of machinery conserved labor, and the addition of plentiful land inputs raised the productivity of both capital and labor. Agricultural implements, which were much more widely disseminated in the North, became to northern farmers what slaves were to southern farmers.

Cotton Textiles

In spite of state and local government subsidies, several attempts to form textile mills in the late eighteenth century failed; most from a lack of efficient machinery. Moses Brown and his three brothers, merchants of Providence, Rhode Island, broke from that pattern (Hedges 1952 and 1968; Perkins 1975; Ware 1931). In 1789, Moses Brown helped finance William Almy (his son-in-law) and Smith Brown (his nephew). The firm of Almy and Brown purchased a spinning jenny and a carding machine, but these replicas of Arkwright's English machinery soon proved inoperative. What made their story different was the entrance of Samuel Slater, an Englishman who had apprenticed under a former partner of Arkwright. Slater believed his chances of owning a factory were much higher in the United States. So, having memorized Arkwright's technology, he sailed to New York, where he quickly determined that the city lacked an appropriate water source to produce textiles. Slater became aware that Moses Brown was looking for a mechanic familiar with the Arkwright's machinery. Early in 1790, he became a partner of Almy and Brown. Slater built the machinery with the smuggled technology; Almy and Brown provided the finance and marketing. The firm proved profitable until, in the aftermath of the War of 1812, the extent of overexpansion in the U.S. textile industry was revealed.[57] When Almy and Brown concluded that financial propriety required that they limit their activities, Slater sought greener pastures. Leadership in the New England textile industry passed to Massachusetts. Over the balance of his working life, Slater was involved in eight partnerships with seventeen partners over four states, but he retained his relationship with Almy and Brown. Their factory only produced cotton yarn; the weaving operations continued to be put out to homes.

The honor of being the first integrated textile firm belongs to the Boston Manufacturing Company, headed by Francis Cabot Lowell, a Harvard-educated merchant. In 1810, Lowell traveled to Great Britain in part to observe power looms in Manchester and elsewhere. He believed New England's growth required that it supplement trade with manufacturing.[58] Returning home in 1812, wary of the war's impact on his trading ventures, Lowell convinced other Boston merchants, including his friend Nathan Appleton and his brother-in-law Patrick Tracy Jackson, to invest $100,000. Working with the aforementioned Paul Moody in late 1813, Lowell successfully tested a water-driven loom based on his memory and smuggled sketches of what he had seen in England. By fall of the following year they demonstrated their loom to other investors before getting a patent. The factory they then constructed in Waltham was the first to turn raw cotton into finished cloth. By 1820, aggregate dividends exceeded the initial paid-in capital, and Lowell was pivotal in obtaining tariff protection from Congress (see Rosenbloom 2004).

The Boston Associates soon came to dominate the New England economy.[59] In 1822, five years after Lowell's death, work began on a new manufacturing center in a town they named Lowell. By 1836, the Associates had located eight major firms at Lowell employing a total of 6,000 workers. All were organized on what has come to be known as the Waltham System, in which all the stages of production were integrated within a large plant that specialized in a single, standardized product. This high-volume strategy required a large capitalization, but it enabled the Associates to realize economies of scale in both production and marketing. The mechanization of production meant that the firm could make use of unskilled labor. Dormitories were constructed adjacent to the factories, and young New England farm girls were recruited (Gibb 1950; Zevin 1971, 1975; Dublin 1979; Jeremy 1981; Dalzell 1987). The textile industry quickly included hundreds of firms along New England's rivers. In 1832, the secretary of the Treasury conducted a survey of American manufacturing.[60] Of the 106 companies with assets of at least $100,000, 88 were textile firms. Claudia Goldin and Kenneth Sokoloff (1982) report that, in 1850, women and children comprised at least 30 percent of the labor force.[61]

Sewing Machines

With the development of a cotton textile industry, and the training of mechanics, it was logical that entrepreneurs would attempt to find a way to mechanize sewing. A French tailor, Barthelemy Thimonnier, is considered to have put the first mechanical sewing device into production. His chain-stitch machine received a French patent in 1830, a British patent in 1848, and a U.S. patent in 1850. But, while the sewing machine was invented in Europe, the crucial innovations came from the United States. The most critical is generally conceded to be Elias Howe's 1846 patent.

Howe developed his interest in sewing machines as a result of machinist work he did for Ari Davis, who made and repaired mechanical devices for mariners and Harvard scientists. All the incentive Howe needed was to overhear a conversation Davis had with a visitor remarking that the person who perfected the sewing machine would profit handsomely. Howe, ignorant of previous work but having watched his wife sew, believed such a machine would have to mimic the human hand. He tried many models, but an 1844 version with an eye-pointed needle, two threads, and a shuttle worked well enough to be patented in 1846. Finding little interest for his machine in the United States, he went to England. Although his machine was adopted, the profit went to William Thomas, an English corset manufacturer, who purchased the English rights to Howe's machine. In order to return home in April 1849, Howe pawned his first machine and patent papers. Upon his return, he learned that during the two years he spent in England, U.S. interest had increased, and a variety of machines, most making use of devices covered under his patent, was being offered for sale. Howe then began a series of lawsuits while manufacturing and marketing his own machine.

The primary suit was against Isaac Singer, whose first machine was constructed in September 1850 and patented less than a year later. Singer, an actor, among other pursuits, aggressively marketed his machine, which had helped popularize the product (Jack 1956). It is generally conceded that Singer's machine corrected the deficiencies in all the earlier machines, including Howe's. Given Howe's lawsuits and the superiority of Singer's machine, relatively few additional firms entered the industry. This was abetted by the arrival of Edward Clark in 1851 to help Singer deal with the patent-infringement suit, the longest court case in United States to that point. Howe won the case in 1854, and Singer alone was forced to pay $15,000 in royalties on previously produced machines and $25 per machine on each machine produced until Howe's patent expired in 1867. The lawsuits, in the view of Grace Cooper (1968), were "choking the sewing-machine industry" (141). The solution, engineered by Clark, was a pooling of the interests of the important patentholders.[62]

In the early years, Singer's primary competition came from the firm of Wheeler and Wilson, which produced a lightweight machine for households. Singer overtook this firm by the 1870s and absorbed them in 1905. A second manufacturer worthy of note is Willcox and Gibbs. In attempting to produce a crude model of a Howe machine from an illustration, James Gibbs produced the first single-thread machine, as he could not tell that the Howe machine used two-threads. Most important, Willcox (the financier) and Gibbs turned to the firm of Brown & Sharpe to manufacture the machines. This sewing machine proved so successful that Brown & Sharpe introduced a new manufacturing process to mass-produce it with interchangeable parts. In the process, as Woodbury (1972) notes, they designed new machine tools that became important to all machine-shop work, not just to sewing machine production.

Mechanicians

What the Erie Canal and other transportation innovations did for the engineering profession, the textile industry and later the small arms industry did for mechanics. It created a group of native-born American "mechanicians" who provided American technological leadership.[63]

Although American entrepreneurs borrowed all the technology they could, early on inventors and innovators created a uniquely American industry, characterized by labor-saving capital and abundant raw materials use. The U.S. economy was short on labor and long on raw material; therefore, entrepreneurs conserved what was scarce and used what was plentiful. As Jonathan Hughes (1986) commented, "One cannot avoid the conclusion that, at the beginning, the character of the Yankee experimenting mechanic, with his craving for efficiency, together with the high price of skilled labor, led Americans to mass-production techniques" (146).

Mass production, as it evolved in the United States, contributed two important innovations: continuous processing and interchangeable parts. The former is most associated with Oliver Evans. In 1784–85, Evans built a flour mill outside Philadelphia run by gravity, friction, and waterpower. Grain was moved from the loading bin throughout the mill's several levels by buckets and leather belts without the intervention of any human effort apart from guiding and regulating. It was an assembly line more than a century before Henry Ford. Evans secured a patent, but, like many others, expended a large amount of time and money defending it.[64] In the decade or so before the Civil War, pork packers in Cincinnati also adopted continuous processing—a disassembly line.

Small Arms Production

Interchangeability appeared first in small arms production, where technology was substituted for skilled workers, armorers, who simply were not available in the United States. In 1798, Eli Whitney received a contract for 10,000 muskets. When it became clear that he wouldn't be able to supply them in a timely way, he proposed to produce the muskets from interchangeable parts. Oliver Wolcott, secretary of the Treasury, who awarded the contract to Whitney wrote, "I should consider a real improvement in machinery for manufacturing arms as a great acquisition to the United States" (quoted in Hughes 1986, 141). The first task was to make the machines that would make the musket parts. Interchangeability had been tried by gunmaker Honoré Blanc in France with no known result. Thomas Jefferson (then in France) talked with him, hoping to get him to emigrate to the United States.[65]

Simeon North, another Connecticut arms manufacturer, more thoroughly developed the idea than did Whitney. North's 1813 contract with the government, in fact, stipulated interchangeability.[66] In addition, a great deal of work was done at the Springfield Armory, a federal facility, under Roswell Lee, who introduced an assembly line and piecework wages. Lee introduced the use of gauges and explicit comparison to a master part into arms-making. Hounshell notes that this converted arms-making "from a craft pursuit into an industrial discipline" (1984, 35). In 1826 at Harpers Ferry, John Hall manufactured what is considered to be the first fully interchangeable parts weapons.

During the 1840s, the federal government no longer purchased arms from contract makers, such as Whitney and North, but instead bought them from producers with patents, such as Samuel Colt, from whom the government could simply purchase revolvers like any other customer. The technology developed by the contract arms-makers and the government armories had proceeded to a point where it no longer needed government subsidization.

Samuel Colt's interest in firearms began in the aftermath of the failure of his father's merchant business and his mother's untimely death. The young Colt conceived the revolver well before he had the means to produce one. In 1835, in his twenty-first year, French and British patents were granted on his revolver during a trip to Europe. The following year he received a U.S. patent. In 1841, through the intercession of Zachary Taylor, the War Department queried Colt about purchasing his revolvers. Lacking the capital to produce the necessary quantity, he subcontracted with Eli Whitney, Jr. The performance of Colt revolvers in the Mexican War, the movement of settlers onto the Great Prairies, and the growing dependence on horseback riding all helped to increase demand.

In 1848, Colt opened a factory in Hartford and hired Elisha Root, an expert mechanic, as factory superintendent. Root, who had mechanized production elsewhere, designed new machines for Colt, many of which were adopted in other industries as well. Hounshell emphasizes that Colt and Root operated from "the proposition that uniformity would be an effect, not an absolute goal, of mechanization." The "pursuit of precision" was subordinate to that of mechanization, volume production, and the substitution of skilled labor with Root machines. Consequently, it is Hounshell's contention that "Colt revolvers were not manufactured with interchangeable parts" (1984, 49). While true interchangeability might have required another step, it was a short step, and the evolution of mechanicians and the machine-tool industry made it one that would inevitably be taken.

Clocks and Watches

In 1816, three years after Simeon North's contract was issued, Eli Terry began mass-producing a low-priced wooden shelf-clock in his Plymouth, Connecticut, shop. His clock revolutionized production as it required redesigning the movements, making them smaller, and, most important, devising machinery to make interchangeable parts. Terry provides an exceptional example of an entrepreneur responding to an opportunity. His clock substituted wood for brass wherever possible, and his innovations fed into the production of brass clocks, watches, and a variety of hardware industries, including machine tools. His shop trained a number of future industry leaders including Seth Thomas, Silas Hoadley, and Chauncey Jerome, who in 1837 applied Terry's ideas to mass-producing brass clocks (Church 1975; Landes 1983; Hoke 1990).

Attempts to apply these ideas to watchmaking began at about the same time, but the job was more difficult as tolerances on the smaller parts were more restricting. Aaron Dennison eventually made the successful innovation. In 1850, Dennison and others formed the Waltham Company to mass-produce watches.[67] In 1853, it took twenty-one man-days to produce a watch in what Landes terms the company's "early, experimental years." This fell to four by 1859 after the company had significantly altered Dennison's initial design. Then came the Civil War, which significantly increased the demand for watches.[68]

The American System

By the 1830s, what came to be known as the "American system" (interchangeability, standardization, and division of labor in lengthy production processes) had begun to permeate industry. The common denominator of this evolution was the use of specialized machines. The result, according to Nathan Rosenberg (1972a), was that efforts such as those of Colt and Root became a separate industry that included firms such as Brown & Sharpe. The machine-tool industry brought together "the skills and technical knowledge essential to the generation of technical change throughout the machine-using sectors of the economy" (257). It dealt with problems and processes common to many industries, thus becoming the locus for transmitting new technological information. Rosenberg (1969) demonstrated a direct line between the introduction of the "American system" in the Springfield Armory at the start of the nineteenth century, the development of the machine tool industry in the middle of the century, and the emergence of the bicycle, aviation, and automobile industries at the end. American entrepreneurs were consistently effective in advancing the economy.

The American South

In contrast to what was happening in the North, antebellum Southern industry has been characterized as "a deplorable scarcity" (Bateman and Weiss 1981). With one-third of the national population in 1860, the South had slightly more than one-tenth of the national output of manufactured goods. There was no shortage of entrepreneurial talent in the South, but the incentive structure there was conditioned by plantation and household production. It was skewed toward agriculture and away from industry. Much of the skilled labor needed for normal manufacturing functions (e.g., blacksmiths, coopers) was bonded labor. This was true even where factories were the locus of production. Virginia's Tredegar Iron Works, the nation's fourth largest in 1860, used slave labor in positions requiring skilled labor. The tradition of household production continued on southern and western farms even as it was disappearing in the North. As was true in the North, the War of 1812 provided an impetus to southern business formation; indeed a few Rhode Island textile manufacturers migrated south after the war, but they were the exception. Census records indicate textile production was as lacking as aggregate industry, in spite of widespread support from politicians, civic boosters, and the press. Conventional wisdom suggests southern entrepreneurs invested their capital where rates of return were highest, but Bateman and Weiss's calculations suggest that rates of return in southern industry were higher than those in cotton. This lends support to their conclusion that "southern industrial laggardness may not have resulted entirely from rational adjustment" (Bateman and Weiss 1981, 16, 18). Given the region's resources, the southern industrial sector necessarily would have been smaller than that in the Northeast, but it could have been much larger than it was. The reason the South did not respond to these possible profit incentives is often attributed to extreme risk aversion in the face of industrialization's presumed dangers. As Eugene Genovese (1965) explained, the planters were concerned about their neighbors' reactions and about the creation of "a class of urban factory slaves or white proletarians" (221). If true, the "deplorable scarcity" was an entrepreneurial failure.

The Effectiveness of Entrepreneurship

This broad overview of entrepreneurship of necessity emphasizes success stories. The innovations discussed underlie the growth of the American economy in the antebellum years. However, not all entrepreneurship was what Baumol (1990) termed "productive," and even successful entrepreneurs sometimes sought wealth through alternative routes.

Among several categories of "unproductive" entrepreneurs were those who violated patent rights. Consider once again how the plow evolved. Forty years passed between Charles Newbold's plow and that of John Deere. The historical record contains the names of several who made crucial improvements that proved patentable, but few names of those whose attempts came up short. Many of the latter group could be discovered by checking court records in which patentholders sought relief from those who sold plows that violated their patents. We know that several plow producers (and those who produced many other goods) expended significant resources defending their patents. There is no simple way of knowing the number of unsuccessful entrepreneurs or how many resources were consumed in their pursuits. However, on balance, the gains must have outweighed the losses as entrepreneurs from Eli Whitney at the beginning of the period to Elias Howe at the end were bedeviled constantly by those who illegally used their patents, and they considered it important to file patent-infringement suits.

A second category of unproductive entrepreneurs was privateers. Although the "golden age" of pirates and smugglers was a century earlier, one notable exception in the antebellum period was Jean Lafitte. Born in France, Jean and his brother Pierre established a blacksmith shop in New Orleans in 1809 that also trafficked in smuggled goods and slaves. A year later, recognizing there was more money in procuring than selling contraband, Lafitte became the de facto leader of the Baratarian pirates, named for their home base in Barataria Bay, Louisiana. When, in September 1814, it seemed likely the British would attack the port of New Orleans, Lafitte assisted the American victory in the Battle of New Orleans. After the war, he returned to piracy from a new base near present-day Galveston, Texas. When the Americans retaliated against his attacks on their ships, Lafitte moved south to the Spanish Main. Some have viewed Lafitte as a successful merchant, but his entrepreneurial methods clearly can be categorized as unproductive. Three decades later, Wall Street's "robber barons" (who will be discussed in the next chapter) began successful financial careers that would also raise ethical issues.

While it is unclear how many people courted entrepreneurial success, it is clear that even successful entrepreneurs occasionally sought wealth through a third approach to unproductive entrepreneurship, rent-seeking. Eli Whitney provides an appropriate starting point. Although Whitney may have had less to do with interchangeability than others, his successful self-promotion, a useful talent for many entrepreneurs, led to his being tied to the idea. In 1797, faced with financial ruin from his gin business, Whitney wrote the federal government offering to produce 15,000 muskets. As noted, he received a contract the following year for 10,000, a far larger quantity than any manufacturer had ever produced. Whitney started from scratch and ultimately completed the contract several years late.

A second rent-seeker was Samuel Morse. What motivated him to work on the telegraph was a series of frustrations in his art career. In particular, he unsuccessfully sought a commission to paint one of the ceiling panels in the U.S. Capitol rotunda. After receiving a patent for the telegraph in 1840, Morse requested government support for his system. Three years later, Congress narrowly passed a $30,000 appropriation. In 1844, after successfully sending a message between Washington and Baltimore, Morse offered to sell his invention to the government for $100,000; instead it financed another year's operations. Thereafter, Morse was satisfied to live off the royalties he received by licensing his patent.

It must not be forgotten that the incentives facing potentially productive entrepreneurs are no guarantee of success. It is also true that relatively unsuccessful entrepreneurs may still earn a profit, and vice versa. Consider the competition between Obed Hussey and Cyrus McCormick, what has been termed "the great reaper war." Both produced a successful reaper in ignorance of each other (and many others). McCormick's name became firmly connected to the reaper in part because his machine was better for reaping grain, and he moved west where grain became the primary crop of the great American prairie. Hussey's machine was better suited to mowing grass/hay, and, he remained in the east. The "war" involved many skirmishes over a few issues. Hussey attempted to make it clear that his device was patented before McCormick's. When Hussey's 1847 application for a patent renewal was late, Hussey was forced to petition Congress; McCormick actively lobbied Congress to refuse Hussey's petition. The following year, when McCormick applied for renewal, Hussey lobbied against it. Curiously, the war continued long after both men passed away. In 1897, the Bureau of Engraving and Printing proposed to commemorate Eli Whitney, "inventor of the cotton gin," and Cyrus McCormick, "inventor of the reaper," on new ten-dollar silver certificates. Hussey's friends protested, and the bills were not issued.[69]

Regardless of McCormick's success, the incentives facing Hussey were still strong as he was working on a steam plow at the time of his death in 1860. His resources remained sufficient to compete in the reaper business for a quarter of a century and to finance the development costs of new inventions, but he did not accumulate the wealth of the McCormicks. Gies (1990) reports when Hussey sold his business in 1858, he claimed in a letter to a friend, "I made no money during the existence of my patent" (27), and that his foreman made more. However, unlike many others who were "runners-up" in competitive battles, Hussey's name is remembered. How much anonymous individuals contributed to entrepreneurial effectiveness may never be known, but it seems clear the competition in which they participated made a significant contribution to economic growth.

Conclusion

The "coming of age" of American entrepreneurship took place at London's Great Exhibition of 1851. Antebellum America was teeming with innovative entrepreneurs. When Britain invited the nations of the world to present their manufactures at this famous exhibition in the Crystal Palace, there was no shortage of American inventors and innovators. American products, not noted for their elegance, were, as Rosenberg (1972b) notes, considered to be practical, affordable, and useful. Five Americans received Council Medals, the Exhibition's highest award.[70] The five included William Cranch Bond for devices applying electricity to instruments making astronomical measurements, Gail Borden for his meat biscuit, David Dick for his antifriction press, Charles Goodyear for his rubber fabrics, and McCormick for his reaper.[71] Almost all the Americans who exhibited played important roles in making sure their products were put to effective use. It was clear that the "American system" had taken over in light consumer goods. Later, it would work its way into heavy industry, into machine-making, and, indeed, into nearly the entire economy.

These five entrepreneurs, like the others discussed above, came from a wide variety of backgrounds. In antebellum America, successful entrepreneurs could rise to the top echelons of society; unsuccessful, unproductive entrepreneurs could become social pariahs. Such individuals were the sons of successful merchants and the sons of farmers. They were graduates of the nation's best universities and grade-school dropouts. Even among the better-educated, more well-to-do of the group, entrepreneurship involved learning by doing (or hiring someone with the requisite complementary skills). America's early engineers, those not formally educated at West Point, were largely products of the transportation sector; early machinists largely, but not exclusively, came from the textile and small arms industries. A well-developed apprenticeship system passed these critical skills to the next generation.

Many entrepreneurs accumulated wealth; others invested their earnings in new ventures or had to protect their rights to an existing one. Time and again, the innovative ideas of these individuals proved so simple that they strained the patent system's ability to protect the holder's right. A good deal of the potential profit was spent protecting those rights. However, the story of those who copied Whitney's gin is little different from the textile technology smuggled from England in the minds of those like Slater and Lowell. In spite of his legal problems, Whitney left an estate in 1825 worth just under $3 million in today's dollars. Isaac Singer, who died fifty years after Whitney, left an estate worth one hundred times that of Whitney. Reputedly, the wealthiest man of the antebellum era was John Jacob Astor. Born in Germany, Astor arrived in the United States shortly after the Treaty of Paris ended the Revolution. He entered the fur trade and, from the start, invested the profits in New York City real estate. By the early 1790s, Astor was the leading American fur trader in the Montreal and London markets, and, with time, helped open the Great Lakes region, the Pacific Northwest, and trade with China. At his death in 1848, Astor was worth over $250 million in today's dollars.

In the antebellum period, the United States was blessed with individuals who helped establish the institutional infrastructure that allowed this growth to compound. The openness of American society, its tie to the common law, and the emergence of a sound financial system contributed to the ability of innovators to bring goods to market. Continued improvements in transportation and communication widened that market throughout the antebellum period. U.S. manufacturing was blessed with a generous supply of curious tinkerers who helped to foster economic growth. The conjunction of entrepreneurial opportunities and an appropriate infrastructure led an agricultural nation to the brink of industrialization over the antebellum years.

Notes

Much of this chapter was completed while the author was visiting the Center for Population Economics at the University of Chicago. He is grateful to Robert Fogel, to the Kauffmann Foundation for financial assistance, and to Marianne Hinds Wanamaker for research assistance nonpareil. He also thanks Will Baumol, Alyse Freilich, Meg Graham, Naomi Lamoreaux, and Joel Mokyr for their comments.

[1] Baumol (1990, 2002) stresses the importance of rules. Murphy, Schleifer, and Vishny (1991), who also emphasize rules, investigate how talented individuals choose between entrepreneurship and rent-seeking.

[2] Dam argues that an independent judiciary, one that controls the bureaucracy, is vital to economic growth and development (2006, 86–87). In particular, "Better-performing courts have been shown to lead to more developed credit markets. A stronger judiciary is associated with more rapid growth of small firms as well as with large firms in the economy" (93).

[3] After 1793, a patent was issued as a result of filing an application accompanied by a fee. Khan and Sokoloff (2006) report that under the 1790 patent law the fee was $3.70 plus copy costs. It was raised to $30 in 1793 and to $35 in 1861. Kenneth Sokoloff (1988) notes the latter was never less than 30 percent of per capita income while it was in force.

[4] Khan 1995. See also Horwitz 1977. Machlup and Penrose (1950) discuss the pro- versus antipatent debates of the mid-nineteenth century in the United States and elsewhere. Michele Boldrin and David K. Levine, *Copy Right: Against Intellectual Monopoly* (available at http://www.micheleboldrin.com/research/aim/anew.all.pdf) is a contemporary antipatent view.

[5] Other organizational structures (e.g., the limited partnership) could have achieved the same end, but, in the early nineteenth century, the corporation was better known.

[6] *Charles River Bridge v. Warren Bridge*, 36 U.S. (11 Pet.) 420, 546 (1837).

[7] Lamoreaux discusses the complex consequences of general incorporation for small and medium-size firms. She argues that, to secure such advantages as limited liability, "businesspeople increasingly had to agree to a particular set of organizational rules" (2004, 34). Wallis (2005) notes that in this period, eleven states adopted new constitutions containing both provisions for general incorporation and procedures for issuing government debt.

[8] The personhood of corporations meant that directors or managers could assert constitutional claims on behalf of the enterprise. The expansion of limited liability, which occurred concurrently, effectively insulated shareholders from most claims against the corporation. This began the gradual separation of ownership from control almost a century before Berle and Means (1932) brought it to the nation's attention. See Lamoreaux 2004.

[9] Born illegitimate in the British West Indies and orphaned at eleven, Hamilton was apprenticed to international merchants. He attended King's College (now Columbia University) and became aide-de-camp to George Washington during the Revolution and, later, one of New York's representatives to the Continental Congress. While there, Hamilton, along with Robert Morris and others, attempted unsuccessfully to develop a revenue source for the national government.

[10] Rolnick, Smith, and Weber (1993) argue the states gave up their right to issue money because they experienced exchange rate variability and came to prefer a monetary union.

[11] Whether U.S. economic growth was "finance-led" remains an open question, but it is clearly the case that these policies facilitated growth. See also Rousseau and Sylla 2005 and Wright 2003.

[12] Only the first five will be considered; for the sixth, which may be as much an outcome as a component of a stable financial system, it suffices to note that in the 1790s states chartered over ten times the number of corporations they chartered in the 1780s (Rousseau and Sylla 2005, 12).

[13] Hamilton's famous "Report on Manufactures" of December 1791 also contained revenue-enhancing recommendations that were adopted (Irwin 2004).

[14] Thomas Jefferson, among others, greatly doubted the extent to which the Revolutionary expenditures of the states had been in the common cause (Hofstadter 1958, part 3, document 3, 155).

[15] The 1782 coinage report of Robert Morris, superintendent of finance, was adopted by Congress. Morris recommended a decimal system based on the Spanish silver dollar, but Jefferson objected to the large size of that basic monetary unit (Ford 1894, 446–47).

[16] Gresham's Law suggests only one metal will remain in circulation. Until the mid-1830s, silver was favored; for the remainder of the antebellum period, it was gold (Studenski and Krooss 1952, 62–63; Martin 1977).

[17] The view that the states used bank charters to get around the prohibition against printing notes has been buttressed by research showing that states not only taxed banks' capital, but sometimes invested in banks. Researchers estimate that, in the antebellum period, states may have raised as much as 20 percent of their finances from bank-chartering (Sylla, Legler, and Wallis 1987).

[18] Wright 2001 is an expanded version; Bodenhorn (2000, chaps. 2–3) reaches a similar conclusion.

[19] Knodell (2003) argues that, by providing both interregional and international exchange services, the bank experienced a "positive synergy" between its private and public business.

[20] According to Martin (1974), Jacksonians faulted the Second Bank for not ridding the country of small-note paper currency.

[21] See Clay's study (1997) of merchant activity in early California.

[22] For early scholarship, see Callender 1902. Hurst (1970) argued that the initiative was governmental; by incorporating transportation companies, political leaders could grant privileges and the rights to claim land, contract loans, and levy tolls to support transportation enterprises.

[23] Given the constitutional prohibition on benefit taxation, Wallis and Weingast (2005) argue that Congress was unable to tax nationally to finance projects that provided benefits to a small number of districts.

[24] Most turnpike companies were small and built fairly short roads; one long-distance route would be served by several companies, each charging tolls on its own sections. Most funds invested in turnpikes were private, even in Pennsylvania, where direct state government turnpike investment was greatest (Fishlow 1972, 472–75).

[25] Fishlow (1972, 474) estimated profit rates of only 3–4 percent.

[26] The most successful of the previous attempts was John Fitch's *Experiment* that operated on the Delaware River from Philadelphia in 1790. Fulton's first working boat traversed the Seine at speeds of less than three miles per hour.

[27] The *North River Steam Boat* was an extremely narrow vessel, 146 feet by 12 feet, with a side waterwheel. The boat was rebuilt with a wider hull and began regular weekly runs between the two cities the following year.

[28] Hunter (1949, 7–11) notes that Fulton recognized the economic potential of the western rivers at the time of the initial Hudson River trial. The partners applied for monopoly grants throughout the west, but only the legislature of "the Orleans territory" obliged.

[29] Mak and Walton 1972, 625. Productivity per ship tended to rise faster than tonnage increased as a result of design improvements, better engines, and better docking facilities (Hughes and Reiter 1958). Per-unit productivity increased by a factor of nearly nine from 1815 to 1860 (Mak and Walton 1972, 637; see also Hunter 1949).

[30] Canal investment from 1815 to 1844 was $31 million, of which 73 percent came from governments. From 1844 to 1860, another $66 million was invested, about 66 percent of which was government money (Goodrich et al. 1961, 215).

[31] By 1829, foreigners had purchased half of the canal's debt (Goodrich 1960, 53–56; Rubin 1961).

[32] To that end, he organized the Patowmack Company to extend the Potomac River as a canal that went up into the mountains (Bernstein 2005, 22–23).

[33] In addition to Wright and Geddes, there was Charles Broadhead about whom little is known (Whitford 1906). The first choice, William Weston, refused to leave England (Bernstein 2005, 58–59; see also Stuart 1871, 48–52). The Americans did "so well as to earn the praise of European experts" (Taylor 1951, 34).

[34] See Goodrich et al. 1961, 30–32. This discussion includes the contrasts drawn between the "Erie route" and the "Ontario route," where Lake Ontario would be used for part of the journey across New York.

[35] Bernstein 2005, 215–16. The canal commissioners promised that White would be compensated for using his patent and his trip expenses to England, but the state legislature refused to honor the agreement.

[36] During the early decades of the nineteenth century, boys acquired skills in many trades through an apprenticeship program. By the Civil War, the proportion of boys serving apprenticeships was declining. This is customarily attributed to the lack of a formal guild system or similar institution.

[37] The following year, Peter Cooper introduced the "Tom Thumb," the first steam locomotive built in the United States to be operated on a common carrier, the Baltimore & Ohio RR.

[38] A road west, the Pittsburgh Pike, was completed in 1817. Although Pennsylvania invested tax funds ($1.8 million by 1825), the Erie presented a new challenge to the state, in general, and Philadelphia, in particular.

[39] Overall, the Main Line Canal earned only 3 percent on the original investment and was sold in 1857 to the Pennsylvania Railroad for $7.5 million (Rubin 1961). For insight into the economic and political difficulties associated with internal improvements in general, see Wallis 2003.

[40] Fishlow 1965. For a brief survey of the conventional view that railroad construction determined fluctuations in the business cycle, see Fogel 1964, 1–10.

[41] Fogel (1964) found that all but 4 percent of the agricultural land that existed in 1890 would have been cultivated in his rail-less system.

[42] Von Gerstner 1997 is a translation of a German book from 1842–43 that looks at both canals and railroads on a geographical basis.

[43] This was more than five times the amount invested in canals (Fishlow 1972, 496).

[44] Gates 1934 contains samples of all the problems associated with mixed enterprises.

[45] Ogden's family lived in New York, upstream of Philadelphia, and supplied that city with lumber. Years later, Ogden's interests included the lumber town of Peshtigo, Wisconsin, which burned over the same days as the 1871 Chicago Fire.

[46] See John 1995, 25ff. The statistics appear on p. 51.

[47] Lakwete (2003) explains the long history of gins. Whitney's gin increased the speed of ginning, but it sacrificed fiber quality for quantity.

[48] In 1812 Congress refused to renew Whitney's patent, but it did express the profound esteem of a grateful nation (Lakwete 2003, 133–34).

[49] Primack (1962, 492) estimates that a sixth of the Midwestern labor force in the 1850s was constantly engaged in clearing land.

[50] The figure comes from "Inventive Were the Pioneers," a webpage maintained by Burlington County, New Jersey, where Newbold was born: http://www.burlco.lib.nj.us/county/history/inventive.html.

[51] Peacock's plow led to a successful infringement suit by Newbold (Hurt 1994, 101).

[52] Predictably, others infringed on Wood's patents, and Wood is reported to have used a large portion of his profits defending them.

[53] Hurt 1994, 134. Since a cast-iron surface had small cavities and did not take a high polish, the moldboard had a tendency to hold prairie soils and slow the plow.

[54] The most extensive history of Deere and his company is Broehl 1984. Among others are Arnold 1995; Clark 1937; and Dahlstrom and Dahlstrom 2005.

[55] Cyrus's father attempted to construct a reaper earlier. Cyrus turned his attention to reaper production as a way to pay off the debts incurred when, in 1836, he and his father purchased an iron foundry ("Cotopaxi") (Hower 1936, 70–71).

[56] As noted, Ogden offered to finance the move. In 1848, McCormick and Ogden became partners in the distribution of reapers in Illinois, Indiana, Michigan, Kentucky, and Tennessee.

[57] In his search for a labor force, Slater is often credited with launching the family system of labor in which children tended machines for their fathers.

[58] According to David Jeremy (1981, 95), Lowell was the optimal vessel of technology transfer.

[59] According to Krooss and Gilbert (1972, 96), "By 1850, they controlled 20 percent of all cotton spindles, 30 percent of Massachusetts railroads, 40 percent of Massachusetts insurance, and 40 percent of Boston Banking."

[60] The McLane Report has many shortcomings, but as Rosenberg (1973) notes, this is the only document that comes close to being a "census of manufactures" circa 1830.

[61] Although it is notoriously difficult to measure the labor participation rate of women working in the home, women and children are estimated to have been about 10 percent of the labor force around 1800, rising to roughly 40 percent around 1830. The rate then declined, but remained above 30 percent through 1850.

[62] Singer could not pay Clark in cash, so he gave him a one-third interest in his patents. Davies (1976) discusses Clark's long career at Singer.

[63] Wallace notes that *mechanicians* was the term then used to describe the skilled workers who designed and made production machines; they were also the inventors and users of machine tools. With specialization, this occupation "merged imperceptibly into that of the blacksmith, the iron master, the machine maker, the engineer, the draftsman, the artist, the inventor, and the natural scientist" (1980, 212).

[64] After 1800 Evans concentrated on high-pressure steam engines that were used for his milling operations as well as for steamboats. See Pursell 1969; and Ferguson 1980.

[65] Hounshell (1984, 25–26) cites General Jean-Baptiste de Gribeauval as the person who introduced the idea to Jefferson.

[66] "The component part of pistols, are to correspond so exactly that any limb or part of one pistol may be fitted to any other pistol" (Hounshell 1984, 28).

[67] Carosso 1949. In 1844, Dennison founded what became the Dennison Manufacturing Company, but he turned over the paper-box business to his brother to enter the watch business.

[68] Landes (1983, 317) notes that the 14,000th watch was produced in 1858 and the 118,000th watch in 1865. Church (1975, 621) reports that the military demand increased productivity by 25 percent.

[69] Greeno 2006. Morse and Fulton appeared together on a two-dollar silver certificate issued in 1896 (Friedberg, Friedberg, and Friedberg 1981).

[70] These were given to but 1 percent of the 13,937 exhibitors (Royal Commission 1851; see also Ffrench 1950 and Moser 2006).

[71] Dick's press was described in one of his advertisements as "an arrangement of mechanical power, by which any given amount of force can be exchanged for any other amount of force…and no material discount lost in the trade for friction…where the simple lever becomes inconvenient" (Reynolds 1938; see also Frantz 1951; Stephens 1989; and Korman 2002).

References

Andreas, Alfred T. 1884. *History of Chicago from the Earliest Time to the Present.* Vol. 1. Chicago: A. T. Andreas.

Arnold, Dave. 1995. *Vintage John Deere.* Stillwater, OK: Voyageur Press.

Atack, Jeremy. 1999. "Quantitative and Qualitative Evidence in the Weaving of Business and Economic History: Western River Steamboats and the Transportation Revolution Revisited." *Business and Economic History* 28, no. 1: 1–11.

Banner, Stuart. 1998. "The Origin of the New York Stock Exchange, 1791–1860." *Journal of Legal Studies* 27, no. 1: 113–40.

Bateman, Fred, and Thomas Weiss. 1981. *A Deplorable Scarcity: The Failure of Industrialization in the Slave Economy.* Chapel Hill: The University of North Carolina Press.

Baumol, William J. 1990. "Entrepreneurship: Productive, Unproductive, and Destructive." *Journal of Political Economy* 98, no. 5: 893–921.

———. 2002. *The Free-Market Innovation Machine.* Princeton: Princeton University Press.

Beard, Charles. 1913. *An Economic Interpretation of the Constitution.* New York: Macmillan.

Berle, Adolf, and Gardiner Means. 1932. *Modern Corporation and Private Property.* New York: Macmillan.

Bernstein, Peter L. 2005. *Wedding of the Waters.* New York: W.W. Norton.

Bodenhorn, Howard. 2000. *A History of Banking in Antebellum America.* New York: Cambridge University Press.

Bodenhorn, Howard, and Hugh Rockoff. 1992. "Regional Interest Rates in Antebellum America." In *Strategic Factors in Nineteenth Century American Economic History*, edited by Claudia Goldin and Hugh Rockoff, 159–87. Chicago: University of Chicago Press.

Broehl, Wayne, Jr. 1984. *John Deere's Company, A History of Deere and Company and Its Times.* New York: Doubleday.

Cain, Louis. 1991. "Carving the Northwest Territory into States." In *The Vital One: Essays in Honor of Jonathan Hughes*, edited by Joel Mokyr, 1–14. Greenwich, CT: JAI Press.

———. 1998. "A Canal and Its City: A Selective Business History of Chicago." *DePaul Business Law Review* 11, no. 1: 125–84.

Callender, Guy Stevens. 1902. "The Early Transportation and Banking Enterprises of the States." *Quarterly Journal of Economics* 17, no. 1: 111–62.

Carosso, Vincent P. 1949. "The Waltham Watch Company: A Case History." *Bulletin of the Business Historical Society* 23, no. 4: 165–87.

Catterall, Ralph. 1903. *The Second Bank of the United States.* Chicago: University of Chicago Press.

Chandler, Alfred J., Jr. 1965. *The Railroads: The Nation's First Big Business.* New York: Harcourt, Brace & World.

Church, R. A. 1975. "Nineteenth-Century Clock Technology in Britain, the United States, and Switzerland." *Economic History Review* 28, no. 4: 616–30.

Clark, Neil M. 1937. *John Deere, He Gave the World the Steel Plow.* Moline: Deere and Co.

Clay, Karen. 1997. "Trade, Institutions, and Credit." *Explorations in Economic History* 34, no. 4: 495–521.

Cooper, Grace Rogers. 1968. *The Invention of the Sewing Machine.* Washington: Smithsonian Institution Press.

Cronon, William. 1991. *Nature's Metropolis: Chicago and the Great West.* New York: W.W. Norton.

Dahlstrom, Neil, and Jeremy Dahlstrom. 2005. *The John Deere Story: A Biography of Plowmakers John and Charles Deere.* DeKalb: Northern Illinois University Press.

Dalzell, Robert F., Jr. 1987. *Enterprising Elite: The Boston Associates and the World They Made.* Cambridge: Harvard University Press.

Dam, Kenneth W. 2006. *The Law-Growth Nexus: The Rule of Law and Economic Development.* Washington, DC: Brookings Institution Press.

Danhof, Clarence H. 1972. "The Tools and Implements of Agriculture." In *Farming in the New Nation: Interpreting American Agriculture: 1790–1840*, edited by Darwin P. Kelsey, 81–90. Washington: The Agricultural History Society.

David, Paul. 1975. *Technical Choice: Innovation and Economic Growth: Essays on American and British Experience in the Nineteenth Century.* New York: Cambridge University Press.

Davies, Robert B. 1976. *Peacefully Working to Conquer the World: Singer Sewing Machines in Foreign Markets, 1854–1920.* New York: Arno Press.

Davis, Lance, and Robert Gallman. 2000. *Evolving Financial Markets and International Capital Flows*. New York: Cambridge University Press.

Downard, William L. 1982. "William Butler Ogden and the Growth of Chicago." *Journal of the Illinois State Historical Society* 75, no. 1: 47–60.

Dublin, Thomas. 1979. *Women at Work: The Transformation of Work and Community in Lowell Massachusetts, 1826–1860*. New York: Columbia University Press.

Ferguson, Eugene S. 1980. *Oliver Evans: Inventive Genius of the American Industrial Revolution*. Greenville, DE: Eleutherian Mills-Hagley Foundation, Inc.

Ffrench, Yvonne. 1950. *The Great Exhibition: 1851*. London: Harvill Press.

Fishlow, Albert. 1965. *American Railroads and the Transformation of the Ante-Bellum Economy*. Cambridge: Harvard University Press.

———. 1972. "Internal Transportation." In Lance Davis, et al., *American Economic Growth: An Economist's History of the United States*, 468–547. New York: Harper & Row.

Fogel, Robert. 1964. *Railroads and American Economic Growth: Essays in Econometric History*. Baltimore: Johns Hopkins University Press.

Ford, Paul Leicester, ed. 1894. *The Writings of Thomas Jefferson*. New York: Putnam's.

Frantz, Joe B. 1951. *Gail Borden: Dairyman to a Nation*. Norman: University of Oklahoma Press.

Friedberg, Robert, Ira S. Friedberg, and Arthur Friedberg. 1981. *Paper Money of the United States: A Complete Illustrated Guide with Valuations*, 10th edition. Fort Lee, N.J.: Coin and Currency Institute.

Gates, Paul. 1934. *The Illinois Central Railroad and its Colonization Work*. Cambridge: Harvard University Press.

———. 1968. *History of Public Land Law Development*. Washington, DC: Public Land Law Review Commission.

Genovese, Eugene. 1965. *The Political Economy of Slavery*. New York: Pantheon.

Gibb, George S. 1950. *The Saco-Lowell Shops*. Cambridge: Harvard University Press.

Gies, Joseph. 1990. "The Great Reaper War." *American Heritage of Invention & Technology* 5, no. 3: 20–28.

Goldin, Claudia, and Kenneth Sokoloff. 1982. "Women, Children, and Industrialization in the Early Republic: Evidence from the Manufacturing Census." *Journal of Economic History* 42, no. 4: 741–74.

Goodrich, Carter. 1960. *Government Promotion of American Canals and Railroads, 1800–1890*. New York: Columbia University Press.

Goodrich, Carter, Jerome Cranmer, Julius Rubin, and Harvey Segal. 1961. *Canals and American Economic Development*. New York: Columbia University Press.

Gordon, John Steele. 1997. *Hamilton's Blessing: The Extraordinary Life and Times of Our National Debt*. New York: Penguin.

Greeno, Follett L., ed. 2006. *Obed Hussey: Who, of All Inventors, Made Bread Cheap*. A Project Gutenberg Ebook available at http://www.gutenberg.org/files/19547/19547-8.txt. (Accessed October 15, 2006.)

Haites, Erik, and James Mak. 1973. "The Decline of Steamboating on the Ante-Bellum Western Rivers: Some New Evidence and an Alternative Hypothesis." *Explorations in Economic History* 11, no. 1: 25–36.

Hammond, Bray. 1947. "Jackson, Biddle, and the Bank of the United States." *Journal of Economic History* 7, no. 2: 1–23.

———. 1957. *Banks and Politics in America from the Revolution to the Civil War*. Princeton: Princeton University Press.

Hedges, James. 1952. *The Browns of Providence Plantations*. Cambridge: Harvard University Press. Providence: Brown University Press.

———. 1968. *The Browns of Providence Plantations*. Providence: Brown University Press.

Hindle, Brooke. 1981. *Emulation and Invention*. New York: New York University Press.

Hofstadter, Richard, ed. 1958. *Great Issues in American History from the Revolution to the Civil War 1765–1865*. New York: Vintage Books.

Hoke, Donald. 1990. *Ingenious Yankees: The Rise of the American System of Manufactures in the Private Sector*. New York: Columbia University Press.

Holdsworth, John, and Davis Dewey. 1910. *The First and Second Banks of the United States*. Washington: Government Printing Office.

Horwitz, Morton. 1977. *The Transformation of American Law, 1780–1860*. Cambridge, MA: Harvard University Press.

Hounshell, David. 1984. *From the American System to Mass Production 1800–1932*. Baltimore: Johns Hopkins University Press.

Hovenkamp, Herbert. 1988. "The Classical Corporation in American Legal Thought." *The Georgetown Law Review* 76(June):1593–1689.

———. 1991. *Enterprise and American Law, 1836–1937*. Cambridge: Harvard University Press.

Hower, Ralph M. 1936. "Cyrus Hall McCormick: American Business Leader." *Bulletin of the Business Historical Society* 10, no. 5: 69–76.

Hughes, Jonathan. 1986. *The Vital Few*. New York: Oxford University Press.

———. 1987. "The Great Land Ordinances: America's Thumbprint on History." In *Essays on the Economy of the Old Northwest*, edited by David C. Klingaman and Richard K. Vedder, 1–18. Athens: Ohio University Press.

———. 1991. *The Governmental Habit Redux*. Princeton: Princeton University Press.

Hughes, Jonathan, and Louis Cain. 2007. *American Economic History*, 7th ed. Boston: Addison-Wesley.

Hughes, Jonathan, and Stanley Reiter. 1958. "The First 1945 British Steamships." *Journal of the American Statistical Association* 3, no. 282: 360–81.

Hunter, Louis. 1949. *Steamboats on the Western Rivers*. Cambridge: Harvard University Press.

Hurst, James Willard. 1970. *The Legitimacy of the Business Corporation in the United States*. Charlottesville: University Press of Virginia.

———. 1978. "Release of Energy." In *American Law and the Constitutional Order: Historical Perspectives*, edited by Lawrence M. Friedman and Harry N. Scheiber, 109–20. Cambridge, MA: Harvard University Press.

Hurt, R Douglas. 1994. *American Agriculture: A Brief History*. Ames: Iowa State University Press.

Irwin, Douglas. 2004. "The Aftermath of Hamilton's 'Report on Manufactures.'" *Journal of Economic History* 64, no. 3: 800–821.

Jack, Andrew B. 1956. "The Channels of Distribution for an Innovation: The Sewing Machine in America, 1860–1865." *Explorations in Entrepreneurial History* 9, no. 3: 113–41.

Jeremy, David. 1981. *Transatlantic Industrial Revolution: The Diffusion of Textile Technologies between Britain and America, 1790–1830s*. Cambridge: MIT Press.

John, Richard. 1995. *Spreading the News: The American Postal System from Franklin to Morse*. Cambridge: Harvard University Press.

Khan, B. Zorina. 1995. "Property Rights and Patent Litigation in Early Nineteenth-Century America." *Journal of Economic History* 55, no. 1: 58–97.

Khan, B. Zorina, and Kenneth Sokoloff. 2006. "Institutions and Technological Innovation during Early Economic Growth." In *Institutions, Development, and Economic Growth*, edited by Theo S. Eicher and Cecilia García-Peñalosa, 123–58. Cambridge: MIT Press.

Kirzner, Israel. 1973. *Competition and Entrepreneurship*. Chicago: University of Chicago Press.

Knodell, Jane. 2003. "Profit and Duty in the Second Bank of the United States' Exchange Operations." *Financial History Review* 10, no. 1: 5–30.

Korman, Richard. 2002. *The Goodyear Story: An Inventor's Obsession and the Struggle for a Rubber Monopoly.* San Francisco: Encounter Books.

Krooss, Herman, and Charles Gilbert. 1972. *American Business History.* Englewood Cliffs, NJ: Prentice-Hall.

Lakwete, Angela. 2003. *Inventing the Cotton Gin: Machine and Myth in Antebellum America.* Baltimore: Johns Hopkins University Press.

Lamoreaux, Naomi. 1994. *Insider Lending: Banks, Personal Connections, and Economic Development in Industrial New England.* New York: Cambridge University Press.

———. 2004. "Partnerships, Corporations, and the Limits on Contractual Freedom in U.S. History: An Essay in Economics, Law, and Culture." In *Constructing Corporate America: History, Politics, and Culture,* edited by Kenneth Lipartito and David Sicilia, 29–65. New York: Oxford University Press.

Landes, David S. 1969. *The Unbound Prometheus.* Cambridge: Cambridge University Press.

———. 1983. *Revolution in Time: Clocks and the Making of the Modern World.* Cambridge, MA: Harvard University Press.

Larkin, F. Daniel. 1990. *John B. Jervis, an American Engineering Pioneer.* Ames: Iowa State University Press.

Lubar, Steven. 1991. "The Transformation of American Patent Law." *Technology and Culture* 32, no. 4: 932–59.

Machlup, Fritz, and Edith Penrose. 1950. "The Patent Controversy in the Nineteenth Century." *Journal of Economic History* 10, no. 1: 1–29.

Mak, James, and Gary Walton. 1972. "Steamboats and the Great Productivity Surge in River Transportation." *Journal of Economic History* 32, no. 3: 619–40.

Martin, David. 1974. "Metallism, Small Notes, and Jackson's War with the B.U.S." *Explorations in Economic History* 11, no. 3: 227–47.

———. 1977. "The Changing Role of Foreign Money in the United States, 1782–1857." *Journal of Economic History* 37, no. 4: 1009–27.

McClelland, Peter. 1997. *Sowing Modernity: America's First Agricultural Revolution.* Ithaca: Cornell University Press.

McGuire, Robert. 2003. *To Form A More Perfect Union.* New York: Oxford University Press.

Miller, Arthur Selwyn. 1972. *The Supreme Court and American Capitalism.* New York: Free Press.

Miller, Donald L. 1996. *City of the Century: The Epic of Chicago and the Making of America.* New York: Simon and Schuster.

Moser, Petra. 2007. "What Do Inventors Patent?" NBER Working Paper No. 13294, August. Cambridge, MA: National Bureau of Economic Research.

Murphy, Kevin M., Andrei Schleifer, and Robert W. Vishny. 1991. "The Allocation of Talent: Implications for Growth." *Quarterly Journal of Economics* 106, no. 2: 503–30.

Niemi, Albert. 1970. "A Further Look at Interregional Lands and Economic Specialization: 1820–1840." *Explorations in Economic History* 7, no. 4: 499–520.

———. 1972. "A Closer Look at Canals and Western Manufacturing in the Canal Era: Reply to Ransom." *Explorations in Economic History* 9, no. 4: 423–24.

Perkins, Edwin J. 1975. *Financing Anglo-American Trade: The House of Brown, 1800–1880.* Cambridge: Harvard University Press.

Primack, Martin. 1962. "Land Clearing Under 19th Century Techniques." *Journal of Economic History* 22, no. 4: 516–19.

Pursell, Carroll W., Jr. 1969. *Early Stationary Steam Engines in America.* Washington: Smithsonian Institution Press.

Ransom, Roger. 1964. "Canals and Development: A Discussion of the Issues." *American Economic Review* 54, no. 2: 365–76.

———. 1971. "A Closer Look at Canals and Western Manufacturing." *Explorations in Economic History* 8, no. 4: 501–08.

Reynolds, John Earle. 1938. *In French Creek Valley*. Meadville, PA: The Crawford County Historical Society.

Rolnick, Arthur, Bruce Smith, and Warren Weber. 1993. "In Order to Form a More Perfect Monetary Union." *Federal Reserve Bank of Minneapolis Quarterly Review* 17, no. 4: 2–13.

Rosenberg, Nathan, ed. 1969. *The American System of Manufacturers: The Report of the Committee on the Machinery of the United States 1855 and the Special Reports of George Wallis and Joseph Whitworth 1854*. Edinburgh: Edinburgh University Press.

———. 1972a. "Technological Change." In Lance Davis, et al., *American Economic Growth*, 233–79. New York: Harper & Row.

———. 1972b. *Technology and American Economic Growth*. New York: Harper & Row.

———. 1973. "Documents Relative to the Manufactures in the United States," review of the 1969 reprint of the McLane report. *Business History Review* 47, no. 1: 106–08.

Rosenbloom, Joshua. 2004. "Path Dependence and the Origins of the American Cotton Textile Industry." In *The Fibre that Changed the World: Cotton Industry in International Perspective*, edited by David Jeremy and Douglas A. Farnie, 365–91. Oxford: Oxford University Press.

Rousseau, Peter, and Richard Sylla. 2005. "Emerging Financial Markets and Early US Growth." *Explorations in Economic History* 42, no. 1: 1–16.

Royal Commission. 1851. *Reports by the Juries on the subjects in the thirty classes into which the exhibition was divided*. London: W. Clowes & Sons.

Rubin, Julius. 1961. "An Innovating Public Improvement: The Erie Canal." In Carter Goodrich, Jerome Cranmer, Julius Rubin, and Harvey Segal, *Canals and American Economic Development*, 15–66. New York: Columbia University Press.

Schlesinger, Arthur H., Jr. 1945. *The Age of Jackson*. New York: Mentor Books.

Schumpeter, Joseph. 1934. *The Theory of Economic Development*. Cambridge: Harvard University Press.

Snowden, Kenneth. 1998. "U.S. Securities Markets and the Banking System, 1790–1840: Commentary." *Federal Reserve Bank of St. Louis Review* 80, no. 3: 99–103.

Sokoloff, Kenneth. 1984. "Was the Transition from the Artisanal Shop to the Nonmechanized Factory Associated with Gains in Efficiency? Evidence from the U.S. Manufacturing Censuses of 1820 and 1850." *Explorations in Economic History* 21, no. 4: 351–82.

———. 1988. "Inventive Activity in Early Industrial America: Evidence From Patent Records, 1790–1846." *Journal of Economic History* 48, no. 4: 813–850.

Sokoloff, Kenneth, and B. Zorina Khan. 1990. "The Democratization of Invention during Early Industrialization: Evidence from the United States, 1790–1846." *Journal of Economic History* 50, no. 2: 363–78.

Stephens, Carlene E. 1989. " 'The Most Reliable Time': William Bond, The New England Railroads, and Time Awareness in 19th-Century America." *Technology and Culture* 30, no. 1: 1–24.

Stuart, Charles. 1871. *Lives and Works of Civil and Military Engineers of America*. New York: D. Van Nostrand.

Studenski, Paul and Herman Krooss. 1952. *Financial History of the United States*. New York: McGraw-Hill.

Sylla, Richard. 1998. "U.S. Securities Markets and the Banking System, 1790–1840." *Federal Reserve Bank of St. Louis Review* 80, no. 3: 83–98.

———. 2003. "Financial Systems, Risk Management, and Entrepreneurship: Historical Perspectives." *Japan and the World Economy* 15, no. 4: 447–58.

Sylla, Richard, John Legler, and John Wallis. 1987. "Banks and State Public Finance in the New Republic: The United States, 1790–1860." *Journal of Economic History* 57, no. 2:91–403.

Taylor, George Rogers, ed. 1949. *Jackson and Biddle: The Struggle over the Second Bank of the United States*. Boston: D. C. Heath.

———. 1951. *The Transportation Revolution*. New York: Holt, Rinehart & Winston.

Thompson, Holland. 1921. *The Age of Invention, A Chronicle of Mechanical Conquest*. New Haven, Yale University Press.

Treat, Payson Jackson. 1962. "Origin of the National Land System Under the Confederation." In *The Public Lands: Studies in the History of the Public Domain*, edited by Vernon Carstensen, 7–14. Madison: University of Wisconsin Press.

von Gerstner, Franz Anton Ritter. 1997. *Early American Railroads*. Stanford: Stanford University Press.

Wallace, Anthony F. C. 1980. *Rockdale: the growth of an American village in the early industrial revolution*. New York: Knopf.

Wallis, John Joseph. 2003. "The Property Tax as a Coordinating Device: Financing Indiana's Mammoth Internal Improvement System, 1835–1842." *Explorations in Economic History* 40, no. 3: 223–50.

———. 2005. "Constitutions, Corporations, and Corruption: American States and Constitutional Change, 1842 to 1852." *Journal of Economic History*, 65, no. 1: 211–56.

Wallis, John Joseph, and Barry Weingast. 2005. "Equilibrium Impotence: Why the States and not the American National Government Financed Economic Development in the Antebellum Era." NBER Working Paper No. 11397, June. Cambridge, MA: National Bureau of Economic Research.

Ware, Caroline F. 1931. *The Early New England Cotton Manufacture: A Study in Industrial Beginnings*. Boston: Houghton Mifflin.

Whitford, Noble E. 1906. *History of the Canal System of the State of New York*. Available at http://www.history.rochester.edu/canal/bib/whitford/1906/Contents.html.

Woodbury, Robert S. 1972. *Studies in the History of Machine Tools*. Cambridge: MIT Press.

Wright, Robert. 1999. "Bank Ownership and Lending Patterns in New York and Pennsylvania, 1781–1831." *Business History Review* 73, no. 1: 40–60.

———. 2001. *Origins of Commercial Banking in America, 1750–1800*. Lanham, MD: Rowman & Littlefield Publishers.

———. 2003. *The Wealth of Nations Rediscovered: Integration and Expansion in American Financial Markets, 1780–1850*. New York: Cambridge University Press.

Zevin, Robert Brooke. 1971. "The Growth of Cotton Textile Production After 1815." In *The Reinterpretation of American Economic History*, edited by Robert Fogel and Stanley Engerman, 122–47. New York: Harper & Row.

———. 1975. *Growth of Manufacturing in Early-Nineteenth-Century New England*. New York: Arno Press.

Chapter 13

Entrepreneurship in the United States, 1865–1920

Naomi R. Lamoreaux

A Period of Rapid Expansion

The half-century or so following the Civil War was a period of extraordinarily rapid economic growth in the United States. Real gross domestic product (GDP) multiplied more than seven times between 1865 and 1920, and real per capita product more than doubled. As the much higher growth rates of total compared to per capita GDP suggest, the economy expanded more by adding new inputs than it did by increasing productivity. Nevertheless, the rate of increase in per capita product (averaging about 1.7 percent per year over the entire period 1870–1920) was higher than ever before in U.S. history, and total factor productivity grew from an index value of 51.0 in 1889, the first year for which figures are available, to 81.2 in 1920 (1929 = 100). These productivity figures, moreover, greatly underestimate the extent of technological progress. Because they are calculated as residuals, they do not capture improvements embodied in capital or other inputs to production (Carter et al. 2006, 3:3, 5, 23–25, 463).

Although many factors contributed to the extensive growth of the period, including high rates of immigration and a substantial rise in the savings rate, perhaps the most important was the expansion and improvement of the nation's transportation and communications network. This development permitted the abundant agricultural and mineral resources of the western parts of the country to be brought into profitable production. It also contributed to the rise of per capita income, most obviously by making it possible to exploit economies of scale and to concentrate production in areas of the country that for one reason or another had a comparative advantage. During this period industry became both more regionally specialized and increasingly dominated by large-scale enterprises (Kim 1995; Chandler 1977).

Another important way in which improvements in transportation raised per capita income was by stimulating technological innovation and entrepreneurship.[1] As entrepreneurs responded to the new opportunities for profit provided by the country's rapidly growing markets, per capita patenting rates soared (see figure 13.1) and technology advanced in directions that were so novel as to constitute a second industrial revolution. Entrepreneurs formed start-up enterprises to exploit cutting-edge developments in new industries such as steel, electricity, chemicals, and automobiles, pushing the frontiers of technological knowledge continually outward and

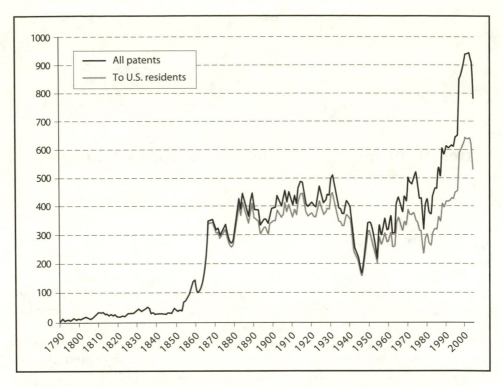

Figure 13.1. Patents Granted by the U.S. Patent Office per Million Residents of the United States. (Source: Susan B. Carter et al., 2006, *Historical Statistics of the United States*, 1:28–29, 3:426–28; U.S. Patent Office, "U.S. Patent Activity: Calendar Years 1790 to the Present," http://www.uspto.gov/web/offices/ac/ido/oeip/taf/tafp.html; U.S. Census Bureau, "Population Estimates, 2000–2006," http://factfinder.census.gov/servlet/GCTTable?_bm=y&-geo_id=01000US&-_box_head_nbr=GCT-T1&-ds_name=PEP_2006_EST&-_lang=en&-format=US-9&-_sse=on.)

dramatically transforming American society in the process. Indeed, so many people came up with so many new technological ideas and founded so many new businesses during this period that it has generally been considered a golden age for both the independent inventor and the entrepreneur (Hughes 1989; Schumpeter 1942).

The Entrepreneur's Status in American Society

If ever there was a time or place when entrepreneurs were the most admired figures in society, it was the United States during the late nineteenth century. Americans knew the names and avidly followed the exploits of the period's "captains of industry." They devoured the rags-to-riches novels of Horatio Alger, poured over P. T. Barnum's *The Art of Money-Getting* and other success manuals, and turned out by the hundreds of thousands to hear the Revered Russell Conwell deliverer his how-to-get-rich lecture, "Acres of Diamonds." There was no higher goal for a young American male to pursue during this period than to become a "self-made man"—to make a great deal of money through dint of his own hard work and "pluck" (Wyllie 1954; Kirkland 1956; Garraty 1968, 16; Cochran 1972, 170–76; Hilkey 1997).

Of course, the number of people who actually rose all the way from rags to riches was very small. Studies of the origins of the country's business leaders showed that the vast majority had middle- or even upper-class backgrounds.[2] Nonetheless, there was significant upward mobility during this period, and the extent of this mobility seems to have been great enough to give real substance to the myth. After studying iron, locomotive, and machinery manufacturers in nineteenth-century Patterson, New Jersey, Herbert Gutman concluded that "so many successful manufacturers who had begun as workers walked the streets of that city" that the idea that "'hard work' resulted in spectacular material and social improvement" was entirely believable.[3] Such examples were powerful incentives to entrepreneurship because they showed that the way to move upward in society was to start one's own business. Indeed, in the late nineteenth century to be an employee (even a genteel, white-collar employee) was to forsake a life of striving for a condition of "dependency"—itself a sign of moral failing.[4]

This was the era when social Darwinist ideas were in the ascendancy, and they were more influential in the United States than anywhere else. According to this view, businesspeople were engaged in a competitive struggle. Only the fittest would succeed. Moreover, because Americans of the time thought the qualities that determined who was fittest were the Protestant virtues of hard work, thrift, and probity, success was taken to be a sign of a man's moral worth (Hofstadter 1955; Wyllie 1954; Hilkey 1997). Judgments of creditworthiness during this period were primarily judgments of character. Men who failed in business had not only proved themselves unfit in a Darwinian sense, they had demonstrated serious moral deficiencies (Sandage 2005; Olegario 2006, 80–118). This idea that failure reflected inner weaknesses was so powerful that movements like the Populists had to rebuild the self-esteem of farmers hit hard by forces beyond their control in order to mobilize them politically. The Populists organized networks of cooperative enterprises in order to relieve farmers' economic distress but also with the aim of substituting an ethic of mutual self-help for the ideal of the self-made man (Goodwyn 1978).

Institutions and the Role of Government in the Aftermath of the Civil War

As the previous chapter emphasized, the Constitution facilitated entrepreneurship by creating the largest free-trade zone in the world, by prohibiting state governments from abrogating contracts or tampering with the value of money, and by giving the federal government the authority to create a system of intellectual property rights. Although the federal government initially undertook to play an ambitious role in the country's economic development, constitutional scruples and sectional politics quickly limited its activities. State governments were not similarly handicapped, however, and from the late eighteenth century on they played an active role in the economy, particularly in the area of transportation improvements. They were especially active during the 1820s and 1830s, investing in, or guaranteeing the debt obligations of, privately organized road, canal, and railroad companies. Some states even built and operated transportation systems as public works.

Some of these projects were ill-conceived, and after several states defaulted on their bonded debt during the depression that followed the Panic of 1837, there was growing political opposition to such a direct role for government in economic development. Although the prevailing sentiment was that infrastructural projects were best left to private enterprise, many state and local governments nonetheless continued to provide financial support to railroad and other transportation companies in the decades that followed (see Taylor 1951; Harz 1948). During the Civil War, moreover, the withdrawal from Congress of Southern legislators (who had vehemently opposed federal transportation projects) freed the national government to resume a promotional role. Congress chartered the Union and Central Pacific Railroads to build the first transcontinental railroad in 1862 and provided the two companies with financial aid in the form of land grants and loan guarantees. A flurry of charters and land grants for additional transcontinentals followed until a series of corruption scandals once again dampened enthusiasm for such governmental initiatives (see Summers 1993).

The most notorious of these scandals involved the Crédit Mobilier Company, a construction company formed by the directors of the Union Pacific to build the railroad. Crédit Mobilier charged its parent company what seemed to be an exorbitant amount for each mile of road it built and made its owners rich. Disgruntled stockholders challenged the arrangement in court, but their suit attracted little attention until the run-up to the presidential campaign of 1872, when a newspaper revealed that the "railroad ring" had bribed influential congressmen by giving them Crédit Mobilier shares. Simple fraud was not front-page news, but bribery was (Bain 1999; see also Summers 1993). The directors of the Central Pacific organized a similar construction company, hired it build their railroad, and handed out railroad passes and other favors to curry political support. Moreover, they and the other railroad "robber barons" misrepresented their companies' finances in order to prop up the value of the securities they issued to raise capital on national and international markets, undermining the stability of the financial system in the process. For example, Jay Cooke's reckless use of his own Philadelphia bank to support the Northern Pacific Railroad's bonds has generally been seen as an important cause of the Panic of 1873 (White 2003).

Historians have taken radically different positions on these activities. Some have viewed them as emblematic of the destructive kinds of entrepreneurship that flourish wherever government largess incites rent-seeking behavior.[5] Others, however, have made the case that without some such shenanigans the railroads would never have been able to raise the capital they needed to finance construction (see Summers 1993). Regardless, there is no question that the railroad scandals awakened deep-seated fears that the nation's democratic institutions were being undermined by economic corruption. Americans traditionally held their politicians in low esteem, and under normal circumstances kept the resources they could command, especially at the federal level, quite limited. The Civil War had necessitated an enormous expansion of the scope of the federal government's activities. By the mid-1870s, however, the Crédit Mobilier scandal combined with lurid reports about corruption in the newly reconstructed state governments of the postbellum South to bring a hasty end, not only to federal transportation projects, but to most of the government's new activities, including Reconstruction itself (Wallis 2006).

Ongoing Promotional Activities of the Federal Government

Although the federal government's involvement in the economy receded in the late nineteenth century, some programs that were conducive to entrepreneurship survived the post-Reconstruction retrenchment. Land policy is a good example. Congress had passed the Homestead Act in 1862, enabling settlers to acquire 160 acres of public land in the western portions of the United States essentially for free on condition that they live on the land for at least five years. Subsequently, the terms of the legislation were liberalized so that under some conditions settlers could acquire greater amounts of land or gain title to their land after a shorter period of residence. Special acts were also passed that granted land to farmers in exchange for planting trees or investing in irrigation. Farmers took entrepreneurial advantage of these favorable incentives to claim on average more than ten million acres of public land each year between 1870 and 1920 (Atack and Passell 1994, 256–60).

Successful cultivation of these western lands required the development of new farming techniques and seed stocks. Here too the federal government played an important role. During the first half of the nineteenth century the states had provided some funding for research on farming practices, and the federal government had joined this effort, sponsoring experimentation with new seed varieties and cultivation techniques under the auspices of the U.S. Patent Office. During the Civil War these programs grew. Indeed, one of the main purposes of the new Department of Agriculture, established in 1862, was to take over the Patent Office's programs and expand them. Similarly, the Morrill Act of the same year created a system of land-grant colleges whose mission was to conduct research on improved farming practices and transmit this knowledge to their students. Government funding for the creation and dissemination of new agricultural knowledge increased further with the passage in 1887 of the Hatch Act, which provided financial support for a system of agricultural experiment stations, and again in 1914 with the Smith-Lever Act, which funded the agricultural extension service (Huffman 1998; Olmstead and Rhode 2002).

As Alan Olmstead and Paul Rhode have shown, this complex of agricultural research institutions provided critical support for the many thousands of farmers who risked everything to move onto the western prairies and plains during the second half of the nineteenth century. Guided by (mostly) government-sponsored research in new seed varieties, farmers tried out new types of grain as they coped with the harsh environmental conditions of the West. Less than 10 percent of the acreage planted in wheat in 1919 consisted of varieties that U.S. farmers had sowed before the Civil War. More than 30 percent was planted in varieties introduced in the 1870s and another nearly 20 percent in types first used during the 1880s and 1890s. Olmstead and Rhode estimate that if farmers had not planted these new seed varieties, yields in western agriculture would have been at least a third lower in 1909 than they actually were and that losses from insect damage and plant diseases would have further reduced output to about half of its actual level. Overall, they calculate, biological innovation accounted for about half of the gain in output per unit of labor that occurred between 1839 and 1909. Most of the rest they attribute to mechanization, particularly of reaping and mowing (Olmstead and Rhode 2002).

The other important economic activity to receive substantial government support in the late nineteenth century was mining. Federal policy encouraged the exploitation of mineral resources on public lands in the West by granting property rights to those who first laid claim to, and worked, ore deposits. This policy was strikingly different from the more common practice internationally of treating mineral resources as the property of the state, and it gave rise to a type of entrepreneur who seems to have been uniquely American—the prospector (Libecap 1979; David and Wright 1997, 217). The government also assisted prospectors by conducting geological surveys that helped them locate valuable resources. As in the case of agricultural research, funding initially came from the states during the first half of the nineteenth century, though the national government financed exploratory expeditions by the army's Corps of Topographical Engineers. After the Civil War the Corps' "Geological Exploration of the Fortieth Parallel" provided assessments of mining methods and equipment in addition to mapping the location of mineral resources. Then, in 1879, Congress expanded these efforts by founding the U.S. Geological Survey. Many of the engineers who staffed the Survey were trained at land-grant colleges, which also supplied experts to private mining companies. The combined stimulus to discovery that these federal policies provided helped catapult the United States into the position of the world's leading mineral producer, with a share of global output that greatly exceeded its proportion of resources in the ground (David and Wright 1997).

Financial Institutions

For a quarter-century after the demise of the Second Bank of the United States in 1836, the federal government neither chartered banks nor regulated them. The exigencies of Civil War finance forced a change in policy, however. Beginning in 1862, Congress passed a series of National Banking Acts that induced most existing banks to exchange their state charters for national ones. The legislation taxed the notes of state banks out of existence, but national banks could issue currency in the form of national banknotes backed by holdings of U.S. government bonds. The federal government thus aimed to achieve two policy goals at the same time: to create a market for its war debt; and to provide the country with a uniform currency that, unlike the hodgepodge of state banknotes that had made up the bulk of the money supply in the antebellum era, would circulate everywhere at par.

Although the creation of a uniform national currency undoubtedly lowered transactions costs and facilitated the growth of a national market, the National Banking System suffered from serious structural flaws that increased the financial instability of the economy. The flaws were a direct result of the political influence that interested groups had exerted during the process of drafting the legislation. For example, at the behest of large northeastern (particularly New York) banks, the legislation specified that ordinary banks could hold their reserves in interest-bearing accounts in banks in designated reserve cities, which in turn could hold their reserves in interest-bearing accounts in banks in New York City (Gische 1979). The result of this pyramiding of reserves was to increase the vulnerability of the entire system to bank failures in New York. Similarly, small banks' efforts to protect themselves against competition from larger banks resulted in a prohibition against branching, denying banks an important tool that they could have used to diversify their portfolios against local shocks (see, e.g., Calomiris 1990). Not surprisingly, repeated crises disrupted the financial system over the next half-century until finally Congress replaced the National Banking System with the more stable Federal Reserve System in 1913 (see West 1974; White 1983; Livingston 1986).

National banks came under the regulatory authority of the U.S. comptroller of the currency, who subjected them to regular examinations to insure that they adhered to mandated reserve requirements. The comptroller also enforced a set of rules that aimed to bolster the soundness of the financial system by limiting banks' business to short-term commercial lending (Lamoreaux 1994, 107–32). Entrepreneurially minded financiers who found the federal rules too restrictive got around them by persuading state governments to charter novel types of financial institutions. The most important were the so-called trust companies. Initially formed to administer the estates of wealthy families, they quickly evolved into intermediaries that played an important role in underwriting securities issues and financing firms in second industrial revolution industries (Neal 1971). A more general consequence of the growth of state-chartered financial institutions was to reduce monopoly power in local credit markets, lowering the cost of borrowing in regions that had previously been underserved by banks and reducing interest rate differentials across states (James 1976). Although this competition between the states and the federal government might thus be seen as conducive to entrepreneurship, it also spurred governments to lower reserve and capital requirements and tolerate more risky lending practices (White 1982).

Banking was subject to at least minimal government regulation during the late nineteenth and early twentieth century. The securities markets were not, and problems of asymmetric information seriously limited the demand for equities. Firms that issued securities generally did not publish financial statements, let alone audited ones, so there was no way of getting reliable information about their performance. Moreover, a number of well-publicized shenanigans drove the lesson home that even the most savvy investors could get taken. In one of the most famous incidents, Cornelius Vanderbilt's attempt to buy control of the Erie Railroad was frustrated by a clever subterfuge that allowed the Erie's treasurer, Daniel Drew, to print a seemingly endless amount of new stock.[6]

The information problems that plagued the securities markets allowed opportunistic entrepreneurs to make money at the expense of the unwary, but they also created opportunities for entrepreneurs who could cultivate investors' trust. During the depression of the 1890s, for example, members of the New York Stock Exchange (NYSE) responded to the declining profitability of their brokerage businesses by instituting important rule changes, most notably requiring firms whose securities traded on the exchange to file annual reports. The new rules made listing on the NYSE an imprimatur of quality, and not surprisingly, paid off in a dramatic rise in the price of a seat on the exchange (Neal and Davis 2007). To give another example, the private banker J. P. Morgan assiduously cultivated a reputation for financial probity and fair dealing, which he was able to exploit when he reorganized a number of bankrupt railroads during the 1890s. Morgan's method in the early stages of a reorganization was to establish a voting trust for investors' stock that would be under his personal control and give him the power to monitor and shape the railroad's business practices. When the trust expired at the end of some agreed-upon period, Morgan continued to protect investors' interests by keeping one of his partners on the railroad's board. During the great merger movement, he played a similar role when he promoted important consolidations such as the United States Steel Corporation.

Shareholders in "Morganized" firms generally earned above-market returns on their investments (Carosso 1987; De Long 1991).

The investments in reputation that men like Morgan and the brokers on the NYSE made seem to have reassured investors, who proceeded to sink increasing amounts of their savings into equities. The value of new corporate shares issued on the New York Stock Exchange rose rapidly. Even before the speculative bubble of the 1920s it reached levels relative to GDP that were higher than those attained in the second half of the twentieth century when investors' interests were protected by the Securities and Exchange Commission (O'Sullivan 2004). In the rough-and-tumble economy of the late-nineteenth-century United States, risks were high and even the most well-informed investors could lose a lot of money. But returns were also high, and intermediaries who were able to elicit investors' trust could earn extraordinary profits.

Incentives to Innovate: The Dissemination of Technological Information

People are more likely to invest time and resources in inventing new technologies if they think they will be able to profit from their discoveries (Schmookler 1966; Sokoloff 1988). They can only profit from their discoveries, however, if they can prevent competitors from stealing them. One obvious way to do this is to keep their ideas secret. Although this strategy can be a profitable one for inventors, it may harm society by inhibiting the dissemination of technological information. Moreover, it may even be suboptimal from the standpoint of individual inventors. In the first place, it may prevent them from acquiring knowledge that could help them surmount technological hurdles more efficiently or devise solutions to problems that otherwise seem intractable. In the second, it may prevent them from profiting from their inventions in other ways—for example, by selling them to individuals or firms better placed to exploit them commercially. Once inventors can extract returns from their ideas by selling them off, they can benefit from a division of labor that allows them to specialize in the creative work they do best.[7]

Patents provided inventors with an alternative way of protecting their ideas from theft. The U.S. patent system, as discussed in the last chapter, enforced inventors' intellectual property rights at quite modest cost. As a result, patentees were able to exchange technological information with each other and with potential buyers for their inventions with comparatively little fear that their ideas would be stolen. Of course, the patent system also stimulated unproductive entrepreneurship by creating incentives for "trolls" to buy up patents and charge extortionate licensing fees. There were certainly instances of such activity during the late nineteenth and early twentieth centuries. In one important example, a businessman bought up a set of brake patents and attempted to use his control of this vital technology to hold up the railroads (Usselman 1991). The general consensus, however, is that during this period of history the U.S. patent system's encouragements to productive entrepreneurship far outweighed these kinds of negative effects.[8]

Moreover, the U.S. Patent Office actively encouraged the dissemination of technological information by offering researchers free and open access to the specifications and models stored in its Washington headquarters, by publishing lists of inventions that obtained patents, and by buying advertisements in private journals that reported information about patents. The most famous of these journals, *Scientific American*, printed lists of patents granted on a weekly basis, featured lengthy descriptions of the most important new technologies, and offered to send its readers copies of complete patent specifications for a small fee. Over time, more specialized trade journals emerged to keep producers informed about patents in particular industries. For example, the *Journal of the Society of Glass Technology* provided detailed descriptions of all patents taken out in the United States and Britain relating to the manufacture of glass (Borut 1977; Lamoreaux and Sokoloff 1999, 2007).

Of course, in order to take advantage of this flood of information, inventors had to be literate and numerate and have enough basic technological and scientific knowledge to translate the words and diagrams on the page into working devices. During the first half of the nineteenth century, when most cutting-edge technologies were mechanical in character, the requisite knowledge was relatively easy to obtain. Basic schooling was widely available at low cost, with the result that most adults had the reading and math skills they needed to learn about new technological developments (Cubberley 1920; Cremin 1980; Kaestle 1983). At the same time, traditional apprenticeships and other ways of acquiring on-the-job training provided practitioners with sufficient technical skills to be able to push out the frontiers of production.[9] During the second half of the century, however, science-based technologies would become more important, and new institutions for transmitting and disseminating knowledge would be needed. The land-grant colleges founded after the Morrill Act were important centers of learning, but much of the growth in higher education during the late nineteenth century was funded by private sources, including businesses seeking to create local pools of expertise to meet their needs. The result was an extensive but decentralized system of colleges and universities in which research was often oriented toward the concerns of local industries (tires in Akron, for example, and mining in Minneapolis) and which gave a larger proportion of the population access to advanced training than anywhere else in the world at that time (Nelson and Wright 1992; Noble 1977; Geiger 1986; Mowery and Rosenberg 1989, 92–95).

Parsing the Flood of Information

The tremendous flood of information about new technologies posed a daunting problem to businesspeople who wanted to invest in promising discoveries. How could they assess the merits of the thousands of inventions patented each year? How could they distinguish inventions that were unlikely to work or would never be economical from those that had the potential to earn significant profits? Unless there was some way of separating important inventions from the mass of patented ideas, the former were unlikely to be put to productive use.

One simple solution was for investors to tap into the discussions that inventors themselves were having about new technologies. During the late nineteenth century certain kinds of enterprises were especially likely to become focal points for such conversations. Hardware stores, for example, were gathering places for people who made and bought the vast variety of gadgets they sold and hence were good places to obtain information about new products and production processes (Lamoreaux, Levenstein, and Sokoloff 2006). Telegraph firms were also magnets for technologically creative people. Early telegraph offices stocked books and journals about electrical technology because operators were responsible for maintaining the equipment as well as for sending and receiving messages. Many of the operators who learned about telegraph technology on the job devised ways to improve it. Thomas Edison is only the most famous example of an inventor who got his start in this way. Western Union executives paid attention to what their employees were doing and often provided them with the financial support they needed to commercialize their discoveries. At the same time, financiers used their telegraph-company connections to learn about promising new technologies. J. P. Morgan's investments in Edison's incandescent lighting project came about, for example, because two of his partners were friendly with Western Union's patent attorney (Israel 1992, 1998; Adams and Butler 1999).

Important firms in the new industries of the period could also become the hubs of overlapping networks of inventors and financiers. A good example was the Brush Electric Company, the pioneer arc-lighting firm established in Cleveland in 1880 (Lamoreaux, Levenstein, and Sokoloff, 2006, 2007). The inventors' network that formed around the Brush enterprise included employees who obtained valuable technical training in the course of their work, learned about opportunities for spin-off enterprises, and used the contacts their position afforded them to launch their own companies. It also included creative individuals who were not Brush employees but who had come there to develop technologies that were complementary to the company's main dynamo and lighting businesses. Sidney Short, for instance, moved to Cleveland and to Brush in order to supervise construction of the custom genera-tors he needed for his electric streetcar invention. He stayed and ran his Short Elec-tric Railway Company out of the Brush factory.

For Short and others like him, the inventors who gathered at the Brush facility provided a useful vetting function. The conversations they had about each other's inventions—which ones were likely to work and which to prove economically valu-able—provided the financiers who plugged into these networks with the information they needed to decide where to put their investments. Thus, Short was able with Brush's help to find financial backing for his enterprise. Similarly, Alfred and Eu-gene Cowles benefited from building their experimental electric aluminum smelting furnace at the Brush factory. Brush had originally scoffed at their ideas, dismissing their smelting process as just an expensive way to burn coal, but after their furnace worked he became a believer and used their aluminum to manufacture his dyna-mos. The conversion of Brush and other observers at the factory helped the Cowles brothers raise capital, as did their ability to invite potential backers to come see their furnace in operation (Lamoreaux, Levenstein, and Sokoloff, 2006, 2007).

Another example of a hub enterprise was the Olds Motor Works in Detroit. Founded in 1901, it was the first automaker to locate in Detroit. It was also one of the earliest volume producers in the industry, and by purchasing large quantities of parts from independent suppliers, it created incentives for other firms to set up in Detroit. Although the Olds Motor Works did not survive the decade as an inde-pendent firm, it played a key role in the growth of the Detroit automobile industry, serving as a source of both technological ideas and spin-off enterprises, including Cadillac, Ford, and Buick (Klepper 2007). According to Steven Klepper, employees tend to leave their positions and form new firms when they have ideas that their employers are not able or willing to exploit. Precisely because of their innovative character, however, spin-offs face problems raising capital from investors who have wealth but lack technological expertise, unless they can rely on people with expe-rience in the industry to convey information about the merits of their projects to potential backers. In addition to employees with new ideas, firms like Olds spawned networks of experts who were able to mediate between financiers and these innovators (Klepper 2007).

Intermediaries in the Market for Technology

A more general solution to the overwhelming flood of information was to rely on expert professionals to assess the merits of inventions offered on the market. The creation in 1836 of the U.S. Patent Office's examination system had fostered the rise of a cadre of patent agents and lawyers who generally had as much or more technical training as they did schooling in law. These professionals could appraise patents for purchasers and evaluate the intellectual property of firms on behalf of potential investors (Lamoreaux and Sokoloff 2003). Their main business, of course, was to process inventors' applications for patents, and as a result they obtained advance knowledge of technologies that would soon be coming out. Serving both sides of the market in this way, they were in a unique position to match inventors who would have patents to sell with businesspeople likely to be interested in purchasing the rights. They were also in a unique position to find investors for new high-tech enterprises being formed.[10]

By cultivating relations of trust with individuals on both sides of the market, moreover, patent agents and lawyers were able to reduce the transaction costs that afflicted trade in technology. Inventors often dealt repeatedly with the same patent attorneys, becoming comfortable enough to run ideas by them at an early stage. Buyers also came to trust the judgment of attorneys they employed over and over and therefore required less information to be revealed about the technology than might otherwise have been the case. Of course, because patent attorneys stood to profit from the sale and licensing of patent rights, there was a risk that they would pursue their own interests at the expense of both sellers and buyers of patents. For this reason the most successful practitioners invested in building reputations for fair dealing. Edward Van Winkle, a patent solicitor in New York City in the early twentieth century, devoted the greater part of each day to cultivating personal relationships by receiving visitors, calling upon colleagues, and meeting with inventors and businessmen over lunch or dinner. He was able in this way to build an extensive network that enabled him to broker numerous agreements between inventors and buyers of their inventions and even organize companies to exploit promising inventions (Lamoreaux and Sokoloff 2003).

Incentives to Innovate: Problems of Corporate Governance

In a legal sense, organizing new companies was relatively easy. As noted in the previous chapter, most of the U.S. states had passed general incorporation laws by the middle decades of the nineteenth century. Simply by registering their enterprises and paying a fee, businesspeople could secure the advantages of the corporate form: concentrated management, owner shielding (limited liability), entity shielding (the enterprise's assets could not be seized by creditors of bankrupt members of the firm), and the ability to lock in capital.[11] Over the course of the late nineteenth and early twentieth centuries, states made the reporting requirements associated with organizing a corporation less burdensome and also put fewer restrictions on what corporations were able to do. New Jersey passed an especially liberal general incorporation law in 1888 that made it possible for corporations to hold stock in other corporations. In other states large-scale businesses were forced to resort to subterfuges such as the trust form of organization in order to merge their enterprises, and so they increasingly shifted to New Jersey charters instead. Some of the states that lost chartering revenues responded by adopting similar statutes or by passing even more liberal laws. Delaware ultimately won this charter-mongering competition (Kuhn 1912; Dodd 1936; Cadman 1949; Grandy 1987; Roy 1997).

The difficult task was not organizing a high-tech enterprise as a corporation, but inducing wealthy businesspeople to purchase equity stakes. Adding to the problem of technological uncertainty was the lack of protection for minority investors during this period. Controlling shareholders could extract more than their fair share of the enterprise's profits in a variety of ways that included electing themselves to lucrative corporate offices, contracting on favorable terms with enterprises in which they had an ownership interest, and borrowing corporate funds at below market rates of interest. Minority shareholders who were disadvantaged by such actions could do little to remedy the situation. By definition, they did not have the votes to secure either a change in policy or the dissolution of the corporation. Nor, except in the most egregious cases, could they secure the intervention of the courts (Lamoreaux and Rosenthal 2006).

Nonetheless, the number of new corporations grew rapidly between the Civil War and the 1920s. Indeed, the increase was so steep that an index of incorporations (1925 = 100) had a value of only about 5 in 1870 (Evans 1948, 34). So long as investors thought they could earn returns that significantly exceeded those available on government securities and other similar instruments, they did not seem to worry about whether controlling shareholders would expropriate some of their returns (Lamoreaux and Rosenthal 2006; Lamoreaux 2006). It is possible, moreover, that the private benefits of control that majority shareholders could command actually increased the incentive for entrepreneurs to form new ventures. Although the lack of protections for minority shareholders may have allowed some entrepreneurs to engage in unproductive extraction, it may also have made it possible for productive entrepreneurs to earn returns commensurate with the extra risk they had to take on.[12]

Protections for creditors were also weak during this period. Except for brief periods from 1800 to 1803, 1841 to 1843, and 1867 to 1878, there was no federal bankruptcy law until 1898. Most state insolvency laws provided that the assets of a failed debtor would be distributed among creditors on a first-come, first-served basis, a method of settlement that advantaged those with inside information and invited collusion between debtors and favored creditors. Many states also discriminated against out-of-state creditors, assigning them lower priority for repayment than in-state creditors (Hansen 1998). When, moreover, these problems were finally solved with the passage of a new federal bankruptcy act in 1898, the law gave debtors much more favorable treatment than was the case in Great Britain or other advanced industrial countries of the time, even allowing them to maintain control of their assets (Skeel 2001).

Nonetheless, the supply of credit expanded steadily. By 1920 net private debt in the U.S. economy totaled $105.8 billion, or 121.5 percent of GDP. Earlier figures are not available, but the change in the magnitude of commercial bank loans during the period before 1920 provides an indication of the steepness of the rise. Total commercial bank loans outstanding increased from $518 million in 1865 (5.5 percent of GDP) to $28,562 million in 1920 (32.8 percent of GDP) (Carter et al. 2006, 3:24–25, 650–51, 774). Here again, it seems, opportunities for profits outweighed the discouragement of weak protection for investors. It is also possible that the lenient environment for debtors encouraged risk taking and hence entrepreneurship (Balleisen 2001).

The Effect of Discrimination on the Incentive to Innovate

The incentives that U.S. institutions provided for engagement in entrepreneurship were greater for some groups in the population than for others. Married women labored under legal disabilities created by the institution of coverture that were only gradually removed over the course of the nineteenth century. Because their economic identity was subsumed under that of their husbands, who had legal control of their property and any income they received, they could not trade on their own account or enter into contracts without their husbands' approval. One might expect these restrictions to have discouraged married women from pursuing entrepreneurial opportunities, and the patent data suggest that this was indeed the case. Taking advantage of variation across states in the pace at which coverture was abolished, B. Zorina Khan found that patenting by women was significantly lower in states where the rules of coverture were still in force and that it increased with the passage of legislation granting property rights to married women (Khan 1996). Even when they were freed from the legal disabilities of coverture, however, women entrepreneurs faced difficulties (for example, in obtaining credit) that put them at a disadvantage relative to men. Not surprisingly, they were most likely to be successful in industries like cosmetics where their understanding of the market and the particular needs of their customers offered counterbalancing advantages.[13]

The situation facing African Americans was in some respects similar. Although the abolition of slavery and the passage of the Fourteenth Amendment to the Constitution granted African Americans the full property rights afforded other citizens, the discrimination they faced in practice made all economic ventures, let alone entrepreneurial ones, more uncertain than they would otherwise be. African Americans were less likely than white Americans of comparable income levels to obtain trade or bank credit, and they were more likely to have the fruits of their labor destroyed or expropriated extralegally. The prospects for African Americans were better in some parts of this period than in others, and one might expect their entrepreneurial activity to have increased in good times and declined in bad. Lisa Cook has argued that patenting by African Americans did indeed track measures of their political status, but it is difficult to get information on inventive activity by African Americans that is not itself affected by the extent of discrimination (Cook 2003). In her landmark study of black business, Juliet E. K. Walker calls the first three decades of the twentieth century the "golden age" of African American entrepreneurship. Black entrepreneurs were particularly successful in the hair care and beauty aids industries and in providing services in other sectors, such as finance, transportation, and entertainment, to members of their communities whose needs were not particularly well served by white businesses (Walker 1998).

Innovation versus Replication

According to Joseph Schumpeter's classic model of entrepreneurship, innovation enables an entrepreneur to earn pure economic profits, and those profits in turn attract imitators until they are competed away (Schumpeter 1934). There is no question that, as soon as an idea proved profitable, businesspeople in the late-nineteenth-century United States raced to copy it. In this dynamic environment, however, replication was often difficult to distinguish from innovation. In the first place, more than one entrepreneur was likely to come up with the same idea around the same time. In the second, followers were often innovators in their own right. Rather than simply copying an idea, they typically improved on it in significant ways. Indeed, forward-thinking entrepreneurs sought ways to benefit from this future stream of innovation, as well as from their original ideas.

A good example of a successful attempt to do both was the Bessemer Association. Henry Bessemer, a British inventor, was only one of several talented individuals who around the same time figured out how to produce steel by blowing hot air or steam through molten iron. In 1863 Alexander Lyman Holley purchased the U.S. rights to Bessemer's patents on behalf of a partnership consisting of himself, an iron-master, and a banker. By that time, Bessemer had already secured control of most of the competing processes, and Holley finished the task, negotiating a settlement with another group of Americans who controlled a set of patents still outstanding. The result was the formation of the so-called Bessemer Association, which pooled the two groups' U.S. patents (Misa 1995, 19–20).

Holley himself was an innovator. He redesigned Bessemer's production process, shrewdly adapting it to the needs of the American railroad market, and then licensed the resulting patents to the Association and, through the Association, to a small number of producers. Virtually all the steel mills built in the United States during the 1860s and 1870s were designed by Holley and used technology licensed by the Association. The licensees in turn were expected to assign to the Association the rights to any improvements they made. For a time Holley and his fellow Associates offered licenses to any producer who paid a $5,000 membership fee. After 1877, however, they began to limit the number of steel mills they admitted to the pool, using their control over the technology to prevent competition from eroding their returns (Misa 1995, 20–21; Temin 1964, 133–38; Meyer 2003). Although few technology-sharing agreements were as successful as the Bessemer Association, firms that licensed valuable patents to other enterprises often included similar clauses in their contracts giving them rights to subsequent improvements.

In other cases, the patent system itself encouraged what might be called innovative replication. Unless they could buy or license the rights, entrepreneurs who learned the details of an innovation by reading patent specifications or reverse engineering a product could only make use of the information they obtained if they could "invent around" it—that is, discover an alternative means to the same end. These efforts often yielded superior results. In electricity, for example, Charles F. Brush, inventor of the pioneer system of arc lighting, protected the various elements of his system with patents. Elihu Thomson knew Brush's system well. Indeed, he had been the judge of a competition at the Franklin Institute that had awarded Brush the prize for the best dynamo. Within a few years of the contest, however, Thomson had developed his own patented system of arc lighting that improved upon his predecessor's in significant ways. Within a decade his company had bought out Brush's (Carlson 1991).

Although competition among firms led to innovative replication, within a single firm there was significant risk that replication would not be accompanied by additional innovation. Entrepreneurs often become enamored of their own ideas and, though they typically subject them to continual improvement, there is a tendency for the changes to become incremental and adaptive over time rather than fundamental and disruptive (see Schumpeter 1934, 1942). Although there are certainly entrepreneurs who are willing to scrap everything when a better idea comes along—Andrew Carnegie was a good example, as was Henry Ford before he built the River Rouge plant—they are relatively rare (Livesay 1975; Hounshell 1984, 217–61). Even as fertile an inventive genius as Thomas Edison was susceptible to this failing. His own electrical lighting system had used direct current, and he was implacably hostile to the new alternating-current (AC) systems that George Westinghouse was developing. In the competitive economy of the late nineteenth century, entrepreneurs wedded to outmoded ideas quickly lost ground to more nimble competitors. In the end, Edison's company was acquired in the General Electric (GE) merger by the Thomson Houston Electric Company, whose lead inventor had responded positively to the AC challenge (Passer 1953, 164–75). Once industries came to be dominated by a small number of very large firms such as GE, the risk that conservatism inside the firm would affect the pace of innovation in the economy as a whole would increase.[14]

The Rise of Big Business

The period 1865 to 1920 witnessed a dramatic change in the size distribution of firms in the U.S. economy as large-scale enterprises emerged to dominate huge swaths of industry. This change would have important consequences for the incentive to innovate, as well as for the way in which innovation was organized. Those consequences, however, would for the most part not be felt until later in the twentieth century and hence will be left for the next chapter. Here the focus will be on the formation of these large-scale organizations, because they themselves were entrepreneurial responses to the conditions and opportunities of the period.

The Railroad

As Alfred D. Chandler Jr. has argued, railroads were the nation's first big businesses. They were the first private enterprises to raise substantial sums of money from the capital markets in New York and abroad and, through their seemingly insatiable demand for funds, stimulated the development of new types of financial intermediaries and instruments that would be important for the economy's subsequent growth. They were also the first businesses to confront coordination problems that were sufficiently complex to induce them to innovate organizationally. By the 1850s, executives such as Daniel C. McCallum of the New York and Erie, Benjamin Latrobe of the Baltimore & Ohio, and J. Edgar Thomson of the Pennsylvania Railroad had realized that it was imperative for both profit and safety to improve control of the rapidly increasing volume of traffic that was flowing over their lines. Over the next several decades they devised organizational charts and manuals that arrayed employees according to a hierarchy of responsibility, clearly specifying the duties of each. They also developed new accounting techniques that enabled them to measure the performance of all the operating units in their dominions (Chandler 1977, 81–121).

The managers who staffed these organizations increasingly thought of themselves as professionals. In the post–Civil War period they flocked into national associations such as the American Society of Railroad Superintendents, subscribed to trade publications such as the *Railroad and Engineering Journal*, presented papers at professional meetings on technical details involving railroad administration, and met with their colleagues to discuss and resolve common problems. Collectively they worked to standardize gauges and railroad equipment so as to facilitate the movement of traffic from road to road. They developed systemwide tracking methods that ensured each company that it would be properly credited for the services it provided. They also agreed on a basic structure of freight charges, classifying hundreds of different types of goods into four basic categories (Chandler 1977, 122–44).

This cooperative ethic spilled over into the arena of technology. In the industry's early years, railroad managers had fostered technological creativity among their employees and encouraged inventors to bring them new devices. The railroads of this era were rarely in direct competition with each other, and managers had freely shared information about new technological developments. These exchanges of information did not stop when railroads' system building made them into rivals. Rather, they became part and parcel of the drive to reduce transshipment costs by standardizing practice across the entire industry. Moreover, as the railroads faced increasing numbers of infringement suits in the 1870s from outside owners of intellectual property, their managers formalized these exchanges by organizing patent pools that could bargain on behalf of all the railroads simultaneously. The pools not only economized on litigation costs but reduced inventors' ability to play one railroad off against another (Usselman 1991, 2002).

This move toward more formal patent pools coincided with an internal shift in railroad managers' attitudes toward innovation by employees. Their previous stance of encouragement gave way to a more conservative effort to control the pace and direction of technological change. Because it was critical to be able to couple cars owned by one railroad to all of the company's rolling stock, as well as to that of other companies with interconnecting tracks, a change in one part of the system could wreak havoc in the functioning of the whole. Hence, at the same time as they cooperated to exploit more fully technologies that were already in place, railroad executives increasingly worked to channel and even contain the innovations of their subordinates. Productivity increased at a rapid pace, but innovation became more incremental and adaptive in character (Usselman 2002; Fishlow 1966).

New Opportunities from the Integration of Production and Distribution

The expansion of the railroad network linked the far-flung regions of the United States into a national market, making it possible for firms in industries characterized by economies of scale to lower their unit costs by concentrating production in large facilities. In such industries the average size of the production unit rose over time and the number of firms declined. At the same time, the level of geographic specialization in the U.S. economy increased (Chandler 1977; Lamoreaux 1985; Kim 1995).

The comparatively rapid speed at which railroads operated also created opportunities for entrepreneurs to found new kinds of business. Before the 1870s, for example, cattle were usually shipped live on railroad cars to eastern cities where they were slaughtered for local consumption. Gustavus Swift, an East Coast butcher who had migrated west to become a cattle dealer in Chicago, realized that he could reap enormous cost savings if he could slaughter cattle in the Midwest and ship the beef to eastern markets in refrigerated cars. Packing meat in Chicago would enable him to capture economies of scale and would obviate having to feed and water cattle in transit. He could avoid paying freight on the inedible parts of the animal (more than half the weight of the carcass) and could escape losses from animals losing weight and even dying on route to markets.[15]

Swift faced a lot of opposition to his plan—not only from butchers and wholesalers whose business he threatened, but also from the railroads, which already had extensive investments in cattle cars and feeding stations. As a result, he was forced to build his entire distribution system from scratch. He sunk all the capital he could raise into the construction of a small fleet of cars, managed to get one railroad to carry them, and plunged into the business. His initial successes gave him the wherewithal to expand into sales. He quickly built a network of wholesale facilities with refrigerated storage space and a sales staff to market the meat to local stores. In addition, by buying rights to harvest ice from the Great Lakes and setting up icehouses along his routes, he protected himself against costly bottlenecks that could have damaged both his product and his business. As a consequence of his skill in system building, Swift's enterprise grew rapidly. Swift made his first shipments of dressed beef in 1877. By 1881 he owned nearly 200 refrigerator cars and shipped something on the order of 3,000 carcasses per week.

Swift's creation of a vertically integrated empire changed the nature of competition in the industry. Before Swift built his system, the meatpacking industry had consisted of hundreds of small local slaughterhouses. Afterwards, the only firms that could meet his low prices were the few that could muster the financial resources to copy his strategy and build their own networks of refrigerated cars, icehouses, and distribution outlets. The industry quickly acquired an oligopolistic structure. By 1888 Swift, and the three firms that built similar systems (Armour, Morris, and Hammond) together accounted for about two-thirds of the nation's supply of dressed beef.

Wholesalers handled distribution for most manufacturing industries during the last third of the nineteenth century, but in some instances they were unable (or, as Swift found, unwilling) to do an adequate job. The problem was particularly likely to arise for technologically complex products such as sewing machines or mechanical reapers. Consumers hesitated to buy these products unless they were taught how to use them and assured that broken machines would be swiftly and cheaply repaired. Independent wholesalers lacked the expertise and incentive to provide such instructional and repair services, so manufacturers had to provide them themselves. Entrepreneurial firms that took the lead in offering such services, such as Singer in sewing machines and McCormick in reapers, rapidly grabbed major shares of the domestic market. The tremendous amount of capital needed to copy their distribution systems kept the number of competitors small, and just as in the case of meatpacking, these industries acquired oligopolistic structures (Chandler 1977; Hounshell 1984).

The Standard Oil Trust

The railroad industry itself had an oligopolistic market structure. Because railroads had enormous sunk costs, wherever multiple railroads served a particular region, they competed vigorously for freight. The railroads attempted to put limits on this competition by forming themselves into cartels, but these efforts were rarely successful, especially before the 1880s.[16] Nonetheless, one particularly entrepreneurial producer was able to take advantage of the railroads' eagerness to fix prices to consolidate his own industry. That entrepreneur was John D. Rockefeller.

During the late 1860s Rockefeller's Standard Oil refinery was the largest in the petroleum industry, but it accounted for only about 4 percent of total industry capacity and did not have any particular advantage in costs. Price competition was eroding profits, and the refiners' repeated attempts to put a stop to it by organizing cartels just as repeatedly failed. In the early 1870s, however, the railroads that served the country's main refining regions collectively offered Standard and other important firms in the industry a deal. The railroads had negotiated an agreement to prevent price cutting in this segment of their business, and they needed the leading refineries to police it. They offered to form them into an association called the South Improvement Company with the task of monitoring oil shipments to make sure that no railroad undercut the agreed-upon prices. In return, the refineries would receive a rebate on their own shipments and also a drawback on those of their competitors (Granitz and Klein 1996).

Although the South Improvement agreement was never implemented,[17] there was a several-month period (after the company was formed but before it fell apart) when prospects seemed dim for refineries not included in the scheme. Rockefeller took advantage of the situation to induce the other firms to sell out. As Elizabeth Granitz and Benjamin Klein have demonstrated, only fear of the effects of the agreement on their competitive position can explain why so many nonmembers sold their refineries to Rockefeller during these months, many of them at distress prices.[18] Emerging from this episode with effective control of the Cleveland segment of the industry, Standard then secretly merged with the original participating refiners in the other production centers. As a result of these acquisitions and mergers, Standard was large enough in and of itself to police the railroads' cartel agreements, and they willingly rewarded it for performing this service with rebates on its shipments. This favored position then allowed Standard to use its ability to "raise rivals' costs" to secure monopoly control of the industry (Granitz and Klein 1996).

The Great Merger Movement

Most capital-intensive industries in the late nineteenth century were more like petroleum than meatpacking or sewing machines. That is, most manufacturers still distributed their products through independent wholesalers, and the intertwined processes of innovation and replication meant that most firms in an industry used essentially the same or comparable technologies. Although there were exceptional cases where entrepreneurs managed to obtain some kind of significant advantage (the crude-steel industry, which Andrew Carnegie dominated, is a case in point), most capital-intensive industries were populated by a relatively small number of evenly matched firms whose fierce competition for market share often drove prices to unremunerative levels. As in the case of petroleum, firms attempted to negotiate collusive arrangements to limit price cutting but were rarely successful. Like Standard, therefore, they turned to mergers for relief, consolidating most or all of the competing firms into a single large enterprise (Lamoreaux 1985).

The petroleum mergers were followed in the 1880s by a small number of others, most notably in the sugar, lead, whiskey, linseed oil, cottonseed oil, and cordage industries. Mergers continued at a slow pace in the 1890s and then took off as the economy rebounded from the depression of that decade. Thirteen multifirm consolidations had been formed during the depression years 1895–97, but in 1898 the number suddenly rose to sixteen and in 1899 to sixty-three. Thereafter the number began to tail off again—to twenty-one in 1900, nineteen in 1901, seventeen in 1902, five in 1903, and three in 1904. All told, between 1895 and 1904 more than 1,800 manufacturing firms disappeared into consolidations, many of which acquired substantial shares (at least initially) of the markets in which they operated. Of the ninety-three consolidations whose market shares it is possible to estimate, seventy-two controlled at least 40 percent of their industries and forty-two at least 70 percent (Lamoreaux 1985, 1–5).

Despite their initially impressive market shares, many of the new consolidations were no more successful over the long run than the collusive agreements they had replaced. The high prices they charged after their formation stimulated an influx of competition, causing virtually all to lose ground and many even to fail. Examining their earnings records for the first third of the twentieth century, Shaw Livermore categorized 37 percent of the mergers as failures, 7 percent as failures that were subsequently rejuvenated, 12 percent as marginal or "limping" concerns, and only 44 percent as successes in the sense that their profit rate at least equaled the average for the manufacturing sector (Livermore 1935).

The survivors transformed the business environment in important ways, however. Consolidations were usually financed by the issue of securities, and the profitability of the most successful ones, as well as the new techniques that their promoters (most notably J. P. Morgan) developed to create markets for their stock, paved the way for other industrial securities to be sold on the national exchanges. As a result of the merger movement, then, large manufacturing corporations gained the same access to national capital markets that the railroads had earlier achieved (Navin and Sears 1955; Baskin and Miranti 1997; De Long 1991).

In industries where they proved successful, moreover, consolidations had a major impact on competitive behavior. The merger of virtually all the firms in an industry created a "dominant firm" that could set prices for the remaining fringe of smaller competitors. Consolidations could only maintain this position over time, however, if there were barriers to entry into the industry or if they had advantages, like Standard Oil's, that allowed them effectively to raise rivals' costs. Otherwise, the high prices they imposed would stimulate an influx of new, more efficient competitors, and their market shares would erode until they no longer had the power to set prices for their industries (Lamoreaux 1985, 118–58).

According to Chandler, the most successful of the consolidations tended to be those that created barriers to entry by integrating forward into distribution. Certainly, there is no question that, by taking control of distribution, the most entrepreneurial of these enterprises were able to exploit new marketing opportunities. Independent wholesalers had typically sold their wares as homogeneous products or sometimes, where it was necessary to signal differences in quality, under their own private brands. Crackers, for example, had typically been distributed in bulk to retailers who dumped them unbranded into barrels in their stores. After the National Biscuit merger, however, the consolidation began to distribute its product in individual packages under the "Uneeda Biscuit" brand, building its own marketing organization to handle and promote the product (Chandler 1977, 331–39).

Once consolidations began to market their own brands, they developed a new concern for protecting them from the encroachments of rival manufacturers. Although brands and trademarks had been a familiar aspect of business activity from time immemorial, protecting these product symbols did not engage the energies of most businessmen until the rise of large-scale organizations at the turn of the century. Not until 1905 did Congress pass a law that protected trademarks in domestic commerce. As Mira Wilkins has argued, the timing of the legislation reflected the new efforts of large firms competing in oligopolistic markets to use product differentiation to preserve and expand their market shares (Wilkins 1992).

The Reorganization of Technological Discovery

In the intensely competitive environment of the late nineteenth century, firms had to stay on the technological cutting edge in order to survive. They could not afford to be foreclosed from promising new technologies by their rivals' control of critical patents, so they had to keep abreast of developments occurring outside the firm and purchase or license the rights to any that were likely to prove important to their businesses.[19] Although many firms had people on staff (or in ownership positions) who engaged in inventive activity, even the largest enterprises of the time were reluctant to put too much weight on internal R & D. Western Union, for example, sometimes financed the development of new technology in-house, but its managers were not convinced that this was the best strategy for staying on the frontier in a time of rapid technological change, and they frequently spun off these enterprises into separate companies.[20] The position of the American Telephone & Telegraph Company (AT&T) at this time was even more extreme. As T. D. Lockwood, head of the company's patent department, explained: "I am fully convinced that it has never, is not now, and never will pay commercially, to keep an establishment of professional inventors, or of men whose chief business it is to invent."[21] Instead, AT&T invested in building the capacity to track and assess inventions generated in the external world. Not until Theodore N. Vail became president of the company in 1907 was this policy reversed (Galambos 1992). More generally, as David Mowery has argued (1995), an important function of firms' early research facilities was to evaluate outside technologies for possible purchase.

The earliest firms to develop in-house R & D laboratories proceeded on a small scale, often for idiosyncratic reasons, until they discovered that the labs brought competitive advantages. During the 1890s, for example, GE faced increasing competition because its basic (Edison) patents on lightbulbs had expired, and inventors elsewhere were developing new, more efficient types of filaments. Charles Steinmetz, a consulting engineer at GE's Schenectady factory, had been trained in Germany and believed that American firms would do well to emulate the R & D labs that German firms had pioneered. He convinced the company to support a modest research initiative (his budget was $15,830) to develop an improved incandescent light. Although Steinmetz did not succeed in his mission (GE ultimately had to purchase the technology from German inventors), the experiment nonetheless established the value of having an in-house R & D facility. The lab had provided important services to other parts of the firm by testing materials and resolving technical problems. More importantly, in the process of experimenting with different kinds of filaments, company researchers had filed a number of minor patents that turned out to be useful—not only defensively, by helping the company protect its product line from infringing competitors, but also offensively, as bargaining chips in negotiations with rivals (Carlson 1997; Reich 1985, 1992; Wise 1985).

AT&T had a similar experience. Under competitive pressure from new wireless technologies (radio) that threatened its control over local voice communications, it focused its energies on building the capacity to provide long-distance service and set up an in-house laboratory to develop an appropriate amplifier. As was the case at GE, the lab failed in this effort, and AT&T had to purchase Lee de Forest's patents. But again the research team proved its usefulness. It made possible the successful inauguration of coast-to-coast telephone service in 1915 by solving a number of technical problems with de Forest's inventions that had to be overcome for the technology to be commercially practicable. Moreover, the lab's accumulation of "a thousand and one little patents" (in the words of the company's president) kept competitors at bay. Companies like AT&T and GE quickly learned that their labs generated patents that were vital to their rivals' competitive position as well as their own and that by cross-licensing technology to each other they could stabilize their industries and erect barriers to entry (Carlson 1997; Reich 1977, 1980, 1985; Lipartito, 2009).

Relatively few large companies invested in full-blown R & D laboratories before the 1920s (Mowery and Rosenberg 1989, 61–65). They had to be convinced that the best strategy for staying on the cutting edge was to develop technology in-house. In addition, talented inventors were reluctant to take positions of employment in large firms, and though they might accept jobs at least temporarily, they could not easily be controlled. George Westinghouse learned this lesson when he contracted with William Stanley to develop a transformer. To his chagrin, Stanley claimed that a related discovery he made while working for Westinghouse was his own property (Wise 1985, 70–71). Less famous inventors could be similarly unreliable, often quitting when they came up with valuable ideas. For example, after two employees of the American Sheet and Tin Plate Company invented a catcher for tinning machines, building the device on company time with company resources and testing it in one of the company's plants, they resigned and contracted with a competitor to develop and commercialize the invention (Lamoreaux and Sokoloff 1999).

Before firms could reap the rewards that might be obtained from internalizing the process of invention, they had to learn to solve a number of important personnel problems. In particular, they had to reduce employee turnover and overcome inventors' resistance to signing their ideas over to their employers. That is, they had to learn how to convince inventors, who had long regarded independent entrepreneurship as the key to upward mobility, that steady employment offered both rewards and opportunities for advancement. In this endeavor, they would be helped by a rise in the amount of capital required for effective invention, a change that made it more difficult for inventors to maintain their independence. They would also be helped by the growing number of college and engineering-school graduates who not only had the requisite scientific training but were also more amenable to the idea of a career in an organization (Lamoreaux and Sokoloff 1999, and 2009).

The movement of inventive activity inside large firms made it possible to bring enormous resources to bear on technological problems and to exploit the power of teams of researchers with differing types of expertise. But it also raised the specter of what had happened on the railroads—that the focus of attention would shift toward incremental and adaptive innovation and that more fundamental and disruptive ideas would be discouraged. As the next chapter will show, few large firms would be able to avoid this danger, though there were outstanding exceptions. Moreover, the shift in the locus of R & D to large firms' in-house laboratories would never be complete. Independent inventors and smaller firms would continue to be fertile sources of radical new technological ideas throughout the twentieth century.[22]

Government Regulation of the Economy

The federal government's regulatory role in the economy was relatively modest in the decades that followed the Civil War. The National Banking Acts gave the U.S. comptroller of the currency responsibility for overseeing banks that held national charters (a declining proportion of the total over time), but there were no other agencies with similar authority over important sectors of the economy. All this would change by the turn of the century. First the railroads and then, with the mergers of the late nineteenth century, enterprises in important parts of the manufacturing sector grew so large relative to most other businesses of the time that they raised fears about the concentration of economic and political power. The ruthlessness with which the "robber barons" of the period pursued their ambitions exacerbated these fears. Moreover, exposés by muckraking journalists undercut the equation of success and virtue that previously had helped to keep hand of the regulator at bay. For example, Ida Tarbell's character studies of John D. Rockefeller, published in contemporary magazines, portrayed the oil magnate as a commercial Machiavellian, "the victim of a money-passion" that drove him to get ahead by any means possible, however dishonorable.[23] Though Rockefeller later gave away an enormous amount of money, he could never completely shake this negative public image, and the Supreme Court later broke up his Standard Oil Company.

The states' efforts to respond to popular concerns about the rise of big business ran up against both economic and legal barriers in the late nineteenth century, and so political pressures mounted on Congress to increase the federal government's role in the economy. The resulting shift in the locus of regulatory authority from the states to Washington likely had contradictory effects on entrepreneurship, encouraging it in some ways but making it more difficult in others. It did, however, open up new rent-seeking opportunities for businesses in at least some regulated industries.

Regulation by State and Local Governments

As William Novak has shown (1996), local governments had long routinely intervened in the economy in numerous ways, enforcing standard weights and measures, setting rules for the conduct of trade, requiring licenses to engage in certain kinds of businesses, and inspecting the purity or quality of products sold to consumers. State governments performed a similar range of functions and more. In addition, their authority to charter corporations enabled them to regulate the business of incorporated enterprises in highly specific ways. Although the U.S. Supreme Court ruled in the famous *Dartmouth College* case in 1819 that corporate charters were protected by the contract clause of the Constitution and could not be altered subsequent to issue, states were able to retain their full authority over corporations by including reservation clauses in charters that gave them the right to change the terms in the future. States used corporate charters to limit the amounts of capital that corporations could raise, the types of activities in which they could engage, and their ability to merge with other enterprises. Special types of corporations were subject to additional regulations. Financial institutions, for example, faced restrictions on their ability to open branches, were required to maintain reserves against deposits, and usually had to submit regular reports on their condition (Novak 1996; McCurdy 1979; White 1983).

During the late nineteenth and early twentieth centuries state governments expanded their regulatory activities in a number of ways and, in the process, came up against the limits of their authority under the country's federal system of government. For example, state efforts to regulate railroads hit a roadblock when the Supreme Court ruled in *Wabash, St. Louis, and Pacific Railway v. Illinois* in 1886 that a state could not regulate rates on shipments that were part of interstate commerce (Hovenkamp 1988). Similarly, empowered by an interpretation of the Fourteenth Amendment to the Constitution that enabled the federal courts to strike down regulatory legislation that went beyond what was necessary to protect the public's health or maintain order, the justices in 1905 in *Lochner v. New York* overturned a New York law setting maximum hours of work in bakeries on the grounds that it was an unconstitutional restraint on workers' right to employment. The Court subsequently ruled against a number of other similar statutes (Kens 1998).

In the case of large-scale businesses, the states' regulatory efforts were stymied more by economic than by political factors. That the power to charter corporations gave states full regulatory authority to proceed against mergers was acknowledged by the federal courts. But this power was not very useful when multiplant giants could respond to state regulation by securing a charter from a friendlier jurisdiction or even by closing down their enterprises in the state. As a result, after a brief flurry of antitrust activity in the 1880s and the early 1890s, the states largely gave up. If there was going to be an antitrust initiative, it would have to come from the federal government (McCurdy 1979; Lamoreaux 1985, 162–69).

Rise of Federal Regulation

By the late 1880s the popular outcry against railroads and other large-scale businesses had spurred the federal government to act. In 1887 Congress passed the Interstate Commerce Act, creating the Interstate Commerce Commission (ICC) and empowering it make sure that railroad rates were "reasonable and just." Although the bill was confusingly written and the ICC was soon hamstrung by the courts, these problems were subsequently remedied by additional legislation, particularly the Hepburn Act of 1906 and the Mann-Elkins Act of 1910. Similarly, in 1890 Congress passed the Sherman Antitrust Act prohibiting combinations in restraint of trade or that monopolized their industries. Although the details of the Sherman Act's application were largely worked out in the courts, Congress supplemented the statute by passing the Clayton Antitrust and Federal Trade Commission Acts in 1914. Other regulatory legislation passed by Congress during this period included the Pure Food and Drug Act of 1906, which prohibited the manufacture, sale, or transportation of adulterated or fraudulently labeled foodstuffs and drugs, and the

Meat Inspection Act of 1906, which created a federal inspection staff to enforce new sanitary standards in the meatpacking industry.[24]

The consequences of all this legislation for entrepreneurship have been the subject of much debate. Some scholars have argued that regulators' refusal to grant adequate rate increases effectively destroyed the nation's railroad network by making it difficult for the roads to raise the capital they needed to improve their track and rolling stock. The underinvestment that resulted forced the government to nationalize the railroads during World War I and, in the long run, led to the railroads' eclipse by the trucking industry (see especially Martin 1971). In Steven Usselman's view, however, the railroad's problems were largely of their own making. Their increasingly rigid focus on exploiting economies of standardization blinded them to changes that were occurring in the transportation sector. Whereas in the late nineteenth century there had been substantial returns to high-volume, long-haul operations, in the twentieth century shippers demanded more flexible services over shorter hauls. Trucks triumphed, according to Usselman, because they meet needs that the railroads were unable or unwilling to fulfill (Usselman 2002, 327–80).

The effects of antitrust law on entrepreneurship were even more ambiguous. In the immediate aftermath of the Sherman Act's passage, prosecutors moved quickly and successfully against cartels and other kinds of collusive arrangements among firms. They found it much more difficult, however, to win convictions against combinations in which competitors had merged to form a single company. Ironically, therefore, the law must be seen as an important cause of the great turn-of-the-century consolidation movement (Chandler 1977, 375–76; Freyer 1995). Similarly, although the courts made certain types of anticompetitive behavior illegal on its face—for example, tying contracts that bound suppliers or customers not to deal with competitors on equal terms—they were rarely willing to proceed against mergers that had much the same consequence. Hence U.S. Steel was able to limit entry into the steel industry by buying up ore reserves, though it would not have been able to negotiate exclusive dealing contracts with ore suppliers. Another problem was that antitrust prosecution depended for its success on complaints from disadvantaged competitors. Such complaints were much more likely to be lodged in industries where large enterprises were competing vigorously than they were where dominant firms enforced price stability. U.S. Steel, for example, was able to insure that competitors would not testify against it in an antitrust suit by guaranteeing that they could operate profitably under its pricing umbrella. It is likely, however, that this guarantee also took away much of their incentive to innovate (Lamoreaux 1985, 159–86). Enforcement of the antitrust laws seems also to have made it more difficult for independent inventors to survive. Because large firms that bought technology on the market were more vulnerable to prosecution than those that developed it in-house, large firms discovered that it was the better part of valor to rely more exclusively on their own laboratories (Mowery 1997).

New Opportunities for Rent-Seeking

Just as the expansion of the federal government during the Civil War era created opportunities for corruption, the ongoing economic activities of state and local governments encouraged rent-seekers to line their pockets at the public expense. The late nineteenth and early twentieth centuries were the heyday of urban "machine" politics. They were also the years, however, when the quality of urban life improved enormously—when cities built roads, utilities, sewers, water purification facilities, and mass transit systems, improving the health and increasing the prosperity of their populations. As Rebecca Menes has explained, the mobility of the population, in combination with competitive pressures exerted through the ballot box and the bond market, constrained governmental officials, whether corrupt or not, to provide high levels of services. As a result, there is no statistical evidence from this period that corruption was bad for growth. All things being equal, there was little difference in the performance of cities governed by corrupt bosses and those that were not.[25]

Corruption, however, was a despised path to wealth during this period. Middle-class Americans associated the rise of machine politics with influxes of impoverished immigrants. Although bosses undoubtedly provided these newcomers with valuable social services in a period when governments were not otherwise meeting their needs, the symbiotic relationship between machines and immigrants increased the ill repute with which both were viewed (Merton 1972). The result was a twin movement to restrict immigration and reform the structure of city governments. Corruption, of course, was never eradicated, but it was rarely the route to high status and social esteem. The heroes of American society were entrepreneurs, not politicians.

The opportunities for rent-seeking that the rise of federal regulation created were probably of greater long-run importance. Here the main beneficiaries, in terms of wealth accumulation, were firms that were able to "capture" the agencies that supposedly oversaw them. Just as the big New York banks had been able to influence the structure of the National Banking System to suit their interests, large-scale enterprises were sometimes able to shape both the content of regulatory legislation and the activities of the agencies entrusted with enforcement. The most important examples of such capture would come later in the twentieth century, however. Although some of the early regulatory initiatives were supported by (and advantaged) large firms, as a general rule they cannot be so easily pigeonholed, and scholars have vigorously debated the extent to which the governmental bodies responsible for their implementation were captured.[26]

Conclusion

Americans have always admired entrepreneurs, but during the years 1865–1920 this attitude was more intense than at virtually any other time in U.S. history. This was the period when the expansion of the railroad network and the incorporation of western lands and resources into the national economy created enormous opportunities for profit, and Americans responded with avidity. Farmers moved out onto the new western lands opened for settlement, prospectors searched for gold or other valuable minerals, inventors patented thousands of new technological ideas, businesspeople embodied these ideas in start-ups and expanded the scope of existing enterprises, and financiers found new ways to meet businesses' growing demand for funds. Although some entrepreneurs accumulated enormous fortunes, in most cases the gains were more modest. Nonetheless, the significant upward mobility that many were able to achieve during this period was an ongoing spur to entrepreneurship.

For most of this period government's role in the economy, especially at the federal level, was mainly promotional in character. The national government made western lands and resources available to those who wanted to exploit them, subsidized transportation, mapped the location of raw material resources, and financed educational and other institutions to supply technological know-how. The U.S. patent system provided strong protection to holders of intellectual property at modest cost and helped to disseminate information about new technologies. The creation of the National Banking System had some unfortunate consequences that increased economic instability, but the system did succeed in instituting a uniform national currency that reduced transactions costs in interregional trade. Moreover, its problems were largely remedied by the passage of the Federal Reserve Act in 1913. State and local governments played a more active regulatory role in the economy, but even at those levels governments mainly intervened in ways that increased the security and transparency of economic transactions, for example by enforcing standard weights and measures and setting rules for the conduct of trade. Only with the rise of big business would governments take on more significant regulatory functions—first at the state level and then the federal.

Although the institutions that Americans inherited from the era of the nation's founding provided a basic security of property rights, protections for external investors in business enterprises did not meet the standards that policymakers today think are necessary for successful economic development. Minority shareholders in corporations had little recourse against exploitation by controlling shareholders, and insolvency and bankruptcy laws disadvantaged creditors. Although these weaknesses may have made it more difficult for businesses to secure equity investments or loans, there was nonetheless an enormous expansion in the number of corporations and in the levels of equity and debt finance relative to the size of the economy. It seems that the opportunities for profit were sufficiently great that those with savings to invest were willing to take the risk that the lower levels of protection entailed. Moreover, entrepreneurs like J. P. Morgan made investments in reputation that elicited investors' trust. Indeed, throughout the economy, whenever information problems made otherwise remunerative transactions difficult, private agents found it worth their while to develop solutions. Thus patent attorneys used the contacts they assiduously cultivated on both sides of the market for technology to match sellers and buyers of inventions and reduce the amount of information they had to reveal to each other. Similarly, businesses like Singer were able to induce consumers to purchase complex and expensive durable goods by investing in local distribution outlets that provided instruction and repair services.

A by-product of this entrepreneurial pursuit of opportunity was the emergence of large-scale businesses with significant market power. Sometimes this market power was a side effect of business decisions made for other reasons—Singer's investments in distribution, for example, helped to make it the dominant producer in the United States—but sometimes, as in the case of Standard Oil, it was deliberately sought. Regardless, the resulting change in the size distribution of firms had enormous consequences. In the first place, it stimulated the state and then the federal government to take on a broader regulatory role in the economy. In the second, it shifted the locus of innovation as large firms built their own in-house R & D laboratories and relied increasingly on internally generated technology rather than buying inventions on the market. How these changes would play out—whether they would be conducive to entrepreneurship or dampen the innovative character of the economy—would not be apparent until much later in the twentieth century. The troubles that the railroad, the first big business, experienced as early as World War I were an important indication that the outcome would not be completely positive. Even in that case, however, the rise of trucking suggested that, in a dynamic economy such as that of the United States, problems in one industry just create opportunities for entrepreneurs in another.

Notes

This chapter benefited greatly from the helpful comments of William J. Baumol, Louis P. Cain, Margaret B. W. Graham, and Joel Mokyr.

[1] For a demonstration using data for an earlier period, see Sokoloff 1988.

[2] See especially the essays by Miller (1962) and Gregory and Neu (1962). For a summary of other studies, see Gutman 1966, 211–14. As Pamela Walker Laird (2006) has shown, most successful businessmen of the period were not really self-made. They received a lot of assistance from established business leaders who took an interest in their careers. Typically, however, they failed to credit this help when they recounted their upward climb.

[3] Gutman 1966, 232. On rates of social mobility more generally, see Ferrie 2005.

[4] On this point, see especially Aron 1987 and Wills 2003.

[5] See especially Josephson 1934; but also White 2003. For a general theory of the circumstances that encourage bad forms of entrepreneurship, see Baumol 1990, 1993.

[6] Adams 1869. More generally, see Baskin and Miranti 1997.

[7] Lamoreaux and Sokoloff 2003, 2007. Under special circumstances information may be shared in the absence of patent protection. See, for example, Allen 1983.

[8] See, for example, Jaffe and Lerner 2004. More generally, on the circumstances conducive to productive versus unproductive entrepreneurship, see Baumol 2002 and 1993. See also Baumol 1990.

[9] For an excellent example, see Cox 1951. More generally, see Stevens 1995.

[10] The first patent agents established their offices in Washington, where they could have frequent contact with examiners in the Patent Office. Very quickly, however, they appeared in other parts of the country, especially in areas like southeastern New England where there were already significant numbers of inventors who could make use of their services. Many of these outlying agents developed correspondent relationships with patent solicitors located in Washington and in other major cities. Relationships with agents in Washington allowed those far away to have a representative on the spot who could check records in the Patent Office for relevant prior art and also get firsthand advice from examiners about the sustainability of patent claims. Relationships with agents in other cities gave them access to information about both the supply of and demand for inventions in different parts of the country (Lamoreaux and Sokoloff 2003).

[11] Freund 1896; Hansmann and Kraakman 2000; Blair 2003. By limited liability I mean a ceiling on shareholders' potential losses from a bankruptcy. Shareholders in specific types of enterprises (such as banks and railroads) were responsible in some states for double or triple the par value of their stock. See Horwitz 1992, 94.

[12] On productive versus unproductive entrepreneurship, see Baumol 1990.

[13] See, for example, Peiss 1998. More generally, see Kwolek-Folland 1998 and Mary Yeager's massive three-volume compilation (1999).

[14] This conservatism will be discussed in the next essay in this volume. On the importance of competition as a driving force for innovation, see Baumol 2002. Schumpeter's views were more ambivalent. On the one hand, he thought that large firms' R & D divisions would routinize innovation and make the entrepreneur increasingly obsolete. On the other, he worried that incumbent firms would shy away from disruptive innovation. See Schumpeter 1942 and 1934.

[15] On Swift's innovation and the development of the meatpacking industry, see Yeager 1981 and Chandler 1977.

[16] Some scholars have argued that after the railroads formed the Joint Economic Committee in 1879, they were much more successful in preventing ruinous price cuts. See Ulen 1980; Porter 1983; and Binder 1988.

[17] The plan collapsed in the face of determined opposition from producers in the oil fields who threatened to enforce with violence an embargo on shipments to the South Improvement Company. See Granitz and Klein 1996.

[18] Under normal conditions, given the petroleum industry's cost structure, refiners would not have been worried by the formation of a cartel, for as outsiders they would have been able to "free ride" on Standard's high prices (Granitz and Klein 1996).

[19] On this point, see Baumol 2002.

[20] For example, Western Union financed the consolidation of the innovative partnership of Gray and Barton with its own machine shop, but the resulting enterprise, Western Electric, operated as an independent firm. When Elisha Gray began work on his harmonic telegraph (essentially the telephone), he resigned his position as superintendent of Western Electric but continued to work in its facilities as an independent inventor (Adams and Butler 1999, 29–38).

[21] Lockwood did hire inventors from time to time but successfully opposed any sustained investment in in-house R & D. Lockwood is quoted in Lamoreaux and Sokoloff 1999, 41–42.

[22] See Baumol 2007, 167–68; and the essays in Clarke, Lamoreaux, and Usselman 2009.

[23] Tarbell's articles are quoted in Chalmers 1966, xv. See also Trachtenberg 1982, 78–86.

[24] For an overview of this first major wave of federal regulation, see Vogel 1981.

[25] Menes 2006. See also the essays collected in Stave 1972.

[26] Contrast, for example, Kolko 1965 and Martin 1971. For a complex view of the forces at play in regulation during this period, see Law and Libecap 2004.

References

Adams, Charles F. 1869. "A Chapter of Erie." *North American Review* 109 (July): 30–106.

Adams, Stephen B., and Orville B. Butler. 1999. *Manufacturing the Future: A History of Western Electric*. New York: Cambridge University Press.

Allen, Robert. 1983. "Collective Invention." *Journal of Economic Behavior and Organization* 4:1–24.

Aron, Cindy Sondik. 1987. *Ladies and Gentlemen of the Civil Service: Middle Class Workers in Victorian America*. New York: Oxford University Press.

Atack, Jeremy, and Peter Passell. 1994. *A New Economic View of American History*. 2nd ed. New York: Norton.

Bain, David Haward. 1999. *Empire Express: Building the First Transcontinental Railroad*. New York: Viking.

Baskin, Jonathan Barron, and Paul J. Miranti Jr. 1997. *A History of Corporate Finance*. New York: Cambridge University Press.

Balleisen, Edward J. 2001. *Navigating Failure: Bankruptcy and Commercial Society in Antebellum America*. Chapel Hill: University of North Carolina Press.

Baumol, William J. 1990. "Entrepreneurship: Productive, Unproductive, and Destructive." *Journal of Political Economy* 98:893–921.

———. 1993. *Entrepreneurship, Management, and the Structure of Payoffs*. Cambridge: MIT Press.

———. 2002. *The Free-Market Innovation Machine: Analyzing the Growth Miracle of Capitalism*. Princeton: Princeton University Press.

———. 2007. "Toward Analysis of Capitalism's Unparalleled Growth: Sources and Mechanism." In *Entrepreneurship, Innovation, and the Growth Mechanism of the Free-Enterprise Economies*, ed. Eytan Sheshinski, Robert J. Strom, and William J. Baumol, 158–78. Princeton: Princeton University Press.

Binder, John J. 1988. "The Sherman Antitrust Act and the Railroad Cartels." *Journal of Law and Economics* 31:443–68.

Blair, Margaret M. 2003. "Locking in Capital: What Corporate Law Achieved for Business Organizers in the 19th Century." *UCLA Law Review* 51:87–455.

Borut, Michael. 1977. "The *Scientific American* in Nineteenth Century America." Ph.D. diss., New York University.

Cadman, John W. 1949. *The Corporation in New Jersey: Business and Politics, 1791–1875*. Cambridge: Harvard University Press.

Calomiris, Charles W. 1990. "Is Deposit Insurance Necessary? A Historical Perspective." *Journal of Economic History* 50:283–95.

Carlson, W. Bernard. 1991. *Innovation as a Social Process: Elihu Thomson and the Rise of General Electric, 1870–1900*. New York: Cambridge University Press.

———. 1997. "Innovation and the Modern Corporation: From Heroic Invention to Industrial Science." In *Science in the Twentieth Century*, ed. John Krige and Dominique Pestre, 203–26. Australia: Harwood Academic Publishers.

Carosso, Vincent P. 1987. *The Morgans: Private International Bankers, 1854–1913*. Cambridge: Harvard University Press.

Carter, Susan B., et al. 2006. *Historical Statistics of the United States: Earliest Times to the Present, Millennial Edition*. 5 vols. Cambridge: Cambridge University Press.

Chalmers, David M. 1966. "Introduction to the Torchbook Edition." In Ida M. Tarbell, *The History of the Standard Oil Company*, ed. David M. Chalmers, xiii–xx. New York: Harper and Row.

Chandler, Alfred D., Jr. 1977. *The Visible Hand: The Managerial Revolution in American Business*. Cambridge: Belknap Press of Harvard University Press.

Clarke, Sally, Naomi R. Lamoreaux, and Stephen W. Usselman, eds. 2009. *The Challenge of Remaining Innovative: Lessons from Twentieth Century American Business*. Stanford: Stanford University Press.

Cochran, Thomas C. 1972. *Business in American Life: A History*. New York: McGraw-Hill.

Cook, Linda. 2003. "Responses in Technical Change to Property-Rights Uncertainty: Evidence from Patenting Activity among African Americans, 1821–1919." Unpublished paper.

Cox, Jacob Dolson, Sr. 1951. *Building an American Industry: The Story of the Cleveland Twist Drill Company and Its Founder*. Cleveland: Cleveland Twist Drill Co.

Cremin, Lawrence A. 1980. *American Education: The National Experience, 1783–1876*. New York: Harper and Row.

Cubberley, Ellwood P. 1920. *The History of Education: Educational Practice and Progress Considered as a Phase of the Development and Spread of Western Civilization*. New York: Houghton Mifflin.

David, Paul A., and Gavin Wright. 1997. "Increasing Returns and the Genesis of American Resource Abundance." *Industrial and Corporate Change* 6:203–45.

De Long, J. Bradford. 1991. "Did J. P. Morgan's Men Add Value? An Economist's Perspective on Financial Capitalism." In *Inside the Business Enterprise: Historical Perspectives on the Use of Information*, ed. Peter Temin, 205–36. Chicago: University of Chicago Press.

Dodd, E. Merrick, Jr. 1936. "Statutory Developments in Business Corporation Law, 1886–1936." *Harvard Law Review* 50:27–59.

Evans, George Heberton, Jr. 1948. *Business Incorporations in the United States, 1800–1943*. New York: National Bureau of Economic Research.

Ferrie, Joseph P. 2005. "The End of American Exceptionalism? Mobility in the U.S. since 1850." NBER Working Paper No. 11324, May. Cambridge, MA: National Bureau of Economic Research.

Fishlow, Albert. 1966. "Productivity and Technological Change in the Railroad Sector, 1840–1910." In Conference on Research in Income and Wealth, *Output, Employment and Productivity in the United States after 1800*. New York: National Bureau of Economic Research.

Freund, Ernst. 1896. "The Legal Nature of the Corporation." Ph.D. diss., Columbia University.

Freyer, Tony. 1995. "Legal Restraints on Economic Coordination: Antitrust in Great Britain and America, 1880–1920." In *Coordination and Information: Historical Perspectives on the Organization of Enterprise*, ed. Naomi R. Lamoreaux and Daniel M. G. Raff, 183–203. Chicago: University of Chicago Press.

Galambos, Louis. 1992. "Theodore N. Vail and the Role of Innovation in the Modern Bell System." *Business History Review* 66:95–126.

Garraty, John A. 1968. *The New Commonwealth, 1877–1890*. New York: Harper and Row.

Geiger, Roger L. 1986. *To Advance Knowledge: The Growth of American Research Universities, 1900–1940*. New York: Oxford University Press.

Gische, David M. 1979. "The New York City Banks and the Development of the National Banking System, 1860–1870." *American Journal of Legal History* 23:21–67.

Goodwyn, Lawrence. 1978. *The Populist Moment: A Short History of the Agrarian Revolt in America*. New York: Oxford University Press.

Grandy, Christopher. 1987. "The Economics of Multiple Governments: New Jersey Corporate Chartermongering, 1875–1929." Ph.D. diss., University of California, Berkeley.

Granitz, Elizabeth, and Benjamin Klein. 1996. "Monopolization by 'Raising Rivals' Costs': The Standard Oil Case." *Journal of Law and Economics* 39:1–47.

Gregory, Frances W., and Irene D. Neu. 1962. "The American Industrial Elite in the 1870's: Their Social Origins." In *Men in Business: Essays on the Historical Role of the Entrepreneur*, ed. William Miller, 193–211. New York: Harper and Row.

Gutman, Herbert G. 1966. *Work, Culture, and Society in Industrializing America*. New York: Random House.

Hansen, Bradley. 1998. "Commercial Associations and the Creation of a National Economy: The Demand for Federal Bankruptcy Law." *Business History Review* 72:86–113.

Hansmann, Henry, and Reinier Kraakman. 2000. "The Essential Role of Organizational Law." *Yale Law Journal* 110:387–440.

Harz, Louis. 1948. *Economic Policy and Democratic Thought: Pennsylvania, 1776–1860*. Cambridge: Harvard University Press.

Hilkey, Judy. 1997. *Character Is Capital: Success Manuals and Manhood in Gilded Ages America*. Chapel Hill: University of North Carolina Press.

Hofstadter, Richard. 1955. *Social Darwinism in American Thought*. Rev. ed. Boston: Beacon Press.

Horwitz, Morton J. 1992. *The Transformation of American Law, 1870–1960: The Crisis of Legal Orthodoxy*. New York: Oxford University Press.

Hounshell, David A. 1984. *From the American System to Mass Production, 1800–1932: The Development of Manufacturing Technology in the United States*. Baltimore: Johns Hopkins University Press.

Hovenkamp, Herbert. 1988. "Regulatory Conflict in the Gilded Age: Federalism and the Railroad Problem." *Yale Law Journal* 97:1017–72.

Huffman, Wallace E. 1998. "Modernizing Agriculture: A Continuing Process." *Daedalus* 127 (Fall): 159–86.

Hughes, Thomas P. 1989. *American Genesis: A Century of Invention and Technological Enthusiasm, 1870–1970*. New York: Viking.

Israel, Paul. 1992. *Machine Shop to Industrial Laboratory: Telegraphy and the Changing Context of American Invention, 1830–1920*. Baltimore: Johns Hopkins University Press.

———. 1998. *Edison: A Life of Invention*. New York: John Wiley and Sons.

Jaffe, Adam B., and Josh Lerner. 2004. *Innovation and Its Discontents: How Our Broken Patent System Is Endangering Innovation and Progress, and What to Do about It*. Princeton: Princeton University Press.

James, John A. 1976. "The Development of the National Money Market, 1893–1911." *Journal of Economic History* 36:878–97.

Josephson, Matthew. 1934. *The Robber Barons: The Great American Capitalists, 1861–1901*. New York: Harcourt, Brace and World.

Kaestle, Carl F. 1983. *Pillars of the Republic: Common Schools and American Society, 1780–1860*. New York: Hill and Wang.

Kens, Paul. 1998. *Lochner v. New York: Economic Regulation on Trial*. Lawrence: University of Kansas Press.

Khan, B. Zorina. 1996. "Married Women's Property Laws and Female Commercial Activity: Evidence from United States Patent Records, 1790–1895." *Journal of Economic History* 56:356–88.

Kim, Sukkoo. 1995. "Expansion of Markets and the Geographic Distribution of Economic Activities: The Trends in U.S. Regional Manufacturing Structure, 1860–1987." *Quarterly Journal of Economics* 110:881–908.

Kirkland, Edward Chase. 1956. *Dream and Thought in the Business Community, 1860–1900.* Ithaca, NY: Cornell University Press.

Klepper, Steven. 2007. "The Organizing and Financing of Innovative Companies in the Evolution of the U.S. Automobile Industry." In *Financing Innovation in the United States, 1870 to the Present*, ed. Naomi R. Lamoreaux and Kenneth L. Sokoloff, 85–128. Cambridge: MIT Press.

Kolko, Gabriel. 1965. *Railroads and Regulation, 1877–1916.* Princeton: Princeton University Press.

Kuhn, Arthur K. 1912. *A Comparative Study of the Law of Corporations with Particular Reference to the Protection of Creditors and Shareholders.* New York: Columbia University.

Kwolek-Folland, Angel. 1998. *Incorporating Women: A History of Women and Business in the United States.* New York: Twayne.

Laird, Pamela Walker. 2006. *Pull: Networking and Success since Benjamin Franklin.* Cambridge: Harvard University Press.

Lamoreaux, Naomi R. 2006. "Did Insecure Property Rights Slow Economic Development? Some Lessons from U.S. History." *Journal of Policy History* 18:146–64.

———. *The Great Merger Movement in American Business, 1895–1904.* New York: Cambridge University Press, 1985.

———. 1994. *Insider Lending: Banks, Personal Connections, and Economic Development in Industrial New England.* New York: Cambridge University Press.

Lamoreaux, Naomi R. Margaret Levenstein, and Kenneth L. Sokoloff. 2006. "Mobilizing Venture Capital during the Second Industrial Revolution: Cleveland, Ohio, 1870–1920." *Capitalism and Society* 1, no. 3, article 5, http://www.bepress.com/cas/vol1/iss3/art5/.

———. 2007. "Financing Invention during the Second Industrial Revolution: Cleveland, Ohio, 1870–1920." In *Financing Innovation in the United States, 1870 to the Present*, ed. Lamoreaux and Sokoloff. Cambridge: MIT Press. Pp. 39–84.

Lamoreaux, Naomi R., and Jean-Laurent Rosenthal. 2006. "Corporate Governance and the Plight of Minority Shareholders in the United States before the Great Depression." In *Corruption and Reform: Lessons from America's Economic History*, ed. Edward L. Glaeser and Claudia Goldin, 125–52. Chicago: University of Chicago Press.

Lamoreaux, Naomi R., and Kenneth L. Sokoloff. 1999. "Inventors, Firms, and the Market for Technology in the Late Nineteenth and Early Twentieth Centuries." In *Learning by Doing in Firms, Markets, and Countries*, ed. Naomi R. Lamoreaux, Daniel M. G. Raff, and Peter Temin, 19–57. Chicago: University of Chicago Press.

———. 2003. "Intermediaries in the U.S. Market for Technology, 1870–1920." In *Finance, Intermediaries, and Economic Development*, ed. Stanley L. Engerman, Philip T. Hoffman, Jean-Laurent Rosenthal, and Kenneth L. Sokoloff, 209–46. New York: Cambridge University Press.

———. 2007. "The Market for Technology and the Organization of Invention in U.S. History." In *Entrepreneurship, Innovation, and the Growth Mechanism*, ed. Eytan Sheshinski, Robert J. Strom, and William J. Baumol, 213–43. Princeton: Princeton University Press.

———. 2009. "The Rise and Decline of the Independent Inventor: A Schumpeterian Story?" In *Challenge of Remaining Innovative: Lessons from Twentieth Century American Business*, ed. Sally Clarke, Naomi R. Lamoreaux, and Steven W. Usselman, 43-73. Stanford: Stanford University Press.

Law, Marc T., and Gary D. Libecap. 2004. "The Determinants of Progressive Era Reform: The Pure Food and Drugs Act of 1906." In *Corruption and Reform: Lessons from America's Economic History*, ed. Edward L. Glaeser and Claudia Goldin, 319–42. Chicago: University of Chicago Press.

Libecap, Gary D. 1979. "Government Support of Private Claims to Public Minerals: Western Mineral Rights." *Business History Review* 53:364–85.

Lipartito, Kenneth. 2009. "Rethinking the Invention Factory: Bell Laboratories in Perspective." In *The Challenge of Remaining Innovative: Lessons from Twentieth Century American Business*, ed. Sally Clarke, Naomi R. Lamoreaux, and Steven W. Usselman, 132-60. Stanford: Stanford University Press.

Livermore, Shaw. 1935. "The Success of Industrial Mergers." *Quarterly Journal of Economics* 50:68–96.

Livingston, James. 1986. *Origins of the Federal Reserve System: Money, Class, and Corporate Capitalism, 1890–1913*. Ithaca, NY: Cornell University Press.

Livesay, Harold C. 1975. *Andrew Carnegie and the Rise of Big Business*. Boston: Little, Brown.

Martin, Albro. 1971. *Enterprise Denied: Origins of the Decline of American Railroads, 1897–1917*. New York: Columbia University Press.

McCurdy, Charles W. 1979. "The *Knight* Sugar Decision of 1895 and the Modernization of American Corporate Law, 1869–1903." *Business History Review* 53:304–42.

Merton, Robert K. 1971. "The Latent Functions of the Machine." In *Urban Bosses, Machines, and Progressive Reformers*, ed. Bruce M. Stave, 27–37. Lexington, MA: Heath.

Meyer, Peter B. 2003. "Episodes of Collective Invention." BLS Working Paper No. 368.

Menes, Rebecca. 2006. "Limiting the Reach of the Grabbing Hand: Graft and Growth in American Cities, 1880 to 1930." In *Corruption and Reform: Lessons from America's Economic History*, ed. Edward L. Glaeser and Claudia Goldin, 63–93. Chicago: University of Chicago Press.

Miller, William. 1962. *Men in Business: Essays on the Historical Role of the Entrepreneur*. New York: Harper and Row.

Misa, Thomas J. 1995. *A Nation of Steel: The Making of Modern America, 1865–1925*. Baltimore: Johns Hopkins University Press.

Mowery, David. 1995. "The Boundaries of the U.S. Firm in R&D." In *Coordination and Information: Historical Perspectives on the Organization of Enterprise*, ed. Naomi R. Lamoreaux and Daniel M. G. Raff, 147–76. Chicago: University of Chicago Presss.

Mowery, David C., and Nathan Rosenberg. 1989. *Technology and the Pursuit of Economic Growth*. New York: Cambridge University Press.

Navin, Thomas R., and Marian V. Sears. 1955. "The Rise of a Market for Industrial Securities, 1887–1902." *Business History Review* 29:105–38.

Neal, Larry. 1971. "Trust Companies and Financial Innovation, 1897–1914." *Business History Review* 45:35–51.

Neal, Larry, and Lance E. Davis. 2007. "Why Did Finance Capitalism and the Second Industrial Revolution Arise in the 1890s?" In *Financing Innovation in the United States, 1870 to the Present*, ed. Naomi R. Lamoreaux and Kenneth L. Sokoloff, 129–61. Cambridge: MIT Press.

Nelson, Richard R., and Gavin Wright. 1992. "The Rise and Fall of American Technological Leadership: The Postwar Era in Historical Perspective." *Journal of Economic Literature* 30:1931–64.

Noble, David F. 1977. *America by Design: Science, Technology, and the Rise of Corporate Capitalism*. New York: Oxford University Press.

Novak, William J. 1996. *The People's Welfare: Law and Regulation in Nineteenth-Century America*. Chapel Hill: University of North Carolina Press.

Olegario, Rowena. 2006. *A Culture of Credit: Embedding Trust and Transparency in American Business*. Cambridge: Harvard University Press.

Olmstead, Alan L., and Paul W. Rhode. 2002. "The Red Queen and the Hard Reds: Productivity Growth in American Wheat, 1800–1940." *Journal of Economic History* 62:929–66.

O'Sullivan, Mary. 2004. "What Drove the US Stock Market in the Last Century?" Unpublished paper.

Passer, Harold C. 1953. *The Electrical Manufacturers, 1875–1900*. Cambridge: Harvard University Press.

Peiss, Kathy. 1998. *Hope in a Jar: The Making of America's Beauty Culture*. New York: Metropolitan Books.

Porter, Robert H. 1983. "A Study of Cartel Stability: The Joint Executive Committee, 1880–1886." *Bell Journal of Economics* 14:301–14.

Reich, Leonard S. 1977. "Research, Patents, and the Struggle to Control Radio: A Study of Big Business and the Uses of Industrial Research." *Business History Review* 51:208–35.

———. 1980. "Industrial Research and the Pursuit of Corporate Security: The Early Years of Bell Labs." *Business History Review* 54:504–29.

———. 1985. *The Making of American Industrial Research: Science and Business at GE and Bell, 1876–1926*. New York: Cambridge University Press.

———. 1992. "Lighting the Path to Profit: GE's Control of the Electric Lamp Industry, 1892–1941." *Business History Review* 66:305–34.

Roy, William G. 1997. *Socializing Capital: The Rise of the Large Industrial Corporation in America*. Princeton: Princeton University Press.

Sandage, Scott A. 2005. *Born Losers: A History of Failure in America*. Cambridge: Harvard University Press.

Schmookler, Jacob. 1966. *Invention and Economic Growth*. Cambridge: Harvard University.

Schumpeter, Joseph A. 1934. *The Theory of Economic Development: An Inquiry into Profits, Capital, Credit, Interest, and the Business Cycle*. Trans. Redvers Opie. Cambridge: Harvard University Press.

———. 1942. *Capitalism, Socialism, and Democracy*. New York: Harper.

Skeel, David A., Jr. 2001. *Debt's Dominion: A History of Bankruptcy Law in America*. Princeton: Princeton University Press.

Sokoloff, Kenneth L. 1988. "Inventive Activity in Early Industrial America: Evidence from Patent Records, 1790–1846." *Journal of Economic History* 48:813–30.

Stave, Bruce M., ed. 1972 *Urban Bosses, Machines, and Progressive Reformers*. Lexington, MA: Heath.

Stevens, Edward W., Jr. 1995. *The Grammar of the Machine: Technical Literacy and Early Industrial Expansion in the United States*. New Haven: Yale University Press.

Summers, Mark Wahlgren. 1993. *The Era of Good Stealings*. New York: Oxford University Press.

Taylor, George Rogers. 1951. *The Transportation Revolution, 1815–1860*. White Plains, NY: M. E. Sharpe.

Temin, Peter. 1964. *Iron and Steel in Nineteenth-Century America: An Economic Inquiry*. Cambridge: MIT Press.

Trachtenberg, Alan. 1982. *The Incorporation of America: Culture and Society in the Gilded Age*. New York: Hill and Wang.

Ulen, Thomas S. 1980. "The Market for Regulation: The ICC from 1887 to 1920." *American Economic Review* 70:306–10.

Usselman, Steven W. 1991. "Patents Purloined: Railroads, Inventors, and the Diffusion of Innovation in 19th-Century America." *Technology and Culture* 32:1047–75.

———. 2002. *Regulating Railroad Innovation: Business, Technology, and Politics in America, 1840–1920*. New York: Cambridge University Press.

Vogel, David. 1981. "The 'New' Social Regulation in Historical and Comparative Perspective." In *Regulation in Perspective: Historical Essays*, ed. Thomas K. McCraw, 155–85. Cambridge: Harvard University Press.

Walker, Juliet E. K. 1998. *The History of Black Business in America: Capitalism, Race, Entre-preneurship*. New York: Twayne.

Wallis, John Joseph. 2006. "The Concept of Systematic Corruption in American History." In *Corruption and Reform: Lessons from America's Economic History*, ed. Edward L. Glaeser and Claudia Goldin, 23–62. Chicago: University of Chicago Press.

West, Robert Craig. 1974. *Banking Reform and the Federal Reserve, 1863–1923*. Ithaca, NY: Cornell University Press.

White, Eugene Nelson. 1982. "The Political Economy of Banking Regulation, 1864–1933." *Journal of Economic History* 42:33–40.

———. 1983. *The Regulation and Reform of the American Banking System, 1900–1929*. Princeton: Princeton University Press.

White, Richard. 2003. "Information, Markets, and Corruption: Transcontinental Railroads in the Gilded Age." *Journal of American History* 90:19–43.

Wilkins, Mira. 1992. "The Neglected Intangible Asset: The Influence of the Trade Mark on the Rise of the Modern Corporation." *Business History* 34:66–95.

Wills, Jocelyn. 2003. "Respectable Mediocrity: The Everyday Life of an Ordinary American Striver, 1876–1890." *Journal of Social History* 37:323–49.

Wise, George. 1985. *Willis R. Whitney, General Electric, and the Origins of U.S. Industrial Research*. New York: Columbia University Press.

Wyllie, Irvin G., 1954. *The Self-Made Man in America: The Myth of Rags to Riches*. New Brunswick, NJ: Rutgers University Press.

Yeager, Mary. 1981. *Competition and Regulation: The Development of Oligopoly in the Meat Packing Industry*. Greenwich, CT: Jai Press.

———. 1999. *Women in Business*. Cheltenham, UK: Elgar.

Chapter 14

Entrepreneurship in the United States, 1920–2000

Margaret B. W. Graham

THE SPECIAL GENIUS OF THE twentieth-century U.S. economy has typically been characterized as the harnessing of technology by entrepreneurs working within the large vertically integrated American corporation, at first wholly a private sector phenomenon, and then in cooperation with an increasingly interventionist federal government.[1] By the 1970s no sector of the U.S. economy, whether public or private, for-profit, or not-for-profit, was unaffected by this regime. Even nonmanufacturing sectors like entertainment and communications bore the stamp of the scientifically enhanced, and regulated, form of industrialization that consolidated the gains of the second industrial revolution.[2]

Closer examination of the twentieth-century experience in the United States, however, suggests a more complicated picture than the simple rule of giant firms.[3] Even the apparent institutionalization of innovation—as a perpetual motion machine embedded in a network of large corporations, supported by complementary institutions—was only part of a more complex story.[4] Less evident, but still important, were the activities of the usually smaller entrepreneurial firm, and of individual inventing entrepreneurs, often working with large corporations. Though the interlocking bureaucracies of what Louis Galambos has termed the "organizational synthesis," which relied on associated professionals, managers, scientists, and government bureaucrats, may have been the dominant mode of the American economy for much of the twentieth century, the impetus for renewal in the American system was grounded in the complementary relationship between the innovating entrepreneur and the enterprising firm, which might be termed the corporate entrepreneur.[5]

Large corporations were well established by the beginning of the twentieth century (as we learned in the previous chapter), but many of them had yet to "corporatize." As historians Olivier Zunz, David Hounshell, and JoAnne Yates have described in detail, the corporatization of America took the form of increasing bureaucratization through standardization, controlled information flow, the investment of impersonal capital, and cultural homogenization.[6] The end of the Great War unleashed a passion for productivity that resulted in a systematic application of scientific management, especially within the large corporation, as well as among its suppliers and institutional collaborators like the labor unions.[7] The institutionalization of the large industrialized corporation also brought with it several new forms of economic coordination—integration of R & D, intercompany associations, and increasing degrees of government regulation (Galambos and Pratt 1988). Together, these changes led to a partial closing of the U.S. innovation system, with the short-term but temporary effect of streamlining technological innovation and harnessing it to national priorities. This highly integrated and compartmentalized innovation system did not drive out the individual entrepreneur entirely, but it formed a different context for entrepreneurship than the open system we saw in previous chapters. The reopening of the system was a development that occurred, not coincidentally, with the spread of information technologies and the third industrial revolution that was fully consummated by the end of the century.

Innovation as a Twentieth-Century Version of Entrepreneurship

It is significant that the Oxford English Dictionary credits Austrian economist Joseph Schumpeter in 1939 with the first use of the term *innovation*, as the essential entrepreneurial act, for in the first half of the twentieth century the term *entrepreneur* became closely associated with science-based innovation. The Schumpeterian entrepreneur's role was to supply the coordination and effort that brought a new process or product to the point of adoption and commercialization, but not necessarily to supply the capital. For this diligent observer of the twentieth-century American economy, entrepreneurs, whether acting on their own, or inside firms, did more than make decisions in the face of change. They responded creatively to change, seeking to shape and use it for their own purposes. Though Schumpeterian entrepreneurs did not have to risk their own capital, entrepreneurship was inherently a risk-taking activity in other ways, one so painful and fraught with uncertainty that it justified the financial returns it generated when it succeeded, even when they were very large.

While Schumpeter initially limited his characterization of the entrepreneur to the creative individual, his later work acknowledged that the advent of the large integrated corporation had changed the American entrepreneurial scene. When scientific research entered the picture, the locus of greatest uncertainty became technological. Firms that integrated invention and research as corporate functions were creating the potential to initiate disruptive innovations that could leave their less well-endowed competitors at a disadvantage. They also acquired the potential to control the rate of change in their industries, and often sought to keep individual entrepreneurs from interrupting the orderly and profitable development of technologies.[8]

Prosperity and Status

No period in American history has celebrated the entrepreneur, and especially the inventing entrepreneur, more wholeheartedly than the period that culminated in the second industrial, or electrochemical, revolution in the 1880s and 1890s. By World War I, however, this revolution had entered a consolidation phase. The wealth and power it generated had also become identified in many quarters with various antisocial activities. When corruption at various levels both in government and firm governance, attracted public attention, the federal government of the Progressive Era instituted social and regulatory policies intended to curb the more antisocial aspects of greed. Regulatory policy was also fashioned to build solid working and middle classes that would be equally resistant to socialism and the solidarity of labor unions.

In this context the corporation adopted a less flamboyant style more in keeping with the public mood and the spirit of science-based efficiency, replacing its hitherto charismatic leaders with professional managers, "the organization men." Large centralized corporations headed by industrial statesmen, like Owen D. Young, chairman of General Electric, would remain a fixture of the twentieth-century business environment, playing a major part in making these classes viable (McQuaid 1978). The role of industrial statesman—an establishment figure, often college-educated, always socially and politically well connected—was rarely open to the entrepreneur. Some that did achieve it, like Samuel Insull, English immigrant, electricity pioneer, and leader of his industry during the 1920s, suffered reversals of fortune for their presumption.[9] For much of the rest of the century, the term *entrepreneur* took on a negative connotation, signifying the eccentric individual who was all too likely to be disruptive to the well-integrated organization.[10]

The new social landscape was shaped by other factors as well, including a narrowing of the disparities in wealth distribution in the society through fiscal policy, and the acquisition of appropriate skills by the broader population. What became known as the "great compression," shrinking the gap between the highest and lowest U.S. income earners, had the effect of reducing the private concentration of investment capital, while giving the federal government more money to spend. The federal income tax, first imposed on the highest income earners in 1913, helped to consolidate the middle class. The income of those in the highest income percentile as reflected in income tax records, dropped from 18 percent of total declared income before World War I to 8 percent of declared income in the early years of World War II. After the wealthiest people saw their marginal tax rate hit 80 percent to help finance the war effort, income inequality hit its lowest level of the century and remained stable well into the 1960s (Piketty and Saez 2003). The midcentury dip was partly accounted for by shifts in tax policy—progressive income taxes, estate taxes, and corporate income tax, which in turn reduced the money payable for dividends. Wage levels for working- and middle-class people were also sustained by big unions and big corporations, as well as by government programs (Fischer 1996, 202–3).

A widening of income inequality levels in the 1970s signaled the start of a new technological revolution, the information revolution.[11] For some, the recurrence of rising income disparities was explained by the failure on the part of the working class, and the unions that represented them, to acquire the new skills required by the shift in technology; for others, they reflected increases in individual entrepreneurship as well as increases in its rewards (Reich 1991). They also reflected the effects of successive waves of financial innovation extending credit to less and less qualified people through the depersonalization and automation of investment at all levels.

Social attitudes toward entrepreneurs corresponded to the income inequality curve. From the late Victorian period to the Roaring Twenties, wealth attained through entrepreneurship or other forms of achievement like entertainment, held celebrity status, but as novels by Willa Cather and F. Scott Fitzgerald demonstrated, the associated materialism and lapses in morality were simultaneously admired and condemned.[12] After the shared sacrifice of World War II, individual power and wealth became suspect, and greater status accrued to those leaders of large organizations, private or public, civilian or military, who knew how to make them productive

(Farber 2002). By the 1990s the tables had turned and entrepreneurs appeared on the front cover of *Time* magazine. Once again the top percentile of the population was in control of over 11 percent of the country's annual income. This time, however, less of the wealth in the top category of taxpayers was accounted for by the rentiers. Owing to striking gains in executive compensation, including stock options, and to massive increases for those whose compensation derived from innovative activities in financial services—venture capitalists, hedge fund managers, and private equity partners—this time more accrued to the working rich, who in turn often used their money to invest in entrepreneurial ventures.

Context and Conditions for Entrepreneurship

The period 1920 to 2000 comprised three distinctly different eras for entrepreneurship. The financially chaotic interwar era of 1920–41, featuring a push for productivity and its consequences for unemployment, ended with the U.S. entry into World War II.[13] For entrepreneurship this period was extremely volatile with many opportunities in fast-growing industries in the 1920s followed by the swift demise of many new companies before and during the Great Depression. The second period from World War II until the long period of inflation beginning with the Vietnam War, 1941–74, involved continuous national mobilization but with a relatively static economic equilibrium emphasizing optimization. In this period innovation was not a high priority for large corporations, or even very welcome in many sectors, except in the designated "high tech" businesses that were needed by the military, and "crossovers" that could translate military technologies into civilian products. The third period, 1975–2000, featured the fluid phase of the information revolution coupled with globalization, combining to become the third industrial revolution. This era saw a resurgence of entrepreneurial opportunity in many different sectors of the economy, especially information technology and new consumer products. Beginning with the economic slowdown characterized as "stagflation," it continued with a revolution in financial institutions that culminated in a series of financial bubbles: the telecoms collapse, the dot-com mania, and the subprime mortgage collapse, the last of which developed after the turn of the new century. Each era for entrepreneurship was characterized by its own unique institutional developments, and in all three eras entrepreneurship played the important but distinctive part that circumstances dictated at the time.

Era One, 1920–1941: Search for Economic Self-Regulation

In the 1920s economic output rose, until in 1929 it achieved a level not to be seen again until 1940 with the ramp-up for World War II. This performance was the result of deliberate attempts to rationalize and achieve efficiency. Besides the focus on productivity, big contributors were social factors generating a new kind of consumption: mobility and suburbanization, rising populations with greater disposable incomes, and more leisure time (Bakker 2003; Melosi 2000, 206–7). Industries that benefited especially from these factors were the several great high-growth businesses that had their start in technological developments before the turn of the century, but drew on wartime demands and financial improvements to achieve postwar scale.

These included two huge changes in transportation, aircraft and automobile production, together with the infrastructure builders and the materials and parts-suppliers that attended those industries; and electrification—comprising also the motorized appliances that electricity made possible, cinema, and consumer electronics, which transformed entertainment and advertising. Entrepreneurs who had driven the development of these industries, both technologically and financially, like Samuel Insull, the electrical pioneer and acknowledged leader of big-city power companies, had already turned to investing the substantial rewards of their prewar activities. Among the high-growth industries of the 1920s, the iconic growth industry was radio, which opened opportunities of many kinds for entrepreneurs, especially inventing entrepreneurs. If the patron industries for nineteenth-century inventors had been the telegraph and the railroads, the patron industries for the twentieth century became automobiles, aviation, electrical appliances for home and industry, entertainment, especially the cinema, and radio. Of these, radio and the electronics that grew out of it became the greatest generator of entrepreneurial opportunity.

Radio: Invention and Innovation

Radio was both science-based and a "crossover" industry, in the sense that its technology base was considered to be strategic from a military perspective as well as important to civilian pursuits. For this reason the U.S. government intervened at the time of World War I to ensure that its technology was not held hostage to the disputes over intellectual property that had plagued it and other emerging technologies in the prior era. Characteristic of this type of intervention was the takeover of American Marconi and its reorganization into the General Electric subsidiary, the Radio Corporation of America (RCA), which was formed to administer a patent pool of radio-related patents drawn from GE, Westinghouse, AT&T, and United Fruit (Aitken 1976; Chandler 2001, chap. 2; Reich 1977). Growth in the industry was fueled by the major social movements of the time. Acculturation of immigrants from prior decades, for instance, was a key growth factor as transplanted populations often speaking and reading no English found community, entertainment, and information about their adopted society in the new medium (Graham 2000, 149–50).

Radio functioned primarily as a point-to-point (i.e., ship to shore) communications medium before the war, but its development was also driven by thousands of ham radio operators who helped to develop the radio art and contributed their expertise in many ways before and during World War I (Douglas 1987). Beginning with radio station KDKA in Pittsburgh in 1920, radio morphed into broadcasting. By 1930 radios could be found in 14 million U.S. households, enjoying a rate of adoption far greater than either electrification or the telephone. Both technologically enabled forms of entertainment, radio and cinema, met with similar rapid increases in use, though sales of radio sets declined in 1926 and again during the Depression. New radio-related opportunities for entrepreneurs ranged from design and production of radio sets and electronic components to dealers and repair shops, advertisers, public relations firms, and entertainment producers. Though the number of companies active in the radio industry declined dramatically in industry shakeouts of the mid-1920s and early 1930s, a few new enterprises survived to become large suppliers of ancillary devices. One factor that inhibited entrepreneurship in radio was the aforementioned control given to RCA over the radio-related patents, for all radio producers were required to license a "package" of patents, whether they could use them all or not. This was a significant liability for smaller enterprises, as was the control of component manufacturing and supply by the electrical companies, GE and Westinghouse (McLaurin 1949).

Dislocation and Innovation

The Roaring Twenties were not just about sudden growth industries, however: the frenzied prosperity masked other forms of economic dislocation, which in turn moved established companies to innovate reactively, often by forming relationships with entrepreneurial enterprises. While overall output rose, employment numbers declined in such previously steady areas as mining, steel, shoes, housewares, and clothing production.[14] Spurred by rapid advances in mechanization achieved during the war years, companies harnessed electricity to replace manpower, and found new uses for internal combustion engines for transport and for agriculture. Homes and farms adopted the new labor-saving devices when their domestic laborers and hired hands took manufacturing and office jobs. At the firm level a new merger movement occurred as companies sought to insulate themselves from change. Many firms that obtained the necessary financing absorbed other firms, especially competitors and suppliers. However, even firms that came out on top in the various industry consolidation movements could not proceed on the basis of scale alone: most could no longer survive by offering the goods they had offered before. For inspiration many embraced social needs, like the movement for sanitary households following the 1918 flu epidemic, or drew on new science bases like home economics for fresh ideas.

The task of keeping up with "The New American Tempo," as it was known by the later 1920s, was not an easy matter. Regina Blaszčyzk has shown that to increase their appeal to a broader spectrum of customers and to compete for a consumer dollar stretched by the purchase of new homes and automobiles, even the most established firms had to change their product lines, often in innovative ways. Companies added new forms of expertise like design and set up new feedback links with their customers. Corporate entrepreneurs like Kohler, the third largest plumbing ware company in the country, abandoned its old channels of distribution dominated by traditional plumbers and plumbing supply contractors, and appealed directly to consumers through a combination of showrooms, designers, and color experts (Blaszczyk 2000). Specialty glass company Corning Glass Works also connected with different markets when it diversified from just selling heat-resistant glassware to laboratories, to selling consumers see-through ovenware and tableware. Even Ford Motor Company tried to adapt its changeless Model T to changing consumer needs, while trying to avoid the appearance of innovating.[15]

Entrepreneurship in general assumed a different shape in this context, in many industries achieving a new symbiosis between large and small enterprises. Large companies that had been forced to innovate reactively settled back into established ways as soon as they dared, but corporate entrepreneurs, like Kohler and Corning, learned from their experience in the 1920s and 1930s to take advantage of economic shock or upheaval by introducing new lines of product or new businesses. Large merchandisers like the department stores and chain stores took on the financing, national advertising and consumer education campaigns, and distribution management challenges of supplying a continental economy, while smaller design and production houses took on the task of making better contact with local consumer fashion needs, while producing higher-quality goods more efficiently and at lower prices.

Despite, or perhaps because of, the fervent efforts of all firms to achieve efficiencies and to strike a balance between innovation and control, the stock market crash in 1929 and the economic collapse that followed it caused many to fear that economic order was not achievable by the private sector alone. Despite the new opportunities that the emergent industries—automobiles, aviation, electrical appliances, and consumer electronic devices—created, there was a net major loss of jobs in the 1930s. For this the public laid the blame on two things: the evident abuses of the public trust that had occurred in their financial institutions, especially the stock market, and the relentless application of new technology to the pursuit of efficiency that had accompanied the institutionalization of R & D.[16]

Institutional Shifts: The Stock Market and Entrepreneurial Funding

Developments in the stock market both enabled the rapid rise of the high-growth industries, and contributed to the subsequent shifts in buying power. The 1920s brought financial innovations of several kinds, creating opportunities for the scrupulous and the shady alike. Important changes had already occurred making it possible for the country's securities markets to offer reliable financing to new companies. According to Mary O'Sullivan, more new stock issues occurred in the 1920s than in any other time in the century (O'Sullivan 2007). Enterprises in the aviation and radio industries, for example, could obtain financing without entrepreneurs having to provide the money themselves. Companies that needed to revamp their businesses, or merge with others, could get the financial backing they needed, while enterprises that had already consolidated could find the financing to acquire others in their industry. If the great merger movement of the 1890s had attempted to organize markets, the merger movement of the 1920s was aimed at changing corporate financial structures, issuing stock, or buying stock back so as to increase the value of the remaining outstanding shares. At a time of postwar consolidation for many industries large companies had better access to capital than small ones.

In addition to the novel forms of equity financing, debt was also important, as the U.S. kept its interest rates low for much of the interwar period, motivating investors to seek out higher-yielding investments. Ivar Kreuger, the Swiss "Match King," made a fortune selling postwar reparations bonds on the behalf of European governments to unwary U.S. investors seeking high yields, and was regarded as a philanthropist until his suicide revealed him to be both a financial entrepreneur and a swindler.[17] Smaller U.S. enterprises often resorted to borrowing to meet their needs. Few twentieth-century entrepreneurs proved to be, like Henry Ford, both completely unwilling to have anything to do with stock markets and allergic to credit (Zunz 1990). Although Ford too had serious difficulties in the downturn following World War I, he avoided going into debt because his suppliers and dealers were willing to do it for him. But according to David Hounshell (1984), he also expressed the belief that sales on credit were harmful to the consumer and "steadfastly refused to consider consumer credit as a legitimate instrument of consumption."

Cheap consumer debt financed buying the new homes in the suburbs and the durable goods that went with them. Towns and cities in turn issued debt of their own to invest in the infrastructure needed to service all the new neighborhoods and homeowners. Middle-class buyers were encouraged to use debt to acquire their cars and houses, and to turn their savings into investments. Many people drained their low-interest bank accounts, and invested their savings in the stock market. Though early in the decade consumer credit was widely available for such purposes, by the late 1920s all forms of investment had become more expensive.

One industry where consolidation was not supposed to take place, at least not across state lines, was banking. But banks, like other enterprises, recognized the development of a national market, and tried to find ways to attain the requisite size needed to take advantage of scale. One banking entrepreneur who later became chairman of the Federal Reserve under Franklin Roosevelt was Marriner Eccles, the first to form a bank holding company, chartered in Delaware, which purchased and owned banks in more than one state, and put together enough of them that it could gain access to eastern banking connections, economies of scale, and large amounts of capital (Hughes 1986).

As consolidations took place in the high-growth industries, however, the amount of trustworthy (blue chip) stock that was available on the market diminished, pushing the prices of remaining stocks to ever greater highs. When the average investor could no longer afford even one share of many high-priced stocks (the Berkshire Hathaways of their day) a few enterprising investment firms adopted the investment trust, imported from England, to offer smaller investors a chance for diversified stock holdings. Most of the management companies that offered these trusts failed quickly, but a few such as those organized by JP Morgan and Goldman Sachs, and the Boston-based independents Mass Mutual and Pioneer, survived. The result was the new mutual fund industry, the innovation of a few entrepreneurial management companies and independent financial entrepreneurs.

Depression Impedes Entrepreneurial Activity

As must be evident from the foregoing account, the Depression that followed the crash of the market in 1929 exposed and exacerbated many kinds of economic weakness: failures of overextended and overleveraged businesses, the interconnectedness of banking institutions, the ready availability of stock market credit. While causality remains a matter of debate in academic circles, one consequence of the Depression was a shift in demand, a decline in buying power for the ordinary citizen. At a meeting with major industrialists convened by President Hoover on November 21, 1929, Henry Ford observed, "American production has come to equal and surpass not our people's power to consume, but their power to purchase" (McElvaine 2003). Paradoxically, upper-middle-class citizens had relatively greater buying power than they had ever had (Szostak 1995). Ordinary consumers who were not utterly destitute continued to buy for the rest of the decade until World War II, but many bought with the help of another financial innovation introduced by a colossal financial and corporate entrepreneur, the General Motors Corporation, the installment plan. After the chaos and wealth destruction of the previous decade the installment plan provided an appealing and reassuring financial discipline.

The war-depression sequence had lasting consequences for the way the American economy would be run. New Deal Democrats secured the White House on promises that the federal government would find solutions to the problems of joblessness and economic instability. The federal government stepped in to coordinate and fund major pieces of the economy, first in the period of the National Recovery Act through public works and later through defense spending. In what has been called the Second New Deal the Roosevelt administration also turned to rigorous enforcement of antitrust legislation, already on the books but seldom enforced, and to other changes in regulatory practice.

If the 1920s provided a heady climate for individual entrepreneurship in chaotic growth—with fluid, rapidly growing new industries, and many new technologies and management techniques being introduced—the conditions of the 1930s worked against starting new businesses and reduced the chances of survival for recent start-ups. In addition to the difficulty of gaining access to capital, the increasing burden of regulation made the minimum effective size for a viable firm harder to achieve. Many firms run by inventor-entrepreneurs were either acquired or driven out of business by larger firms. Business failures, especially among small and medium-sized companies occurred with increasing frequency, peaking in 1933, but continuing at substantial levels until World War II. For the most part the New Deal administration's several disjointed efforts to coordinate economic recovery stalled, leaving fear and pessimism in their wake (Raff 1991; Hughes 1986).

Large firms that had not taken on excessive debt were better able to weather the prolonged downturn and many took the opportunity to pursue entrepreneurial opportunities or to sponsor entrepreneurial ventures.[18] To prudently managed firms, the Depression offered a chance for a new kind of corporate entrepreneurship, anticipating and diversifying into long-term business opportunities drawing on research-based invention, rather than relying on immediate demand.[19] BF Goodrich investigated artificial rubber; RCA pushed to achieve a working television system; Alcoa looked into structural aluminum for housing and large buildings; Corning Glass produced new high-purity glasses and large telescope mirrors; and DuPont pushed ahead with nylon and other artificial fibers.[20] For these companies and many others, the respite from the unrelenting demand pressures of the 1920s was a chance to pursue the long-term research for a program of new products and services. While some firms that had recently opened research departments closed them as an economy measure, firms that kept their R & D laboratories open and working during the Depression built the knowledge bases and acquired the skills that laid the foundation for new business growth for the next several decades.[21]

In the early 1930s many observers blamed the onset of the Great Depression on the drive for efficiency through industrial research. Even such a consequential member of the New Deal administration as Secretary of the Interior Harold Ickes believed that technological unemployment was an unavoidable consequence of invention (National Resources Science Committee 1937, quoted in Rhodes 1999). Scientist-statesmen like Karl Compton, president of MIT, and Frank Jewett, CEO of the Bell Telephone Company, were anxious to counter this technological pessimism and to convince the public to make a different connection between science, jobs, and prosperity. They argued that, contrary to popular opinion, well-funded and organized science-based innovation could be a purposeful spur to growth, far more reliable than the trial-and-error "imagining" they attributed to independent inventors like Thomas Edison. Their campaign to redeem science in the public mind claimed for industrial research an essential role in future economic growth and set the stage for huge increases in public funding for science in companies and research universities alike.[22]

Effects of Industrialized Research on Entrepreneurs

Industrial research was institutionalized, in two senses, after World War I. First, the large corporation brought research in-house, to occupy a special place in the corporate hierarchy. Second, the corporate laboratory formed the nexus of a set of relationships and practices with other organizations beyond the boundaries of the firm that has been called the U.S. national innovation system.[23] The resulting set of close and interactive relationships never completely excluded inventor entrepreneurs of a previous era, but it did push them to the periphery, outside the expanding boundaries of the more formal knowledge networks formed by large firms and research universities.

As discussed in the previous essay, only a few exceptional pioneering corporate research laboratories were established in the United States before World War I.[24] According to surveys conducted by the National Research Council, more than 500 firms set up corporate laboratories in the decade after World War I.[25] Most believed that a lead in industrial research had given Germany advantages during the war, especially in advanced war materiel, in weaponry, and poison gasses. Because in-house research required significant investment and only the largest firms in any industry had the scale to support it, those that did the research and were willing to share or license their results were creating knowledge resources for entire industries. The federal government actively encouraged private investment in R & D. Especially during the Coolidge administration the funding of industrial research by companies was treated as justification for technology-based firms like RCA to behave as sanctioned technical monopolies (Sturchio 1985).

If the large corporation as an institution had become homogeneous and monolithic by the 1920s, this newest part of the firm had not (Zunz 1990). Industrial research laboratories recruited leaders with charisma as well as recognized scientific achievement to hire stables of distinguished scientists in the United States and from abroad. Corporate laboratories were seldom the first laboratories that a company possessed, but they differed from the others already in use. Before corporate laboratories appeared, there were works laboratories, sales laboratories, experimental mills, licensing laboratories, design studios, and testing laboratories. Like corporations in their formative years a generation earlier, their technical staffs were filled with eclectic groups of people, from many disciplines and occupations. Earlier laboratories were not so remote as to be unreachable by ordinary employees, nor so secretive as to be off-limits to customers, licensees, and suppliers, many of them entrepreneurs. When corporate laboratories proliferated and became increasingly involved with government-funded research, however, the R & D function took on a different character—increasingly remote, campus-like, and protected from the daily interruptions that close connections with production sites were likely to involve.

During the 1920s corporate research laboratories formed connections with other industrial laboratories, university departments, scientific societies, and government bureaus such as the National Bureau of Standards (NBS) and the Patent Office.[26] By World War II these networks had developed further, but also narrowed into vital links with government funders and a select group of research-performing universities, forming an integrated, self-sufficient, and increasingly closed innovation system.[27] Well-established relationships between experienced inventors and certain large and medium-sized companies survived the 1930s, but the time passed when companies in high-growth industries welcomed the product ideas of amateurs and tinkerers (Hintz 2007, Douglas 1987, Israel 1992, conclusion).

After the war corporate laboratories were expected to fill a new role for large corporations—serving their strategic purposes, creating long-term opportunities, acting as arbiters and standard setters between different divisions of the corporation. Many corporate laboratories gained control of the entire R & D agenda of their respective firms, sometimes closing or integrating the other laboratories and often changing their modus operandi (Graham and Pruitt 1990). In some cases a laboratory became the organizational surrogate for the company's leader, institutionalizing innovation. In 1951 RCA's CEO David Sarnoff made this mission quite explicit by renaming the corporate research laboratory after himself.

Era Two: War and the Innovation System

For U.S. policymakers World War II offered a powerful example of what the economy could accomplish if directed and optimized by the federal government. Direction and optimization were most efficiently accomplished through large corporate entities, which might in turn rely on, or even start from scratch, smaller entrepreneurial companies. In the era that began with World War II successful entrepreneurs and entrepreneurial companies had to become skilled at dealing with politicians and procurement officers to such an extent that economic historian Jonathan Hughes called them procurement entrepreneurs.[28] Large corporations that were chiefly government suppliers were known as *prime contractors*, and supported their research mainly with government research contracts, farming out smaller projects to subcontractors. For military business the primes frequently served as mediators and shields for smaller entrepreneurial enterprises that could not handle the demands of government bureaucratic controls, as well as for other large companies that did not want to deal directly with the government for fear of compromising their intellectual property rights.

The effort to convert the economy to a war-fighting mode reinforced patterns that had already become embedded in the large technology-dependent firms in the late 1930s. Firms like General Motors and Ford Motor Company had just returned to profitability when preparations for World War II and Lend Lease forced them to redirect their efforts, and convert their capacity to war production. Large corporations with working R & D laboratories like Westinghouse, General Electric, and RCA contributed members of their engineering and research staffs as well as project management expertise to several huge, secretive, science-based projects for which the war became known—radar at MIT, radio at Harvard, the Manhattan Project at University of Chicago and Los Alamos. These interdisciplinary programs involved corporate researchers working together with research faculties at universities and recruited as well from other institutions. Both the interdisciplinary approach they used and the inventions they generated were early forms of university entrepreneurship and created a reservoir of opportunities for development after the war.

In World War I the primary mobilization challenges had been for uniform manufacturers, food suppliers, and the makers of munitions and vehicles, but World War

II posed more difficult choices for many U.S. manufacturers. When mobilization time was short, large established firms obviously had the advantage over smaller firms, and there was no time for start-ups. The new military procurement programs needed technically demanding goods: artificial substitutes for essential raw materials that came from overseas or belligerent countries—rubber for shoes and tires, critical ingredients for medical supplies. Established firms could continue to produce their regular products in the face of unpredictable demand, or they could choose to ramp up production for different products that had a definite military need, and for which the government promised a new and innovative compensation arrangement—"cost-plus" reimbursement. In the rubber industry for instance BF Goodrich chose to stick with rubber while Goodyear chose to become an aircraft manufacturer in response to the defense program (Blackford and Kerr 1996). Corporate executives went to Washington on behalf of their companies partly to do their patriotic duty and partly because they found that service on the War Production Board and other coordinating agencies could yield valuable information both about current demand and about competition as it might be shaping up for the postwar era. Nevertheless, privately bearing the cost of conversion to new military programs, as some entrepreneurial firms tried to do to avoid government claims on intellectual property, could mean sustaining serious losses from arbitrary program discontinuations.

War preparation created opportunities for brand new entrants, but rarely for small concerns. The U.S. military, with its long-established preferences for large concentrated suppliers that could provide items at large scale and lowest cost, naturally looked for new entrants that had already demonstrated the necessary management and organizational skills. Such a case was Henry Kaiser, steel magnate and friend of Franklin Roosevelt's, who was persuaded to enter the aluminum business when the government doubted both the capacity and the willingness of the Aluminum Company of America (Alcoa) to supply all its needs. The antitrust case against Alcoa as a monopolist had already been tried, and under these circumstances the company was unlikely to want to add on still greater capacity. Biographer Steven Adams calls Kaiser a new kind of government entrepreneur (Adams 1997). Other types of entrepreneurs that would emerge in the postwar and Cold War eras were variations on Jonathan Hughes's procurement entrepreneurs—technology-based entrepreneurs with expertise in defense-related technologies, and university entrepreneurs who developed new businesses from their research projects, often while continuing to hold academic appointments. For these new kinds of entrepreneurs government sponsorship provided not only access to funding and expertise, but also steady, predictable, and often cost-indifferent demand.[29] The downside, of course, was a creeping form of lock-in owing to complementary bureaucratization in government agencies and the companies with which they dealt.

Role of Government, Equilibrium, and Democratization

Entrepreneurship looked decidedly different in the period after World War II than it had looked before, or during, the war. If the logic of the 1930s had been focused on science-based innovation—to invent new products that would get the economy going again—the logic of the postwar period was to optimize output from existing plants. Many new products marketed in the postwar era were based on invention and development undertaken in the prewar era. Process modifications were required to meet unforeseen levels of demand and to bring costs down, especially in consumer goods, and product invention took a back seat to process development (Hayes and Abernathy 1980).

Exceptions in the civilian economy were for products that were funded by government programs aimed at improving living standards for, and the productivity of, returning servicemen. Federal housing loans, for instance, made it possible for many people to buy houses for the first time, and entrepreneurial opportunities in housing construction, epitomized by the Levittowns in the Middle Atlantic region and Daly City in San Francisco, could be seen in suburbs all over the country. For the postwar nuclear family with the mother at home another important growth area was mass entertainment—television and popular music recording. Entrepreneurial opportunities abounded around television advertising, production, and recording, as well as dealerships and repair services.

For two decades (1950–70) 70 percent of the U.S. workforce was employed by large enterprises serving the relatively predictable needs of other large corporations and the mass consumer. Whether these enterprises supplied steel, aluminum, construction equipment, televisions, computers, chemicals, or pharmaceuticals, they appeared capable of maintaining a stable equilibrium and controlling their own destiny. When so much demand existed for existing products, why risk inventing new ones, an irrational phenomenon known as self-obsolescence? There was one sector of the economy, however, where the market for innovation was inexhaustible—the federal government and especially the military.

ROLE OF GOVERNMENT: FUNDING "BIG SCIENCE"

The three-way establishment that had come into being during World War II—the co-evolution of administrative government, university, and private industry—coalesced in peacetime under a decidedly military command-and-control model (Balogh 1991; Roland 2001). The designated technologies that ultimately fed into military, institutional, and consumer product markets—were funded through a newly organized system of intermediaries that came to be known as "Big Science." As we have previously established, the corporate research laboratory formed a vital link in this new innovation system.

After a divisive political debate between those holding different visions of how government resources should be allocated and by whom, the 1950s offered in the main the picture of economic stability that had been promised. The general population believed that science had had a vital role in winning the war, and the scientific community continued to serve military priorities first. Prewar industrial laboratories had mainly focused on industrial and consumer products—artificial fibers, telephone systems, lighting, photography, and glassware. In the postwar era, a relatively smaller portion of the nation's industrial scientific capacity was directed at civilian purposes, while a much-expanded portion was allocated to defense applications, with the DOD and the various branches of the military controlling the research agenda. Thanks to a Congress whose members saw that the most promising way to secure jobs for their constituents was through military funding, and a populace that feared the ongoing threat of renewed international conflict, the U.S. Defense Department had the loudest voice in determining what scientific disciplines and problem areas would receive funding and through what channels. Convinced also of the need for American self-sufficiency in science and the belief that focused investments in basic scientific knowledge would pay off in a cornucopia of new applications, government funding was allocated to a defined and relatively narrow set of scientific disciplines and technologies, many of which related to discoveries made in the large wartime projects. Funding went to research performers in three different settings: research universities, government laboratories, and major companies with R & D laboratories that were equipped to tie their research to new military products (Graham 1985; Mowery and Rosenberg 1989, 143). Many high-tech entrepreneurs of this Cold War period had their start in one leading laboratory or another. On the East Coast MIT-connected Lincoln Laboratories, Bell, and RCA spawned the entrepreneurs that built Route 128 around Boston. On the West Coast, a particular development target of the federal government, many high-tech entrepreneurs got their start as radio amateurs producing electronic components. Numerous companies started out like the Varian brothers, who set up their pioneering Silicon Valley company to produce microwave tubes, or Hewlett and Packard that started with scientific instruments, and later Robert Noyce and Gordon Moore who left the Shockley West Coast laboratory to form Fairchild Semiconductor, a division of the East Coast firm Fairchild Camera, and then left Fairchild to form Intel with Andy Grove (Lécuyer 2006).

Defense mobilization coordinated through the prime contractors in turn formed the context for various forms of civilian enterprise. Many of the designated technologies in the postwar era were crossovers—aircraft and avionics, computers and controllers, electronics and communications, nuclear power, and solid-state materials. Though the rhetoric of political economy in the United States held that governments could not dictate winners and losers, the defense budget, and the untold millions of dollars in federal funding allocated to the intelligence community, in effect selected and created the technology-based industries that would attract and concentrate most of the country's dynamic resources. Consumer electronics drew on the same knowledge base and shared many of the same production processes as military electronics. Even major investments in infrastructure were justified by reasons of defense—the national highway system, the investments in education at all levels including an interest in foreign languages, all were tied in some way to federal defense priorities.

Enthusiasm for government funding for science was on the wane, however, when in 1957 the USSR launched the world's first satellite, Sputnik, ensuring that U.S. government funding for defense mobilization would increase rapidly. The concerns that this raised were best articulated by President Eisenhower, one of the country's most prominent wartime military leaders, who in his farewell address to the nation in 1961 warned of the unwarranted influence of the "military-industrial complex" in the councils of government (Kevles 1978, 393).

Navigating the ever-growing government bureaucracies of the postwar era required an organizational skill that was as much a form of government entrepreneurship as qualifying to be a government contractor. Jonathan Hughes points to figures like Mary Switzer, who fought successfully for federal mental health programs, and Marriner Eccles, who redesigned the Federal Reserve, as government entrepreneurs who changed the course of the U.S. government as effectively as Thurman Arnold was to change federal antitrust policy. Although all three were successful at creating new programs and finding the organizational means to make them effective, none of them relied simply on enlarging the bureaucracy. All three found ways to promote legislation or embed in executive practice procedures that catalyzed parts of the established economy and society outside Washington to achieve the reforms they believed were needed.

Nonmilitary agencies of the federal government were nevertheless in an expansion mode for most of the rest of the century, and they garnered huge investments that called for procurement entrepreneurs in peacetime: data-processing systems for big agencies like Social Security, the Internal Revenue, and later NASA, Medicaid, and Medicare. High-tech companies might not all be entirely focused on supplying government, but for most of them government was a significant and lucrative part of their overall business. Once obtained, the business was easy to keep and with the cost-plus funding formula, the risk was low. In these conditions it was hardly surprising that high-technology businesses were the source of most of the dynamic activity on Wall Street in the 1950s and 1960s.

In the context of continuous defense preparedness and the rapidly expanding federal government of the Cold War, the nature of government procurement created narrower, more technology-focused opportunities for individual and corporate entrepreneurship than had existed in the earlier part of the century. But opportunities for procurement entrepreneurs were attractive in all the designated technologies—communications, electronics, advanced materials, and computer technologies (Mowery and Rosenberg 1989; see also Galison and Hevly 1992; Galambos and Pratt 1988; Dyer 1998; Dyer and Dennis 1998). Computers and computer-based technologies in particular, later known collectively as information technology, extended across all boundaries (Coopey 2004). While early uses of computers were primarily for missile development, within a decade computer technology had found broader and more mundane uses, filling data centers in government bureaus and large enterprises alike, as well as providing automated controls for manufacturing processes.

The Computer, Basis of the IT Revolution

While all of the large science-based projects created entrepreneurial opportunities for established companies, most were connected with industries that in the United States were traditionally regulated, and had been classed by regulatory theorists as "natural monopolies," like electric power and communications. They were also extremely capital intensive in the equipment needed for research and even more for the massive investments needed for development—nuclear particle accelerators, nuclear fuel processing facilities and power plants, electronic components manufacturing for radar and radio. The greatest area of opportunity for new entrants and smaller enterprises clustered around the information appliance that was first known as a calculator (Galison and Hevly 1992).

As Campbell and Aspray point out, the technology that ultimately led to the multifaceted information technology industry at the heart of the information revolution needs to be understood as drawing on that vast web of technologies, systems, and practices collectively known as systematic management, that had developed in the first half of the twentieth century. Nevertheless, the modern computer itself was the device without which the rest of the system would not have existed. As developed for military purposes, the computer was the parallel wartime "invention" of several teams of inventors at different universities—Harvard's Aiken Laboratory,

MIT, Penn, and Princeton all developed analog versions of the so-called electro-mechanical calculator designed to do the challenging computational tasks required for World War II weaponry (Yates 2000; Campbell-Kelly and Aspray 1996).

Though all were university entrepreneurs, few of the inventors involved in the initial development of the computer recognized that the new high-speed calculators might also have commercial applications apart from the weapons systems that funded them, many of which would be obsolete before the computers themselves could be completed. The exception was the team of Eckert and Mauchly at the University of Pennsylvania's Moore School, who recognized that these devices were not just mathematical calculating machines but would make possible the automation of huge information-processing tasks already needed to keep the large corporations, and the rapidly expanding government bureaus and agencies with their ever greater requirements for information, operating. The market for such devices—costing millions of dollars to develop—would for the foreseeable future be confined to the large organizations that already employed thousands of people processing massive amounts of information, or for advanced weapons systems with performance requirements in which speed and information capacity were essential (Yates 2005). In the United States there was a five-year window of opportunity (1948–53) when the amounts of money required to get into the business were small enough to allow new entrants to gain a foothold before larger, more established firms with better access to money and established distribution networks seized on the opportunity and the newly defined capability. Given their propensities for technological inertia, on the other hand, it is doubtful that the larger firms would have been so quick to invest had there not been active new entrants.

Three kinds of firms were candidates for entering the new computer industry—electronics firms, business machine firms, and entrepreneurial start-ups. In the first round the entrepreneurs were eight firms (IBM and the Seven Dwarves). Of these, in addition to the Eckert and Mauchly Computer Corporation, the two start-ups were CRC and DEC. IBM was the one existing business machine firm to make the entrepreneurial transition, and four electronics firms—RCA, GE, Burroughs, and Sperry Rand, which bought Eckert and Mauchly—stayed in the business long enough to help reshape their own industry by creating the new one (Cortada 2000; Fabrizio and Mowery 2007; Usselman 2007). Very different in size, experience, and endowments, all three types of firms were innovators in their respective industries and deserve to be called corporate entrepreneurs.

The Eckert and Mauchly experience demonstrated what difficulties small entrepreneurs of all kinds, and especially high-tech entrepreneurs, faced in the postwar environment. Chief among them was securing financing for their new ventures. Needing vast and unpredictable amounts of money, and lacking buyers who believed in the product and were willing to spend the money, early developers of all sizes took on a combination of military contracts and commercial orders to finance the initial development of their machines. All grossly underestimated the amount of time and effort it would take and what the most challenging aspects of the project would be. Eckert and Mauchly, who had tried to attract financial backing even before the end of the war, could raise only shoestring financing, and that for only a fraction of the development needed. None of the sources they approached for funding, mostly established companies, were willing to advance them even the inadequate amounts they asked in their optimism, let alone the vastly greater amounts they would actually spend on development of their computer, the ENIAC. In the end the commercial version of the ENIAC was financed by several civilian contracts, only kept afloat by a major diversion to a couple of military contracts.

The company that eventually succeeded in dominating the computer industry during the 1950s and 1960s, IBM, prevailed not because it was the technology leader, but because it designed a managerial and technological support system for users that gave them what they needed to make computer investments profitable. For decades this system operated effectively as a monopoly, impenetrable by competitors, and closed to outside suppliers. So the courts concluded in the 1970s when IBM agreed to operate differently by opening the development part of its business, and the less profitable products like the IBM Personal Computer, to outsiders.

IBM spawned its own set of spin-off entrepreneurs like H. Ross Perot, for several years IBM's leading salesman, who left in 1962 to set up his own company, Electronic Data Systems, supplying data-processing services primarily to government agencies. In the 1980s EDS made Perot a multibillionaire when he merged it with General Motors and later sold it outright when the entrepreneurial behaviors and attitudes of his EDS employees working inside GM struck automotive executives as intolerably disruptive.

Other entrepreneurial businesses that IBM inadvertently helped to develop arose out of its need to play catch-up with Apple's personal computer in the 1980s after IBM had already done badly in the competition for minicomputers with entrepreneurial companies like DEC. Unable to wait until it could generate all the necessary components and softwares inside, and unsure of hitting the winning combination if it did, IBM outsourced the operating system for its PC to a new software start-up run by Harvard dropout Bill Gates and his partner Paul Allen, and simultaneously gave the microchip design to the Fairchild spin-out Intel. Both companies soon achieved larger book values than IBM itself, as Big Blue, like many other high-tech companies of an earlier era, went through a period of downsizing and restructuring.

Institutions in the Closed Innovation System

As early as the 1920s vocal critics of the U.S. patent system were complaining that the institution created to ensure fair compensation for inventors had been co-opted by large corporations (Noble 1977). As Leonard Reich has demonstrated, with armies of patent lawyers and deep pockets, corporations like AT&T and GE pursued the defensive strategy of buying up and suppressing any patents that threatened their control of technological change in their industry. They could either refuse to license the patents they held, or they could charge such high royalties or attach such onerous conditions to their use that the technology was not worth obtaining. At the same time, they could vigorously prosecute anyone that either infringed or tried to invent around their patents.

A similar irony attended the antitrust regime, intended to maximize intercompany competition and to keep prices low for consumers; when vigorously enforced, it resulted in unintended consequences. Midcentury efforts to offset the negative effects of these interacting institutions, so important to innovation and entrepreneurship, actually reinforced the closing of the U.S. innovation system, where access to ideas and research became more restricted and where secrecy and exclusivity prevailed for much of the rest of the century.

PATENTS AND ANTITRUST

As indicated in the two previous chapters, the regimes for patenting and antitrust were both well established in previous eras (Khan 2005). The U.S. patent system was established at the birth of the Republic to encourage inventive activity, while the time-limited nature of patents was intended to prevent their misuse as a form of technological restraint of trade, or block to continued innovation. Low fees charged to file patents were intended only to cover administrative costs and to encourage entrepreneurial activity, an arrangement that continued until the 1990s. Antitrust legislation, especially the Sherman Act of 1890, applied to patent monopolies as well as to other forms of restraint of trade. The U.S. patent system had functioned for a century without any rules about monopoly to offset it, but when companies rather than individuals became patent-holding entities, the system became subject to widespread abuse (Markham 1966).

The controversial case of radio-related patents exemplified the broader problem and continued to be an issue well into the 1950s (Aitken 1976, 1985; McLaurin 1949; Lécuyer 2006). On the one hand RCA's unified control over the pool of "radio-related" patents enabled rapid advances in this important communications technology for military purposes and also for the wholly unforeseen emergence of radio broadcasting. But the ability of RCA to control all radio-related patents provoked bitter opposition throughout the interwar period by numerous smaller electrical companies like Raytheon. Electronics companies like Philco that expanded their own research during the war, when licensing royalties were suspended, struggled under the burden of paying RCA's substantial "package licensing" fees after the war.[30]

A big shift in antitrust policy and enforcement began in the 1930s and continued into the 1970s, though it was suspended during World War II, when Yale law professor Thurman Arnold was appointed to head the Antitrust Division at the Roosevelt administration Justice Department. Arnold, a classic government entrepreneur in the sense that he quickly reorganized and expanded his department and set it on a very different course, was an avowed skeptic about the value of U.S. antitrust laws, but soon surprised the business community by enforcing them. Arnold held that despite the American distrust of bigness, it was not large size, but the deliberate action of large companies that failed to pass on savings from efficiencies to consumers, that was the greater evil. To make his point Arnold adopted the practice of filing simultaneous civil and criminal suits, offering company executives the consent decree as a way of avoiding personal time in jail. Starting in 1938, the Department of Justice launched hundreds of investigations, prosecuting whole industries—building and construction, tires, fertilizer, glass, motion pictures, electric companies, petroleum and transportation, to name only a few. The new vigor with which the law was upheld proved effective at creating uncertainty, and changed the shape of industrial competition, but partly because of the larger business environment of the era, its effect on innovation was inconclusive.[31]

Although antitrust prosecutions were suspended during World War II, postwar administrations continued enforcement actions and gradually broadened their scope. In spite of their importance to the war effort, RCA, Alcoa, AT&T, GE, and many technology-based companies in the 1950s had antitrust actions concluded against them, resulting in the compulsory licensing of many thousands of patents—either royalty-free or at very low cost. Alcoa was forced to license its latest technology to competitors, Kaiser and Reynolds, aluminum companies that the government had created during the war. AT&T was compelled to license its key transistor and semi-conductor patents to all comers royalty-free.

Well into the 1960s it was generally believed that antitrust policy had been an effective spur for R & D investment and therefore, naturally, for innovation. When there was a conflict between patent policy and antitrust policy, antitrust prevailed more often than not as the courts proscribed price-fixing clauses in license agreements and set higher standards of patentability. Yet although Steve Usselman, looking at IBM, maintains that a strength of the U.S. antitrust system was that it was not coordinated with other parts of the regulatory system, large corporations still found ways to adjust to the regulatory system, with the effect of harming smaller companies' interests and limiting their access to technology (Usselman 2004). Companies subjected to compulsory licensing often chose to rely on secrecy rather than patenting as a way of protecting their intellectual property. In this they were aided by the Cold War security regime that gradually extended well beyond the range of military contractors (Markham 1966).

Even though Thurman Arnold forced a sea-change in the ways companies could share technology, the suppression of patent monopolies produced unintended consequences for the patent system. AT&T's forced licensing of its patent holdings still allowed for cross-licensing, which amounted to a barter system that gave AT&T a dominant position in many key areas. Xerox, when deprived of its patent monopoly of xerographic technology earlier than originally anticipated, turned to a practice of wholesale patent exchange with its Japanese arch-rival Canon. RCA, when ordered to discontinue its package licensing arrangements in the United States, simply shifted its licensing regime to Japanese licensees, thus helping to speed up the development of the Japanese consumer electronics industry (Graham 1986).

In the 1970s the number of patents filed fell off dramatically, partly because of changes described above and partly because of cutbacks in the funding of the Patent Office. Reforms in the U.S. patent system in the early 1980s—extending the duration of patents, designating specialized courts to deal with patent cases, allowing patent protection for software inventions—shifted the odds once again in favor of patent-holders, rather than those who would sue them for antitrust. In the 1990s the Patent Office became self-supporting when patent filing fees increased, under the rationale that a large proportion of filers under the U.S. system were no longer U.S. citizens or taxpayers. By this time improvements in information technology made the ability to search patents and claims much easier, and power shifted dramatically in favor of patent-holders whether they were "practicing" the patents or not. Companies called "patent trolls" acquired suites of patents that they had no intention of using, holding them until a large company with related technologies could be sued for patent infringement. Whether large companies had infringed or not, they often preferred to settle patent suits rather than delay their product introductions for years while the suits made their way through the court system. A celebrated case of this kind arose at the end of our period around the new email equipment and service provider Research in Motion (Canadian maker of the Blackberry), which was sued by patent-holding company NTP, Inc. for violating certain of its patents on retrieving email. Many other companies such as AT&T and Verizon simply settled for substantial sums, but RIM ignored NTP's demands and ended up settling a few years later for nearly half a billion dollars after having fought the infringement charges through many layers of appeal.

Laboratories as Corporate Entrepreneurs

Corporate research as an institution rarely achieved the reality of the surrogate innovators that leaders like David Sarnoff intended they should become. One among many corporate divisions, they seldom achieved the standing to overcome conflicting interests among bureaucratic peers. As a means of self-defense in internecine squabbles, and as a way of attaching measurable value to their work, they often resorted to attaching a monetary value to their work through patenting and licensing.

For many large technology-based companies, including Texas Instruments and RCA, licensing revenues for proprietary technologies became as important, sometimes more important, than the innovations the patented discoveries were intended to generate or support (Graham 1986; Jelinek 1979). Eventually this practice made formerly innovative companies vulnerable to smaller more innovative and nimbler corporate entrepreneurs that did not view intellectual property as a source of revenue or a means of control. When AT&T faced the challenge of achieving a radical increase in its system's bandwidth in the 1970s and 1980s, for instance, it proved to be no match for the more flexible and entrepreneurial Corning Glass Works. Corning, by innovating in optical fiber in the 1970s, and supplying it first to AT&T's mortal enemy, MCI in 1984, forced AT&T to acquiesce in the optical fiber revolution twenty years earlier than it would otherwise have chosen to do (Graham 2007).

Founded in 1970, Xerox PARC (Palo Alto Research Center) started out as a countercyclical example of the closed innovation model of corporate laboratory many companies had pursued successfully in the 1930s, but instead it became an unintended exemplar of the reopening of the U.S. innovation system. Located in the heart of Silicon Valley, PARC was a corporate laboratory with a special long-term mission that proved to be a highly effective incubator for inventor-entrepreneurs at a time when they were generally finding it hard going. PARC had been set up as a ten-year strategic investment by Xerox chairman Peter McCullough to invent "The Office of the Future" as a planned successor to the patent-protected Xerox photocopier. At a time when high interest rates and even higher inflation rates caused many corporations to question the value of research, Xerox hired an exceptionally talented set of researchers from some of the leading physics and computer science departments and think tanks, many of them already known to each other as part of the Department of Defense's DARPA (Defense Advanced Research Project Agency) program. By deliberately hiring researchers who were both brilliant and hands-on, people who wanted to use what they made, the laboratory managed in a much shorter time than expected to produce enough inventions, and entrepreneurial individuals with ideas, to make a serious contribution to the growth of Silicon Valley. Adobe, Small Talk, Apple Computer, Microsoft, and eventually even Google—all owed their existence or at least their innovative success in part to the technological fecundity of Xerox's small West Coast laboratory. Not expecting or even wanting such an early payoff for its investment, the parent corporation reaped little reward from this creative activity. Only a few years after its founding, inventors started leaving PARC for more flexible opportunities in the Bay Area. By then, as discussed below, conditions were changing and the institutions were forming to support their various individual attempts to develop and sell pieces of the emerging office of the future. Later it was acknowledged at Xerox that the company would have earned far more from its investment in PARC had it arranged to benefit from the laboratory's many spin-offs.

Era Three: The Third Industrial Revolution

The third era for entrepreneurship in the twentieth-century United States is only beginning to be digested by historians, though other social scientists have offered some sweeping, provocative, and often conflicting propositions that need to be tested not only against the aggregate data, but against more disaggregated and more qualitative evidence.[32]

In this era, beginning in the 1970s, conditions for entrepreneurship were shaped by the twin forces of the information revolution and globalization, forces that combined to become the third industrial revolution. The linking of global financial markets with the growing liberalization of markets and the deregulation of formerly regulated industries in the United States followed closely the model already introduced in Thatcher's England.[33] Historians agree that it ushered in a level of international trade and competition by no means unprecedented, but not seen since before World War I (Osterhammel and Petersson 2005). For U.S. entrepreneurs, especially individual entrepreneurs, these developments, combined with the relaxation of antitrust enforcement and the deregulation of several formerly regulated industries, created opportunities of an intensity and variety not open to individuals since the Roaring Twenties.

One long period of economic shock put an end to the way U.S. business had been conducted since the 1940s. Although the period consisted of an almost unrelenting series of setbacks, the most serious was an unprecedented combination of high inflation and slow economic growth—known as "stagflation." Coping with these shocks rather less well than some international rivals, American businesses confronted international competition in manufactured goods in the very industries that had been mainstays of the U.S. economy since the 1920s—automobiles, electronics, and consumer electronics.[34] Venerable U.S. industries like machine tools, protected in the previous era by their importance to defense mobilization, disappeared altogether in the early 1980s. The basis of the new international competition was not simply price, but quality and performance as well. Europe and Asia had rebuilt their manufacturing plants after the war, especially in basic industries like steel, using the latest manufacturing technology and adopting the most up-to-date management practices. American manufacturers were thus condemned to endure more than a decade caught in what was later termed a "productivity dilemma" (Abernathy 1978; Abernathy, Clark, and Kantrow 1983).

The United States experienced a general decline in productivity growth rates from the 1970s to the mid-1990s. Popular candidates for causes of the decline included the shift from one set of base technologies arising out of the electrochemical revolution to a new set of information technologies that had come into widespread use but had yet to yield improvements in productivity and lower returns to R & D expenditures. The numbers also reflected a fundamental shift from manufacturing to service as the basis of the U.S. economy. In retrospect, although these developments were interpreted as aspects of the shift from the industrial economy to the knowledge economy, they might also have pointed to several decades of suppressed independent entrepreneurial activity. If, as we have seen, such shifts foreshadowed impending trouble for many large corporations and their employees, for entrepreneurs outside the corporation and eventually outside the country, they opened many attractive and accessible opportunities.

The Decline of Corporate Entrepreneurship

Corporate entrepreneurship among large corporations became the exception rather than the rule even for technology-based companies during the 1970s as the Cold War system began to come apart under a combination of centrifugal forces and outside pressures. As Spurgeon and Leslie have argued, the Silicon Valley model of entrepreneurial development, usually thought of as the icon for private entrepreneurship in the United States, had its roots deep in the wartime program of the federal government to develop the West Coast defense industries, and continued along with Stanford University to be dominantly related to the military business until well into the 1980s (Sturgeon 2000 and Leslie 2000).

As the Cold War settled into familiar patterns, with guaranteed returns based on a cost-plus formula in the military sector, companies controlling fundamental patents hiding behind patent protection, and regulated companies turning their regulatory position to their advantage, investors became enamored of "high-tech" firms. Lacking serious competition in a world of oligopolies and cost-plus contracts, hightech companies seemed to show that the rewards for corporate entrepreneurship could be had without the risks.

But completely private entrepreneurial opportunities arose with increasing frequency as large companies and government agencies sold or divested their technologies, restructured, reengineered, and downsized, and even demolished their stockpiles as the costs of maintaining them in a high interest rate environment became too high and the returns for keeping them too low (Sullivan 1997).

Meanwhile inside the prime contractors, government-funded research, with its heavy and complicated reporting requirements, evoked a corresponding bureaucratization in companies that pushed innovators and innovation to the margins. At the height of the Cold War it was the rare corporate laboratory that could tolerate real mavericks, and when it could it was likely to develop a counterculture that drove a wedge between the laboratory and the rest of the company (Graham 1985). Creeping bureaucratic procedures slowed many industrial programs to a crawl. The burden of procedure was so great that a program manager at Lockheed, the big California aeronautics and space contractor, developed the Skunkworks to get things done. This pared-down, tight-knit collection of the most flexible and dedicated employees was committed to starting and completing a new development program on time and within budget. If the Skunkworks came to symbolize creativity and effectiveness within the large corporation, its rapid spread through government contractors was testimony to how hard it was to pursue innovation in the context of the ever more tightly interlinked bureaucracies (Arthur 1989).

Ironically, the corporate laboratory's role as chief innovator eventually undermined the capacity of many larger firms to be entrepreneurial, and revived their need for the role of external entrepreneur. One critical factor affecting the ability to innovate commercially was the new stricter security provisions attached to military R & D during the Cold War, and the restrictions they placed on the circulation of scientific knowledge.[35] Another was an innovation in corporate structure, the multi-divisional, or M-form, which helped to establish the pattern of the corporate laboratory as a prime mover in innovation in the first place. In a celebrated act of corporate entrepreneurship through organizational change, DuPont pioneered the M-form to facilitate diversification, out of weapons manufacture into civilian products, and then into starting new ventures. Many other corporations followed DuPont's example after World War II, but the new organizational form could and often did lead to destructive internal competition between different corporate divisions vying for resources.

Over time strategic planning and resource allocation that required each corporate division to excel on its own worked against coordinated initiatives and undermined effective corporate entrepreneurship. The consequences of this shift were especially evident in the risk-avoidance that shaped the conglomerate movement in the 1960s and 1970s. The growing tendency toward risk aversion and short-term maximization of returns to technology, which was driven by a financial community that demanded ever more frequent reporting and punished surprises, eventually led to the downfall of many large, formerly innovative firms. The organizational problems posed by corporate research and the divisional structure were not lost on those who started their careers in corporate research. Indeed the founders of one of the most successful entrepreneurial corporations of the next generation, Intel, organized R & D very differently, hiring many Ph.D.s, but putting them on the production floor and spreading their research locations throughout the operation.

Despite the clear attractions of corporate laboratories after World War II—the stable, well-compensated employment, the attractive facilities, locations, and resources for travel and equipment—many of the most brilliant inventors and scientists, especially those with entrepreneurial leanings, opted to pursue their ideas and their aspirations in less comfortable surroundings. Early technological entrepreneurs received funding from large, mostly eastern, firms that wanted to diversify into government business, like Remington Rand or Fairchild Camera. Many leading industrial researchers—computer scientists and materials scientists—discovered their own entrepreneurial inclinations, and were moved to start their own companies after watching executives at parent companies reap most of the rewards. Starting out, they got the resources they needed from friends, family, and other contacts, followed by procurement contracts from larger enterprises. In cases that were rare at first they gained support from a new form of financing, venture capital. In Silicon Valley especially, where the climate allowed for outdoor work much of the year, more than a few garage shrines mark the spots where famous high-tech companies got their start. William Hewlett and David Packard, Steven Jobs and Steve Wozniak, Paul Allen and Bill Gates, and eventually Michael Dell, as well as many less well known kit-makers and experimenters like Ed Roberts, designer of the Altair computer kit, laid the groundwork for new "high-tech" enterprises in driveways, garages and dorm rooms.

The conglomerate movement of the 1960s signaled an inflexion point in corporate behavior, effectively putting an end to the mid-twentieth-century approach to large corporate entrepreneurship. In the conglomerate form, technology-based companies discovered the comfort of countervailing risks, and financial speculation and manipulation of assets offered a lucrative alternative to the harder work of entrepreneurship. Technology-based companies that had suffered from volatile stock prices because of the uncertainties of innovation were seduced by the persuasive powers of investment bankers, often on their boards, into acquiring unrelated businesses with different risk characteristics. Smaller growth companies began to manage themselves to be good targets for acquisition. Acquiring firms soon found that unrelated acquisitions with different management characteristics and different requirements for capital undercut their ability to carry out the steady product innovation they needed to renew their core businesses. Corning's acquisition of the Fairchild spin-off Signetics in the 1960s was an example of the kind of transaction that posed a significant diversion from the acquirer's core business (Lécuyer 2006; Graham and Shuldiner 2001). Even companies like Northern Telecom that in the 1970s acquired smaller companies they considered technically related and strategically vital had trouble managing them to profitability. Many other acquisitions, motivated by narrower aims of rapid financial gain and acquired for stock, encountered even worse problems. When RCA acquired a handful of companies in services and consumer goods in the 1960s, stockholders protested loudly, suspecting that such unrelated operations would undercut the ability of the large technology firm to continue to play the role of lead entrepreneur for consumer electronics. RCA's attempts to prove its detractors wrong, and to introduce the VideoDisc as the next generation consumer electronics product, led to a decade of costly missteps and culminated in eventual failure in 1984 (Graham 1986).

RCA was not alone. Other large technology-based companies that had formerly been reliable corporate entrepreneurs failed in the 1980s when trying to introduce innovative mass-market products, including Eastman Kodak with its disc camera, AT&T with its picture phone, and Polaroid with its repeated attempts to innovate in electronic cameras. Even in the more predictable institutional business, the traditional leaders lost traction. DuPont waited many years to find uses for Kevlar. IBM dominated mainframe computers, but did not compete successfully with new entrants DEC or Data General in minicomputers, failed to invent around Xerox in copying machines, and lost its supercomputer designer Seymour Cray, who set up an independent supercomputer business. Even Ampex, a smaller company that did not carry the same baggage and that had the steady commitment of its innovative institutional customer, the ABC broadcasting network, lost out to Sony in professional portable video cameras (Florida and Kenney 1990; Graham 1982; Rosenbloom and Freeze 1985).

To be sure, a few established companies continued to act as corporate entrepreneurs in nonmilitary technologies throughout the distressed decades of the 1970s and 1980s. Minnesota Mining and Manufacturing (3M) was renowned for the number of new products it brought to market by encouraging researchers to become entrepreneurs inside the framework of the firm. Hewlett Packard with its HP Way encouraged creativity and a new version of corporate entrepreneurship by keeping its units small and delegating substantial authority to eager young managers. Corning Incorporated introduced a wide range of technically challenging new products based on novel combinations of glass formulations and patented processes. But after numerous failure experiences involving significant R & D and new ventures, innovation fell out of fashion and the financial markets no longer rewarded established "high tech" companies to the same degree (Lazonick, forthcoming). In almost all the science-based industries it was new entrants, spin-offs or start-ups, that seized and held the advantage over large corporations where innovation was concerned.

After several decades of funding the designated technologies at accelerating rates, with returns that were at best hard to measure, U.S. society in general turned against the practice of concentrating so much of its collective spending in science and weapons technology. When public opinion, and also much scientific opinion, turned against the military uses of science, the younger generation of researchers fostered in the DOD research system were motivated to find civilian uses for their work. The latent commercial opportunities that might have been generated by the remaining 40–50 percent of federal research funding each year that was not performed by industry had been mainly bottled up in a handful of research universities in nine states and in several government laboratories (Mowery et al. 2004; Mowery and Rosenberg 1989).

The Consumer Movement: Scale for Entrepreneurs

A rebellion among American consumers also marked the transition that started in the late 1960s. The baby boom generation born after World War II, which came of age resisting the war in Vietnam, associated big business with destructive uses of technology like the production of chemical warfare agents, and a military procurement system run amok (Roland 2001). Reacting against an increasingly entrenched economic system and a bureaucratic form that was starting to show its weaknesses, the baby boomers rejected the hierarchy and diminishing security of the large corporation, and with it the boring sameness of the products it produced. As Daniel Yergin has shown, they reacted by welcoming variety from smaller producers and lower prices from imported products and deregulated industries, while at the same time demanding a greater degree of social regulation: clean water and clean air, consumer protection, product safety, and various environmental controls. In tune with these developments in the marketplace the federal government responded by downsizing funding for military R & D and shifting the focus of government regulation to energy and lifestyle issues, turning to a regulatory regime focused on health, safety, and equal opportunity employment. The ensuing deregulation of such industries as airlines, communications, and utilities attracted entrepreneurial ventures that soon challenged previous industry leaders and exploited niches that in some cases, like MCI telecommunications and Southwest Airlines, grew into dominant positions.[36] Deregulation of telecommunications not only gave rise to entrepreneurial concerns like MCI, but to legions of new suppliers, when telecommunications equipment was no longer dominated by Western Electric.

Minor cracks had appeared in the facade of the stable regulated postwar economy as early as the 1950s, when imports like the Volkswagen Beetle and the pocket-sized transistor radio from Sony found a surprising number of willing buyers in the United States. But the transition that signaled the end of the long period of postwar stability began when first imported radios and televisions and then imported cars from Japan gained a following in U.S. markets. A sudden sharp recession in consumer electronics in 1971 revealed that the United States was in the process of losing one of its strongest manufacturing businesses. Soon large and well-heeled companies like General Electric and RCA were failing in the high-growth parts of the electronics business as well, unable any longer to meet either the managerial or the financial demands of the fast-growing computer business (Coopey 2004, introduction).

For the first time since the 1930s a generation questioned the central premises on which the country's economy was based—the twin pursuits of growth and scale. What appeared to be merely youthful social rebellion, soon outgrown, developed economic "legs." The critique of the "beats" and the "hippies" may have seemed utopian, but the enterprises they started in university dormitories and garages, and even on collective farms, occupied niches that could be developed. Though these alternatives hardly seemed to be credible business entities at first, over time the pursuit of the small-scale goods—natural foods, herbal medicines, natural fibers, new sources of energy like biomass, wind and solar, even personal computers—gave rise to substantial businesses capable of competing with the large corporations. Some existing companies recognized the alternatives as the wave of the future and bought them out, while others weakened or transferred into other lines of business.[37]

The information revolution got its second wind when computers moved from institutional to consumer products. While large companies like IBM, AT&T, and Xerox still controlled the mainframe and full-service parts of the office machine and computer hardware business, they soon lost control of successive waves of smaller machines. Independent software and peripherals, home computers, and computer games took the entire computer business in such different directions that by the end of the century, few of the original companies were still in the business. Software, when made independent of hardware, became for a few years the easiest entry point in the IT industry and also one of the first to create entrepreneurial opportunities in the U.S. market for developing countries (Campbell-Kelly and Aspray 1996, 181–205; Coopey 2004, 300). By the latter 1980s information technology had started to penetrate other industries' products and processes, not just their systems. Artificial intelligence emerged in robotics, and new robotics firms sprang up to challenge machine tool companies.

One place the combinatorial tendency of information technology showed up most clearly was in pharmaceuticals, where the Human Genome Project, launched in 1990 and funded by $3 billion of federal government money, involved the kind of data manipulation and record keeping that was only possible with massive increases in computer power. Genomics, seemingly an extension of macrobiology, became another field ready for entrepreneurial activity.

Opening the Innovation System

Entrepreneurial opportunities based on emerging technologies in biotech, new materials, and of course advanced software and applied forms of information technology like Infomatics opened more widely as Congress directed government laboratories to share their discoveries with private enterprise. Under the provisions of the Bayh-Dole Act passed in 1980, universities were allowed to patent discoveries made with government funding. A handful of research universities, starting with Columbia and Stanford, were soon collecting large licensing royalties, and the financial stakes for research universities became much higher when a younger entrepreneurial generation of researchers began to patent their work and to seek out investors to partner with them in start-ups (Mowery et al. 2004). In parallel, numerous industrial laboratories adopted the practice of selling their proprietary technologies rather than holding them for development.

Technologies that had long been sequestered in government laboratories became available to private investors along with the expertise of many of the more enterprising researchers who had worked on them. When the Cold War came to an abrupt end in the late 1980s, declassified technologies of extraordinary power—database technologies, computer imaging for animation and gaming, supercomputers, satellite technologies and spacecraft—were ready to be commercialized by entrepreneurial firms, often started by experienced entrepreneurs in serial start-ups, such as ousted Apple entrepreneur Steve Jobs's new companies, Next and Pixar.

A few industries benefited from increased federal funding for non-military-related research. Chief among these funded fields were agriculture, through land-grant colleges and university research stations, long supported at the state level, and drug and disease research through the National Institutes of Health. In these areas the U.S. innovation system was never as tightly closed even during the Cold War as it was in the designated technologies. Funding for agricultural research, one of the most important forms of public funding in the earlier periods, continued in amounts that were nowhere near as high as the designated technologies, but they continued to benefit communities across the country and the companies that served them. Meanwhile, as Galambos and Sturchio have written, the pharmaceutical industry, which was always international to some degree, relied on a network of sources for ideas and investment, including not only public funding for research, but also both private and public research performers at government, university, and industry laboratories (Galambos and Sturchio 1996).

Even though networks were a major part of the innovation system for the entire twentieth century, entrepreneurial activity was primarily closed and corporate until the developments that opened the U.S. innovation system more generally. Only in the 1980s did it become commonplace for biotech start-ups like Genentech and Amgen to grow to become major players in pharmaceuticals. Genentech received a boost by forming an alliance with Corning Incorporated, called Genencor, that accepted stock in place of investment money (Dyer and Gross 2001). Alliances like Genencor, which had been out of favor for decades because of the antitrust focus on technology sharing, became a much more common way for small and start-up companies with high-tech specialties to team with large corporations and yet remain independent. For university entrepreneurs like Craig Venter, who started Celera Genomics with a $300 million investment by the Perkin Elmer Corporation, to compete with the government-sponsored Human Genome Project, conditions to support research based start-ups were well in place in the 1990s.

Notably, the international pharmaceutical industry, which benefited both from a variety of types of research funding and from the vigilant regulation of the Food and Drug Administration, became one of the few advanced industries in which even leading European companies chose to locate their headquarters and their research laboratories near leading U.S. research universities rather than remain in their home countries or outsource to Far Eastern developers and producers. This was a sign that the access to the discoveries funded by the National Institutes of Health and to start-up companies headed by university entrepreneurs created especially attractive conditions for pharmaceutical and medical device investment. Similarly, Japanese, Taiwanese, and Korean companies specializing in information technologies, especially producers of microprocessors, elected to start up advanced industrial research laboratories near major U.S. research universities like Stanford and MIT.

As human capital and social capital became more important than fixed capital toward the end of the twentieth century in the developed countries, the prevailing forms of successful organization changed from hierarchy to network in other industries as well, benefiting companies that were less hierarchical and more open. Early signs that open standards were the wave of the future were Xerox's Ethernet standard, licensed free of charge in the 1980s, and IBM's open-code approach to generating software for its PC that helped to give it the advantage over what was generally considered the superior technology of Apple's personal computers. Even before the Internet gave them the means to adopt it more fully, the open software movement and the success of companies like AOL, Apple, Amazon, eBay, Cisco, and eventually Google were signs that the U.S. innovation system was at least as open, and possibly more open, than it had been since the nineteenth century.

By the early 1990s it was widely recognized that companies that were forming strategic alliances with smaller technology-based companies and formal research relationships with university researchers were developing much faster and more effective approaches to acquiring new skills and new business opportunities than companies that still relied on their own in-house capabilities. Pharmaceutical companies that needed to make a rapid transition to genomics and to replenish their drug pipelines, telecommunications companies that needed new devices and new software, and many companies that needed workforces that were up to date with the new technologies, looked to start-up companies, as either acquisitions or collaborators, but primarily as agents of renewal.

Entrepreneurial Fraud

As cultural priorities shifted away from defense toward poverty alleviation and alternative consumer lifestyles, and as the innovation system became less controlled and more open, new arenas opened not only for legitimate entrepreneurship, but also for the kinds of imaginative fraud not seen since the financial speculators of the 1920s or the military contracting profiteers of the middle decades. Following on the heels of the new government legislation providing health care—Medicare and Medicaid—came private enterprises offering ways to outsource services like laboratory testing. Many such enterprises turned out to be incubators for sophisticated attempts to defraud the federal government. Other lifestyle-related opportunities took mass entertainment in new directions, anticipating the predicted leisure time that would be released by the increased use of computer automation. Such pursuits not only increased the sales of new consumer electronics devices like VCRs both domestically and internationally, but laid the groundwork for huge new illicit lines of business when the Internet was commercialized in the early 1990s—for online gambling and trafficking in pornographic images and in drugs. Many such businesses were too unsavory for large centrist organizations to touch, leaving a large market that nimbler and less socially vulnerable enterprises could exploit by operating outside the law—including pirate radio stations, organized crime, and Native American reservations.

Similar developments occurred in the financial community. Once deregulated, savings-and-loan institutions, for instance, took advantage of Federal Deposit Insurance covering accounts up to $100,000 to make imprudent investments in search of higher yield. By 1988 more than 500 S&Ls had achieved the dubious distinction of insolvency. Government bailouts of S&Ls in the late 1980s, which deepened an already huge federal deficit, led not to greater financial probity, but to even greater abuses of the public trust toward the end of the twentieth century. Outside the protected area defined by ever-weakening government banking regulations, financial entrepreneurs explored new financial instruments and vast new investment vehicles known by the all-purpose term *hedge funds*, designed once again to earn spectacular yields with minimal exposure to actual risk.

Financial Entrepreneurship

Just as the volatility of the interwar period had yielded tremendous innovative activity on the part of companies seeking to adjust to the major changes and new uncertainties of that period, so the difficult financial markets of the third era of the twentieth century sparked new waves of financial innovation.

As alluded to earlier in the discussion of high tech and the conglomerate movement, the investments made with stock and paper profits in the 1960s often caused the acquiring companies to lose value themselves a decade later. Small investors withdrew from the stock market. Double-digit inflation, intensifying the inflation already under way from the Vietnam War, followed the Breton Woods collapse and the loss of the gold standard. A dearth of capital coupled with very high interest rates provoked urgent attempts to try innovative approaches to financing new ventures. Weakened by the loss of millions of ordinary investors, the equities markets concentrated on less risky kinds of investments.

It was in this context that Michael Milken, still one of the most controversial financial entrepreneurs, emerged on Wall Street. Recognizing that normal corporations were finding it very difficult to finance their internal development, Milken invented a new issues market for high-yield bonds. Milken's employer, Drexel Burnham Lambert, as only a minor player among Wall Street giants in corporate finance, was willing to give something novel a try. With Milken's invention, companies with low credit ratings, and little hope of securing financing on the corporate bond market, could issue what were called "junk bonds." The new market was enabled in part by the new Rule 415 that allowed underwriters to speed the bonds to market. Junk bonds were risky for underwriters, but they were also very profitable.

Savings-and-loan institutions were permitted to buy the bonds, and jumped at the chance to find higher interest rates, overlooking the bonds' risky quality. After several years of enthusiastic acceptance of his junk bonds, Milken became the highest-paid Wall Street employee ever, rumored to have accumulated over $3 billion in personal wealth. Unfortunately, initial buyers of junk bonds were inflating the already high prices before selling them to investors and then kicking a portion of the cash back to Drexel. Milken went to jail and Drexel shut its doors, but the junk bond market continued, after a minor pause for the stock market crash of 1987.

A financial innovation that depended on the availability of junk bonds was the leveraged buyout, using debt to take over companies, strip their assets, conduct layoffs, and then sell the companies to other investors, having realized major profits.[38] The vast sums of money accumulated in private hands in the 1980s and early 1990s provided in turn new pools of capital that could, given the right institutional arrangements, be made available to finance new enterprises. Led by the best-known corporate takeover firm, Kolberg, Kravits, Roberts, many takeover specialists took over and broke up lethargic companies that had succumbed to poor management, and some that were just unlucky, and created a boom in leveraged buyouts, the mainstay of investment banks and private equity firms alike. Many large bureaucratic companies that had been celebrated for their longevity and staying power either disappeared or were downsized and reorganized, releasing expertise and other resources into the market to be picked up by more entrepreneurial leaders with their own investments at stake.

Extending free-market solutions to social and environmental problems that had previously been tackled by government regulation became another area of entrepreneurial activity, often by academic entrepreneurs wanting to apply their ideas in the marketplace. In some instances their efforts proved highly successful. When the Clean Air Act was passed in 1990 with the objective of reducing acid rain by means of attaching a cost to emissions, Richard Sandor, former Berkeley economics professor, set up the Chicago Climate Exchange to implement a "cap and trade" system, making it more expensive for electric power companies to pollute than to install scrubbers to control sulfur dioxide emissions. The Environmental Protection Agency credits the new system with reductions in emissions of many millions of tons annually, as well as savings in reduced lung disease and other related illnesses (Specter 2008). The acid rain problem has indisputably improved. In effect, financial entrepreneurs, like Sandor, have superseded government entrepreneurs in their efforts to address such problems as clean air and climate change, while creating large new investment opportunities in the financial markets.

Institutionalizing Venture Capital

Private banks and wealthy individuals, members of the top percentile of income recipients until the 1940s—had been providing investment money for start-up ventures well before the twentieth century, but venture capital in its twentieth-century form began after World War II. On both coasts concerns about a shortage of risk capital gave rise to new forms of financing. Boston and the San Francisco Bay Area led the way. In 1946 a group of Boston civic leaders headed by General George Doriot, a professor at the Harvard Business School, formed American Research and Development—a nonfamily venture capital organization organized as a closed-end fund with an investment focus on opportunities in electrical and medical electronics (Kenney and Florida 2000, Ante 2008). AR&D, which both loaned to and invested in start-up companies around Boston for twenty-five years, had some notable successes with a number of high-tech companies spawned at MIT, but by far its greatest money-spinner was Digital Equipment Company (DEC).

The region that had received the largest portion of federal defense funding in the Cold War era was California. In the San Francisco Bay area around Stanford a number of small concerns started up and, lacking the necessary ability to raise capital for expansion, sold out to large East Coast firms (O'Sullivan 2007). The first real financial breakthroughs for an alternative course of financing came in the mid-1950s when first Varian and then Hewlett-Packard floated successful public offerings on the New York Stock Exchange. In the 1960s some of the larger high-tech firms like Fairchild and DuPont looked to investments in corporate new ventures based on new technologies as a way of diversifying when they were constrained by antitrust action from growing larger in their core businesses.

In 1958 Congress passed the Small Business Act, followed by the establishment of the SBIC (small business investment company.) Not only did this make more money available, but it allowed entrepreneurs to reduce their own personal liability. By the early 1960s private investors, including some of General Doriot's students, started family SBICs, so that by the early 1960s substantial amounts of money became available to high-technology start-ups outside the framework of the large established eastern firms. As the SBICs developed full-time staffs of professional investors, they became important organizational stepping stones to the full-blown venture capital funds that emerged in the 1970s and 1980s.

Various investment funds formed on the West Coast, but it was with the "limited partnership" that venture capital hit upon a form that worked. This form of organization had greater upside potential for investors than the SBICs, and from then on the limited partnership prevailed. Between 1968 and 1975 as many as thirty venture capital firms formed or reformed in Silicon Valley alone. Coinciding with the semiconductor revolution, and the shift from transistors to integrated circuits, this wave of investment activity awarded high returns to early venture capitalists, causing northern California to prosper while older industrial parts of the country were mired in industrial transition. The success of a few major deals—Xerox's payment of a billion dollars for SDS (Scientific Data Systems), Fairchild and Intel, the Apple II computer and others—did much to establish venture capital during the late 1970s and early 1980s.

While in the aggregate only small amounts of money were involved in venture capital until the 1980s, returns on the investments made in general were quite high (20–30 percent). A serious turning point for the industry came in the late 1970s when two important events occurred. The year 1978 brought a significant reduction in the capital gains tax, and in 1979 ERISA legislation governing pension investing was reinterpreted to say that it was "prudent" to include more risky investments in a portfolio as long as it wasn't too great a percentage. This opened the way for pension funds to invest in venture capital and shifted the focus of venture capital money-raising from wealthy families to institutions. From then on certain VCs raised funds on a regular basis, though the amount they were able to raise in any given year depended heavily on recent performance and on capital gains tax rates, which in turn also affected the opportunities that were available for investment (Gompers et al. 1998).

After a decade or so of variable experience, professional venture capitalists became important sources of entrepreneurial funding, not just because they supplied hard-to-find early-stage capital, but because they also became an important source of business expertise for inventor entrepreneurs. Venture capitalists sat on the boards of each company they invested in and guided their investment companies until they could go public (Hambrecht 1984). One consequence of this form of control was the increased importance of intellectual property. Venture capitalists, needing tangible evidence of achievement—something to sell when an investment went sour, evidence for their investors that their investment was sound—insisted on the early filing of a patent portfolio, and patents and venture capital became ever more tightly linked.

While venture capitalists were becoming professionals in their own right, venture capital was being institutionalized. In those areas where it was well established, like Boston and the West Coast, but increasingly in other "high tech" areas such as

New York, New Jersey, and Texas, law firms and accounting firms and various other professional service firms developed related kinds of expertise. Naturally this could only happen where the volume of venture capital investment was large enough to support such an infrastructure, and for this reason venture capital remained concentrated in a few locales to the end of the century.

According to studies by Kortum and Lerner (2000), venture capital money was three times more potent as a source of capital for innovation than simple R & D even though it accounted for only 3 percent of all the R & D money expended between 1983 and 1992. Given the growing reliance of venture capitalists on patents as part of the investing process, the growth in venture capital funding had a leveraging effect on patenting. Toward the end of our period well-established VC firms were reviewing far more proposals than they could ever consider funding, yet having patents in place was one of the conditions start-ups had to meet for having a proposal considered.

Over time venture capital covered the entire spectrum of funding from main stage funding to seed funding, but ironically, as venture capital became an industry, it also adopted a lower risk profile. In some instances this meant less willingness to offer early-stage funding; very often it meant reducing the risk through syndication. As the first generation of professional VCs retired, very few well-established firms continued to take on full investments themselves, a change that diluted the quality of experienced advice available to start-ups. Only a few of the early venture firms, like Sequoia Partners and Hambrecht and Quist, were still in business by the year 2000.

As young inexperienced people poured into the business toward the end of the century, technology areas considered "hot" attracted disproportionate amounts of money, while solid, more conventional brick-and-mortar investments were spurned as "old economy." Not surprisingly, there were many failures for every successful start-up. Paradoxically, in the later stages of "irrational exuberance" as chairman of the Federal Reserve Alan Greenspan called it, dot-com companies that did not receive VC financing were more likely to survive than those that did (Goldfarb, Kirsch, and Miller 2007). While many failed, a few spectacular Internet company successes like Amazon and eBay pursued a business model that supported the efforts of thousands of small-time entrepreneurs to reach markets previously unreachable. Once again, established businesses were persuaded to invest their own money in response to the new model businesses, as retail giants of all kinds added the new forms of distribution to keep up with the dot-com enterprises.

By the end of the century, having gone through the tremendously volatile period of dot-com investments, venture capital had matured from an institution to an industry. In the areas in which it was most concentrated it supplied up to a third of all the capital used for start-ups. Viewed from this perspective, this version of the networked firm, initially motivated by the demand for higher-yield investments and better-informed advice, provided an important alternative to the large bureaucratic firm as a backer of entrepreneurial ventures, at least in some industries. On the other hand, would-be entrepreneurs in biosciences found it harder and harder to find early-stage money from venture capitalists, and recent start-ups also had a hard time refinancing to grow their businesses. Venture capitalists were also seeking secure returns and ever higher yields without risk-taking.

Ironically, even as the venture capital industry gathered steam, a movement arose to oppose it. For all the researchers, hobbyists, and amateurs who eventually took their passion to market, there were many others who objected to what they considered a perversion of the original purposes of their enterprises. Toward the end of the century, invigorated by the Internet, the open software movement took on new life, which in turn gave rise to further voluntarist movements such as Wikipedia. These movements could be seen as forms of collective entrepreneurship—introducing a technology into widespread use—for free—with the intention of collecting money for collateral activities like advertising or services. Although these movements were controversial, the open software movement challenged the basic business model of many software companies in ways that would have profoundly transformative effects on whole industries in the next century (Lazonick, forthcoming).

Conclusion

This overview of entrepreneurship in the twentieth century points to some important continuities in the U.S. economy—legal, financial, and communications-related—that were critical to encouraging entrepreneurial behavior and continued to be important. The protections of the Constitution—the sanctity of contracts and the protection of private property—continued, while corporate law evolved within the common-law tradition. The patent system and a robust public education system reaching an ever broader spectrum of society continued in force throughout the century, though both the patent system and public education had their ups and downs. New financial instruments evolved, but the basic principles remained firm. New forms of transportation and communication developed, reducing costs and eventually making most industries "footloose," but place continued to matter.

Multiple and diverse, though largely uncoordinated, public and private funding sources for technology development—state governments, private foundations, and patron industries like agriculture, the railroads, and the telegraph—also endured, although the focus of invention shifted in the new century to different patron industries—electronics, automobiles, and aviation. The federal government intervened after World War II to select and allocate resources to the highest potential technologies for defense and the public welfare.

While important institutions and patterns endured, some features of the twentieth-century economy departed markedly from earlier eras, and these changes had a profound effect on the context for entrepreneurship. As much innovation became more scientifically linked, entrepreneurs needed more education, or at least better-educated employees, and access to greater resources. With the institutionalization of the regulated corporation and the integration of R & D as a central corporate function, entrepreneurship became both more linked to technological innovation and more subject to corporate influence. When antimonopoly laws were prosecuted vigorously, as they were from the 1930s to the 1980s, and corporations were prevented from growing by simply absorbing competitors or running them out of business, the corporation integrated many entrepreneurial functions that had previously been conducted outside its walls.

During the generation or so when innovation and development and national defense were compelling and unifying national goals, and the security of a career in a large, solid organization was most appealing, the corporation served as the prime recruiter of entrepreneurial talent, and the chief developer of new businesses. While these developments did not suppress independent research and invention altogether, they did have the effect of funneling entrepreneurial activity toward a few core technologies. The result for technologies that had military priority, even for crossover technologies that had applications for civilian purposes as well, was a closed innovation system—with access to applications and to funding—limited, classified, and performed in restricted areas.

As we have seen, a few key technologies like agriculture and medical research remained more accessible to the public and more subject to entrepreneurial activity, even global entrepreneurial activity. Nevertheless, during the middle years of the century entrepreneurship was very much associated with "high tech" ventures, and much of the funding it relied on came from publicly supported research and development, and publicly funded procurement contracts. Fundamental research performed in universities was not as restricted, but because it was separated from commercial exploitation by the values of scientific purity, it did not flow readily into entrepreneurial channels.

With the concentration of knowledge, the scarcity of private investment capital, and the large capital demands of many of the core technologies where opportunities were greatest, the scope of independent inventor-entrepreneurs in the midcentury was reduced, though they never disappeared altogether. Even in areas like agriculture where sources of innovation were widely distributed and remained more accessible, high-growth companies like Pioneer Hybrid moved to consolidate their position by integrating R & D and forming more restrictive networks with a few key universities.

A great deal remains to be understood about the revival of individual, private sector entrepreneurship in the 1970s that began the reopening of the innovation system. Indeed, whether it was the opening of the innovation system that promoted entrepreneurship, or an eruption of entrepreneurial energy that opened the innovation system, is not easy to determine. Opportunities for entrepreneurs arose with the continuing decline in the cost of information technologies and their spread into smaller and civilian applications. The combinatorial aspects of new computer-based information technologies also generated many new application areas for entrepreneurs to exploit.

Important social changes like the demands for clean air and water, for lifestyle improvements, and consumer and product safety protections shifted the focus of government expenditure, and opened up a new category of entrepreneurship, first working within government and then working from outside to change it. Government entrepreneurs were largely replaced by those in the private sector who wanted to bring about change using free-market mechanisms.

By the 1980s the core technologies fuelling the third industrial revolution would extend beyond IT to embrace macrobiology, miniaturization, and many new and hybrid materials and processes. Globalization also offered new markets and reinvigorated migration patterns that opened entrepreneurial opportunities linked to trade. Technologies like software and many of the new countercultural alternatives were far less demanding of capital than their midcentury predecessors, making high-tech investments the source of "irrational exuberance." By the end of the century several emerging technologies, like genomics, with tremendous promise for growth, and with enthusiastic entrepreneurial involvement, had become more capital intensive, so that neither private investors nor capital markets seemed capable of supporting them.

In sum, the most important finding from this overview has to do with the multi-faceted and often complementary relationship that developed in the twentieth century between entrepreneurs and the large corporation.[39] By the 1960s the large corporation showed itself to be too prone to bureaucratic lock-in to be entirely self-sustaining and self-renewing. Though the large corporation had displayed a temporary capacity during the Depression for spontaneous entrepreneurship, the tendency toward growing bureaucracy and risk-averseness in the postwar period gradually made genuine entrepreneurial personalities unwelcome in all but the most enterprising firms. When they abandoned the corporation, entrepreneurial employees took their expertise and their zest for innovation with them. Recognizing their ever-greater need for new ideas, and only rarely prevented by antitrust, some corporations formed alliances with enterprising firms, while others resorted to buying them, but sporadic bursts of financially motivated acquisition seldom resulted in productive outcomes.

With more capital available in private hands, and investors seeking ever higher yields, toward the end of our period new entrepreneurial ventures were growing rapidly, gaining knowledge and expertise through networks, and challenging the established corporations directly, sometimes putting them out of business. Nevertheless, to corporations that recognized their need for transformation, enterprising firms offered not only candidates for outsourcing and sources for innovative products, but exemplary business models as well. Finally, globalization altered the geography of U.S. entrepreneurship just as it altered the geography of business generally. While it has been appropriate to speak of American entrepreneurship in the twentieth century as a distinct phenomenon, it seems very unlikely that historians of the twenty-first century will be able to identify any such thing.

Notes

[1] Servan-Schreiber 1968; Galbraith 1967; Thurow 1999; Chandler and Cortada 2000. Oddly, Chandler and Cortada downplay the role of government, except as funders of R & D.

[2] Gerben Bakker (2003) points to the entertainment industry as an example of an industry that was not regulated, but was still affected by the parts of the economy that were.

[3] Alfred D. Chandler's (1977) portrayal in *The Visible Hand* of the rule of large firms as the only important story of U.S. industry has recently been challenged from several quarters: Philip Scranton (1997) on the one hand, and Naomi Lamoreaux, Daniel M. G. Raff, and Peter Temin (2003) on the other.

[4] Lance Davis and Larry Neal (2007) maintain that it was the mixed systems of large and small firms that account for the timing of both the second and third industrial revolutions.

[5] Eric S. Hintz (2007) notes that nearly 50 percent of total patents were still granted to independent inventors, outside the corporation, through the 1950s.

[6] Zunz 1990; Hounshell 1984; Yates 1989. According to Olivier Zunz, Thorstein Veblen in *The Engineers and the Price System* (1921) blamed corporate finance for turning the management of the corporation into a bureaucratic practice that was confining to the engineer. Veblen saw engineers and entrepreneurs, whom he associated with the profit motive, as inherently opposed, and saw Taylorism as a way to free "technological man" from the captains of finance. Zunz notes that Veblen did not take into account "tinkerers" like Henry Ford, whom we would call inventor-entrepreneurs.

[7] Aitken 1960, 237. Though the labor unions at government arsenals rejected scientific management after a few early experiments, unions embraced the movement after World War I as an arena where labor-management cooperation could yield major gains in productivity. See the study by Robert Kanigel (1997), who shows that Taylorism became embedded in American manufacturing during World War I, and spread like wildfire thereafter.

[8] See McCraw 2007. More recently William Lazonick (2007) has extended the theory of the innovative firm to distinguish between firms that optimize and firms that allocate resources to innovation, while Nathan Rosenberg (2000) has stressed the critical point, noted in the last chapter, that the most radical

and disruptive innovations are brought to fruition by further development by many parties, who should legitimately be considered part of the innovation process, though they may not be entrepreneurs. Also see Reich 1980.

[9] Samuel Insull, who started his career as secretary to Thomas Edison and went on to become a major electricity innovator, organizer of the network in Chicago, and leader of his industry, was scapegoated during the Depression, and died a broken man, having been tried and acquitted for securities fraud.

[10] Yergin and Stanislaw 1998. Managing the maverick well became a hallmark of the innovative firm—see Graham and Shuldiner 2001.

[11] B. M. Friedman (2007) summarizes this argument and its social implications.

[12] In F. Scott Fitzgerald's *The Great Gatsby*, published in 1925, the main character both idolized the riches and glamour of the Jazz Age and felt uncomfortable with its materialism and morality. Similar attitudes were shared by the characters in Willa Cather's *The Professor's House*, also published in 1925.

[13] Szostak 1995. Economists today dispute the push for productivity as a contributing factor to the Depression, but few deny that a net loss of jobs occurred in established industries, and contemporary observers were convinced that the obsession with efficiency had led to conditions of oversupply. See Rhodes 1999.

[14] Galambos and Pratt (1988) quote John Kendrick, the classic source for productivity figures.

[15] Graham and Shuldiner 2001; Hounshell 1984, 263–77. Hounshell points out that many Model T owners valued its changelessness, so to make visible modifications was tricky.

[16] Archibald MacLeish writing in *The Nation*, 1933, cited in Rhodes 1999, 116. MacLeish was writing at the depths of the Depression trying to find hope in the productivity story. See also Pursell 1981. For a recent account of the financial innovator whose exposure did much to spur banking regulation in the depths of the Depression see "The Match King," *The Economist*, December 19, 2007, 115–17.

[17] "The Match King."

[18] O'Sullivan 2006. GE bought back its own shares and drew down its debt burden, while Westinghouse repeatedly overextended itself.

[19] Field (2003) shows the numbers that reflect the success of these developments.

[20] Blackford and Kerr 1996; Graham 1986; Graham and Pruitt 1990; Dyer and Gross 2001; Hounshell and Smith 1988. It was observing companies like these that led Schumpeter to observe that innovation was now the activity of large companies.

[21] Mowery and Rosenberg 1989. This is consistent with Alexander J. Field's (2003) argument that despite severe unemployment the period 1929 to 1941 was the most economically progressive decade of the century.

[22] Edwin F. Mansfield (1968) summarizes the campaign to ensure scientists of full employment. He cites Dupree 1957 as the original history of these events.

[23] David C. Mowery and Nathan Rosenberg (1993) depict the relationships between research performers and institutions as developing in systematically different ways in different industrialized countries.

[24] Reich 1985; Wise 1985; Hounshell and Smith 1988. The best and most balanced summary of the evolution of industrial research in the United States is Hounshell 1996.

[25] National Research Council, Bulletins 16 and 60 (1919 and 1927); Herbert Hoover 1926, quoted in Rhodes 1999.

[26] David Noble (1977) discusses this developing set of relationships. See also Graham 2008.

[27] David C. Mowery and David J. Teece (1996) summarize the increasingly inward-looking nature of postwar industrial research.

[28] Hughes 1986. Recognizing this new reality, one of Corning's most important directors in the period after World War II was General Walter Bedell Smith, who had been General Eisenhower's chief procurement officer during the war and who later became chairman of the AMF Corporation.

[29] Mowery and Rosenberg (1989, 123–68) point to the vast increases in funding of university research through the National Science Foundation; to the National Defense Education Act, passed in 1958; and to several other important pieces of legislation on the supply side, as well as to focused procurement on the demand side.

[30] Kevles 1978. Raytheon, where Vannevar Bush spent his early career, was one of many small firms that had nearly been forced out of business by RCA's discriminatory allocation of vacuum tubes and high licensing fees.

[31] Whether rigorous antitrust enforcement did in fact force growth-seeking activities into the narrow channel of innovation when other avenues like acquisitions were foreclosed remains a matter of controversy. See also Miscamble 1982; Markham 1966; Waller 2004.

[32] Manuel Castells, who asserts that the information revolution enabled global networking for the first time, is contradicted by many historians of international business who see this change as less a qualitative shift than a return of modes of behavior that began in the Middle Ages and were last seen in the early twentieth century. Historians' attempts to digest and rethink this period include Galambos 2005; Lamoreaux, Raff, and Temin 2003; and Lazonick 2007.

[33] For the conventional economic interpretation, see Yergin and Stanislaw 1988.

[34] Ironically, in consumer electronics the rise of Japanese competition in consumer electronics was partly due to the efforts of the leading innovator in the United States, RCA, which successfully replaced its revenues from domestic package licensing by shifting the practice of package licensing to Japanese electronics companies (Chandler and Cortada 2000, introduction).

[35] Mowery and Teece (1996, 113) state a point that is often overlooked, that the trend toward remote "campuses" was above all a security move on the part of the many corporate laboratories that received government funding for research on the condition that it would be conducted on a classified basis and under tight security.

[36] Yergin and Stanislaw 1998. Deregulation of the airlines provided the right conditions for upstarts like Peoples Express and Southwest Airlines. MCI challenged AT&T in telecommunications and attracted suppliers that competed aggressively and successfully with the old Western Electric—for example Corning, which achieved a dominant position in optical fiber.

[37] The bible of this movement, according to Steve Jobs, was Stuart Brand's *The Whole Earth Catalogue*.

[38] *Wall Street Journal* op-ed on Wolfson, innovator of the corporate buyout, January 16, 2008.

[39] See Jones 2007, who notes the importance of understanding entrepreneurship in its larger historical context, and the need furthermore to understand more about the changing nature of skills, behavior, and personality that have been needed in different contexts.

References

Abernathy, William J. 1978. *The Productivity Dilemma: Roadblock to Innovation in the Automobile Industry*. Baltimore: Johns Hopkins Press.

Abernathy, William J., Kim B. Clark, and Alan M. Kantrow. 1983. *Industrial Renaissance: Producing a Competitive Future for America*. New York: Basic Books.

Adams, Stephen B. 1997. *Mr. Kaiser Goes to Washington: The Rise of a Government Entrepreneur*. Chapel Hill: University of North Carolina Press.

Aitken, Hugh G. J. 1960. *Taylorism at the Watertown Arsenal: Scientific Management in Action, 1908–1915*. Cambridge: Harvard University Press.

———. 1976. *Syntony and Spark: The Origins of Radio*. New York: Wiley.

———. 1985. *The Continuous Wave: Technology and American Radio, 1900–1932*. Princeton: Princeton University Press.

Ante, Spencer E. 2008. *Creative Capital: Georges Doriot and the Birth of Venture Capital*. Boston: Harvard Business Press.

Arthur, W. Brian. 1989. "Competing Technologies, Increasing Returns, and Lock-in by Historical Events." *Economic Journal* 99:116–31.

Bakker, Gerben. 2003. "Entertainment Industrialized: The Emergence of the International Film Industry." *Enterprise and Society* 4:579–85.

Balogh, Brian. 1991. *Chain Reaction: Expert Debate and Public Participation in American Commercial Nuclear Power, 1945–1975*. Cambridge: Cambridge University Press.

Blackford, Mansel G., and K. Austin Kerr. 1996. *BF Goodrich: Tradition and Transformation, 1870–1995*. Columbus: Ohio State University Press.

Blaszczyk, Regina Lee. 2000. *Imagining Consumers: Design and Innovation from Wedgwood to Corning*. Baltimore: Johns Hopkins University Press.

Campbell-Kelly, Martin, and William Aspray. 1996. *Computer: A History of the Information Machine*. New York: Basic Books.

Cather, Willa. 1925. *The Professor's House*. New York: Knopf.

Chandler, Alfred D., Jr. 1977. *The Visible Hand: The Managerial Revolution in American Business*. Cambridge: Belknap Press of Harvard University Press.

———. 2001. "Consumer Electronics: The United States." In *Inventing the Electronic Century: The Epic Story of the Consumer Electronics and Computer Science Industries*, 13–49. New York: Free Press.

Chandler, Alfred D., Jr., and James W. Cortada, eds. 2000. *A Nation Transformed by Information: How Information Has Shaped the United States from Colonial Times to the Present*. Oxford: Oxford University Press.

Compton, Karl T. 1949. "Foreword." In W. Rupert McLaurin, *Invention and Innovation in the Radio Industry*. New York: Macmillan.

Coopey, Richard, ed. 2004. *Information Technology Policy: An International History*. Oxford: Oxford University Press.

Cortada, James W. 2000. "Progenitors of the Information Age: The Development of Chips and Computers." In *A Nation Transformed by Information: How Information Has Shaped the U.S. from Colonial Times to the Present*, ed. Alfred D. Chandler Jr. and James W. Cortada, 177–212. New York: Oxford University Press.

Douglas, Susan. 1987. *Inventing American Broadcasting, 1899–1922*. Baltimore: Johns Hopkins University Press.

Dupree, A. Hunter. 1957. *Science in the Federal Government: A History of Policies and Activities to 1940*. Cambridge: Belknap Press of Harvard University Press.

Dyer, Davis. 1998. *TRW: Pioneering Technology and Innovation since 1900*. Boston: Harvard Business School Press.

Dyer, Davis, and Michael Aaron Dennis. 1998. *Architects of Information Advantage: The Mitre Corporation since 1958*. Montgomery, AL: Community Communications.

Dyer, Davis, and Daniel Gross. 2001. *Generations of Corning: The Life and Times of a Global Corporation*. Oxford: Oxford University Press.

Fabrizio, Kira R., and David C. Mowery. 2007. "The Federal Role in Financing Major Innovations: Information Technology during the Postwar Period." In *Financing Innovation in the United States, 1870 to the Present*, ed. Naomi R. Lamoreaux and Kenneth L. Sokoloff, 283–316. Cambridge: MIT Press.

Farber, David R. 2002. *Sloan Rules: Alfred P. Sloan and the Triumph of General Motors*. Chicago: University of Chicago Press.

Field, Alexander J. 2003. "The Most Technologically Progressive Decade of the Century." *American Economic Review* 93:1399–1413.

Fischer, David Hackett. 1996. *The Great Wave: Price Revolutions and the Rhythm of History*. New York: Oxford University Press.

Fitzgerald, F. Scott. 1925. *The Great Gatsby*. New York: Charles Scribner's Sons.

Florida, Richard L., and Martin Kenney. 1990. *The Breakthrough Illusion: Corporate America's Failure to Move from Innovation to Mass Production*. New York: Basic Books.

Friedman, Benjamin M. 2007. "Comment on 'Sustaining Entrepreneurial Capitalism' by William J. Baumol, Robert E. Litan, and Carl J. Schramm." *Capitalism and Society* 2, no. 2, article 1.

Galambos, Louis. 2005. "Recasting the Organizational Synthesis: Structure and Process in the Twentieth and Twenty-first Centuries." *Business History Review* 79:1–38.

Galambos, Louis, and Joseph Pratt. 1988. *Rise of the Corporate Commonwealth: U.S. Business and Public Policy in the Twentieth Century*. New York: Basic Books.

Galambos, Louis, and Jeffrey Sturchio. 1996. "The Pharmaceutical Industry in the Twentieth Century: A Reappraisal of the Sources of Innovation." *History and Technology* 13, no. 2: 83–100.

Galbraith, John Kenneth. 1967. *The New Industrial State*. Boston: Houghton-Mifflin.

———. 1994. *The World Economy since the Wars: A Personal View*. London: Sinclair-Stevenson.

Galison, Peter, and Bruce W. Hevly, eds. 1992. *Big Science: The Growth of Large-Scale Research*. Stanford: Stanford University Press.

Goldfarb, Brent D., David Kirsch, and Daniel Miller. 2007. "Was There Too Little Entry during the Dot Com Era?" *Journal of Financial Economics* 86, no. 1: 100–144.

Gompers, Paul A., Josh Lerner, Margaret M. Blair, and Thomas Hellman. 1998. "What Drives Venture Capital Fundraising?" *Brookings Papers on Economic Activity: Microeconomics*: 149–204.

Graham, Margaret B. W. 1982. "Ampex Corporation: Product Matrix Engineering." Harvard Business School Case Series.

———. 1985. "Industrial Research in the Age of Big Science." In *Research on Technological Innovation, Management, and Policy*, vol. 2, ed. Richard S. Rosenbloom, 47–89. Greenwich, CT: Jai Press.

———. 1986. *RCA and the VideoDisc: The Business of Research*. Cambridge: Cambridge University Press.

———. 2000. "The Threshold of the Information Age: Radio, Television, and Motion Pictures Mobilize the Nation." In *A Nation Transformed by Information: How Information Has Shaped the U.S. from Colonial Times to the Present*, ed. Alfred D. Chandler Jr. and James W. Cortada, 137–75. New York: Oxford University Press.

———. 2007. "Financing Fiber." In *Financing Innovation in the United States, 1870 to the Present*, ed. Naomi R. Lamoreaux and Kenneth L. Sokoloff, 247–82. Cambridge: MIT Press.

———. 2008. "Technology and Innovation." In *The Oxford Handbook of Business History*, ed. Geoffrey Jones and Jonathan Zeitlin, 347–73. New York: Oxford University Press.

Graham, Margaret B. W., and Bettye H. Pruitt. 1990. *R&D for Industry: A Century of Technical Innovation at Alcoa*. Cambridge: Cambridge University Press.

Graham, Margaret B. W., and Alec T. Shuldiner. 2001. *Corning and the Craft of Innovation*. Oxford: Oxford University Press.

Hambrecht, William R. 1984. "Venture Capital and the Growth of Silicon Valley." *California Management Review* 26, no. 2: 74–82.

Hayes, Robert H., and William J. Abernathy. 1980. "Managing Our Way to Economic Decline." *Harvard Business Review* 58, no. 4: 67–77.

Hintz, Eric. 2007. "Independent Inventors in an Era of Burgeoning Research and Development." Presented at the Business History Conference, Cleveland. Available at http://www.thebhc.org/publications/BEHonline/2007/hintz.pdf.

Hounshell, David A. 1984. *From the American System to Mass Production, 1800–1932*. Baltimore: Johns Hopkins University Press.

———. 1992. "DuPont and Nylon." In *Big Science: The Growth of Large-Scale Research*, ed. Peter Galison and Bruce W. Hevly, 236–64. Stanford: Stanford University Press.

———. 1996. "The Evolution of Industrial Research in the United States." In *Engines of Innovation: U.S. Industrial Research at the End of an Era*, ed. Richard S. Rosenbloom and William J. Spencer, 13–85. Boston: Harvard Business School Press.

Hounshell, David A., and John K. Smith. 1988. *Science and Corporate Strategy: DuPont R&D, 1902–1980*. Cambridge: Cambridge University Press.

Hughes, Jonathan. 1986. *The Vital Few: The Entrepreneur and American Economic Progress*. 2nd ed. New York: Oxford University Press.

Israel, Paul. 1992. *From Machine Shop to Industrial Laboratory: Telegraphy and the Changing Context of American Invention, 1830–1920*. Baltimore: Johns Hopkins University Press.

Jelinek, Mariann. 1979. *Institutionalizing Innovation: A Study of Organizational Learning Systems*. New York: Praeger.

Jones, Geoffrey. 2007. "Entrepreneurship." In *The Oxford Handbook of Business History*, ed. Geoffrey Jones and Jonathan Zeitlin, 501–28. New York: Oxford University Press.

Kanigel, Robert. 1997. "The Great Diffusion." In *The One Best Way: Frederick Winslow Taylor and the Enigma of Efficiency*. New York: Viking Press.

Kenney, Martin, and Richard Florida. 2000. "Venture Capital in Silicon Valley: Fueling New Firm Formation." In *Understanding Silicon Valley: The Anatomy of an Entrepreneurial Region*, ed. Martin Kenney, 98–123. Stanford: Stanford University Press.

Kevles, Daniel J. 1978. *The Physicists: The History of a Scientific Community in Modern America*. New York: Knopf.

Khan, B. Zorina. 2005. *The Democratization of Invention: Patents and Copyrights in American Economic Development, 1790–1920*. Cambridge: Cambridge University Press.

Kortum, Samuel, and Josh Lerner. 2000. "Assessing the Contribution of Venture Capital to Innovation." *Rand Journal of Economics* 31:674–92.

Lamoreaux, Naomi R., Daniel M. G. Raff, and Peter Temin. 2003. "Beyond Markets and Hierarchies: Towards a New Synthesis of American Business History." *American Historical Review* 108:404–33.

Lanham, Richard A. 1993. *The Electronic Word: Democracy, Technology, and the Arts*. Chicago: University of Chicago Press.

Lazonick, William. 2007. "Business History and Economic Development." In *The Oxford Handbook of Business History*, ed. Geoffrey Jones and Jonathan Zeitlin, 67–95. New York: Oxford University Press.

———. 2009. "Restructuring the Old Economy Corporation." In *Sustainable Prosperity in the New Economy? Business Organization and High-Tech Employment in the United States*. Upjohn Institute for Employment Research.

Lécuyer, Christophe. 2006. *Making Silicon Valley: Innovation and the Growth of High Tech, 1930–1970*. Cambridge: MIT Press.

Leslie, Stuart W. 2000. "The Biggest 'Angel' of Them All: The Military and the Making of Silicon Valley." In *Understanding Silicon Valley: The Anatomy of an Entrepreneurial Region*, ed. Martin Kenney, 48–67. Stanford: Stanford University Press.

Mansfield, Edwin F. 1968. *The Economics of Technological Change*. New York: Norton.

Markham, Jesse W. 1966. "The Joint Effect of Antitrust and Patent Laws upon Innovation." *American Economic Review* 56:291–300.

McCraw, Thomas. 2007. *Prophet of Innovation: Joseph Schumpeter and Creative Destruction*. Cambridge: Belknap Press of Harvard University Press.

McElvaine, Robert. 2003. "Review of *Rainbow's End: The Crash of 1929* by Maury Klein." *Business History Review* 77, no. 2, 319-321.

McLaurin, William Rupert. 1949. *Invention & Innovation in the Radio Industry*. New York: Macmillan.

McQuaid, Kim. 1978. "Corporate Liberalism in the American Business Community, 1920–1940." *Business History Review* 52:342–68.

Melosi, Martin V. 2000. *The Sanitary City: Urban Infrastructure in America from Colonial Times to the Present*. Baltimore: Johns Hopkins University Press.

Miscamble, Wilson D. 1982. "Thurman Arnold Goes to Washington: A Look at Antitrust Policy in the Later New Deal." *Business History Review* 56:1–15.

Mowery, David C., Richard Nelson, Bhaven Sampat, and Arvids Aiedonis. 2004. *Ivory Tower and Industrial Innovation: University-Industry Technology Transfer before and after the Bayh-Dole Act in the United States*. Stanford, CA: Stanford Business Books.

Mowery, David C., and Nathan Rosenberg. 1989. *Technology and the Pursuit of Economic Growth*. Cambridge: Cambridge University Press.

———. 1993. "The U.S. National Innovation System." In *National Innovation Systems: A Comparative Analysis*, ed. Richard Nelson, 29–75. New York: Oxford University Press.

Mowery, David C., and David J. Teece. 1996. "Strategic Alliances in Industrial Research." In *Engines of Innovation: U.S. Industrial Research at the End of an Era*, ed. Richard S. Rosenbloom and William J. Spencer, 111–29. Boston: Harvard Business School Press.

National Research Council. Multiple Years. *Bulletin of the National Research Council*. Washington, DC: National Research Council of the National Academy of Sciences.

Neal, Larry, and Lance E. Davis. 2007. "Why Did Finance Capitalism and the Second Industrial Revolution Arise in the 1890s?" In *Financing Innovation in the United States, 1870 to the Present*, ed. Naomi R. Lamoreaux and Kenneth L. Sokoloff, 129–61. Cambridge: MIT Press.

Noble, David. 1977. *America by Design: Science, Technology, and the Rise of Corporate Capitalism*. New York: Knopf.

O'Sullivan, Mary A. 2006. "Living with the U.S. Financial System: The Experiences of General Electric and Westinghouse Electric in the Last Century." *Business History Review* 80:621–56.

———. 2007. "Funding New Industries: A Historical Perspective on the Financing Role of the U.S. Stock Market in the Twentieth Century." In *Financing Innovation in the United States, 1870 to the Present*, ed. Naomi R. Lamoreaux and Kenneth L. Sokoloff, 163–216. Cambridge: MIT Press.

Osterhammel, Jürgen, and Niels P. Petersson. 2005. *Globalization: A Short History*. Princeton: Princeton University Press.

Piketty, Thomas, and Emmanuel Saez. 2003. "Income Inequality in the United States, 1913–1988." *Quarterly Journal of Economics* 118:1–39.

Pursell, Caroll. 1981. *Technology in America: A History of Individuals and Ideas*. Cambridge: MIT Press.

Raff, Daniel M. G. 1991. "Making Cars and Making Money in the Interwar Automobile Industry: Economies of Scale and Scope and the Manufacturing Behind the Marketing." *Business History Review* 65:721–53.

Reich, Leonard S. 1977. "Research, Patents and the Struggle to Control Radio: A Study of Big Business and the Uses of Industrial Research." *Business History Review* 51:208–35.

———. 1980. "Industrial Research and the Pursuit of Corporate Security: The Early Years of Bell Labs." *Business History Review* 54:504–29.

———. 1985. *The Making of American Industrial Research: Science and Business at GE and Bell, 1876–1926*. Cambridge: Cambridge University Press.

Reich, Robert. 1991. *The Work of Nations: Preparing Ourselves for 21st-Century Capitalism*. New York: Knopf.

Rhodes, Richard. 1999. *Visions of Technology: A Century of Vital Debate about Machines, Systems, and the Human World*. New York: Simon and Schuster.

Roland, Alex. 2001. *The Military-Industrial Complex*. Washington, DC: American Historical Association.

Rosenberg, Nathan. 2000. *Schumpeter and the Endogeneity of Technology: Some American Perspectives*. New York: Routledge.

Rosenbloom, Richard S., and Karen J. Freeze. 1985. "Ampex Corporation and Video Innovation." In *Research in Technological Innovation Management and Policy*, vol. 2, ed. Richard S. Rosenbloom, 113–85. Greenwich, CT: JAI Press.

Scranton, Philip. 1997. *Endless Novelty: Specialty Production and American Industrialization, 1865–1925*. Princeton: Princeton University Press.

Servan-Schreiber, Jean-Jacques. 1968. *The American Challenge*. New York: Atheneum.

Specter, Michael. 2008. "Big Foot." *New Yorker* 84, no. 2: 44–53.

Sturchio, Jeffrey L. 1985. *Corporate History and the Chemical Industries: A Resource Guide*. Philadelphia: Center for History of Chemistry.

Sturgeon, Timothy J. 2000. "How Silicon Valley Came to Be." In *Understanding Silicon Valley: The Anatomy of an Entrepreneurial Region*, ed. Martin Kenney, 15–47. Stanford: Stanford University Press.

Sullivan, Margaret Cox. 1997. *The Hostile Corporate Takeover Phenomenon of the 1980s*. Washington, DC: Stockholders of America Foundation.

Szostak, Rick. 1995. *Technological Innovation and the Great Depression*. Boulder, CO: Westview.

Thurow, Lester C. 1999. *Building Wealth: The New Rules for Individuals, Companies, and Nations in a Knowledge-Based Economy*. New York: HarperCollins.

Usselman, Steven W. 2004. "Public Policies, Private Platforms: Antitrust and American Computing." In *Information Technology Policy: An International History*, ed. Richard Coopey, 97–120. Oxford: Oxford University Press.

———. 2007. "Learning the Hard Way: IBM and the Sources of Innovation in Early Computing." In *Financing Innovation in the United States, 1870 to the Present*, ed. Naomi R. Lamoreaux and Kenneth L. Sokoloff, 317–63. Cambridge: MIT Press.

Veblen, Thorstein. 1921. *The Engineers and the Price System*. New York: B. W. Huebsch.

Waller, Spencer W. 2004. "The Legacy of Thurman Arnold." *St. John's Law Review* 78: 569–613.

Wise, George F. 1985. *Willis R. Whitney, General Electric, and the Origins of U.S. Industrial Research*. New York: Columbia University Press.

Yates, JoAnne. 1989. *Control through Communication: The Rise of System in American Management*. Baltimore: Johns Hopkins University Press.

———. 2000. "Business Use of Information and Technology during the Industrial Age." In *A Nation Transformed by Information: How Information Has Shaped the U.S. from Colonial Times to the Present*, ed. Alfred D. Chandler Jr. and James W. Cortada, 107–35. New York: Oxford University Press.

———. 2005. *Structuring the Information Age: Life Insurance and Technology in the Twentieth Century*. Baltimore: Johns Hopkins University Press.

Yergin, Daniel, and Joseph Stanislaw. 1998. *The Commanding Heights: The Battle between Government and the Marketplace That Is Remaking the Modern World*. New York: Simon and Schuster.

Zunz, Olivier. 1990. *Making America Corporate, 1870–1920*. Chicago: Chicago University Press.

*Chapter 15*_____

An Examination of the Supply of Financial Credit to Entrepreneurs in Colonial India

Susan Wolcott

In 1968 William Baumol called for a renewed focus on the "determinants of the payoff to entrepreneurial activity." Understanding the allocation of entrepreneurial talent was crucial, as "the entrepreneur is the key to the stimulation of growth." In a 1990 paper, on a less optimistic note, he argued that an inappropriate payoff structure, one that rewards unproductive entrepreneurship, is empirically associated with very slow growth.

India, particularly colonial India, is a fascinating case study of slow economic growth. Post-1948 India developed slowly, most obviously because of bad government policies that stifled growth in obvious ways. The recent removal of some of those policies has accelerated development. But colonial India also had slow growth, despite very good government policies. Taking the last two centuries as a whole, then, the Indian economy has been characterized by widespread poverty unparalleled in the world's industrialized countries. What is the role of entrepreneurial payoffs?

Discussions of the limited nature of India's economic development frequently attribute a major role to the difficulty of obtaining funding for the creation of new enterprises, or for the expansion of established firms. Yet, as is demonstrated in this chapter, India has possessed a profusion of well-functioning financial institutions, both before it achieved independence and since then. Indeed, there is a striking similarity between the structure and functioning of these financial institutions in India and those that were prevalent in the United States in the middle of the nineteenth century. Since that situation evidently did not prevent economic growth in the United States, inaccessibility to capital in India must be ruled out as an impassible obstacle to entrepreneurship and growth in India.

There was one important difference in the U.S. and the Indian systems. The provision of financial capital in India remained largely "informal." Most financial capitalists chose to operate as private entities even though Indian financial entrepreneurs operated under a British colonial legal system that permitted incorporation and limited liability, and there were incorporated banks in India as well as stock and security markets. I argue that this propensity for informality may have been a consequence of the caste system. In the nineteenth century Max Weber famously argued that the Hindu social system failed to reward entrepreneurism and it was this misaligned payoff structure that stifled capitalist growth (Weber 1958). He noted that the Hindu caste system was tied to an acceptance of an immutable world order, and this, coupled with an expectation of reincarnation, led to disinterest in the mundane. While much of Indian business scholarship has been devoted to correcting the view that Indians were unconcerned with material gain, scholars have been forced to acknowledge that Indian business networks are affected by the caste system. In 1955 Helen B. Lamb observed that the vast majority of Indian entrepreneurs were drawn from just three communities: the Marwaris of Rajasthan, the Vanias of Gujarat, and the Parsis.[1] This pattern continues even today, with every study showing that these same three communities control the lion's share of India's industries. The only change is that three other communities, Punjabi Khatris, Chettiars, and Maharashtrians have been added to the list as lesser, but still important groups (Khanna and Palepu 2004, 14).

The prevalence of these groups strongly suggests that the payoffs to entrepreneurism differed somehow across caste lines. The historical record suggests that wealth was not viewed negatively by any caste.[2] The payoff structure of the caste system, however, gave members of moneylending and trading castes a good way to enforce contracts through reputation, and so made legal enforcement less necessary among these caste members. Caste membership itself deterred cheating. I will argue that India's formal financial sector remained undeveloped because the informal sector worked so well, at least within these groups. On the other hand, it is possible that by retarding the growth of less personal credit systems, India's informal systems may have lessened the payoff to entrepreneurism for nonmembers of these groups.

My chapter proceeds as follows. Briefly, I describe the sense in which colonial India's economic policies were good, but its economic development was not. I then describe colonial India's financial markets. I define the sense in which India's markets were more informal than those of the antebellum United States. Next, I examine data to measure the performance of the Indian system relative to the U.S. system. In the fourth section I argue that this informality may be linked to the caste system. I then discuss how the caste-based financial system that supported India's commerce and trade evolved into a caste-based managerial agency system that supported India's industries. The chapter concludes by speculating on potential connections between India's personal system of finance and its limited development.

The Institutional Environment and Economic Development of Colonial India

A major new research program—exemplified by the work of Stanley Engerman and Kenneth Sokoloff, and Daron Acemoglu, Simon Johnson and James Robinson—suggests that a key institutional characteristic is "the breadth of access to opportunities for social and economic advancement—the ability to own land, obtain schooling, borrow, and innovate." What is crucial, in this view, is that laws and government policies promote broad participation in entrepreneurism. It is claimed that such a breadth explains the odd fact that the United States and Canada surged ahead of other American countries that were more resource rich (Hoff 2003, 207 and 208, respectively). It may seem surprising, but many of the U.S. and Canadian characteristics cited as growth enhancing reasonably describe the colonial Indian economy.

When Indians took over the governance of India in 1947, the main policymakers were determined not to repeat what they perceived to be the mistakes of the British. T. N. Srinivasan and Suresh D. Tendulkar write that the Nationalists thought that the British policies of laissez-faire and free trade were the major reasons for India's lagging industrial growth. They quote Nehru as describing world trade as a "whirlpool of economic imperialism." The Nationalists replaced the British policies with what came to be known as the "License Raj." This system required entrepreneurs to obtain a permit for any large industrial investment. Though it was originally put in place in an attempt to control and direct the economy for the public good, this system "degenerated into a tool for political and other patronage dispensation" (Srinivasan and Tendulkar 2003, 13 and 14, respectively). Moreover, licensing limited capacity and restricted supply. Firms could sell anything they could produce to domestic consumers, and thus had little incentive to improve quality or lower price. Labor management policies were also strictly circumscribed by government dictums. Independence meant that the mass of Indians gained the right to vote, a right that has been associated with good economic policies in many countries, says the new research agenda. For whatever reasons, however, the Indian electorate supported economic policies that clearly stifled entrepreneurism and innovation.

Compare this with the colonial regime. Though in terms of absolute numbers there were many educated Indians, the majority of Indians were illiterate, and that was almost certainly not good for growth. In addition, native Indians were largely excluded from government. Enfranchisement was limited, and the politicians who were elected primarily had advisory roles (Chaudhary 2006b). On the other hand, the policies that Britain imposed upon its colony most economists would describe as growth enhancing, such as the laissez-faire and free trade decried by the Nationalists. Sir George Rankin, a former chief justice of Bengal, described the legal structure of colonial India, in particular the law of contracts, as an improved version of British civil laws. The Indian Contract Act of 1872 was a simplified and codified version of existing British practices. When the British codified their own laws by the statutes of 1890 and 1893, "Sir Frederick Pollock had before him the [Indian] Commission's draft of 1866" (Rankin 1946, 93ff. and 97, respectively). The Indian law was modified in turn by the Indian Act of 1932 to bring it more exactly in line with British statutes, but, once again, Rankin argues, certain components of the Indian Act, in particular how it treated firms, were an improvement in clarity and completeness over existing British laws. Another point in favor of growth was that Indians were, largely, landowners. There were certainly many large estates and plantations in India, but the vast majority of Indian agriculturalists owned at least some land.

Thus Indians were given good policies and good laws, and through their landownership should have had access to credit. The large literate population, at least, should have been poised to innovate. Still, was their subordinate status in their own country an impediment to growth? Some authors, such as Subramanian Swamy (1979) and Amiya Bagchi (1972), have claimed the British government "placed hurdles" in front of native Indian entrepreneurs. But these authors' complaints are not that the British placed actual hurdles, but rather that the British failed to help entrepreneurs with subsidies and protective tariffs. More modern scholars—and certainly those concerned with productive paths of institutional development—would probably argue that the British failure in this regard during their tenure as rulers of India was actually the best help that could have been given to Indian entrepreneurs.

And in absolute terms, there was a great industrial expansion in India in the early twentieth century. Rajat Ray has shown that by 1939–40 the paid-up capital of joint-stock companies registered in India had increased fourfold from its 1914 level. It increased an additional 50 percent beyond the 1939–40 level by 1946. The annual rate of increase between 1914 and 1946 was 16.85 percent (Ray 1979, table 9, p. 39). The joint-stock companies included industrial firms, but also were involved in banking, transport, plantations, mines, and estates. Bagchi notes, however, that as India had no indigenous machinery manufacturers, imports of machinery give an accurate index of physical investment specifically in industry. Denominated in 1929–30 rupees, the accumulated total gross physical capital imported into India across the first four decades of the twentieth century was nearly 4 billion rupees (Bagchi 1972, table 3.2). In this absolute sense, then, there was certainly impressive industrial investment.

Still the industrial sector remained small relative to India's overall economy. Net investment in the colonial period constituted only 2 to 4 percent of national income, as opposed to an average of around 23 percent of Indian GDP in recent years. Machinery investment in the colonial period was especially low in relative terms, only 0.5 percent of national income.[3] Even by independence in 1947, despite the wartime surge in company registrations, the manufacturing sector represented just 16 percent of India's net product, and the largest part of that, 8.9 percent, was small-scale manufacturing (Heston 1982, table 4.3B). Between 1911 and 1951, the share of India's workforce in manufacturing actually dropped, from 10.1 to 8.7 percent. It should be noted, however, this was primarily due to a fall in female laborers in manufacturing. The percentage of male laborers in manufacturing was relatively stable: 9.5 percent in 1901 and 9.1 percent in 1951 (Krishnamurty 1982, table 6.2).

What is perhaps more important, productivity growth was minimal. Heston gives figures for the change in value added between 1900 and 1947 in all of the major sectors of the Indian economy (1982, table 4.4). Heston estimates that agriculture, which constituted about 70 percent of employment and GDP, may have even had a slightly negative annual growth in real value added per worker in this period. Manufacturing and commerce growth in real value added per worker was only about 1 percent. From this perspective, India hardly represented a dynamic economy.

Tirthankar Roy argues that India's resource endowments explain both the low investment levels and resulting lack of productivity growth. According to Roy, the scarcity and resulting high cost of capital and skilled labor in India meant that Indian industry was best suited to be, and was, "a vast world of traditional manufacturing, consisting of tool-based industrial production performed in homes or small workshops" (2002, 118). His argument echoes that of Morris Morris. Morris points out that though the official figures suggest that small-scale industry was both a bit larger and a bit more dynamic in terms of productivity than large-scale industry, because of serious underreporting in workshop activities in the interwar period, it may even have been more dynamic than the official figures would suggest. Further, the fact that Indian entrepreneurs were focusing on such workshops was not an indication of backwardness:

> The introduction of modern (if often technically "outmoded") machinery into a workshop context was the rational and quite efficient response by private entrepreneurs to cost and demand conditions as they existed over wide parts of the Indian economy. (1992, 221)

According to Roy and Morris, India was developing. It was just that India's development path was a bit different from that of Western economies, and that difference was due to the much greater cost of establishing modern industrial plants in India.

Morris adds another reason for Indian entrepreneurs' avoidance of large-scale industry, and that is their much greater familiarity with commerce and workshops. Morris's most recent statement on the development of industry in India was a 1987 article, but he has long claimed that the uncertainties of large-scale manufacturing were too great given the lack of infrastructure in India. Although Morris never cites Frank Knight directly, Morris is obviously referring to Knightian uncertainty, the distinction between "risk" (randomness with knowable probabilities) and "uncertainty" (randomness with unknowable probabilities) (Knight 1921). Morris points out that developed countries have "futures markets, statistical and other forms of specialized services that reduce risks and minimize uncertainties" (1992, 202). Indian entrepreneurs had, according to Morris, no such services.

> Thus, a new enterprise had to promise a very high rate of return not only to meet the cost of scarce capital but also to allow for the greater risks. The higher the rate of return required to offset the general uncertainties of novel enterprises, the fewer were the opportunities that promoters and investors found promising. (1982, 557)

Morris's statement, however, highlights the need for financial entrepreneurs in India. The main purpose of well-functioning financial markets is to minimize risk to individual savers so as to facilitate the use of capital. There is greatest need for them when the payoffs to investments are most uncertain. Consider, for example, the theoretical model of Jeremy Greenwood and Boyan Jovanovic (1990). The job of the bank in this model is to accumulate costly knowledge on the uncertain aggregate state of technology. As banks are relatively large players, they have more incentive to pay the research costs than individuals, and they can offset risks among individual projects. For both reasons, in an economy with well-functioning credit markets there is more saving and more growth.

This line of argument suggests that colonial India would not have been a congenial environment for innovative entrepreneurs if there were insufficient financial entrepreneurs to take on the task of researching the unknown, or if for some reason financial entrepreneurs performed their task inefficiently. On one point Morris is obviously misjudging the sophistication of the Indian economy. Futures markets for cotton had been widespread in northern India since at least the very early nineteenth century (Bayly 1992, 395). By the end of the century there were deep futures markets for all agricultural products in all parts of India, which appear to have been the exclusive domain of native merchants (Ray 1988). But what of other forms of "intelligence gathering"?

Financial Markets of Colonial India

When the Europeans arrived in India in the sixteenth century, they found a sophisticated financial market already in place. Few writers describing this market fail to quote the following colorful observation by the great seventeenth-century traveler Tavernier.

> The Jews engaged in money matters in the Turkish Empire are usually considered to be exceptionally able, but they are scarcely fit to be apprenticed to the money changers of India. (Tripathi 2004, 21)

The Indians had developed a system to transmit large sums across the great distances of India and even further. It was called the *hundi* system. A *hundis* was "a sort of bill of exchange drawn by a party on his agent or correspondent elsewhere, asking the latter to pay to the drawee a specified sum of money the equivalent of which the drawer must have already received" (Tripathi 2004, 18). By 1700 this system covered all of India and a market for salable *hundis* was developing. The network stretched from Surat to Dacca, and in the other direction over the Persian Gulf and the Red Sea to Makha" (Ray 1988, 265). Both the *shroffs*, or professional private bankers, and merchants were involved in selling and accepting *hundis*. It is thought that this system may have originated with the need of the many regional rulers of India to pay their troops.[4] This network continued to operate under the British. The 1931 Central Banking Enquiry Committee estimated that 90 percent of India's inland trade was financed by indigenous bankers (Chandavarkar 1982, 798).

Official descriptions of India's informal credit network break the system into three levels: village moneylenders, town moneylenders, and, at the apex, private bankers. Bankers are typically distinguished from moneylenders in that the former accept deposits and the latter do not. However, this is not a hard-and-fast rule, and can be broken on either side.[5] The most prominent caste groups of bankers include the Marwaris, who were originally from the northwest regions, but spread to all parts of India, and were especially prominent in eastern India; the Chettiars of Madras, who were also the main financial agents in Burma; the Khatris and Arora bankers of the Punjab; and finally the Bohras of Gujarat and the Multanis of Sind. (Note that with the exception of the Parsis and Maharashtrians, these are *exactly* the communities that have continued to dominate Indian entrepreneurism.) Timberg writes that the seminal treatment of the indigenous banking system of India remains L. C. Jain's 1929 book, an outgrowth of his Ph.D. thesis at the London School of Economics. Jain, a Marwari himself, gives the following description of indigenous bankers' activities.

> Their offices and branches are spread all over the country in important centres like Calcutta, Bombay, Delhi, Rangoon, etc., where they have their *munims* and *gumashtas* or agents, who look after their business. The munims are invested with very wide powers. They are not highly paid, but their industry, integrity, and efficiency are remarkable and proverbial. They submit periodical returns and reports of their doings to their head offices and receive from them occasional instructions. Some of the bankers even have correspondents outside India, at Aden, Djibuti in Africa, Addis Ababa in Abyssinia, Paris, in Japan and other places. (1929, 36)

Even among the bankers, there were divisions between the large and the small. In a discussion of the Marwari diaspora, Tripathi notes that the migrants from Rajasthan were as a rule the small operators. The big bankers, who enjoyed the patronage of the Rajput chiefs, stayed in place, and their family members set up branches in other centers (Tripathi 2004, 86). Timberg likens this latter group to the Rothschilds studied by David Landes or the New England merchant migrants studied by Bernard Bailyn who founded their businesses on lines of credit from their "London creditor-relatives" (Timberg 1978, 102). The small operators were those who perhaps started as clerks to a larger house, accumulated capital, and then set up in business for themselves.

The indigenous bankers of India performed many of the same functions a formally incorporated bank would perform. They bought and sold *hundis*. (It is perhaps indicative of the dominance of indigenous bankers that in India all bills of exchange were referred to as *hundis*, even those sold by joint-stock banks and the Imperial Bank, the latter being the quasi-government bank of India.) Indigenous bankers offered lines of credit to their customers. Much of this business was done on personal account. They usually took deposits. Consider the example of Motiram Narasidas of Surat, interviewed by the Bombay Provincial Bank Enquiry Committee 1929–30. He was a pure banker in that banking was his only business. He received deposits, for which he paid 4½ percent. (The joint-stock banks were paying, according to Mr. Narasidas, 5 percent at this time.) He loaned only against personal security. His rate to other *shroffs* was also 4½ percent, going to 5½ percent at times, to merchants at 9 percent, and to agriculturists at 6–9 percent. Narasidas, though a private individual, reported that he issued annual balance sheets (Provincial Banking Enquiry Committee [Bombay] 1930, 1:152–57). The indigenous bankers were unlike more formal banks in that they typically operated chiefly from their own capital, even if they took deposits. Further, they rarely issued checks, and when they did, those checks were not accepted by formal banks, that is, the joint-stock banks and the Imperial Bank (Jain 1929, 43). These characteristics, however, were not unlike the private U.S. bankers studied by Richard Sylla, or even the early New England banks studied by Naomi Lamoreaux. She noted that for these banks, both banknotes and deposits held a "relatively insignificant position" among banks' liabilities. The bulk of their liabilities, as in Indian indigenous banks, was the bank's own capital (Lamoreaux 1994, 3; Sylla 1976).

Another difference between indigenous banks and formally incorporated banks was that indigenous bankers typically also carried on other business. Narasidas, referred to earlier, is somewhat unusual in that he was a "pure" banker. Jain writes that most indigenous bankers were simultaneously engaged in another "allied business," and these included virtually every line of industry, trade and commerce. "They are grain dealers, general merchants, commercial agents, brokers, goldsmiths, jewelers, land-owners, industrialists and traders" (Jain 1929, 43). Ray notes that the two largest family owners of cotton textile mills in the Gujarat center of Ahmedabad, the Sarabhais and Kasturbai Lalbhai, continued with their indigenous banking business despite adding industrial pursuits to their portfolios. And the very wealthy Birla Brothers, who were jute mill owners, among other industrial activities, engaged in trade and most especially spot and forward transactions in the bazaar in the 1930s that were at least as large as their industrial interests (Ray 1992, 59). In both of these latter two cases, the financing available from their close connections to the indigenous banking sectors were instrumental in financing their industrial activities. I will return to the link between indigenous banks and Indian industrial financing in a later section, but here I want to note the similarities of this Indian system with the banks of New England described by Lamoreaux (1994). She argued that buying commercial bank stock in antebellum New England amounted to joining an "investment club" in which members' savings were sent to the enterprises of the directors of the bank.

Each Indian firm acted independently, according to Jain. They did, however, have guilds, sometimes called *mahajans*. These institutions were part caste *panchayat*, or council, and dealt with religious and social matters, and part trade dispute and insolvency courts.[6] In some parts of India, the *mahajans* evolved in the interwar period into "associations," but performed exactly the same role that the medieval Indian guilds had performed. Jain notes that the Bombay Shroffs' Association settled between twenty and twenty-five disputes a day. They had a form in which all of the details of the case were noted, including the parties to the dispute. The secretary of the association investigated, and handed down a decision. Jain writes that these decisions were accepted by all. On the few occasions when the parties took the dispute to a formal court, the decision of the association was typically upheld, as it had been arrived at from "personal knowledge." In Gujarat, also in western India, the association set the *hundi* rate, by which all members abided. The setting of intra-shroff rates was apparently also the practice of the Bombay Association.[7]

The Nakarattar Chettiars had the most formalized overarching organization of all of the communities of indigenous bankers (Rudner 1994). The Nakarattar Chettiars were and are a caste based in Chettinad in Madras. They were the main financiers of this region, but were even more famous for their widespread operations in Burma, Ceylon, and Malay. At least before the 1930s, the bulk of their collective funds was employed outside of India. The Nakarattar Chettiars held monthly meetings to discuss the current financial situation and set interest rates, as did other groups. The Chettiars, unlike other banking groups, were a single caste rather than a caste group, and the meetings were held at their temple. The caste panchayats of the Chettiars were used to settle disputes between Nakarattar businessmen over payment of interest on loans, return of deposits, or other business matters. The Chettiars were unlike other banking groups in another way. There were two formal layers of bankers. A small number of Chettiars, Rudner estimates something like 10 percent, were designated as *adathis*, or parent bankers (1994, 128ff.). They acted as clearinghouses between individual Nakarattar Chettiar bankers, much as a large New York or Philadelphia bank might have served as a correspondent bank for small rural banks in the antebellum United States. Two bankers did not have to know one another if they had a common *adathi*. Further, excess funds could be deposited with an *adathi* who would have the most up-to-date and complete commercial knowledge.

These organizations of bankers would in many ways have mitigated the uncertainty of business operations in India. Colonial Indian businesses were not operating completely without commercial information. The British administration in India had produced unusually good information for a poor country on agricultural prices and population since the 1870s. In the 1920s, labor bureaus were started in the various administrative centers and researched and published all information that was considered relevant to the labor markets (Mehrban 1945). Still, it is likely that there was a lack of formal private or government-sponsored commercial intelligence relative to more developed contemporaneous countries. And because India remained till well past independence dominated by small workshops and farmers who were only partly producing for the market, the economy was almost certainly less knowable than those same developed contemporaneous countries. The organizations of bankers, however, had contacts in every part of India, and in the case of the Chettiars, in many other parts of Asia as well. Their meetings were opportunities not just for setting interest rates and settling disputes, but also for exchanging information. Rudner claims that caste gatherings at weddings and funerals were just as important for learning of new business opportunities as they were for cementing social ties. The organizations themselves would not have conducted the "research" Greenwood and Jovanovic envisioned for commercial banks, but it seems unlikely that any good industrial opportunity that presented itself to any individual indigenous banker would lack for funds, even if he alone could not supply the investment capital. Individual indigenous bankers were independent, but not isolated.

The informal nature of India's financial system did not harm its ability to support agricultural production and commerce. In an important article, Ray gives a thorough discussion of the workings of the "bazaar" credit system for financing India's agricultural trade in the interwar period. He cites one example pulled from the records of the Bihar and Orissa Provincial Banking Enquiry Committee of 1929–30 that is a particularly nice description of how the system worked. The Province of Bihar and Orissa was just west of the Province of Bengal. Coconuts were one of the main crops of the Puri district, and were sold to confectioners, chiefly in the nearby Central Provinces (CP).

> Four coconut dealers at the railhead, one Marwari and three Oriyas, bought up the coconuts from local Brahman agriculturists who collected the produce of other ryots and moved the nuts by road to the railhead. The four coconut dealers financed one quarter of the nuts by advances which carried no stipulation of exclusive right of purchase and they paid cash down for the other three-quarters. When the *mandi* [market town] merchant at the railhead filled an order from a CP confectioner by railing the ordered coconuts, he telegraphed the buyer, who wired back that he should draw a *hundi* on a particular merchant in Bombay or Calcutta. The coconut merchant drew a *hundi* accordingly and sold it locally in Puri to a merchant willing to remit money to either Calcutta or Bombay. He usually got a premium for a *hundi* drawn on Calcutta, to which plenty of merchants wished to remit. By contrast, he had to sell *hundis* at a discount in Bombay where fewer merchants wanted to remit money. (Ray 1988, 288)

Thus the *mandi* merchants were first engaged in financing the coconut growers, and then participated in the financing of the final sales through the *hundi* market. Ray argues that the system, while "unorganized" by Western standards, was perfectly suited to the "monsoon economy and rural production organisation of India." According to Ray, the greater riskiness of agriculture in India meant that it was necessary to spread out the risk over many different agents.

This system was, in fact, not unorganized or particular to India. It seems very similar to the way cotton production, for example, was financed in the nineteenth-century United States. Harold Woodman describes a two-tier system (1968, esp. 76–83). For large planters in the antebellum period, there were agents who supplied credit beforehand, and sold the cotton after the harvest. Like the Marwaris and Oriyas of India, they had no legal right to market the crops, but often did. These were called factors. Smaller planters appear to have dealt more with the local store-owners, who supplied credit, and then sold the crops. These store owners themselves typically received credit from a factor. It is true that Indian farmers did not rely on commercial banks for agricultural credit, but then neither did farmers in the antebellum or postbellum U.S. South.

The mainstay of Indian rural credit were the rural moneylenders—the bottom rung of India's credit ladder. These were an extremely diverse group. Jain writes, "So far as money-lending is concerned, any one and every one takes to it. A member of any caste who may have a little money in hand can hardly resist the temptation of lending it out to neighbours" (1929, 28). This is a common theme in official documents. Peter J. Musgrave quoted an early1860s statement of the deputy commissioner of Rae Bereli, which is in the United Provinces, north India, on this point: "Almost every man appears to be in debt, and he who saves a rupee puts it out upon interest" (1978, 219).

Efficiency of Colonial India's Financial Markets

To provide financial capital efficiently for both industry and agriculture, the Indian system would have to have been integrated across its layers and across geographic distances. There was the appearance of different spheres and, thus, a separation between the formal and the informal sector. Still, there were channels for funds to flow across functional spheres.

The Imperial Bank, exchange banks, and joint-stock banks were at one extreme. They handled the export trade. There are also indications that they handled the less risky parts of Indian business. Consider the evidence of Rai Surana before the Bihar and Orissa Provincial Banking Enquiry Committee on October 26, 1929. Surana was the manager of the Bhagalpur branch of the Benares Bank. The Benares Bank was founded in 1901, and this branch was founded in 1909. This branch collected about one-third of the bank's total deposits. Surana reported that the main business of the bank was to lend money against pronotes (promissory notes) and *hundis* and give cash credits and overdrafts. It also sold government securities. When there were no good prospects locally, the branch put idle funds at deposit at the Imperial Bank in Calcutta. The bank financed neither agriculture nor industry, but it did lend to traders and to zamindars, the landlords of large estates in British India. In particular, the branch did not fund the local tannery. Surana noted, "The tannery in Bhagalpur was refused accommodation even by the Director of Industries because tanneries are not regarded as sound business" (Provincial Banking Enquiry Committee [Bihar and Orissa] 1930, 3:160–64).

The indigenous bankers operated in a somewhat different sphere than the formal banks. Like the Benares Bank, many indigenous bankers held deposits at the Imperial Bank. They periodically received accommodation from that bank and other formal banks. They were different in that they had a wider circle of personal knowledge, and were willing to have borrowers deemed too risky by the formal banks. Baker in his study of Madras found that the Imperial Bank had a list of "approved" Chettiar bankers. Baker writes that these bankers frequently borrowed from the Imperial Bank, tacked on 0.5 percent, and lent to an "unapproved" banker who was known to the Chettiar banker (Baker 1984, 287). The other branches of the Imperial Bank had similar lists of approved indigenous bankers in most provinces. The Central Banking Enquiry Committee reported that though indigenous bankers only indirectly loaned money to agriculturists, except in Burma, they "always maintained a close personal touch with the trader and the small industrialist" (Indian Central Banking Enquiry Committee 1931, 1:105 and 99, respectively). The tannery in Bhagalpur, spurned by Surana's Benares Bank as well as the colonial government, was probably financed by an indigenous banker. Indigenous bankers, however, were not unconnected to larger-scale industry. Tripathi notes that the bankers frequently purchased mill shares, and Jain notes that the indigenous bankers would leave large deposits with the large cotton mills of Indore in central India, though this largely constituted short-term lending (Tripathi 2004, 132; Jain 1929, 48).

Though the connections between the formal and indigenous banks to agriculture were indirect, funds from the commercial and indigenous banks were channeled to agriculture as well as industry. There were two ways. Sometimes the traders who had been loaned money themselves would subsequently lend money to the agriculturalists. Baker writes that the produce of Madras Province was sold to village dealers. Production and credit expanded "as more and more village dealers became known in the urban market and were able to borrow extra funds from the indigenous bankers" (1984, 258). The connection running between the Imperial Bank and the indigenous banker who lends to the local dealer is well summarized in the following quote from a witness before the Madras Provincial Bank Enquiry Committee.

> Indigenous bankers can be said to be practically helping agriculture, trade and industry in the district [Tanjavur], say to the extent of 60%.... The indigenous bankers generally start with a very small capital. The Imperial Bank of India and joint-stock companies [banks] help them to a certain extent. They easily influence the public and get deposits which, in some cases, rise to several times the capital. There are instances where private bankers started business with a nominal capital of Rs. 10 or 20 thousands and transacted more than Rs. 15 lakhs [1.5 million rupees] within a period of fifteen years. Finally when the accounts were closed they had a surplus of Rs. 1, 2 or even 3 lakhs in some cases. (Baker 1984, 287)

Another channel through which the funds of the indigenous banker reached agriculture was that the bankers would lend money to smaller moneylenders (small relative to the banks), who loaned to agriculturists. Musgrave relates the story of a rich agriculturist in Chakerji, a village in Etah in the United Provinces. The agriculturist, named Narayan Singh, lent from his own profits. He found this so lucrative that he borrowed 2,000 rupees in 1885 from a Bohra banker in Kasganj, paying interest at 12 percent per year and lending out at 3.125 percent per month (Musgrave 1978, 218). The evidence of the indigenous bankers before the Bombay PBEC report suggests that this was common practice even in 1929. The rate at which moneylenders could borrow from the *shroffs* had not changed much from Musgrave's example (Provincial Banking Enquiry Committee (Bombay) 1930, 1:200, also 3:483).

Of course large agriculturists could borrow directly from the bankers, as in the case of the Gujarat banker Narasidas mentioned earlier. And all of these bankers and moneylenders might themselves be brokers or traders, or in fact even agriculturists. It was an extremely fluid system with no legal segregation, and the traditional occupational segregation among these productive activities was much more fluid than one might have supposed.

Ray argues that the integration was incomplete. While he acknowledges that "there was a large downward flow of credit," he claims that the connection between formal banks, the bazaar, and the rural economy was weak.

> The sphere of the bazaar is thus clear: it operated at the tier of the marketing hierarchy where *hundis* were in circulation. This excluded at one end the village shandies which had no sources of mobile credit, and at the other end the international ports-of-call which possessed the higher but entirely alien financial instruments of the exchange banks. (Ray 1988, 278)

The evidence Ray gives to support his claim is twofold. On the disconnect in the system between the formal banks and the bazaar, he argues that there is no connection between the *hundi* rates of the bazaar and the Imperial Bank call money rate. The second disconnect, what Ray terms the "cleavage within the indigenous system," occurred because there were no "negotiable instruments" in use connecting the *shroffs* to the *sowcars*, or moneylenders. Funds moved between these two groups through the "clumsy use of book credits," which were unable to ease the seasonal credit shortages in the country caused by the monsoon growing season. In many areas of India there are two cropping seasons. The monsoons come in the early summer months. The *kharif*, or rainy season crop, is put in the ground during the monsoons, and harvested in December. Then the *rabi* crop is sown, and grown on residual moisture from the monsoon. It is harvested before the monsoons come, and

TABLE 15.1
Annual Bank and Bazaar Rates in India

Year	Imperial Bank rate	Imperial Bank Calcutta call rate	Imperial Bank Bombay call rate	Imperial Bank *hundi* rate	Calcutta bazaar *hundi* rate	Bombay bazaar *hundi* rate
1922				6.00	8.00	10.58
1923				6.71	7.15	9.69
1924				6.96	5.79	10.00
1925	5.33	3.08	3.53	5.92	9.10	9.77
1926	4.92	2.48	2.91	4.42	10.13	8.22
1927	5.58	3.45	4.19	5.54	9.75	8.72
1928	6.17	3.85	4.55	6.13	9.81	8.31
1929	7.33	5.38	6.71	7.50	11.33	10.23
1930	5.56	3.29	3.56	5.56	8.61	7.54
1931	6.92	4.29	5.35	7.00	7.58	5.36
1932	5.17	2.67	3.42	5.17	7.08	4.59
1933	3.58	0.73	1.23	3.58	6.58	3.38
1934	3.50	0.75	1.69	3.50	6.58	4.50
1935	3.46	0.88	1.69	3.46	6.50	5.50
1936	3.00	0.41	0.38	3.00	5.50	4.13
1937	3.00	0.25	1.08	3.00	5.50	5.25
1938	3.00	0.64	0.47	3.00	6.83	4.83
1939	3.00	2.33	2.58	3.00	6.50	5.38

Source: Annual Reports of the Comptroller of the Currency, India, various years. The bazaar rates are not official rates, but only informed estimates.

is typically the larger crop. Ray writes, "From May to August rural creditors needed funds to make advances to the cultivators for sowing the kharif. The funds lying idle in the bazaar could not find congenial employment in the mofussil precisely when there was stringency there" (1988, 277–78).

Ray's claims are testable. Starting in 1922, the comptroller of the currency of India published monthly estimates of the bazaar *hundi* rate for Calcutta and Bombay, as well as the Imperial Bank bank rate, the Imperial Bank call money rates for Calcutta and Bombay, and the Imperial Bank *hundi* rate. Annual values for these are given in table 15.1. There is typically, though not always, a wedge between the rates of the Imperial Bank and the bazaar. But, as discussed above, the bazaar

TABLE 15.2
A Comparison of the Integration of the Indian and U.S. Financial Capital Markets

A. Correlation coefficients between monthly rates in Indian centers, 1922–39

	Bank rate	Call rate, Calcutta	Call rate, Bombay	Imperial *hundi*	Calcutta bazaar	Bombay bazaar
Bank rate	1					
Call rate, Calcutta	0.92	1				
Call rate, Bombay	0.90	0.93	1			
Imperial *hundi*	0.99	0.92	0.90	1		
Calcutta bazaar	0.65	0.68	0.63	0.43	1	
Bombay bazaar	0.62	0.68	0.65	0.73	0.54	1

B. Correlation coefficients between annual average commercial paper rates in various U.S. cities, 1836–59

	Boston	New York	Philadelphia	Charleston	New Orleans	Cincinnati
Boston	1					
New York	0.87	1				
Philadelphia	0.82	0.90	1			
Charleston	0.09	0.67	0.54	1		
New Orleans	0.58	0.85	0.74	0.60	1	
Cincinnati	0.84	0.80	0.50	0.23	0.81	1

Sources: For Indian data see table 15.1. The U.S. data are from Bodenhorn 2000, table 4.7.
Note: Note that all Pearson correlation coefficients were statistically significant at less than the 0.1 percent level.

took on riskier clients. There are also differences between the Bombay and Calcutta rates.

We can formally test for integration using correlation coefficients. The results of this test are given in the top panel of table 15.2. All measures are statistically significant, suggesting that these were not separate markets. To interpret these numbers, we need to put them in perspective. Howard Bodenhorn reports the interest rates on commercial paper in various U.S. cities. Though he does not use them for this purpose, I have constructed correlations, which are reported in the lower panel of table 15.2. The northeast centers of Boston, New York, and Philadelphia are more integrated than Indian centers. On the other hand, cities such as Charleston, and even New Orleans, are not more tightly linked to each other or to the major financial cities than were Bombay and Calcutta.[8]

The reported bazaar rates also let us examine the issue of seasonality. Ray argued that his reading of the official documents suggests that after the *rabi* harvest, from May to August the bazaar funds were idle when they could have been used by the rural sector to advance monies for the *kharif,* or rainy season crop. Table 15.3 reports the results of regressions testing for the degree of seasonality in the Bombay and Calcutta bazaar rate data. The data do suggest strong seasonality in the bazaar rates. Rates appear to rise between one and two percentage points in the first six months of the year. The seasonality is greater in the Bombay bazaar.

Once again, we should put these numbers in perspective. The United States, in fact all gold standard countries, experienced seasonality of money demand in the nineteenth century, with rates peaking just after the harvest in September and rising through January, though it is also true that in the United States, this seasonality lessened considerably after the creation of the Federal Reserve System in 1914. Truman Clark reports estimates of the degree of seasonal rate differentials

TABLE 15.3
Regressions of the Seasonal Pattern of Bazaar Rates in India, 1922–39

A. Dependent variable is the monthly Calcutta bazaar *hundi* rate			
Variable	Coefficient	Standard error	*p*-value
Intercept	7.30	0.24	<.00001
1st quarter dummy	0.57	0.36	0.117
2nd quarter dummy	1.00	0.36	0.007
3rd quarter dummy	−0.14	0.41	0.739
B. Dependent variable is the monthly Bombay bazaar *hundi* rate			
Variable	Coefficient	Standard error	*p*-value
Intercept	5.92	0.33	<.00001
1st quarter dummy	1.96	0.51	0.0002
2nd quarter dummy	2.15	0.51	0.0001
3rd quarter dummy	0.13	0.58	0.8257

in the United States for various measures including the call money rate, 60–90-day commercial paper, and the 90-day time money rate. Between the years 1890 and 1913, the peak differences between these rates was between December, the peak, and January, the trough. The average differences are 2.28 percent for call money, 0.50 percent for commercial paper, and 0.88 percent for time money (Clark 1986, table 2). While these rate differentials, except for call money, are a bit lower than the seasonal differentials seen in India, they are of the same order of magnitude. Thus, if India suffered from a seasonal change in money demand, it suffered no more than had the United States in the nineteenth century. Further, because the drop in rates postharvest is similar to what was experienced in the United States, it seems unlikely that the Indian rural-urban financial market integration was any less than the U.S. rural-urban integration.

Caste and Colonial Indian Credit Markets

The analysis thus far has shown the similarities between the Indian credit system and the mid-nineteenth-century U.S. financial system. But there were significant differences, including the extent to which informal credit exceeded formal credit, and the widespread involvement of many individuals in rural lending. The cultural institution of caste played an important role in the Indian credit system and may partly explain these two oddities of the Indian credit system. Though caste has many aspects, most economists have focused on just two: the hereditary assignment of some occupations such as priests and manure collectors or sweepers, and the hierarchy that separated, socially and economically, the high castes from the lower castes. However important these may be for both the speed and the morality of Indian economic development, they are not my focus. I want to concentrate on a different aspect of caste. Whatever else it was, caste is an extended, somewhat formalized kinship network. M. N. Srinivas argues that despite the scorn heaped upon it, few Indians would want to abandon the caste system, as "joint family and caste provide for an individual in our society some of the benefits which a welfare state provides for him in the industrially advanced countries of the West."[9] Continued membership in the network required meeting certain obligations. If a member failed to meet his obligations, he, *and his family*, would be formally outcasted, and lose all benefits of membership. In India, there were accepted, formal means of adjudicating cases in which members failed in their obligations to the social network. Each caste had its own panchayat, or council, over which the headman of the caste officiated. Cases taken up by the caste panchayat dealt with personal matters that would lower the reputation of the caste, such as irregular unions and family quarrels; with land disputes; and with other disputes between caste members. The panchayat had other functions such as planning community festivals, or reforming the subcaste, or *jati*, customs (Kolenda 1978, 89). The decisions of the panchayats are upheld by the group. The punishment meted out for grievous violations of caste rules is to "deprive a casteman of the right to receive water, or the tobacco pipe, from the hands of his fellow castemen and forbids them likewise to receive it from them." This effectively expels him from the community. He will not receive help in time of difficulty. There will be no one for his children to marry. Kolenda writes that the resulting "social control of members is unusually strong and effective" (1978, 11).

Credit contracts are by definition an exercise in trust. The larger the funds involved, the longer the time period between borrowing and repayment, and the more geographically distant the parties, the greater must be the trust to induce both parties to enter the contract. Lamoreaux believes that the fact that businessmen and bankers were related by blood or marriage in early nineteenth-century New England facilitated the development of credit networks. Those who either defaulted on loans, or used funds improperly, "risk[ed] ostracism from the kinship group and the loss of both their claims on family resources and the connections vital to business success" (Lamoreaux 1994, 26).

Caste extends the kinship network to include more individuals and increase its benefit, and simultaneously raises the cost of transgressing the social norms by formal outcasting. Both Rudner (for the Chettiars in the nineteenth and twentieth centuries) and Bayly (for north Indian merchants of the seventeenth) argue that if a businessman acted unscrupulously, not only would he lose business connections, his children would become unmarriageable (Rudner 1994, 128; Bayly 1992, 375). More formally, Bendor and Swistak determined that in an evolutionary game theory framework, some degree of cooperation may be sustained in the absence of binding institutional supports if there is a sufficiently dense social network so that everyone knows who has cooperated and who has not, if there are sufficiently severe penalties for cheating, and if punishment is multilateral; a failure to cooperate with any one individual must lead to retaliation by the entire group. The level of cooperation chosen will depend upon what players expect other players to do, and the levels of punishment (Bendor and Swistak 2001). As the caste system provided all of these criteria—communication, multilateral punishment, and harsh penalties for defection, theoretically it should have been capable of sustaining a much higher degree of cooperation than a less extensive, less formal network. On a more empirical basis, Timberg writes, "It may be that many institutions, such as the joint family and strong, particularistic caste loyalties are the secret of success in Indian business and industry." In particular, he argued that it was the Marwaris' wide resource group that was the secret of their commercial and industrial success (Timberg 1978, 17 and 98, respectively). Other analysts were impressed with the integrity of Indian financial intermediaries. Cooke, describing Indian private banking in 1863, was impressed by a system in which, "although millions were invested, the loss of bad debts, arising out of the dishonour of the instruments at maturity, was a most insignificant fraction per cent" (Ray 1988, 305). Seventy years later the authors of the Bihar and Orissa PBEC wrote:

> The word of the shroff is better than an expensive bond. None of the large *mathudhar* transactions—transactions which are carried on daily by shroffs amongst themselves by word of mouth without any written record or document—are ever denied. The slightest rumour of unfair dealing with clients will impair such sensitive credit.

It is not only the chief bankers who maintained a reputation for probity. The Bihar and Orissa reports give the following account of an establishment of indigenous bankers.

> The employees of the [indigenous bankers] are generally poor relations and caste men imbued with the traditions and well acquainted with the practices of the profession. As such they are thoroughly amenable to the social influence of the caste *panchayat*, which is always more effective in securing honesty than any legal penalty. (Provincial Banking Enquiry Committee [Bihar and Orissa] 1930, 193 and 195, respectively)

I noted earlier that the decisions of the Bombay shroff association were considered binding and just by its members (Jain 1929). The Indian financial network may have remained informal because this informality had so little cost in India, given the private incentives for honesty.

This argument suggests a never fully explored role for the concentration of entrepreneurship among certain Indian castes. Kripa Freitas has speculated on the role of caste in sustaining contracts (Freitas 2006). Analysts describing the indigenous banking sector certainly suggest that caste ties were important deterrents to cheating. Such arguments suggest that certain castes were more likely to engage in entrepreneurism, not because of any cultural predisposition, but rather because, if the business network in part depended on caste connections, members of different castes when choosing a career had different ex ante relative profit expectations. This is not to say that business activities and support were restricted to intracaste ties, which the empirical record shows to be patently false, but rather that intracaste ties had an additional means of contract enforcement that seems likely to have affected relative payoffs.

The Indian Financial Market and Indian Industrial Organization

Peter Rousseau and Richard Sylla (2005) argue that the expansion of the formal banking system in the United States spurred the development of a liquid securities market, and that this in turn spurred incorporation. For the United States, they argue, the development of formal, liquid financial markets exploiting limited liability induced investment by both domestic and foreign investors.

A similar pattern did not occur in India, even though all of the legal apparatus was in place: there was a formal banking sector, a securities market, and incorporation. Instead, managing agencies evolved as a hybrid of family firms and incorporation. Caste networks of trust in India's financial systems could be responsible for the development of this uniquely Indian form of industrial finance. Many of the most important managing agency firms of the colonial period were offshoots of the family firms of indigenous bankers, such as those of C. N. Davar, who built the first Indian cotton mill, and J. N. Tata and G. D. Birla (Lamb 1955). But while indigenous bankers remained completely outside of the formal, regulated system, managing agencies adopted some aspects of the formal system. The Indian managing agency remains today a legally distinct firm that promotes, finances, and acts as the "decision-making unit" of one or more other "legally separate and presumably independent" firms (Brimmer 1955). Typically the operating unit was a joint-stock company. Sometimes the managing agency was publicly traded as well.

Though Lamb and Brimmer attribute the invention of the managing agency structure to English entrepreneurs in India, Tripathi claims that its structure is Indian: "For shorn of details, the managing agency structure represented an adaptation of the joint family system, still a prominent feature of the Indian social structure, for managing a business enterprise" (2004, 113). Partnerships, according to Tripathi, were too risky for "cautious Indian investors," and the managing agency "was an organizational fiction" that allowed private control while utilizing the joint-stock system. If Morris is correct and unknowable uncertainty was the main deterrent to Indian industrialization, then the managing agency was a brilliant adaptation. It allowed the entrepreneur to manage and finance a firm while also protecting himself from full exposure to the risks of new enterprises. Brimmer found many managing agencies that controlled just one independent firm. He also found some individuals who controlled more than one independent firm, but did so using a distinct and separate managing agency for each firm. Though Brimmer did not believe he had a completely satisfactory explanation for this pattern, he thought it was linked to the wealthiness of individuals controlling the managing agency, and at least in 1951, to the fact that the bulk of that wealth had been generated through trading. The industrial concerns were relatively small parts of the overall operations of the individual's or family's business interests. By having a separate "firm" manage each company, only the assets invested in that firm were at risk. The managing agency would have all of the benefits of flexibility associated with vertical and horizontal industrial integration, while risks would remain compartmentalized by limited liability.

The Indian managing agency has not escaped criticism. Some detractors believed that it had not evolved sufficiently far from its family-firm origins. Lamb, for example, thought there were two tiers of managing agencies. Those who "rationalize their operations, publish adequate records, maintain plant, deal effectively with labor and delegate authority to professional staffs," and those who maintain company secrecy, rely too heavily on family members and 'fellow castemen,'" and emphasize quick profits (Lamb 1955, 108). Brimmer is even more damning, arguing that English managing agencies overwhelmingly comprise the first group and Indian managing agencies the second. Brimmer especially faults the Indian managing agencies for secrecy and nepotism.

Small firms facing relatively large risks may have relied on a limited labor pool for the extra advantages that kinship connections brought, such as greater trustworthiness, but the ill effects of nepotism in managing agencies were moderated as the firms expanded. Lamb notes that as firms grew larger, they consistently reached out beyond caste and community boundaries so that the boards of the largest and most successful firms would have representatives of several mercantile communities (1955, 110). It is important to realize that this was not a modern phenomenon stemming from a movement away from traditional attitudes. Christopher Bayly studies the business communities of eighteenth-century north India. As mercantile interests became more politically secure, caste connections were supplemented with other types of connections. It was not that caste connections disappeared, but rather that they were bound into larger units. He argues that "caste and religion provided the building blocks out of which mercantile and urban solidarities were perceptibly emerging." Bayly believes these multicaste groups were stronger because each part within the whole was held together by caste ties (1992, 177ff.).

The role of caste connections in corporate governance and finance has not faded away since independence despite the expansion and development of the Indian economy. Khanna and Palepu study the evolution of the structure of control of India's modern industries between 1939 and 1997. They have found that family-run business groups continue to dominate Indian industry. These family groups—such as that of the Tatas or the Birlas—are direct descendants of family-run managing agencies. At least in the early 1990s, while there were roughly as many non-group-affiliated private firms as family-group-affiliated private firms listed on the Bombay Stock Exchange, the group-affiliated firms' average sales were almost four times as large. The entrepreneurial families behind these groups tend to be drawn from the communities of the Marwaris, Parsis, Gujarati Banias, and Chettiars, as was true of the indigenous bankers and industrialists in the colonial period.

Khanna and Palepu claim that the personal nature of business practices in India has its uses. In developing countries some markets are missing, such as the market for venture capital and that for managerial talent. Family groups have superior knowledge of and access to financial capital and people. They can utilize these resources as substitutes for the nonexistent impersonal, arm's-length markets. Of course, there are obvious potential moral hazards when one group has superior access to resources, but such potential inefficiencies are less of a problem when there are many rich families, each with access superior to the bulk of the population, but not relative to one another. In their study Khanna and Palepu find there was more turnover among India's top fifty firms than among the top fifty U.S. firms over the same time period, and thus they conclude that though Indian markets are dominated by recognizable families, competition across these families is probably sufficient to punish inefficient nepotism and secrecy. Their arguments are similar to Lamoreaux's claim that in early-nineteenth-century New England, a small group of "insider" bankers with their superior knowledge of available opportunities could more efficiently finance investor projects than could an ill-informed market. She argues that though these insider bankers had superior access to resources, the outcome was efficient because entry to the banking sector was easy. Competition among the insiders provided the necessary discipline.

There is, however, one striking dissimilarity between the Indian case and New England. While personal finance of industry persists in India even today, insider lending disappeared in New England by the late nineteenth century (Lamoreaux 1994). It was replaced by professional bankers with no business interests to impair their "objectivity and impartiality." Banks ceased to act as interested investors, and simply became collectors and dispersers of savings.

I think these very different trajectories may be the key to understanding how India's culture has affected the development of Indian industry over the twentieth century. While it seems reasonable to argue that competition among a fairly large set of entrepreneurs, even if it is a limited set, might lead to a socially efficient allocation of a fixed level of financial resources, it is still possible that the limits of the set might affect the accumulation of financial resources over time. Many years ago George Akerlof speculated that because each Indian managing agency can "be classified according to communal origin" or caste, the group could use communal social sanctions to encourage honesty. He also argued, however, that such a structure might lead to expropriation of the return of any investor in the managing agency who was not of the same caste community, and thus discourage saving. As evidence he pointed to the more heterogeneous mix of stockholders in British-owned managing agencies in India relative to Indian-owned managing agencies (Akerlof 1970). More recently, Mobius and Szeidl presented a model that highlights the trade-offs between the trust generated by tight networks, and the limits to the network maintaining trust requires. Their model was meant to examine the provision of informal credit in less developed countries "where legal contract enforcement is unavailable or costly" (Mobius and Szeidl, 2007, 1). The interesting insight for my purposes is that when the need for trust is greatest, such as diamond merchants in New York City, social welfare is highest in tightly connected societies, but in contrast, when the stakes are lower, such as borrowing for a bicycle or a car, social welfare is highest in more diverse communities. First let me note that legal contract enforcement is always costly, even in modern societies with formal financial institutions. One might then interpret impersonal commercial banks and finance through impersonal stock offerings as a "low trust" system and indigenous banks and family dominated managing agencies as a "high trust" system, that is, a system in which trust rather than legal enforcement plays a relatively important role. Commercial banks keep extensive public records, as do publicly traded companies. Indigenous banks are repeatedly described as secretive, as were traditionally oriented managing agencies. Secrecy requires greater trust, and thus caste ties were necessary to maintain honesty. Secrecy also undoubtedly has some advantages. Resources can flow with great flexibility and minimum transactions cost along such networks.[10] But theory suggests that secrecy has a cost too: the limitation of the network of participants. Given that both systems have advantages, one cannot say absolutely which is better. The contrasting experience of widespread growth in the nineteenth-century United States and the limited scope of wealth accumulation in twentieth-century India, however, would at least a priori suggest the advantages of financial transparency and diffuse participation.

Restriction of Entrepreneurship?

My thesis would suggest that the chief Indian industrialists should all have had similar backgrounds. Consider as an initial sample the head of the nineteen Indian family groups Markovits identifies among the top fifty-seven Indian business groups in 1939. Markovits gives a thumbnail sketch of each of the main industrialists at the end of the colonial period (Markovits 1985). These sketches allow me to identify the caste affiliation of seventeen of the nineteen large business groups he identified. There are seven firms from the Bania caste of moneylenders and traders. Six of these are from Gujarat. There are four firms with Parsis connections, and four firms with Marwari connections. The firm of Thackersey is from a family of Cutchi Bhanias, a trading caste that originated in Sind, now Pakistan. Another firm was headed by Mafatlal Gagalbhai, a Patidar Kanbi from Gujarat, a Shudra. We can add to this list the Indian partners of Martin Burn, the second-largest business group in India in 1939. Markovits identifies this firm as English because the largest shareholders, with 40 percent, were the English Martin family. But there were two significant Indian partners: Mukerjee, who held 37 percent, and Banerjee, who held 17 percent (Herdeck and Piramal 1985, 210). Their share of Martin Burn places them in a category of business importance similar to the other Indians I have listed. Mukerjee and Banerjee were Bengali Brahmins.

Since this is a small list of entrepreneurs, perhaps we might also consider the thirteen whose biographies are highlighted in the book *Indian Industrialists*, by Gita Piramal, now a recognized expert on Indian business families, and her coauthor, Margaret Herdeck. This book identifies some of the giants of Indian industrialization from the late colonial and early independence period. The authors claim to have pulled these names almost at random from the major industrialists of the era, but most scholars would, I think, consider this a fairly representative list of important entrepreneurs. Several entrepreneurs highlighted in this work overlap those included in Markovits's list of the fifty-seven large business groups in 1939. These were Tata, Birla, and Mafatlal Gagalbhai. The others are Bajaj, Goenka, Modi, Ambani, Oberoi, Thapar, K. C. and J. C. Mahindra, Kirloskar, and T. T. Krishnamachari. The first two were Marwaris; Modi was an Agarwal from Uttar Pradesh, a related caste. Ambani is a Gujarati Bania. Thapor, Oberoi, and the Mahindra brothers were all Punjabi Khatris, another moneylending, trading caste. Kirloskar and T. T. Krishnamachari were both Brahmins.

Thus all but one of these entrepreneurs were either from moneylending, trading castes or Brahmins. Only one, Mafatlal Gagalbhai, was of a lower caste. (Shudras are the lowest of the four varnas, but they are above the so-called untouchables.) Gagalbhai's father was an artisan, and he himself began life peddling his own handwoven gold lace, carrying his wares in a sack on his back. Mafatlal proves that it was not impossible for an artisan to rise to wealth without family connections, but he is the only example of a nontrading caste, non-Brahmin entrepreneur.[11] To appreciate how limited the network appears to have been, note that in the census of British India in 1931, only seven million, or slightly less than 2 percent of Indians, identified themselves as belonging to traditional merchants and traders castes, a group that included Baniya, Bhatia, Chetti, Khatri, Komati, and Vaishya.[12] Brahmins constituted a further 15 million, or 4.3 percent of the population. In a 1997 article in the Indian magazine *Business Today*, Gita Piramal argued against the notion that Marwaris alone dominated Indian industry. She wrote: "A closer look allows us to throw out this hoary notion. There are more Sindhis, Parsis, Punjabis, Chettiars and Brahmins than ever before in the Top Fifty [Indian business groups]. If there is a trend, it points to a more broad-basing of entrepreneurship in Indian than ever before" (Piramal 1997, 22). Since even this wider group is still just a small share of India's overall population, I would respectfully suggest that the description "broad-basing" in this case is quite relative.

Of course, I am not arguing that one had to be from a trading caste or a Brahmin to be an entrepreneur in India in the colonial period or today. I have already mentioned Mafatlal Gagalbhai. Also, there were at least a few Muslim textile mill owners in colonial Bombay. But the preponderance of trading caste members and Brahmins, especially the former, among important entrepreneurs, given their quite small share of the Indian population as a whole, is certainly suggestive that there was some factor that afforded these individuals superior access to opportunity.

I will add one more fact that I think is relevant to the question of whether trading caste members themselves believed they faced different ex ante opportunities. Primary education was in large part privately funded in colonial India (Chaudhary 2006a). Thus, if an individual was literate, it was at least in part driven by his parents' demand based upon an assessment of his expected return. The 1931 census gives rates of literacy for some select castes. Among the general Indian population five years and older, only 15.6 percent of males were literate. Among Brahmins five years and older, 23 percent of males were literate. But among the Baniya, 54.4 percent of males were literate. Among the Chetti, 44.7 percent of males were literate. And among the Khatri, 45 percent of males were literate.[13] There was something clearly different about India's trading castes.

Conclusion

Was India's unusual credit system a hindrance to economic growth in the colonial period? If it were, it was not due to obvious problems such as an absolute scarcity of capital or a lack of sophistication. And if Indians were lacking for resources, Indians as they began their industrialization path were no more constrained for financial capital than U.S. entrepreneurs had been as that country was industrializing in the mid-nineteenth century. But Indian credit, unlike the U.S. financial system, was largely provided informally. I have argued that caste appears to have provided an enforcement mechanism alternative to formal laws. Caste connections among financial firms thus decreased the costs of remaining outside the formal sector, and allowed Indians the relative freedom of continuing as private firms.

The more personal financial markets of India did not preclude entrepreneurship and investment. Many huge industrial concerns were launched in the 1920s and 1930s. These include Tata Iron and Steel Company, which had an average gross block capital in the years 1924–25 to 1934–35 of 227 million rupees. G. D. Birla floated Hindustan Motors with a paid-up capital of 49.6 million and Textile Machinery Corporation with a paid-up capital of 10 million rupees. Walchand managing agency set up Premier Automobiles with a paid-up capital of 22 million rupees (Ray 1992, 61). These amounts for single companies are large compared with Bagchi's figure that I cited previously, for total cumulative investment in industrial machinery from 1900 to 1939 of 4 billion 1929–30 rupees. But all of these firms were begun by families who already had extensive commercial interests. Financing of very large concerns was restricted to those with family connections.

The amounts I quoted in the previous paragraph point to another fact. While it is not clear if the Indian economic system generated an optimal degree of entrepreneurism, it clearly generated large returns for at least some entrepreneurs. This chapter has largely focused on informal financial activity in India, as it was the preserve of indigenous Indians. The Marwari caste cluster as well as Gujarati Banias and south Indian Chettiars had been known and admired for their financial prowess for centuries. The Parsis emerged as financiers and intermediaries when the British came to India. Members of each of these groups garnered enormous wealth in the colonial period, say business historians. But it is difficult to measure the wealth associated with private, informal banking and trading. Many of the banking families, however, added industrial concerns to their holdings by the end of the colonial period, and these are more easily measured. The Tata's are the most well known of the Parsis entrepreneurial families. In 1939, the family's publicly held industrial holdings were worth 620 million rupees (equivalent at the time to US$207.5 million). This was the single largest business group in India of any nationality. It remains so today. The next richest Indian family group, then and today, is that of the Marwari Birlas. The family industrial holdings were worth 40.9 million rupees in 1939. The Gujarati Banias were represented by Lalbhai Kasturbai, among others. His family's holdings were 23.3 million rupees in 1939. The families were the main shareholders in these companies, but not the only ones. On the other hand, the value of publicly traded companies represent just a subset of each family's wealth. Consequently I believe these values are a rough indicator of the orders of magnitude of Indian family wealth.[14]

This chapter began with the statement that India was and is poor. The wealth of individual families does not contradict that assessment. It does, however, suggest a puzzle. If the legal and government institutions put in place by the British in colonial India cannot be responsible for the general level of poverty, at least in that period, and if during the colonial period India had a large, integrated financial structure, and a supply of clever, well-remunerated entrepreneurs, what limited Indian growth? I cannot answer that question completely. But the evidence presented here suggests several points that are important. First, the caste system, despite being so widely condemned, probably facilitated the initial industrial development of India by providing financial and managerial resources at low transactions costs to an absolutely large number of entrepreneurs. At the same time, however, the personal, caste-based nature of the Indian system almost certainly hindered the involvement of a much larger set who could have potentially become entrepreneurs. It was not that individuals were restricted from being entrepreneurs because they had been born to the "wrong" caste. The Indian social system was actually much more fluid than many people suppose, and wealth and success were valued by all, and in some sense, open to many. Members of trading castes, however, would have had preferred access to the informal financial networks of India. Their preponderance among early-twentieth-century industrialists suggests that that access gave them an advantage. As I mentioned earlier, there is an emerging interest among economists in the effect of institutions that provide wide access to opportunity. A prime historical example of its good effect is the, appropriately described, broad-based nature of entrepreneurism in early economic growth in Holland, as documented by the chapter in this volume by Oscar Gelderblom. India may well represent the obverse. Thus, one potential explanation for India's slow growth is that limited access to financial capital for the great majority of Indians may have led to a misdirection of their energy and talent. India has had many justly famous entrepreneurs. Perhaps what may have been more important in India's past record of slow growth is the many anonymous individuals who remained outside the network, and thus faced lower ex ante payoffs and, therefore, lessened incentives for entrepreneurism.

Notes

This chapter was originally prepared for the History of Entrepreneurship conference held at New York University, October 19–21, 2006, organized by William J. Baumol, David Landes, and Joel Mokyr, and sponsored by the Kauffman Foundation. I wish to thank Howard Bodenhorn as well as all participants for useful comments.

[1] Lamb 1955. Parsis are Zorastrians and not Hindus. But the caste system so permeated traditional India that the social relations of even non-Hindu groups exhibited certain caste-like features. Thus scholars speak of Moslem "castes" and Christian "castes" in India.

[2] A major work by Tripathi (2004) discusses the history of entrepreneurship in India from the sixteenth to the twentieth century. His book well illustrates the position of power and respect enjoyed by successful businessmen in India.

[3] Roy 2002; for the colonial data and International Monetary Fund, *International Financial Statistics Online* for the data 1994–2002.

[4] Ray writes that though some had thought that the term *hundi* was a corruption of *Hindi* or *Hindu*, that is incorrect, and that the word is instead a derivative of the Sanskrit *hundika*, which itself is derived from the root verb *hund*, meaning "to collect" (Ray 1988, 305).

[5] Jain notes that some moneylenders took deposits from their "clients" though this was on a very small scale (1929, 35). Before the Assam PBEC, an agriculturist moneylender noted that he accepted deposits (Provincial Banking Enquiry Committee [Assam] 1930, 2:158). Baker notes that in evidence before the Madras PBEC, it was reported that local moneylenders accepted deposits "as a social obligation," not because they needed them for their business (1984, 280).

[6] Tripathi notes that one difference between the *mahajans* and a caste panchayat is that the bankers were actually from several different castes. The panchayat, though, was the model for the *mahajan* (Tripathi 2004, 22 and n. 28).

[7] Jain 1929, 39–42 for Gujarat; Provincial Banking Enquiry (Bombay) 1930, 3:506. This might suggest that the guilds acted as cartels. Perhaps they did. As will be discussed in a later section, however, the rates they set were strongly influenced by the rates of the Imperial Bank of India.

[8] Bodenhorn 2000. I have borrowed the concept of comparing correlations from Bodenhorn, who attributes it to McCloskey. The idea is that we a priori identify an "integrated market," and then compare the degree of integration of the market for which we are less certain about to the degree of integration we have a priori identified as "integrated." I should also note that the Indian data are monthly, and Bodenhorn's annual. I also constructed annual correlations for the Indian data, and as one would expect, these correlations are even larger.

[9] Srinivas 1962, 70. I should note that I use the word *caste* because it is the one more familiar to the general reader. But throughout, I am referring to one's obligations to *jati* members, as was Srinivas in this quote. The caste system is loosely based on the four varnas of Brahmanas (priests), Kshatriyas (warriors and aristocracy), Vaishyas (merchants) and Shudras (the servants of the others). Castes either belonged to one of these four, or were below these in the hierarchy; these latter are the so-called untouchables, or scheduled castes. In practice, these four varnas are less important than were the relationships among and between the quite numerous subcastes, or *jatis*. While one would typically find a member of each of the four main castes in each village in India, the subcastes were specific to each region. The jatis were the true functional unit of the caste system. They were, for example, the endogamous unit. And the obligations of jati members to each other were much stronger than were the obligations of caste members more generally. (See, among others, Hutton 1963.) I should also mention that the caste system was not a monolithic institution. It operated differently in the different parts of India. But the characteristics I am interested in, i.e., one's obligation to the group and the punishment for violating group norms, are fairly universal.

[10] The authors of the Bihar and Orissa Provincial Bank Enquiry Committee report noted that many individuals, especially those who were "jealous of their credit," preferred the secrecy of dealing with an indigenous banker to exposing their transactions to a "low paid employee of a bank." Further, his clients reciprocated the discretion with which an indigenous banker treated them. The authors of the report wrote, "They will stand by him in his hour of difficulty even at some personal sacrifice and will not press for payment when he is embarrassed. *This enables him to carry on his business with lower cash balances than his unlimited liability and the nature of his deposits would warrant*" (Provincial Banking Enquiry Committee [Bihar and Orissa] 1930, 193).

[11] There are also no Chettiars on this list. In his study of Chettiars, Rudner (1994) gives some information on the life of the important Chettiar industrialist Sir Annamalai Chettiar. It seems industry remained a relatively small part of this families activities, which concentrated on banking and politics. In Khanna and Palepu's 1969 list of prominent business groups, origninally compiled by Gita Piramal, there are several groups from south India, including one I was able to identify as Chettiar, Murugappa. This family had begun investing in India only after they dismantled their holdings in Burma.

[12] The population of India, including the princely states, in 1931 was 352.8 million. There were only 238.6 million Hindus. But the caste data include anyone who identifies their caste, which would include some Muslims and Christians as well as Hindus. Note also that the "Marwaris" are not a caste. They are Baniyas who originally came from Rajasthan. The caste data are from Table XVII, India. 1933. Census of India, 1931. Part II. Imperial Tables. Delhi: Manager of Publications.

[13] Census of India, 1931, Part II, "Imperial Tables," Tables XIII and XIV.

[14] The data for this paragraph are drawn from Markovits 1985, appendix 1.

References

Akerlof, George. 1970. "'The Market for Lemons': Quality Uncertainty and the Market." *Quarterly Journal of Economics* 84:488–500.

Bagchi, Amiya. 1972. *Private Investment in India, 1900–1939*. Cambridge: Cambridge University Press.

Baker, Christopher John. 1984. *An Indian Rural Economy, 1880–1955: The Tamilnad Countryside*. Oxford: Clarendon Press.

Baumol, William J. May, 1968. "Entrepreneurship in Economic Theory." *American Economic Review* 58:64–71.

———. 1990. "Entrepreneurship: Productive, Unproductive, and Destructive." *Journal of Political Economy* 98:893–921.

Bayly, Christopher A. 1992. *Rulers, Townsmen, and Bazaars*. Oxford: Oxford University Press.

Bendor, Jonathan, and Piotr Swistak. May 2001. "The Evolution of Norms." *American Journal of Sociology* 106:1493–1545.

Bodenhorn, Howard. 2000. *A History of Banking in Antebellum America: Financial Markets and Economic Development in an Era of Nation Building.* Cambridge: Cambridge University Press.

Brimmer, Andrew F. 1955. "The Setting of Entrepreneurship in India." *Quarterly Journal of Economics* 69:553–76.

Chandavarkar, A. G. 1982. "Money and Credit." In *Cambridge Economic History of India*, ed. Dharma Kumar, 2:762–803. Cambridge: Cambridge University Press.

Chaudhary, Latika. 2006a. "Determinants of Primary Schooling in British India." Working paper, Stanford University.

———. 2006b. "Social Divisions and Public Provision: Evidence from Colonial India." Working paper, Stanford University.

Clark, Truman A. 1986. "Interest Rate Seasonals and the Federal Reserve." *Journal of Political Economy* 94:76–125.

Freitas, Kripa. 2006. "The Indian Caste System as a Means of Contract Enforcement." Working paper, Northwestern University.

Greenwood, Jeremy, and Boyan Jovanovic. 1990. "Financial Development, Growth, and the Distribution of Income." *Journal of Political Economy* 98:1076–1107.

Herdeck, Margaret, and Gita Piramal. 1985. *India's Industrialists.* Washington, DC: Three Continents Press.

Heston, Alan. 1982. "National Income." In *Cambridge Economic History of India*, ed. Dharma Kumar, 2:376–462. Cambridge: Cambridge University Press.

Hoff, Karla. 2003. "Paths of Institutional Development: A View from Economic History." *World Bank Research Observer* 18, no. 2: 205–26.

Hutton, John. 1963. *Caste in India: Its Nature, Function, and Origins.* 4th ed. Bombay: Oxford University Press.

Indian Central Banking Enquiry Committee. 1931. *Part 1. Majority Report.* Government of India Central Publication Branch.

Jain, L. C. 1929. *Indigenous Banking in India.* London: Macmillan.

Khanna, Tarun, and Krishna Palepu. 2004. "The Evolution of Concentrated Ownership in India Broad Patterns and a History of the Indian Software Industry." NBER Working Paper No. 10613, June. Cambridge, MA: National Bureau of Economic Research.

Knight, Frank H. 1921. *Risk, Uncertainty, and Profit.* Boston: Houghton.

Kolenda, Pauline. 1978. *Caste in Contemporary India: Beyond Organic Solidarity.* Menlo Park, CA: Benjamin/Cummings.

Krishnamurty, J. 1982. "The Occupational Structure." In *Cambridge Economic History of India*, ed. Dharma Kumar, 2:533–52. Cambridge: Cambridge University Press.

Lamb, Helen B. 1955. "The Indian Business Communities and the Evolution of an Industrialist Class." *Pacific Affairs* 28, no. 2: 101–16.

Lamoreaux, Naomi R. 1994. *Insider Lending: Banks, Personal Connections, and Economic Development in Industrial New England.* Cambridge: Cambridge University Press.

Markovits, Claude. 1985. *Indian Business and Nationalist Politics, 1931–39.* Cambridge: Cambridge University Press.

Mehrban, N. A. 1945. "The Work of the Labour Office." In *Some Social Services of the Government of Bombay*, ed. Clifford Manshardt, 32–54. Bombay: D. B. Taraporevala Sons.

Mobius, Markus, and Adam Szeidl. 2007. "Trust and Social Collateral." NBER Working Paper No. 13126, May. Cambridge, MA: National Bureau of Economic Research.

Morris, Morris D. 1982. "Large-Scale Industrial Development." In *Cambridge Economic History of India*, ed. Dharma Kumar, 2:553–676. Cambridge: Cambridge University Press.

———. 1992. "Indian Industry and Business in the Age of *Laissez Faire*." In *Entrepreneurship and Industry in India, 1800–1947*, ed. Rajat Kanta Ray, 187–227. Oxford: Oxford University Press.

Musgrave, Peter J. 1978. "Rural Credit and Rural Society in the United Provinces, 1860–1920." In *The Imperial Impact: Studies in the Economic History of Africa and India*, ed. Clive Dewey and A. G. Hopkins, 216–32. London: Athlone Press for the Institute of Commonwealth Studies.

Piramal, Gita. 1997. "Legends of the Maharajahs." *Business Today*, December 9.

Provincial Banking Enquiry Committee (Assam). 1930. *Report, 1929–30*. Government of India Central Publication Branch.

Provincial Banking Enquiry Committee (Bihar and Orissa). 1930. *Report of the Bihar and Orissa Provincial Banking Enquiry Committee, 1929–30*. Government of India Central Publication Branch.

Provincial Banking Enquiry Committee (Bombay). 1930. *Report*. 3 vols. Government Central Press.

Rankin, George Claus. 1946. *Background to Indian Law*. Cambridge: Cambridge University Press.

Ray, Rajat Kanta. 1979. *Industrialization in India: Growth and Conflict in the Private Corporate Sector, 1914–47*. Oxford: Oxford University Press.

———. 1988. "The Bazaar: Changing Structural Characteristics of the Indigenous Section of the Indian Economy before and after the Great Depression." *Indian Economic and Social History Review* 25, no. 3: 263–318.

———. 1992. "Introduction." In *Entrepreneurship and Industry in India, 1800–1947*, ed. Rajat Kanta Ray. Oxford: Oxford University Press.

Report of the Comptroller of the Currency. Various years. Bombay.

Rousseau, Peter L., and Richard Sylla. 2005. "Emerging Financial Markets and Early US Growth." *Explorations in Economic History* 42, no. 1: 1–26.

Roy, Tirthankar. Summer 2002. "Economic History and Modern India: Redefining the Link." *Journal of Economic Perspectives* 16, no. 3: 109–30.

Rudner, David West. 1994. *Caste and Capitalism in Colonial India: The Nattukottai Chettiars*. Berkeley and Los Angeles: University of California Press.

Srinivas, M. N. 1962. *Caste in Modern India and Other Essays*. New York: Asia Publishing House.

Srinivasan, T. N., and Suresh D. Tendulkar. 2003. *Reintegrating India with the World Economy*. Washington, DC: Institute for International Economics.

Swamy, Subramanian. 1979. "The Response to Economic Challenge: A Comparative History of China and India, 1870–1952." *Quarterly Journal of Economics* 93:25–46.

Sylla, Richard. 1976. "Forgotten Men of Money: Private Bankers in Early U.S. History." *Journal of Economic History* 36, no. 1: 173–88.

Timberg, Thomas A. 1978. *The Marwaris: From Traders to Industrialists*. New Delhi: Vikas.

Tripathi, Dwijendra. 2004. *The Oxford History of Indian Business*. Oxford: Oxford University Press.

Weber, Max. 1958. *The Religion of India: The Sociology of Hinduism and Buddhism*. Trans. and ed. Hans H. Gerth and Don Martindale. Glencoe, IL: Free Press.

Woodman, Harold D. 1968. *King Cotton and His Retainers: Financing and Marketing the Cotton Crop of the South, 1800–1925*. Lexington: University of Kentucky Press.

Chapter 16

Chinese Entrepreneurship since Its Late Imperial Period

WELLINGTON K. K. CHAN

UNTIL THE LAST DECADE, the image of China for most of us was that of a country full of people, underdeveloped, poor, and communistic. Indeed, for at least one century, from the late nineteenth to the late twentieth centuries, China's share of the world's gross product dropped precipitously, from around 8 or 9 percent to no more than 4 or 5 percent, while its population as a share of the world's total stayed fairly constantly at approximately 20 to 24 percent. Yet from at least the late sixteenth to the early nineteenth centuries, China alone accounted for between a quarter and a third of the world's gross output (Frank 1998, 108–16, 165–74, 297–320; Maddison 1995, 19–31). Late imperial China's agriculture was far more productive and commercialized than the contemporaneous West's, while its urban markets were bigger, and in many ways, just as sophisticated.

What happened was that by the early nineteenth century the Chinese agrarian economy was already heading toward a major crisis. And added to it was a second damaging development related to foreign trade and the state's relations with the outside world. The import of opium, starting in the late eighteenth century, turned the Chinese gain in silver from its exports into a deficit by the early nineteenth century. The drain on silver bullion was further exacerbated by several military defeats in wars and a treaty system with Western powers that denied China the right to conduct trade and foreign affairs on an equal basis. As for the revolution that ushered in a republican China early in the twentieth century, it did not help much; for the country was consumed by warlordism, civil war, and during the 1930s and 1940s, by Japan's invasion that destroyed its domestic trade and industry (Fairbank 1986).

The latest resurgence of China's economic performance did not come about by the Marxist-Leninist style of central planning that characterized the Chinese economy since it became a communist state in 1949. In 1978, the new party leader Deng Xiaoping announced a major economic restructuring. This has led to incredible successes, such that after thirty years of extraordinarily rapid growth, often at double digit annual growth rates, China's GNP has just overtaken all of Europe's to become the third largest economy in the world, just behind the United States and Japan. It has opened up millions of private or semiprivate enterprises, some having become so large as to reach multinational scale, such as China International Trust and Investment Corporation (CITIC), Lenovo and Haier, and others remaining mostly small to medium in size. And operating them are an equally large number of entrepreneurs.

Indeed, the Chinese economy now and in the late imperial period shares remarkable patterns of continuity despite a hiatus of almost two centuries.

Who are these entrepreneurs of the post-Mao era? How have they emerged after a period of thirty years, from 1949 to 1978, when the very notion of entrepreneurship was banned? Are these new entrepreneurs different from those in the past? Do they share similar social background and hold comparable views and values about entrepreneurship? What sort of institutional support or hindrance confronts them? What kind of social positions do they occupy? And how do their roles fit into a state and society that is led by a Communist party? Before we turn to these issues, however, we would need to examine those aspects of the Chinese traditional society and economy pertinent to the functioning of entrepreneurs and their spirit of enterprise. We need to find out what ideological and institutional impediments beset the merchant class, and how they overcame those hurdles, for example, how China's political authoritarianism affected entrepreneurial activities in times of troubles. We should also examine how merchants took advantage of certain economic conditions, such as the need of the average farm household to engage in subsidiary handicraft work on textiles to make ends meet, and social institutions, such as the common native place associations, to better their entrepreneurial spirit and social station. Finally, we shall discuss the different types of merchants, and the different kinds of business organizations such as the family firm and the partnership, formats, and environment in which they functioned as entrepreneurs.

Pertinent Features of the Economy in Late Imperial China

Since the Chinese civilization began as an agricultural society several thousand years ago, there existed social and cultural biases against merchant activities. But there was also recognition of its necessity, as one of the oldest canonical texts clearly pointed to the existence of a market and the essential role it performed.[1] The four-class social ranks, with officials first, followed by farmers, artisans, and merchants last, appeared during the Han dynasty (206 BC–AD 220). But for much of the period before and after, there was general grudging toleration of merchants because a large agricultural society that included many different regions of varying fertility for growing different crops and other produce needed commerce, if only for reasons of comparative advantage or to help balance unequal distribution. In some periods, such as during parts of the Tang (618–907), the Southern Song (1127–1279) and the Mongol (1279–1368) periods, bustling urban life and rather unregulated rural markets, as well as relative ease of long-distance travel, allowed trade, including those on the Silk Route through Central and western Asia, to blossom.

Moreover, by around AD 900, the Chinese had already made a wide range of scientific and technological discoveries that had considerable impact on the economy. They included the compass, printing, and paper, as well as chain pumps for irrigation, double-acting piston bellows for high-temperature kilns and for blast furnaces to turn cast and wrought iron into steel, canals with sophisticated locks and segmented arch bridges for easy transport of goods, driving belts and pulleys for various mechanical devices, and spindle or quilling machines for silk and other fabrics. From the tenth to the fourteenth centuries, technological improvements in the various mechanical fields continued, and even branched into early ripening seedings, better fertilizers, and new crops, to the point that they appeared to approach the threshold of some systematic experimentations. They coincided with the increasing popularity of woodblock printing, and the concurrent arrival of the Northern Song's (960–1127) scholars-officials, whose widespread postings allowed the printed manuals to disseminate the latest technological information all over the empire (Temple 1981).

The Turn to Commodity Markets

But the dominant agrarian-based ideology remained, marginalizing technological improvements, and treating mercantile interests as inherently in conflict with those of society and the state. The founding emperor of the Ming dynasty (1368–1644), having risen from the peasant class, emphatically favored an agrarian economy in which every village is self-sufficient and self-sustaining, with local commerce kept to a minimum, and regional exchanges in goods and services limited to instances of real necessity. Yet it was during the Ming period that the Chinese economy took a significant turn to developing commodity produce for the market. A number of unplanned factors conspired to bring this about. First was the state's successful revitalization of the farm, allowing some farmers to accumulate surpluses while others went into specialization of cash crops. Second was the construction of two new national capitals under the founding Hongwu emperor and his son Yongle. They also built major highways as well as the reinstallation of the Grand Canal that linked the north with the prosperous Lower Yangzi. Furthermore, the Ming continued to be concerned with the Mongols in the north and northwest, and with the Japanese piracy along the eastern seaboard. This led to the building of a network of post roads and post stations across the country to move official documents speedily (cf. Brook 1998b, 65–79; 1998a, 580–81, 670–72).

Third, the market mechanism was stimulated by the seven major maritime expeditions, each involving a hundred and more ships and thousands of marines, sent to Southeast Asia and the Indian Ocean by the Yongle emperor between 1403 and 1433. Although the goal was mostly political, they introduced the goods and trading practices from that part of the world to China. More importantly, they charted maps, added logs of new sea lanes, or improved on old ones. While this expansive policy of the Ming came to a sudden and complete halt in 1433, to be replaced by a new policy to ban all overseas trade or travel, it did not prevent some Chinese along the coast from migrating to or trading with that entire region of Southeast and South Asia, doing so clandestinely or, more accurately, with the unofficial sanction of the local authorities (Levathes 1994; Ng 1983; Tian 1956).

A fourth factor that promoted the markets was the rise of population in China between 1400 and 1600, from a base of about 75 million to probably 150 million. A long period of peace, internal migrations to the southwest, and the introduction of new crops from the New World all contributed to it. Along the Lower Yangzi River in the region south of its bank called Jiangnan, from the late fifteenth century on, the family farm became smaller while the family grew larger, and handicraft work in silk and cotton began to enter as subsidiary industries. Their increasing production, based almost exclusively on individual farming families, seems to have greatly benefited from newly invented spinning wheels that had once been less efficient quilling machines but were now fitted with driving-belts and connected to larger wheels to provide speed. And as these new producers searched for new markets for their commodities, they were helped by the expansion of silver ingots and copper cash coins from Japan, and by the massive imports of silver pesos and guilders from European traders, whose first ship reached Canton (Guangzhou) by 1519. Both the Japanese and the European traders were exchanging their bullion for Chinese goods. Tokugawa Japan put a stop to their silver outflow in the early 1600s. But the silver imports from Europe continued into the early 1800s, by which time more than two-thirds of the silver Spain took from the New World had come to China. At about 1500, the Ming government also converted what used to be various taxes in kind, usually in grains and in corvee labor, into silver and copper (Pomeranz 2000; Atwell 1977).

The monetization of the Chinese economy by the late sixteenth century allowed more and more farm-produced commodity goods to go into the market. We see that in the rapid growth of rural and urban markets. In the Jiangnan region, by the early 1500s, each of these markets was only a few miles apart, and their growth can be documented by each new edition of the local county gazetteers—these editions usually updated every twenty-five or thirty-five years. Several gazetteers from the Lower Yangzi counties included accounts of local commercial activities, as well as the presence of wholesale and retail merchants from outside the county and region (Brook 1998b, 117–19). We also see it in the spread of commercial crops, of cotton, mulberry, sugar cane, tobacco, and tea into other parts of China. Thus, by the late 1500s, the Jiangnan farmers' proximity to market appears to have allowed many of them not only to go into specialization of cash crops or of the handicraft industry as a source of subsidiary income, but also to turn them into full-fledged family enterprises (Xu and Wu 1985; Huang 1990; Brook 1998a).

These farm-produced goods then joined with other forms of commodities, including tea and Chinese medicinal herbs that traveled over long distances, to support not just foreign trade, but also a thriving domestic urban market. By the late Ming, conspicuous consumption by the urban well-to-do, stimulating the exchanges between rural and urban markets, just like going on the road for business or leisure, became a common everyday scene totally unlike what society had envisioned at the beginning of the dynasty.

New Institutions Supportive of Entrepreneurship

The Qing dynasty (1644–1912), which followed the Ming, carried on the same general policy of laissez-faire toward the merchant class. Commercial taxes were light, except for certain monopolies and such as those collected from European merchants for the imperial household by the Cohong merchants. The state remained uninterested in regulating the economy and left the merchants to govern themselves by setting up rules and guild associations. Indeed, the growing presence of these guilds based on trade categories or common places of origins in major cities by the beginning years of the Qing reflects the increasing prominence of long-distance merchants who built these associations and made use of these institutions to network and to authenticate their professional credentials with the local authorities. Indeed foundation tablets of guild halls are replete with names of merchant founders and of retired officials whom they invited to serve as guild directors (Liu 1987, 33, 44–46).

Meanwhile, the rural economy was gaining in size and maturity mainly as a result of an unrelenting pressure of population growth from around 1700, so that China's numbers doubled within the eighteenth century, rising from about 150 million to over 300 million by the early 1800s. With larger and larger populations to support, there was an intensification of land reclamation, a broader specialization of cash crops and more diversification of cropping patterns. A growing fragmentation of the landholding also meant that the average farm, managed by tenants and owner cultivators, continued to become even smaller. In the rich and highly populated Jiangnan, the largest estates rarely exceeded several hundred mou, or about one hundred acres. The only larger tracts of land were likely to be part of the newly reclaimed mountain land managed by merchant partnerships who rented out individual tracts to work gangs hired by subcontractors to open new fields.

These activities were again supported by a bigger spread of the handicraft processing sector that came almost exclusively from the same family farms whose small size often meant that they had to take on handicraft work, peddling, or porterage to keep the family above subsistence. Moreover, they were linked with a very lively network of markets, extending from periodic and standard ones in the rural areas to very large ones in urban centers, engaging in local and regional trade and, for those in specialized trades such as rice and dried seafood products, with the international markets of Southeast Asia. Finally, there were the long-distance traders who traversed the country on designated routes, and specialized in specific products such as silk, timber, and herbal medicines (Zelin 1991).

Much of the success of such a highly commercialized, yet rural-based, economy, however, came from critical support provided by regional towns and central cities. Besides those already mentioned, such as the coordination of traffic flow and of long-distance trade, or the social networking among merchants and officials through guilds and common place associations, there was increasing sophistication in commercial and financial instruments, institutions, and practices. Even though the Qing government continued its policy of not formulating new laws to regulate these new developments, officials everywhere allowed commercial contracts to be taken to court for adjudication and enforcement. This led to greater complexity in various forms of contracts, from mortgaging or leasing of land, to partnerships with various forms of profit-sharing, and to new corporate entities such as lineage trusts, thus opening up large areas for innovative financial arrangements and business ventures (Xu and Wu 1985).

These developments, when combined with the presence of an openly accessible market, allowed even those individuals who had little or no surplus capital to start small-scale, often family-run, business operations. And since the fragmentation of farms meant that the majority of households lived at or near subsistence level, such a turn to entrepreneurship in fact involved mostly this type of households, so that risk-taking of this sort became a common practice, and in this way, probably gave rise to the common term *mousheng* (lit. "seeking a living") to mean "going into business." In any event, the use of written enforceable contracts, and their application to cover a growing range of situations, meant that entrepreneurs could access greater institutional support in defining their rights and responsibilities in conducting their business.

The Absence of Technological Support and Why

Given the enormous scale—and the apparent success—of the agrarian and market economy in late imperial China as discussed above, one question that compels some answers, even if tentative, is why the promising starts made by technological improvements early on did not lead to some transformational breakthroughs similar to what happened in England in the mid-eighteenth century. We know, for example, that major advancements in the textile machine continued during the eleventh and twelfth centuries. One silk-reeling machine had a treadle that could draw a large number of filaments directly from boiled silkworm cocoons and lay them out in broad bands on a rotating reeling frame, and in this way, resulted in producing the work of several older reeling machines. By the thirteenth century, the same type of machines was adapted for spinning hemp threads and cotton yarns. But this kind of inventiveness seems to have ceased from the late fourteenth century on, so that old discoveries remained fairly static, or fell into disuse (Elvin 1973, 194–99).

Many scholars have blamed it on a new form of Neo-Confucianism that became dominant during the Ming dynasty. When it began in the Northern Song as a direct rejection of the Buddhist notions that all life and things are illusionary and transient, Neo-Confucianists celebrated the goodness and meaningfulness of life and of nature. And its greatest exponent, Zhu Xi (1130–1200), exhorted his followers to go out and intellectually conduct "the investigation of things" as a central part of one's education process. Since Confucian learning was, however, intricately tied to one's self-cultivation and moral understanding, the principles that governed human behaviors in society and those that ruled nature could become commingled. Thus, from its inception, Zhu's exhortation was challenged by others who emphasized meditation and introspection. By mid-Ming, arguments by Wang Yangming (1472–1529) that nature and all other phenomena existed only in man's consciousness had won general acceptance. By blurring the distinction between subject and object, his view suggested there was no longer a philosophical reason to investigate the external world. What mattered was subjectivity, introspection and intuition. And even though the seventeenth century saw a new philosophical movement that emphasized a return to careful evidential studies and practical statecraft, the damage to science and scientific experiments had already been done. In the end, in spite of its long and distinguished record of scientific knowledge and practical applications, China did not advance to modern science, which would have been needed if it were to break into modern technology on its own (Elvin 1973, 225–26; Ronan 1978).

But there were other causes for the absence of technological support as well. From the early sixteenth to the late nineteenth centuries, or from mid-Ming to the late-Qing periods, the Chinese population had probably more than tripled from a base of about 130 to over 400 million. This was also the period that China was, at various times, approaching involution. Certainly with farm yields already at very high levels, and with each added capital resource to improve the land also reaching severe diminishing returns, the needs of the additional population had to rely on new land reclamation. But that too was often insufficient, and in any case, approaching its limits by the end of the eighteenth century. Moreover, the market was running quite optimally; and judged by their respective yields, the tools each used, and the management of their farms, the level of technology the Chinese farmers were using in about 1750 was probably as good as their contemporaries' in western Europe. Thus, it seems quite unlikely that the Chinese economy could acquire meaningful new wealth from some increment in productivity. Indeed, it is more likely that the Chinese economy would be unable to accept the kind of technological breakthroughs that came to western Europe at this time, for how was one to justify the relatively high costs of labor-saving machines when labor in China was so cheap and so overly abundant? Furthermore, without the ability to drastically increase the availability of raw materials such as cotton, what good would those new machines powered by new sources of energy such as steam be? One recent study has shown that Europe's technological inventiveness in the eighteenth century might not have made much difference had there not been several crucial accidental factors that occurred at the same time. They included proximity of coal mines to canals, the juxtaposition of coal and steam engine, and perhaps most critically, the very large new sources of raw materials and other resources from North American colonies (Pomeranz 2000, 67–68).

Innovation Stimulated by Contact with the West

A new area of change, however, began to emerge at about the same time. Starting in 1759, the Qing state authorized a small number of licensed merchants, the Cohong merchants, to trade exclusively with a group of chartered European merchants under the Canton trade system. While scholars still debate the net pluses and minuses of Western trade and investment in China from the mid-eighteenth to the mid-twentieth centuries, there is no question that the various groups of Chinese merchants who came in touch with these foreigners acquired new skills, new forms of organizational principles, and new ideas for starting and managing a business. Western merchants have also introduced new sources of capital with the arrival of Western banks, and new rules, such as the practice of Western legal and administrative systems. They provided additional tools and fresh perspectives for the Chinese entrepreneur (Hao 1986). Others who later on went to the West to engage in business would also pick up similar ideas and practices, and many would return home to form new businesses as well (Chan 1996; 1999).

During the second half of this period, from 1842 to 1945, the Chinese economy was subject to Western exploitation under the unequal treaty system. For example the European powers imposed tariff limitations on imported goods; their merchants received preferable treatment by putting undue pressure on the weak Chinese authorities, and restricted at times their credit to Chinese borrowers. As a result, Chinese factory owners and traders often could not compete on equal terms against their Western counterparts. However, other Chinese entrepreneurs fought back successfully, often by making use of their extensive social networks, superior knowledge, and more up-to-date information on the domestic market to access and control sourcing and distribution of goods and services (Cochran 2000).

Impediments from Bureaucratic Domination

Throughout Chinese history, political control over all aspects of business activities has always been a given even though merchants had significant autonomy so long as they did not infringe upon the power of the state. In times of political strife or of weakened central authority, official domination—especially of the type emanating from the provinces—seems to have strengthened, Thus, soon after several private merchants who had worked for Western firms and were familiar with Western business practices responded to a government call to set up and manage China's first group of Western-style industries during the 1870s, regional governors-general took advantage of their supervisory role by appointing other managers who came from a bureaucratic background. Then, as these official managers gained experience, they asserted their power to take over management control by forcing out the private managers and by converting government funds, which had been on loan to serve as working capital, into privately owned shares (Chan 1978).

During the first two decades of the twentieth century, several of those who moved in and out of official posts became very successful in turning these companies into major businesses. Sheng Xuanhuai and the China Merchants' Steam Navigation Company, Yen Xinhou and the Imperial Bank of China, Zhang Jian and the Dasheng Mills, and Zhou Xuexi and the Chee Hsin Cement Company are just a few examples of officials who had left their official positions but were able to continue using their political networking to maintain their control as well as bring new business for their companies. The industries they ran all shared varying degrees of Western-influenced corporate entities such as joint-stock ownerships with limited liability and modern management style for the factory floor and the general office. But their accounting or central office, where major decisions were made, remained traditional. Zhang Jian, who had strong moral ideals that led him to run a modern corporation and to accomplish much in bringing modern amenities to the region where his factories and ancestral home were located, did not follow proper corporate procedures, such as assigning depreciations of plant facilities, while his central office mixed private and corporate uses of company funds as if he were running his own family firm.[2]

This pattern of close affiliation between officials and semiofficial merchants continued throughout the republican period (1912–49), as provincial governors and governors-general were replaced by regional warlords or their factional groupings. And even though both the Qing dynasty in its final years and the early Republic set up a modern legal framework for corporate entities and commercial practices, a majority of the larger enterprises, be they industrial, financial, or commercial, had to have some close political backing in order to survive.

This situation did not improve much during the Nanjing government period (1927–37), for the Nationalist Party leader, Chiang Kai-shek, maintained at best an ambiguous relationship with the big-business community. While there was some growth in the modern economic sectors, the government provided only limited support for market-based economic development. Many wealthy owners of enterprises were forced to buy national bonds or to give other forms of monetary contributions (Coble 1980). In any case, the Nanjing government was pushed out by Japan's invasion of China. A full-scale civil war between the Nationalists and the Communists then followed the war with Japan. In 1949, the establishment of the People's Republic brought an end not just to the civil war, but also any form of private business or market economy.

Changing Social Status of the Entrepreneur

Since, as noted above, China had a thriving market by the late imperial period, would it be likely that most or all of its merchants managing it enjoyed little or no social prestige, as was called for in theory? In practice, those rules that limited merchant activities and access were often not rigidly enforced. While conservative scholar-officials continued to equate education and learning with the acquisition of virtue, and to look down on merchants who usually had no training in the classics, society as a whole gradually took on progressively positive attitudes toward them and the roles they played.

Changing Perspectives on the Merchant Class during Song and Ming

By the Song dynasty (960–1279), when Chinese society experienced both a ratio-nalization of social and ethical principles through the rise of Neo-Confucianism as well as an upsurge of the domestic market and interregional trade, the merchant class's social status improved. Indeed, some of the Neo-Confucian scholars no lon-ger came from aristocratic or literary elite families, but were sons of merchants. The preeminent Neo-Confucian scholar, Lu Xiangshan (1139–92), came from such a background. Little wonder, then, that he was among the first to observe that all the four classes of commoners were capable of doing what is morally right, while a learned person could turn his learning to unethical use (Yu 1987, 85–86). By thus acknowledging that everyone could act morally and ethically, he was in fact arguing against the old notion that only the old ruling elite of aristocrats and scholars were worthy of respect, and proposing a new notion that all classes of people, including merchants, while they had different functions to perform, were capable of goodness and were, therefore, honorable.

It was not until some 325 years later, from the early sixteenth century on, how-ever, that one begins to find writings by scholars and merchants commenting on the blurring of social ranks between their two social classes. Perhaps the most dramatic example came from the writings of Ming's most famous Confucian official and phi-losopher, Wang Yangming (1472–1529). In an obituary dated 1525 and carved on the tombstone of Fang Ling, who had begun his career as a scholar but later fol-lowed his wife's family to become a merchant, Wang commented that the "four classes of commoners (*simin*) pursue different professions (*ye*), yet share the same commitment of the Way (*dao*)" (Yu 1987, 104–5). Wang's sentiments were echoed by another Confucian scholar-official Gui Youguang (1507–71), who wrote approv-ingly, "In ancient times the four classes of commoners had their distinct functions, but in later times the status distinctions among scholars, peasants, and merchants have become blurred" (quoted in Brook 1998b, 143). A number of factors explain this transformation, but the keys are the economic changes discussed above, espe-cially the expansion of the domestic and overseas trade and the monetization of the Chinese economy by the end of the sixteenth century.

The same century also saw the growing importance of groups of merchants from specific locales; the earliest to emerge included those from Huizhou and Shanxi, whose long-distance trade and control in monopolies such as salt, as well as their role as depositories of government funds, made them rich and important to officials. Probably even more conducive to merchant-official interaction was the growing trend of well-to-do merchant families developing occupational diversification within each family (Fu 1956, 41–44; Ho 1964, 50). Under such a strategy, many merchants' sons and nephews who showed aptitude for book learning were groomed to study and to take the state's civil examinations. Successes in such a strategy brought fur-ther success, since their business activities would thereby win official protection, while those sons who became officials would gain an economic base of support that further helped their official careers.

Such a development was also reflected in the growing presence of printing houses. At least in the Jiangnan regions, where wealth and the quota for exami-nation successes were most abundant, many rich merchant households held large private library collections, each consisting of several thousands of volumes (*juan*).

These merchant collections served not only as an index of their rising social status, but also the useful function of supporting their sons' education (Brook 1998b, 129, 134–35). By late Ming, the biographies of scholar-officials openly admitted records of merchant antecedents, or the support of commercial wealth in making their way into officialdom (Brook 1998a, 581–82).

Closing of the Gap in Social Class between Officials and Merchant Elite

This symbiotic arrangement between these two social classes became very evident throughout the Qing dynasty (1644–1912), as is demonstrated by the genealogy of forty-two well-established scholar-gentry lineages. Each of them held to a tradition of dividing scholarly and mercantile functions among their members over many generations (Chang 1962, 181–88, 280–87). The significance of such a trend did not escape the notice of many contemporary scholars. One nineteenth-century scholar, Shen Yao, observed that a member of the scholar-gentry must first gain economic independence before he can maintain personal dignity and individual character (Fu 1956, 41–44; Yu 1987, 97–98, 100–101).

Perhaps the highest compliments accorded the merchant class during the Qing were given by two emperors, the Kangxi (r. 1662–1722) and Qianlong (r. 1736–96) emperors who chose to stay at the private estates of salt merchants in Yangzhou several times during their tours to the Lower Yangzi region, and received lavish hospitality. Like other wealthy merchants elsewhere, these Yangzhou merchants had fathers or other family members who were scholar-officials, and because of their enormous wealth, they were able to live a scholar-gentry lifestyle surrounded by books, literati paintings, and other art collections. It appears that the salt tax as well as the contributions of the salt merchants became a major source of revenue during the early Qing period, when vast portions of the farmland were in crisis, and the state needed additional funding to finance the quelling of the Three Feudatories' rebellions. The personal relationships thus formed between these two emperors and the Yangzhou merchants generated a system of mutual support lasting almost to the end of the dynasty. Meanwhile, the merchants also benefited from the added opportunities to make money by serving as bankers and investment agents of the Imperial Household. In addition, through a special examination quota called "merchant registration," the state provided extra slots and venues for their sons to pass the state civil exams (Finnane 2004, 119–21).

While there is general consensus on the closing gap between officials and elite merchants by the eighteenth century, scholars do differ on the degree to which the gap remained, or if there was a blurring of social status between the two. For example, one recent study on merchant philanthropy observes that from the growing use of the term *shenshang* (lit. gentry-merchants), there was not only an increasing blurring of their social class distinction, but also a clear indicator that "merchants *as merchants*" were increasingly visible and respectable (William 1984, 98–106, 246–47; Smith 1998, 422). Other scholars do not accept the conclusion that the two classes' boundaries had blurred. One famous mid-eighteenth-century painting, which records a scene from a fashionable garden party given by one of the famous salt merchants in Yangzhou, has been used to demonstrate that the two social classes have blended because the guests depicted were known personalities of the local merchant and official elite. But a more recent study reveals that such an inference may be incorrect, for that same gathering actually shows a social grouping in which almost everyone's ancestry came from Huizhou area, and belonged to the Huizhou merchant group, whose families have since Ming times become residents of Yangzhou. The author concludes by arguing that social distinctions between the two classes remained, and is evidenced by "the salt merchants' continuing aspirations to literati status." As for the term *shenshang*, it probably meant no more than the two social categories of "gentrymen and merchants" (Finnane 2004, 253–64).

In my own study on a similar topic for the late nineteenth and early twentieth centuries, I note that the difference in social status separating ordinary merchants and officials was still great. Many officials, for example, had taken up business ownerships, but would remain anonymous by using made-up or "such-and-such house" (*mouji*) names, and assumed passive roles by hiring managers to carry out the actual operations and entrepreneurial decisions. However, the low social esteem meted out to merchants was no longer so onerous, for many unsuccessful or impoverished scholars were switching to commerce by pleading the need to make a living, or because of ill health during critical periods when taking civil service examinations. As for the rich merchants running large shops, they were unquestionably successful and influential members in their communities. They collaborated freely with officials, even though many of the same officials still publicly called the merchant profession *mo'ye* (insignificant occupation) (Chan 1977, 22–24).

Modern Industry and a New Business Class

The really significant qualitative change in the relative social status and social interchange between officials and merchants came during the second half of the nineteenth century as the nation began its serious effort to adopt modern technology as well as Western industrial organization and management as part of its "Self-Strengthening Movement." Senior officials who advocated these progressive reforms as a way to protect China from further Western encroachments quickly discovered that only Chinese compradors, that is, those Chinese merchants who had work experience with American and European merchants and had acquired knowledge of Western business practices, were willing and ready to put up their own capital and to manage these new enterprises. Because the first set of Western-style factories and steam-powered shipping established under official patronage in the early 1870s was hitched to the "Self-Strengthening" campaign, the private managers, all of whom were former compradors, took on a new elevated social status. And when they were referred to by the same old term, *shenshang*, that term had already transformed itself to mean a blended gentry-merchant.

This first group of comprador-industrialists was quickly followed by many others, including former officials and others who had not been compradors, as they, too, launched their own modern-style industry; and a new term, first coined in Japan for their modern industrialists, soon came into use to refer to them. Such a person, an industrialist, is now officially known as a *shiyejia*, connoting an aura of high respect and social distinction (Chan 1977, 25–29, 49–52, 34). Between 1903 and 1907, the central government offered awards of various official ranks, including status of nobility, to anyone who set up large-scale capital investments in modern enterprise. And in order to safeguard their investments, the government in 1904 also issued the first set of company laws ever promulgated in China for private citizens to set up joint-stock companies and partnerships of both limited and unlimited liabilities (Chan 1977, 180–83, 187–95; Kirby 1995). In place of the traditional merchant, the modern entrepreneur had indeed arrived.

The rising social status of the merchant class as well as its increasing interactions with the official class during late imperial China had a major impact on the degree to which entrepreneurs were able to function throughout this period. When their social status was far apart, and contact infrequent, it would be hard to imagine major merchant initiatives succeeding, because of uncertainty of official support or exploitation, for as pointed out above, political decisions have always taken primacy in Chinese society. But when there was a mutuality of interest, as when merchant families sent some children to school to try pass the civil service examinations, and others into business, networking across the social divide became possible and was often practiced. Then, when the state promoted modern industry and encouraged private participation, cooperation or intervention reached new heights. However, in addition to acquiring the proper social status and gaining access to the political elite, individual talents and cultural propensity toward sound entrepreneurship are just as important in the making of successful entrepreneurs. It is to these issues that we must now turn.

The Entrepreneur in Cultural and Historical Contexts

Given China's traditional disdain for the culture of the marketplace and its particularistic penchant for extending trust to those who share kinship and native place, it is hard to imagine the presence of a well-run and dynamic market managed by a body of merchants growing in size and social status during the late imperial period, as described above. The missing component is insight into the roles and actions carried out by the merchant leadership, for without it we cannot learn if there was a place for entrepreneurs who, in Joseph Schumpeter's classic formulation, could act as visionaries with the ability not only to form "new combinations," but also to do things "in a new way?" (1947, 151). In what follows, we examine how the Chinese entrepreneur is affected by personal characteristics, social networking, and the firm.

The Role of Personal Characteristics

The findings of a recent survey conducted on 400 entrepreneurs and 550 nonentrepreneurs in contemporary China show that the entrepreneurs place a high value on work and drive, accept reasonable risks, and, compared to the nonentrepreneurs, have a greater number of family members as well as childhood friends who also become entrepreneurs. They also tend to be more optimistic about the economic institutions with which they work (Djankow et al. 2006). Studies on the earlier periods tend to emphasize the poverty-stricken nature of the home environment that induced entrepreneurs to be bold, work hard, be frugal, and migrate to other parts of the country or overseas, where they could build networks based on common native origins and lineage. Moreover, they place a high premium on keeping their word, preserving trust, and practicing *shangde* (merchant virtue). These studies demonstrate high continuity in the talents and values possessed or aspired by Chinese entrepreneurs past and present, for essentially the same values are affirmed by merchants as early as fifteenth-century Shanxi merchants who became prominent salt merchants and long-distance traders in Yangzhou and elsewhere, by Cantonese migrants to California and Australia in the nineteenth century, and, even today, by the latest wave of emigrants from Fuzhou to New York and Europe (Zhang et al. 1995, 13–14; Guo 1960).

If we accept these personal characteristics as common among Chinese entrepreneurs from past to present, then we can see that they readily share that part of the Schumpeterian vision which entails the blazing of new paths. But do they share the remainder of Schumpeter's picture: innovative activity, testing of new ways of doing things, and forming new combinations? Here, the records are quite clear. From the Shanxi merchants to today's Fuzhou emigrants, Chinese entrepreneurs have carried out these efforts successfully, as will be discussed in a later section. What seems different from the Schumpeterian model is the Chinese strong emphasis on networking and on heavy reliance on family and kin. This has led to several consequences: for example, preference for the family firm, its relatively small size, and a focus on personal networking and management. In this regard, it appears that cultural values such as social norms and political principles can have important influences on how the entrepreneur acts (Berger 1991; Redding 1990). Chinese political institutions, social norms, and value systems have been quite different from those of the West, and remain so today.

The Role of Social Networking

All enterprises must involve some exchange of goods or services between individuals or corporate entities. An aspiring Chinese entrepreneur needs to establish different kinds of associations with various individuals. He usually turns to family members, kinsmen, or those who share his native place to form family firms or partnerships. He also seeks others who have other affinities to expand his circle of association, for in his view, they are the principal building blocks with which to start any business relationship. Beyond these obvious but limited choices the entrepreneur also needs to cast a wider web, seeking eligible candidates, including nonkin, for associates.

In that regard, the observations of several anthropologists are particularly helpful. One argues that personal relationships can develop just as much on another set of criteria (Freedman 1957). They involve the gradual development of *xinyong* (trustiness, reliability in pledging commitments and in fulfilling obligations) and of *ganqing* (sentiments) between individuals, within associations, and among a business community. In this way, business relationships become dynamic, placing a premium on a combination of personal connection and networking that is often referred to as *guanxi* (lit., relationships), and while *guanxi* can be among kin, it is more often extended to all nonkin, including strangers. A second anthropologist notes that Chinese social ties are often triadic, "involving a third person serving as introducer, go-between, mediator and sometimes as guarantor" (DeGlopper 1995, 31). Such a pattern in forming of associations is probably best explained by a third anthropologist, who contends that unlike Western organizations, whose members follow clearly defined rules and relationships to one another, and which have fixed boundaries, Chinese organizations are composed of overlapping networks of individuals linked by differentially categorized relationships with one another. They are also discontinuous, for they center on each individual's relationship with another, and their boundaries are flexible and indistinct (Fei 1992, 60–64, 20–21).

The Role of the Firm

These cultural characteristics have greatly influenced the size and organizational structure of Chinese enterprises throughout history. Because the relationship between owner and key employees is best when it is personal, and since kinship ties remain fundamental, most enterprises stay relatively small to median in scale. Entrepreneurs who run them are most likely sole or partial owners, working on behalf of their families or partnerships. And even in situations where raising the requisite capital is not an issue, there appears to have been a real resistance against the development of multiunit, multitiered, and gigantic corporate entities that, as so ably shown by Alfred D. Chandler Jr. (1977), characterizes the history of American business.

In recent decades, with the growth of transnational operations and professional management in a multitude of specialized fields, many Chinese corporations have also increased their size and organizational complexity, probably in order to attain sufficient economies of scale for effective competition. But none has grown to the size attained by their counterparts in Japan or South Korea. In addition, the establishment of a modern legal framework and the membership in international trading organizations, such as the World Trade Organization, has afforded Chinese firms and their owners better protection against official and state encroachments. Historically, the state's arbitrary confiscations of wealth as well as excessive extortions by officials have been a major reason why merchants tried to keep their establishments rather small and inconspicuous. However, for the large multiunit, multinational firms today, in the areas of ownership and the decision-making process at the top, the traditional structure and strategy have remained relatively unchanged.

In addition to size, questions have also been raised about the longevity of the Chinese family firm. Because the Chinese did away with primogeniture during the Qin dynasty (255–206 BC), all sons have inherited the family's assets more or less equally. In this way, during the lifetime of a father-entrepreneur, the family firm would likely grow and prosper, and all or most of the sons would be working together in the family business. After the father was gone, the married brothers would often opt to keep the family firm together. But in time, there were apt to be brothers who disagreed with one another over business strategy. When that happened, the family was likely to close the firm or partition it. This has led one sociologist to postulate the model of a four-stage life-cycle for the family firm over the course of two or three generations, dividing it into the following phases: emergent, centralized, segmented, and disintegrating (Wong 1985). This is, however, not necessarily the norm. The rise and fall of family firms probably follows more complex patterns that defy neat generalization.

My own research suggests that several successful family firms have started with teams of two brothers who complement each other in talent and personalities: one brother excelled in vision, innovation, and risk-taking, while the other provided organization, systemized the books and other operations, and nurtured the staff and networks with a wide circle of associates. During the early years of the twentieth century, two major establishments in Hong Kong and Shanghai, the Wing On Department Store and the Shenxin group of textile and flour mills, owed their successes to their two sets of founder brothers (Chan 1996). But the pattern also shows that this type of cooperation and complementarity often does not recur in future generations, for the new sets of brothers or cousins are likely to have their own dynamics in sorting out who minds the store and who leaves. This is demonstrated by the example of another company, the Kin Tye Lung Company of Hong Kong, with affiliates all over Southeast Asia, during the course of a hundred years. Here, brothers and cousins competed, so that over the generations, one branch of the extended family dominated while other branches faded out, and then, through continuing restructuring, the dominant branch weakened, while a third one that had faded regained its leadership in the company. In this way, a family firm can disintegrate and regenerate in turn (Choi 1995).

Although the family firm was the preferred form of Chinese enterprise, both the capital resources and the broad range of business available to any one family were usually quite limited. This would lead an aspiring entrepreneur to examine several partnership options, with kin or nonkin, such as lineage trusts, with neighbors or even strangers brought in by middlemen. As it turned out, a good many of them were not true partnerships. The most common type was one made up of a senior managing partner with one or a few minority partners. The latter were rentiers who collected dividends but had no voice in the business. There were also firms that were in fact solely owned family businesses, which gave out several small sets of minority shares to friends and other related parties as part of building networks among a circle of friends. Another variant had the managing partner owning a few nominal shares while the silent partner was the true principal shareholder. He remained anonymous most likely because, as a local official, he was not allowed to run a business in the area under his jurisdiction. Late-nineteenth-century novels are filled with stories of such entrepreneurial officials. Indeed, since ownership of businesses was not in the names of individuals, but in the names of families, or more frequently, in fictive entities, for example, such and such estate (*tang*) or business house (*hao, ji*), senior officials such as Li Hongzhang invested in many businesses using such a device to conceal their identity (Chan 1977, 60–62).

There were obviously many true partnerships in which several working partners combined their resources and talents to make their enterprises work. But just as brothers and cousins could disagree among themselves, partners, too, often found themselves at odds with one another, and their breakups occurred even more frequently than those of family firms. In any case, the lesson that can be drawn from this seems to be that, regardless whether they are family firms or partnerships, each firm must regenerate its spirit of entrepreneurship with each generation or each set of leadership.

In another study on the nature of the Chinese enterprise, I have laid out the following list as representative of their core features:

1. Small-scale, relatively simple organizational structure

2. Close overlap of ownership, control by individuals linked by family and kinship ties, or by partnerships among kin and family friends

3. Centralized decision-making

4. Personal and family networking that encourages opportunistic diversifications, cutting across regional and national boundaries to expand membership of affiliate firms and to reduce transaction costs in sourcing, capital acquisition, and contracts

5. A high degree of strategic adaptability (Chan 1998)

I shall next examine the various types of merchants who have performed a wide range of entrepreneurial tasks from the late imperial period to the present.

The Merchant Groups in Historical Context

In late imperial China, the merchant profession was grouped in several ways. One major divide was between those who had some form of official status and those who ran private enterprises. Among the former there were at least three main types: those officially licensed for a specific line of trade or industry, such as salt merchants; those assigned the exclusive right to conduct certain business activities, such as the Cohong merchants who alone could have relationships with the Western merchants at the port of Canton during the period from 1759 to 1834 when the Canton trade system was in operation; and finally, the generic *yahang* (brokerage or commission agency) merchants who had official sanction to serve as guild officers or, more broadly, as middlemen. They regulated the rules of trade, helped collect taxes, and officiated in various forms of exchange.[3] As for the private merchants, their groupings were far more untidy and numerous, ranging from the rural family operators who tried to make ends meet by taking their farm produce and subsidiary handicraft products to market, to brokers with innovative ways of promoting transactions, and prominent entrepreneurs who owned and managed several lines of businesses, some of which would have required them to obtain official licensing.

The intermingling of official and private businesses in the wide-ranging roles played by the same individuals was part and parcel of the growing phenomenon, discussed earlier, of the blurring of social distinction between officials and merchants. It also reflected the social reality that political consideration took precedence over economic activities other than the most basic. On the other hand, its multilateral networkings encouraged the strengthening of *guanxi* across social classes and, as we have seen, allowed official and semiofficial merchants to perform as entrepreneurs.

Another way of classifying merchant groups or bands (*shangbang*) has been by common geographical origins, such as specific provinces or urbanized regions. There have been ten major bands during the late imperial period.[4] The most influential ones included the *shangbang* from Shanxi, Huizhou, Ningbo, Fujian and Guangdong. A second group was trade or industry specific, such as those in salt, tea, medicine, piece goods, and finance. A third group was the compradors who worked both as independent merchants and as managers-cum-agents for Western firms located in the treaty ports. Then, as we move to the twentieth century, there arose a new group of modern industrialists and also owners and managers of modern-style corporations, including some who built modified models of what they had seen overseas. Finally, there are emergent types of entrepreneurs in post-Mao China, including those who are party and former party bureaucrats.

The Entrepreneur's Activities

The Shanxi Merchants: New Markets and Innovative Partnerships

With the range of Chinese merchant groupings since the early Ming dynasty having been outlined, what follows are examples taken from the various groups to show how individual merchants or groups of merchants performed their tasks as entrepreneurs. We shall begin with the Shanxi merchants; they were probably the earliest group to become wealthy and influential. And as officially licensed salt merchants, they controlled the most lucrative salt distribution markets in Ming and Qing China. Yet their semiofficial status and monopoly of an essential consumers' good did not prevent them from being entrepreneurial. They came largely from three neighboring counties in the southern part of Shanxi where the landscape was rugged and the soil poor, a location that placed them next to the major highway connecting Beijing in the east with China's strategic northwest corridor in Gansu. They claimed that their barren physical environment spurred them on to hard work, frugality, and drive, while their access to a major highway made them more open-minded so that they were able to make use of the opportunity it offered to venture out for business that involved long-distance travels. Furthermore, they were also close to the northern borders where the Ming emperor kept large garrison commands to deter Mongol military incursions. Starting in 1370, when the government began the policy of offering salt certificates to merchants in exchange for transporting grain and horses to these frontier commands, merchants from these Shanxi counties quickly responded by leaving their homes, many setting up residences and shops in Yangzhou to be close to the salt market. Others, drawn by their cultural propensity to look out for kin and neighbors, followed them to Yangzhou and soon found themselves entering into the same line of work (Zhang 1995, 1–17; Brook 1998a, 680–81).

From that beginning, and as they gained a reputation for trust (*xinyong*) and strong networking among themselves, they grew in wealth and status. They also developed innovative strategies and established a new organizational structure. Thus, they reduced the cost of their grain contributions by opening up new farmland near the garrison command posts, thus cutting out much of their transportation costs. This type of experience probably helped them later on to invest in large tracts of mountain land in northern and western China to develop into farm- or timberland, or plantations for commercial crops such as tea, edible fungus, and medicinal herbs. It required them to hire capable managers, and to bring in workers and large numbers of immigrants to serve as tenant farmers. It also involved working out difficult management problems of coordination and control (Fu 1956).

Meanwhile, their readiness to travel allowed them to trade in a wide range of goods, including foodstuffs, tea, medicine, silk, cotton, piece goods, and iron, and in the process, to establish long-distance networks throughout the country. They also went into more traditional investment by buying land and setting up pawnshops. Then when the state changed its policy in 1492 to allow salt certificates to be exchanged for cash, Shanxi merchants quickly took advantage of the growing need to transport silver bullion and branched into banking. By the Qing period, many Shanxi merchants, especially one particular group from the central region, had developed into the state's deposit banks for tax revenue as well as the private savings of senior officials (Zhang 1995, 19–26). By the early nineteenth century, they so dominated the banking industry throughout the country that several of them turned themselves into remittance banks (*piao hao*), allowing them to issue bank drafts that could be cashed at their interprovincial branches and affiliates all over the country's commercial centers (Zhang 1995, 69–80).

To manage a growing number of branches in numerous lines of trade in various distant parts of the country, the Shanxi merchants owed their success to tight management teams, sound reputation, and, above all, a system to recruit and retain large bodies of able and trusted staff. On recruitment and retention, many owners found an innovative way to form partnerships with senior employees by providing them with special partnership shares for which they did not have to put up any capital. In this way, a symbiotic relationship was formed between the original owners and the new partners, with the former retaining the long-term service and loyalty of capable assistants and the latter gaining entrée into a business that was already well established and had strong financial resources. These partners would then be assigned to branches to serve as managers, with full power to run those business units, but with periodic reviews every few years, and to share the profits—quite probably about 30 percent—with the former owners (Zhang 1995, 15–16, 46–47). Such an operational framework in profit sharing and management authority seems to have been the first of its kind and became a model for others to follow (Wu 1923, sec. 7, pp. 1–24).

Reufuxiang: Chain Stores and Merit Profit Sharing

We see fuller expressions of this practice in traditional firms in Beijing and in Shanghai down to the early part of the twentieth century. But just as in the sixteenth century, when the Shanxi merchants started the practice to meet the challenge of new market conditions, changing market conditions in the late nineteenth century forced at least one highly respected piece goods company, the Ruifuxiang of Beijing, to modify both its profit-sharing plan and its business strategy. This family firm, which had begun in the seventeenth century in a county seat in the Shandong province selling native cloth, had gone into decline during the eighteenth century, but was revived during the 1870s by a new family member, Meng Luoquan (1850–1939). By the mid-1880s, Meng, serving as both owner and chief manager, began to add new imported fabrics, cosmetics, and other foreign luxuries to its traditional lines of piece goods and expand his shops to Beijing, Shanghai, and other cities in Shandong, so that at its height in the 1920s, his chain grew to twenty-six stores in five cities with about 1,000 employees.[5]

Meanwhile, although each branch followed the traditional practice of being treated as a separate unit with its own accounting of profits or losses, Meng, with the help of an able assistant, developed his own system of coordination and centralized control by grouping the branches into clusters. Each cluster, usually including the branches in each city, would be headed by one of the branch managers doubling as district manager. The latter would be responsible for daily tours as well as joint conferences with all the other branch managers in his district. He would also coordinate inventory control and sales, and every five days make written reports to Meng. At the same time, Meng reassigned the 30 percent shares that had been set aside for each branch manager by combining them into one large pool. He then divided it into 300 bonus points in two sets: a main set of 220 to 240 points to be distributed among the managers and other senior staff, and a second set consisting of the remaining 60 to 80 points, apparently held in reserve, to be used to supplement regular staff salaries and as periodic bonuses. In this way, Meng turned the old formula of giving away 30 percent of profit to benefit just a few, into a merit system for the many. As a result Meng, the owner, maintained his personal relationships with all his senior to midlevel staff. Indeed he was known to appoint two kinds of employees: those with talent and those with particularistic ties to him and entrusted to keep checks on others.[6]

Impediments Deriving from Modern China's Political Disorder

It is no accident that despite their differences, both the Shanxi merchant group and the Ruifuxiang eventually declined and failed for much the same reason—because of events related to China's turbulent political crises. Some other factors also led to their decline; for example, the growing difficulty for both the Shanxi merchants and the aging Meng Luoquan to keep up with the more modern forms of their industry. But the critical factor was political. For the Shanxi salt merchants and those engaged in several lines of long-distance trade, the mid-nineteenth-century Taiping Rebellion that decimated much of the wealthy Jiangnan region, south China, and mid-Yangzi provinces, cost them their market. Their banking group struggled on, and indeed those who had specialized in remittance banks reached their peak years around 1900 as their bank drafts achieved their maximum usage.

But the same years also saw the rise of modern-style commercial banks and the founding of an official bank by the central government that took away almost all the tax revenue deposits that used to go to Shanxi merchants' banks. Moreover, because of their prominence and their close relationship with the government, the Shanxi merchants and bankers as a group were subject to repeated demands for large monetary contributions by the faltering Qing state and by the growing number of corrupt officials, which became an unsustainable drain on their working capital (Zhang 1995, 93–100). As for the Ruifuxiang, it owed its rapid growth into a big chain of shops not just to Meng's innovative organizational and strategic reforms, but also to personal networking with several groups of political leaders. They included marriage alliances with several Beiyang warlords. When they, too, lost power by the mid-1920s, the Mengs did not have connection with the new political leadership led by the Nationalist Party, and the company fortune began to decline (Chan 1982, 226).

We have seen how private merchants, such as Meng Luoquan, and the Shanxi merchants, both as officially licensed salt merchants and as private traders, were able to make use of their entrepreneurial skills to create and accumulate considerable wealth. At the same time, we have also seen how wealth can be lost through the state's confiscatory policy or in times of political turmoil. These two groups of merchants were not the only Chinese entrepreneurs who suffered losses in this way. Because these kinds of political crises occurred almost continually, from the Opium War that began in 1839 to the founding of the People's Republic in 1949, losses from political causes, carrying with them failed enterprises and other forms of interrupted entrepreneurial aspirations, became a constant occurrence in modern Chinese history.

Brokers as Innovators

There was one other major form of entrepreneurs in late imperial China that requires our attention. They assumed multiple names, but in reality they were all middlemen or brokers—that third party without whom *guanxi* or networking between the first two parties would not have been possible. Recent studies have noted their proliferation in urban centers beginning in the seventeenth century, especially as officers of trade and native place guilds, and in rural northern China where private brokers used innovative ways to promote business transactions (Mann 1987; Duara 1988). Even back in Ming China, those long-distance traders did not transport their goods by themselves. They would seek out special brokers, called *baoren* (lit. guarantors), and pay them a fee to arrange for the hiring of reliable boatsmen and their boats to carry their goods along specific river routes, and of master porters and their crew on overland routes. Thus, a well-respected *baoren* was someone very knowledgeable about the transportation market and the carriers, so that in exchange for his fees, he offered the prospect of safe delivery of the consigned goods, and agreed to reimburse the traders for losses due to negligence (Brook 1998b, 67). In such a case, the *baoren* combined his brokerage role with his entrepreneurial role as an insurance agent.

Probably the best-known brokers in nineteenth- and early-twentieth-century China were the compradors. They began as licensed clerks and distributors of goods working for the Cohong merchants, but with the demise of the Canton trade system, the European and American companies in the Chinese treaty ports hired them to be their resident brokers, treasurers, and guarantors of their Chinese staff. Their role as guarantors then extended to all business transactions between their foreign employers and any other Chinese merchants who conducted business with their foreign firms. Like the *baoren* of the transportation business, the compradors had to have sound knowledge of the market, good networks, and a fine business sense to succeed in these roles. And, therefore, it is not surprising that as they grew in importance alongside the growth of foreign trade, they became better known as wealthy independent merchants conducting business of their own while remaining in the service of the foreign firms. Yet even as independent merchants, they continued their brokering role in helping other Chinese investors adapt Western-style managerial practice and a factory production system to their modern-style enterprises (Hao 1986).

Most private brokers, however, performed the more ordinary task of bringing together various individuals, some with particular skills, others with capital or a combination of both, to form partnerships. Several good examples of this type are illustrated by the salt wells and natural gas extraction industry in Sichuan during the nineteenth and early twentieth centuries, when the demand for Sichuan salt suddenly doubled in the mid-nineteenth century because the Taiping Rebellion had just taken over large areas of the Yangtze valley, blocking off the Huguang region from its normal sources of supply. Since most of the Sichuan brine and gas operators were rather small, and since the time between drilling and full-scale production could extend to many years, landowners needed to select partners who had the skill to site wellheads and the gas furnaces (used in tandem to evaporate the brine into salt) properly, and the financial resources to get through the drilling. Many turned to retaining the services of special brokers called *chengshouren*, not just in putting together the initial partnerships, including the land leases that the landowners signed in exchange for a specified percentage share of the salt extracted, but also in providing several vital functions throughout the course of the project (Zelin 2005, 38–42).

It appears that these *chengshouren* brokers were highly skilled in the technical side of managing salt wells, as well as knowledgeable in finding partners who had financial sources to pay for the drilling. Some *chengshouren* were also financially well off and became capital-contributing partners as well as getting a percentage share from managing the salt yards. Then, as these projects were likely to have many dry years in between drilling and production, so that the original set of partners might run out of money to keep the drilling going, an elaborate system of new partnerships was set up to bring in successor partners to take over or, more likely, to split the percentage shares with the predecessor partners. Through the extensive networking of *chengshouren* brokers, this type of shares transfers appears to have been quite common by the late nineteenth century. And in many cases, these transfers were extended to a second set of successor partnerships. By the early twentieth century, this mix of partners who joined the partnership at different times and carried different portfolios would need management teams to address their concerns, just as those wells that reached full production would look for new leadership to direct distribution and deal with other marketing issues. At such a juncture, brokers were again called in or commissioned from among the partners to help set up a new central office with its own hired professional staff (Zelin 2005, 42–46, 53–54).

A complicated slate of partners with varying percentage sharing of profits when their salt wells finally reached full production obviously required a highly sophisticated and well-tested set of legally enforceable contracts. The partnerships in these Sichuan salt yards, by making use of the traditional contracts for land purchasing and leasing as templates, were able to incorporate their specific requirements into new contracts that accurately reflected each party's rights and obligations. Furthermore, local officials, already used to dealing with these and other commercial contracts, actively engaged in adjudicating lawsuits that involved them. The multitude of available partners for the Sichuan salt wells taking different risky profit-sharing positions, the ingenious roles of the *chengshouren* brokers operating through their extensive networking, and the existence of working official rules and regulations to settle disputes, all point to a vigorous market in which entrepreneurs could function and thrive.

Adapting Innovation from Western Models

Up to now we have followed a chronological review of the principal kinds of entrepreneurs from Ming to Qing. As the twentieth century approached and left late imperial China behind, one distinctive feature stands out among modern China's larger firms, and that is their adapting of Western business organization and practices to fit the new market conditions in China. Two notable examples are the premier modern-style department stores founded in Hong Kong in 1900 and 1907. They then moved on to Shanghai where, again, they followed one another to open even grander stores in 1917 and 1918. Ma Yingbiao and Guo Luo respectively were the founders of these two establishments, the Sincere Company and the Wing On Company. They also shared similar backgrounds: both had migrated to Sydney, Australia, as young men from Zhongshan county, just next to Macau, and both had worked in farms and Chinese groceries and export businesses until they each had earned their way to become partners in their companies. And both were impressed by Sydney's flagship department store, Anthony Hordern & Sons, and its array of goods and services all in one large building. Upon returning home, each decided on Hong Kong, a British enclave with a sizable Chinese middle class already exposed to Western goods, as the place to begin the experiment.[7]

Ma, the first to try, took several years to convince his partners that he would spend much of their initial capital just to decorate the sales floors so that he could artfully display all kinds of high-quality goods, mostly imported, all to be sold in fixed prices. Moreover, he would provide attentive service to all customers. These ideas were very different from the traditional way of selling high-end products. Quality stores sold only a small range of specialized goods, and they would display only the cheaper goods at the store front, where prices for each item could be negotiated, while the more expensive items would be stored away in private rooms and opened only to wealthy and well-established customers. Ma and Guo also added their own ideas that fitted into the needs of their clientele. For example, they each added a deposit and remittance bank department, to help customers who, like them, had relatives in Australia who would be sending home money as remittances. They also turned part of their buildings into amusement parks to attract more visitors; at the same time, they offered Western-style hotel and dining facilities to provide an aura of modernity. Each also made use of Hong Kong's British corporate laws to register as joint-stock limited liability companies—legal protection that extended to their Shanghai establishments, since they situated them inside Shanghai's International Settlement.

They planned their entry into Shanghai—by then China's most cosmopolitan and richest city—with great care. Each erected a big palatial edifice for his store on Shanghai's most fashionable street, Nanjing Road. When they opened, one after another, in 1917 and 1918, their emporiums set a new standard of modernity and opulence for all of China (Chan 1999).

Guo Luo's and Ma Yingbiao's enthusiasm in adopting Western organization and practice, however, did not extend to the boardroom or even to the senior management. Both relied on kinship and native place origins to recruit their entire staff, and ran their business dealings through their personal networks. This did not change when Guo expanded to the textile industry, to specialized manufacturing to supply the department store, and to several other branches in Guangzhou and elsewhere. In this way, not unlike the traditional family firms, these two large and modern-looking establishments continued to run their business empires by personal management. They did not build a Western-style impersonal hierarchical corporate structure.

The preference for the Chinese style of networking and personal management remained a ubiquitous feature of Chinese enterprises throughout the first half of the twentieth century. It continued to be true for the two largest Chinese industrial groups of this period: the Shenxin Cotton Mills, founded by Rong Zongjing and his brother Rong Desheng, and the China Match Company, founded by Liu Hongsheng. Rong Zongjing, the older brother, ran the cotton mills as well as flour and cloth mills under a central holding office in Shanghai, using his extensive networking with political leaders, business associates, and labor foremen to run the business empire. Like the traditional merchant, he relied heavily on particularistic ties. However, he also dared to confront the anger of family and kin when he decided to move his factories from his hometown of Wuxi, where his business had started, to Shanghai, where he could establish wider networks including such features as credit lines from Japanese bankers.

Liu Hongsheng, who graduated from the American Episcopalian St. John's University in Shanghai and for a time worked for the British-owned Kailuan Mining Corporation, started out rather differently, for he tried to use his networking skills only selectively in building up his industrial projects in shipping and in woolen mills. He was also known to favor Western-style management, and while he made use of his Ningbo-native place connections, he was strict about hiring nonkin exclusively on their merits for his staff. By 1930, he already succeeded in putting together a professional team of managers when he started to acquire other match factories and merged them with his own to create the largest match-making company in China.

But around 1935, as his thirteen sons and daughters—all having completed their college or professional studies in the United States, Britain, or Japan—started to return home, he reorganized his top management, let go his nonkin professionals, and replaced them with his own children (Cochran 2000; Chan 2006).

In reviewing how successful Chinese entrepreneurs have functioned over the last several hundred years, it is striking to note that no matter what the size or the structure of their operations, they seem to thrive best when they work via their personal relationships. Of course, their success has also relied on a well-run management. But the core emphasis on networking has not become less intense in recent times even as entrepreneurs come into contact with Western-style organization and management. Indeed, building networks and borrowing Western models have gone hand in hand as Chinese entrepreneurs have adopted and adapted certain Western features such as the organization of the factory production process, hiring of professionals for advice and for day-to-day management, and new marketing strategies to cater to the needs of a consumer-driven economy.

Entrepreneurs in Post-Mao China

Entrepreneurs with Official Connections

Among the people in business in today's China, the great divide is between those who have access to the ruling Communist party and its political support and those who do not. A merchant's access to the ruling elite is just as important now as it was in the past. Indeed, the relationship between political power and economic success is most evident in the case of the Rong family, currently headed by Larry Rong of CITIC-Pacific. Ironically, the Rongs come from a group of families the Communists dub as "national bourgeoisie" because they owned large industrial complexes during the republican period. Since most of this "national bourgeoisie" fled to Taiwan, Hong Kong, and elsewhere around 1948, only a very small number of them have survived in China. Around 1978, Deng Xiaoping asked his friend Rong Yiren, who was Larry Rong's father, to form CITIC as a financial company to invest in foreign trade and in infrastructure projects. Rong senior—son of Rong Desheng, mentioned earlier as a cofounder of republican China's largest textiles group, the Shenxin Textiles Company—made good use of Deng's backing, his family's old networks, and personal entrepreneurial skills to create the largest financial conglomerate in all of China by the time he died in 2005.[8]

His son, Larry Rong, migrated to Hong Kong from Shanghai in 1978 and joined CITIC's Hong Kong branch in 1987. Through his quick grasp of international business and finance, he rapidly acquired and merged other companies with the CITIC branch, so that by the mid-1990s he had already changed the company into an affiliate and renamed it CITIC-Pacific. It has also become a major multinational property and utility conglomerate. Over the last several years, his name consistently has appeared in *Forbes*' list as one of the three or four richest men in China.[9]

One group that has equally strong access to power is made up of the sons and daughters of prominent national party leaders, such as those of former president Jiang Zeming, former premier Li Peng, former vice president Wang Zhen, and others. However, these so-called princelings have not become major powerhouses either in terms of sheer size or of percentage control of any sector of the economy. None of them, for example, has made *Forbes*' list of the ten richest persons in China since that annual list was first compiled in 1999. Their relative lack of success most likely comes from the deficiency of their entrepreneurial skills. And now that the new party leadership under President Hu Jingtao frowns on their activities, they probably will become even less successful.

The far larger group of individuals in business with strong *guanxi* (relationships) with the political authorities consists of local and regional party leaders who have quit their party posts to go into business. More commonly, it is family members— sons, daughters, spouses, in-laws, or close relatives—who run the business and rely on their kinship connections for help when needed. Others stay on in their official posts and are able to direct collective enterprises as well as to invest in privately owned business. One example is illustrated by the party secretary of Lin Village, formerly a suburb but now incorporated into one of Xiamen's municipal districts. Party secretary Ye started a brickmaking factory as a collective enterprise of his production brigade. This was early in the 1980s and an opportune bit of timing, for his factory was starting to produce bricks just as a building boom in private houses in Xiamen was under way. In the mid-1980s, as the government encouraged privately owned enterprises, Ye, with his keen sense of what the market needed and his skillful use of networking to assure sources of supply for his materials, led a group of eight fellow villagers jointly to invest in a red brick factory of higher quality. His own investment brought him handsome returns, and so, by 1990 he had launched yet another venture after careful market study. He formed a joint partnership among his own municipal district's governing board, Xiamen city's Electricity Bureau, and a zinc-plating company from another province, to build the first electrified zinc-plating factory in his province (Huang 1998, 139–40, 192–93, 214–15).

All the while, Ye has remained party secretary, and has continued to do well, living in a big mansion that he built from his investment. The main difference between him and those officials who have quit their posts is that Ye has not become a full-time entrepreneur. He delegates to others the management of all the companies, both private and collective, that he helped to get started, even though he has kept them under his constant supervision. Those who have resigned from their posts do so to spend full time in private business. Yet they, too, have to spend considerable time networking with their former colleagues in government.

Entrepreneurs without Official Connections Initially

Those who start their business with no party or other official relationships make up the largest group of individuals. They often have very small capital put together from family savings or with the help of friends and kin. Yet many of them have overcome their initial handicaps so well that they make up most of the business leaders today, including a majority of *Forbes*' ten richest Chinese entrepreneurs.[10] We have some data on the total number of individuals who have tried, and also on those who have failed. According to one set of data, from the early 1980s to the end of 2004 there were just over three million private businesses registered with the government. More than 90 percent of these companies are family owned, and most of them are also family managed. Since the 1990s, some 150,000 new businesses have been formed each year, while at the same time, some 100,000 businesses have also closed each year. It appears that 60 percent of the registered companies are likely to go bankrupt in 5 years, and the average life-span of the contemporary Chinese business is only 2.9 years.[11]

These numbers, however, refer to those more formally organized enterprises with issued stocks and limited liability. If we include the street-corner shops, the mom-and-pop stores, and other small businesses, such as those providing auto repairs and rental service, which require just a simple license to do business, the number nationally was estimated to be almost 24 million at the end of 2005, and that number is said to be growing at 15 to 20 percent annually (Loyalka 2006). What do such numbers tell us? First, the average life-span of current Chinese firms, at 2.9 years, is unusually short, and probably reflects the relative lack of entrepreneurial skills of most of the people who start businesses. Second, while the total number of businesses may not seem large for a country of 1.3 billion people, it does represent a remarkable turnaround when we consider that no private business was allowed until about twenty-five years ago.[12]

In this regard, it appears that this latest surge into the market is similar to those in the sixteenth and the eighteenth centuries. In both the past and the present, they were and are led by families that need the additional income, and by individuals who have drive and who dare to take risks. Most of them carry out what might be called "replicative entrepreneurial activities," in the sense that they follow a common pattern, starting very small, perhaps with a stand on a busy sidewalk or a small store that sells specific items like clothing, or provide some form of service. Many would fail within a year or two, but many more would start essentially the same things over again. Others who also try would likely grow to somewhat bigger shops and move to better locations. In time they acquire a stable clientele, and many of them earn their living in this way.

Then there are others from the same group who have also started small, but through daring moves, helpful networkings, and special insight, have become national business leaders by finding new ways to market their goods or services. An example is the success story of Huang Guangyu, chairman and owner of the Gome Electric Appliance Enterprise Group, the largest in China's chain-stores industry. Huang's family was so poor that he could not afford to finish his junior high school before he and his brother left home in southern China to go to Inner Mongolia as traveling salesmen. One year of hard work rewarded them with small savings of 4,000 yuan and the friendship of a Communist party official whose help was critical for them in finding a small shop in Beijing. This was in 1986 and Huang was just seventeen years old. Probably with the support of the same official, the two brothers were able to secure a loan of 30,000 yuan, so that with a total working capital of just over US$4,000, they opened a retail business in electric appliances in 1987 (Situ 2006, 83–96).

At that time, private retail business was just starting in China, and the first group of business owners had not yet learned about good customer service or competitive pricing. Huang soon developed a strategy of providing fair service and selling his goods at an extremely low markup. This won him a high local reputation and large turnovers in sales, which, in turn, allowed him to launch several chain stores in different districts of Beijing by 1993. As his revenue grew, he used the funds to branch into the real estate market. Then during the late 1990s, as Huang noticed that there was a full range of domestically produced appliances under a few major brand names and that they performed well, he negotiated with the manufacturers to assure him the lowest pricing of their products in exchange for his stores giving their appliances prominent display, while he cut back on foreign imports. By then, his chain stores were spreading to other cities, and they quickly made the Gome company name synonymous with low price, honesty, and courteous service all over China. In 2004, he launched his first store in Hong Kong; the following year, he doubled the number of his chain stores to over 500, targeting a majority of the 600 Chinese cities with 400,000—500,000 population. His new goal was to branch out overseas, setting up stores in Southeast Asia first. When the *Forbes* list of China's richest appeared in March 2006, he and Larry Rong shared first place, each with personal assets estimated at US$1.7 billion.[13]

Roles of Officials as Patrons and Facilitators

Huang's success story is not unique, as China goes through its early phase of development into a modern industrial society. His rags-to-riches story, his uncanny ability to seize market opportunities, and his ability to accumulate enormous personal wealth are entrepreneurial elements experienced by others in other societies going through their comparable developmental stage. However, what seems peculiarly critical in today's China is that for any Chinese entrepreneur who starts out with no access to the political elite, as was Huang's case, to exceed minimal business operations requires the help of a patron with political power. This seems to be a necessary gateway so long as the sources and distribution of material supplies and of financing are controlled or greatly influenced by the Communist party or the state. In my own interviews conducted in the Pearl River Delta region during the summer and late fall of 2005 with several entrepreneurs who operate private businesses with annual receipts ranging from US$1 million to US$6 million, I found that they all had official patrons before they moved up from positions of office worker, peddler, or mom-and-pop storekeeper.

This brings us to the role played by these party officials and bureaucrats, for one way to judge their help is to see their role as facilitators. In two of the cases I interviewed, officials used their power to assure the supply of needed materials for businesses: in one case, construction materials for two successful companies, one in construction and the other in plumbing supplies; and in the other, carton paper for a carton box factory. Later, the first facilitator resigned from his official post and became a partner in the business. The second stayed on his job, and without any formal agreement, the factory entrepreneur made sure that he was sent lavish gifts on all the big festivals on the Chinese calendar.[14] Thus, both political patrons have gained personally. In the first case, his help provided a bridge for him to become an entrepreneur. In the second case, his help led to a form of corruption that is very prevalent in China today. But the gifts are more than a nonproductive, redistributive form of entrepreneurship, for while the patron has received redistributive wealth, he has also created new wealth for the entrepreneur.

To further muddy the role played by these political facilitators, consider the story of a middle-level party member and official bureaucrat, nicknamed Big Bluffer Ye by the *Washington Post* reporter John Pomfret. In 1995, as deputy chief of Nanjing's fashionable district, the Drum Tower District, Ye decided to turn the run-down main street back to its former luster. So he raised the rents charged the owners of seedy stores, fined the street peddlers, and confiscated their wares, all in an effort to chase them out. He widened the street and decorated it with lights to attract pedestrian traffic. When this attracted the peddlers to return and a few of them challenged the police, he applied a municipal code that allowed him to put them in labor camp for two years. The unusually harsh punishment made its point. In less than three years, the street has become a high-end shopping area with nice boutiques and fancy restaurants. It created well-paying jobs and a cash cow in the form of new tax revenue for the city. Ye, too, has benefited personally; he won promotion to the position of party secretary of his district, and has acquired sufficient financial resources to send his son abroad for education (Pomfret 2006, 182–85, 228–33, 258). Here is a situation where the official used his power to create new wealth for the community and for himself. In this way, both Big Bluffer Ye and the patron of the carton factory have transformed themselves from redistributive bureaucratic facilitators to productive bureaucratic entrepreneurs.

It is tempting to suggest that so long as they do not become overly greedy, there may be a place for this kind of bureaucratic entrepreneurship in China. But any system that denies accountability and the basic requirements of the rule of law cannot last long without dragging down the entire system. To lessen or even to do away with the need for bureaucratic entrepreneurs, government reforms are required to allow free market forces to determine the flow of goods and services, and of credit and finance so that officials no longer hold the administrative power to decide who gets what and when. But the problem probably goes deeper, since new forms of official corruption and of collusion continue to proliferate even as credit and resource allocations have opened up greatly, while corporate governance and state regulations are far more sophisticated in today's China.

Aside from an increased need for official patronage, particularly by the small and medium-sized business operations, today's entrepreneurs in China do not seem to be different from those in the past. Their social backgrounds and personalities, the rationale for going into business, the values they hold, and their focus on social networking, are all quite similar. Even in social status they have regained the respectable position they finally attained during the republican period. Since 2002, when the Communist party ratified former party secretary Jiang Zeming's "Three Represents" formula, which accepts capitalists as part of the advanced ranks of the people, successful business leaders have been admitted to membership in the party.

Conclusion

Chinese entrepreneurship has always been an inherent part of Chinese history and tradition, despite the fact that its large number of practitioners had to endure long historical periods of ideological disesteem, even social marginalization. During the late imperial period, they gradually gained proper recognition and acceptance. The position of entrepreneurship, however, remains fragile, for politics remains as central as it has ever been. In China today, having no access to party officials remains a critical institutional impediment to any successful entrepreneurial operation. As for the traditional times, although the state did not intrude on merchants' day-to-day business, no large-scale enterprise was allowed without some form of state control or participation. That has led to a tradition of keeping enterprises at a modest size, so that they are less likely to attract unwanted official attention, and can remain flexible and nimble. The import of Western legal structure together with China's participation in international agreements has lessened the fear of arbitrary action by the state, but those fears still persist today.

In terms of characteristics, the Chinese entrepreneur does not deviate much from what Schumpeter has defined for the Western entrepreneur—those qualities of boldness and vision and of innovation and new combinations. Thus, when the Shanxi merchants devised new ways of profit sharing with their managers, that practice spread, then was standardized and later refined by others like the Ruifuxiang of Beijing. Brokers, too, such as the specialized ones involved in the salt yards in Sichuan, showed tremendous ingenuity and extensive market networks in structuring a great variety of partnerships customized for that industry's specific needs. No institution, political or religious, has tried to block these activities. Instead, they have been supported by officials and merchant guilds through their adjudication of court and arbitration cases.

What seems to set the Chinese entrepreneurs apart from Schumpeter's is their focus on building networks. Because of the Chinese concepts of association and of one's relationship with the group, Chinese management styles and setups remain rather different from those of the West. But that does not seem to have affected the Chinese entrepreneurs' ability to adapt certain parts of Western models and still use their own business structure and strategy effectively.

There is little doubt that entrepreneurship has been the most productive means of accumulating wealth. Incomes generated by officials might have surpassed those earned and saved by entrepreneurs at various times in Chinese history. But a good deal of what the officials acquired in the process must be interpreted as distributive entrepreneurship; and that was mostly taken from entrepreneurs illegally or by sheer administrative intervention. However, we have also seen that officials' role as facilitators for individual entrepreneurs and communities can generate new wealth, so that the net result is rather more clouded. Some officials take advantage of their established networks to go into business themselves, clandestinely, doing it part time or by quitting their official posts. This seems to have been quite common since the late imperial period. It is even more so today, probably because the rapidly expanding economy creates more opportunities to make use of relationships for substantial gains. Bureaucratic entrepreneurship that became quite important in late Qing and republican China did more harm than good for productive entrepreneurs. It is likely to produce similar results under the present regime.

In sum, Chinese entrepreneurship and entrepreneurs continue to thrive in China. If their past record is a guide, they will overcome future challenges that come their way.

Notes

I wish to thank my colleague Lynn Dumenil for her helpful comments during my writing of this chapter.

[1] *The I-Ching or Book of Changes* (1967).
[2] For Sheng Xuanhuai, see Feuerwerker 1958; for Yen Xinhou and Zhou Xuexi, see Chan 1977, 51–52, 218–19, 110–18; for Zhang Jian, see Koll 2003.
[3] On salt merchants, see Finnane 2004; on the Cohong merchants, see Wakeman 1978; on the *yahang* merchants, see Mann 1987.
[4] Cf. the ten-volume work (one on each of the ten *shangbang*) Zhang et al. 1995.
[5] *Beijing Ruifuxiang* 1959; *Jiu Shanghai Xiedaxiang choubu shangdian di "diangui"* 1966.
[6] *Beijing Ruifuxiang* 1959; Chan 1982.

[7] Chan 1981; *The Sincere Company, Limited. Hong Kong: Diamond Jubilee 1900–1975* (n.d.) (Hong Kong: n.p.).

[8] "Rong Yiren: An Obituary," *The Times* (London), November 1, 2005, 61.

[9] Xiao 1999, 272–81; for his listing in *Forbes'* list, see *Singtao Daily* (Los Angeles), October 10, 2006, B1.

[10] "*Forbes'* List of China's Richest Entrepreneurs," *Singtao Daily* (Los Angeles), April 29, 2005, A1.

[11] "Report on the Development of China's Private Enterprises, 2005" conducted and published by All-China Federation of Industry and Commerce, cited by the *Financial Express* (India), July 5, 2005.

[12] A total of 24 million business enterprises is small for a population of 1.3 billion, for it means that only about 3 percent of the adult Chinese population sets up business of its own. If we use as a guide the recent annual reports compiled by thirty-four country-based research reports sponsorship by the Swiss- and American-based Global Entrepreneurship Monitor (GEM), the 3 percent figure would place China among the least active countries in entrepreneurial participation. However, the same report also shows that Shenzhen, the metropolis next to Hong Kong, has 11.4 percent of its adult population in business, making it the tenth highest among thirty-four economies. See *Research Studies of Hong Kong and Shenzhen for the Global Entrepreneurial Monitor* (2004) (Hong Kong: Centre for Entrepreneurship, Chinese University of Hong Kong).

[13] See "Forbes' List of Richest Entrepreneurs in China," *Singtao Daily* (Los Angeles), March 10, 2006, A1. Early in 2009, Huang was stripped off his chairmanship and jailed by the government for malfeasance and bribery. Huang's clash with the law is not an isolated incident among those whose names have appeared on the *Forbes* list. Many of them have also been charged and convicted, and their wealth confiscated. See "Original sin: The stigma of wealth in China," *The Economist* (New York), Sept. 5–11, 2009, 70.

[14] This paragraph relies on the author's interviews with the two entrepreneurs in Dongguan, China, on November 3, 2005.

References

Atwell, William S. 1977. "Notes on Silver, Foreign Trade and the late Ming Economy." *Ch'ing-shih wen-t'i* 3, no. 2.

Berger, Brigitte, ed. 1991. *The Culture of Entrepreneurship*. San Francisco: Institute for Contemporary Studies Press.

Brook, Timothy. 1998a. "Communications and Commerce." In *The Cambridge History of China*, vol. 8, part 2, ed. Dennis Twitchett and Frederick W. Mote, 579–707. New York: Cambridge University Press.

———. 1998b. *The Confusions of Pleasure: Commerce and Culture in Ming China*. Berkeley and Los Angeles: University of California Press.

Chan, Kai Yiu. 2006. *Business Expansion and Structural Change in Pre-War China: Liu Hongsheng and His Enterprises, 1920–1937*. Hong Kong: Hong Kong University Press.

Chan, Wellington K. K. 1977. *Merchants, Mandarins, and Modern Enterprise in Late Ch'ing China*. Cambridge: East Asian Research Center, Harvard University, distributed by Harvard University Press.

———. 1978. "Government, Merchants and Industry to 1911." In *The Cambridge History of China*, vol. 11, part 2, ed. John K Fairbank and Kwang-Ching Liu, 416–62. Cambridge: Cambridge University Press.

———. 1982. "The Organizational Structure of the Traditional Chinese Firm and Its Modern Reform." *Business History Review* 56:218–35.

———. 1996. "Personal Styles, Cultural Values and Management: The Sincere and Wing On Companies in Shanghai and Hong Kong, 1900–1941." *Business History Review* 70: 141–66.

———. 1998. "Tradition and Change in the Chinese Business Enterprise: The Family Firm Past and Present." *Chinese Studies in History* 31, nos. 3–4: 127–44.

———. 1999. "Selling Goods and Promoting a New Commercial Culture: The Four Premier Department Stores on Nanjing Road, 1917–1937." In *Inventing Nanjing Road: Commercial*

Culture in Shanghai, 1900–1945, ed. Sherman Cochran, 19–36. Ithaca, NY: East Asia Program, Cornell University.

Chandler, Alfred D., Jr. 1977. *The Visible Hand: The Managerial Revolution in American Business*. Cambridge: Belknap Press of Harvard University Press.

Chang, Chung-li. 1962. *The Income of the Chinese Gentry*. Seattle: University of Washington Press.

Choi, Chi-cheung. 1995. "Competition among Brothers: The Kin Tye Lung Company and Its Associate Companies." In *Chinese Business Enterprise in Asia*, ed. Rajeswary A. Brown, 98–114. London: Routledge.

Coble, Parks M., Jr. 1980. *The Shanghai Capitalists and the Nationalist Government, 1927–1937*. Cambridge: Harvard University Press.

Cochran, Sherman. 2000. *Encountering Chinese Networks: Western, Japanese, and Chinese Corporations in China, 1880–1937*. Berkeley and Los Angeles: University of California Press.

DeGlopper, Donald R. 1995. *Lukang: Commerce and Community in a Chinese City*. Albany: State University of New York Press.

Djankow, Simeon, Qian Yingyi, Gérard Roland, and Ekaterina Zhuravskaya. 2006. "Entrepreneurship in Development: First Results from China and Russia." Paper presented to the Annual Meeting of the Allied Social Science Associations, Boston, January 6–8.

Duara, Prasenjit. 1988. *Culture, Power, and the State: Rural North China, 1900–1942*. Stanford: Stanford University Press.

Elvin, Mark. 1973. *The Pattern of the Chinese Past: A Social and Economic Interpretation*. Stanford: Stanford University Press.

Fairbank, John K. 1986. *The Great Chinese Revolution, 1800–1985*. New York: Harper and Row.

Fei, Xiaotong. 1992. *From the Soil: The Foundations of Chinese Society*. Berkeley and Los Angeles: University of California Press.

Feuerwerker, Albert. 1958. *China's Early Industrialization: Sheng Hsuan-huai (1844–1916) and Mandarin Enterprise*. Cambridge: Harvard University Press.

Finnane, Antonia. 2004. *Speaking of Yangzhou: A Chinese City, 1550–1850*. Cambridge: Harvard University Asia Center, distributed by Harvard University Press.

Frank, Andre Gunder. 1998. RΕΟRΙΕΝΤ: *Global Economy in the Asian Age*. Berkeley and Los Angeles: University of California Press.

Freedman, Maurice. 1957. *Chinese Family and Marriage in Singapore*. London: Her Majesty's Stationery Office.

Fu, Yiling. 1956. *Ming Qing shidai shangren ji shangye ziben* (Merchants and commercial capital in the Ming and Qing periods). Beijing: Renmin chuban she.

Guo, Chuan. 1960. *Yong'an jingshen zhi faren ji qi changcheng shilue* (A brief history of the origin and development of the Wing On spirit). N.p.

Hao, Yen-ping. 1986. *The Commercial Revolution in Nineteenth-Century China: The Rise of Sino-Western Mercantile Capitalism*. Berkeley and Los Angeles: University of California Press.

Ho, Ping-ti. 1964. *The Ladder of Success in Imperial China: Aspects of Social Mobility, 1368–1911*. New York: John Wiley and Sons.

Huang, Philip C. C. 1990. *The Peasant Economy and Rural Development in the Yangzi Delta, 1350–1988*. Stanford: Stanford University Press.

Huang, Shu-min. 1998. *The Spiral Road: Change in a Chinese Village through the Eyes of a Communist Party Leader*. 2nd ed. Boulder, CO: Westview Press.

The I-Ching, or Book of Changes. 1967. Trans. Cary F. Baynes. 3rd ed. Princeton: Princeton University Press.

Jiu Shanghai Xiedaxiang choubu shangdian di "diangui" (The "Shop Regulations" of the Xiedaxiang Clothing Shop in old Shanghai). 1966. Shanghai: n.p.

Kirby, William C. 1995. "China Unincorporated: Company Law and Business Enterprises in Twentieth-Century China." *Journal of Asian Studies* 54, no. 1: 43–63.

Koll, Elisabeth. 2003. *From Cotton Mill to Business Empire: The Emergence of Regional Enterprises in Modern China*. Cambridge: Harvard University Asia Center, distributed by Harvard University Press.

Levathes, Louise. 1994. *When China Ruled the Seas*. Oxford: Oxford University Press.

Liu, Kwang-ching. 1987. "Jianshi zhidu yi shangren" (Institutions of the recent period related to the merchants). In Yu Ying-shih, *Zhongguo jianshi zongjiao lunli yi shangren jingshen* (Religions, ethics, and the spirit of the merchants in late imperial China). Taipei: Lianjing chuban.

Loyalka, Michelle D. 2006. "A Chinese Welcome for Entrepreneurs." *Business Week*, January 6.

Maddison, Angus. 1995. *Monitoring the World Economy, 1820–1992*. Paris: Development Centre, Organisation for Economic Co-operation and Development.

Mann, Susan. 1987. *Local Merchants in the Chinese Bureaucracy, 1750–1950*. Stanford: Stanford University Press.

National Bureau of Statistics of China, comp. 2004. *China Statistical Yearbook, 2003*. Beijing: Zhongguo tongji chuban she.

Ng, Chin-keong. 1983. *Trade and Society: The Amoy Network on the China Coast, 1683–1735*. Singapore: Singapore University Press.

"Original sin: The stigma of wealth in China." 2009. *The Economist*, September 5–11, 70.

Pomeranz, Kenneth. 2000. *The Great Divergence: China, Europe, and the Making of the Modern World Economy*. Princeton: Princeton University Press.

Pomfret, John. 2006. Chinese Lessons: Five Classmates and the Story of the New China. New York: Henry Holt.

Redding, S. Gordon. 1990. *The Spirit of Chinese Capitalism*. New York: Walter de Gruyter.

Research Studies of Hong Kong and Shenzhen for the Global Entrepreneurial Monitor. 2004. Hong Kong: Centre for Entrepreneurship, Chinese University of Hong Kong.

Ronan, Colin A. 1978. *The Shorter Science and Civilisation in China: An Abridgement of Joseph Needham's Original Text*. Vol. 1. Cambridge: Cambridge University Press.

"Rong Yiren: An Obituary." 2005. *The Times* (London), November 1.

Rowe, William T. 1984. *Hankow: Commerce and Society in a Chinese City, 1796–1889*. Stanford: Stanford University Press.

Ruifuxiang, Beijing (The Ruifuxiang of Beijing). 1959. Beijing: Zhonghua shuju.

Schumpeter, Joseph. 1947. "The Creative Response in Economic History." *Journal of Economic History* 7, no. 2: 149–59.

Shanghai Yong'an gonsi de shansheng fazhan wo gaizao (The birth, development, and reconstruction of the Wing On Company of Shanghai). 1981. Shanghai: Renmin chuban she.

The Sincere Company, Limited, Hong Kong: Diamond Jubilee 1900–1975. N.d. Hong Kong: n.p.

Situ, Wei. 2006. *Zhongguo tiaoji fuhao juanqi* (An unofficial account of China's superrich). Vol. 4. Hong Kong: Xiafei'er chuban youxian gongsi.

Smith, Joanna Handlin. 1998. "Social Hierarchy and Merchant Philanthropy as Perceived in Several Late-Ming and Early-Qing Texts." *Journal of Economic and Social History of the Orient* 41:417–51.

Temple, Robert. 1981. *The Genius of China: 3,000 Years of Science, Discovery, and Invention*. New York: Simon and Schuster.

Tian, Rukang. 1956. "Shiqi shiji zhi shijiu shiji zhongye Zhongguo fanchuan zai dongnanya zhou fanyun wo shangye de diwei" (The commercial importance of the junk trade in Southeast Asia from the seventeenth to the mid-nineteenth century). *Lishi yanjiu* 8.

Wakeman, Frederic, Jr. 1978. "The Canton Trade and the Opium War." In *The Cambridge History of China*, vol. 10, part 1, ed. John K. Fairbank, 163–212. Cambridge: Cambridge University Press.

Wong, Siulun. 1985. "The Chinese Family Firm: A Model." *British Journal of Sociology* 36, no. 1: 58–72.

Wu, Guizhang. 1923. *Zhongguo shangye xiguan daquan* (A complete handbook on Chinese commercial customs). Shanghai: Shangwu chuban she.

Xiao, Yanden. 1999. *Zhongguo meiyou qiyejia* (China does not have entrepreneurs). Chengdu, China: Jiangyun Industrial Culture Development Co.

Xu, Dixin, and Chengming Wu. 1985. *Zhongguo zibenzhuyi de mengya* (The sprout of capitalism in China. Vol. 1. Beijing: Renmin chuban she.

Yu, Ying-shih. 1987. *Zhongguo jianshi zongjiao lunli yi shangren jingshen* (Religions, ethics, and the spirit of the merchants in late imperial China). Taipei: Lianjing chuban.

Zelin, Madeleine. 1991. "The Structure of the Chinese Economy during the Qing Period: Some Thoughts on the 150th Anniversary of the Opium War." In *Perspectives on Modern China: Four Anniversaries*, ed. Kenneth Lieberthal, Joyce Kallgren, Roderick MacFarquhar, and Frederic Wakeman Jr., 31–67. Armonk, NY: M. E. Sharpe.

———. 2005. *The Merchants of Zigong: Industrial Entrepreneurship in Early Modern China*. New York: Columbia University Press.

Zhang, Haiying. 1995. *Shanxi shangbang* (The merchant group of Shanxi). Hong Kong: Zhonghua shuju.

Zhang, Haiying, Zhengming Zhang, Jianhui Huang, and Qunping Gao. 1995. *Zhongguo shida shangbang* (The ten merchant groups of China). 10 vols. Hong Kong: Zhonghua shujia.

Chapter 17

Entrepreneurship in Pre–World War II Japan: The Role and Logic of the Zaibatsu

SEIICHIRO YONEKURA AND HIROSHI SHIMIZU

THIS CHAPTER IS THE STORY of the path followed by an economy that came to be characterized, if not dominated, by a relatively small number of very large firms, the zaibatsu. Part of the story is the burst of growth that followed a long period of isolation, in a country suddenly opened up by the military threat of an invading force—the 1853 incursion of Admiral Perry and his fleet. This was followed by a thorough reconfiguration of the structure of government as a critical step toward elimination of the country's technological lag. The account here will describe the relatively modest entrepreneurial origins that can underlie even formation of such giant enterprises.

The uniqueness of this development process offers a number of significant insights. One illustration is a program undertaken during the Meiji Restoration period, showing how restructuring of the prevailing institutions can affect entrepreneurial activity. There, reformers chose to commute peasant rice payments to the samurai into government bonds and tax the peasants in money to pay the interest on the bonds. The samurai were encouraged to become bankers and investors (with the Tokyo and Osaka Stock Exchanges founded in 1878, almost at the same time as the issue of the bonds). Thereby, the samurai were led to eschew combat and to become entrepreneurs and capitalists.

The growth of the zaibatsu also helps to explain the reputed comparative advantage of Japan in innovation that is incremental rather that radical. For that is also a characteristic of large innovative enterprises in other countries. Their innovation activity tends to be conservative and characterized by effort to minimize risk, presumably because of their relatively complex managerial organizations and the responsibility that is imposed by substantial asset size.

In the history of the zaibatsu, entrepreneurs were the key drivers of development. Under the enormous institutional changes and social upheavals, they developed organizational forms of innovation that enabled young engineers and college graduates to be recruited and assigned to positions of power. Their innovative activity tends to be characterized by efforts to employ new knowledge in their businesses and to make multiple use of scarce resources.

In recent years, *entrepreneurship* has become a popular and seductive term even in Japan. The word, however, tends to be bandied about somewhat randomly. Some people use it in reference to individuals who set up businesses, others to describe an individual who introduces new technologies or business models. In this chapter, following the pioneering works of Joseph A. Schumpeter, we define entrepreneurship as the ability to carry out innovation that constructively destroys the status-quo and leads to new economic development (Schumpeter 1934). In short, the capacity to "innovate," we believe, is a core concept of entrepreneurship.

While Schumpeter implied that innovation is not necessarily limited to technological innovation, many previous studies have gravitated toward this aspect of the subject. As Alfred D. Chandler Jr. showed, however, organizational innovation has made an important contribution to economic growth throughout history (1962, 283–323). Chandler asserted that entrepreneurs played an important role in carrying out organizational innovation in the modern business world, thereby laying the foundations for the establishment of large modern enterprises. This assertion has even greater validity for developing countries. Entrepreneurship is deeply embedded in the historical context. Entrepreneurs in different social contexts face different challenges and must utilize different resources. Those in less advanced countries, for example, are likely to access cheap labor more readily than their counterparts in the developed world. However, of necessity, such entrepreneurs are required to develop their businesses in an environment where resources are limited and social and human capitals are generally underdeveloped.

As the latecomer to the modern capitalist world, the need to introduce, rather than to develop, advanced technology and institutional structures, was particularly pressing for Japan, and was precipitated by the desire to catch up with the advanced nations of the West. In this sense, the core competence of entrepreneurship in prewar Japan involved the accumulation of "organizational capability" to facilitate modernization.

Beginning in the late eighteenth century, the Industrial Revolution brought fundamental change to social, political, and economic structures in continental Europe, Britain, and the United States of America. The economic system evolved from feudalism through mercantilism to industrial capitalism. This process was not automatic or smooth; instead, it was a rough and uneven evolution that transpired over the course of a century.

By contrast, social, political, and economic change hit Japan with the force of a hurricane. Japan moved from feudalism to capitalism in a very short space of time. It had insufficient resources for industrialization, however, and its political foundations were still fragile. Moreover, Japan's 200-year-old closed-door policy meant that scientific and technical knowledge lagged far behind that of other nations, and the international community of the day was not particularly receptive to latecomers either. Imperialistic attitudes prevailed and the countries of the West were greedy and possessive.[1]

In this chapter, we define entrepreneurship as the ability to bring about innovation and discuss the development of Japan's vast business conglomerates, the zaibatsu, an event that occurred during the 1870s when the feudal system had only recently been dissolved and the infrastructure vital to economic growth had yet to be developed. It focuses on the methods employed by Japan's entrepreneurs to achieve organizational breakthroughs and develop big business conglomerates that were then deployed in the development of important institutions in the fields of international trade, shipbuilding, security markets, modern banking, and railways, thereby promoting economic growth in prewar Japan.

The Effectiveness of Entrepreneurship in Accumulating Wealth: The Role and Importance of the Zaibatsu

European trade relationships with Asia have a history that dates back to the Age of Discovery in the early fifteenth century. Direct contact, however, remained peripheral. During the 250 years of the Tokugawa era when Japan's ports were closed to all but a few Dutch and Chinese traders, the economy developed along highly feudalistic lines and, although capitalism had gained some hold, Japan's knowledge of science and technology lagged far behind that of the West.

The First Opium War of 1839 to 1842 marked the beginning of European imperial hegemony in Asia. The incursions of foreign imperialism reached Tokugawa Japan in the 1850s when, on July 8, 1853, Commodore Perry of the U.S. Navy sailed a squadron of black-hulled warships into the harbor at Edo (now Tokyo). Perry brought with him a letter from U.S. president Millard Fillmore addressed to the emperor, demanding the opening of ports and various other concessions from Japan. The U.S. show of force led to Japan's acceptance of the Convention of Kanagawa on March 31, 1854. These events shocked the Japanese authorities into an awareness that the country was technologically backward as compared to the West and that it needed to industrialize if it was to retain its autonomy. This realization culminated in the Meiji Restoration of 1868, the chain of events that led to administrative modernization of the government and to rapid economic development thereafter. The advent of industrialization in Europe was accompanied by dramatic increases in the demand for Asian raw materials, and the Long Depression of the 1870s saw industrialized Europe turning increasingly to Asia in its search for new markets for European industrial products. The depression also affected the way in which Western powers approached this new market, moving from trade and indirect rule to unequal trade and formal colonial control.

The Meiji Restoration was the catalyst for industrializing Japan's feudal economy and triggered the nation's rise as a military power under the slogan "Rich Nation, Strong Army."[2] The Meiji government rushed headlong into the development of national industry in a bid to catch up with the West and safeguard its political autonomy. However, Japan lacked infrastructure, capital, human resources, science, and technology, as well as political stability, all of which were critical to industrialization. Angus Maddison has estimated that Japan's per capita GDP in 1900 was US$677, which was only about one-fourth of that of the UK (2,798) or the United States (2,911) and on a par with Thailand and Mexico (Maddison 1995, 23–24).

While industrialization was a national priority, Japan first needed to tackle its serious resource shortages, a hurdle that needs to be surmounted by any country seeking to develop modern industries. The breakthrough for Japan came in the form of conglomerates, or zaibatsu, an organizational innovation that had the dual benefit of concentrating managerial resources and allowing them to be put to multiple uses.

The policies carried out by the Allied Powers after World War II demonstrate that the zaibatsu had become increasingly active in the national economy. Japan's military resources were mobilized at the outbreak of the war with China in July 1937 and remained in action until Japan was defeated in August 1945. On August 15 of that year, the Japanese government conceded unconditional surrender to the Allied powers.

The Supreme Commander of the Allied Powers (SCAP) then set about reweaving the social, economic, and political fabric of Japan. SCAP implemented various political and social policies, imposing constitutional democracy and introducing land and labor reforms as well as women's rights. SCAP's primary concerns were demilitarization and democratization. Economists working for SCAP produced an analysis of the Japanese economy and argued for fundamental democratization of all economic institutions as a precursor to future peace and normalcy.

In order to achieve the goals of democratization and demilitarization, SCAP began the process of breaking up the zaibatsu, which were regarded as monopolistic and a seedbed for social injustice and fascism,[3] by freezing the assets of the four big conglomerates—Mitsubishi, Mitsui, Sumitomo, and Yasuda. In 1946, the General Headquarters (GHQ) of SCAP established the Holding Company Liquidation Commission (HCLC). GHQ transferred the stock of the zaibatsu to HCLC, which in turn sold it off to the public in increments. Then in 1947, GHQ set up an antitrust law that was designed to prevent the reconstruction of the zaibatsu. That year also witnessed a purge of political establishments and business leaders, who were examined by GHQ and the Japanese government and removed from office if found to have actively supported war, nationalism, or fascism. These policies imply that the zaibatsu played a significant role in both the national economy and militarism in the run-up to, and during, the war.

The term *zaibatsu*, which literally means "financial cliques," refers to the widely diversified big-business conglomerates that gained significant concentration during the Meiji era. Morikawa defined zaibatsu as "a group of diversified businesses owned exclusively by a single or an extended family (1992, xvii). Table 17.1 presents the zaibatsu of the Meiji era.

Using data relating to the paid-in capital of joint-stock companies in Japan, Morikawa showed that in 1928 the amounts contributed by the subsidiaries of the seven leading zaibatsu, Mitsui, Mitsubishi, Yasuda, Asano, Sumitomo, Okura, and Furukawa, accounted for 16.5 percent of the aggregate figure for all joint-stock companies (1992, xvii). Until SCAP stepped in with its 1947 dissolution policy, these zaibatsu together with newly formed zaibatsu such as Nissan and Nitchitsu had spent years steadily increasing their presence in the national economy. Table 17.2 shows the extent to which these zaibatsu businesses dominated the key industries that fueled Japan's rapid industrialization, contrasting the paid-in capital of fourteen zaibatsu subsidiaries with that of all commercial entities in Japan in 1947.

The prevailing wisdom on zaibatsu, a position that frequently reflects the predominantly Western view of these conglomerates as feudal monopolistic family businesses, can be summarized in the following terms:

1. They established and maintained close relations with government officials and exploited these political and personal connections in conducting business.

2. They further diversified their business activities by capitalizing on their monopolistic financial and political power.

TABLE 17.1
Zaibatsu of the Meiji Era

	Founder	First business	Capital[a]
Mitsui	Mitsui Hachirobei Takatoshi	Draper's shop in 1673	849,136
Mitsubishi	Iwasaki Yataro	Shipping and trading in 1873	592,943
Yasuda	Yasuda Zenjiro	Exchange house in 1863	248,647
Sumitomo	Sumitomo Masatomo and Soga Riemon	Copper smelting and processing in 1590	187,513
Asano	Asano Soichiro	Coke trade in 1876	167,488
Okura	Okura Kihachiro	Military supply in 1868	149,206
Kawasaki	Kawasaki Hachiemon	Bank in 1876	95,885
Furukawa	Furukawa Ichibei	Mining in 1877	71,478

Sources: Morikawa 1992; Takahashi 1930.
[a] Total amount of capital contributed by group firms in 1928 (in thousands of yen).

TABLE 17.2
Paid-In Capital, Fourteen Zaibatsu Subsidiaries

	Capital (% of Japanese total)	Total in Japan
Manufacturing and mining	10,440,200 (47.2%)	22,089,231
Heavy industries	8,020,289 (55.6%)	14,430,619
Metal	1,655,406 (43.2%)	3,829,681
Machinery	4,302,777 (56.4%)	7,632,409
Chemical	1,961,402 (66.1%)	2,968,529

Source: Yamazaki 1979, 252.
Note: The fourteen zaibatsu are Mitsui, Mitsubishi, Sumitomo, Furukawa, Asano, Okura, Yasuda, Nomura, Nissan, Nitchitsu, Nisso, Mori, Riken, and Nakajima.

3. This practice went on to become a seedbed of corruption and social injustice that led to social unrest and class disputes.

Strictly speaking, the key to the success of the zaibatsu in prewar Japan lies in the extent to which these firms expanded on early organizational innovations in the process of evolving into modern businesses. Early in the modernization process, the Japanese government had attempted to set industrialization in motion by establishing state-owned enterprises. The increased burden on state coffers and rising inflation, however, forced the Meiji government to switch from direct action to an indirect policy of intervention, and it began promoting private sector involvement in public businesses such as banking, shipping, cotton spinning, and mining. Some merchants responded, but the opportunity was not restricted to the merchant class; instead, it was open both to established firms—those that went into business in the Edo era and survived the social upheaval of the Meiji Restoration—and to those that had only recently launched businesses, following restoration of imperial rule. Only those that were prepared to accumulate the necessary organizational capabilities were able to respond. The core requirement was human resources, since in the face of the rapid introduction of modern capitalism, only flexible and talented people could adapt to external changes and find new opportunities in the flood of economic events.[4]

Relevant Institutions: Meiji Restoration and Institutional Change

When Douglass North indicated that institutions play a significant role in determining economic performance, both economists and economic historians began turning their attention to formal and informal establishments (North and Thomas 1973).

The Meiji Restoration was one of the most radical institutional changes experienced by Japan before World War II (Lockwood 1954, 3–37). This chain of events was set in motion by the government's abolition of the 200-year closed-door policy, which then led to the modernization of Japan's feudalistic economic, political, and social systems.

The first task for the Meiji government was to revolutionize the political system. Feudal clans were abolished and a centralized, modern political system introduced, with the establishment of local administrative offices in 1871. The cabinet system came into being in 1885, while the Constitution of the Empire of Japan was enacted in 1889. This charter provided for a form of constitutional monarchy that was based on the Prussian model, in which the emperor of Japan would be an active ruler wielding considerable political power that was to be shared with an elected legislature (known as the Diet).

The government then set about reforming the nation's social institutions. One of the most radical changes was the abolition of the four divisions of society, a term used to refer to the social model introduced early in the seventeenth century. The four social classes were warriors (the samurai), farmers, artisans, and merchants. Their abolition promoted social mobility and the utilization of social capital. As will be shown later, many of the zaibatsu entrepreneurs were lower-ranking samurais; the abolition of traditional social divisions gave them the means to mobilize managerial resources and establish their own businesses.

The government also endeavored to transplant from the developed nations of the West advanced science and technology, and political, legal, economic, and social institutions. To assist in Japan's modernization, it hired some 2,300 foreign engineers and teachers with expertise in fields as diverse as agriculture, medical science, law, economics, military, natural science, and engineering.[5] A mission comprising political leaders was also dispatched to advanced countries such as the United States, Britain, and France with instructions to study the political, legal, and economic systems of these nations. Many students were also sent overseas during the years 1871 to 1873.[6] The resulting inflow of scientific and technological knowledge was to become an important foundation for the industrial development of Japan.

The reforms of the educational system instituted during the Restoration were also to play an important role in entrepreneurial activity in Japan. The goal was to develop human capital, especially in engineering, and skilled labor. Established in 1871, the Ministry of Education founded public elementary, junior high, high schools, universities, and vocational schools under the banner of compulsory education for all. Nine Imperial Universities were created in 1886. Keio University had been founded in 1858 and Hitotsubashi University in 1875. Both these universities provided advanced training in economics, business accounting, and business management. The Imperial Universities, such as the universities of Tokyo and Osaka, together with the Tokyo Institute of Technology, founded in 1881, were to become the main suppliers of vocational school teachers, engineers, and floor supervisors. In fact, many of the entrepreneurs who played important roles in the industrialization of Japan were educated at these universities.[7]

Japan's commercial law was formulated on the basis of German commercial law and enacted in 1893. Introducing a joint-stock, limited partnership, and general partnership company system, this law institutionalized limited liability for entrepreneurs. The adoption of the commercial law was to result in a rise in the number of joint-stock companies. At the same time, the government began to establish state-owned factories such as Tomioka Silk Manufacturer, under the slogan "rich country, strong nation." It also set up a new monetary system, introducing the yen in 1871, the country's first standard currency. The national bank acts were laid down in accordance with the U.S. national bank system, and four national banks established in 1872. Many national banks were subsequently established following the amendment of the national bank acts in 1876, and these were to become an important funding source for Japan's entrepreneurs.

These institutional changes provided an environment favorable to entrepreneurs. As has been pointed out extensively in the literature, these changes played a significant role in the industrialization of the national economy. However, it would be facile to suppose that the mass entrepreneurship and vigorous industrial development that ensued were the direct corollary of these institutional changes. In fact, the reverse is true: bureaucratic reform was the outcome of entrepreneurial activity. It was the entrepreneurs who designed and executed the institutional reforms that were to create key infrastructure and transform the national system from a feudal to a market economy.

Entrepreneurial Activity: Organizational Innovation and Zaibatsu

This section examines how multiple uses of scarce resources and the reconciliation of conservative family interests with entrepreneurial ventures led to organizational innovation, by looking at the two largest zaibatsu groups: Mitsui and Mitsubishi. Although the trajectories followed by these two zaibatsu differed, in tracing their histories a certain logic to the organizational innovations pursued by these two conglomerates will become evident.

The origins of the Mitsui zaibatsu, one of the oldest and largest zaibatsu in Japan, date back to 1673 and the opening of a drapery in Tokyo (then Edo) by Mitsui Takatoshi. The Mitsubishi zaibatsu, meanwhile, emerged from the upheaval of the Meiji Restoration. Entrepreneurs in early Meiji lacked capital resources and social infrastructure and were also hampered by Japanese ignorance of contemporary science and technology. However, while the old zaibatsu such as Mitsui and Sumitomo were buttressed by their accumulated wealth and reputation as venerable traditional merchants, the newly developed zaibatsu such as Mitsubishi and Yasuda had no such resources to draw on and were required to procure human and financial assets from scratch. The tasks confronting the old and new zaibatsu were thus very different. This section analyzes the challenges faced by the entrepreneurs of Mitsui and Mitsubishi, the innovations that were introduced by these zaibatsu and the methods they employed to develop their business concerns.

Organizational Innovation at Mitsui

Mitsui Takatoshi was the fourth son of the Mitsui merchant family.[8] He was born in 1622 in Matsuzaka city in Western Japan, where he opened a small kimono shop (the Japanese drapery) and later engaged in money exchange. At age fifty he decided to open a kimono shop called Echigoya in Edo, Japan's capital and its most prosperous market. When Takatoshi started his business, the large traditional kimono merchants did not use fixed prices; in other words, all transactions were negotiation based, credit was the only currency, and their clientele was limited to feudal rulers and wealthy merchants. Takatoshi, on the other hand, targeted the rank-and-file middle class and introduced what was a highly innovative style of merchandising for its time. He rejected the ill-defined and ambiguous pricing practices of the established kimono purveyors, attaching affordable, nondiscountable, and fixed prices and accepted only cash. His new style of business quickly gained popularity among the middle classes, and the proceeds from the trade enabled Takatoshi to establish a money exchange service in 1683. His business with the middle classes had given Takatoshi the means to develop a close relationship with the Tokugawa shogunate, and both the draper's shop and the exchange house were later appointed official purveyors to the administration. Takatoshi's businesses grew as Edo flourished, and he went on to open a shop in Osaka, the second largest city in Japan. He died in 1694 at age seventy-three.

By the mid-eighteenth century the population of Edo had passed one million, making it one of the world's largest cities. Takatoshi's sons decided not to split their inheritance; instead, they used it as a collective fund to establish, in 1710, an unlimited liability partnership, the Mitsui Omotokata (a kind of holding company) to regulate the affairs of the extended Mitsui family.[9] The Mitsui Omotokata, which consisted of nine families (later eleven), controlled the finances and management of the drapers' shops and money exchange houses; the investments made by the Mitsui family were repaid in the form of biannual cash dividends (a fixed percentage of their business proceeds). Developing rapidly, the family's businesses transformed the Mitsui into one of the most powerful merchant families of the Edo era.

SOCIAL UPHEAVAL AND NEW MANAGERS

By the middle of the nineteenth century, however, the nascent conflict between new economic activities and the feudal system had reached critical proportions, and the excessive debts and rampant defaulting of the samurai and farmer classes had become a major social issue. Serious crop failures, meanwhile, brought famine, and, in 1855, Edo was struck by a major earthquake. Economic stagnation caused Mitsui's draper business to fall behind in its payments, and the money exchange service with the shogunate and other *daimyos* (clans) became a significant burden on its financial resources (Yasuoka 1998).

Mitsui's business concerns were also affected by the social upheavals sparked by the incursion of Western powers. The opening up of several trade ports in the late 1850s plunged the Tokugawa shogunate into financial crisis consequent upon the outflow of gold and a coup d'état of the feudal clans, whose slogan was "Revere the Emperor and Expel the Barbarians." The shogunate later approached large merchants requesting financial support in its fight against the rebellion. Since the Mitsui family had already committed substantial amounts to the shogunate, however, it decided to seek outside assistance from an entrepreneurial merchant, Minomura Rizaemon. Minomura was born in 1821 and became son-in-law to a relatively small vegetable oil and sugar merchant. He met Oguri Tadamasa, one of the shogunate's top officials, while running a traditional business in Edo and, with the Mitsui family, went on to become an important shogunate financier. Minomura's sharp-wittedness and powers of negotiation had impressed the Mitsui family. It was this that led them to solicit his help in dealing with their financial trials. Through hard negotiation and his accumulated network of political ties he succeeded in reducing—to one-third their original level—the shogunate's financial demands on Mitsui, and, in 1866, the Mitsui family gave him an official position as the chief executive of its money exchange business.

When Minomura joined Mitsui, Japan was in social and political turmoil. It had been forced by the Treaty of Amity and Commerce to open two ports, Shimoda and Hakodate, to the United States in 1853, and then five more (Hakodate, Nagasaki, Yokohama, Niigata, and Kobe) for international trade in 1859, at which point the country began to engage in international trade. Besides the United States, the shogunate was forced to conclude unequal treaties with Great Britain, France, the Netherlands, and Russia, pacts that included extraterritoriality, the loss of tariff autonomy, and most-favored-nation status. The outflow of gold caused by forced international trade resulted in rapid inflation. Japan, like China and several other Southeast Asian countries, seemed destined to become a quasi-colony. The mismanagement of international treaties raised doubts about the shogunate's capabilities and fueled sympathy for those advocating reverence to the emperor and the expulsion of foreigners. Besieged by foreign powers and internal disaffection, the Tokugawa shogunate began to lose political control over Japan. Meanwhile, the new youthful leaders of comparatively remote clans, such as Choshu and Satsuma, were planning to overthrow the Tokugawa shogunate and unite Japan under the emperor's rule.

Although the House of Mitsui was a purveyor to the Tokugawa shogunate, Minomura forewarned of the demise of Tokugawa regime and the emergence of a new government and advised the Mitsui family to provide financial backing to this new government and to renounce Tokugawa. As Minomura had anticipated, Tokugawa Yoshitsune, the fifteenth Tokugawa shogun, returned his political power to the emperor in 1867, and the Meiji government was established the following year. The newly established Restoration government had limited fiscal and political power, but it needed to achieve rapid industrialization and to develop a strong military. Minomura subsequently succeeded in establishing close political ties with the new government under the aegis of Inoue Kaoru, an influential Restoration player, and went on to secure an important position in finance, exchange, and trade. The close relationship with the new government, however, was a financial liability for Mitsui because the government's fiscal foundations were so weak. From the outset, the government faced a succession of financial crises and in 1870, it asked Mitsui to provide 300,000 ryo (the old currency unit) in funding to widen its revenue base. This was an enormous sum, even for the wealthy Mitsui family. Notwithstanding, had Mitsui declined, the government would have fallen, and Japan potentially would have been subjugated to Western control. Minomura elected to sell a number of Mitsui properties in order to free up the necessary funds, thereby wining the trust of the Restoration government and gaining stronger and more powerful political connections for Mitsui.

Business Opportunities and Impediments to Innovation

With consumer production stagnating and import costs still high, it was imperative for the Meiji government to lay the foundations for a modern capitalistic economy as quickly as possible. The prompt establishment of a stable monetary and banking system was a particularly urgent priority. In order to balance its trade, the government also had to create industries capable of competing with their foreign counterparts. Minomura realized that it would be necessary for Mitsui to restructure its traditional businesses; however, none of its existing managers and engineers understood the importance of modernizing, nor were they capable of executing the necessary reforms. Minomura therefore recruited a number of new staff members from outside the family, men who possessed the knowledge and entrepreneurial skills necessary for developing new business. The new recruits included Takashi Masuda, the founder of Mitsui Bussan (the domestic trading arm of the Mitsui business) and Nakamigawa Hikojiro, a leading reformer of Japan's banking business. The Mitsui family, however, remained skeptical of the changes and opposed the reorganization of their businesses. The traditional merchants preferred holding real estate, which was regarded as a safe asset, to developing new, untried fields of business (Yasuoka 1998, 494). This risk-averse attitude was a problem for the entrepreneurs who required a certain amount of capital investment to fund their new business ventures. With this in mind, Minomura undertook an important organizational innovation—attempting to establish a limited-liability holding company that would allow the capital of the traditional merchants to be harnessed for new ventures. The following section elucidates the process via which these innovations were effected.

In the early 1870s, Minomura conceived a plan to establish a bank and sent seven of its personnel to the United States to study modern banking techniques. New banking regulations established by the Meiji government in 1872, however, required that any national bank be founded cooperatively. Thus it was that, in 1873, Dai-ichi Kokuritu Ginko (Daiichi National Bank), Japan's first national bank, came into being. The bank was capitalized through public subscription and contributions from the House of Mitsui and Ono Gumi, another leading exchange house that had begun operating during the Edo era.

Minomura, however, had not abandoned his plans for an independent Mitsui bank. In order to concentrate Mitsui's financial resources on banking, he believed that it would be necessary to separate the languishing kimono business from Mitsui's portfolio. Japan had no joint-stock company system as yet, and the Mitsui family could not avoid its unlimited obligations to guarantee the liabilities of the shops in its possession. By introducing managerial independence and limiting financial support, Minomura attempted to halt the decline in capital and to clarify the responsibility and accountability of the kimono business.

Mitsui Omotokata, the organization controlling the family's business concerns, had unlimited liability in the draper's shop business (Mitsukoshi); and so, the bank and the Mitsui family might have been harmed had this business failed. Business enterprises in the Edo era had either been general partnerships, that is, associations of individuals, or unincorporated companies, the owners of which were all personally liable for any legal action filed against the company and debts owed. As already stated, no commercial law was enacted until 1893, and there were no laws granting limited liability to the stockholder during the 1870s. The separation of the draper's shop business from Mitsui Omotokata was thus designed to mitigate the risk of failure on the bank that Minomura was planning to establish. He submitted his proposal to the finance minister, Okuma Shigenobu, who granted permission on one condition: that the bank's stockholders would have unlimited liability. Minomura accepted this condition and, in 1876, established Mitsui Bank, the first private bank in Japan. Having accepted unlimited liability in the new bank, Minomura needed to minimize any risk to the Mitsui family posed by the Mitsukoshi business, even while retaining managerial control, and Mitsui thus appointed several of its personnel to the board.

This organizational innovation had two goals: to enhance the individual potential fields of the new businesses while minimizing the business risks of individual firms for the family assets. Since the joint-stock structure had yet to be recognized under existing Japanese laws, there were no regulations governing limited liability, and the entrepreneurs thus hoped to achieve these two goals simultaneously. This organizational setup had the unintentional benefit of furthering the separation of ownership (capital) and management and gave the entrepreneurs a freer hand to develop new businesses.

Minomura's plans for a private bank also included a proposal for the formation of a trading company. Since international trade was new to Japan, expertise in this area was severely limited, and Minomura singled out Masuda Takashi to manage the new trade enterprise. Masuda had served as an interpreter and had worked for the Ministry of Finance following the Meiji Restoration. He joined Senshu-sha, the trading company found by Inoue Kaori, in 1874, the year of its inception.[10] When Masuda was hired to establish a trading company for Mitsui, international trade was dominated by the West. Minomura believed that in order to achieve rapid industrialization, it was necessary for Japan to import advanced technology and promote exportation to acquire foreign currency. He recognized that there was money to be made from international trade. When Inoue returned to the political stage in 1876, Minomura offered Masuda the presidency of Mitsui's newly formed trading enterprise: Mitsui Bussan. The Mitsui family was not particularly interested in international trading since the business was totally unfamiliar to these old merchants; their concern was risk. Once again, Minomura—this time with Masuda's assistance—needed to devise an organizational setup that would not impose the obligation of unlimited liability on the Mitsui family.

The newly established Mitsui Bussan was a nominal unlimited partnership between two very young family members of Mitsui (the seventh son of Takafuku, the head of the family, and the third son of his brother, Takayoshi), but it had no ties either to Mitsui Omotokata or to Mitsui Bank. The necessary initial investment came in the form of a loan from Mitsui Bank, instead of from Mitsui Omotokata, which was reluctant to commit resources to the trading company. Masuda became operational president but had no capital commitment to the company. The key undertaking for Minomura and Masuda was to ensure the financial security of the Mitsui family (Takahashi 1968, 14). With sixteen employees, however, Masuda quickly established a head office in Tokyo and three branch offices in Yokohama, Osaka, and Nagasaki. The separation of capital and management also gave him the freedom to promote college graduates from top universities, such as Tokyo Higher Commerce School (now Hitotsubashi University) and Keio University without bothering the family. This locking-in of human resources and advanced knowledge (specifically, English and accounting) was instrumental to the development of the nascent but growing business in international trade (Abe 1995, 110).

Masuda continued to pursue the restructuring initiative following the death of Minomura in 1877. The finances of Mitsui Bank were severely tested in 1885, however, when the Meiji government requested all private chartered banks, Mitsui included, to return the delegated functions to the central bank (namely, the right to print money) together with their paid-in capital, in connection with the establishment of the Bank of Japan. The bank's financial standing had already deteriorated because it had been forced to establish many branches in less economically important locations to carry out its designated public duties. Drastic reform became inevitable.

New Skilled Managers for New Business Ventures

After struggling with this problem for several years, in 1891 the Mitsui family and Masuda decided to appoint a young businessman, Nakamigawa Hikojiro, to reform Mitsui Bank. Nakamigawa had spent three years in London studying Western political, economic, and business systems. After returning to Japan, he became president of Sanyo Railways, a railroad company that was established in 1887. His appointment was supported by Inoue Kaoru, who, as already stated, was a member of the oligarchy ruling Meiji Japan.

Nakamigawa began by introducing new blood, employing undergraduates from Keio University, his alma mater. At that time, many of the bank's administrative and managerial personnel were local government officials; Nakamigawa, however, delegated important managerial decisions to his team of talented young mangers and introduced a performance-based pay system. His second accomplishment was to reposition Mitsui Bank's business domain from public agency to private banking. He believed that the web of associations inside government was preventing Mitsui from sloughing off old traditions and modernizing its businesses. Although Nakamigawa had been recommended by a leading politician, he severed his connections with the Restoration government and set about cleaning up Mitsui's public agency businesses. His goal was to improve the bank's finances by modernizing the business itself.

Both Nakamigawa and Masuda were engaged in a bid to transform Mitsui's businesses from government-affiliated traditional merchants into modern conglomerates and the search for economies of scope, a process that involved taking advantage of the government's privatization policy. Matsukata Masayoshi, who took over as minister of finance after Okuma Shigenobu was ousted in 1881, pursued a policy of financial austerity that ran directly counter to the inflationary policies of his predecessor. These were the years of the so-called Matsukata deflation and were marked by rigid budget constraints, the withdrawal of unconvertible money, and further privatization of public businesses. Many public works and mines were sold to private companies; the majority was snapped up by the zaibatsu.[11] In April 1888, the government called for bids for the state-owned Miike Mines, one of the largest coal mines in Japan, which had been under government control since 1873. With the expectation that the energy industry would play a central role in the industrialization of Japan and in light of the fact that Mitsui Bussan had had an exclusive contract with Miike coal since 1879, Masuda was convinced that the mines would be vital both to Mitsui Bussan and to the Mitsui zaibatsu. As government-appointed agent for coal exports, Masuda also understood the potential advantage of acquiring the Miike mines, since he was in a position to assess the exact extent of the deposits at Miike. When Masuda voiced his intention to tender a bid on behalf of Mitsui, Mitsubishi—which had a flourishing steamship business and had already purchased other national coal mines—stated that it would also participate in the bidding. Although Mitsui Bank was immersed in Nakamigawa's reform program, Masuda offered 4,555,000 yen, an unprecedented amount of money at that time. Mitsui's winning bid was only slightly higher than the offer tendered by Mitsubishi: 4,552,700 yen.[12]

The public was highly skeptical about Mitsui's ability to manage the mines, and Masuda was labeled "insane" for offering such an exorbitant bidding price. Knowing how scarce talented human resources were, however, Masuda said that the price included the cost of Dan Takuma, the chief engineer at Miike. Dan had studied mining engineering at the Massachusetts Institute of Technology and returned to Japan in 1878. After teaching at Osaka Engineering School and the University of Tokyo as an assistant professor, he moved to the Ministry of Engineering in 1884 and began working for Miike Mines. Masuda's plans to buy the mines were hatched at a time when primitive, traditional mining methods remained widespread. There was no incentive to improve efficiency, because cheap labor was abundant. Most of the miners were outcasts and convicts from local prisons. Masuda recognized that the introduction of advanced mining technologies would potentially increase productivity. He was convinced that Dan would play an important role in the modernization process. In fact, Mitsui Bussan accrued enormous profits from the technology-fueled development of the Miike mines. Moreover, like Alfred Sloan at GM, an MIT graduate with engineering background, Dan went on to make a huge contribution to the entire Mitsui conglomerate as the head of Mitsui Holding in the early twentieth century.[13]

As we have seen from this brief history of the Mitsui zaibatsu, while the traditional merchant families tended to be risk-averse in their attitude toward new ventures, they were forced to rely on entrepreneurs in order to survive in the transitional economy; in fact, disputes did occasionally erupt between family members and the professional managers they hired. Even Mitsui Takayoshi, who championed the reforms put forward by Minomura, sometimes opposed the changes proposed by his protégé (Yasuoka 1998, 497). The development of organizational structures that would reconcile the conflicting requirements of family hostility to risk, especially in untried business enterprises, and the absence of legal provision for limited liability partnerships, became an imperative. Mitsui began disengaging ownership from management and diversifying into new businesses somewhat earlier than other zaibatsu, which, as Berle and Means pointed out, is an important element of the modern corporate structure (Berle and Means 1932). This separation had the unintended effect of allowing the Mitsui zaibatsu to hire and promote young and talented personnel with a good grasp of the new business modalities and technologies in trade, finance, and mining, without fanning family anxiety. Mitsui actively recruited accomplished human resources with new knowledge from outside the company and charged them to adapt to the changes occurring in the wider environment. Several of these professional managers, Masuda, Nakamigawa, and Dan, for example, also promoted college graduates to further the development of the conglomerate. Nakamigawa, in particular, hired many graduates from Keio University to modernize and develop Mitsui Bank (see table 17.3). These young businessmen went on to diversify Mitsui's operations into department stores, paper manufacturing, textiles, and so on.

Running counter to the multidivisional organizations being developed in the United States, Mitsui developed a holding company type of conglomerate. From the point of view of transaction cost theory, this structure appears costly since each individual subsidiary was required to have redundant indirect functions, such as

TABLE 17.3
Salaried Managers Promoted at Mitsui

Name	University	Position[a]
Fukuhara Eitaro	Keio University	Mitsui Bussan
Majima Yoki	Tokyo Higher Commerce School (Hitotsubashi University)	Mitsui Bussan
Komuro Sankichi	Tokyo Higher Commerce School (Hitotsubashi University)	Mitsui Bussan
Fukui Kikusaburo	Tokyo Higher Commerce School (Hitotsubashi University)	Mitsui Bussan
Fujise Masajiro	Tokyo Higher Commerce School (Hitotsubashi University)	Mitsui Bussan
Asabuki Eiji	Keio University	Oji Paper (moved from Mitsubishi), chairman
Fujiyama Raita	Keio University	Oji Paper, executive director
Muto Sanji	Keio University	Kanebo, president
Wada Toyoharu	Keio University	Kanebo, Tokyo Head Office manager
Ikeda Shigeaki	Keio University	Mitsui Bank, executive director
Hibi Osuke	Keio University	Mitsukoshi, chairman
Fujiwara Ginjiro	Keio University	Oji Paper, president
Kobayashi Ichizo	Keio University	Hankyu, Chairman

Source: Abe 1995, 110.
Note: Main position held at Mitsui following promotion by Iwasaki Yataro.

corporate strategy planning, personnel, general affairs, financing, and so on (see Williamson 1975 and Chandler 1962). Rationally, the multidivisional structure (the M-form), centralizes the indirect functions of each division and makes it possible to allocate managerial resources for an entire organization and thus to eliminate redundant costs. However, organizational structure is not always determined by rationality; it is often dictated by dependency on historical paths.

Mitsui's choice of the holding company structure was motivated by three factors. The first was the conflict between family traditionalists and the new business entrepreneurs. The Mitsui family's aversion to risk dated back two hundred years, but in order for the family to survive the Meiji Restoration and the social and economic upheaval that accompanied this transition, it was necessary to bring in talented entrepreneurs from outside the company. The entrepreneurs, on the other hand, saw the Restoration as a great opportunity to launch new businesses. The second contributor to Mitsui's decision was the paucity of knowledge of modern business and technology, which left the old merchants with no choice but to give their managers a free hand to embark on new business ventures; so it was better for the entrepreneurs to be separate from the holding company. Finally, the range of business opportunities available in early Meiji was enormous, ranging from banking to railroads, trading, mining, shipping, shipbuilding and textiles, among others. However, the competition among old and new business groups was fierce, as was evidenced by the bidding for the Miike mines. The emphasis was on speed, and it was thus easier for the zaibatsu to establish subsidiaries under the holding company form than to internalize through divisions.

Mitsubishi: Multiple Uses of Resources[14]

Mitsui and Sumitomo established their business in the Edo era, going on to become giant conglomerates and to play significant roles in the industrialization of Japan. Mitsubishi, meanwhile, constitutes a comparatively new zaibatsu, since its first business was not founded until 1870. It took the company just fifteen years, however, to become one of the biggest business conglomerates in Japan.

Mitsubishi, however, faced challenges different from those faced by the zaibatsu whose businesses dated back to the Edo era; because it was a late entrant, Mitsubishi lost out to Mitsui and Sumitomo in important areas such as banking and mining.

This section examines how Mitsubishi succeeded in becoming one of Japan's four largest conglomerates in such a short space of time. Mitsubishi tried to avoid competition by breaking into new business areas. The company also diversified, making multiple uses of scarce resources accumulated in its core business.

SHIPPING BUSINESS: NEW GROWING DEMAND

Iwasaki Yataro was born in 1835 in Kochi Prefecture (then Tosa province), a region located on the south coast of Shikoku. He had humble status as a result of his father's position as a master-less samurai, but he became a follower of Yoshida Toyo, a politician committed to innovating the clan's political and economic bases, and was promoted rapidly, becoming a high-ranking official in the Tosa clan by 1870. That year, Yataro was assigned to operate the Tosa clan's shipping business, in which position he learned international trade. He then borrowed three ships from the clan and commenced shipping operations between Osaka and Tokyo and Kobe and Kochi. In

1873, Iwasaki bought the ships from the Tosa clan and established his own shipping firm, which he named Mitsubishi Shokai. He headquartered the company in Tokyo, and since no other company had moved into the shipping business, was able to gain a competitive advantage against his forebears.

At that time, the Meiji government was attempting to convert its fleets from sail to steam to expedite the industrialization and modernization of the economy. Foreign shipping companies had begun to open regular lines to Japan (Mishima 1981, 41–42). A British company, Peninsular and Oriental Steam Navigation (P&O), for example, had opened regular services between Nagasaki and Shanghai in 1859 and introduced the Yokohama, Shanghai, Hong Kong route in 1867. A French shipping company, Messageries Impériales, meanwhile introduced large steamships and opened a new route between Yokohama and Shanghai in 1867. Pacific Mail Steamship, an American company, opened a new route from San Francisco to Shanghai via Yokohama in 1865 and introduced a new service between Yokohama and Shanghai via Kobe and Nagasaki. Clearly, mass transport on land and sea would be essential to industrialization. The Meiji government thus established a shipping company in 1870. This state-run shipping company was unsuccessful, however, and was dissolved after ten months because of poor management (Mishima 1981, 43–44). The government established a new shipping company to provide regular services between Tokyo and Osaka in 1871. This company also failed and was dissolved in 1875.

Beginning in 1874, Yataro developed his shipping business by capitalizing on military demand. The modernization policy of the Meiji government had abolished privileged social classes and the samurai class in particular. In 1873, for example, the government announced that samurai stipends were to be taxed on a rolling basis, and this policy led to a series of samurai rebellions that culminated in 1874, when three thousand samurai, led by Eto Shinpei, rose up against the government in Saga (Kyushu). The government asked Mitsubishi for the use of its vessels in dispatching government forces to Saga, and it was owing to the swiftness of the Mitsubishi fleet that the Meiji government was able to subdue this insurrection.

The punitive expedition to Taiwan by Japanese military forces in 1874 was the first overseas deployment of the imperial Japanese military. The government decided to send 3,000 soldiers to Taiwan, and since its goal was to develop the domestic shipping industry for international trade, it ordered Mitsubishi to transport these men to Taiwan, awarding the company thirteen vessels for this purpose, which Mitsubishi was permitted to retain once the Taiwan expedition was completed. Mitsubishi's shipping capacity thus expanded, and the company opened an international route between Yokohama and Shanghai, becoming one of the largest shipping firms in the country.

Mitsubishi's shipping business grew through the aggressive use of discounting. In the growing process, Iwasaki promoted a number of professional managers who had graduated from top universities with a view to internalizing the advanced knowledge necessary to developing Mitsubishi's business concerns (see table 17.4).

Mitsubishi had supported large urban business interests and used its government subsidies to dominate the shipping industry. However, Mitsubishi now had many rivals in the shipping business. Foreign vessels had commenced operating out of Japan and several zaibatsu groups were moving into the field. Price competition intensified. Moreover, the growth of Mitsubishi was accompanied by a rise in anti-Mitsubishi sentiment. Opponents criticized its relationship with the Constitutional Progressive

TABLE 17.4
Salaried Managers Promoted in Mitsubishi

Name	University	Position[a]
Soda Heigoro	Keio University	Mitsubishi Goshi, general manager
Yoshikawa Taijiro	Keio University	Nippon Yusen, president
Toyokawa Ryohei	Keio University	Mitsubishi Goshi, director of Bank Division
Asabuki Eiji	Keio University	Oji Paper (moved to Mitsui), chairman
Kondo Renpei	University of Tokyo	Nippon Yusen, President
Yamamoto Tatsuo	Mitsubishi Commerce School	President of Bank of Japan
Suenobu Michinari	University of Tokyo	Tokyo Marine Insurance, president
Kato Takaaki	University of Tokyo	Prime Minister of Japan
Isono Kei	University of Tokyo	Meijiya, founder
Hasegawa Yoshinosuke	Columbia University	The Public Steel and Iron Manufacturing, Foundation Committee
Nanbu Kyugo	Columbia University	Mitsubishi Goshi, director of Mining Division

Source: Abe, "Kindai Keici No Keisei (Formation of Modern Business)," p. 109–110.
Note: Main position held at Mitsubishi following promotion by Iwasaki Yataro.

Party, one of the main political parties, which was the recipient of Mitsubishi funding. Then, in 1883, Shibusawa Eiichi, an industrialist who later established Shibusawa zaibatsu, launched a shipping company in partnership with Mitsui: Kyodo Unyu Kaisha (Joint Shipping Company), to compete with Mitsubishi.

The aggressive price war between the two shipping companies—a battle that lasted for two years—damaged the financial standing of both firms. The government proposed that these two firms merge on equal terms to form a new company. Agreement was reached and in 1885, a new company, Nippon Yusen Corporation (NYK), was born. Iwasaki Hisaya, Yataro's eldest son, became the first shareholder, and though Mitsubishi had theoretically lost its shipping company, in practice, it had won the pricing war against Kyodo Unyu Kaisha and secured the managerial initiative in the newly established company.

The shipping business played two important roles in Mitsubishi's development. As stated at the beginning of this section, key businesses, like mining and finance, were already dominated by veteran businesses such as Mitsui and Sumitomo when Mitsubishi founded its shipping business in the 1870s, but the older zaibatsu had no hold on marine transport. With the government's support, the shipping business enabled Mitsubishi, a comparatively new zaibatsu, to accumulate capital and to grasp business opportunities for diversification.

DIVERSIFICATION: MULTIPLE USES OF RESOURCES

From the mid-1880s, Yataro began to diversify and to shift the focus of Mitsubishi's business from shipping to heavy industry. He began by internalizing businesses that were complementary to shipping, and then spun off the internalized resources once they became independently capable of servicing the main business. This process brought unused managerial resources to light. In Penrose's words, the diversification of Mitsubishi was based on the utilization of unused resources (Penrose 1980).

In the 1880s, coal was the main fuel for vessels, and the shipping business needed to maintain ample supplies. The growth of the industry, however, raised questions about the feasibility of securing sufficient coal resources and in April 1881, Yataro began operating a mining business in Wakayama to supply the Mitsubishi fleet. The supply of coal from Wakayama was not enough to meet the demands of Mitsubishi's growing shipping business, however. At the time, Mitsubishi was also buying coal from the Takashima coal mine in Nagasaki, and in March 1881 Yataro decided to bring this mine into the Mitsubishi fold. The Takashima coal mine was bought by Mitsubishi with the assistance of Fukuzawa Yukichi because Yataro anticipated that the business would not only provide a stable supply of energy for the Mitsubishi shipping arm, but that it could also profit handsomely from the exportation of excess. Yataro's predictions proved correct, and Mitsubishi began shipping its spare coal to Shanghai, Hong Kong, and Singapore. Yataro overcame one of the obstructions hampering the Mitsubishi shipping business and created a complementary and synergistic relationship between coal mining and shipping through backward vertical integration.

Another stumbling block for Mitsubishi was the lack of a ship repair facility at its main port, Yokohama, and the company was thus forced to send damaged ships to Shanghai or London for repair. Yataro therefore established the Mitsubishi Engine Works in partnership with Boyd & Co., which financed half of the capital for the ironworks in 1875. In 1876, the Engine Works began taking repair orders from other shipping companies. In December 1879, Yataro acquired Boyd & Co.'s interest in the Mitsubishi ironworks, and while the Mitsubishi Engine Works were not used for shipbuilding, it did become the largest privately owned ship-repair dock in Yokohama and one of Mitsubishi's most important.

Mitsubishi then began surveying the shipbuilding business. The Tokugawa shogunate had established a ship-repair dock in 1857 and, in 1863, had constructed facilities for building battleships in Nagasaki. The Meiji government bought Kosuge Ship Repair Dock, which was established 1868 with the introduction of advanced ship-repairing technology from Britain. These facilities, known as Nagasaki Shipyard, became an important center for shipbuilding. However, with the locus of the shipping business shifting from Nagasaki to Kobe and Osaka, the government decided to privatize its Nagasaki shipping concerns. In June 1884, Mitsubishi, at that time competing with Kyodo Unyu Kaisha, made a successful bid to lease the premises from the government. Shoda Heigoro invested to upgrade the dockyards and their plant facilities so that the Nagasaki Shipyard could build large and technically advanced ships and Mitsubishi deployed advanced engineers from the Mitsubishi Engine Works to Nagasaki. It also employed new graduates from the Tokyo Technical School (later the Tokyo Institute of Technology) and Imperial College of Engineering (later the University of Tokyo). These skilled engineers and the upgraded facilities at Nagasaki Shipyard gave Mitsubishi's shipbuilding business the leading position in the industry.

Mitsubishi later began offering fringe services to the shipping business. From the outset, the company had faced stiff competition from foreign shipping. One of its rivals, P&O of the United Kingdom, was increasing its market share by moving into the financial sector and had won a transport contract with Osaka's wholesale association. Yataro believed that if Mitsubishi also offered financial services such as documentary bills (i.e., bills attached to bills of landing, assuring their payment), it could increase its own market share. He launched this service for shipments between Tokyo and Osaka in March 1876, then extended it to cover every branch in Japan in 1879. In 1880, Iwasaki Yataro established the Mitsubishi Exchange Office (Mitsubishi Kawase Ten), later called Mitsubishi Bank, which became the main bank of the Mitsubishi conglomerate. Yataro also developed another peripheral service with its warehouse and cargo business. By developing a transport network that covered Japan and providing financial services to shippers, Mitsubishi connected dispersed markets and remote regions such as Tohoku and Hokkaido with the central markets and Osaka. In other words, Mitsubishi extended the market frontiers of Japan.

In addition, Yataro attempted to develop a marine insurance business, but the government refused permission since the peerage association of the former clan lords had already begun establishing such insurance agencies, utilizing the capital of old feudal lords and court nobles. Nonetheless, Mitsubishi was invited to join the business by Shibusawa Eiichi, one of the organizers of this project, who believed that the company would be one of its largest customers. Mitsubishi decided to participate and provided 11,000 yen in capital (more than one-sixth of the total capital); it also became the first shareholder. The business, named Tokyo Marine Insurance, began operating in 1878.

ADVANCED KNOWLEDGE AND FURTHER DIVERSIFICATION

As the scale and scope of the business grew, it was necessary for Mitsubishi to expand its pool of human resources with advanced expertise in the new growing businesses. It began by employing foreign engineers and introducing advanced technology from abroad. A British engineer sent by Boyd & Co., for instance, played an important role in introducing advanced technologies at the Mitsubishi shipbuilding plants (Iwasakike Denki Kankokai 1979, 2:200). Foreign engineers additionally played a leading role at Nagasaki Shipyard. Mitsubishi also sent its engineers to Britain and the United States to learn advanced technology.

As already stated, Yataro also hired new graduates from the Tokyo Technical School and the Imperial College of Engineering. He additionally established two schools that were intended to supply human resources to Mitsubishi's growing businesses. His first school, the Mitsubishi Merchant Ship School in Tokyo, was opened in 1875 with government assistance. It was designed to produce skilled crew. In 1878, Yataro established a business school, Mitsubishi School of Commerce, also in Tokyo. He was convinced that there was a shortage of workers capable of understanding the new business environment and of leading innovation in emerging sectors and believed that Mitsubishi needed to take responsibility for producing the human resources that would be needed for its business concerns. At this school, one hundred students studied English, mathematics, bookkeeping, economics, history, and geography. Iwasaki Hisaya, Yataro's oldest son, was one of them. Although it closed after six years owing to the financial constraints of competing with Kyodo Unyu, the Mitsubishi School of Commerce did make a contribution to human resource training. Toyokawa Ryohei, the senior lecturer at Mitsubishi School of Commerce, was instrumental in the hiring of many entrepreneurs for Mitsubishi. It was he who, in 1875, recruited Shoda Heigoro, a teacher at Keio University. Shoda introduced cost accounting for Mitsubishi's shipping business, a practice that was unheard of at the time. He was also involved in the establishment of Tokyo Marine Insurance and Meiji Life Insurance and supported three Iwasaki entrepreneurs, Yataro, Yanosuke, and Hisaya.

The shipping business was central to Mitsubishi's concerns, and Yataro diversified with a view to establishing complementary ventures. Diversification took the form of both backward and forward-vertical integration, which was a rational strategy given the scarcity of available resources. Yataro's death in 1885 altered this trajectory. His eldest son, Hisaya, was still young, so Yataro's younger brother, Iwasaki Yanosuke, took over Yataro's position at Mitsubishi. Yanosuke positioned the Nagasaki Shipyard and Takashima Coal Mine at the center and created a new diversification strategy with the slogan "From the sea to the land." His first major step was to buy the Nagasaki Shipyard, which, at the end of the 1880s, was primarily used for repairs; Yanosuke wanted to use it for shipbuilding.

Yanosuke bequeathed the presidency to Yataro's oldest son in 1893. Hisaya had studied at the University of Pennsylvania from 1886 and returned to Japan in 1891. Although both Yanosuke and Hisaya acceded to the presidency of Mitsubishi by succession, it does not follow that Mitsubishi's pattern of promotion was based solely on family lineage. Hisaya had studied English, accounting, law, and economics at Mitsubishi School of Commerce. After assuming the presidency of Mitsubishi, he modernized Nagasaki Shipyard, investing huge amounts in infrastructure and equipment and recruiting advanced engineers, and installed advanced equipment so that the shipyard could produce large, custom-built vessels. The first vessel built at the Nagasaki Shipyard was a 206-ton vessel for the coal mines. By the end of the 1900s, the shipyard had become one of the most advanced shipbuilding facilities in the world. In 1905, Mitsubishi established Kobe Shipyard. Many industrial firms were spun off from the two shipyards, as Mitsubishi developed related businesses, such as Mitsubishi Ironworks in 1917, Mitsubishi Internal-Combustion Engine Manufacturing in 1920, and Mitsubishi Electric in 1921, all of which were to become important elements of the parent company.

There was a certain pattern to the diversification strategies employed by Mitsubishi. The company started by internalizing complementary resources to gain competitiveness in its core business. This accordingly took the form of vertical integration. Second, when these internalized businesses reached the point at which they could provide services to non-Mitsubishi firms, they were spun off from the core business. In other words, when unused resources emerged, the core business began to provide services to other firms. Top management spun-off noncore businesses to create independent enterprises that would enable newly empowered entrepreneurs to make strategic decisions and increase their commitment to the businesses under their command. This diversification into related areas made the best use of available resources, especially when they were scarce, scattered, or had been taken by forerunners. It is worth noting that in early Meiji, Mitsubishi had entered fields such as silk manufacturing and copper mining, neither of which was closely related to any of its existing businesses. None were successful, however. It was the businesses with links to existing ventures that contributed to the development of the Mitsubishi conglomerate.

ORGANIZATIONAL INNOVATION: MULTIDIVISIONAL FORM

Much of the previous literature on the Mitsubishi zaibatsu has pointed out that the strong entrepreneurial leadership demonstrated by Iwasaki Yataro, Yanosuke, and Hisaya played an important role in the company's development.[15] In 1875, Mitsubishi made it clear that the Iwasaki family would have managerial control and responsibility for all its business concerns (Iwasakike Denki Kankokai 1979, 2:152). In clear contrast to Mitsui, the Mitsubishi entrepreneurs faced no obstacles in allocating family capital to new ventures.

However, as Mitsubishi diversified, it became difficult for the family to monitor and control individual concerns. With this and the restructuring of the central office in mind, Yanosuke established the Mitsubishi Sha in 1886. Even though Yanosuke was the power behind this organizational change, he introduced divisional managers to monitor individual businesses. The problems were aggravated by further expansion in the mid-1890s, and in 1893 Mitsubishi reorganized its portfolio, giving financial and managerial autonomy to the coal-mining and mining arms. The coal mine, mining, and shipbuilding businesses were turned into limited partnerships. Mitsubishi adopted a multidivisional form to control diversified business, as is discussed by Chandler (1962). Based on this organizational shake-up, individual divisions were converted to joint-stock companies, and the central office became a holding company in 1917. As Morikawa (1981) has indicated, this transformation allowed the respective firms to raise capital and avoid business risks, and their leaders were given managerial autonomy over strategic decisions.

Conclusions

Entrepreneurship is the ability to carry out innovation that leads to economic growth. In 1853, Japan opened its society after a period of seclusion that had extended over two centuries. It needed to achieve rapid industrialization in order to catch up with the West. It had little or no industrial and social infrastructure, however, and its knowledge of science and technology lagged far behind that of the developed world.

Note again that the government played a crucial role in this process. There was a substantial group of innovative entrepreneurs in the Meiji period. As we discussed, many of the zaibatsu entrepreneurs were lower-ranking samurai. There were four social classes, which originated in the mid-sixteenth century, namely samurai, peasants, artesian and merchants. This social class system was generally rigid and immobile in the Edo period, though there was a certain level of social mobility among rank-and-file people. The nation enjoyed a period of peace and prosperity for more than 250 years. Under this period of peace, samurai became courtiers, bureaucrats, and administrators in the Edo period. The class system was abolished in 1869 with the fall of Tokugawa regime. This was one of the important institutional changes that promoted entrepreneurial activity. The abolition of the class system gave the nation a great social mobility. Based on this increased mobility, the lower-ranking samurai developed their personal networks and entered into new businesses. Regardless their ex-social class, the able managers and skilled engineers were recruited and assigned to positions of power in the fields of growing businesses. The Meiji government adopted a strong industrialization policy and promoted the industrial development of firms, luring skilled engineers from Britain and France with the promise of high salaries. The educational reforms instituted by the Meiji government to provide highly skilled engineers and business experts were also important institutional changes for entrepreneurial activity. The government set up public manufacturing facilities, including shipyards and ironworks as well. These institutional changes provided an environment favorable to entrepreneurs.

However, it was the entrepreneurs that were the key drivers of the transformation from feudalism to industrial capitalism. Entrepreneurs such as Minomura Rizaemon and Iwasaki Yataro internalized scarce resources and developed vertically integrated enterprises by putting the resources thus accumulated to multiple use.

The Mitsui families were leading traditional merchants who went into business during the Edo era and faced stagnation in the immediate aftermath of the Meiji Restoration. Mitsui was compelled to reform its traditional ways by the deep-seated changes in society that came with the Meiji Restoration; it brought in capable entrepreneurs such as Minomura and Masuda to implement radical change. In the process of reconstructing the Mitsui business, these entrepreneurs frequently ran counter to the family's interests and risk-averse preferences, but the absence of mature financial markets necessitated the use of family capital. They thus developed a style of corporate governance that would permit capital resources to be utilized without imposing unlimited liability obligations on the family. This style of governance sheltered other businesses from risk and encouraged investment in new ventures. Based on organizational innovation, the entrepreneurs empowered college graduates, with advanced expertise and business acumen, to make strategic managerial decisions.

As the late Edo latecomer, Mitsubishi did not encounter such problems. It did, however, have to compete with its predecessor and operate with scarce resources. Mitsubishi tackled these challenges by establishing a shipping business—a field free of competitors—as its central concern. Its lack of resources led the company to buy public assets from the government and to internalize resources that were complementary to its core business. Once these resources had reached a certain scale, the company began to diversify. The roles played by Mitsubishi's leaders, including Iwasaki Yataro and Iwasaki Yanosuke, in the rapid expansion of the company have been discussed. It is, however, important to note again that their managerial decisions were based on economic reasoning. The pattern of Mitsubishi's development was the result of diversification and multiple uses of accumulated resources.

A key strategy central to the success of both zaibatsu was the creation of organizational structures that enabled young engineers and college graduates to be recruited and assigned to positions of power (Yonekawa 1984). Mitsui and Sumitomo had also delegated some limited managerial authority over daily administrative tasks to their employees during the Edo era, but they retained control over strategic managerial decisions. As industrial businesses grew in scale and scope, it was necessary for top management to promote capable engineers and managers to make use of new advanced knowledge. The entrepreneurs thus adopted a multidivisional structure that would give such personnel the necessary authority to make key decisions, and the big business conglomerates began promoting college graduates. Until the 1920s, the main businesses of the zaibatsu were shipbuilding, ironworks, and coal mining. In the decades that followed, new conglomerates increased their competitiveness in industries such as automobiles and chemicals by employing engineering graduates with knowledge of new technologies in these growing industrial sectors. They were operating in different fields from their predecessors, but the techniques they employed were identical with those espoused by Mitsui and Mitsubishi.

It is noteworthy that throughout the Meiji era, not only the zaibatsu families but also their entrepreneurial managers could get both financial and social rewards from their business activities. For example, Yanosuke Iwasaki, the second president of Mitsubishi and one of the richest men in prewar Japan, became the fourth president of the Bank of Japan and devoted his time to national financial policy. Nariaki Ikeda, the general manager of Mitsui Holdings after Takuma Dan, became the fourteenth president of the Bank of Japan and served the Konoe cabinet as the minister of both Finance and Commerce and Industry from 1938 to 1939.

Zaibatsu have been significant players in the Japanese economy since the Meiji Restoration. They reached their zenith in terms of size and influence in the 1930s. The five zaibatsu holding companies (Mitsui, Mitsubishi, Sumitomo, Yasuda, and Fuji) were dissolved by GHQ as a part of the "democratization and demilitarization" policy after 1946. With their holding companies shut down, in the 1960s the zaibatsu began restructuring their businesses (known as *keiretsu*) by developing cross-share holdings, and their economic influence remains strong in many industrial and financial sectors of Japan.

The organizational innovations that enabled the promotion of skilled personnel in new business ventures and the multiple uses of resources that led to their rapid growth in scale and scope played an important role in the Japanese economy at a time when tremendous new business opportunities were widespread and the resources to understand and exploit these opportunities were scarce and dispersed. The zaibatsu was the organizational innovation adopted by Japan at this particular stage in its economic development.

Appendix: Japan

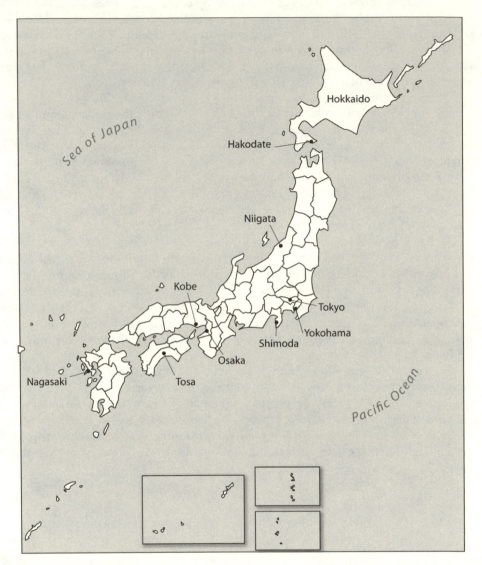

Figure 17.1. Map of Japan.

Notes

[1] For more information on the economy of the late Tokugawa period, see Lockwood 1965, 17–44.

[2] On the slogan, see Samuels 1994.

[3] For further information on the zaibatsu dissolution, see Bisson 1954. Regarding the economic reforms following World War II, see Teranishi and Kosai 1993 and Nakamura 1981.

[4] Examples in other countries of family-controlled conglomerates that have grown rapidly by concentrating national resources can be found in South America, India, and, more recently, Korea and Russia. These business groups are observed to have emulated the strategies employed by Japan's zaibatsu in the transformation to industrial capitalism. For more information on comparative studies of family business conglomerates, see Yasuoka 1985.

[5] On the foreign engineers, see UNESCO Centre for East Asian Cultural Studies 1975.

[6] For information on the governmental project to send students abroad in this period, see Takahashi 1968, 351–55.

[7] For details on vocational education and development, see Hayashi 1990, chap. 12. Both Hayashi and Hirshmeier (1964) point out that a new positive image of business emerged during the Meiji era.

[8] About the Mitsui zaibatsu, see Yasuoka 1982, 1998; and Roberts 1973.

[9] On the Mitsui business and role of Omotokata, see Yasuoka 1998.

[10] For details on Senshu-sha and the founding of Mitsui Bussan, see Nihon Keieishi Kenkyu Sho 1978.

[11] On the privatization of public works and mines, see Kobayashi 1977.

[12] For information on this bid, see Nagai 1989.

[13] For details on Alfred Sloan, see Sloan 1963. In 1914, Dan became head of Mitsui Holdings, succeeding Masuda Takashi and leading Mitsui to become Japan's largest conglomerate. In 1932 he was assassinated by right-wing nationalists, in front of the newly built general office.

[14] For details on the Mitsubishi zaibatsu, see Mishima 1981, 1989.

[15] For example, see Mishima 1981, 210–12.

References

Abe, Takeshi. 1995. "Kindai Keiei no Keisei" (Formation of modern business). In *Nihon Keieishi: Nihongata Kigyokeiei no Hatten Edo kara Heisei e* (Business history of Japan: The development of Japanese business management, from Edo to Heisei), ed. Miyamoto Matao and Kikkawa Takeo. Tokyo: Yuhikaku.

Berle, Adolf A., and Gardiner C. Means. 1932. *The Modern Corporation and Private Property*. New York: Commerce Clearing House.

Bisson, Thomas Arthur. 1954. *Zaibatsu Dissolution in Japan*. Berkeley and Los Angeles: University of California Press.

Chandler, Alfred D., Jr. 1962. *Strategy and Structure: Chapters in the History of the Industrial Enterprise*. Cambridge: MIT Press.

Hayashi, Takeshi. 1990. *The Japanese Experience in Technology: From Transfer to Self-Reliance*. Tokyo: United Nations University Press.

Hirschmeier, Johannes. 1964. *The Origins of Entrepreneurship in Meiji Japan*. Cambridge: Harvard University Press.

Iwasakike Denki Kankokai. 1979. *Iwasaki Yataro Den* (Biography of Iwasaki Yataro). Tokyo: University of Tokyo Press.

Kobayashi Masaaki. 1977. *Nihon no Kogyoka to Kangyo Haraisage* (Japan's industrialization and the sales of governmental works). Tokyo: Toyo Keizai Shimpo Sha.

Lockwood, William Wirt. 1954. *The Economic Development of Japan: Growth and Structural Change, 1868–1938*. Princeton: Princeton University Press.

———. 1965. *The State and Economic Enterprise in Japan: Essays in the Political Economy of Growth*. Princeton: Princeton: Princeton University Press.

Maddison, Angus. 1995. *Monitoring the World Economy, 1820–1992*. Paris: Development Centre of the Organisation for Economic Co-operation and Development.

Mishima, Yasuo, ed. 1981. *Mitsubishi Zaibatsu.* Tokyo: Nihon Keizai Shimbun Sha.

———. 1989. *The Mitsubishi: Its Challenge and Strategy.* Greenwich, CT: Jai Press.

Morikawa, Hidemasa. 1981. "Mitsubishi Zaibatsu no Keiei Soshiki" (Managerial organization of the Mitsubishi zaibatsu). *Keiei Shirin* 7, no. 7.

———. 1992. *Zaibatsu: The Rise and Fall of Family Enterprise Groups in Japan.* Tokyo: University of Tokyo Press.

Nagai, Minoru, ed. 1989. *Jijo Masuda Takashi Oden* (Autobiography of Masuda Takashi). Tokyo: Chuo Koron Sha.

Nakamura, Takafusa. 1981. *The Postwar Japanese Economy: Its Development and Structure.* Tokyo: University of Tokyo Press.

Nihon Keieishi Kenkyu Sho, ed. 1978. *Kohon Mitsui Bussan Kabushiki-kaisha 100 nen-shi* (A 100-year history of Mitsui Bussan). Tokyo: Nihon Keieishi Kenkyu Sho.

North, Douglass C. 1990. *Institutions, Institutional Change, and Economic Performance.* New York: Cambridge University Press.

North, Douglass C., and Robert Paul Thomas. 1973. *The Rise of the Western World: A New Economic History.* Cambridge: Cambridge University Press.

Penrose, Edith T. 1980. *The Theory of the Growth of the Firm.* New York: Sharpe.

Roberts, John G. 1973. *Mitsui: Three Centuries of Japanese Business.* New York: Weatherhill.

Samuels, Richard J. 1994. *"Rich Nation, Strong Army": National Security and the Technological Transformation of Japan.* Ithaca, NY: Cornell University Press.

Schumpeter, Joseph A. 1934. *The Theory of Economic Development: An Inquiry into Profits, Capital, Credit, Interest, and the Business Cycle.* Trans. Redvers Opie. Cambridge: Harvard University Press.

Sloan, Alfred P. 196. *My Years with General Motors.* Garden City, NY: Doubleday.

Takahashi, Kamekichi. 1930. *Nihon Zaibatsu no Kaibo* (Analysis of zaibatsu in Japan). Tokyo: Chuo Koron Sha.

———. 1968. *Nihon Kindai Keizai Keiseishi* (History of the modern Japanese economy). Vol. 2. Tokyo: Toyo Keizai Shinpo Sha.

———. 1973. *Nihon Kindai Keizai Hattatsushi Dainikan* (Development of the modern Japanese economy). Vol. 2. Tokyo: Toyo Keizai Shinpo Sha.

Teranishi, Juro, and Yutaka Kosai, eds. 1993. *The Japanese Experience of Economic Reforms.* Basingstoke, Hampshire: Macmillan; New York: St. Martin's Press.

UNESCO Centre for East Asian Cultural Studies. 1975. *Shiryo Oyatoi Gaikokujin* (Historical record: Foreign employees). Tokyo: Shogakkan.

Williamson, Oliver E. 1975. *Markets and Hierarchies, Analysis and Antitrust Implications: A Study in the Economics of Internal Organization.* New York: Free Press.

Yamazaki, Hiroaki. 1979. "Senjika no Sangyo Kozo to Dokusen Soshiki" (Industrial structure and monopolistic organization in wartime). In *Senji Nihon Keizai* (The wartime Japanese economy), ed. Yamazaki Hiroaki and Tokyo Daigaku Shakai Kagaku Kenkyujo, 217–89. Tokyo: University of Tokyo Press.

Yasuoka, Shigeaki, ed. 1982. *Mitsui Zaibatsu: Nihon Zaibatsu Keieishi* (Mitsui zaibatsu: Business history of zaibatsu). Tokyo: Nihon Keizai Shinbun Sha.

———. 1985. "Zaibatsu no Hikakushiteki Kenkyu no Sobyo" (Historiography of comparative studies of zaibatsu). In *Zaibatsu no Hikakushiteki Kenkyu* (Comparative study of zaibatsu), ed. Yasuoka Shigeaki, 2–36. Kyoto: Mineruva.

———. 1998. *Zaibatsu Keiseishi no Kenkyu* (Formation of zaibatsu). Kyoto: Mineruva.

Yonekawa, Shinichi. 1984. "University Graduates in Japanese Enterprises before the Second World War." *Business History* 26, no 2: 193–218.

Chapter 18

"Useful Knowledge" of Entrepreneurship: Some Implications of the History

WILLIAM J. BAUMOL AND ROBERT J. STROM

THE TERM "USEFUL KNOWLEDGE" in the title of our chapter is not meant to imply that the utility of historical study of entrepreneurship is in any sense questionable. Rather, we seek to remind the reader that our orientation in this book mirrors the interest of Ben Franklin, America's first great entrepreneur-inventor, in knowledge that has practical applications. Just as Franklin sought to promote useful knowledge that would improve the quality of life in a new land,[1] so we seek in this book to derive practical lessons regarding entrepreneurship and its relationship to economic growth from the historical accounts in this volume. Indeed, it is our contention that these histories give us much to think about and much to guide those who seek to formulate pertinent policy—policy to encourage economic growth via the use and dissemination of innovation and policy for the containment and even the elimination of poverty. This concluding chapter seeks to extract some of the noteworthy implications that emerge from the material offered by the eminent historians who wrote the earlier chapters of this book.

Before we proceed, a caveat must be brought to the attention of the reader. We must make clear that neither of the authors of this chapter can claim any professional qualifications as economic historians (or as historians of any other stripe). Our comments can only be interpreted as observations of very interested but very amateur onlookers.

We begin this chapter by arguing that history may well provide the most fertile field for the germination and gathering of ideas for policy. Far more than other topics in economics, the study of entrepreneurship must turn to nonstatistical history for the bulk of its evidence. There are essentially three sources of evidence that one can use to analyze an economic activity such as entrepreneurship: statistics, theory, and history. For empirical evidence, as one would expect, economists generally prefer statistics to history. Much as one can learn from historical circumstances and events, they are always complex, and their form and operations are subject to the interactions of an array of multifaceted influences. History offers nothing that resembles the *ceteris paribus* cleanliness of a controlled experiment.

Yet statistical analysis depends on the availability of a multiplicity of identical items that can be added together, averaged, or correlated with other variables. While we can calculate the number of laptops of a given model produced by a factory, an R & D establishment's inventions must all be different from one another if they are indeed to qualify as inventions. It is this fundamental heterogeneity that prevents these inventions from being added together or otherwise analyzed statistically. Recent statistical work has certainly offered significant illumination on the realities of entrepreneurship, telling us, for example, a great deal about the earnings of entrepreneurs. But the inherent diversity of the activity and its products remains a daunting obstacle to the econometric approach.

The theoretical approach runs into analogous obstacles. First, standard theory depends heavily on mathematical calculation of optimal decisions. This process is generally possible, however, only when one can deal quantitatively with interrelated variables, such as the amount of electric power and other inputs used and the magnitude of the resulting quantifiable output. For the reasons indicated in the previous paragraph, the fundamental heterogeneity of the entrepreneurship terrain makes this sort of calculation impossible.

Furthermore, the bulk of the useful knowledge contributed by standard microeconomic theory (in contrast to the rapidly expanding macroeconomic growth literature) is stationary in character and focuses on the properties of static equilibria. But such an equilibrium excludes the activities of the innovative entrepreneur, whose role is to bring to market (or to some other place in the economy) something that previously was not there. In the implicit scenario of a static model, the entrepreneur has been replaced by the manager, and the entrepreneur has moved on to bring changes to a new destination.

In short, here, as in few other parts of economics, we are driven to history for insights, despite all of the complexities of the phenomena it reports. It is true that historical analysis draws its inferences from messy examples that bear no resemblance to controlled experiments. Particularly apropos is the old Yiddish proverb, "*For example* is not a proof." Yet, as a means to consider the validity of hypotheses, it is not as powerless as this adage might seem to imply. A series of examples may not prove convincingly that an inference is true, but we must also recognize the validity of the converse: an example (or, rather, a counterexample) can indeed be a disproof.

This volume, then, seeks to use the study of history to illuminate useful knowledge regarding entrepreneurship and entrepreneurship policy. Each chapter of this volume describes the particularities and idiosyncrasies of entrepreneurship in a single time and place. Taken together, these chapters reveal wide variation, from the features of the economy and the entrepreneurs' status in the society, to the society's institutions and even the nature of entrepreneurial activity in that time and place. A consideration of these chapters also, however, reveals commonalities in the development of a culture of entrepreneurship, the institutions that foster this activity, and the relationship between entrepreneurial activity and economic growth.

These commonalities offer us an opportunity to draw inferences and hypotheses regarding entrepreneurship in our own time. For example, we may consider the evidence provided in the preceding chapters to suggest what inferences one can draw on the pertinence of productive entrepreneurship for economic growth, whether its abundance is indispensable for achievement of that goal, and whether it is very effective in promoting it. And we may review the implications of historical accounts of the influences that promote productive entrepreneurial activity. We must evidently proceed with caution in reliance on history as a guide to policy. The passage of time changes attitudes, constraining circumstances and even the goals and preferences of the community. Yet, treated with care, history can offer some relevant and valid insights pertinent to current policy issues on which other sources of evidence are scarce or even unavailable.

The Role of Culture in the Activities of the Entrepreneur

It must be recognized that some of the influences we encounter in these historical accounts do not lend themselves to encouragement by policy programs. Historians and others, notably Max Weber, Douglass North, and David Landes, have emphasized the role of religion and of the community's culture more generally, as key determinants of the intensity of that society's productive entrepreneurial activity and the size of its body of entrepreneurs. Many of the contributors to this volume also illustrate this powerful influence of culture on the vigor and character of entrepreneurship activity throughout the course of history.

Religion is perhaps one of the strongest cultural influences on the activities of the entrepreneur throughout history. Max Weber's seminal work, *The Protestant Ethic and the Spirit of Capitalism* (1904–5), articulates this relationship most memorably, but the authors of this volume also illustrate these effects, going as far back as Mesopotamia. Cornelia Wunsch, for example, articulates the dependence of Mesopotamian society's religious institutions upon economic support from mercantile activities. And both she and Michael Hudson note that this relationship resulted in a society that was considerably more conducive to mercantile entrepreneurship than ancient Greece and Rome. Similarly, Timur Kuran reports that the Muslim religion initially encouraged entrepreneurial activity. While Muhammad's own merchant activities may have led to the approbation of entrepreneurial activity in these early years, the religion has since evolved in directions less hospitable to such economic activity. Finally, John Munro discusses the relationship between Protestantism and the origins of modern capitalism and, with Murray, addresses the relationship between the usury doctrine for Protestants and Catholics and entrepreneurship.

John Munro also offers a different perspective on the role of religion on a society's entrepreneurial activity in his illuminating discussion of the very great contribution of the British religious dissenters and the Scots to the outburst of invention that arguably underlay the eighteenth-century Industrial Revolution in the British Isles. Here, as in other arenas such as those encompassing the Huguenots and the Jews, religion fostered entrepreneurial activity not only through the educational activities encouraged by these religious belief systems but also through the religious discrimination and exclusion these religious groups faced from a variety of economic positions.

Other Cultural Influences

While religion clearly plays a powerful role in the encouragement or discouragement of entrepreneurial activity, faith is far from the only cultural influence on entrepreneurship. This volume also describes a profusion of secular cultural influences. Joel Mokyr, for example, discusses the importance of informal institutions (codes of behavior, patterns of beliefs, and trust relations) to entrepreneurship during the Industrial

Revolution in Britain. He suggests that the cultural value placed on trustworthiness among gentlemen was an indispensable requirement for the rise of modern banking, along with such financial instruments as bills of exchange. Trust between gentlemen allowed for transactions with strangers in distant locations, in which the shipper of merchandise trusted the recipient to provide payment and the recipient trusted the shipper to send the promised items. Susan Wolcott also looks at the role of culture in shaping the financial system, focusing on the caste system in India.

There are equally powerful examples of cases in which culture discouraged entrepreneurial activity. The focus on military activity in ancient Rome, for example, meant that the importance and potential of nonmilitary inventions were underestimated. The Romans valued inventions that facilitated the conduct of warfare, including road-building improvements, aqueducts, and advances in the design of weapons, but they (and notably Vitruvius) failed to see the promise of the water mill or the steam engine. Similarly, the opportunities for corruption that plagued the culture of medieval China discouraged entrepreneurship. This corruption, compounded by the growing influence of Buddhism, is held to be responsible, in part, for the Chinese failure to commercialize the profusion of inventions during the Tang and Sung dynasties. Movable type, the blast furnace, the spinning wheel, the wheelbarrow, and the oft-mentioned gunpowder, among others, were effectively allowed to languish.

Entrepreneurs and Economic Growth: On Definition and Taxonomy

Culture undoubtedly plays a primary role in the development of an entrepreneurial society and, therefore, in economic growth. As a guide to growth policy, however, such observations are a council of despair. We know little about effective ways to influence and modify the culture of a society, and we are in no position, for example, to change a nation's religious beliefs to stimulate economic growth. While illuminating and important, the impact of culture and religion on entrepreneurship cannot be included in the domain of *useful* knowledge, for there is little or nothing that can be done to modify their current makeup or degree of profusion.

In this recapitulation, then, we will focus on other institutions of the society—those influences that do constitute opportunities for the adoption of programs that encourage growth and attack poverty, even if it can be argued persuasively that their influence is less powerful that that of other variables that resist deliberate modification and, therefore, are absent from our account. Ultimately, we will seek to derive from the studies in this volume what it is possible to deduce from the history about entrepreneurship policy. Given the importance of history to the study of entrepreneurship, the apparent absence of any volumes such as this one represents an important opportunity so far overlooked.

We necessarily begin with a few remarks on terms as they are used here (although other authors may have used them in different ways elsewhere in this book). First and foremost, we see an *entrepreneur* as anyone who undertakes some economic activity on her own initiative on the basis of alert observation of an opportunity to enhance her wealth, power, or prestige. Particularly in more recent times, this activity most often involves the creation and organization of a new business firm. But the activity did not always take this form and, indeed, does not always assume this form today.

This definition of entrepreneurship, even when limited to the creation of firms, encompasses a wide range of different activities. It is, therefore, useful to divide this activity further into two categories. The first includes all firms that are replicative or engage in activities very similar or identical to those of firms already in place. The creation of yet another retail shoe emporium serves as an excellent example of this type of replicative firm creation. Innovative entrepreneurs, by contrast, create firms that offer new products, use new production processes, enter new markets, or adopt new forms of organization. The innovative entrepreneur's primary role is not invention. Rather, these individuals ensure the utilization of promising inventions by conceptualizing their best use and bringing them to the market.

These entrepreneurs may be further divided into productive entrepreneurs, those who contribute to economic growth, and unproductive entrepreneurs, those who contribute little or nothing to the growth of the economy and sometimes, in fact, detract from it. Perhaps surprisingly, it seems that there is little if any association between replicative entrepreneurship and growth, and that the correlation may even be negative. A plausible explanatory hypothesis is that absence of rapid technical change and the associated growth results in a scarcity of jobs and the resulting unemployed are then forced to open small shops or become itinerant peddlers in order to earn a living.

Innovative entrepreneurship, on the other hand, can be either productive or unproductive. Innovative, unproductive entrepreneurs are those enterprising individuals who employ new approaches to rent-seeking, criminal, and other unproductive or even socially damaging activities. These are the entrepreneurs who seek to obtain a larger slice of the pie for themselves, rather than increasing the size of the pie for everyone. Prototypes include the enterprising individual who finds an unrecognized avenue to enter the bribe-taking bureaucracy or the lawyer who recognizes an opportunity to undertake a novel and potentially lucrative lawsuit. Even more extreme examples are the creators of firms that are part of organized crime or the warlords who create private armies. These individuals may be as innovative as the founder of a factory engaged in manufacturing legitimate products, but they fail to contribute to the economy and may even detract from its output.[2]

Such an orientation of the unproductive entrepreneur is easily understandable, particularly from a historical perspective. For much of human history, there was no guarantee that the individual whose efforts enhanced the magnitude of the pie would reap rewards. Indeed, history is replete with examples of the opposite. In many cultures, the monarch theoretically owned everything, and, in some societies, the king chose to transform this theory into reality quite often. Likelihood of expropriation is surely the ideal disincentive to productive effort. It is so much surer to organize a powerful private army, use it to grab away the neighbor's goods and chattel, and then employ that same army to prevent the nominal ruler from exercising his claim to expropriation rights. If a baron stole horses from a neighbor, the increase in the size of his cavalry could be far more certain than if he had tried to discover better methods of breeding, knowledge that even if acquired successfully might strengthen enemies more than it contributed to their discoverer.[3] To a degree, the limitations of the reward of the inventor and his productive entrepreneur partner continue today, as Professor Nordhaus (2004) has shown so dramatically.

Furthermore, unproductive entrepreneurship contributed to enhanced social status in many societies. The violent activities of the aggressive warriors were often perceived as heroic, and the rent-seeking achievement of close friendship with the king was inherently status-enhancing. By contrast, the dirty work of running an innovative enterprise has seemed mean and unglamorous by comparison through much of history. Indeed, the notion that contribution to productive capacity and production itself can be a meritorious activity is a rather subtle idea that has been overlooked or even despised in many societies. Even today, prestige is a reward of many of the occupations whose goal is redistribution rather than creation of wealth.

While many of the preceding chapters address the pervasiveness of innovative, unproductive entrepreneurship through history, our focus here is on the evidence of innovative, *productive* entrepreneurship in the histories offered in this volume. Innovative, productive entrepreneurship is the unique phenomenon that has driven and continues to drive much of the economic growth and productivity increases in the modern world. While economists have long seen this strong association between productive entrepreneurship and economic growth as self-evident, it must be conceded that this conclusion rests on little more than (somewhat informed) judgment and impressionistic deduction. There is little conclusive and direct evidence that demonstrates the influence of innovative, productive entrepreneurial activity upon growth. Yet, as we will show, there is a good deal of historical evidence that makes the absence of such a relationship highly implausible. And it is widely believed and highly plausible that innovative entrepreneurship not only contributes to growth but also plays a vital role.

An example will bring this out. There were a number of predecessors of James Watt who built earlier steam engines. Indeed, there was a working steam engine invented by Heron of Alexandria, likely in the first century AD. This invention, however, was used only for amusement (Abraham Lincoln [1858] called it "a toy"), and, evidently, it was never used for any of the myriad productive purposes for which it was launched at the end of the eighteenth century. This was probably attributable to the fact that this early engine was of simple design that offered very little power, and did not provide the reciprocal (up and down) motion that is needed for tasks such as driving of a pump. But, in addition, Heron, unlike Watt, did not have access to entrepreneurs to commercialize his invention, for the entrepreneurs of his time saw their avenue to gain as primarily military activity or the sponsorship of military invention.

James Watt, in contrast, benefited from his relationship with Matthew Boulton, a senior partner and an inventor himself, who served as Watt's entrepreneur. While Watt's early steam engine was used primarily to pump water out of mines, Boulton soon discovered that this market was saturated. It was Boulton's suggestion that Watt transform the up-and-down motion of the steam pump into rotary motion that could serve many other purposes, and that he invent a way to do so that did not use the already-known device used for the purpose: the long-understood crank, whose use had recently been blocked by a patent. Watt, in turn, responded by reportedly getting his assistant to invent the sun and planet gear that was used in subsequent Boulton-Watt engines and was, in fact, the prime power source of the Industrial Revolution. Boulton, then, was surely not the inventor, but he was alert to the opportunities for the invention's use, and he recognized the adaptation it required. He ensured that Watt's engine, unlike Heron's, did not languish. Rather, he brought it to market and put it to productive use—a perfect example of the role of the innovative entrepreneur and his contribution to economic growth.

Productive Entrepreneurship throughout History

There is a general impression that this type of innovative, productive entrepreneurship is relatively new. Many believe that at least until the Renaissance, and perhaps until the approach of the Industrial Revolution, entrepreneurs were predominantly unproductive. The histories of the Italian condottiere, the bribe-taking mandarin members of the Chinese judiciary, and the British royal favorites certainly contribute to this misconception if considered only by themselves. The work of the historians in this book also suggests, however, that all of the different types of entrepreneurs in our taxonomy have long been with us. There were, in fact, productive entrepreneurs relatively early in the period of recorded history.

In order to illustrate the appearance and development of productive entrepreneurship, we bring together the accounts of this volume into a single—necessarily brief—account of entrepreneurial activity since the very beginnings of history. As Hudson's and Wunsch's chapters suggest, the beginnings of productive entrepreneurship may be found in Mesopotamia. The confluence of the Mesopotamian rivers and their centuries of deposition of rich soil permitted the society to produce a surplus, perhaps for the first time. Furthermore, the geology of the area provided no stone or metal and little lumber, making distant trade mandatory for the production of weapons and for construction of buildings, including palaces. The society, therefore, needed productive entrepreneurs to organize these activities, and it needed appropriate incentives that would induce individuals to pursue this entrepreneurial activity effectively. The arrangement under which religious institutions derived much of their funding from the activities of these entrepreneurs, for example, offered Mesopotamian entrepreneurship an apparent respectability that made it attractive to would-be entrepreneurs. Mesopotamia, it seems, was the first, brief, early period of productive entrepreneurship.

Early Muslim communities, too, experienced and evidently valued productive entrepreneurship. As Timur Kuran explains, the respectability of productive entrepreneurship in this time derives in part from the fact that Muhammad himself was a merchant. In the early period after his death, entrepreneurs who followed the example of Muhammad's mercantile activities were in good repute.

The Roman and medieval eras, however, may be characterized as destructive entrepreneurship at its most manifest. In this golden age of redistributive and destructive entrepreneurship, it was profitable (and honorable) to accumulate wealth by violent means. The possibility of productive entrepreneurship, it seems, was not even considered. The Roman conquests are prime examples of efforts to acquire the possessions of others by violent means, and the history of medieval China also offers insight into the bribes and corruption that typified that period.[4] As Hudson writes, "One looks in vain [in Roman writings] for the idea that profit-seeking enterprise might drive society forward to achieve higher levels of production and living standards." The approach to acquisition of wealth was fundamentally redistributive, using means, often violent, to garner a larger slice of the pie, rather than doing anything that would make the pie larger. Arguably, the destructive entrepreneurship of this period may even serve as part of the explanation for the fall of Rome[5] and the poverty of the "dark ages."

Ironically, it was the very success of this unproductive entrepreneurship that led to the evolution of the institutions that underlay productive entrepreneurship in the later Middle Ages.[6] The innovative success of the destructive entrepreneurs entailed cumulative military invention, and the kings of this time needed continually to make purchases to acquire these innovative military technologies and protect themselves from others who would use them. As a result of these costly military innovations, coupled with an increasing reliance on paid armies to enhance the size of military forces, these kings—for whom aggressive warfare was arguably the primary occupational activity[7]—were often, indeed almost always, seriously short of funds. For whenever they did manage to scrape up enough to proceed on their military enterprises with little financial hindrance, the arms race was opened yet another notch. By the inherent character of the game, any amount that seemed sufficient on one day was sure to be woefully inadequate on the next.

The kings, then, found themselves perpetually underfinanced, heavily in debt, and unable to find willing lenders. They were reduced to distasteful expedients, begging for a bit here, wheedling or extorting a bit there. Indeed, much of medieval history is a story of battles—not the supposedly glorious clashes of arms, but battles between the kings and the subjects from whom the monarchs hoped to draw their funding. As some historians have put it, they were "pauper kings."

These kings, particularly in the British Isles, were forced to turn to their nobles for financial support. And the nobles, in exchange, extracted royal agreements for the earliest institutions to protect productive entrepreneurship in the future, from the sanctity of property to the rule of law more generally. The "pauper kings" reluctantly acceded to the nobility's demands for protections against arbitrary exactions and abuse in order to receive their funds and other forms of support. In continental Europe, it was not so much the nobles as the merchants, the master craftsmen, the primitive bankers, and the others who acquired wealth from economic activities in the towns to whom the monarchs turned for financing, and in exchange offered a degree of freedom in the towns.

The Renaissance saw further changes that would encourage entrepreneurial activity. During this time, the kings were able to use their financial resources and their improved weaponry and tactics to curb the violent redistributive entrepreneurial activities of their nobility, thereby forcing the nobility to seek new sources of wealth. From the suppression of private armies to the termination of royal power to grant monopolies to favorites, the foreclosure of opportunities for rent-seeking and other forms of unproductive entrepreneurship were key to fostering productive entrepreneurship.

At the same time, the continuing growth of institutions favorable to productive entrepreneurship—the sanctity of property (though it may sometimes have impeded "creative destruction"), the enforceability of contracts, the system of patents, and the rise of banking—all helped to provide inviting opportunities to entrepreneurs for whom rent-seeking and independent military violence had become far more difficult. It is this set of institutions, in fact, that helped to clear the path to industrial revolution and modern innovative (and productive) entrepreneurship. This period between the Renaissance and the Industrial Revolution, then, can be seen as the birth of widespread productive entrepreneurship.

On this view it was only when the king became sufficiently powerful to suppress the activities of independent military entrepreneurs, and when other actions such as the British Statute of Monopolies of 1624[8] curbed royal grants to rent-seeking companions, that entrepreneurs in substantial numbers turned to productive activities and contributed a critical element to the explosion of productivity that underlay the Industrial Revolution and its sequel.

Institutions That Have Promoted Innovative, Productive Entrepreneurship through History

As this brief history illustrates, and as Douglass North has long emphasized, it is the institutions of the society that arguably have served to reallocate entrepreneurial activity to a considerable extent from rent-seeking and military violence to innovation and production. We offer below a more detailed account of the evolution of some of these key institutions—the patent system, antitrust law, and bankruptcy protection laws. These are just a few of the institutions that have played a role in encouraging productive entrepreneurial activity in the past, can be altered by government, and, therefore, are promising paths to reform.[9] The evolution of this rule of law, in fact, was perhaps the most important contribution to the flourishing of productive entrepreneurship and the birth of capitalism.

Patent System

The patent system is evidently an institution that effectively promoted innovative entrepreneurship not only via the reward of a temporary legal monopoly, but also by making it possible to transform access to such intellectual property into a salable commodity. Patents offer the entrepreneur an additional means to acquire wealth for herself and her associate inventor while simultaneously ensuring widespread use of her invention. Yet, it is noteworthy here, according to the evidence provided by historians, that in practice patents seem to have had little effect in encouraging innovation during the earlier period of their existence.

A consideration of the curious history of patents reveals, however, that while the early "letters patent" were intended to foster greater utilization of intellectual property, they originally offered no protection or incentives for the creators or inventors themselves. In fact, letters patent were issued in England to encourage the transfer of intellectual property (IP) to new countries, and, for this reason, they were granted to producers who would steal ideas from their own countries and bring them to England where their patent gave them a monopoly over the production and sale of the item for a specified period. The first notable example of a patent occurred in England, at least as early as 1331, when England gave John Kemp, a Flemish weaver, a patent[10] monopoly to pursue his trade in England (see North and Thomas 1973, 147). The patent, in effect, gave a workman who mastered a trade initially carried out only in another country permission to migrate to England and set up this new trade there. North and Thomas indicate that this practice was hardly rare:

> This policy of encouraging foreigners to bring in new innovations from the continent was extended to many other areas [beside weaving]; mining, metal working, silk manufacturing, ribbon weaving, etc. Of the fifty-five grants of monopoly privilege made under Elizabeth, twenty-one were issued to aliens or naturalized subjects. (1973, 153–54)

This early use of patents, then, was not designed to offer protection to creators of intellectual property but, quite the contrary, as an incentive for transfer of the intellectual property and to contribute to the enhancement of productivity in the new country.

The patent only later became an instrument to protect inventors, in the wake of parliamentary anger over royal misuse of letters patent to reward royal favorites, and for other purposes having no connection with good IP management. The Statute of Monopolies brought the modern usage of patents into English law. And the explicit incorporation of patents in the Constitution of the United States is an extraordinary act that may well have substantially facilitated the rapid progress of this country toward its position of economic leadership.[11]

Antitrust Law

Antitrust law and the competition it fosters have also played important roles in encouraging innovation in the past century. These laws helped to ensure the intensity of competition among oligopolistic firms that makes innovation a life-and-death matter for them, inspiring their undeviating attention to the marketing of new products and the adoption of new productive processes. Such competition also led to the creation of R & D divisions within the enterprise, working systematically to provide the innovations that firms require in a continuing stream in order to retain their position in the market.

Bankruptcy Protection

Yet another institution that has worked in this direction is bankruptcy law, which offers a degree of protection to entrepreneurs who experience failure in an undertaking. Because innovation, with its lack of clear precedent, is inherently a very risky activity, bankruptcy protection is surely a significant encouragement of innovative efforts. These laws were implemented relatively early in the history of the United States,[12] and it has been argued that the relatively strong penalties that were—and continue to be—exacted for failure in the Old World, such as effective denial in much of Europe of funding to individuals who have once experienced failure, help to explain the failure of the major European economies to catch up with that of the United States, despite their short-lived superiority in rate of growth after World War II. This observation also raises questions about the advisability of recent modification of the American bankruptcy laws that have increased the cost of a failed undertaking.

Banking System

The rule of law and its associated institutions described above are most often cited as those that are critical for the availability of an abundance of productive entrepreneurial activity. But the current volume also repeatedly draws our attention to the role of the banking system and, in particular, its creation of instruments such as bills of exchange. The role of this institution seems self-evident, but there is more here than is contained in the usual story.

The problem is the size of the business firm created by the entrepreneur and the size of the market in which he operates. In activities that can provide scale economies, efficiency and growth clearly favor firms that are large and markets that are extended. But these markets require time-consuming transportation of products from the place of production to the retailer's location. If producer A delivers to distant retailer B, either B must pay for the shipment before having received it, or B must have shipped the products before receiving payment, or both. Evidently, without a bank, this transaction will work only if A and B are well acquainted and have reason to trust one another fully.

Before the intervention of the banks, these limitations largely confined such transactions to family and friends, and generally prevented firms from growing beyond the minuscule. Then, in Italy and the Netherlands, banks made their appearance and served as the instrument that solved the resulting problem. An established bank that had nurtured a reputation for trustworthiness could accept a cash deposit from the merchant who was to receive a shipment, holding it until the merchandise had been obtained. In that way, both parties could be sure of receiving what they had been promised, and extensive transactions among distant individuals who did not even know one another could proceed without the previous handicap. This development was supplemented by the invention and adoption of such practices as double entry bookkeeping and new court-enforced rules admitting such recorded material as legitimate evidence of unpaid debt. With the appearance of such institutions, a firm basis for growth of the firm and the market had been provided, and with it the early prosperity of northern Italy, the Netherlands, and, soon after, the United Kingdom.[13] On the general subject, see Joel Mokyr's chapter on the growth of a culture of cooperation through reputation. Mokyr and Casson and Godley also show that in England there was another institutional development that dealt with the problem of trust in distant transaction: the acceptance of the idea in the eighteenth and nineteenth centuries that trustworthiness was an indispensable characteristic of a "gentleman" and an absolute requirement for his acceptance as such by society.

How Institutions That Induce Productive Entrepreneurship Arise

While our discussion here supports the conclusion that the institutions of a society create the incentives that lead entrepreneurs to allocate their capacities to activities that contribute to production, it leaves an important question unanswered: How do these institutions arise? We will argue next that they can arise, and often have, as a matter of historical accident. It would seem that the nations who were affected by the right accidents grew most rapidly. This may appear to be a council of despair, but it is not. For by studying those accidents, one can hope to replicate them or their analogs through appropriate policy. And, of course, the accidental developments that are about to be described are only part of the story and sometimes only a secondary part, but it is contended here that they nevertheless did have an instructive and significant role to play.

This volume is replete with examples of historical accidents that helped to introduce the institutions responsible for a nation's entrepreneurial success. In this chapter alone, we have alluded to the fact that it was the very financial desperation of the monarchy that gave rise to the property rights that protect entrepreneurs, and that patent law was originally conceived to encourage the transfer of intellectual property rather than protect it. In the discussion that follows, we offer a detailed discussion of the unintentional development of institutions that supported entrepreneurship in medieval England and the Dutch Golden Age.

Medieval England[14]

The evolution of the rule of law in Britain serves as a prime example of the accidental creation of institutions that support entrepreneurship. The Magna Carta and the charters that followed it, in fact, were the direct result of the British kings' concessions to the nobility. Like the other medieval kings, those in the British Isles faced an ongoing arms race in which the ante was constantly raised. They were truly the "pauper kings" we described earlier, facing continually rising costs and increasing financial pressures. This story may begin when King John of England's territories were attacked by Phillip Augustus, the Capetian king of France. John found himself, like his brother Richard I and father Henry II before him, embroiled in French combat. Furthermore, he faced military problems in Wales, Scotland, and Ireland. Desperate for funds, he resorted to a variety of expedients such as heavy taxes on noble widows that bought them immunity from enforced remarriage, particularly to men beneath them in social status, and large payments required of heirs on reaching maturity before they were allowed to obtain their bequests. These taxes, combined with the loss of Normandy by the Plantagenets at the Battle of the Bovines (1214), led to widespread discontent among the Magnates (the earls and barons). The Magna Carta was agreed to in 1215 as a compromise between the king and the Magnates, restricting the king's power and giving the Magnates protections against the financial exactions and related abuses they had experienced in the past. And while this charter was not truly the confirmation of liberty and democracy that it is sometimes reputed to be, it was clearly a step in a direction that the country would move much further in the next century.

These rights were extended further when King John's son Henry III faced a similarly desperate situation. Like his father, Henry III was notoriously short of funds. Facing a simultaneous need to defend what was left of his father's Angevin territories in France and to intervene in quarrels between the papacy and the Holy Roman emperor in Sicily, Henry, as was to happen again so many times, adopted financing measures that re-elicited the anger of the barons. The barons finally rose in what was in effect a revolt. In a Parliament held at Oxford in 1258, they forced the king to agree to a new charter that enhanced the rights provided in Magna Carta, more fully curtailing the means that could be used by the monarch in raising funds. More important, to deprive the king of support among the commons, which included many knights and royal officials, the Oxford charter committed the magnates to extend to the (upper) commons rights similar to those that the nobles had extracted from the king for themselves. Once out of the power of the barons, however, Henry sought to invalidate his oath by appealing to the Louis IX, king of France, who ruled that the agreement, extracted by force, was invalid.

Finally, King Henry's son Edward extended these rights even further. Edward's reign was marked by warfare in Wales, Scotland, and France, and he was predictably beset by the usual cash shortage. In 1296 he accepted a new charter, providing guarantees against arbitrary taxation, a key step toward acceptance of the idea that there should be no taxation without representation, something not fully settled until the "Glorious Revolution" of 1688 and the end of the male Stuart line of kings. In the reigns of each of these kings, their financial pressures forced them to extend the property and other individual rights to the nobility—and eventually to what we may consider the upper middle class—that laid the foundation for future productive entrepreneurial activity.

Dutch Golden Age

A consideration of the remarkable Dutch Golden Age, discussed in more detail by Gelderblom, reveals a similar story of fortuitous accidents that led to model institutions, flourishing innovation, and prosperity. The Netherlands, so insignificant in size, led the world economy for four centuries, from the beginning of the fifteenth century until the last years of the eighteenth century. And the country remained one of the world's most prosperous nations even after its economic leadership came to an end.

The role of inventors and entrepreneurs in the country's prosperity cannot be underestimated. Not only did the Dutch invent new methods of construction for canals and dykes, but they designed ships better adapted to the needs of trade and created trading posts in places as far and exotic as New Amsterdam (New York). They designed new architectural forms that were imitated in parts of England and in New England, and they created new financial institutions, including the establishment of the Central Bank in the Amsterdam Exchange Bank early in the seventeenth century (1635). This novel institution preceded both the Bank of Sweden and the Bank of England by years and preceded Alexander Hamilton's bank and the Federal Reserve System by more than a century.[15]

Just as many of the British institutions favorable to entrepreneurship were created accidentally, the Dutch accomplishment can be credited, in part, to at least three apparently catastrophic historical phenomena. First, the massive breakthrough of the seas on November 1, 1170, created the 200-square-mile Zuider Zee, terrifyingly, in a single day. The flooding undermined grain cultivation and drove a portion of the agricultural labor force to migrate to the towns. At a time when the urban population of Europe was perhaps 10 percent, that of the Netherlands was closer to 50 percent. This move to the towns led to expanded handicraft and primitive manufacturing activities, bringing with them the need and incentives for entrepreneurial activity. Furthermore, the towns in the Middle Ages served as oases of freedom of thought and conscience, including freedom from serfdom, and this freedom arguably played an important role in Dutch prosperity. Some have also emphasized a relatively early Dutch propensity to undertake *cooperative* (as contrasted with "individualistic") activities such as dam construction that protected the community and the economy from the unrelenting threat from the sea.

The Spanish capture of Brussels and Antwerp serves as a second example of a seemingly calamitous event that turned out to be an economic blessing for the Netherlands. Following the Spanish capture, the Dutch succeeded in cutting Antwerp off from the Baltic for two centuries, thereby protecting the trading position of Amsterdam and encouraging enterprising foreign trade. In addition to enabling economic growth in the city, the Spanish victory brought an exodus of enterprising Calvinist refugees, fleeing Spanish oppression. These refugees joined others, such as the Jews who had fled from Spain, in bolstering Amsterdam's entrepreneurial activity. This expulsion of talent to other countries, can, of course, be seen many times in history, from Louis XIV's expulsion of the Huguenots from France, to Hitler's expulsion of the Jews,[16] to the exodus of members of the middle class from Castro's Cuba.

These stories, like the accidental and intentional successes of so many other entrepreneurial nations, illustrate the importance of the society's institutions to the creation of an entrepreneurial climate. While the institutions that support productive entrepreneurship may have arisen quite by accident in previous periods, these tales offer us insights that can help to create policies that will foster the same institutions in our society today. As Landes emphasizes in the introduction to this volume—and as the later chapters of this book and a look at current events indicate, many opportunities for change remain. Wolcott and Chan explain, for example, that the shortcomings of the banking systems of India and China continue to plague their economies. In both countries, it is at least highly plausible that the widespread failure to go beyond business based on family and close friends is a major handicap to their expansion and to growth of their economies. Those who foresee uninterrupted continuation of the spectacular growth of both these economies have not taken into account those and other institutional handicaps. One need only recall how, only a few decades ago, the common wisdom foresaw that the U.S. economy would shortly be surpassed by Japan and Germany, to recognize how tenuous such forecasts can be. The continuing abundance of rent-seeking opportunities throughout the world serves as another prime example of the policy work that remains to be done. The prevalence of corruption is well recognized, and it is striking that the much-publicized recent scandals entailing corporate misbehavior in the United States still leave that country far behind much of Africa, Latin America, and the Far East as havens of bribery and other associated phenomena. We still have noteworthy examples of rent-seeking through misuse of the law, notably through attempts at remunerative sham litigation, as when an inefficient business firm sues a more efficient rival on antitrust grounds. There remains also the enterprising activity of crime syndicates as a glaring example of continuing unproductive entrepreneurship.

In short, the lessons of history remain pertinent and show us directions that are promising avenues for amelioration of the economic conditions of the impoverished countries of the world, as well as the measures that the world's successful economies can adopt to help them retain their rate of economic progress. Such insight into appropriate policy is hardly the only object of this book, but it is surely not something of little value.

Notes

[1] Franklin 1743. Professor Mokyr notes, in correspondence with the authors of this chapter, that *useful knowledge* is a term that was in wide use in Enlightenment Europe, and goes back to Bacon and the Baconians.

[2] Some illuminating recent examples are provided by Graham in this volume.

[3] For a more detailed discussion of this type of entrepreneurship, see Hudson and Wunsch in this volume.

[4] See Chan in this volume for a broad discussion of the history of entrepreneurship in China.

[5] Here Professor Mokyr comments: "There is no question that both Rome and medieval China were corrupt and heavily rent-seeking, but the picture is not quite *that* bleak.... Michael Hudson clearly cannot find much in Roman *writing* that would suggest profit-seeking enterprise, but the fact remains that Roman law and relative peace in the Mediterranean enforced by Roman armies contributed to the flourishing of a very high level of international trade (in grains, wine, olive oil, perfumes, and high-end textiles across the *mare nostrum*). Somebody clearly saw profit opportunities somewhere. In the end, ... it's not so much that nobody at all tries to engage in productive entrepreneurship as much as ... that predatory behavior of those who control the means of violence eventually kills the geese that lay the golden eggs. But that is not instantaneous, and we see in most eras some successful entrepreneurship."

[6] See Murray in this volume for a more broad discussion of entrepreneurship in medieval Europe.

[7] Of the eighteen English reigns starting with William the Conqueror and ending before Henry VII, the first Tudor, there was substantial warfare in virtually every one.

[8] Professor Mokyr comments: "I am not sure if the causality runs from that statute to entrepreneurs turning increasingly to productive activities or the other way around: more and more opportunities through trade and manufacturing had given these people the power of the purse, and they wanted to consolidate that and place constraints on what the executive could do."

[9] Examples of other changes in institutions that facilitated entrepreneurship can be found throughout this volume, from the zaibatsu in Japan described by Yonekura and Shimizu, the establishment of joint-stock companies in England described by Munro, and the establishment of a central bank in the U.S. described by Cain, to Murray's discussion of the creation of the bill of exchange.

[10] The term comes from *letters patent*, or letters issued by the monarch meant to be visible (patent) to all (as distinguished from confidential *letters close*).

[11] See Wengenroth in this volume for a discussion of intellectual property rights in Germany and their impact on innovation, and Cain in this volume for a discussion of patent law in antebellum United States. Gelderblom discusses the patenting system in Holland.

[12] See Lamoreaux in this volume for a discussion of U.S. anti-trust law and bankruptcy law (enacted in 1898).

[13] See, for example, the chapters in this volume by Gelderblom and Mokyr.

[14] Again, see Murray in this volume for a more broad discussion of entrepreneurship in Medieval Europe.

[15] See Cain in this volume for a discussion of Hamilton's policies.

[16] See Wengenroth in this volume for a discussion of the expulsion of Jewish state employees from their positions and the loss of the scientific elite, including twenty Nobel laureates.

References

Franklin, Benjamin. 1743. *A Proposal for Promoting Useful Knowledge among the British Plantations in America*. Philadelphia: Printed by Benjamin Franklin.

Lincoln, Abraham. 1858. "Lecture on Discoveries and Inventions."

Nordhaus, William D. 2004. "Schumpeterian Profits in the American Economy: Theory and Measurement." NBER Working Paper No. 10433, April. Cambridge, MA: National Bureau of Economic Research.

North, Douglass C., and Robert Paul Thomas. 1973. *The Rise of the Western World: A New Economic History*. Cambridge: Cambridge University Press.

Contributors

WILLIAM J. BAUMOL
Department of Economics
New York University

LOUIS P. CAIN
Department of Economics
Loyola University Chicago and
Northwestern University

MARK CASSON
Director, Centre for
Institutional Performance
Economics Department
University of Reading

WELLINGTON K. K. CHAN
Department of History
Occidental College

OSCAR GELDERBLOM
Department of History
Utrecht University

ANDREW GODLEY
Centre for International
Business History
University of Reading
Business School

MARGARET B. W. GRAHAM
Desautels Faculty of Management
McGill University

MICHEL HAU
Université Marc Bloch

MICHAEL HUDSON
Institute for the Study of
Long-Term Economic Trends

TIMUR KURAN
Departments of Economics and
Political Science
Duke University

NAOMI R. LAMOREAUX
Departments of Economics and
History, School of Law
University of California, Los Angeles

DAVID S. LANDES
Department of Economics
Harvard University

JOEL MOKYR
Departments of Economics and History
Northwestern University and the
Eitan Berglas School of Economics,
Tel Aviv University

JOHN MUNRO
Department of Economics
University of Toronto

JAMES M. MURRAY
Director of the Medieval Institute
Department of History
Western Michigan University

HIROSHI SHIMIZU
Institute of Innovation Research
Hitotsubashi University

ROBERT J. STROM
Director, Research & Policy
Ewing Marion Kauffman
Foundation

ULRICH WENGENROTH
Munich Center for the
History of Science and Technology

SUSAN WOLCOTT
Department of Economics
Binghamton University

CORNELIA WUNSCH
School of Oriental and African
Studies
University of London

SEIICHIRO YONEKURA
Institute of Innovation Research
Hitotsubashi University

Index